OFTEN WRONG

THE OFTEN WRONG, VOLUME ONE. First printing. October 2019. Published by Image Comics, Inc.
Office of publication: 2701 NW Vaughn St., Suite 780, Portland, OR 97210. Printed in the USA. For information regarding the CPSIA on this printed material call: 203-595-3636. For international rights, contact: foreignlicensing@imagecomics.com. ISBN: 978-1-5343-1352-1.

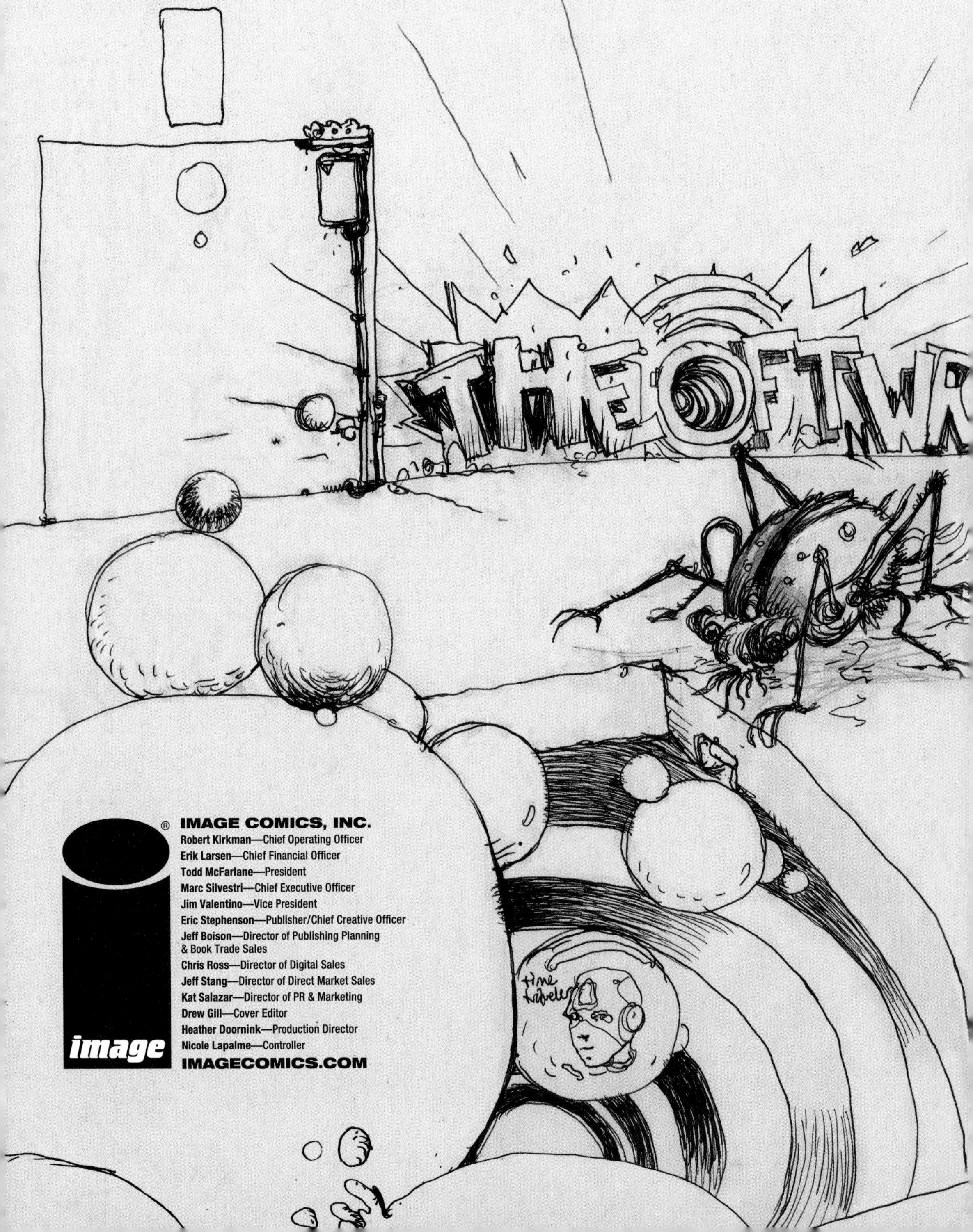
THE OFTWR

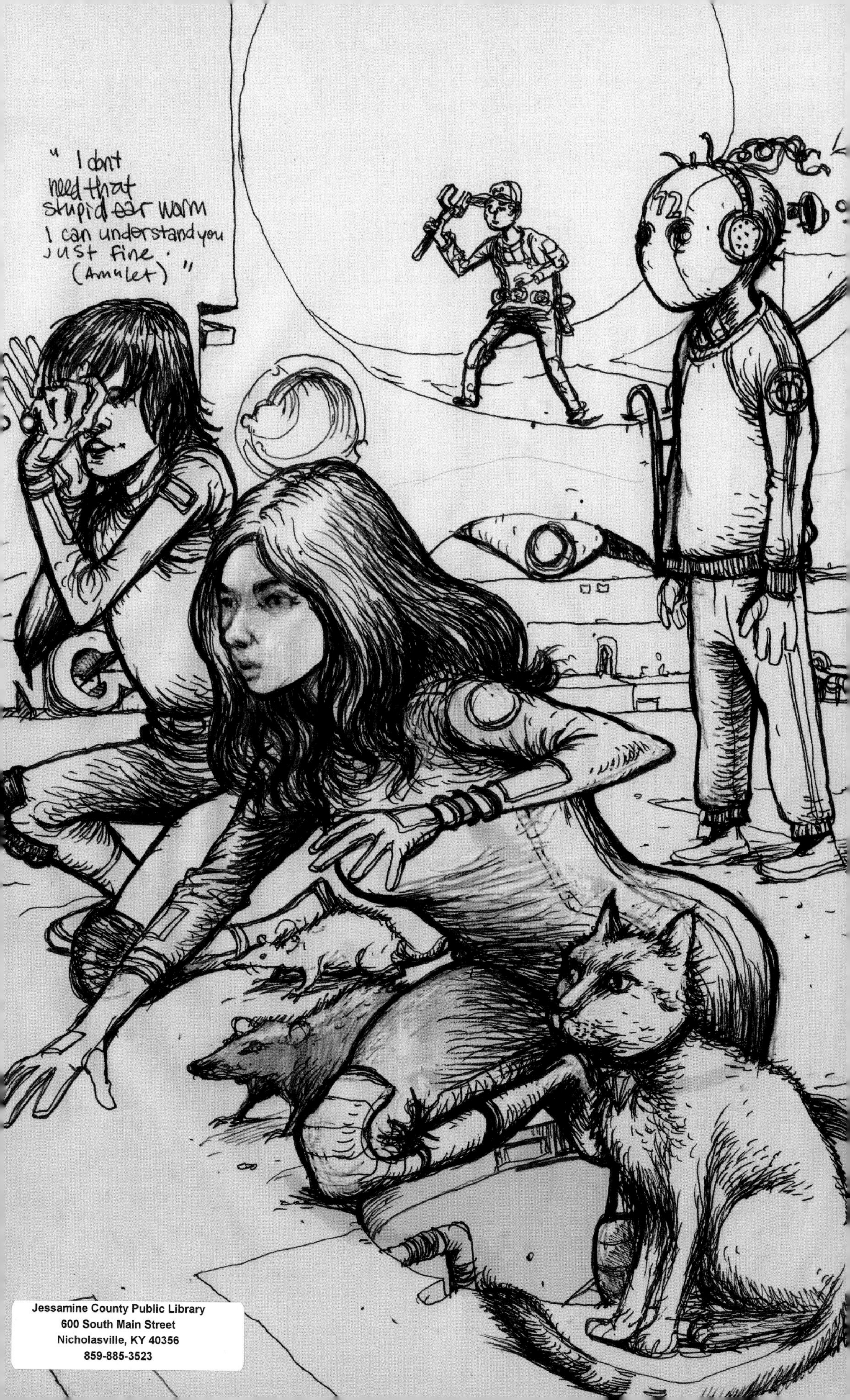
" I don't need that stupid ear worm I can understand you just fine. (Amulet) "

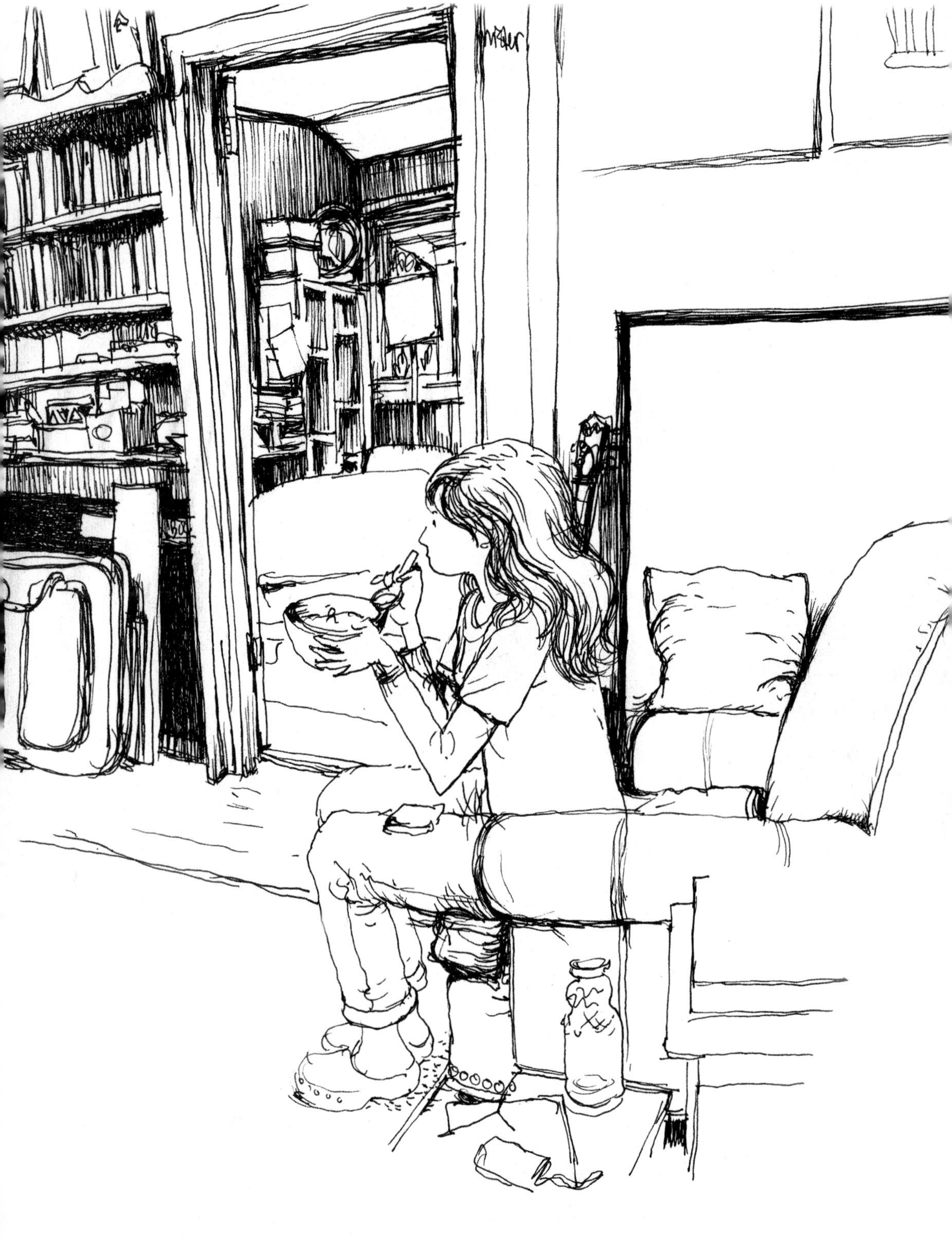

SW portland, OR Dec 2014

Mac Nenditch

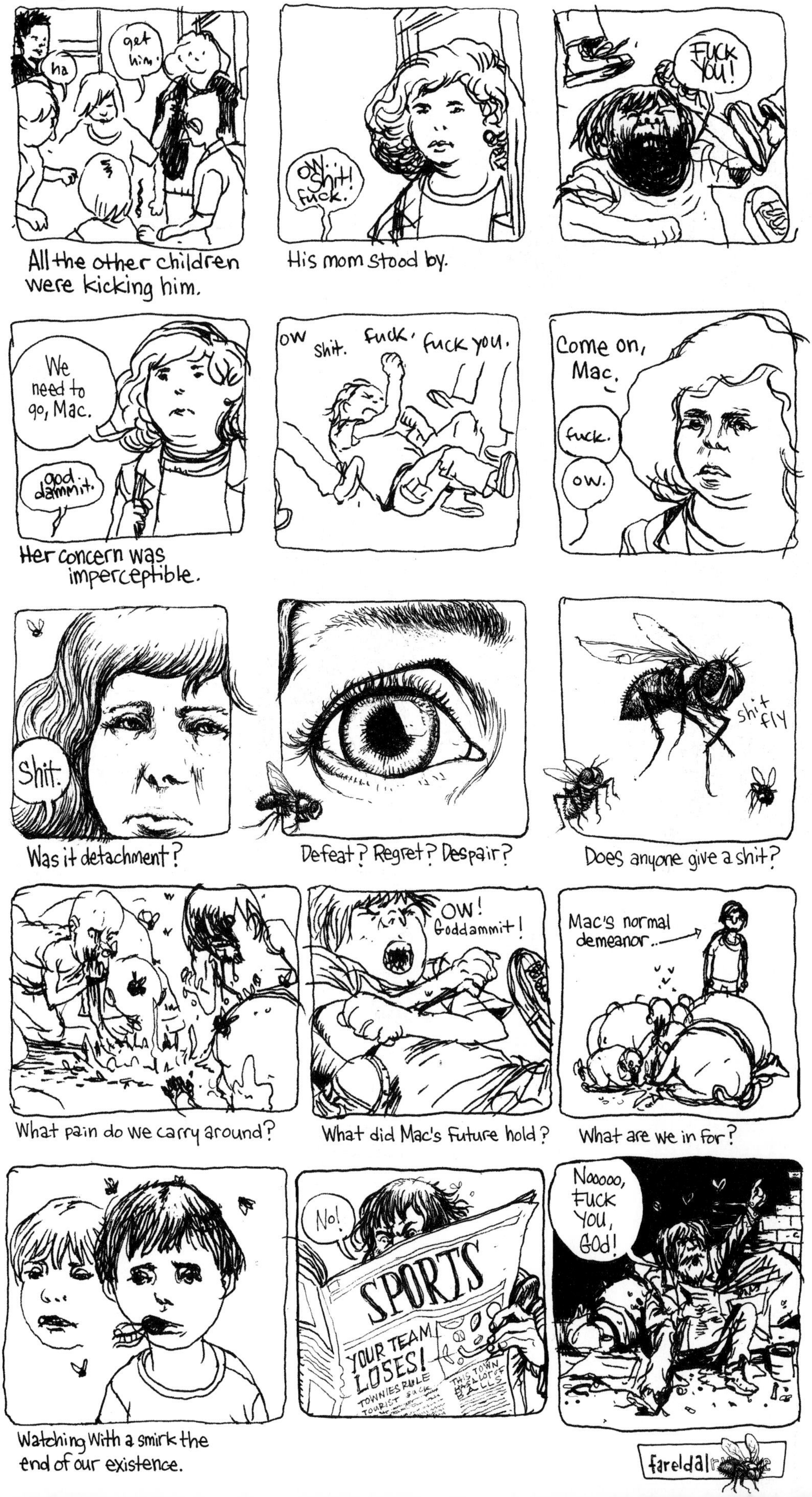

ha
get him.
All the other children were kicking him.
Oh... Shit! fuck.
His mom stood by.
FUCK YOU!
We need to go, Mac.
god dammit.
Her concern was imperceptible.
ow
shit.
fuck.
fuck you.
Come on, Mac.
fuck.
ow.
Shit.
Was it detachment?
Defeat? Regret? Despair?
shit fly
Does anyone give a shit?
What pain do we carry around?
OW! Goddammit!
What did Mac's future hold?
Mac's normal demeanor..
What are we in for?
Watching with a smirk the end of our existence.
No!
SPORTS
YOUR TEAM LOSES!
TOWNIES RULE
THIS TOWN HAS A LOT OF BALLS
Noooo, FUCK YOU, GOD!
fareldal

the Wrenchies

THE WRENCHIES is a paranoid dystopian fantasy
comic book published by First Second Books in 2014.

The idea came from a 15-page story I did for
the MEATHAUS S.O.S. ANTHOLOGY about brothers
transformed after entering a Shadowsmen cave.
One of the brothers, Sherwood, sees his
entire dark future in an instant.

Another story in that same issue of MEATHAUS
by one of my favorite artists, Tom Herpich,
really got me thinking about a post-apoctolyptic,
psychedelic quest kind of thing mixed with
the 1979 film OVER THE EDGE.

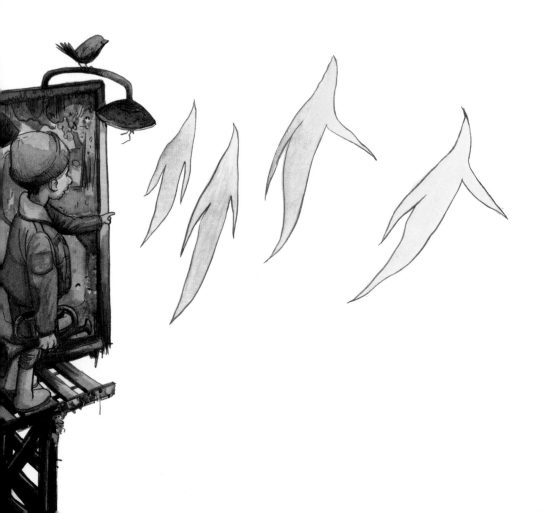

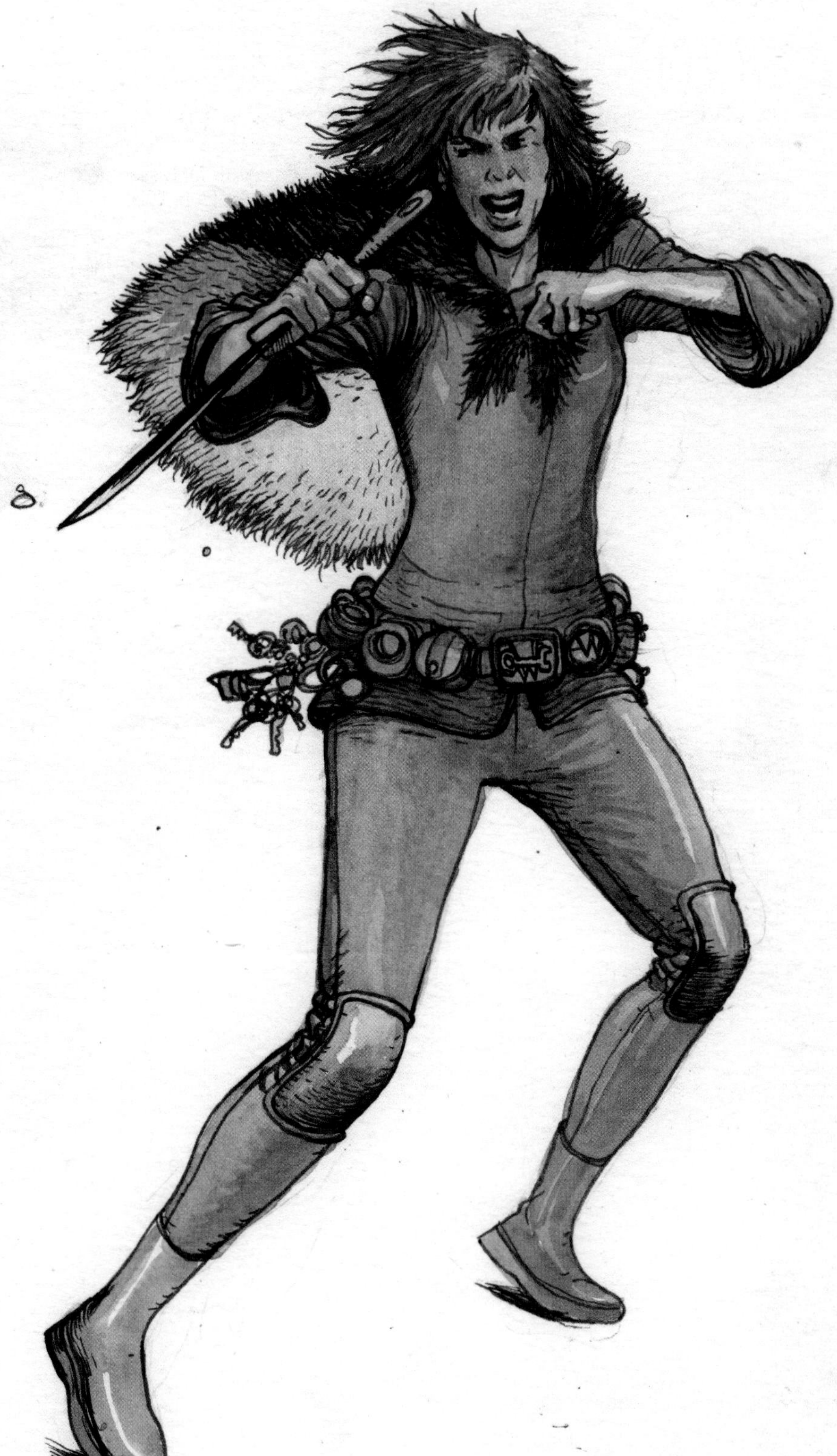

Diamond Day: Smart and strong leader of the Wrenchies.

both of
my sisters
are still
alive in
my head.

Vivian and Virgayle Taylor are
sisters, born two of three.
Their powers are telepathic
and telekinetic, and more
controllable while they
are holding hands.

Their other sister, Emery,
died when going into an amulet.
Her spirit is still in communication
with them when the girls hold hands
and she operates as a ghost spy.

She leaves
group
before
finding sharon
the Wrenchies

She
and

later
meets up
with
SEPT
in
IWAH

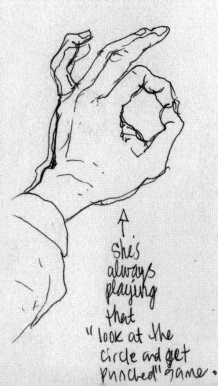

A
She's
always
playing
that
"look at the
circle and get
Punched" game.

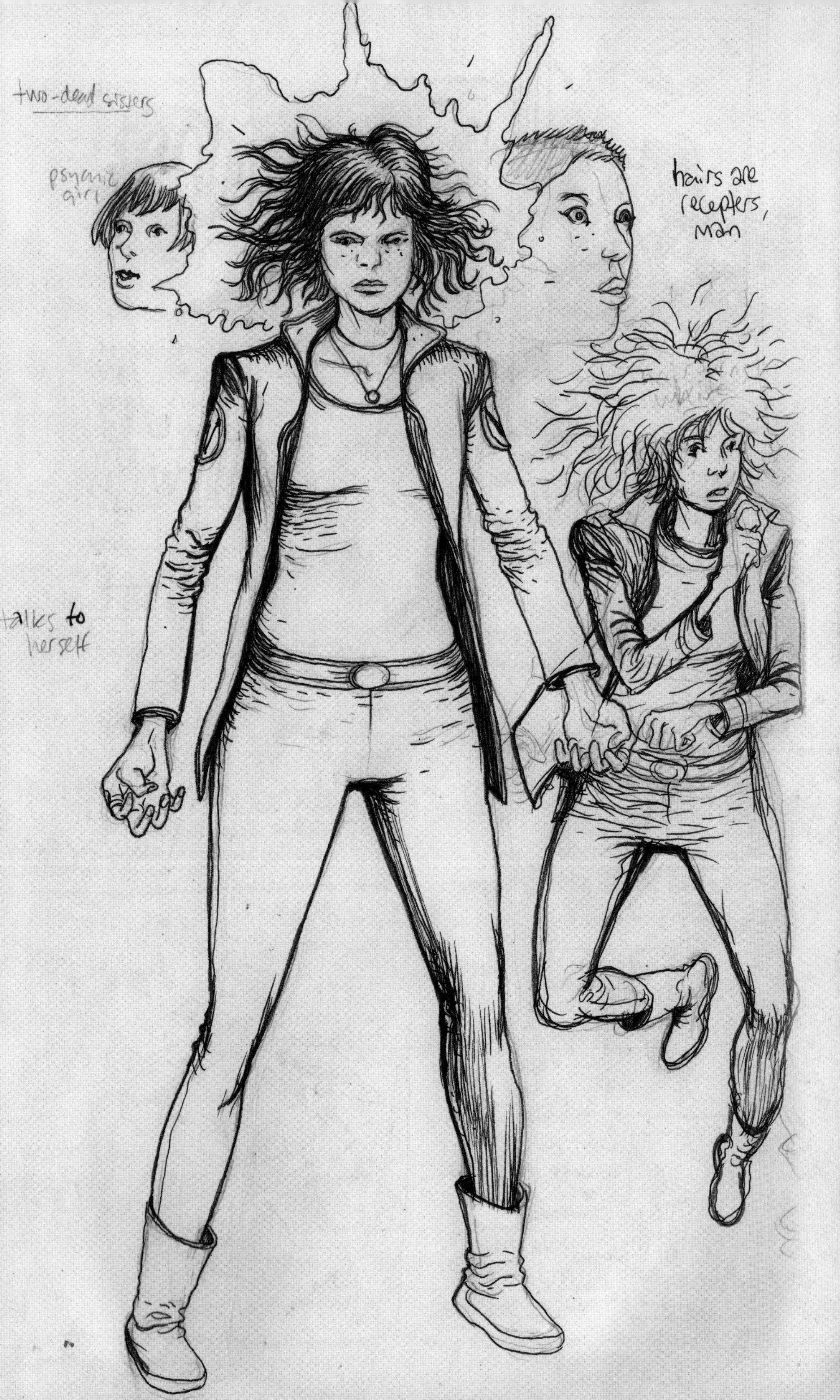
two-dead sisters
psyanic girl
hairs are recepters, man
talks to herself

LeKing Snipes: Expert with mystically charged hellfire pistols.
An evil bug crawled into his ear and transformed him into a horrific
beast, and rather than eat his teammates he ran away.

The following comic, originally published on TOR.com,
is a scene that happens just after the end of THE WRENCHIES.
It was created mostly in a sketchbook with some Photoshop assembly and coloring.

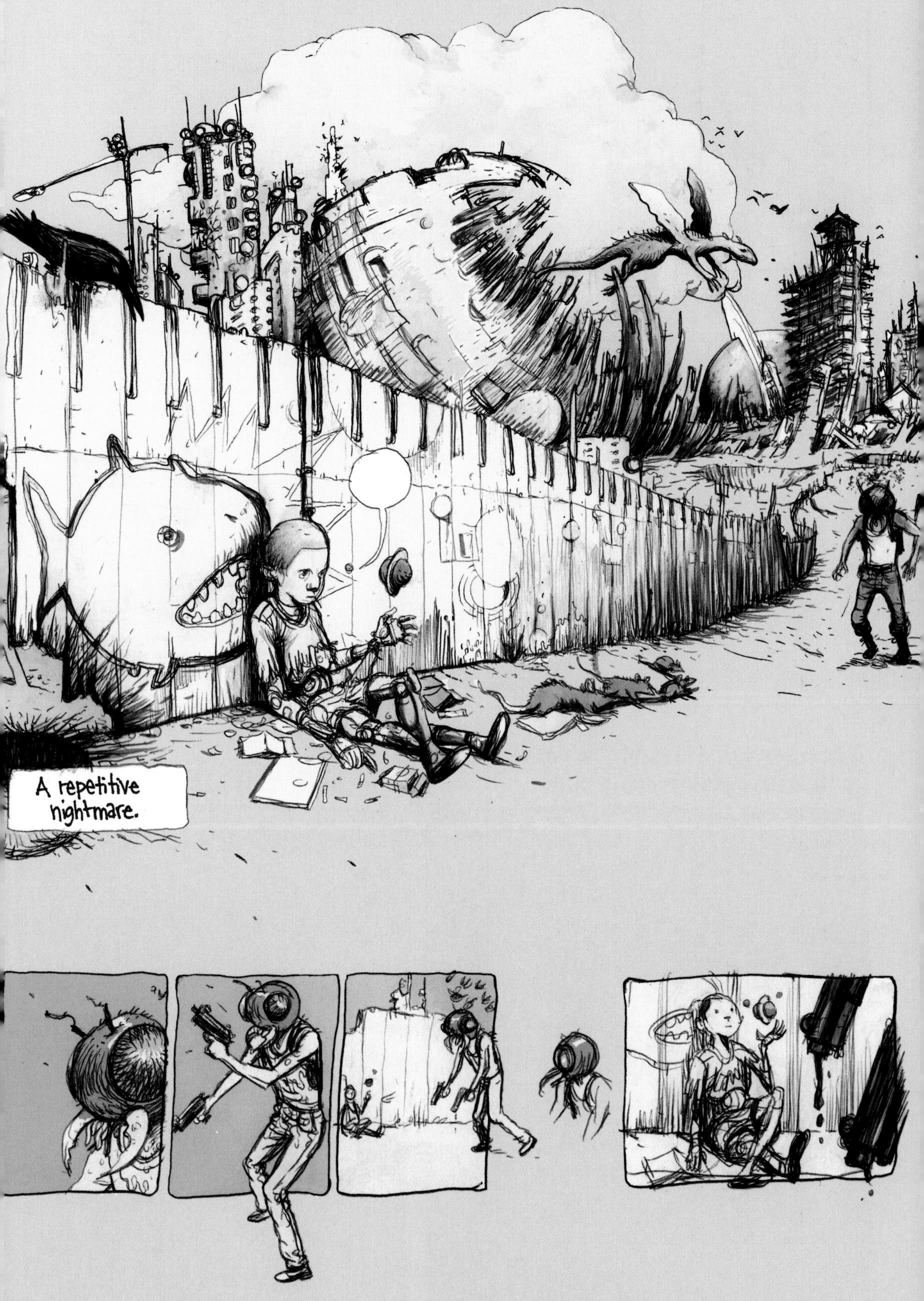
A repetitive nightmare.

Remainder, A 'Wrenchies' tale.

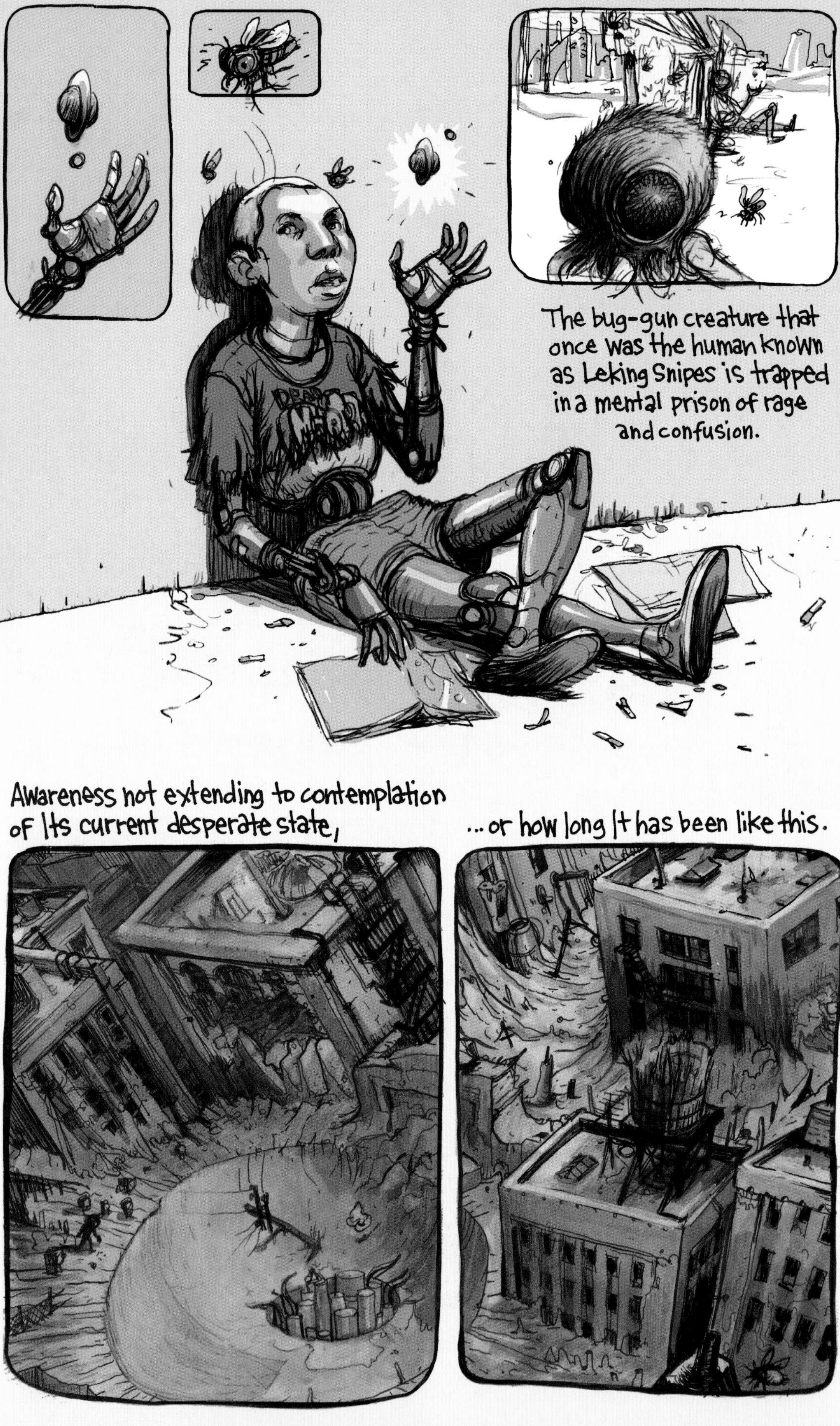
The bug-gun creature that once was the human known as Leking Snipes is trapped in a mental prison of rage and confusion.
Awareness not extending to contemplation of Its current desperate state,
...or how long It has been like this.

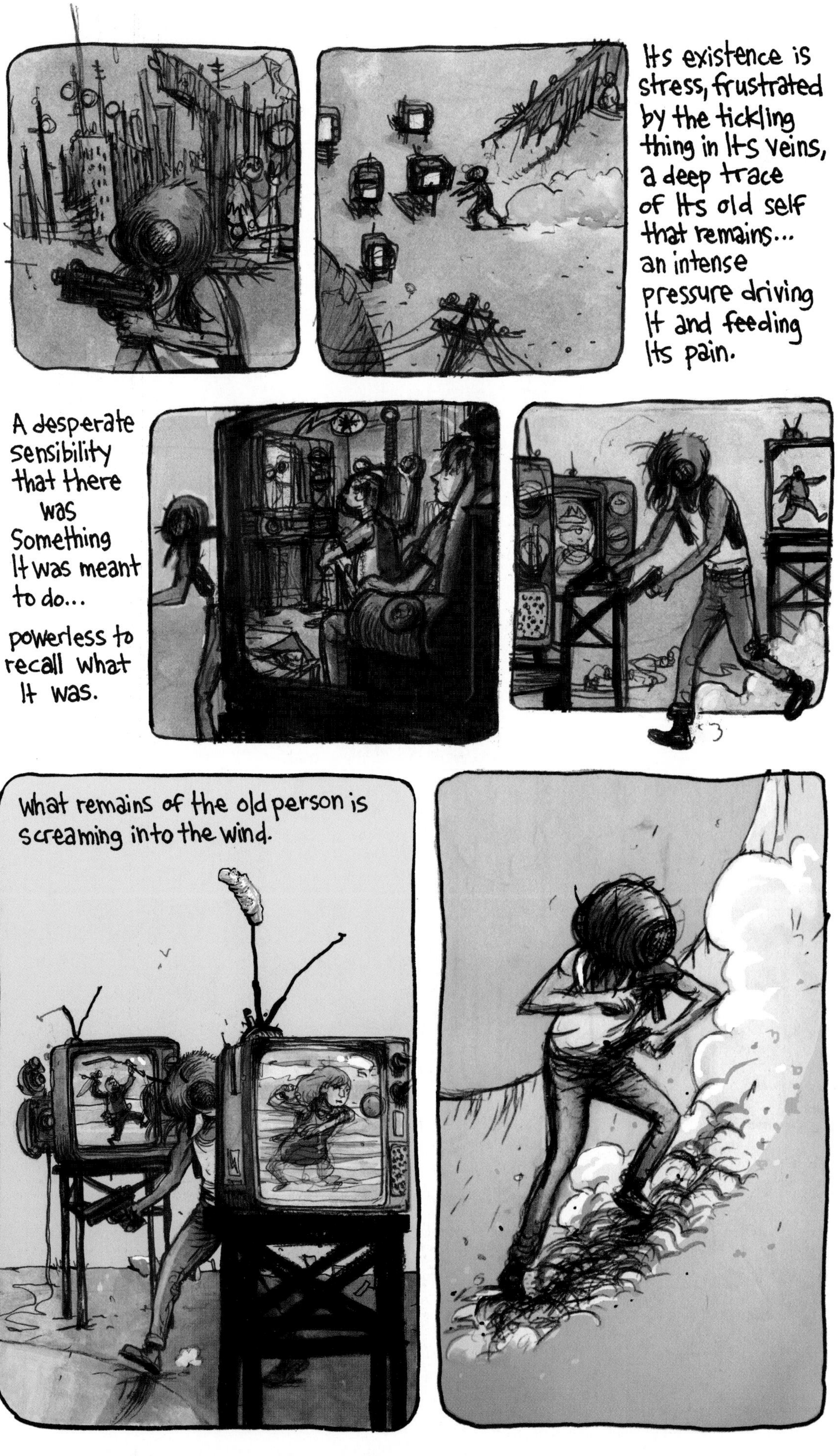
Its existence is stress, frustrated by the tickling thing in Its veins, a deep trace of Its old self that remains... an intense pressure driving It and feeding Its pain.
A desperate sensibility that there was Something It was meant to do...
powerless to recall what It was.
What remains of the old person is screaming into the wind.

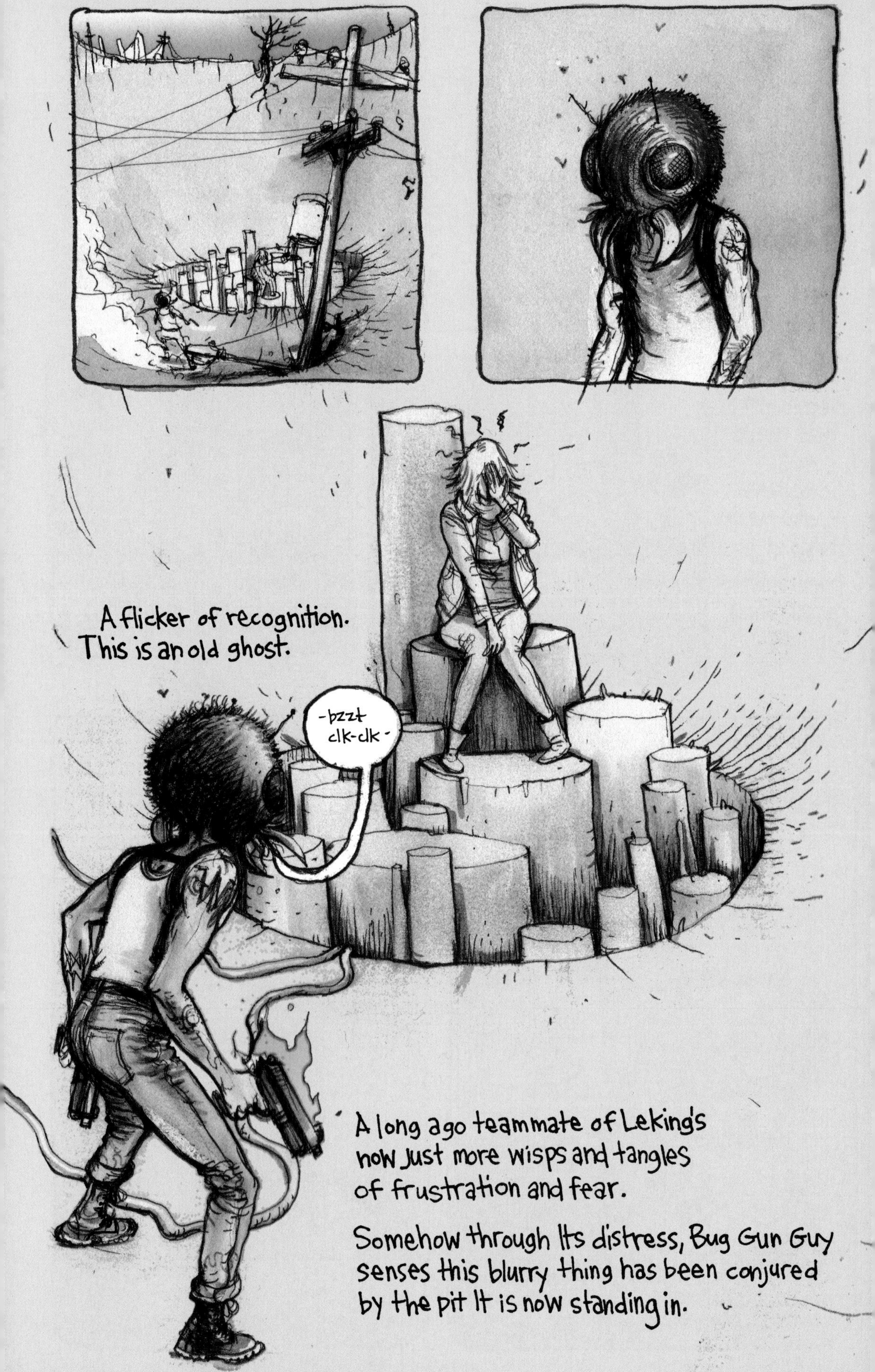
A flicker of recognition.
This is an old ghost.
-bzzt clk-clk-
A long ago teammate of Leking's now just more wisps and tangles of frustration and fear.
Somehow through Its distress, Bug Gun Guy senses this blurry thing has been conjured by the pit It is now standing in.

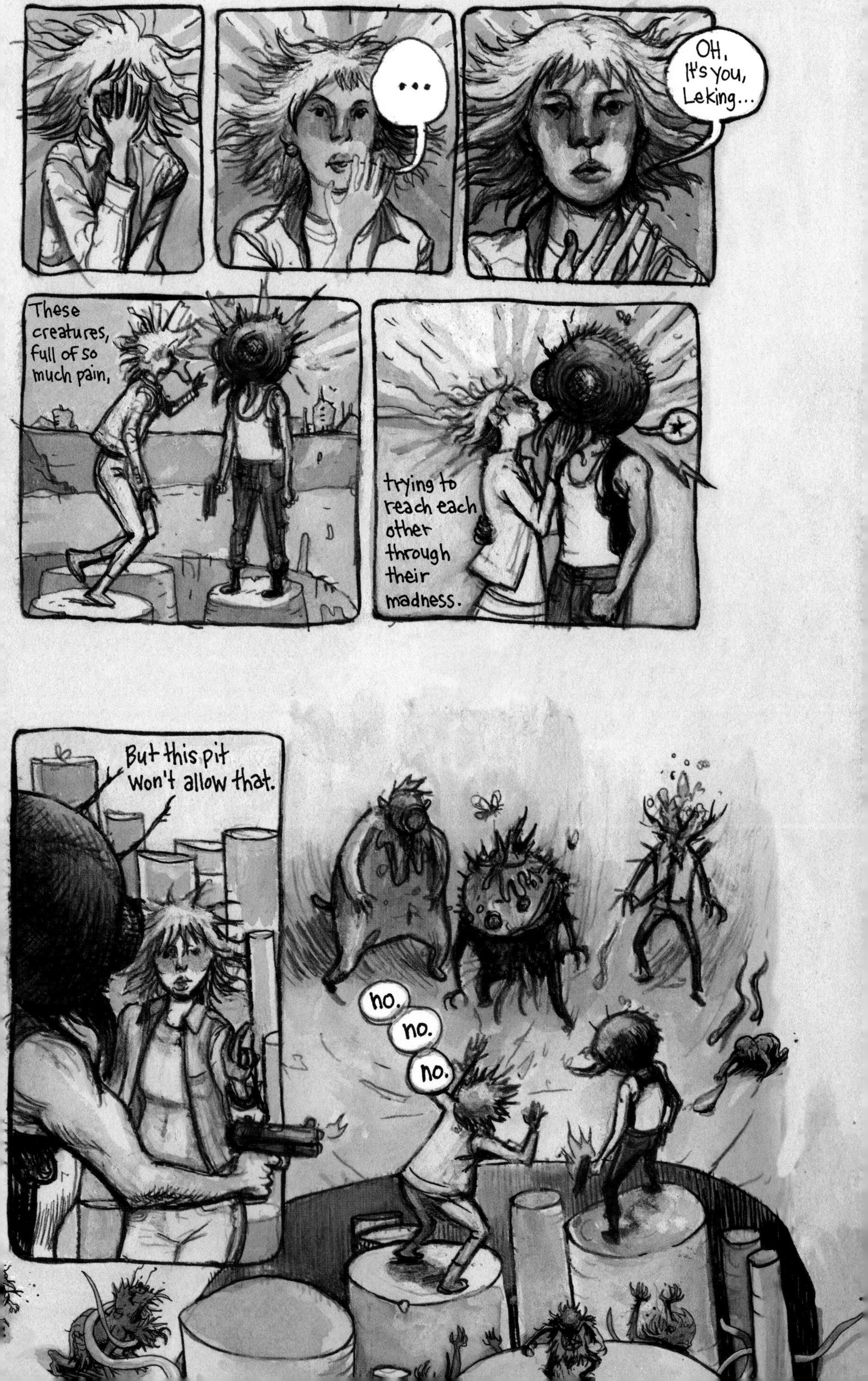
...
OH, It's you, Leking...
These creatures, full of so much pain,
trying to reach each other through their madness.
But this pit won't allow that.
no.
no.
no.

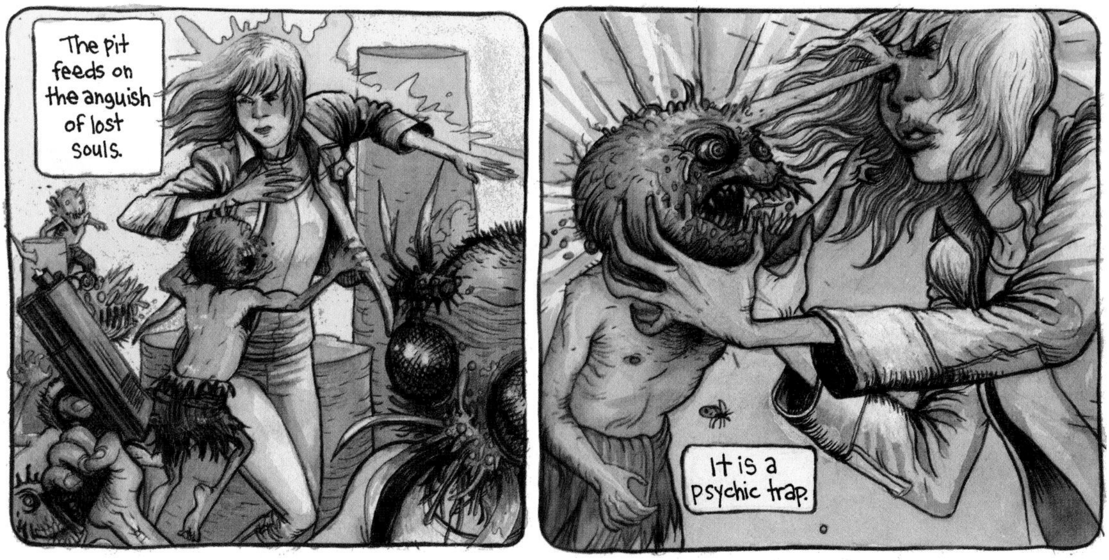
The pit feeds on the anguish of lost souls.
It is a psychic trap.

The bug creature feels like this has all happened many times before, finding momentary relief from the despair of this existence by engaging in violent conflict.

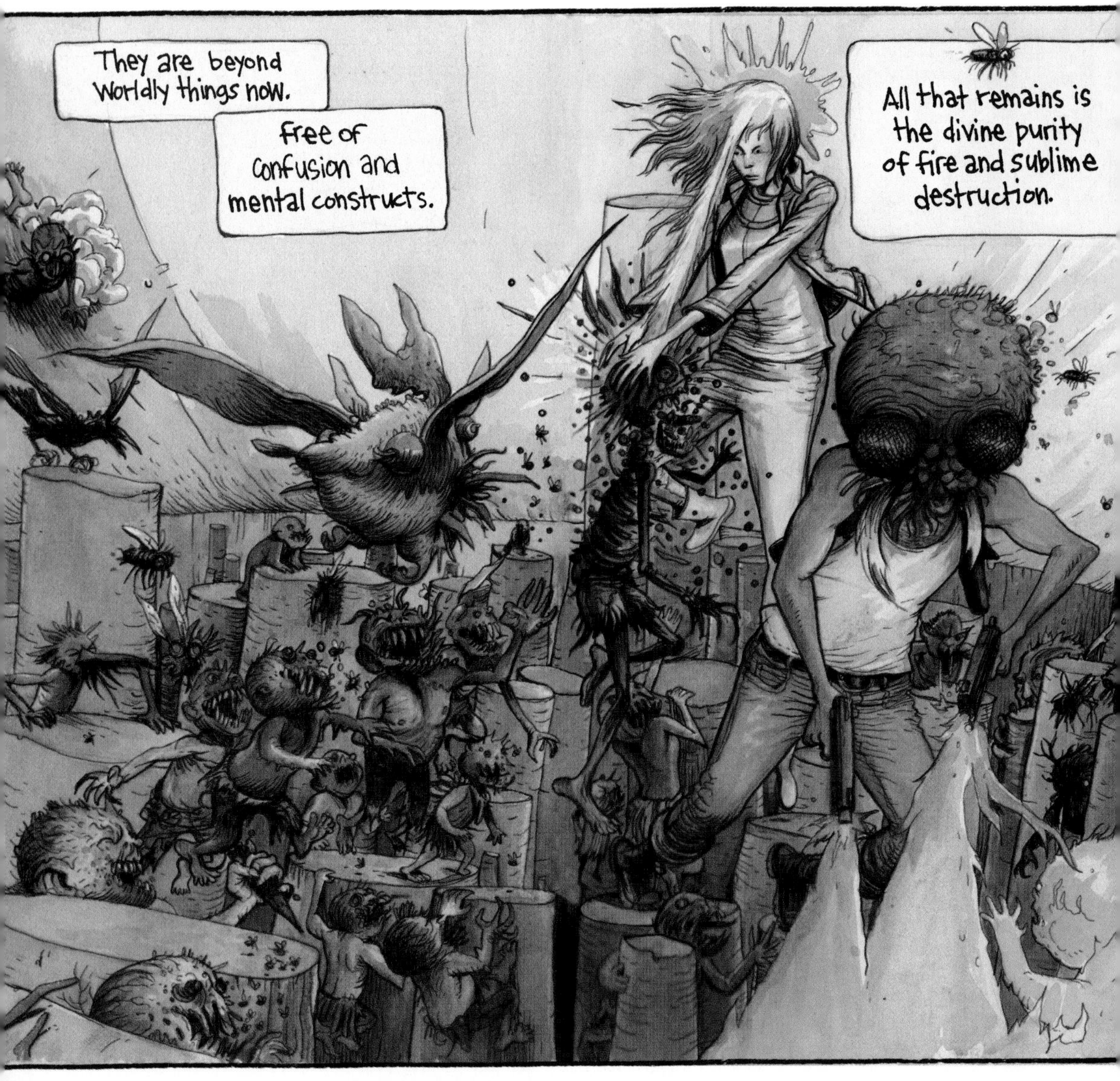
They are beyond worldly things now.
Free of confusion and mental constructs.
All that remains is the divine purity of fire and sublime destruction.

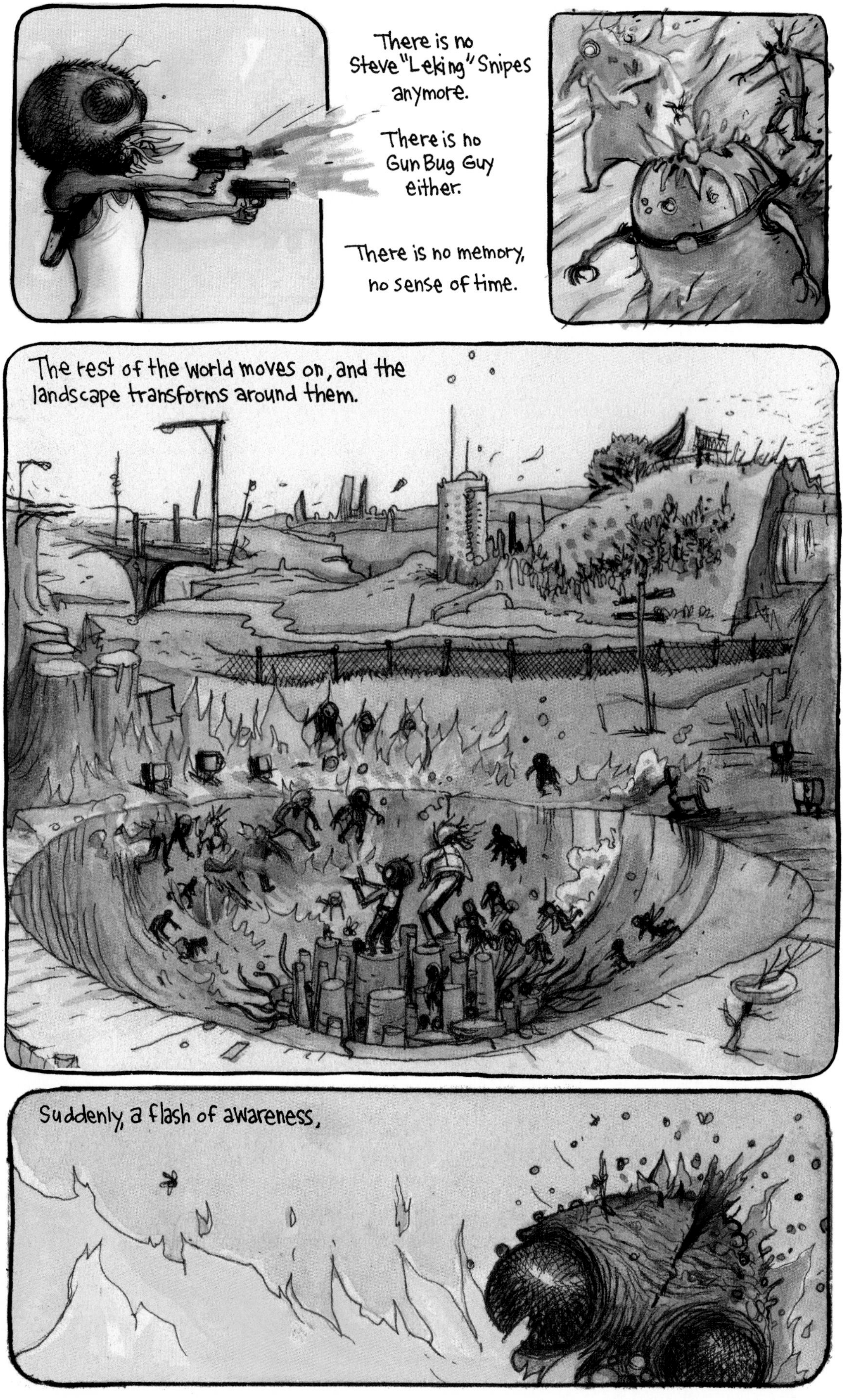
There is no Steve "Leking" Snipes anymore.
There is no Gun Bug Guy either.
There is no memory, no sense of time.
The rest of the world moves on, and the landscape transforms around them.
Suddenly, a flash of awareness,

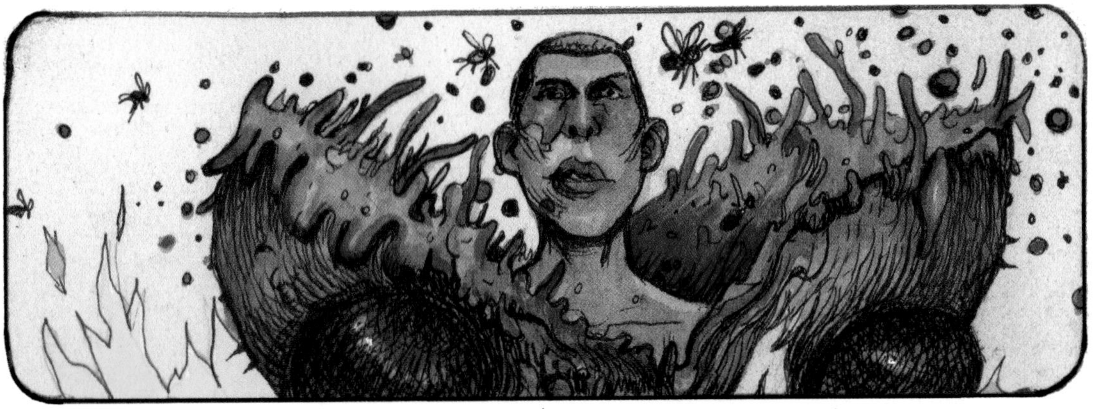

The Sight of the ancient boat resonates, and triggers more specters from Leking's old life.

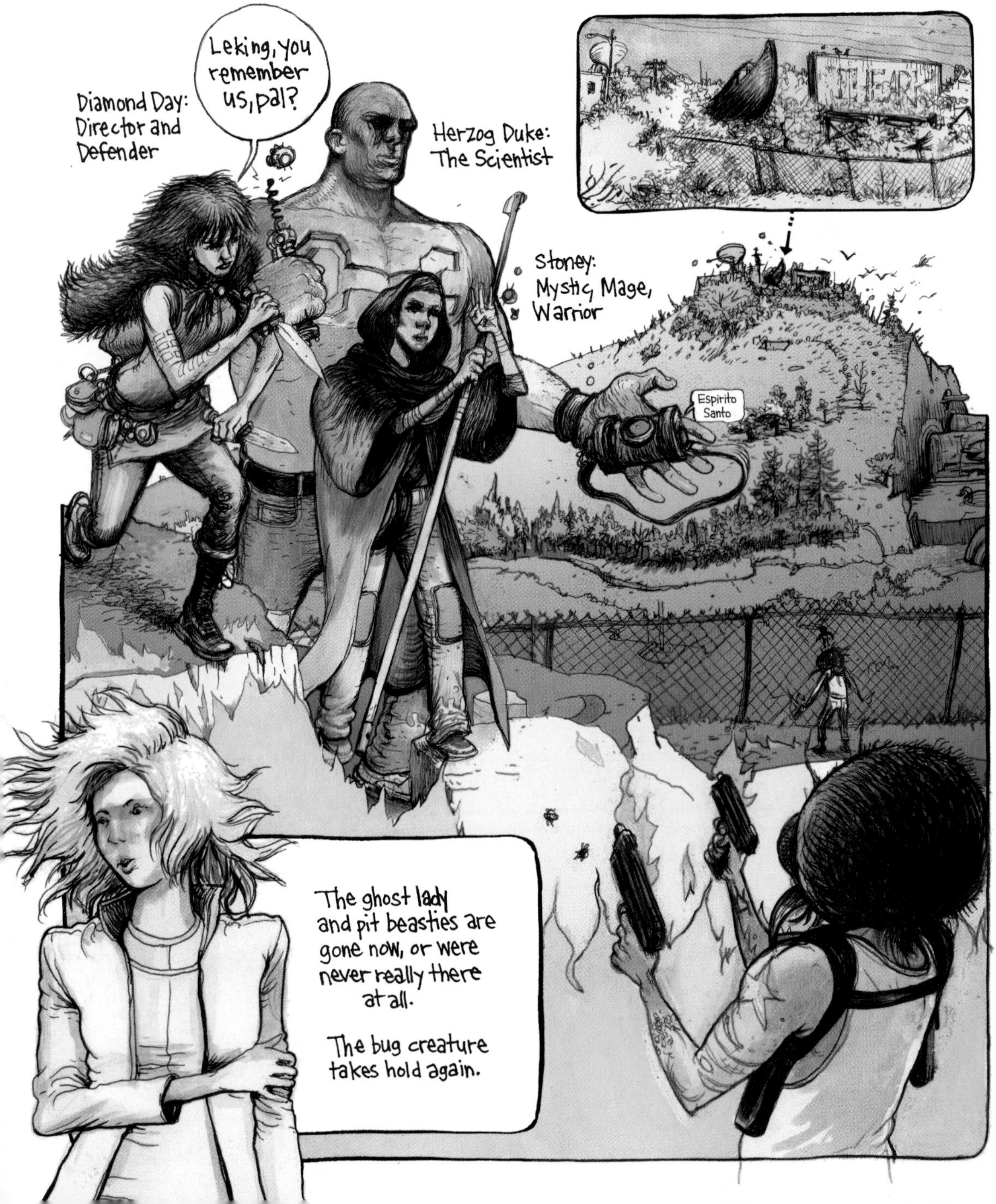

Diamond Day:
Director and
Defender
Leking, you remember us, pal?
Herzog Duke:
The Scientist
Stoney:
Mystic, Mage,
Warrior
Espirito Santo
The ghost lady and pit beasties are gone now, or were never really there at all.
The bug creature takes hold again.

The terror hits It again, and It must Flee.

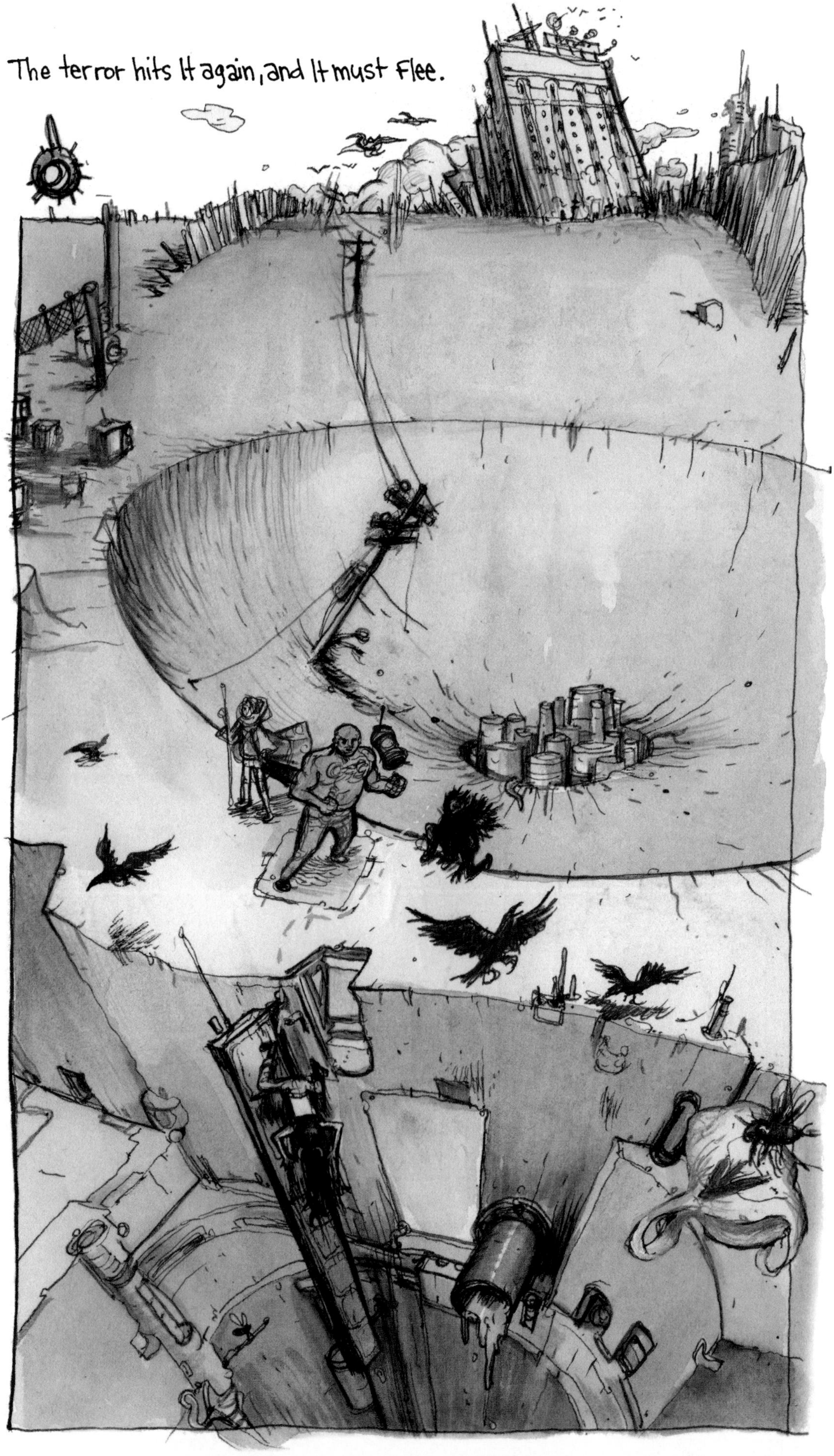

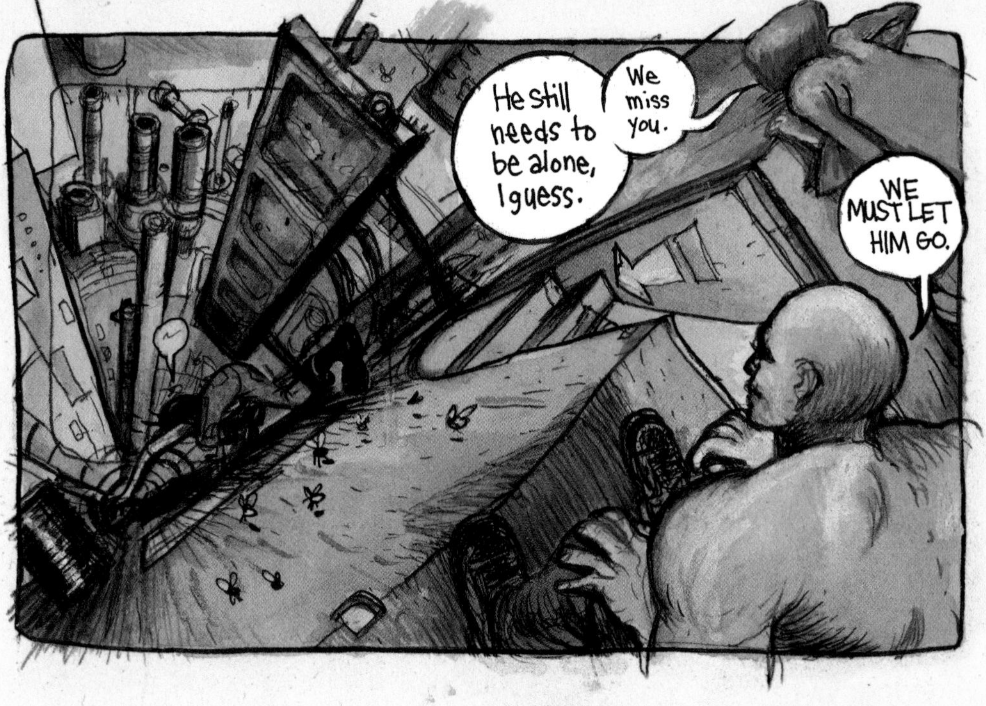
He still needs to be alone, I guess.
We miss you.
WE MUST LET HIM GO.

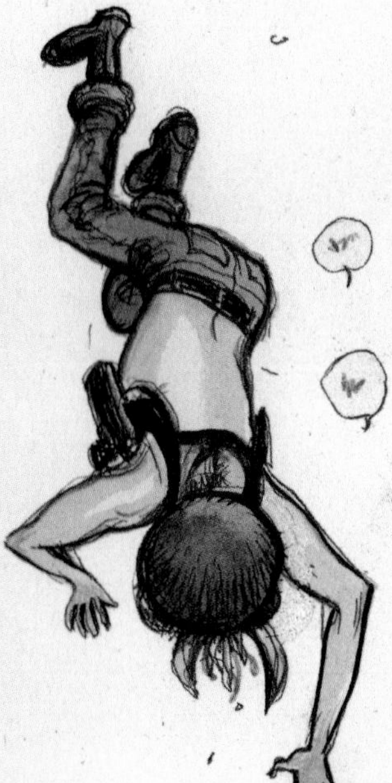

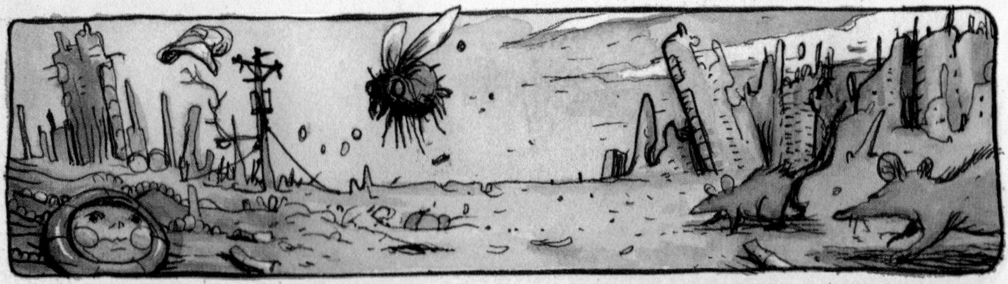

We see it through in time.

Stoney is another character inspired by *OVER THE EDGE*.
She is the mystical misguided counselor of the group.

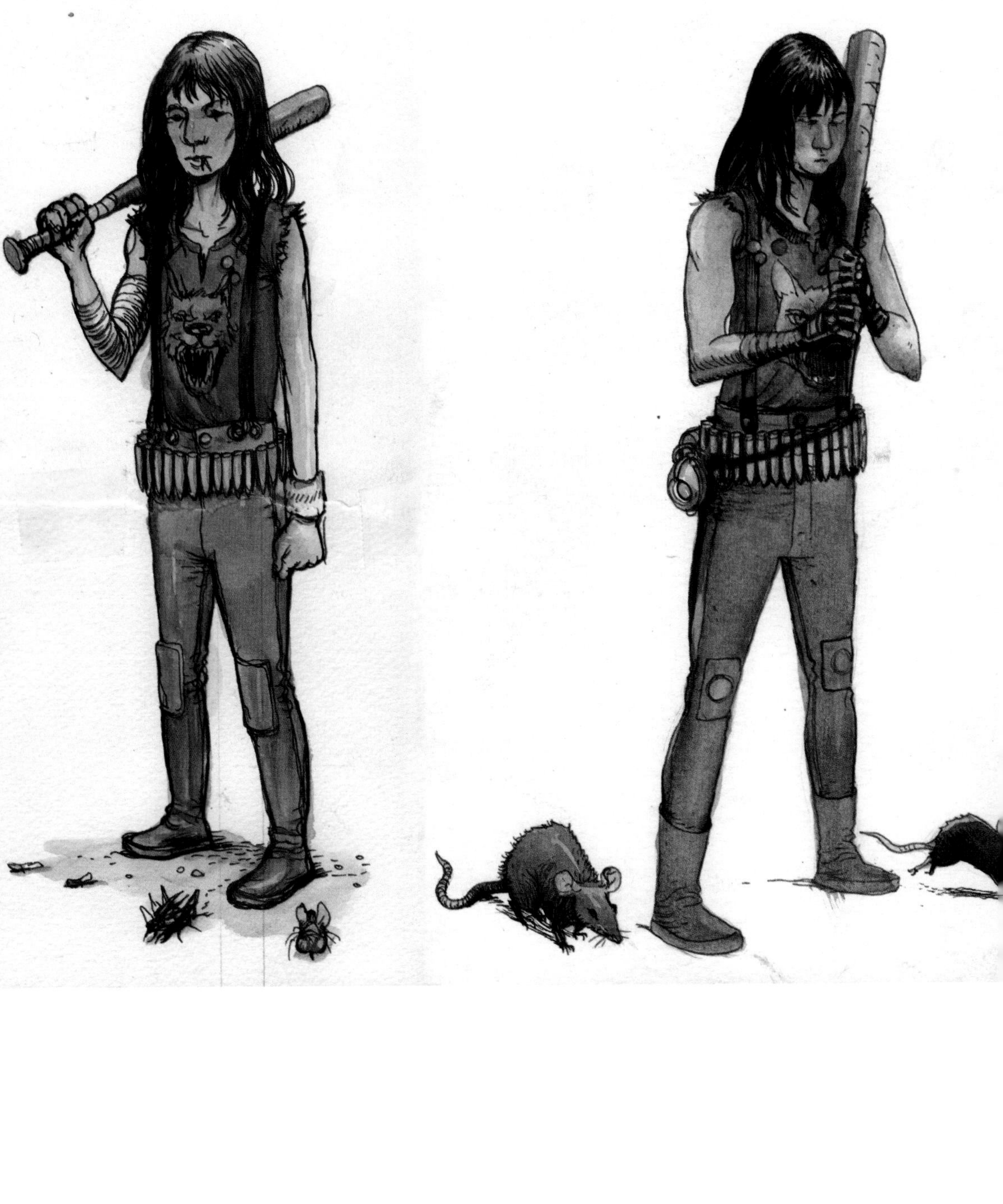

Jad is the cool and charismatic leader of the young Wrenchies,
big brother to Tad, and future husband to Spectarla.

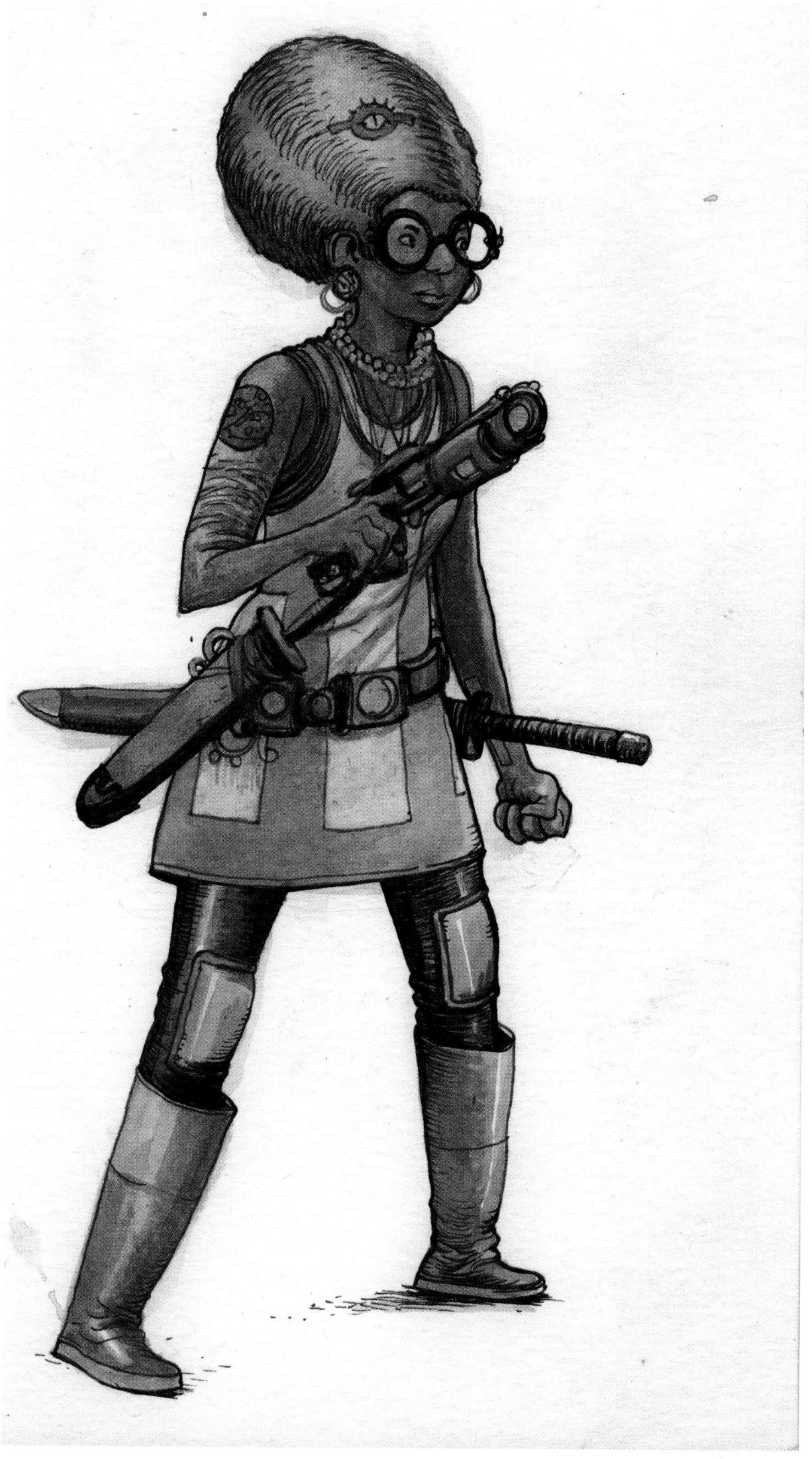

Spectarla Sabina is Shakey's cool and sarcastic older sister.

The Scientist

Herzog Duke has golem-like body of that contains the brain of a 21st-century scientist who transferred his consciousness from his old frail body to this new powerful and seemingly immortal one. He constructed the body during his imprisonment on Proxima Centauri, where he also first met the teenage Sherwood Breadcoat.

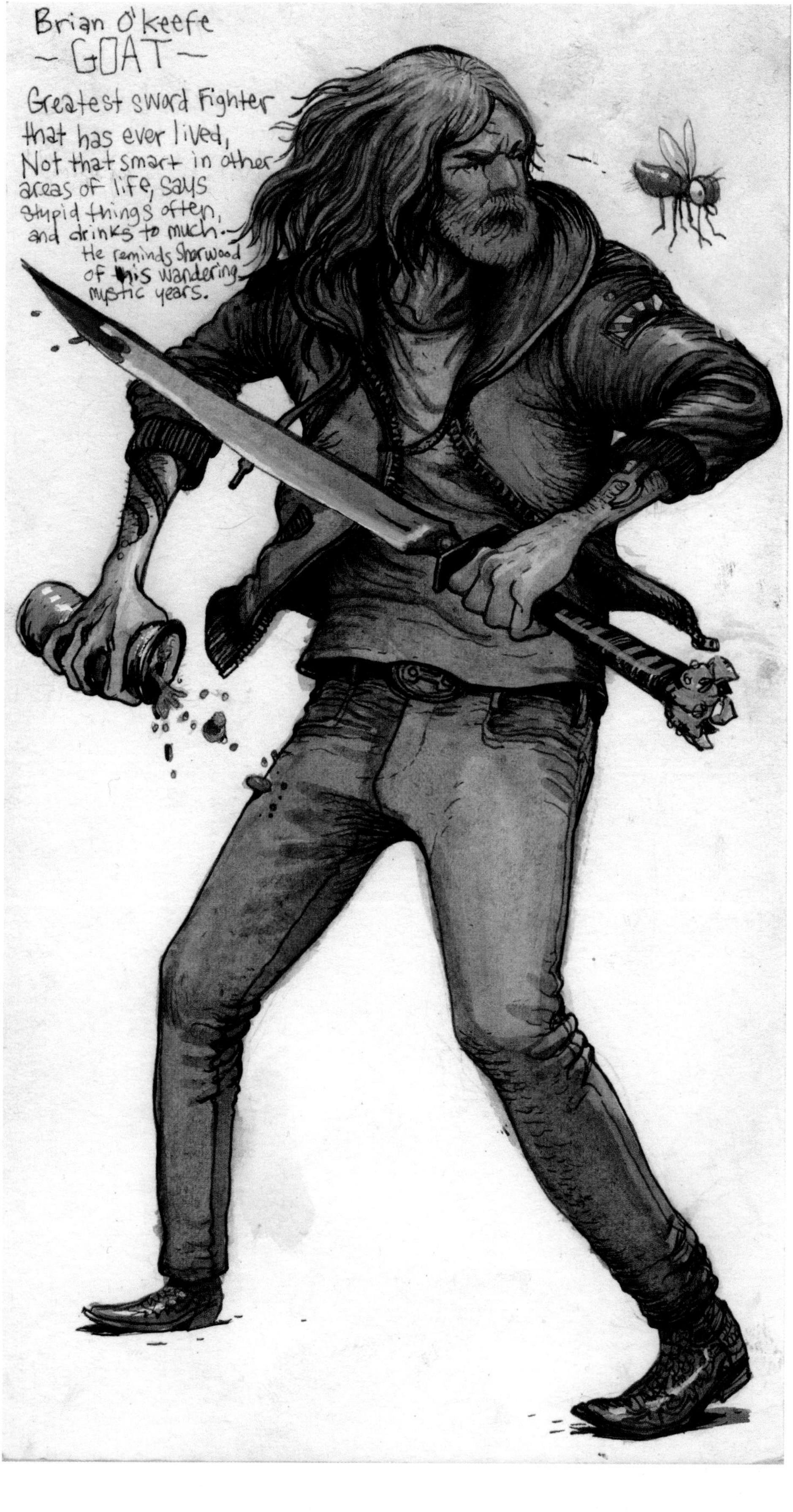
Brian O'Keefe
~ GOAT ~
Greatest sword Fighter that has ever lived, Not that smart in other areas of life, says stupid things often, and drinks to much.
He reminds Sherwood of his wandering mystic years.

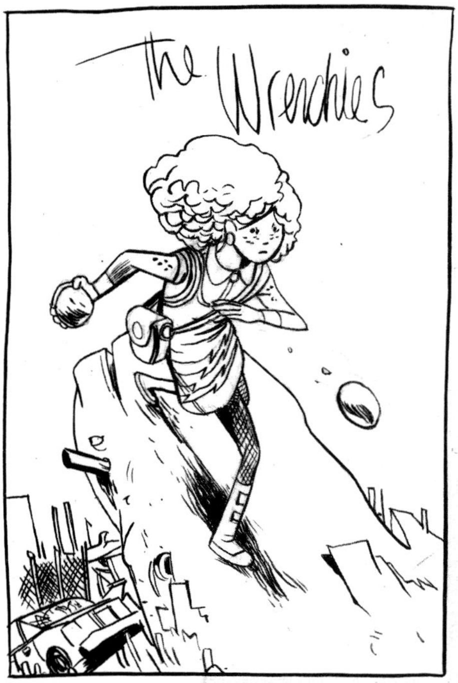
The Wrenchies

Marci is really good at throwing rocks and wisecracks. Her future self is a ghost named Parasol that is a friend to the teenage Sherwood Breadcoat.

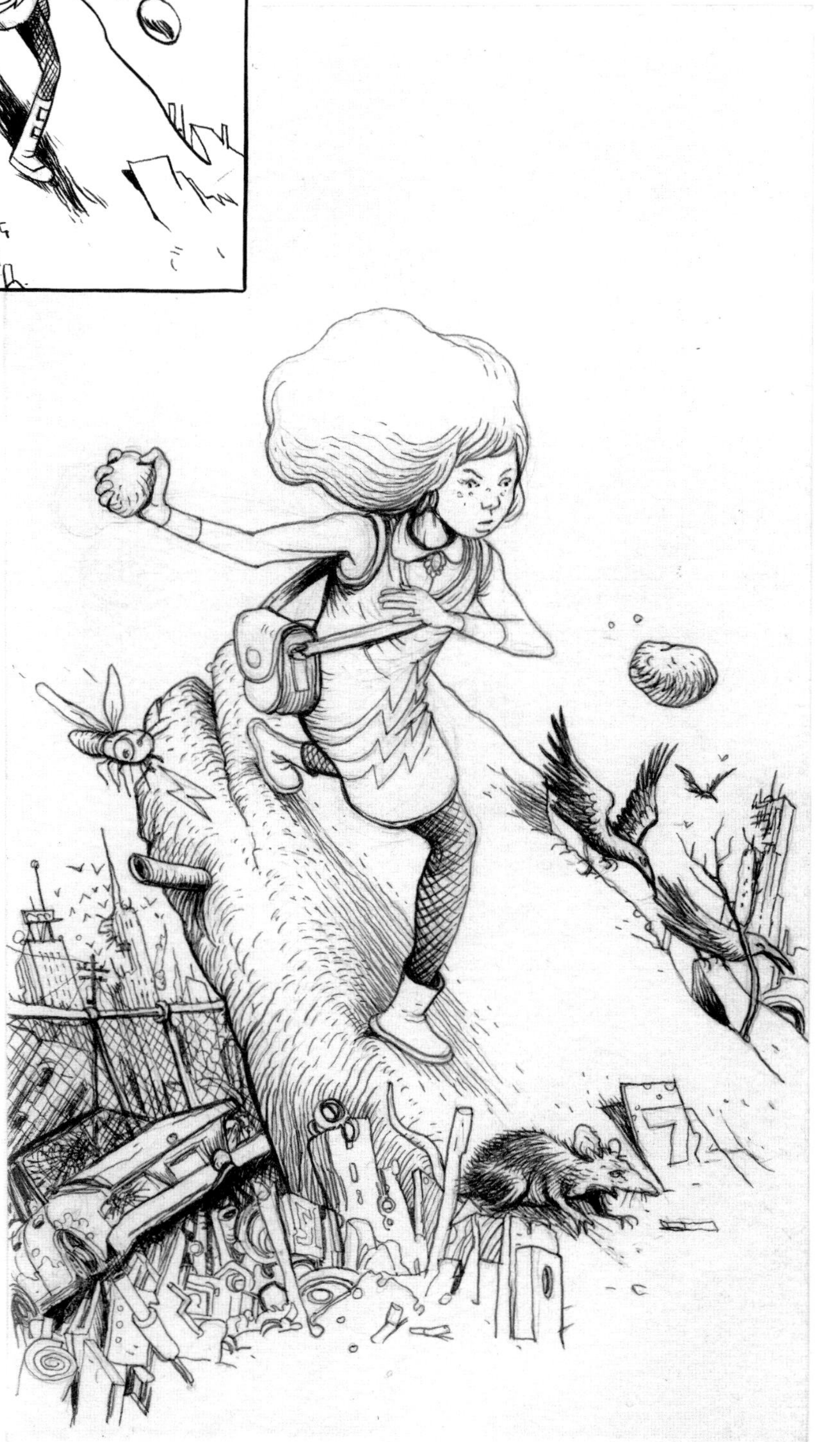

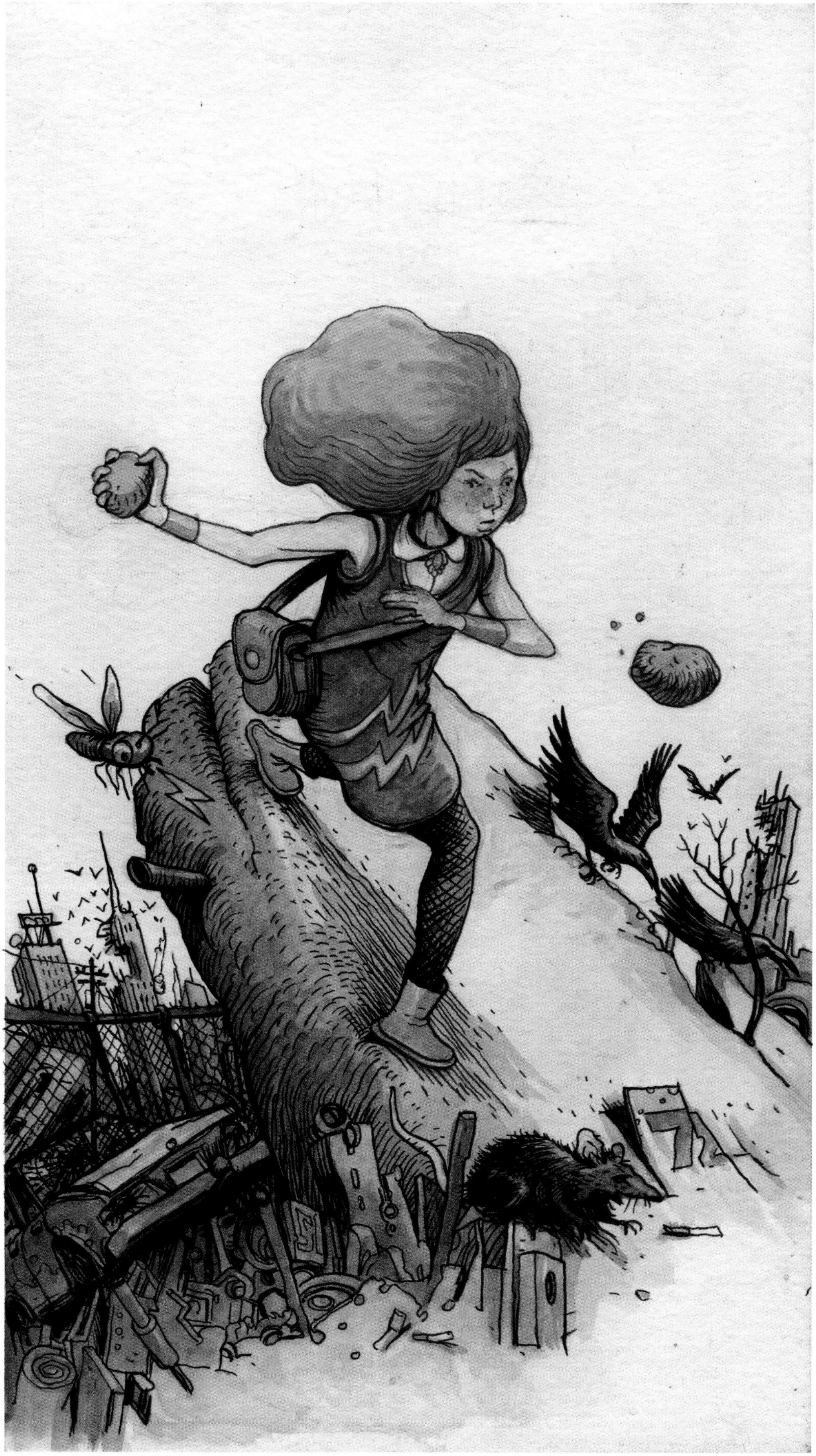
7

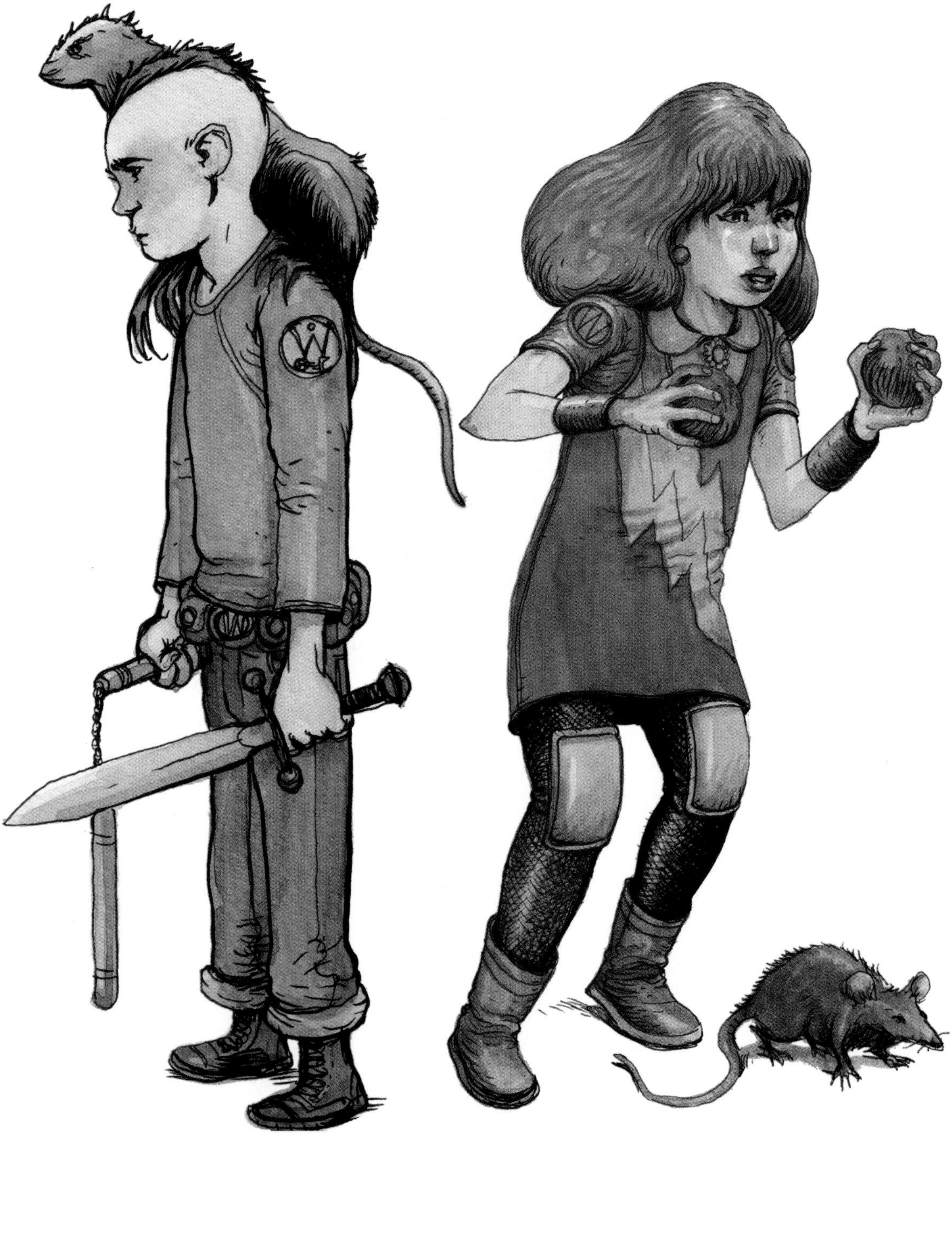

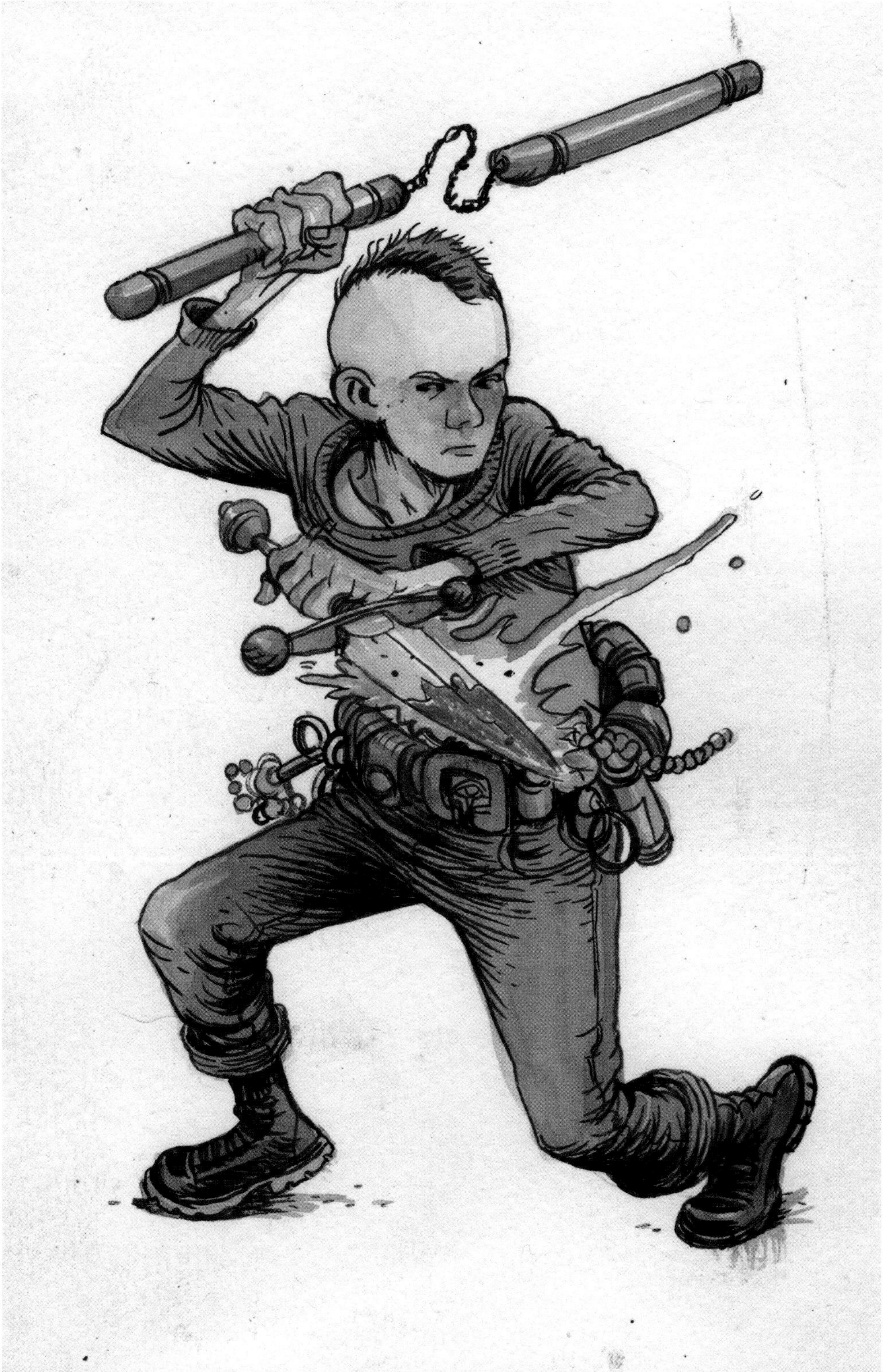

Bance is silent and serious, he is the best fighter out of all the Wenchies, young and old.

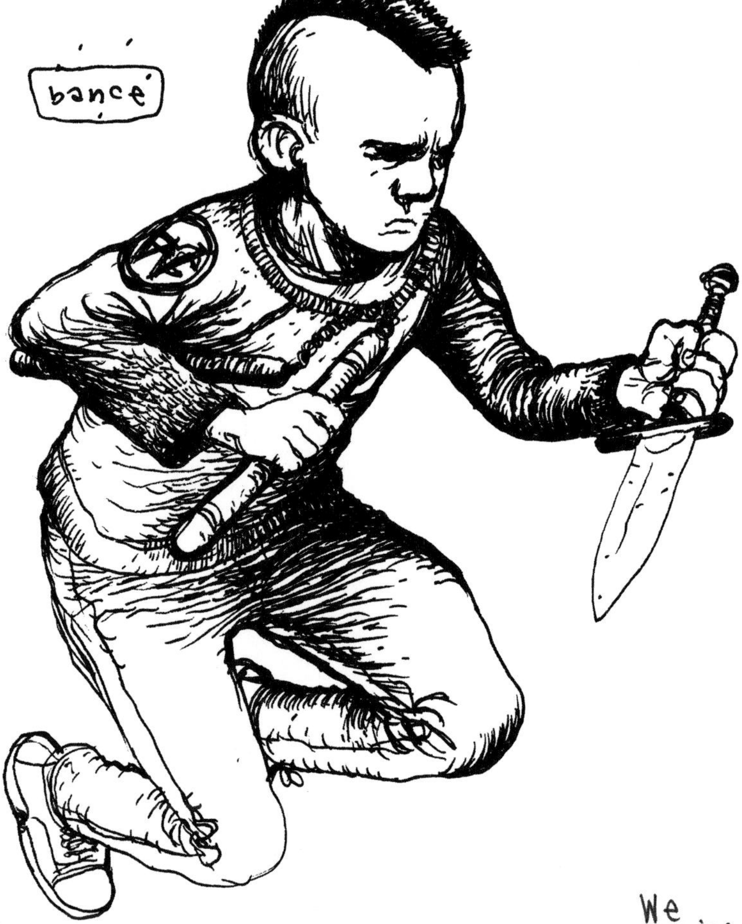
bance

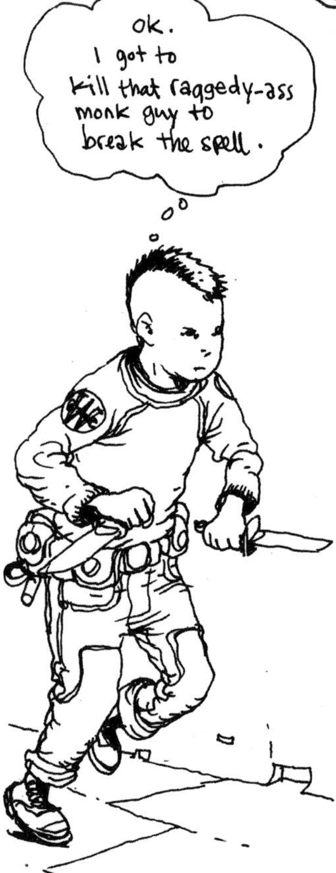
ok.
I got to
kill that raggedy-ass
monk guy to
break the spell.

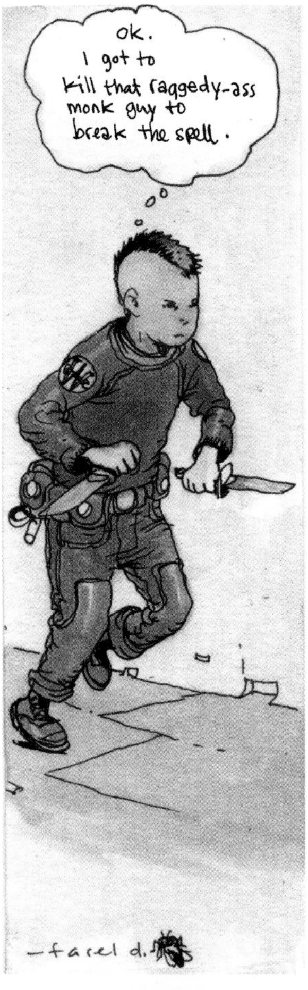
ok.
I got to
kill that raggedy-ass
monk guy to
break the spell.
-farel d.

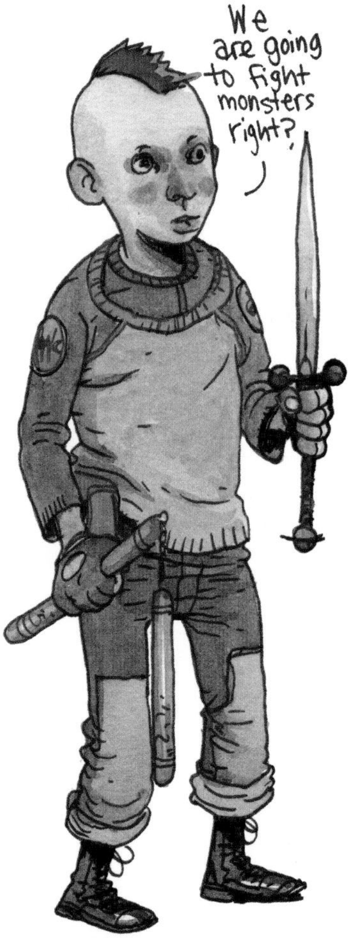
We
are going
to fight
monsters
right?

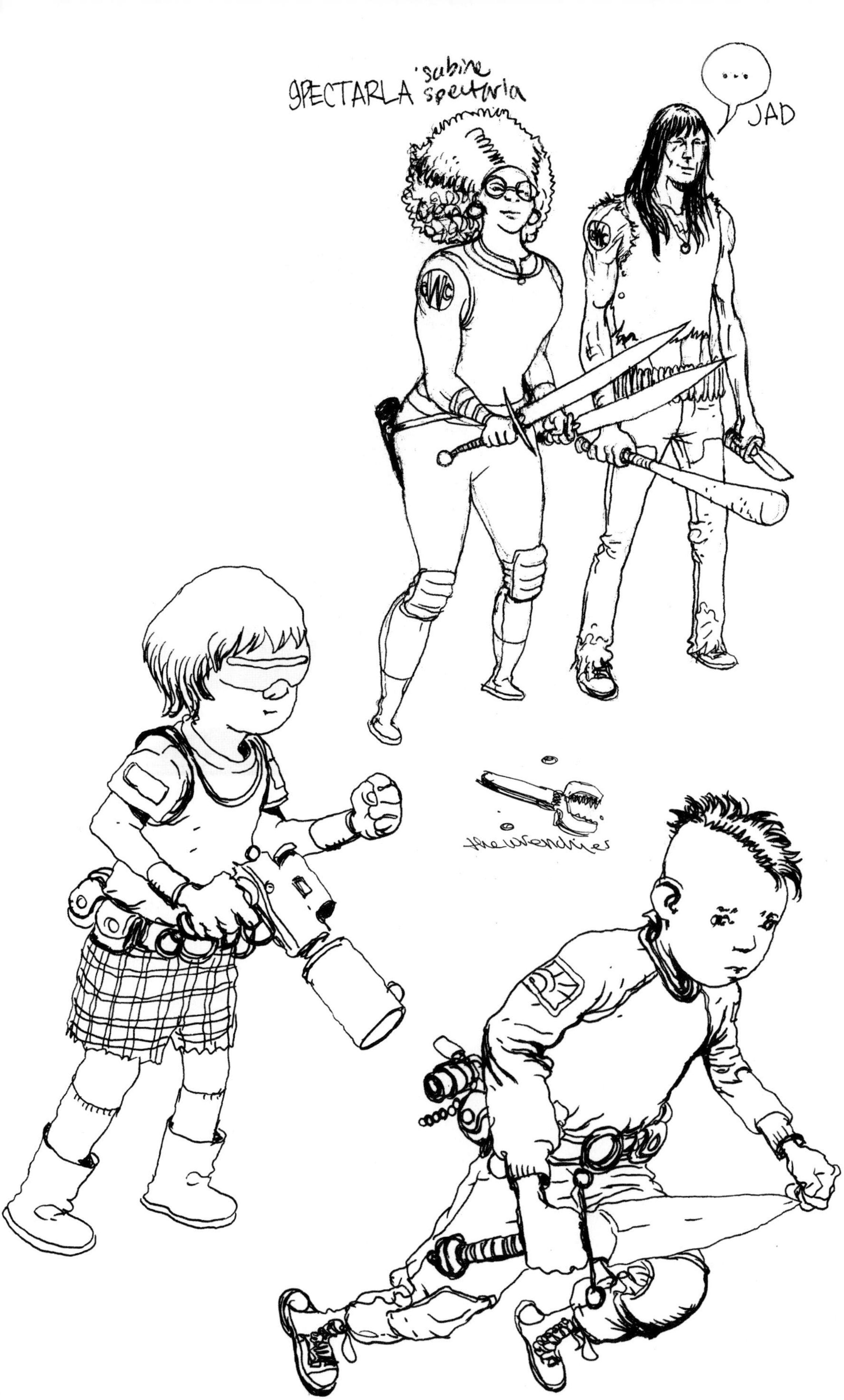
SPECTARLA
'sabine spectarla
...
JAD
the wrenchies

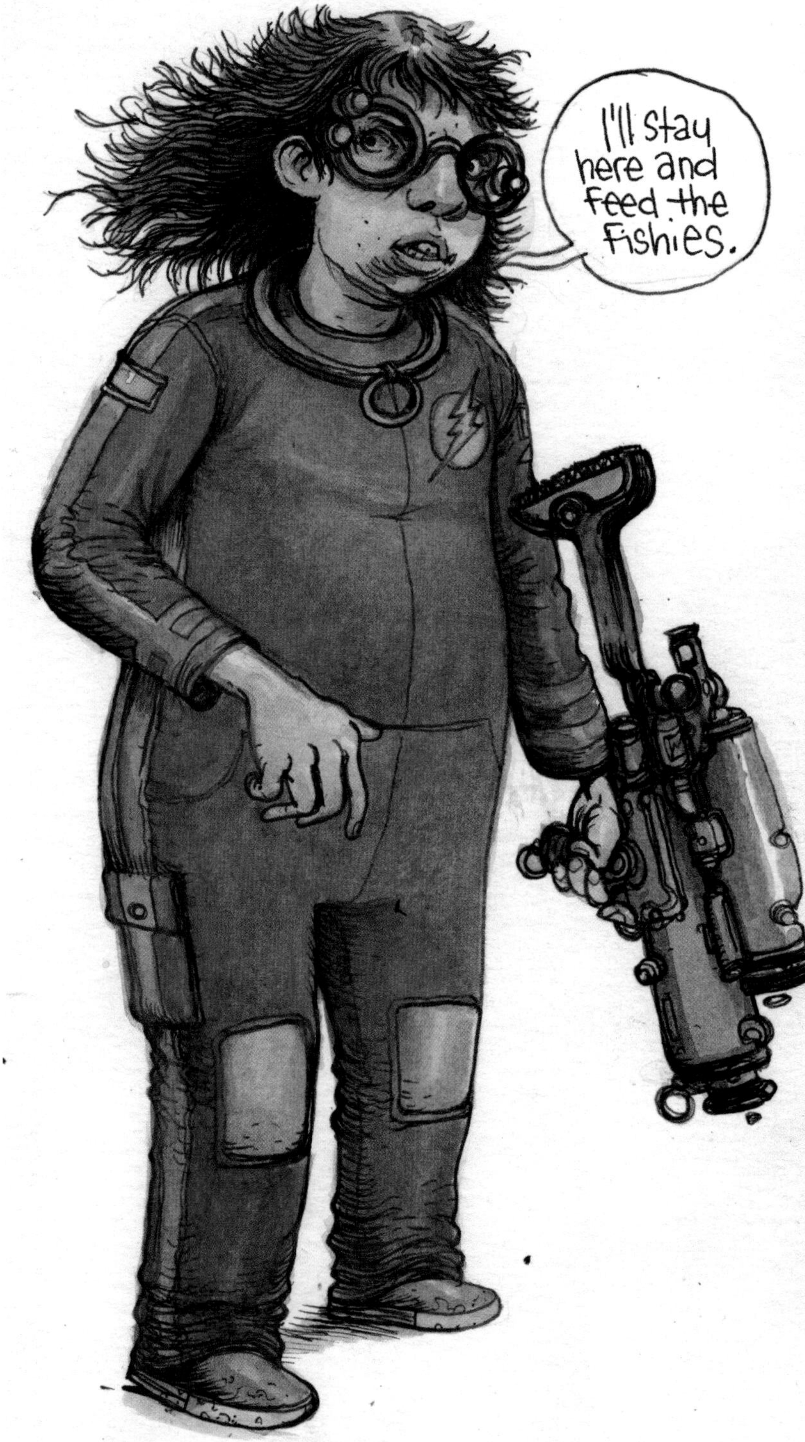
I'll stay here and feed the fishies.

Olweyez is nearly as smart and capable as the
Scientist but has no taste for adventure or heroics.

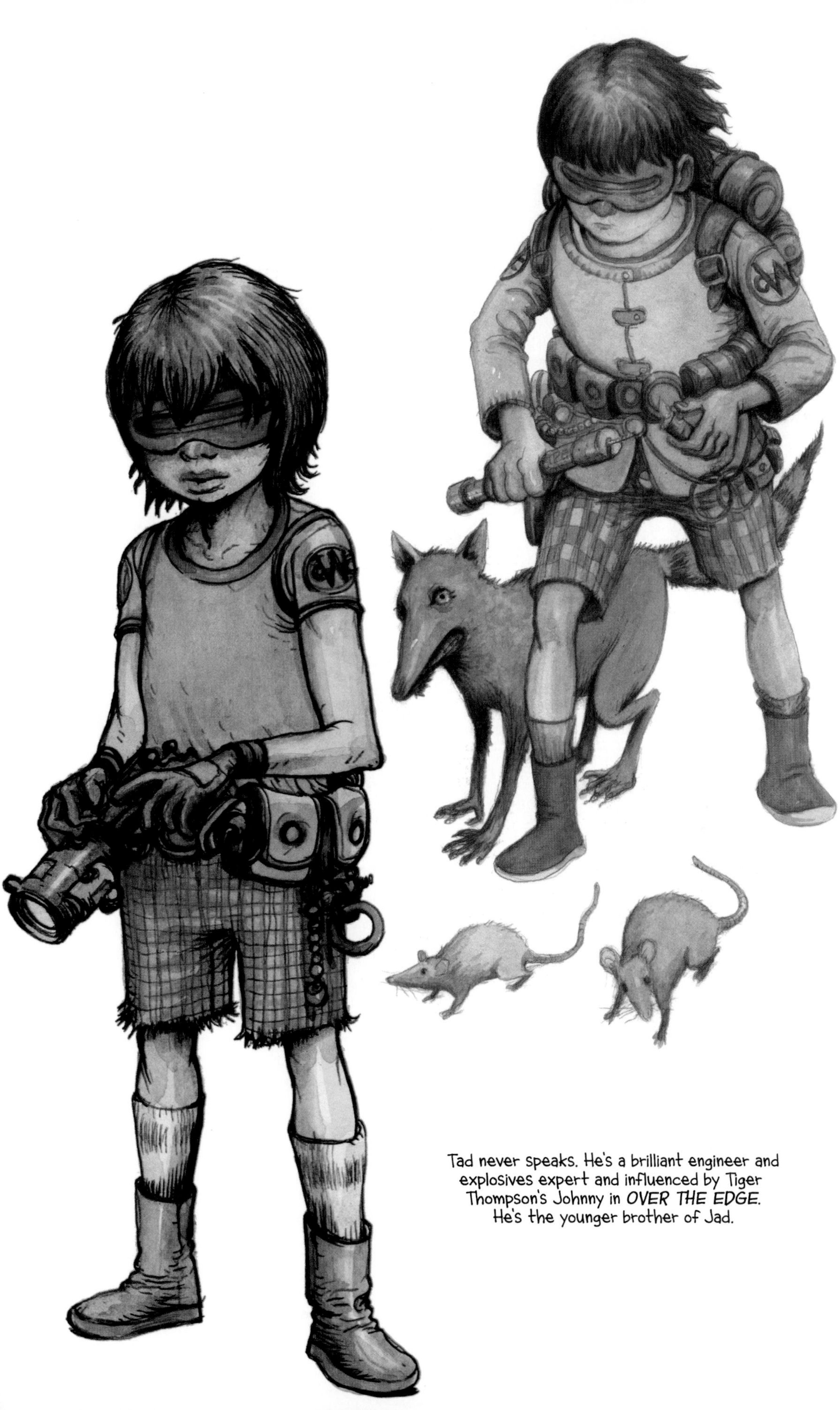

Tad never speaks. He's a brilliant engineer and explosives expert and influenced by Tiger Thompson's Johnny in *OVER THE EDGE*. He's the younger brother of Jad.

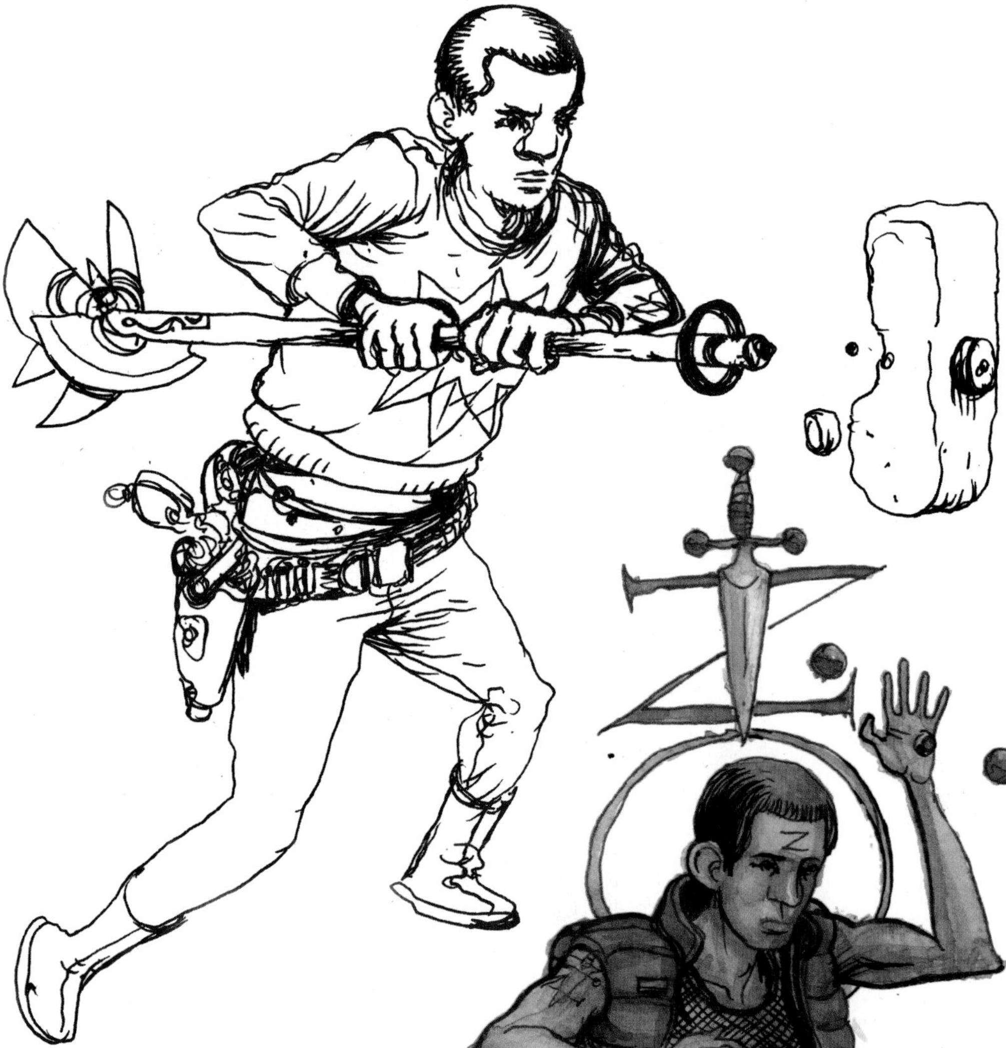

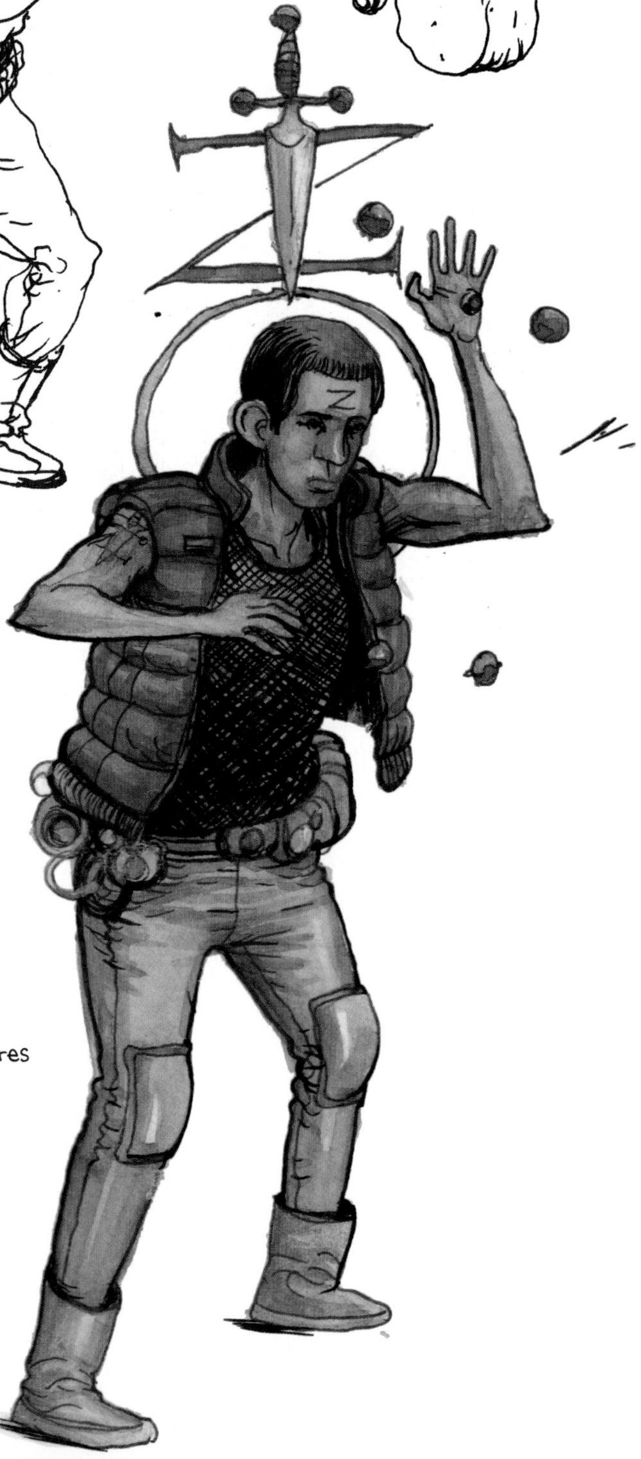

Shakey is a real wizard and has magical spheres that will do whatever he wants them to.

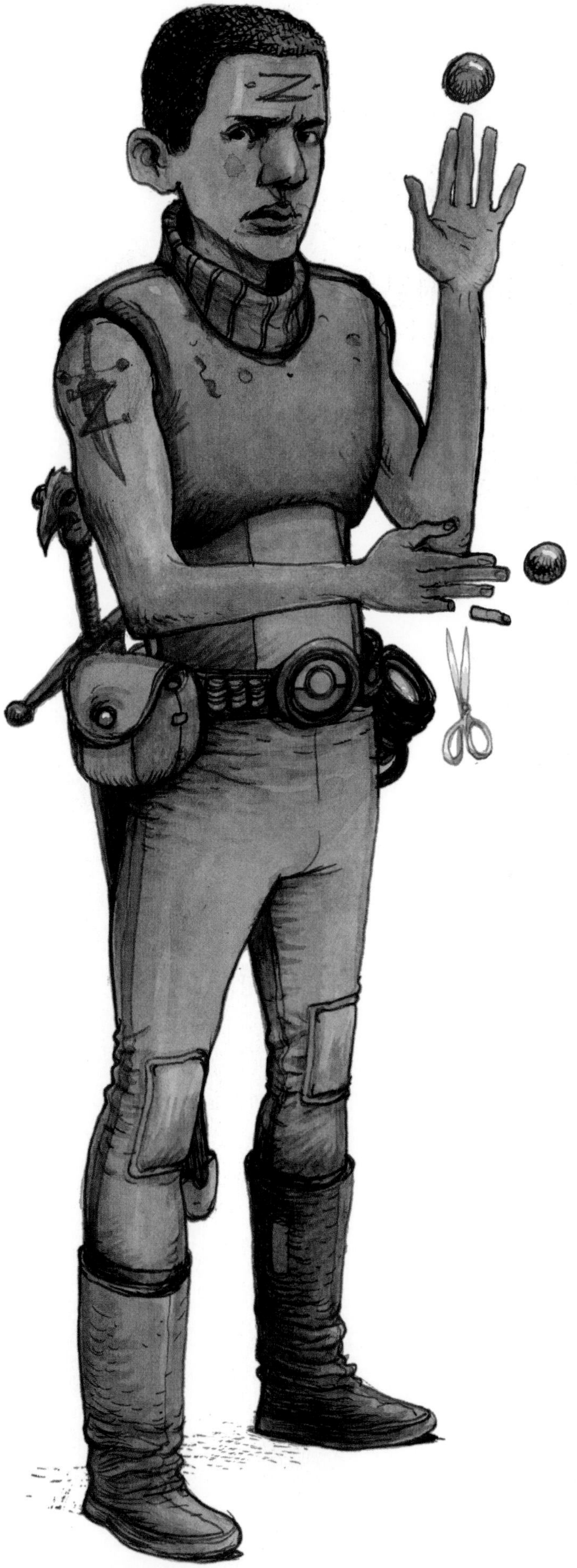

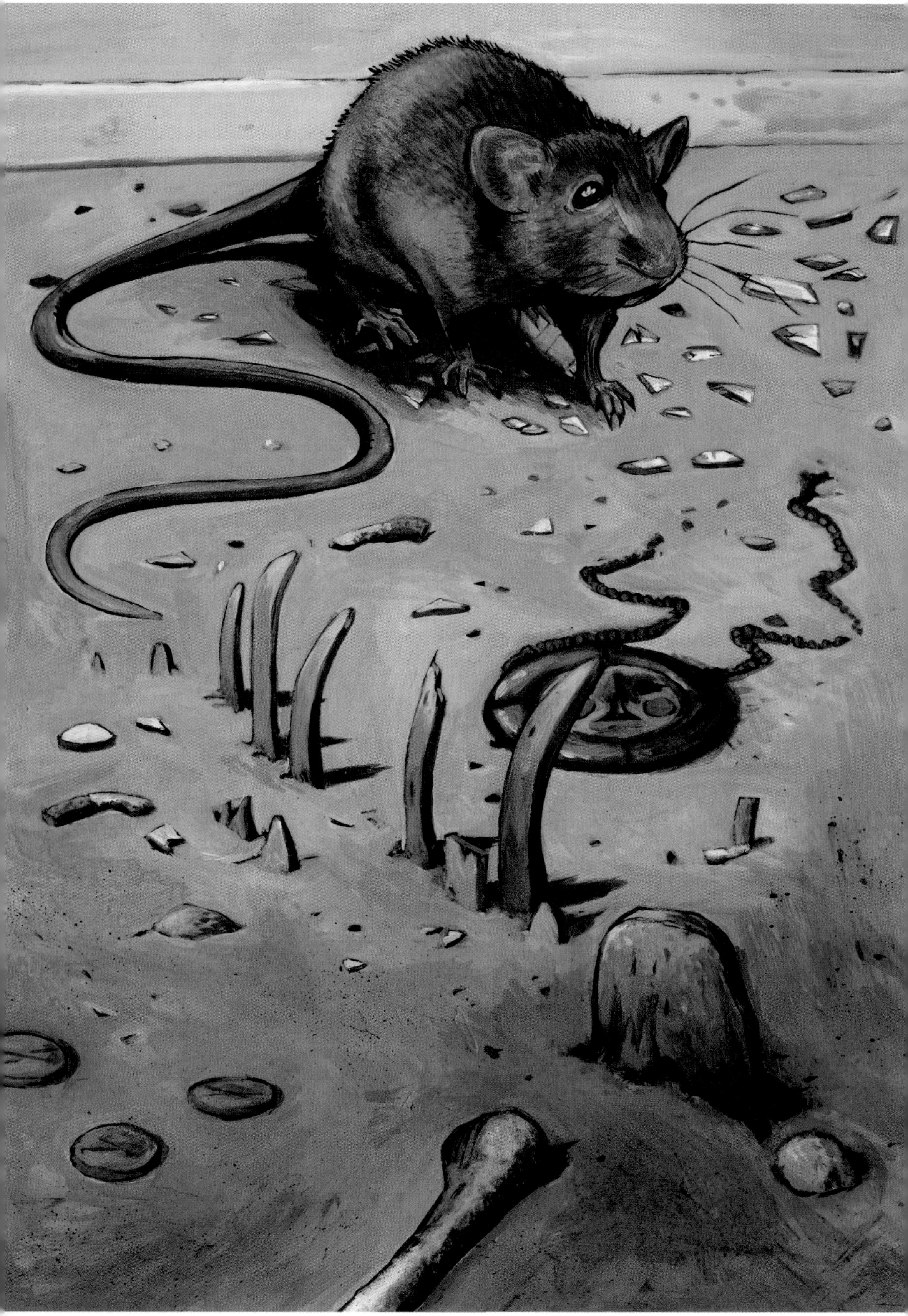

Hollis and Sherwood were
once neighbors and friends.

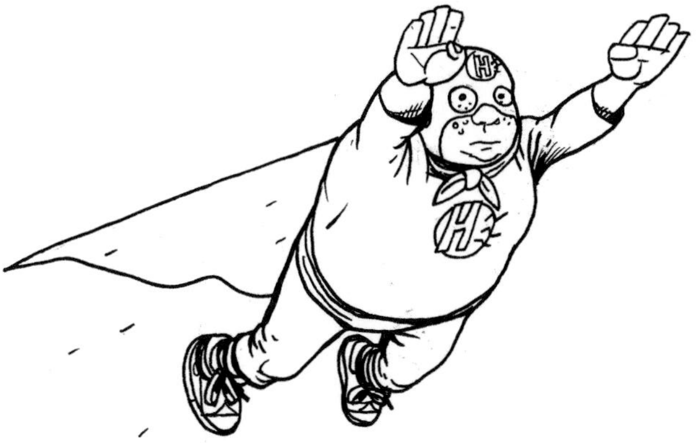

Hollis is the heart
of the Wrenchies.

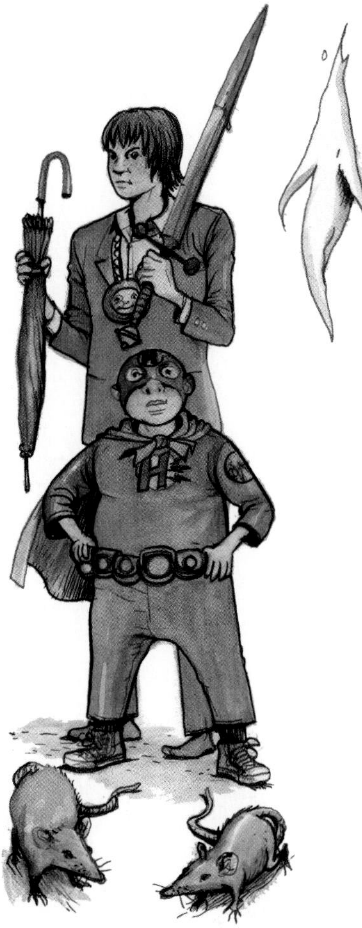

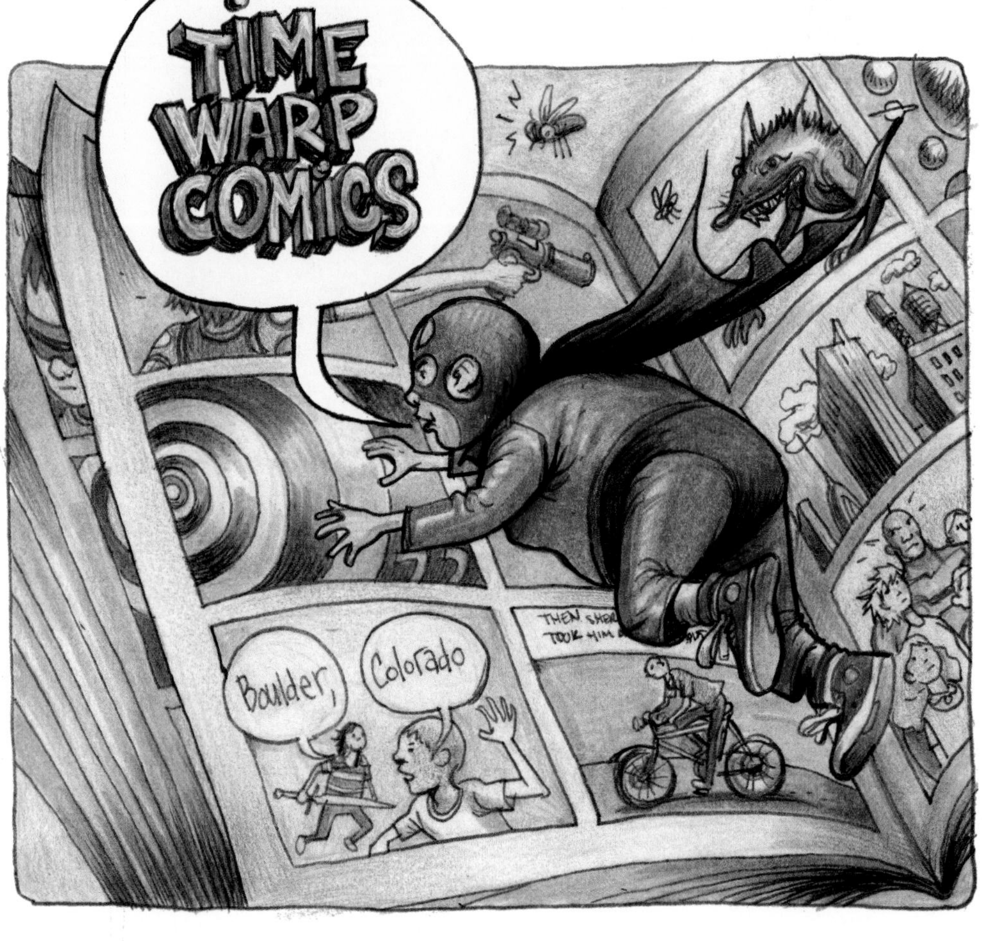
TIME WARP COMICS
Boulder,
Colorado

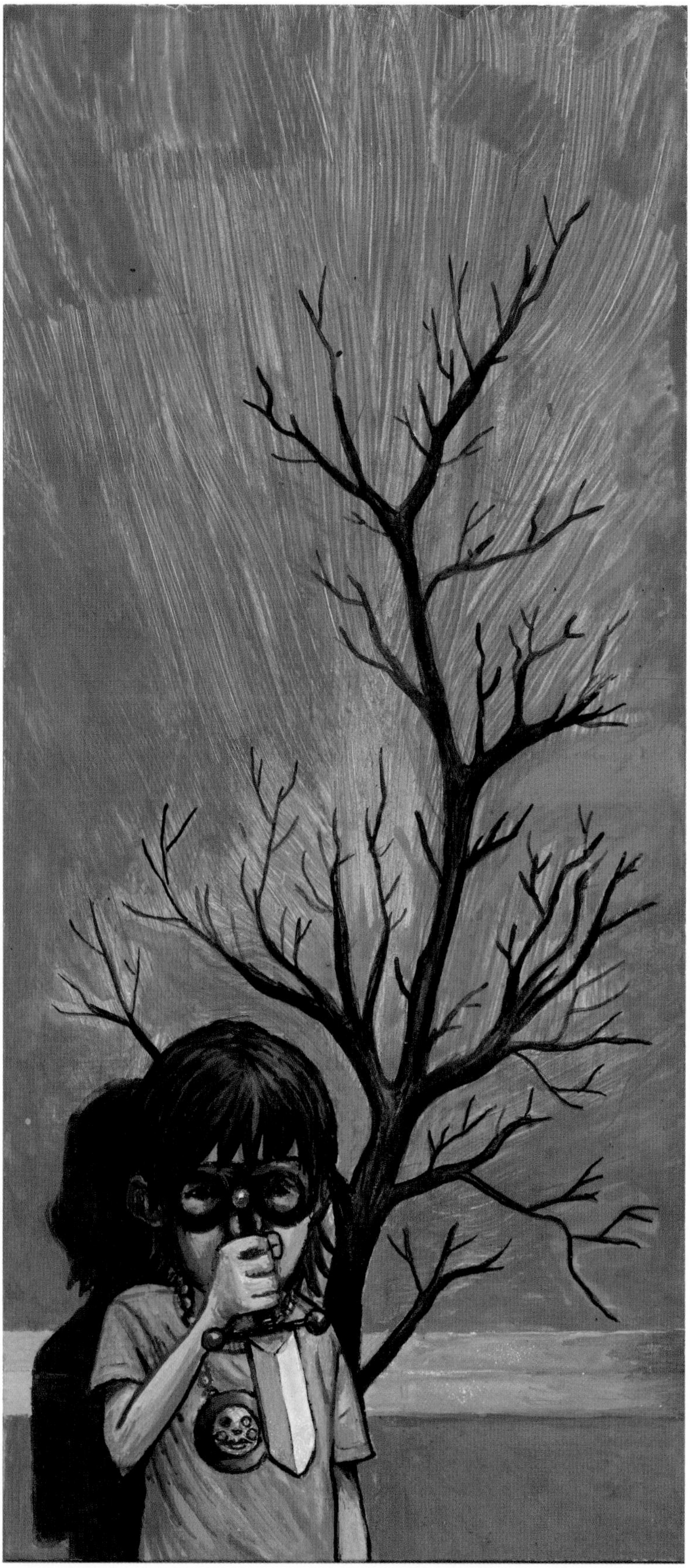

Young Sherwood Presley Breadcoat.

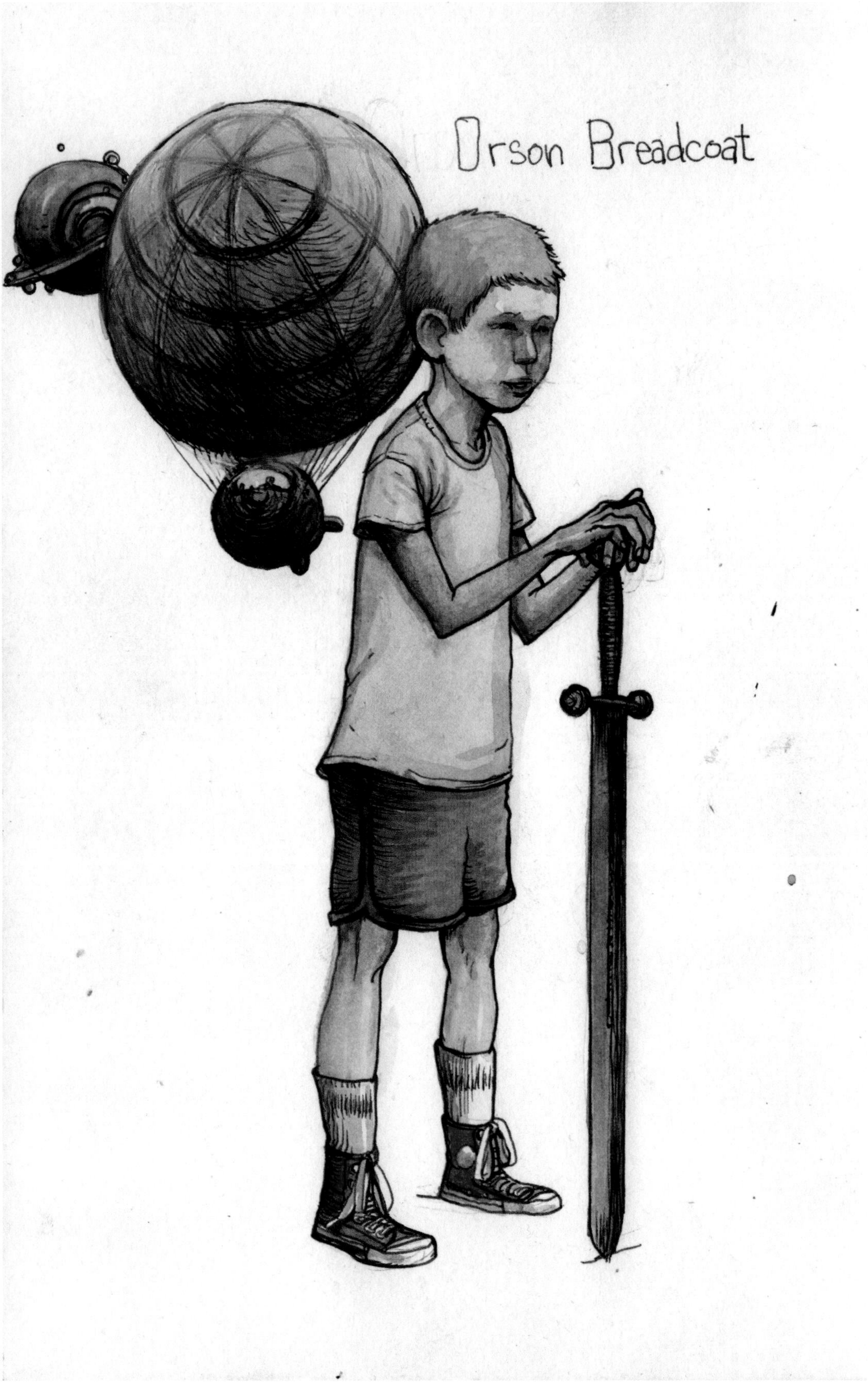
Orson Breadcoat

Sherwood's younger carefree brother is talented at just about everything. He is a bit of a bully to Hollis on Proxima Centauri.

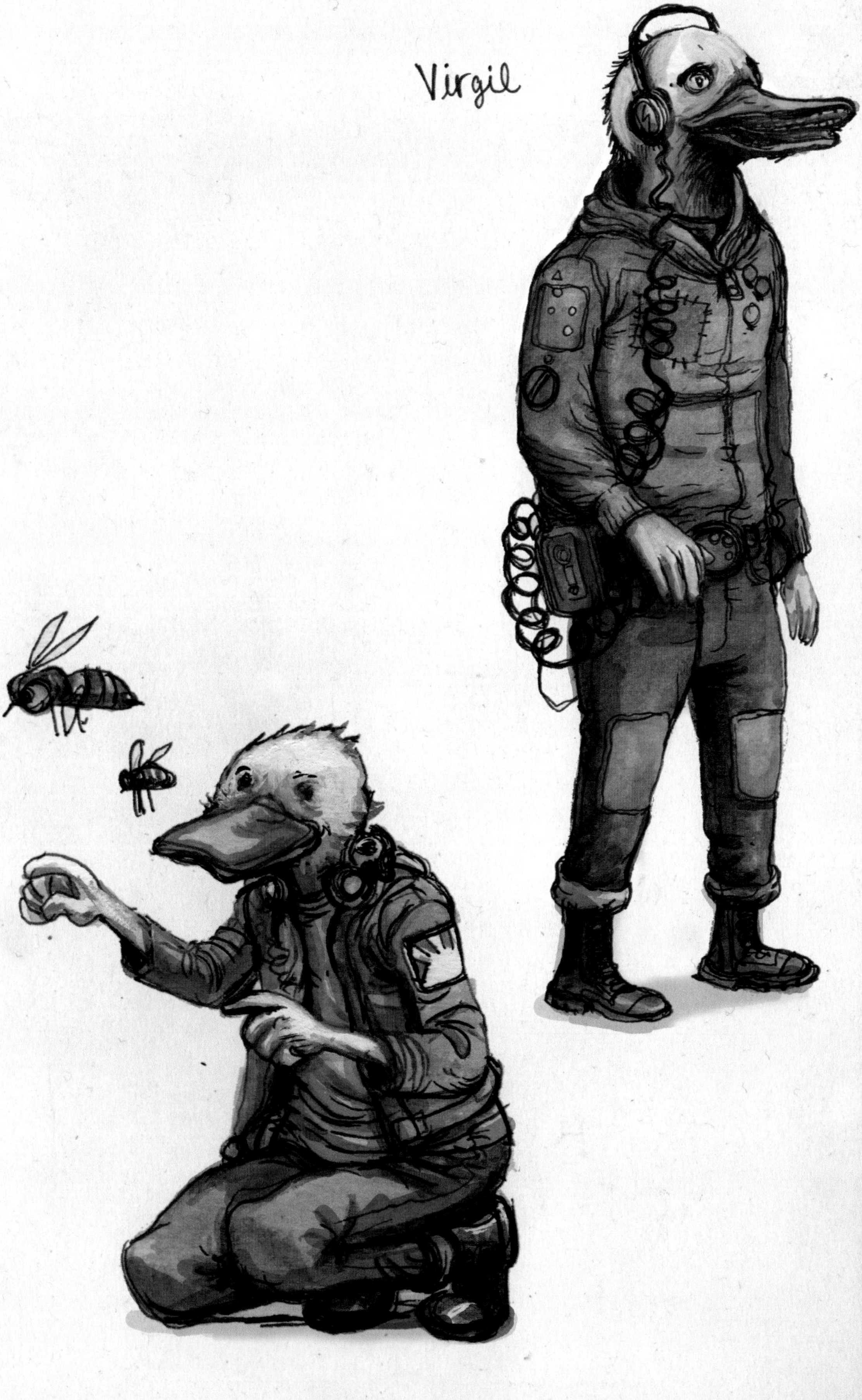
Virgil

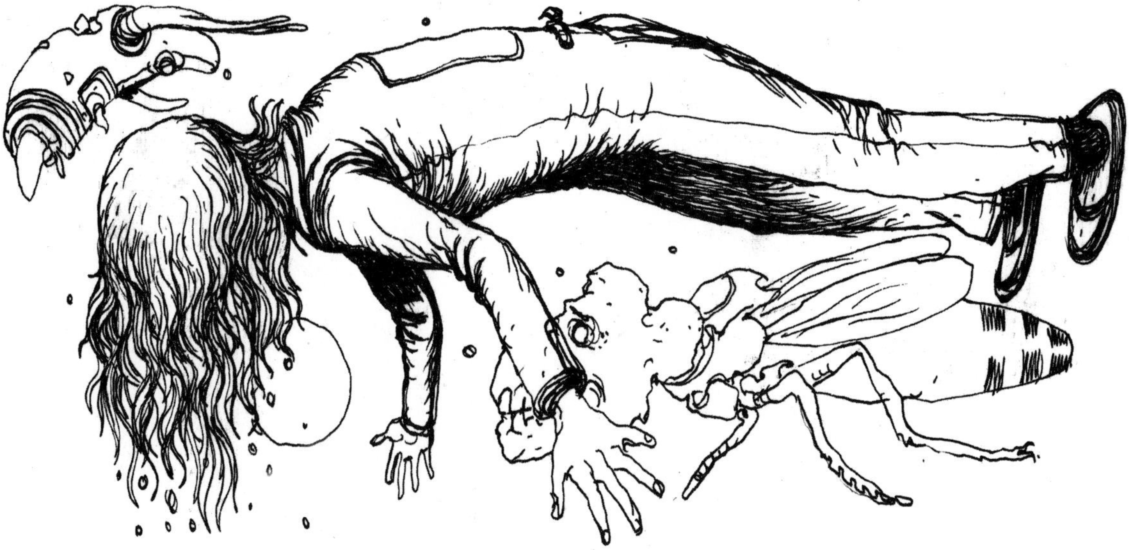

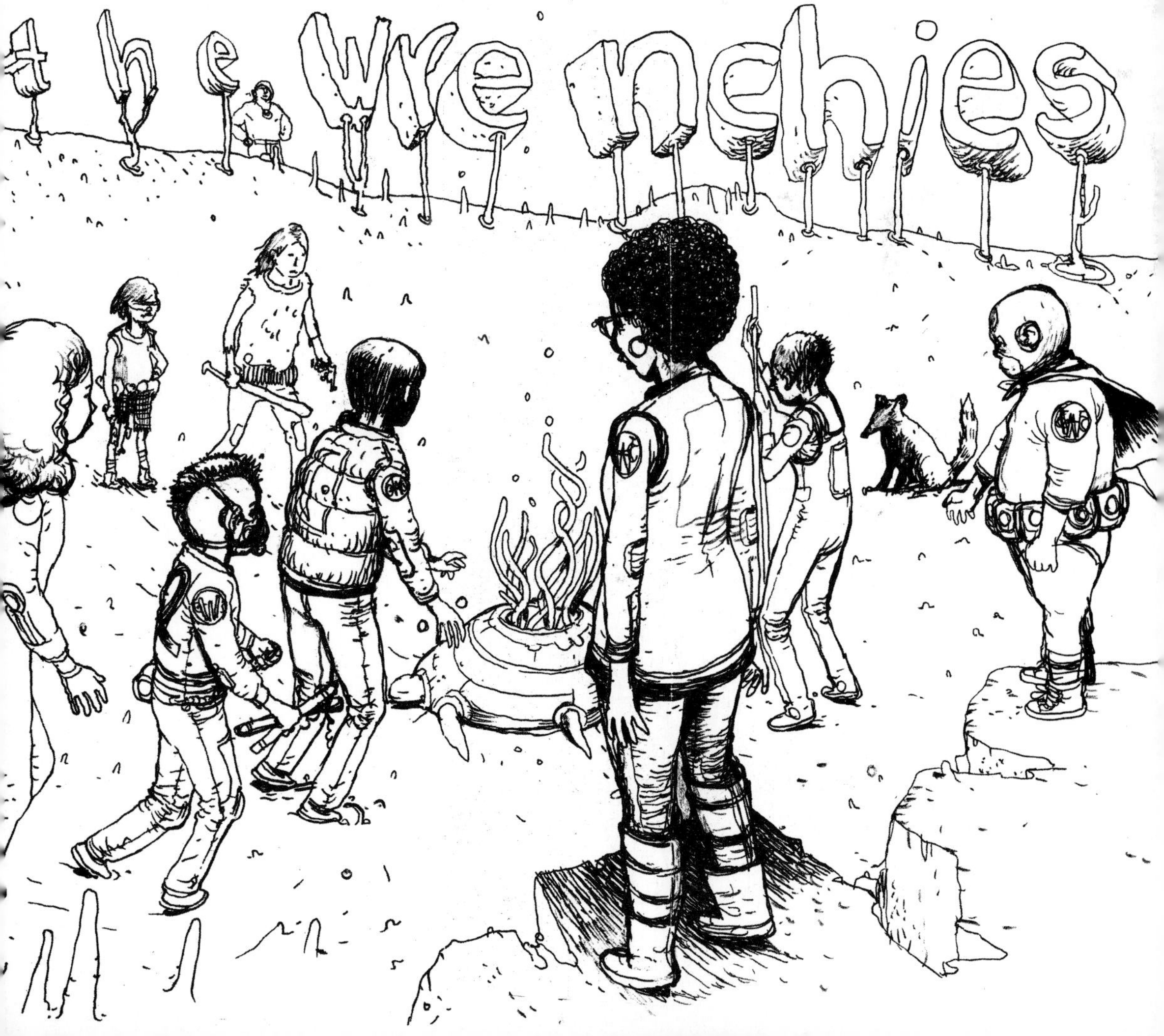
the wrenchies

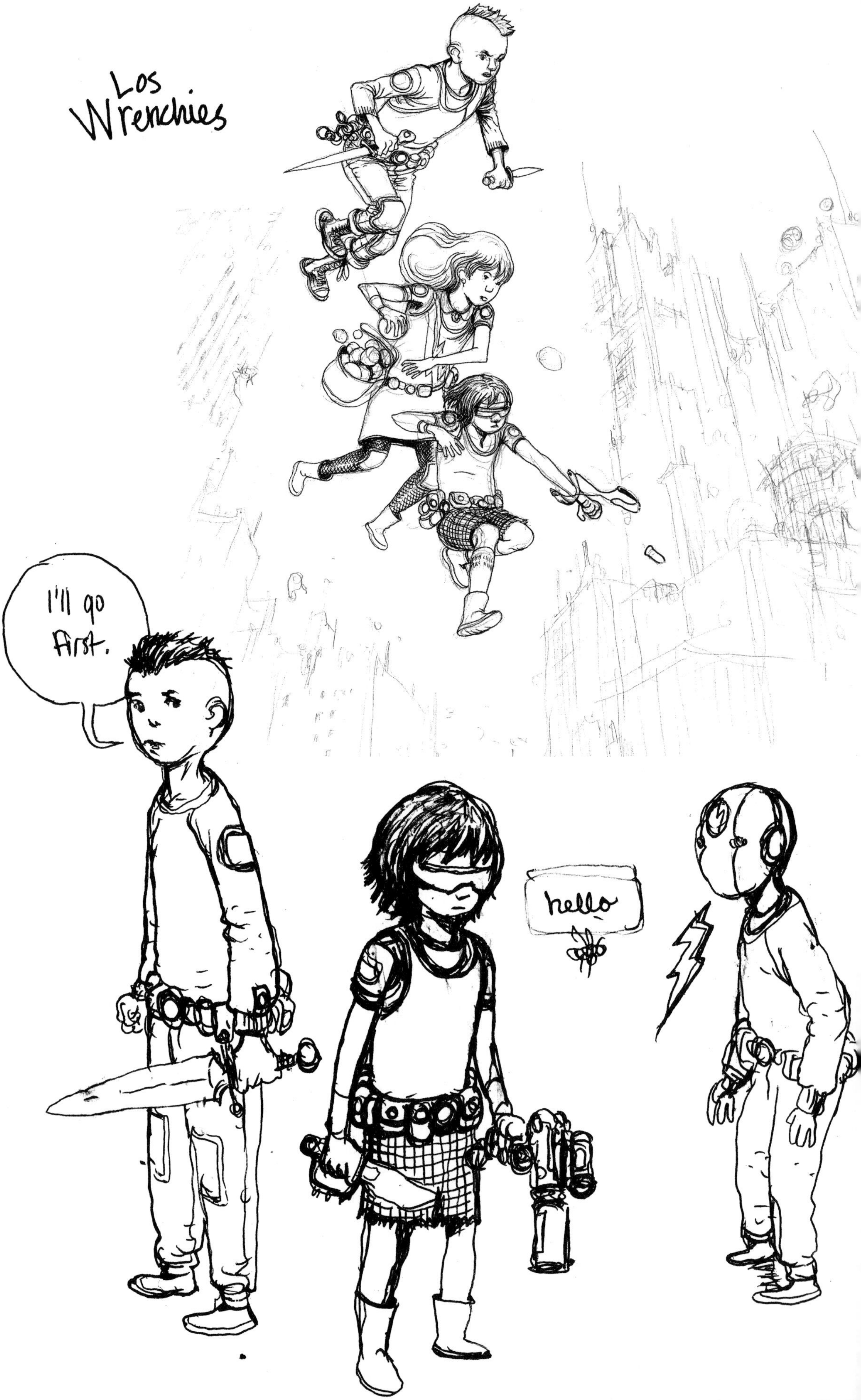
Los Wrenchies
I'll go first.
hello

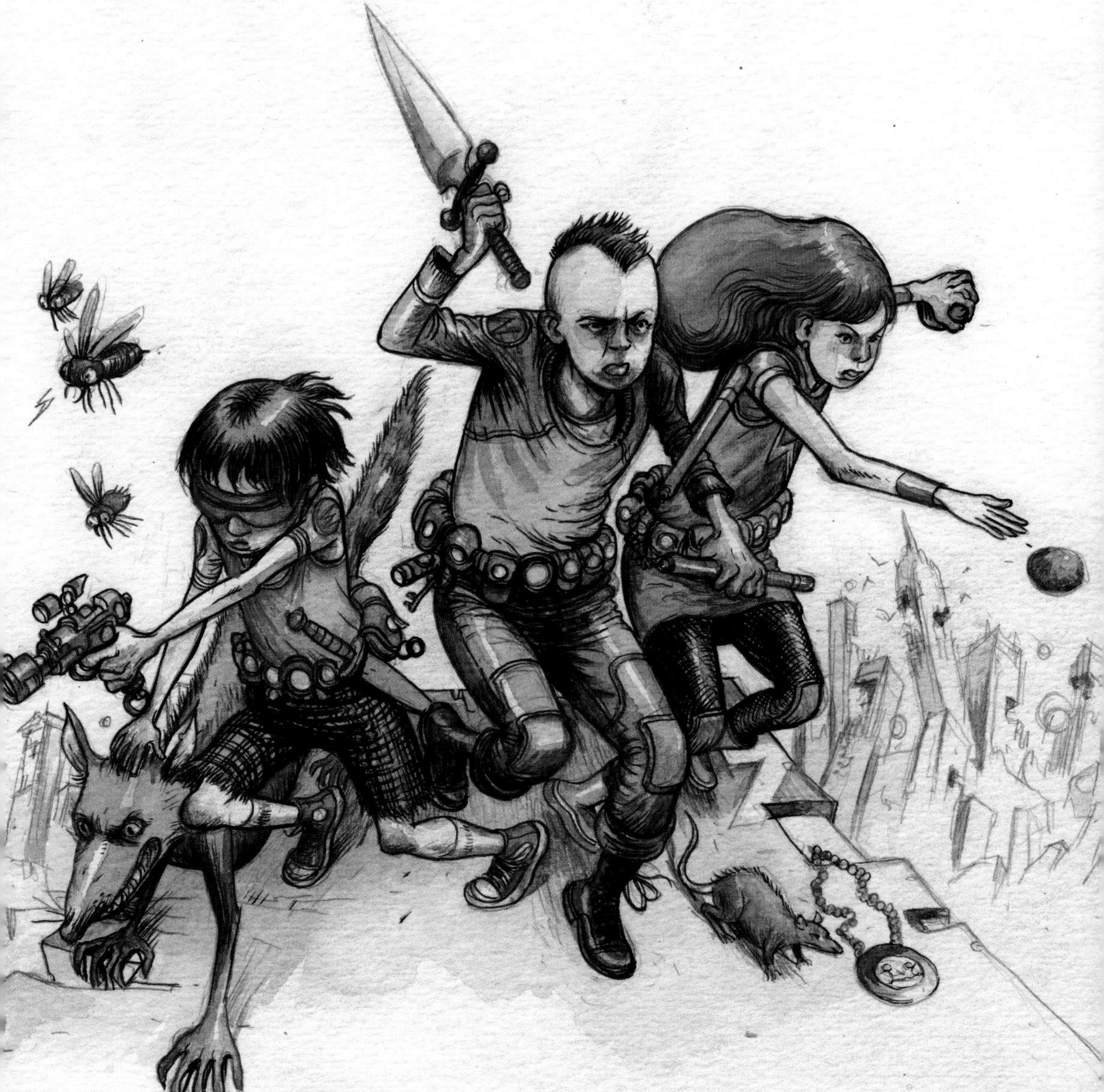

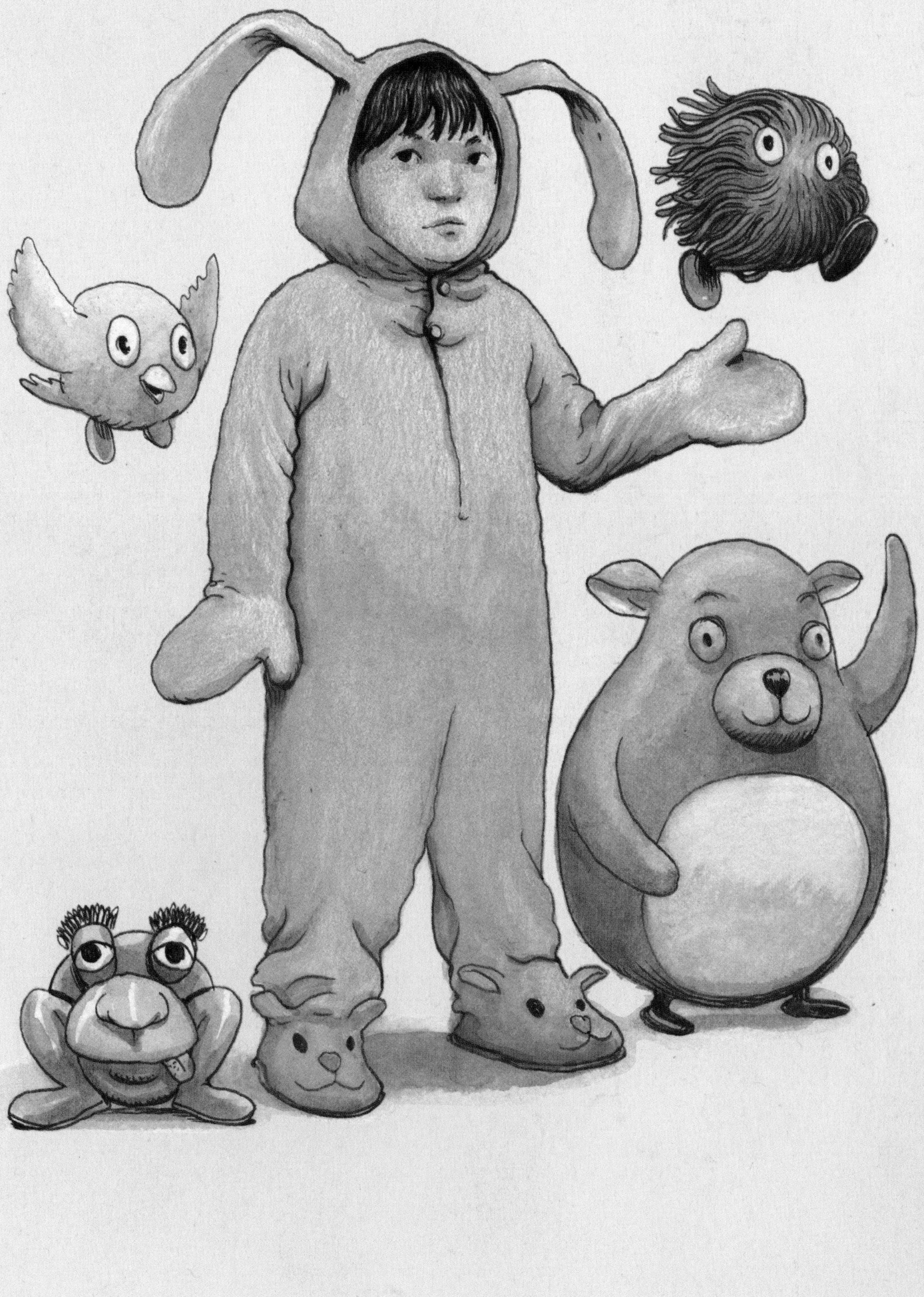

Pin-up of OP6 from *TREMOR DOSE* by Michael Conrad and Noah Bailey.

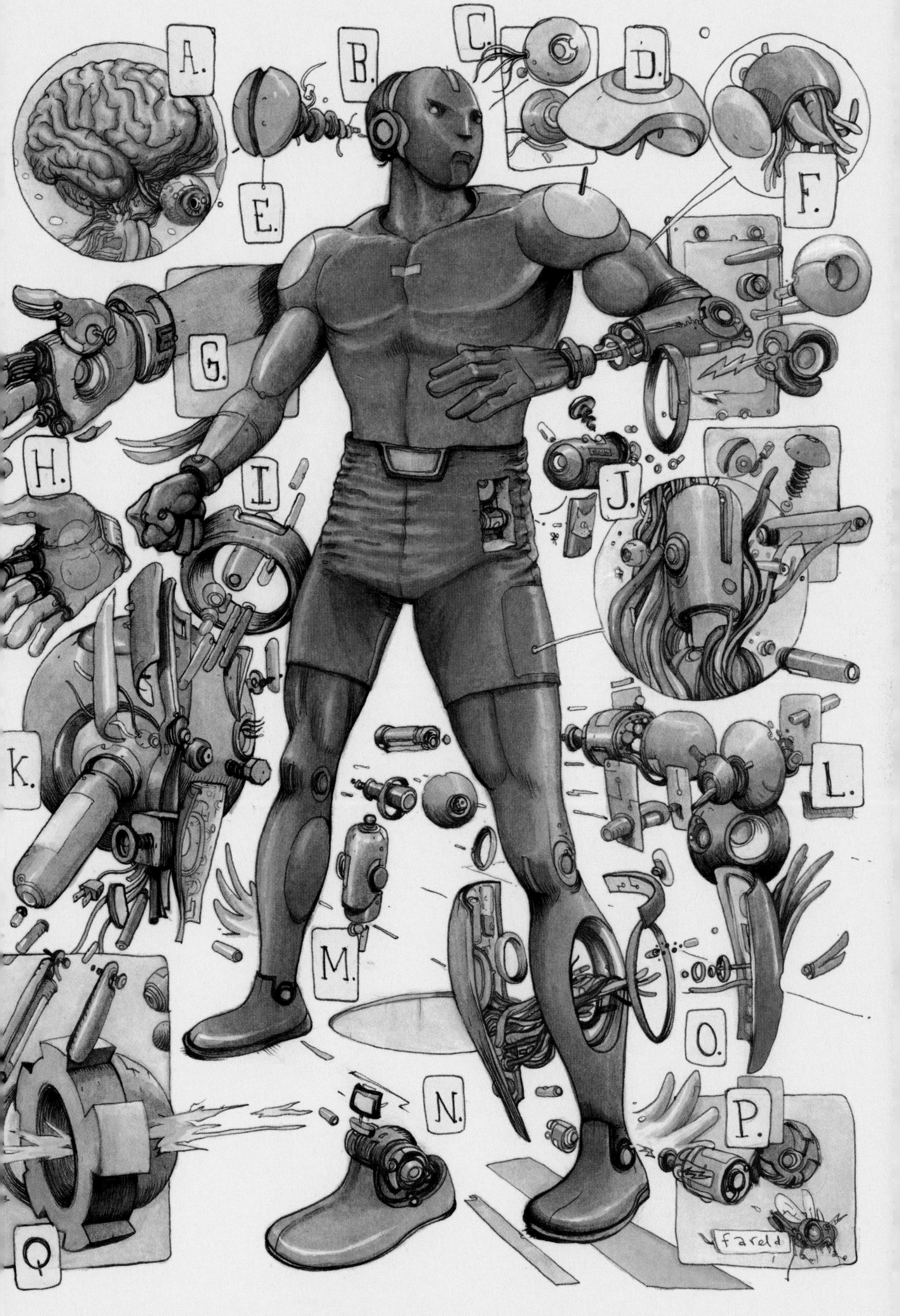
A.
B.
C.
D.
E.
F.
G.
H.
I.
J.
K.
L.
M.
N.
O.
P.
Q
fareld

Splash page from the upcoming book, *BETTER PLACE* by Duane Murray and Shawn Daley.

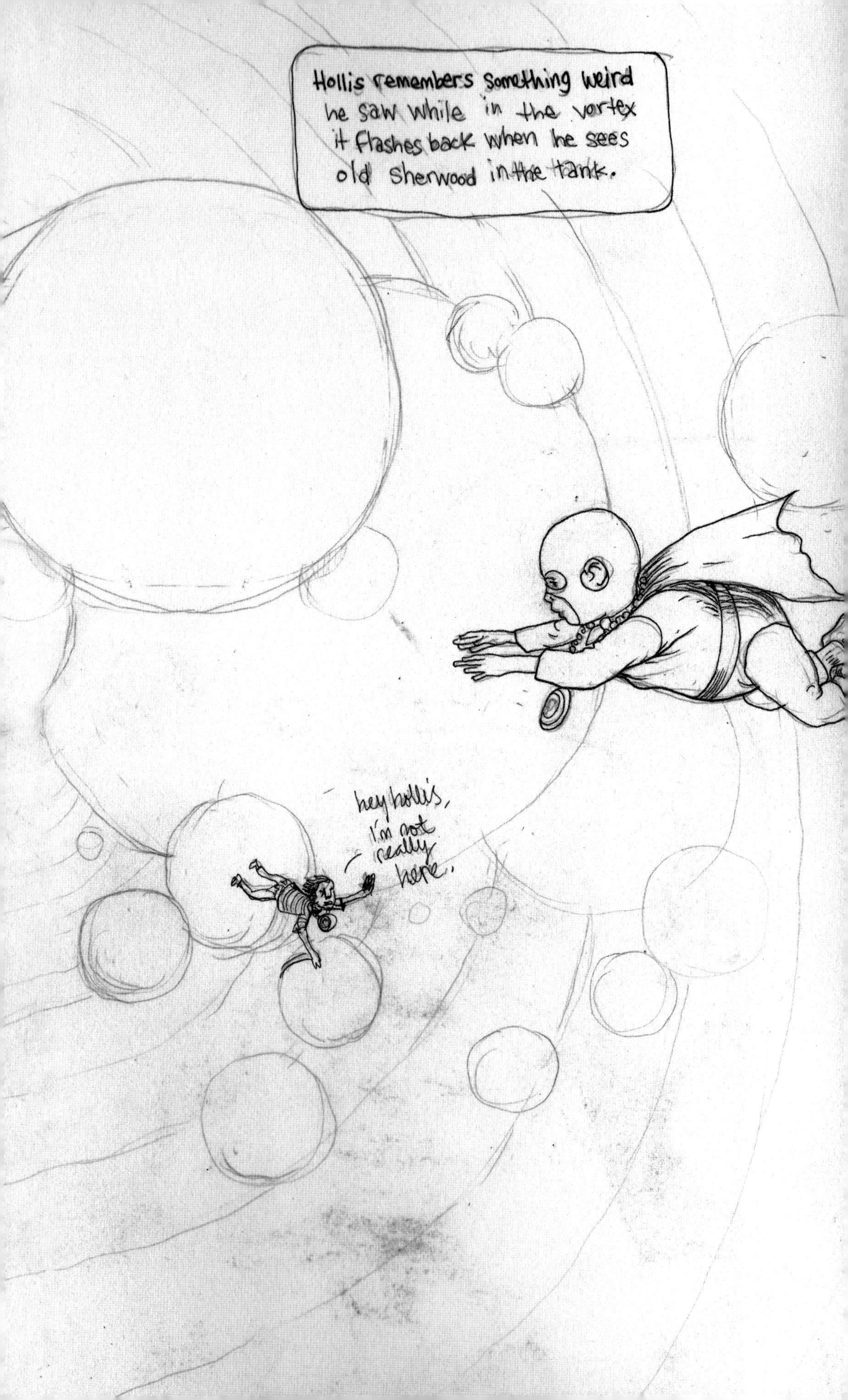
Hollis remembers something weird he saw while in the vortex it flashes back when he sees old Sherwood in the tank.
hey hollis, i'm not really here.

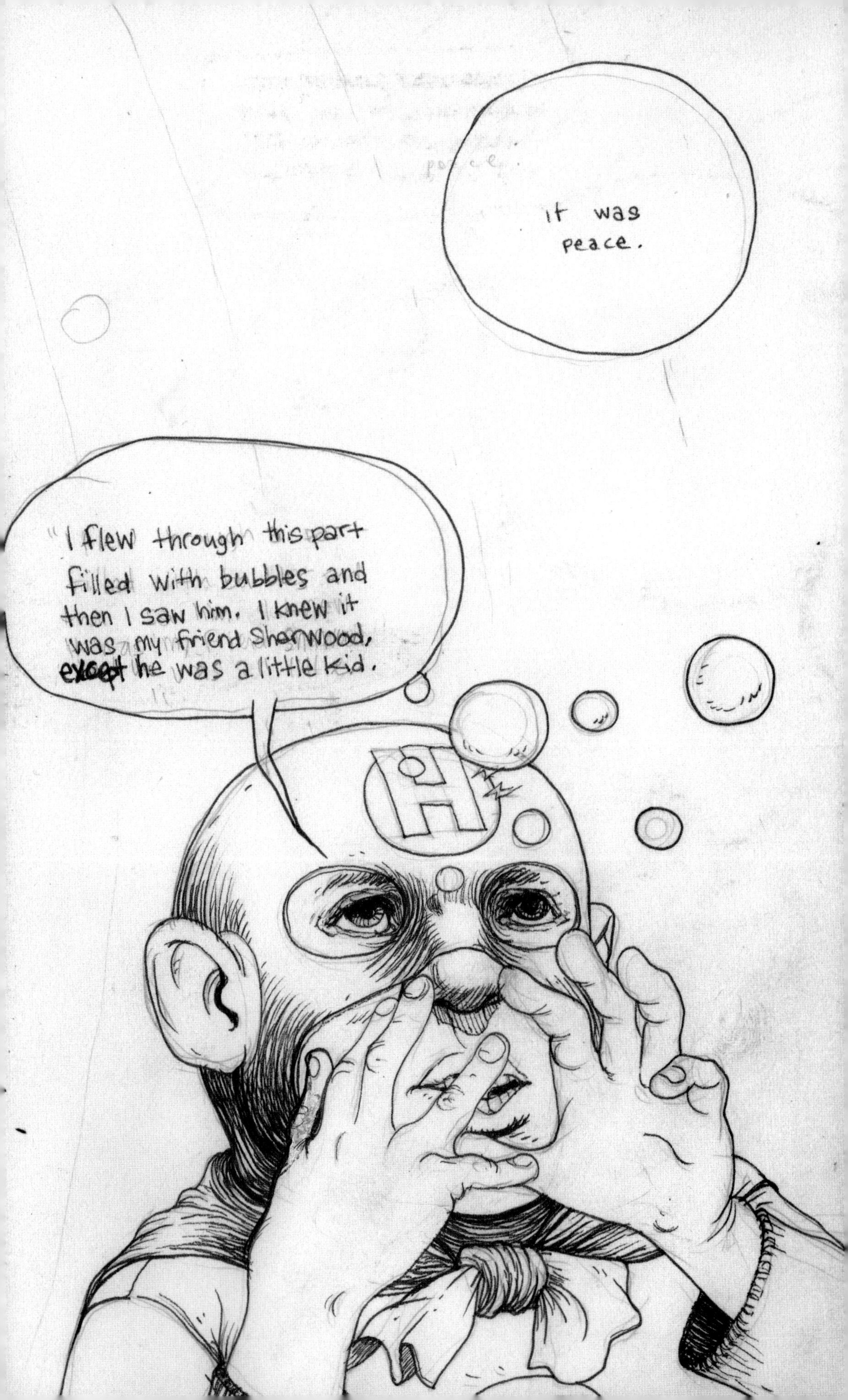
it was peace.
"I flew through this part filled with bubbles and then I saw him. I knew it was my friend Sherwood, except he was a little kid.

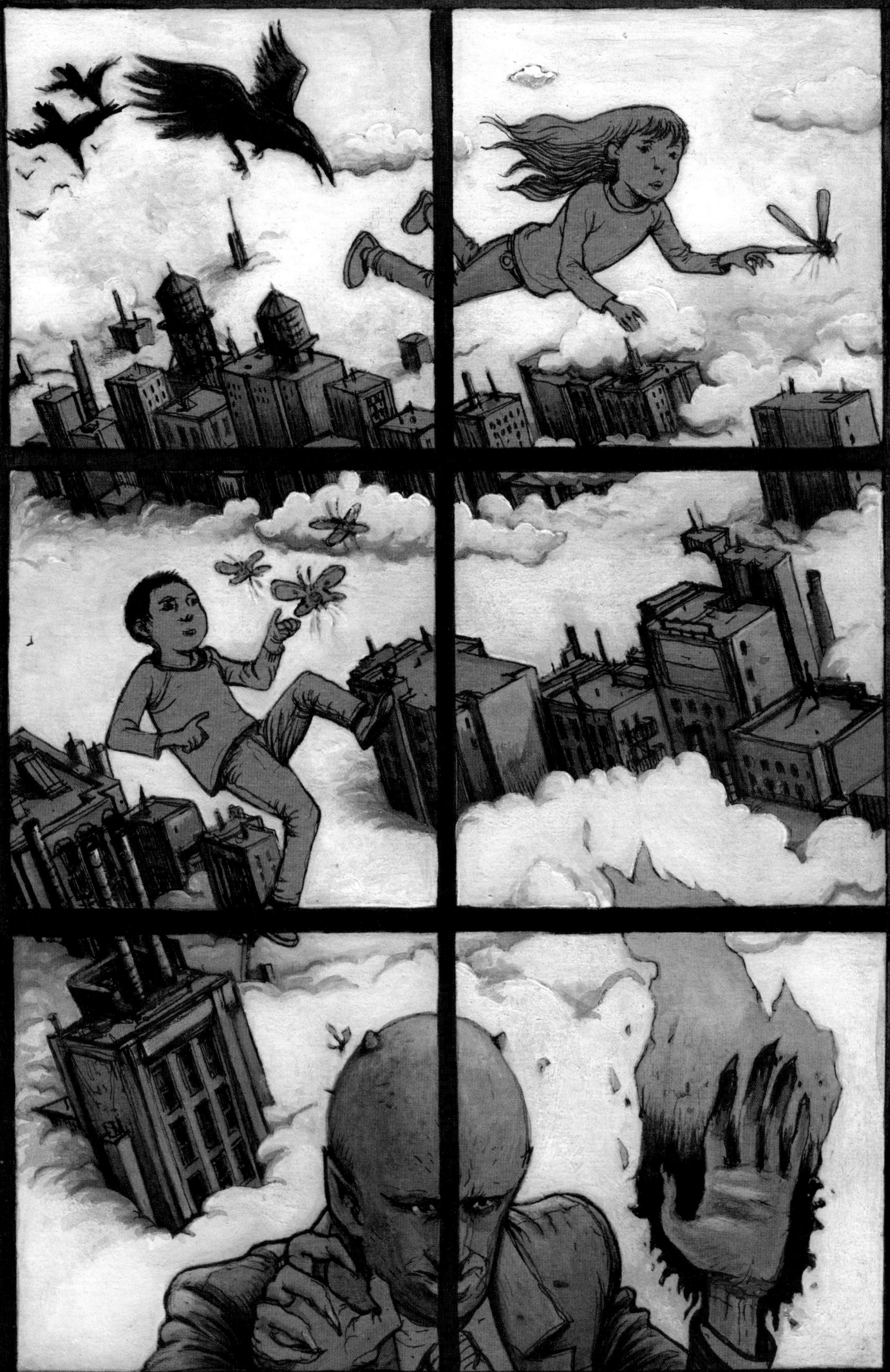

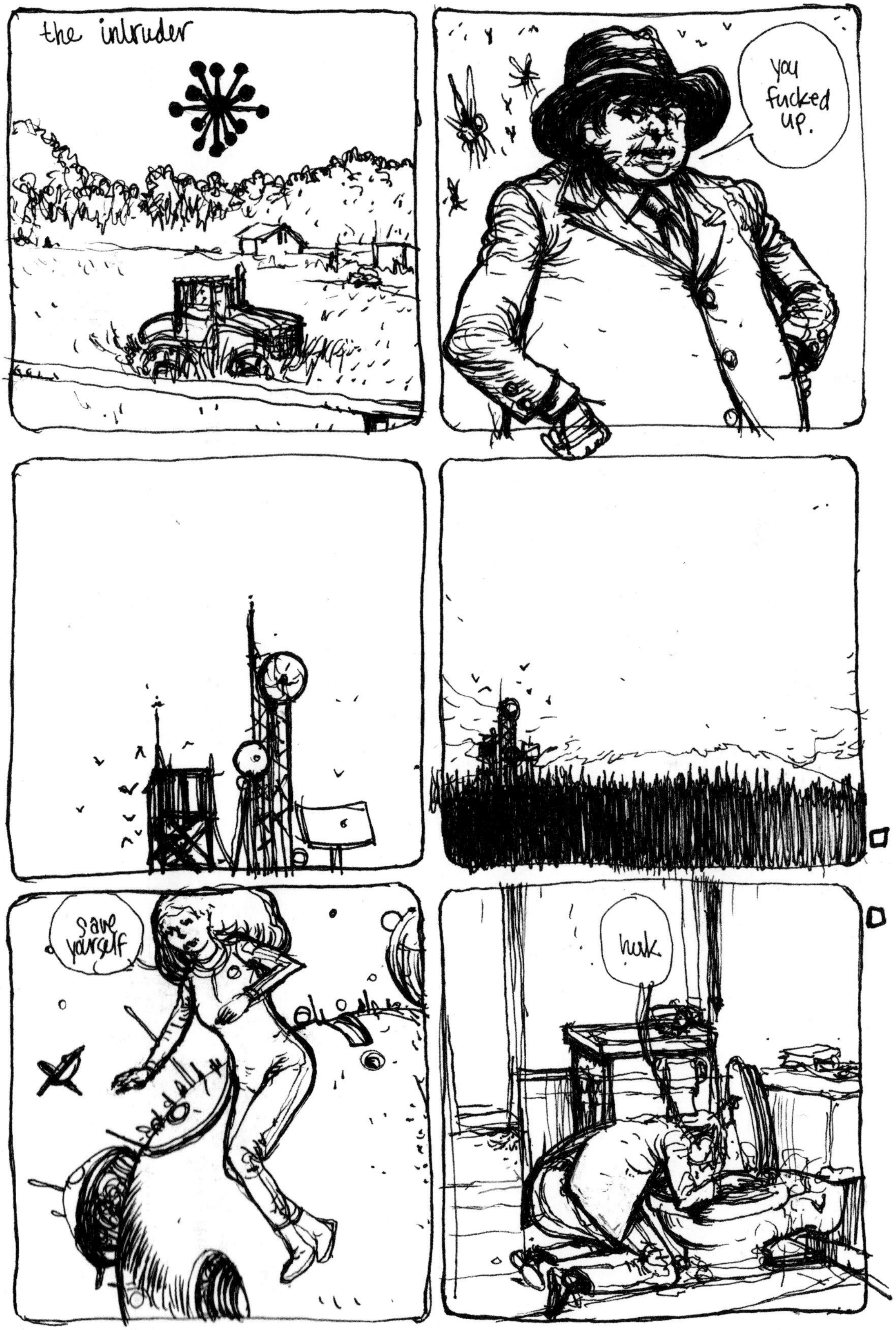
the intruder
you fucked up.
save yourself
hurk.

This page and the next few were discarded pages and panel ideas from *THE WRENCHIES.*

amulet page

on the amulet.

marci marci parasol.

space lady

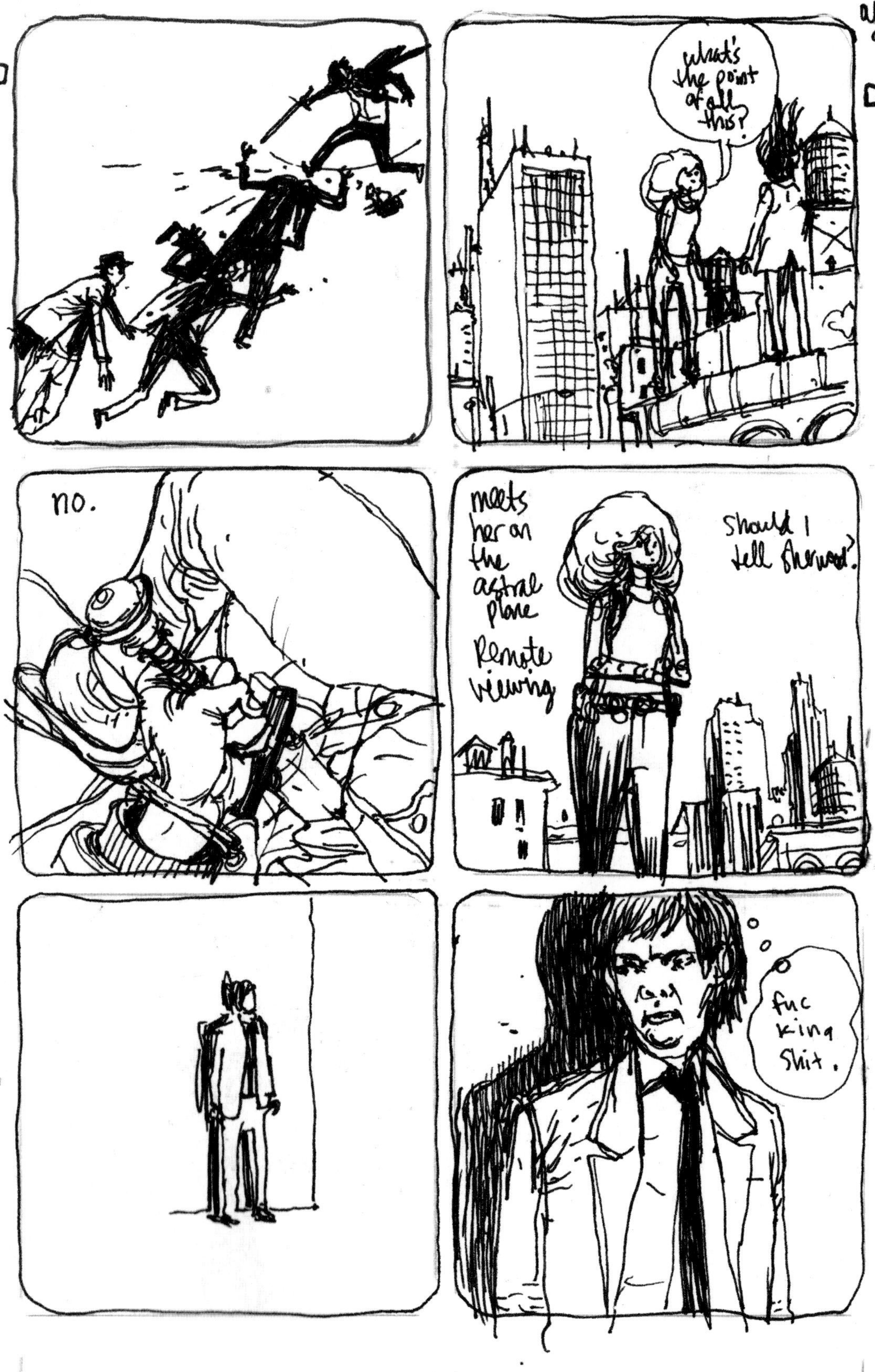
what's the point of all this?
no.
meets her on the astral plane
Remote viewing
should I tell Sherwood?
fuc king shit.

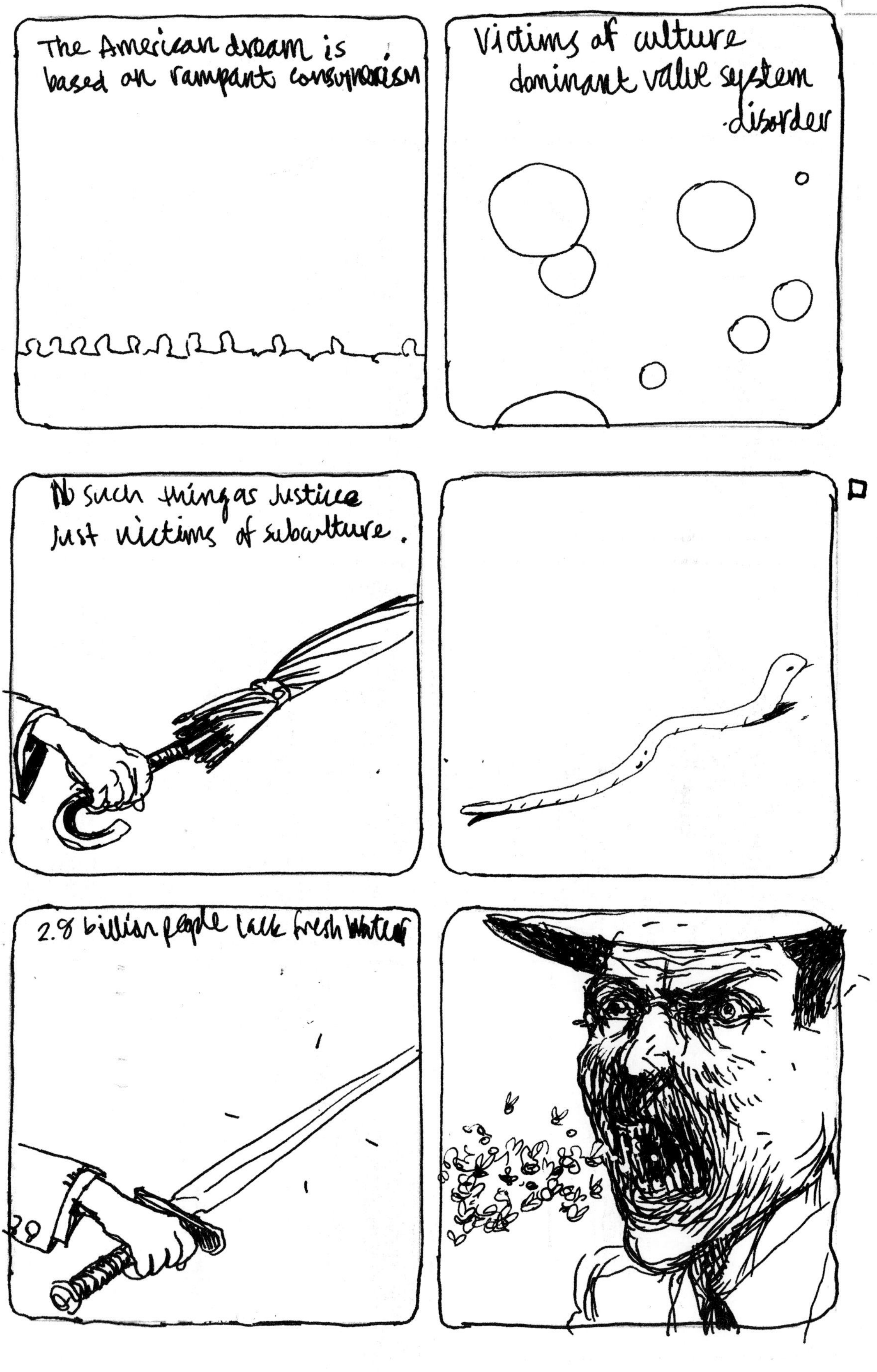
The American dream is
based on rampant consumerism
Victims of culture
dominant value system
disorder
No such thing as Justice
Just victims of subculture.
2.8 billion people lack fresh water

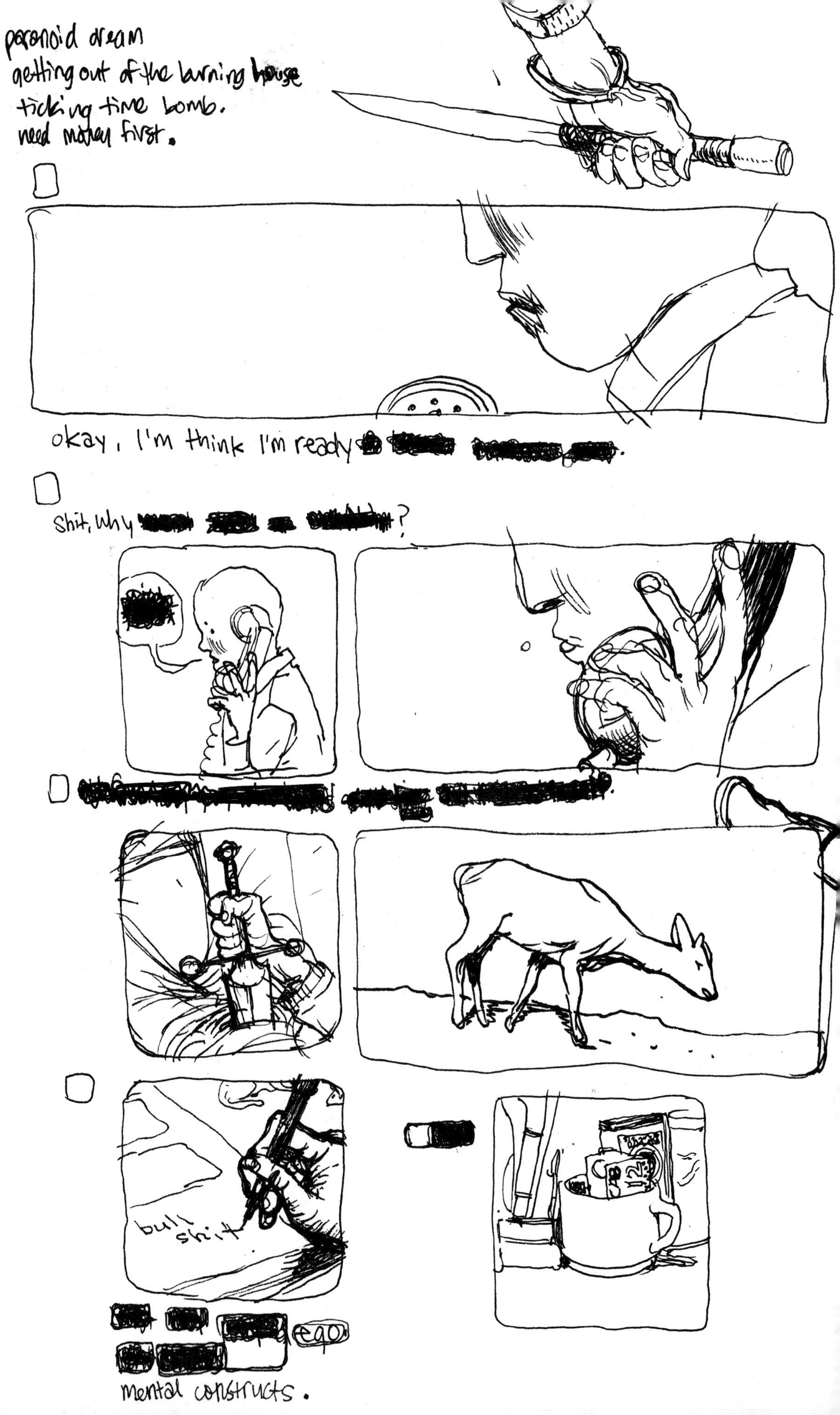
paranoid dream
getting out of the burning house
ticking time bomb.
need money first.
okay, I'm think I'm ready [redacted].
shit, why [redacted]?
[redacted]
[redacted]
bull shit
[redacted]
[redacted] ego
mental constructs.

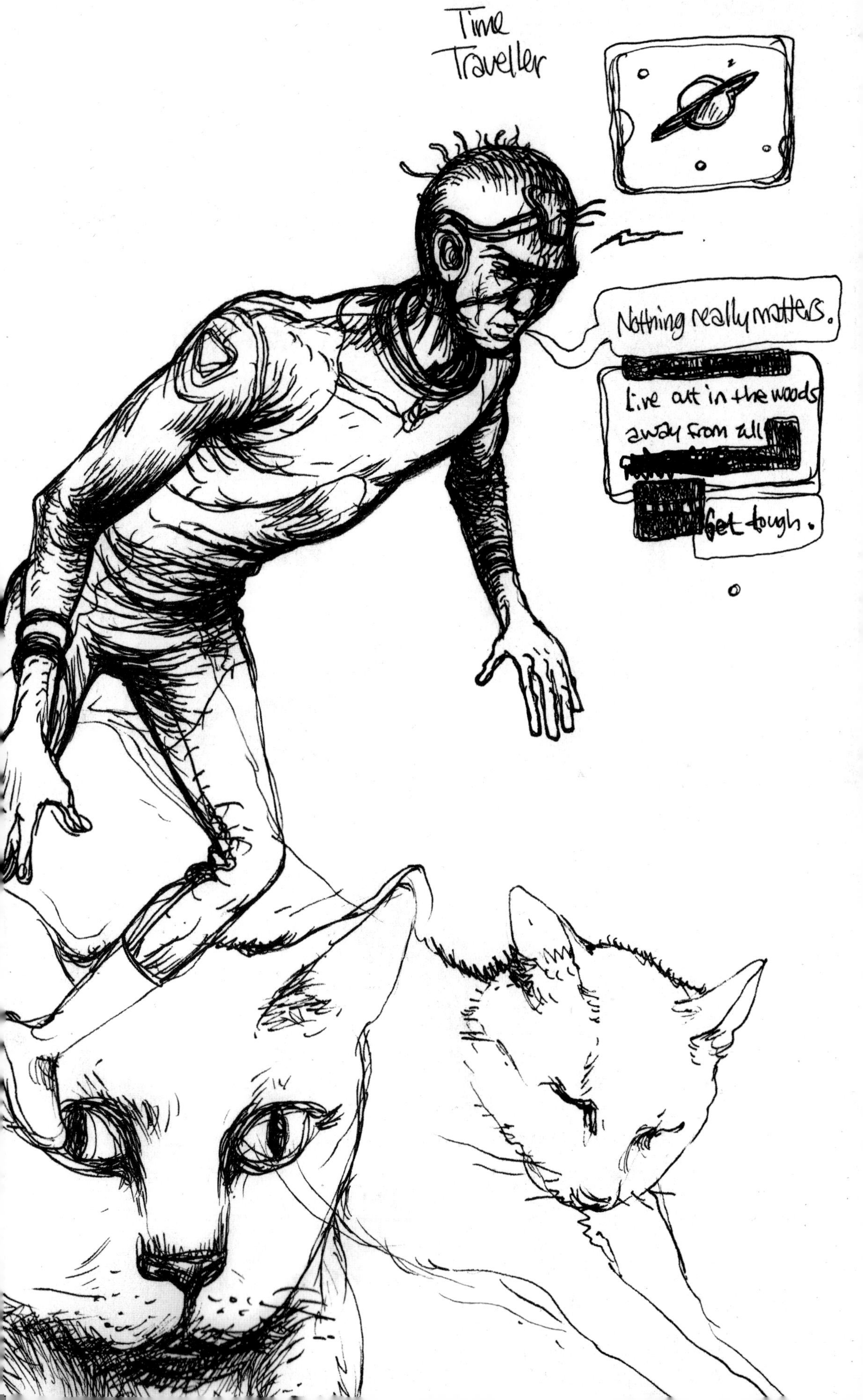
Time Traveller
Nothing really matters.
[redacted]
Live out in the woods away from all [redacted]
[redacted] Get tough.

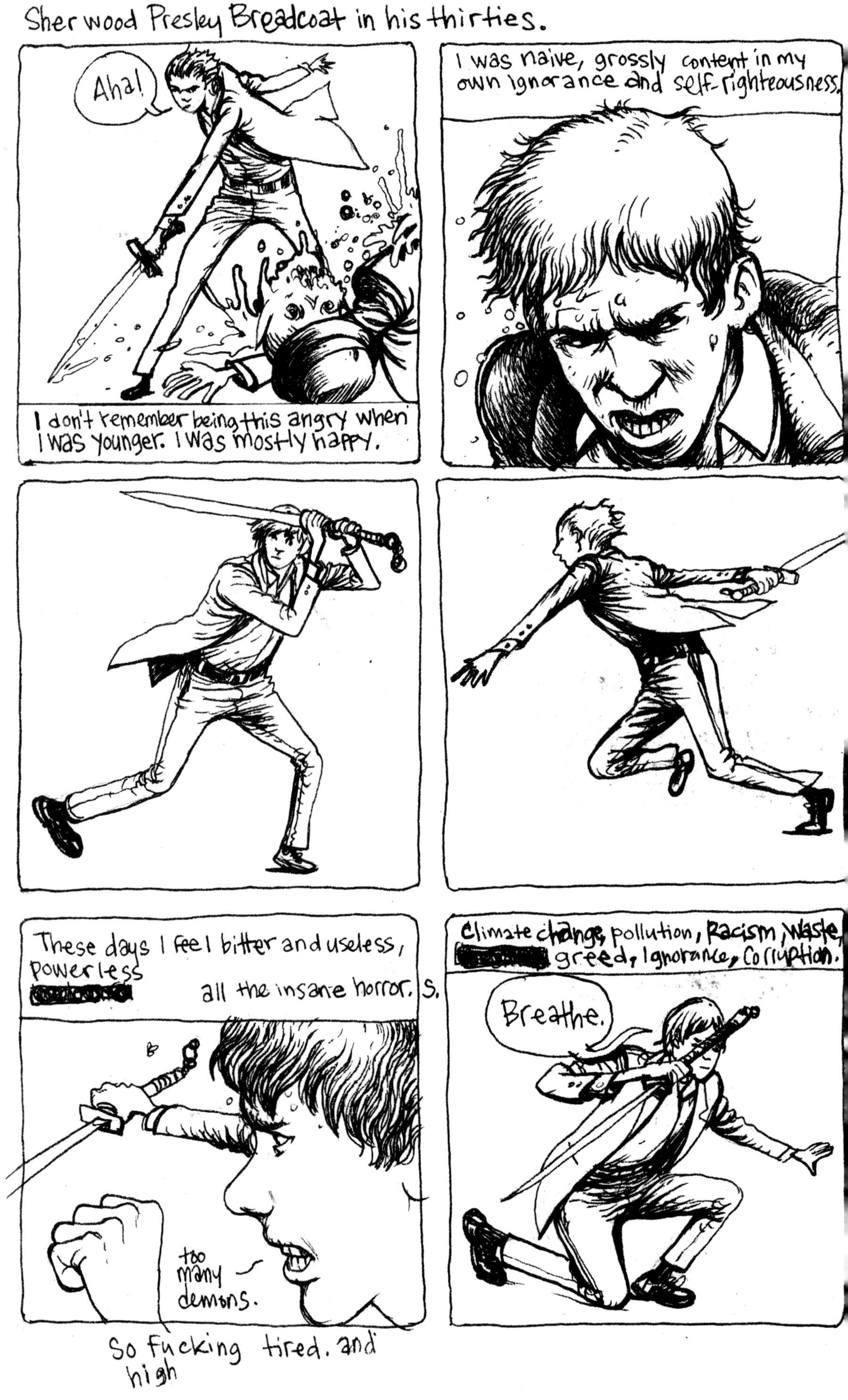

Sherwood Presley Breadcoat in his thirties.
Aha!
I don't remember being this angry when I was younger. I was mostly happy.
I was naive, grossly content in my own ignorance and self-righteousness.
These days I feel bitter and useless, powerless [redacted] all the insane horror. S.
too many demons.
So fucking tired. and high
Climate change, pollution, Racism, Waste, [redacted] greed, Ignorance, Corruption.
Breathe.

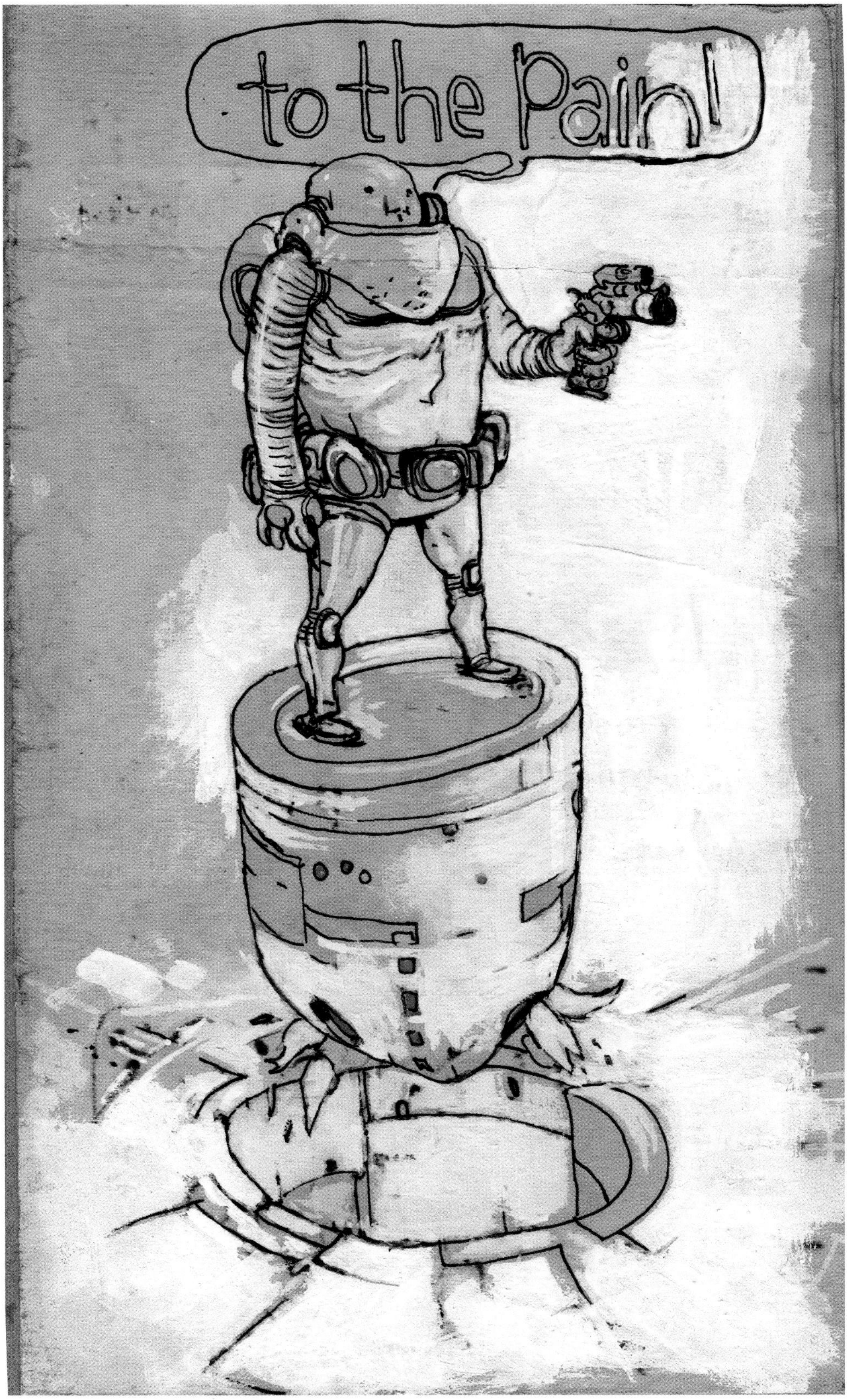
to the Pain!

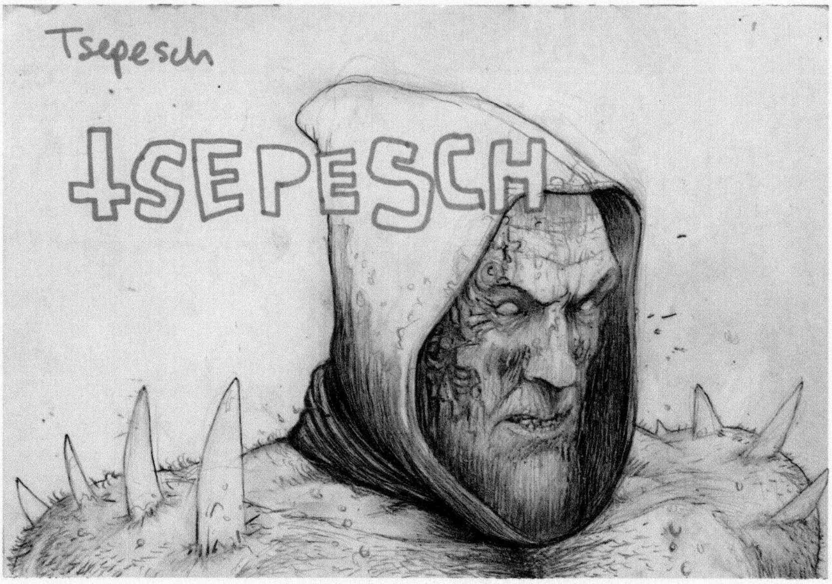
Tsepesch
TSEPESCH

DOOMSDAY CLOCK - 2.5 minutes until

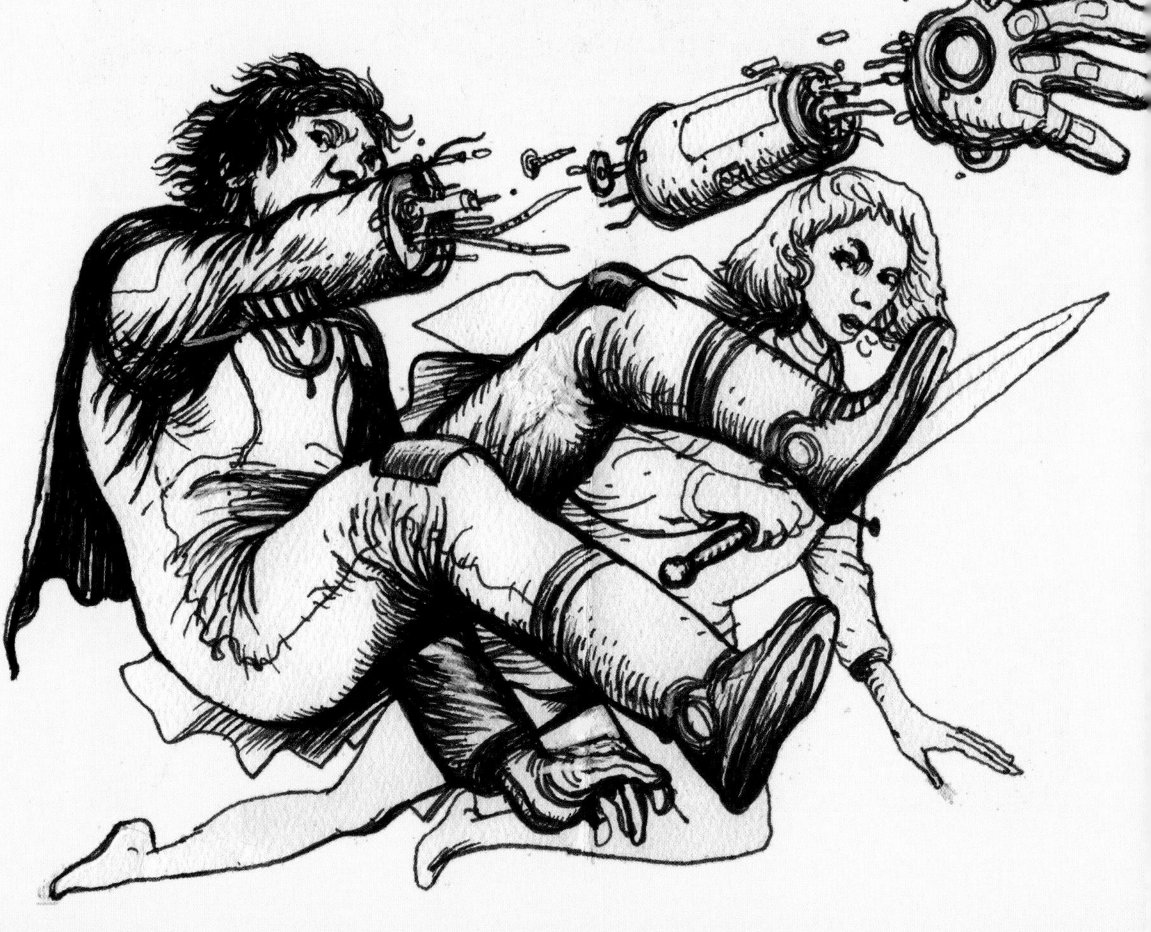

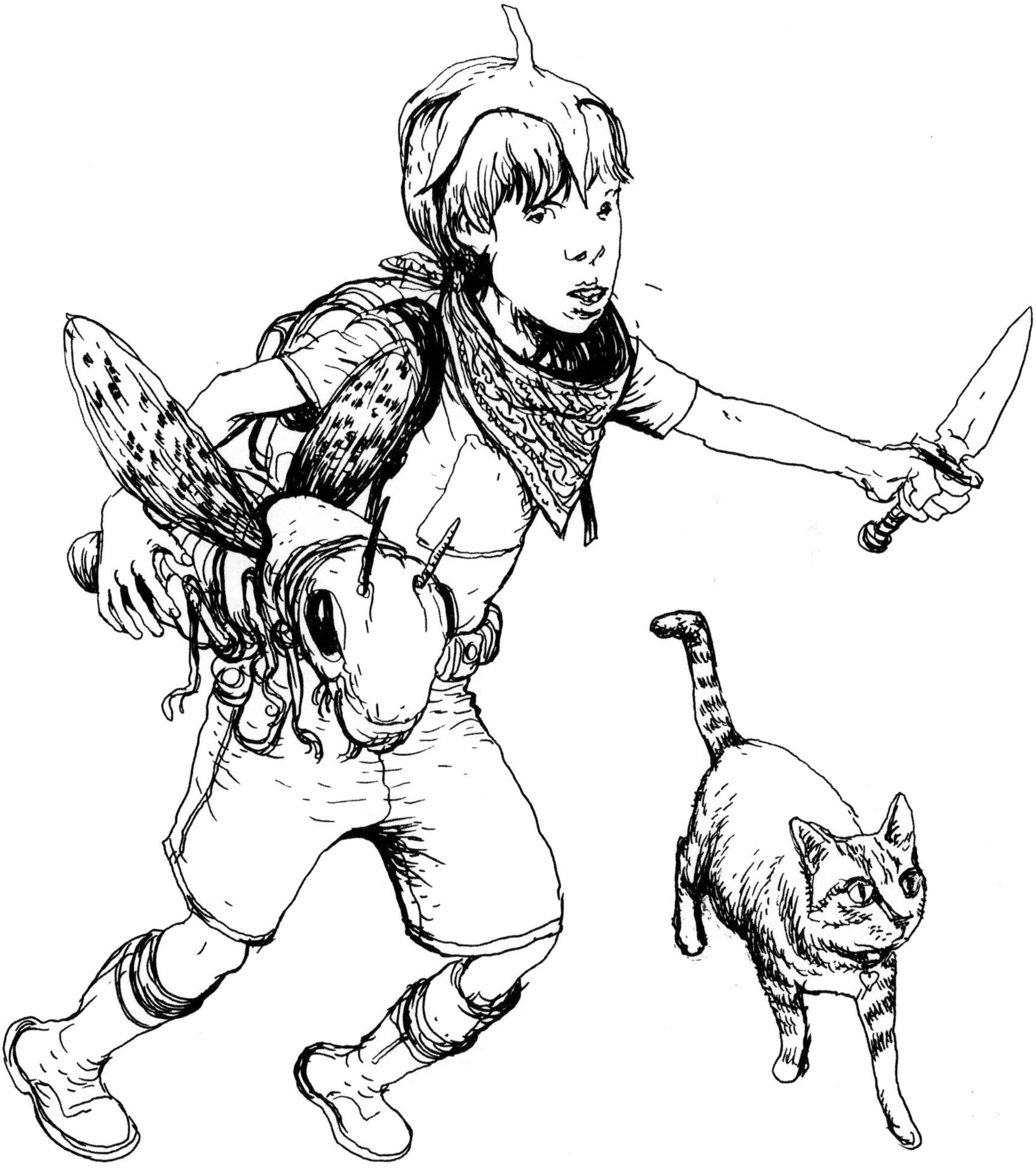

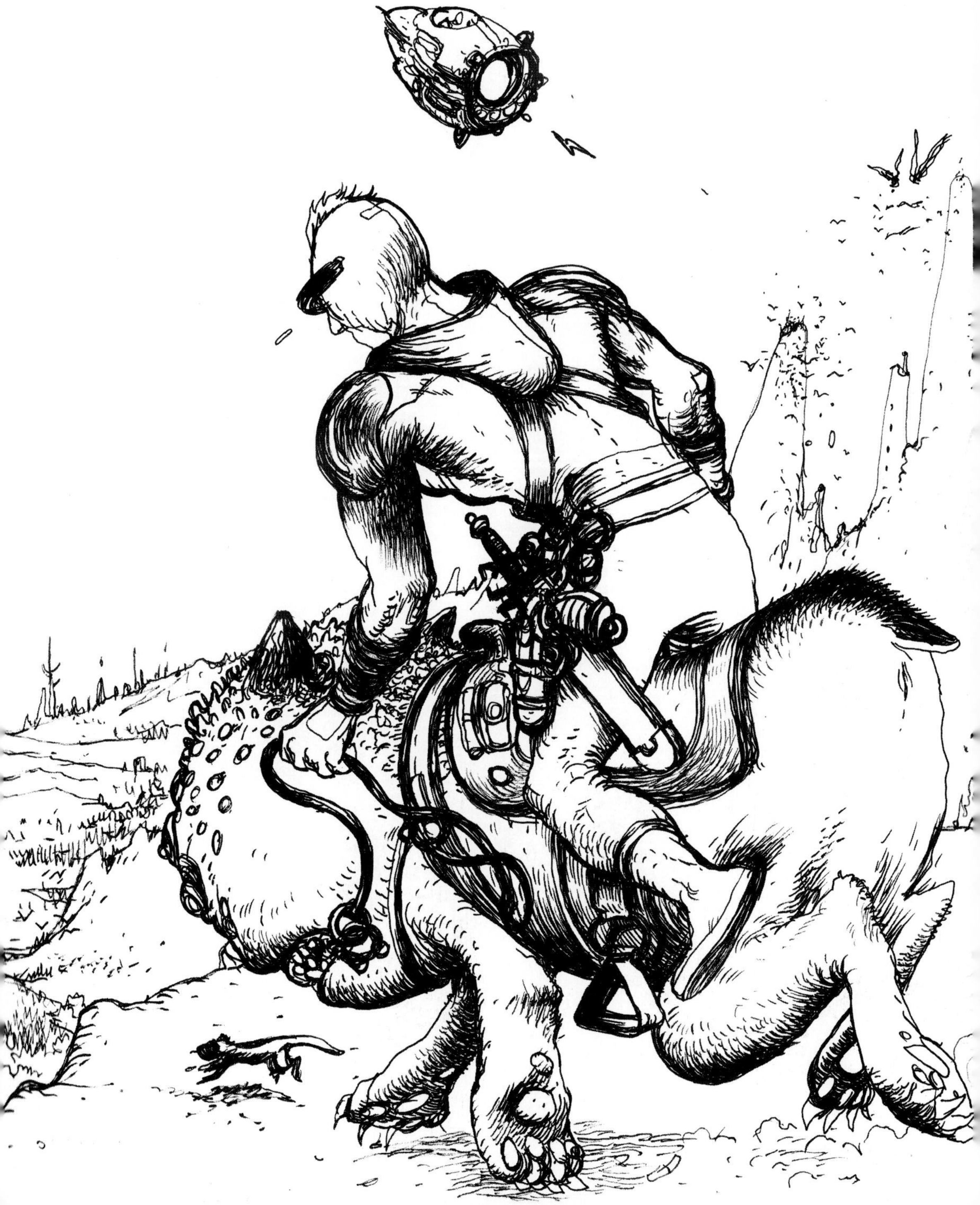

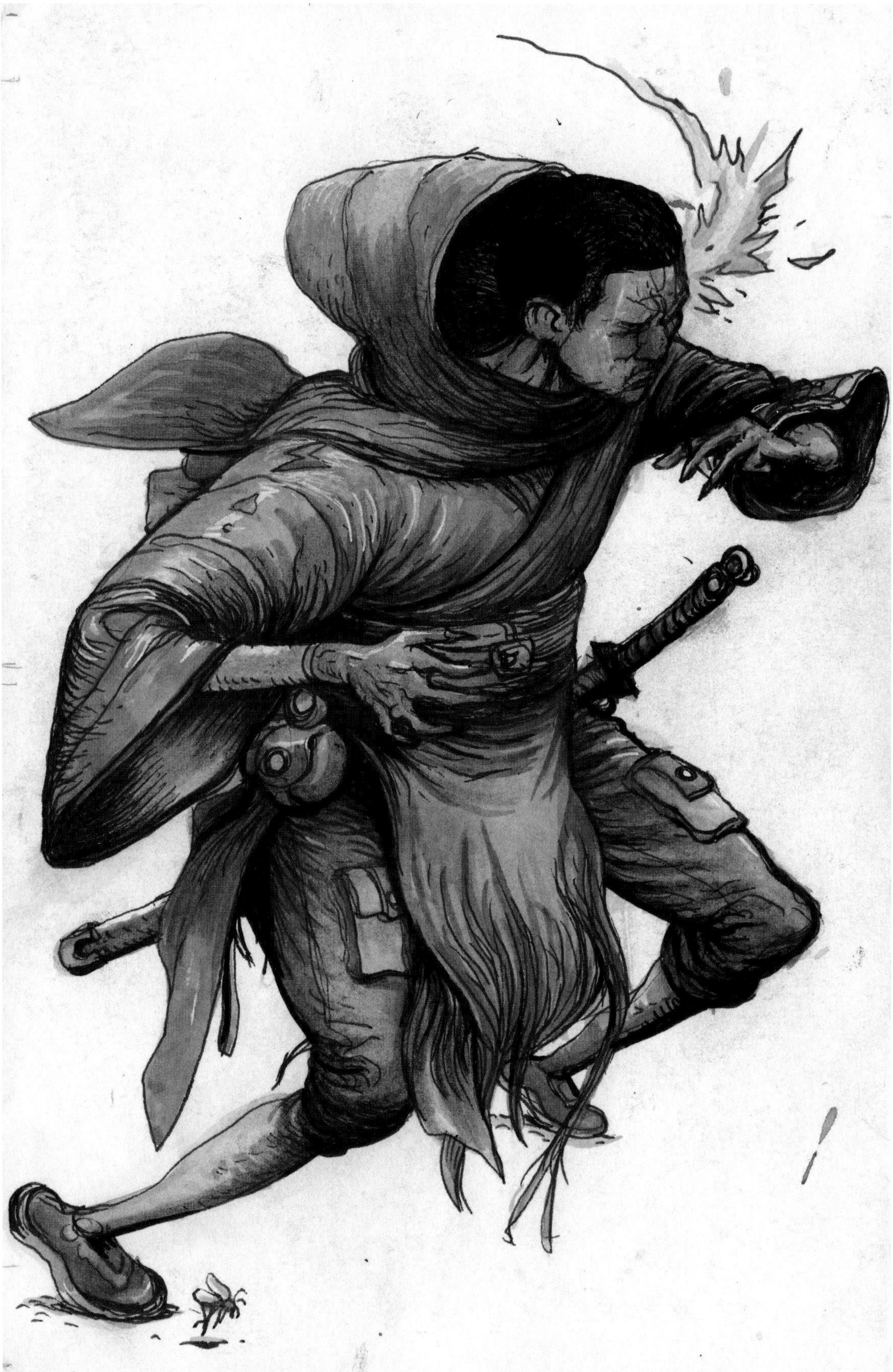

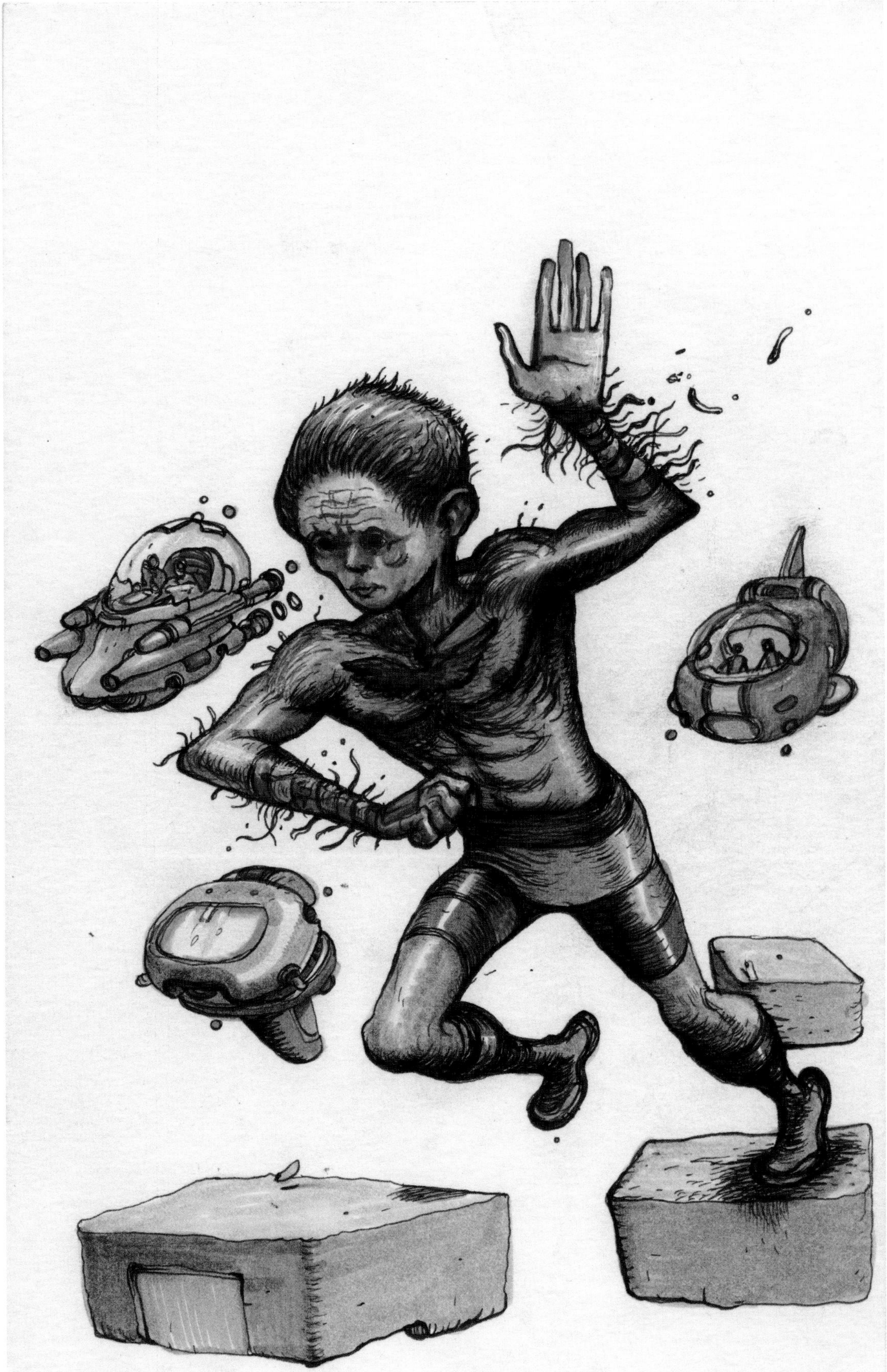

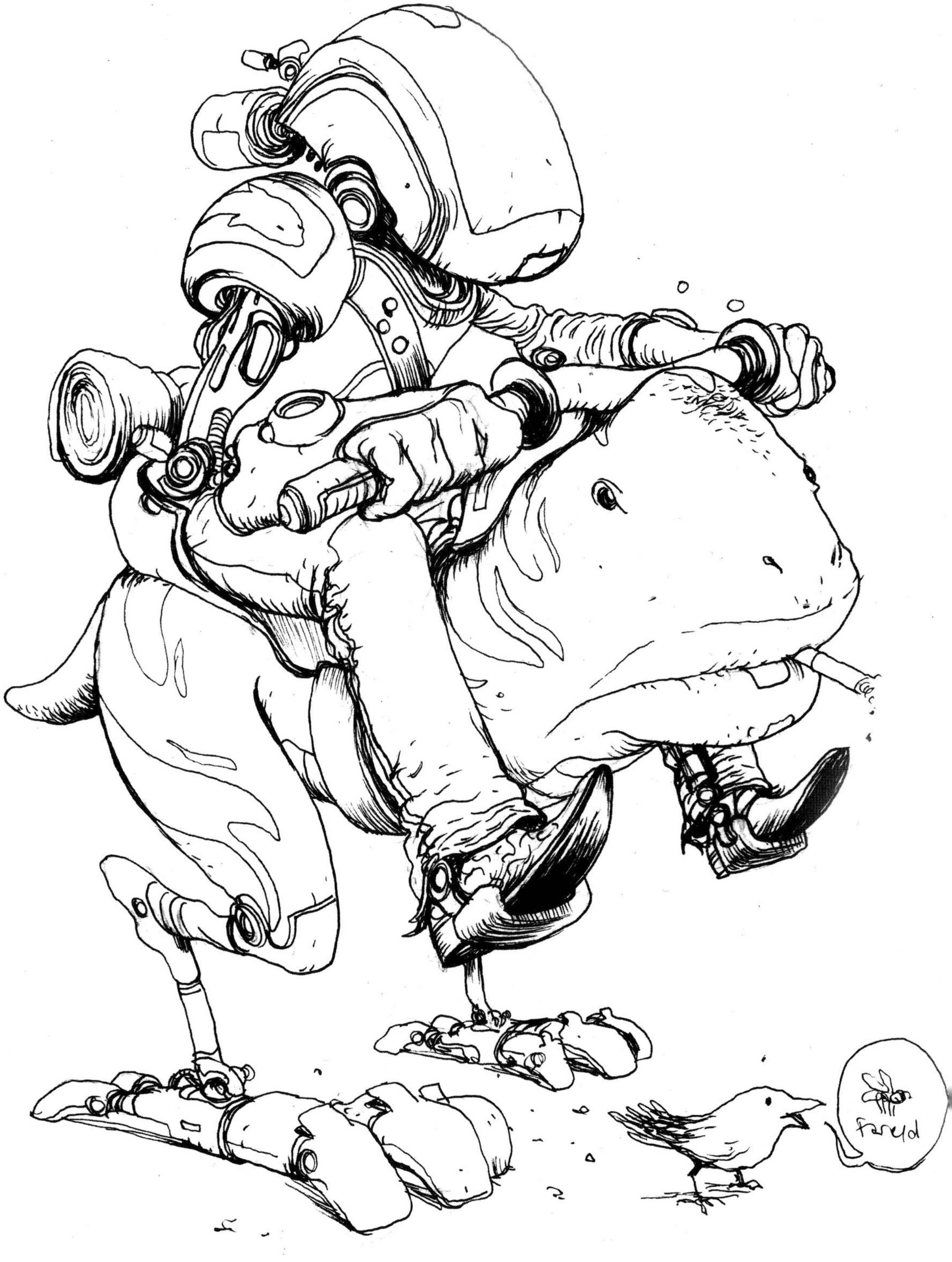

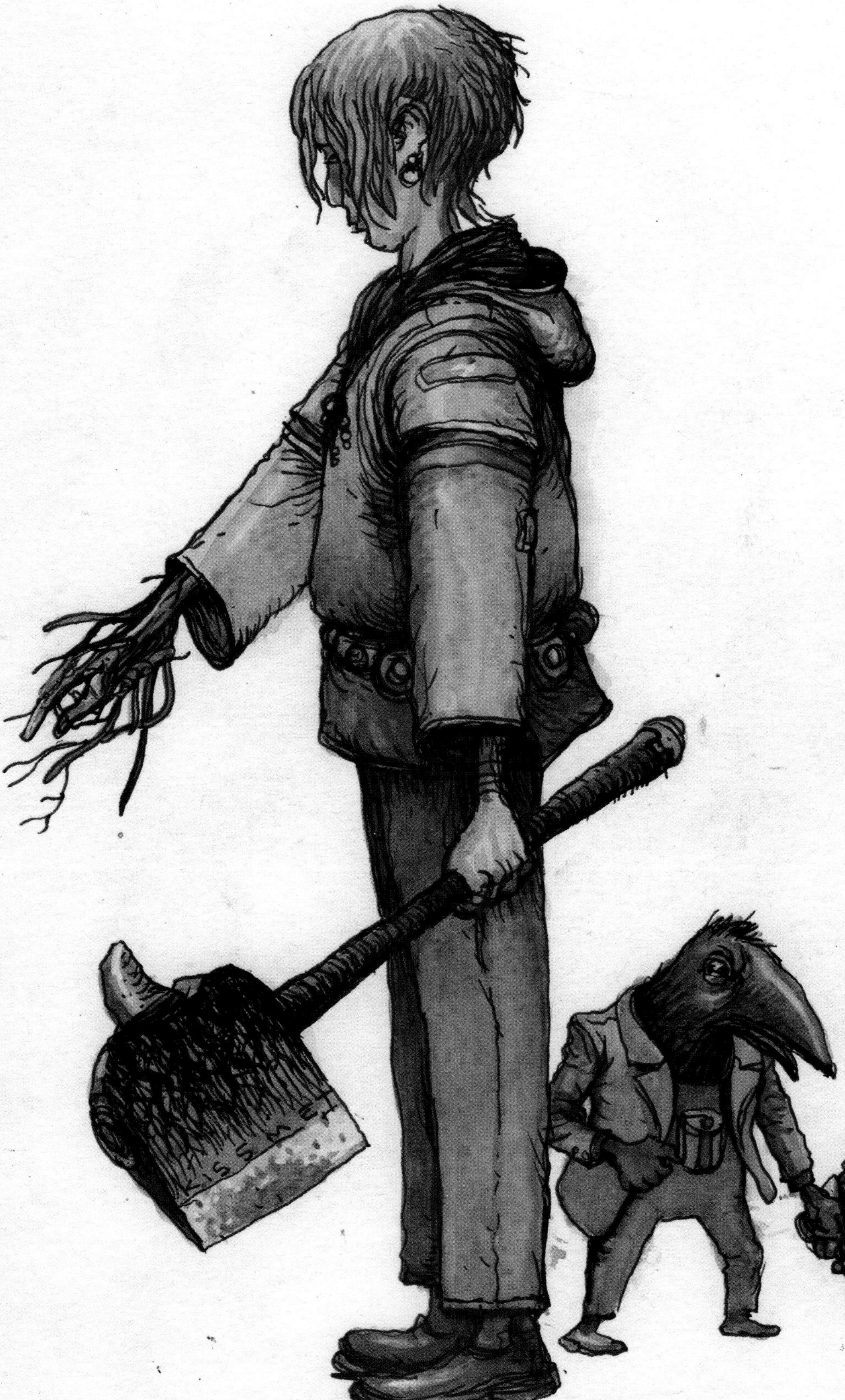
KISS ME

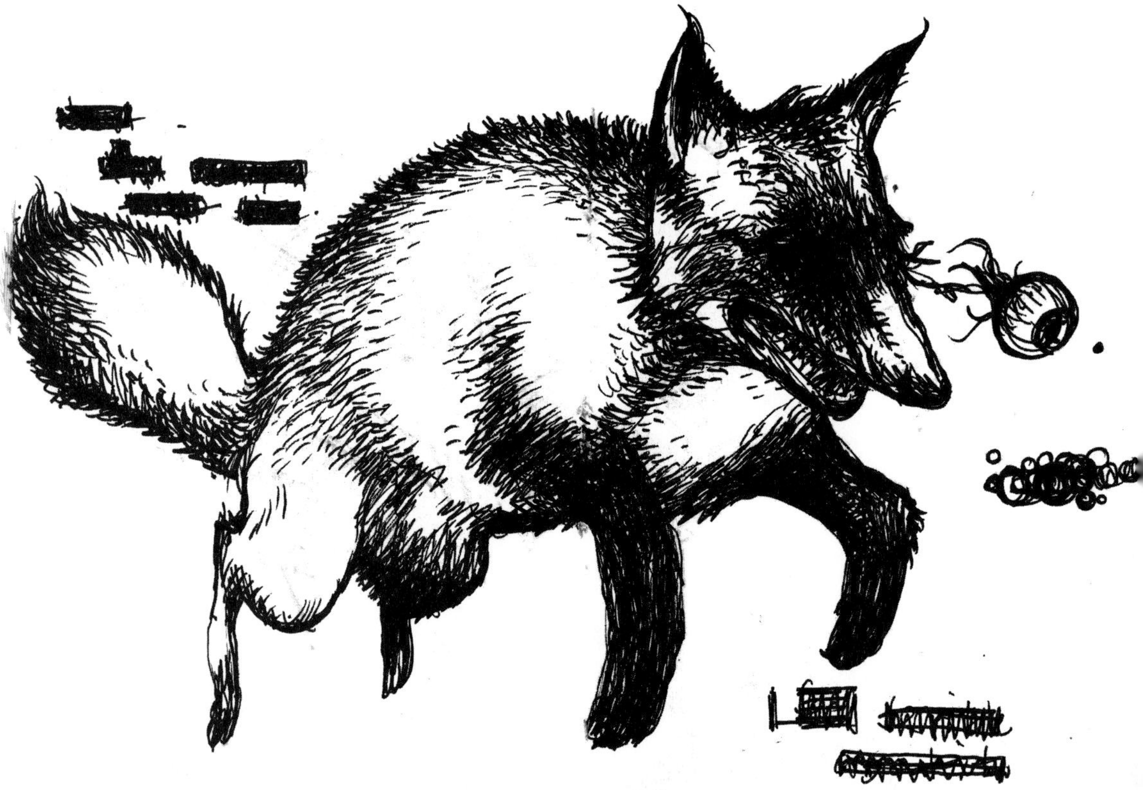

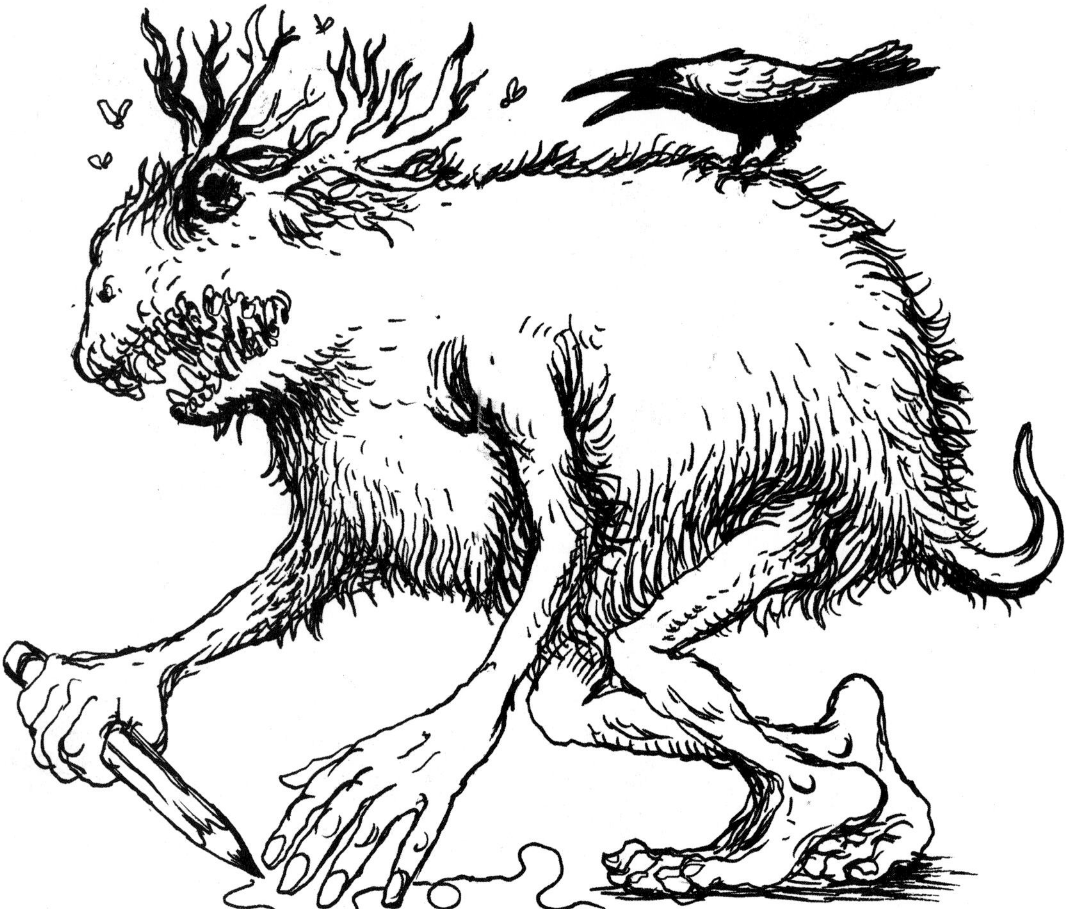

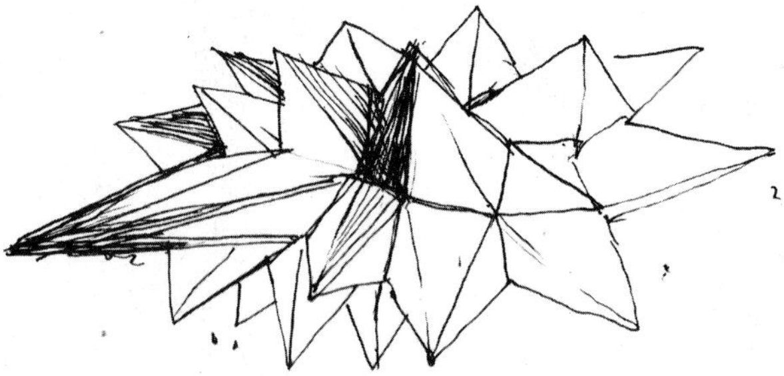

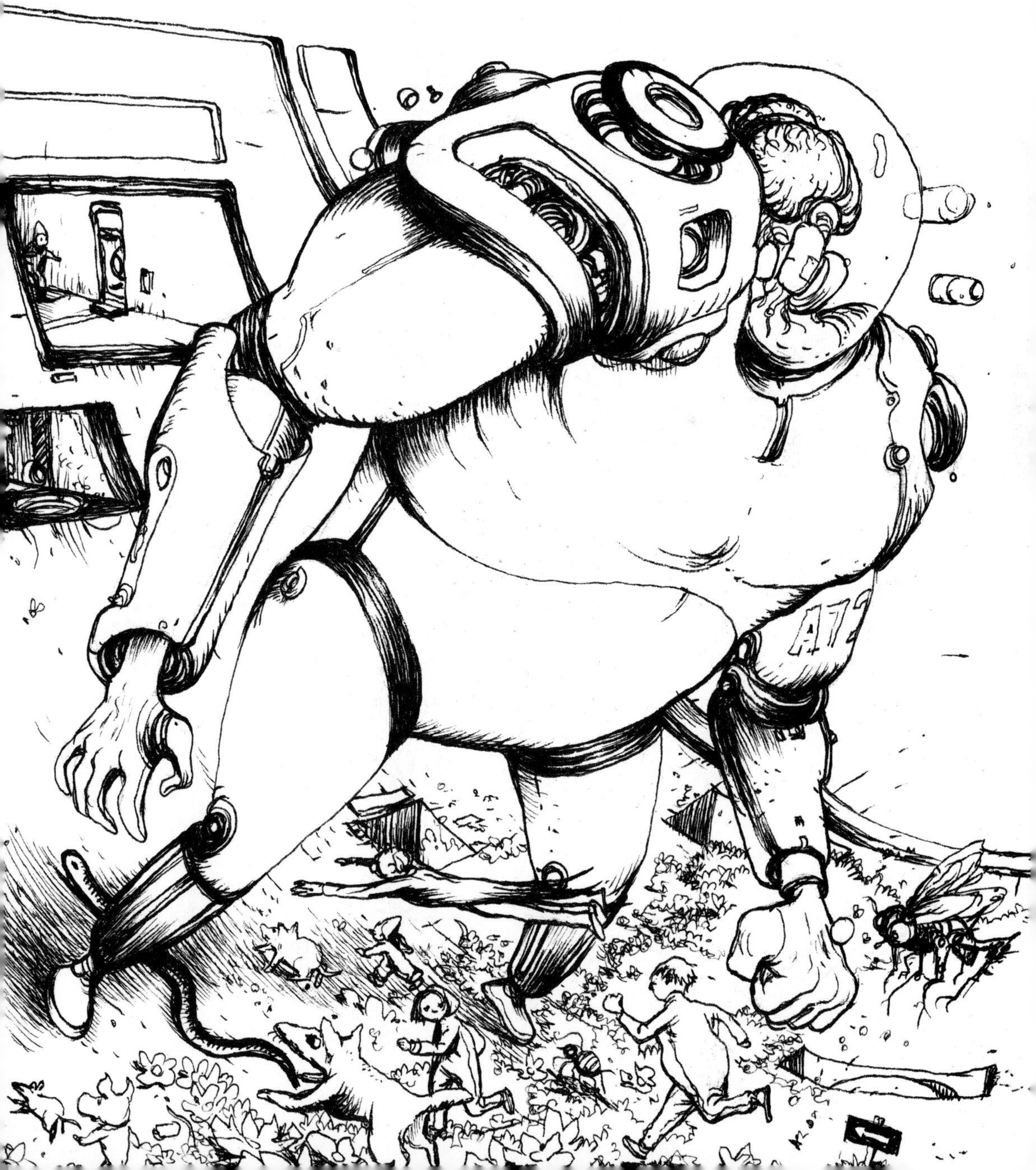

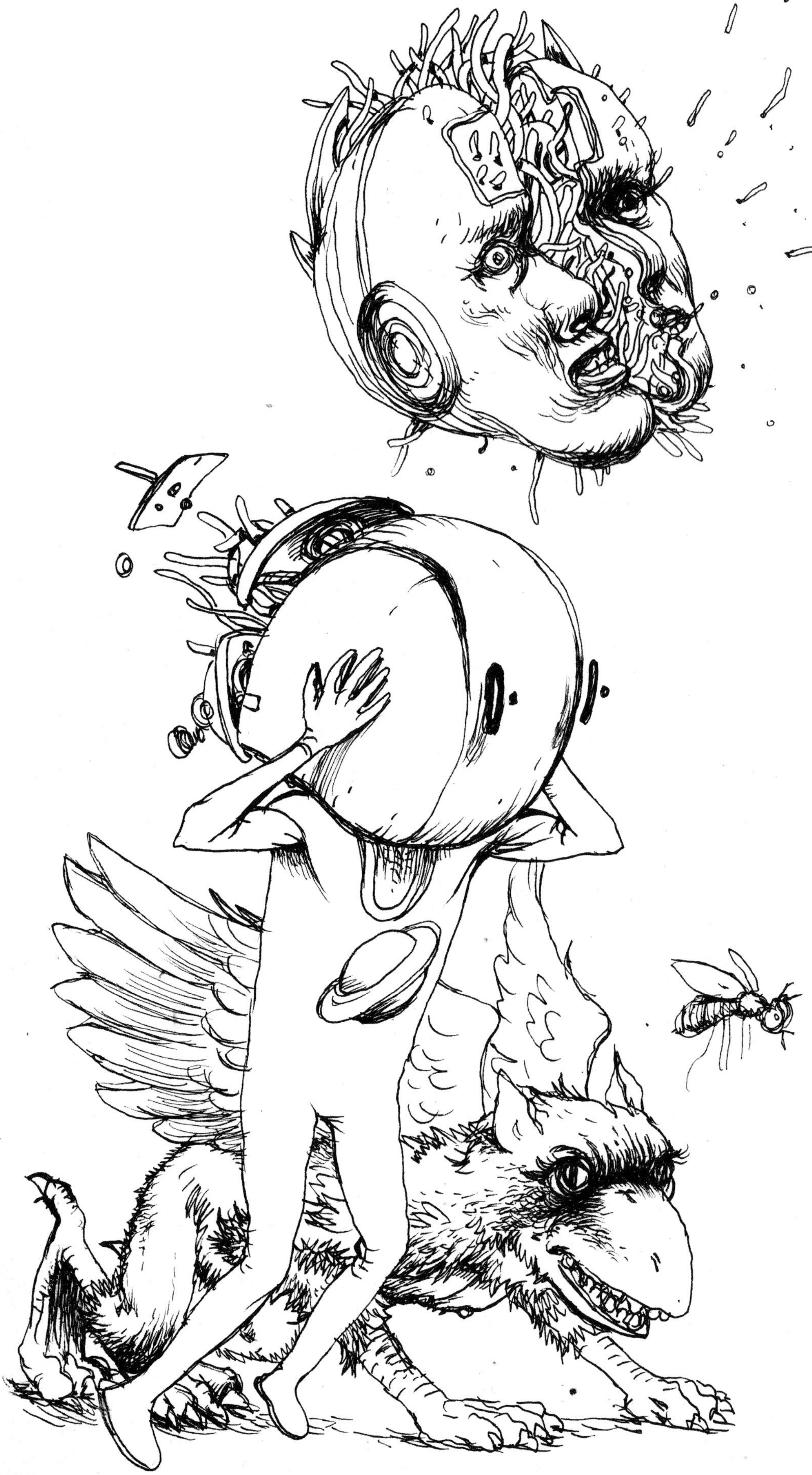

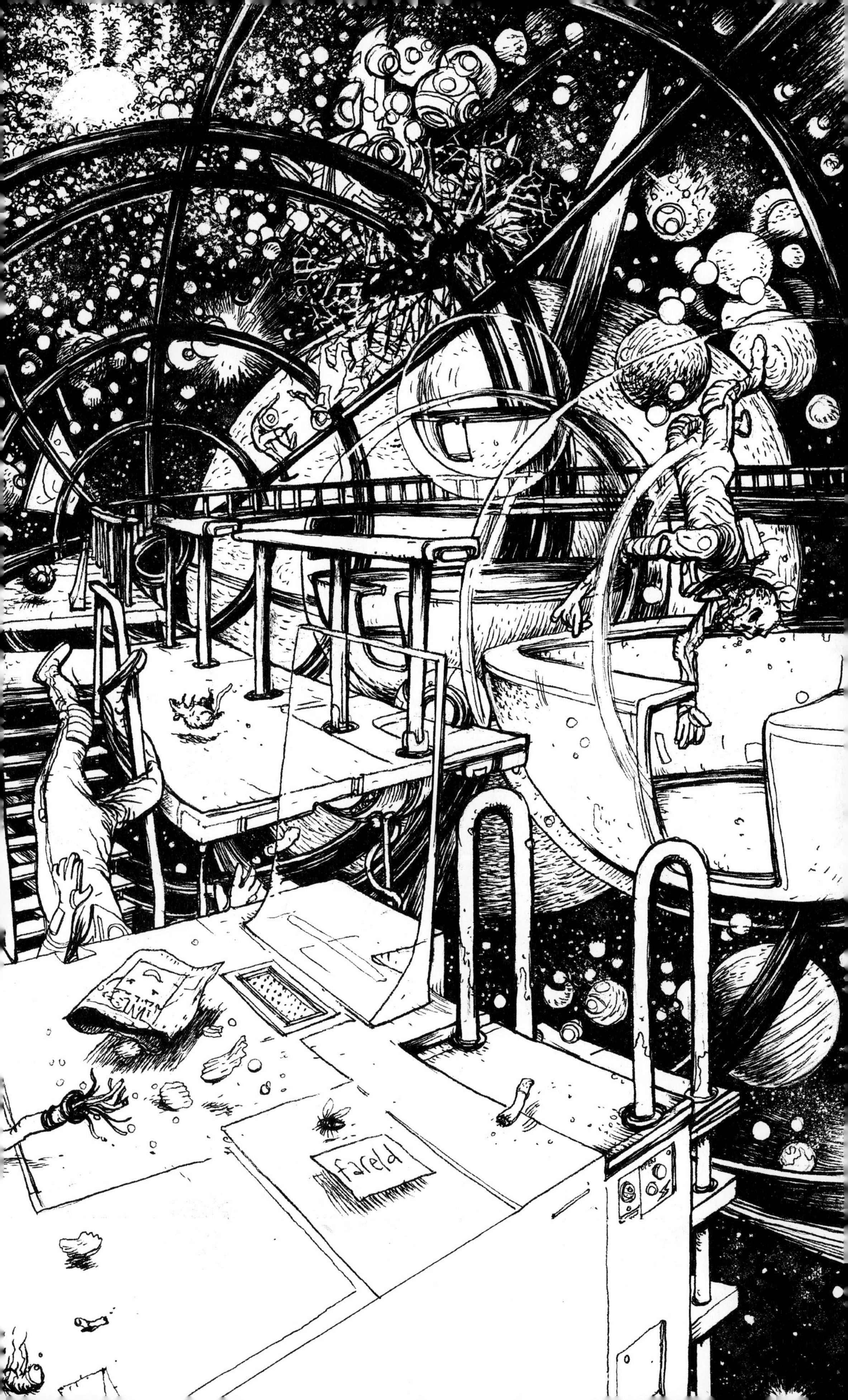
fareld

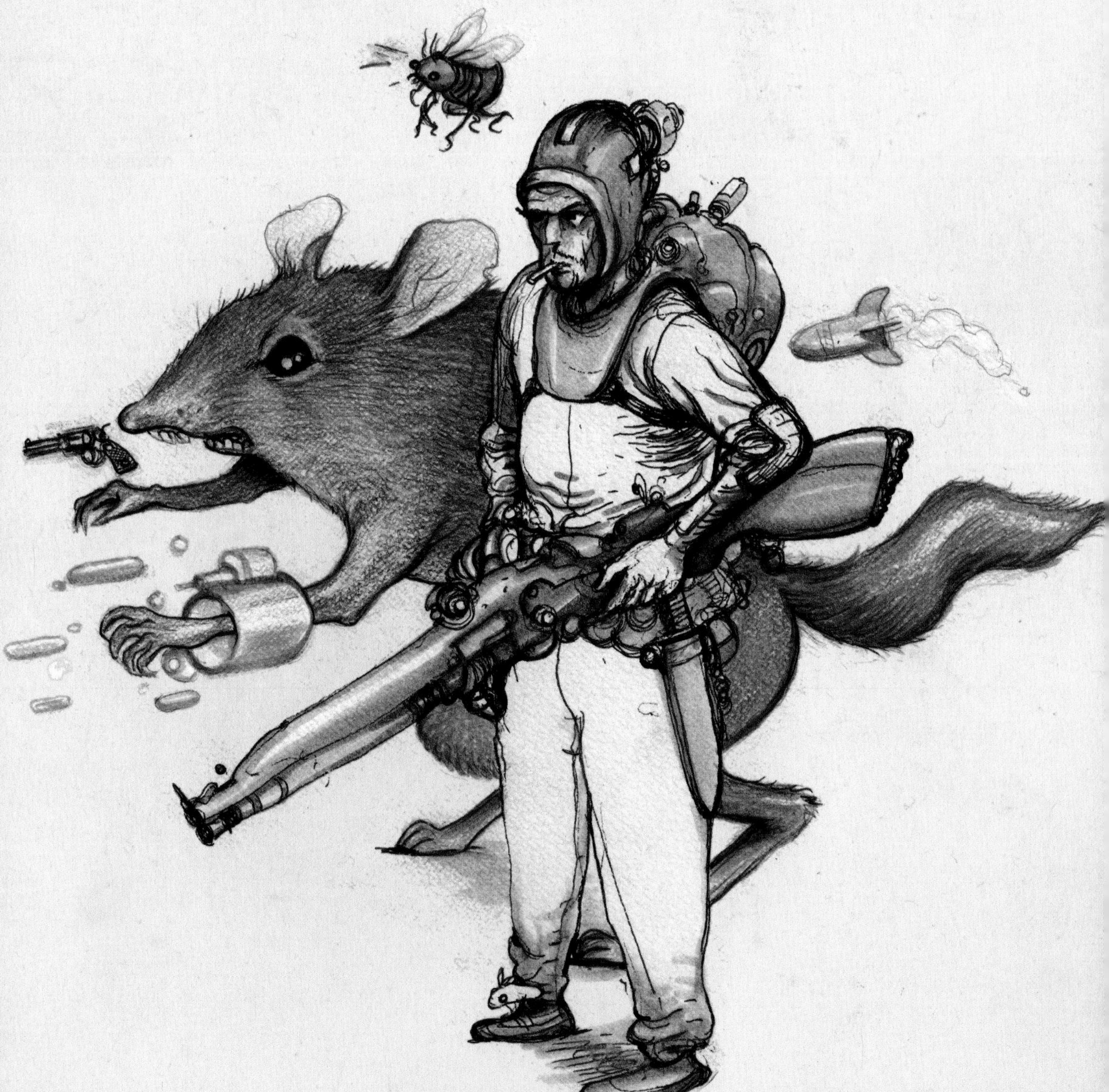

f a m i l y

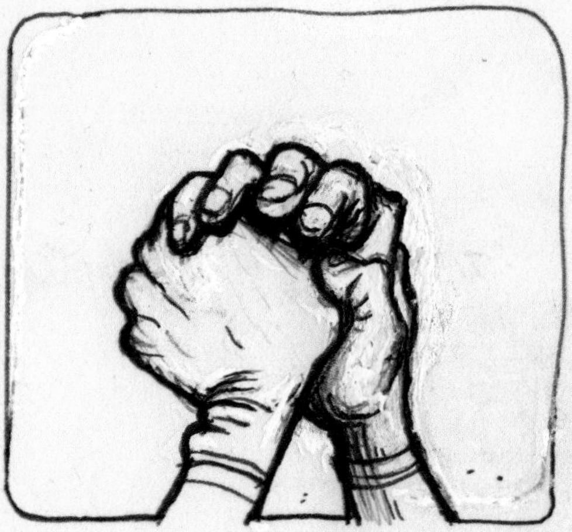

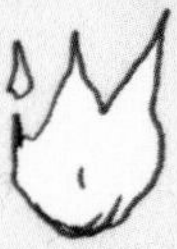

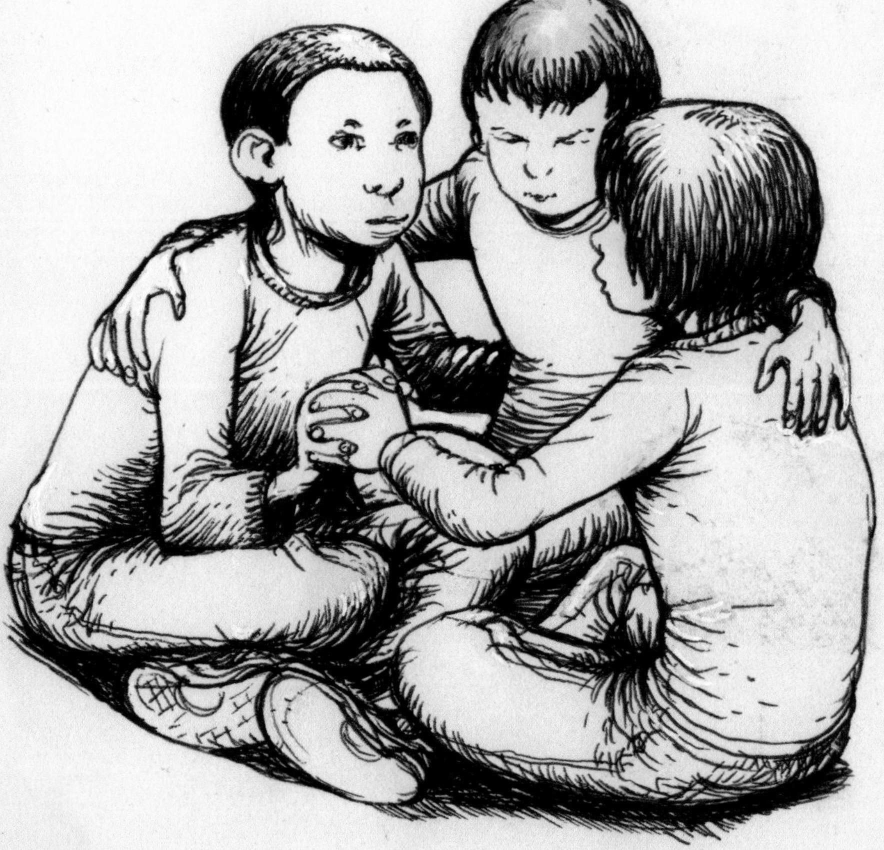

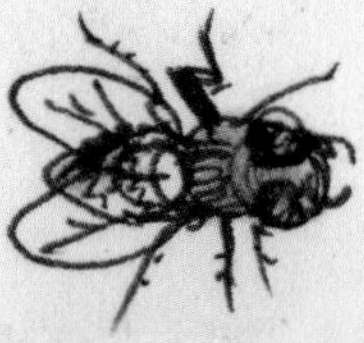

-[redacted]-

[redacted] little buildings [redacted]

[redacted].

[redacted] two [redacted].

[redacted]. [redacted]

[redacted]

also [redacted]

[redacted]

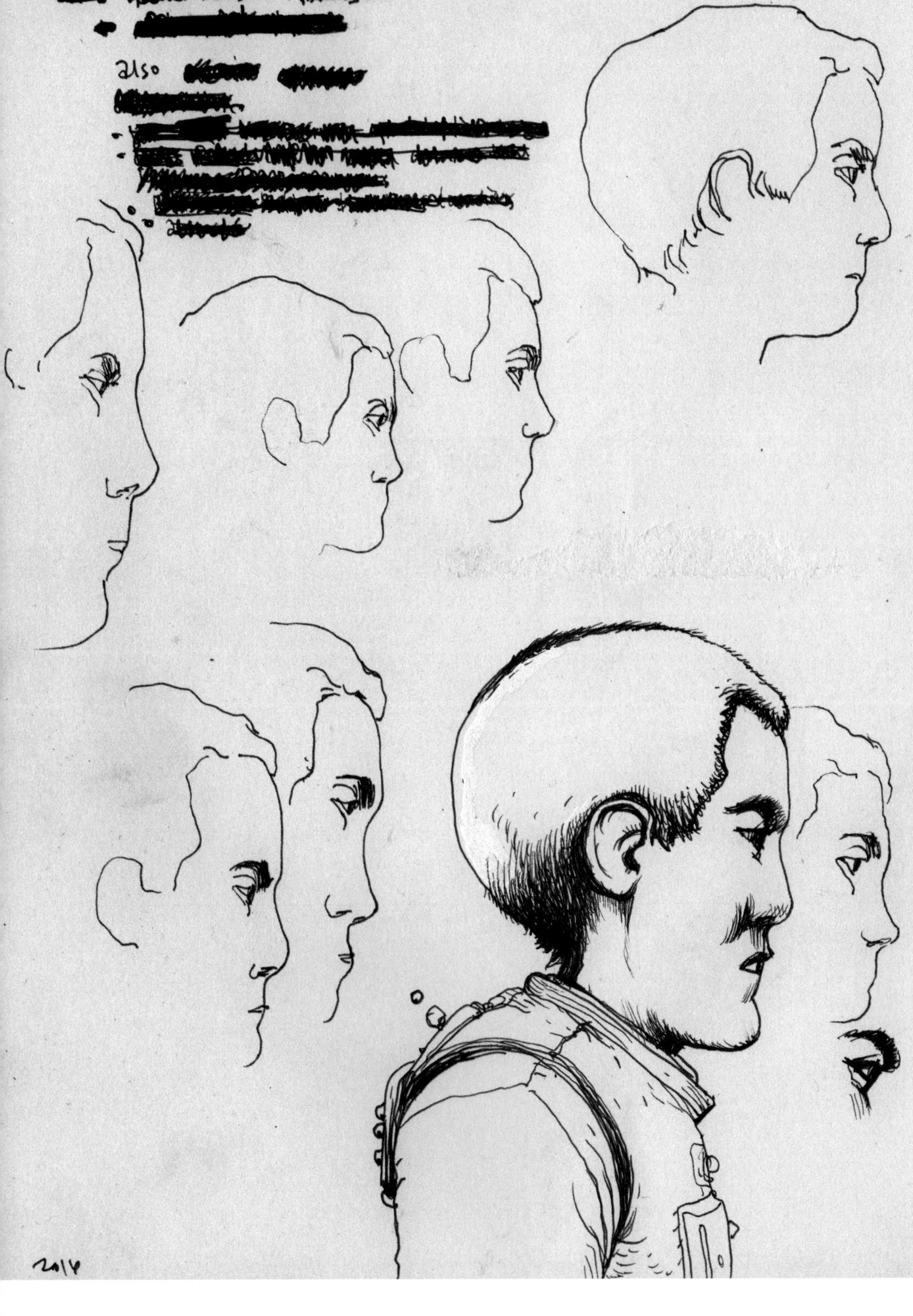

2014

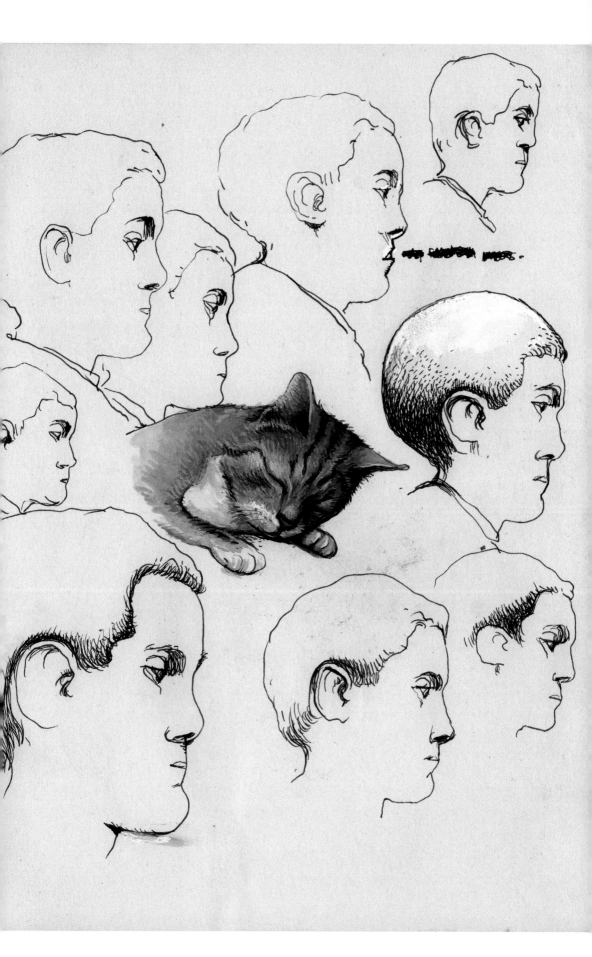

i will survive

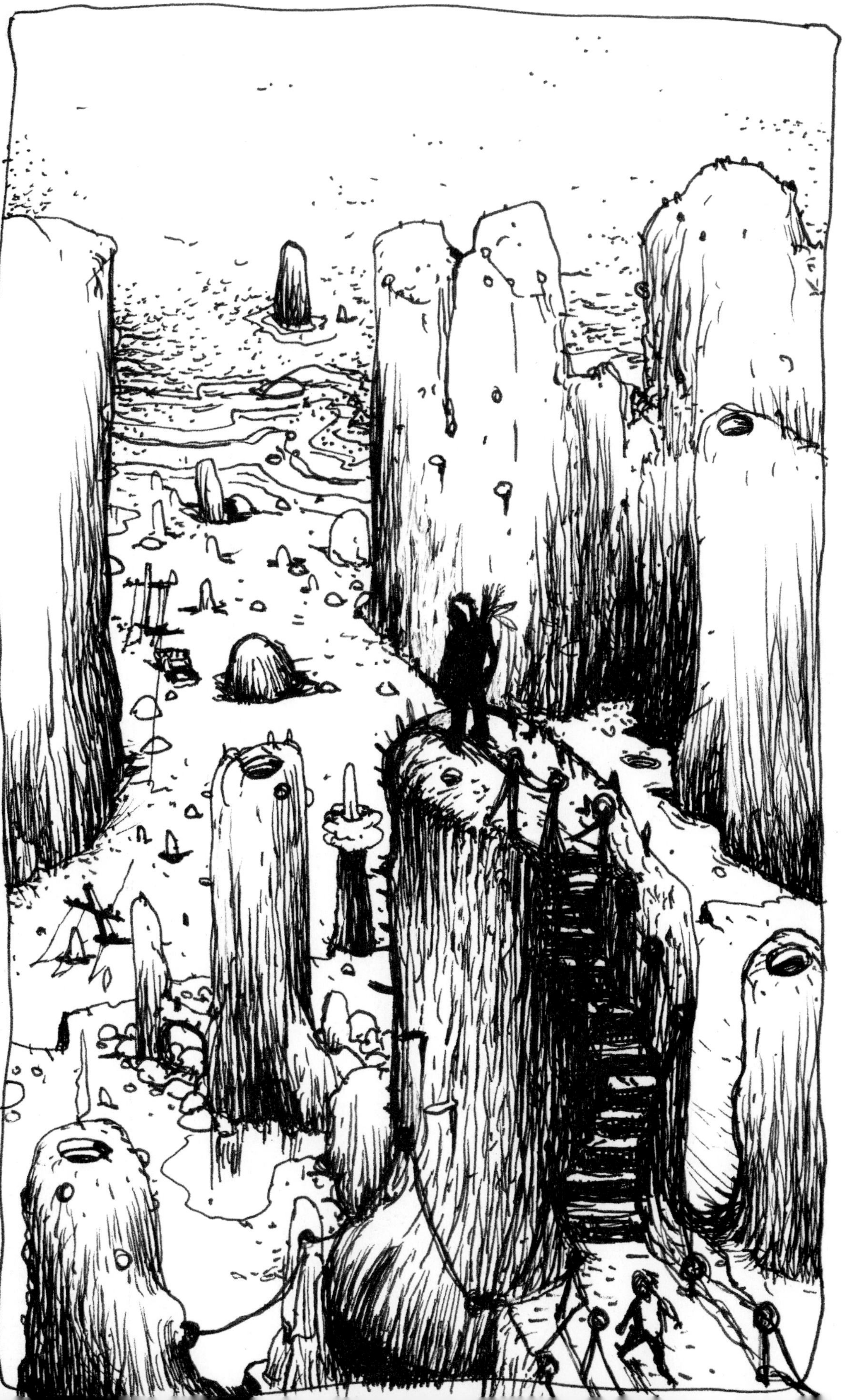

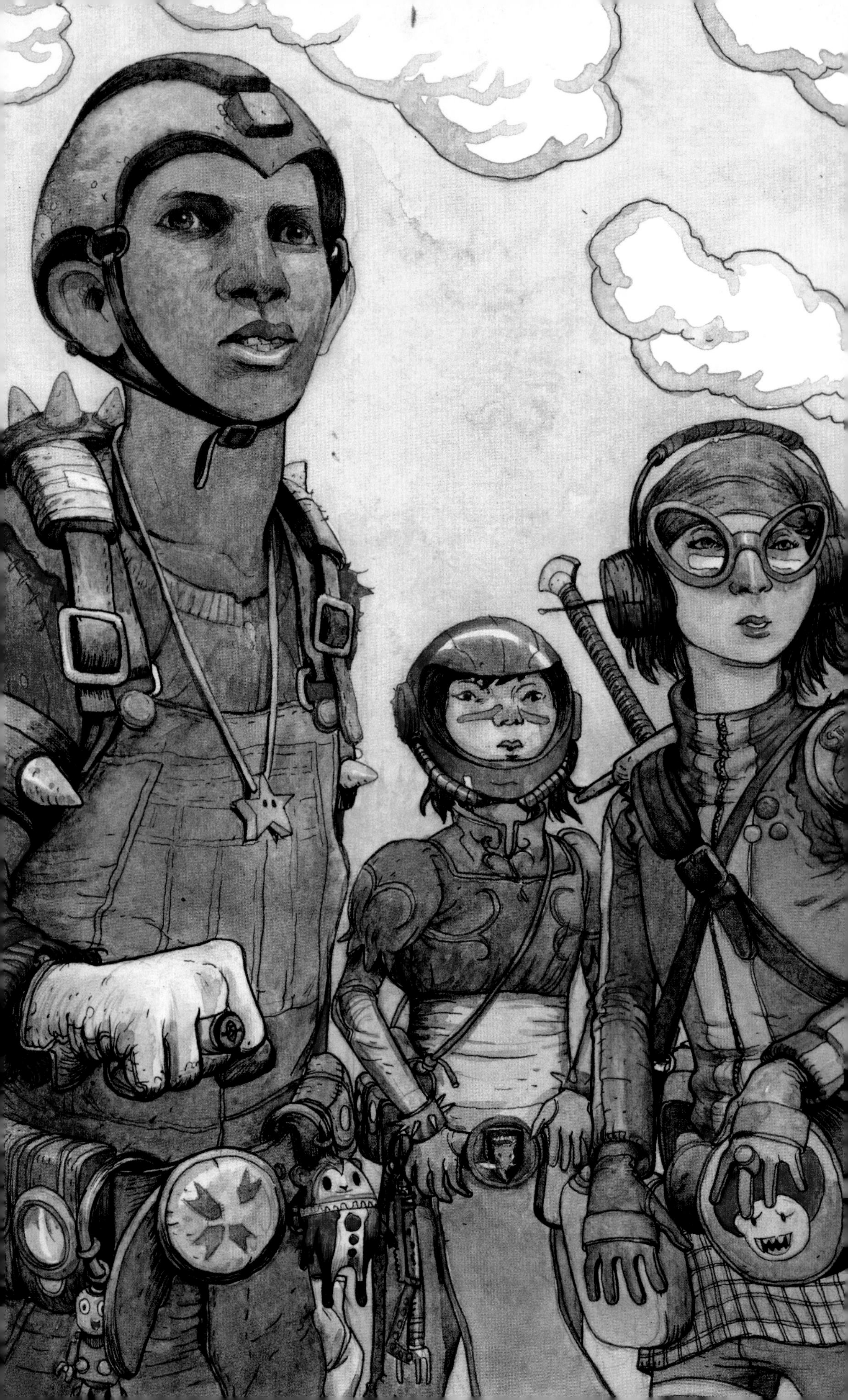

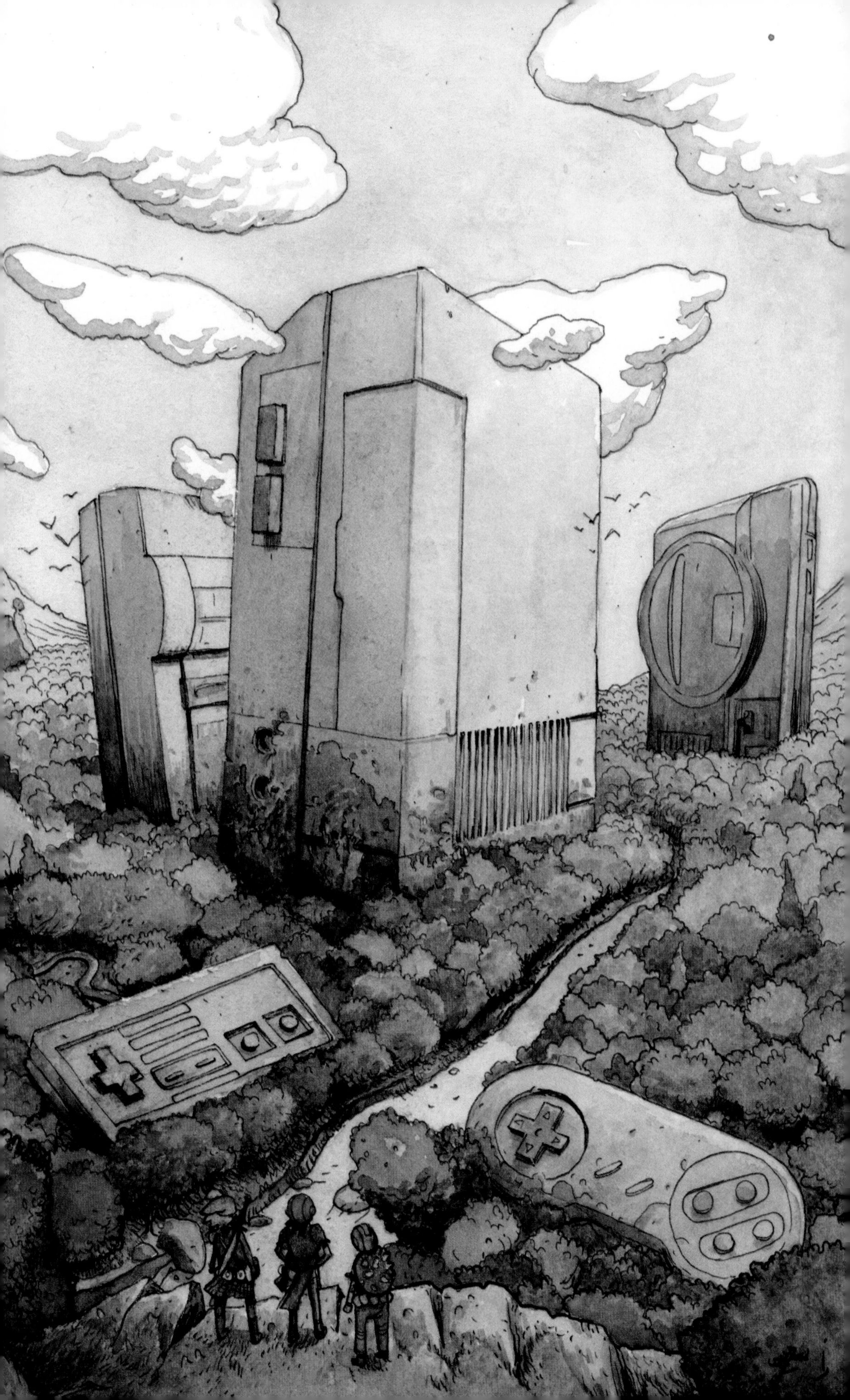

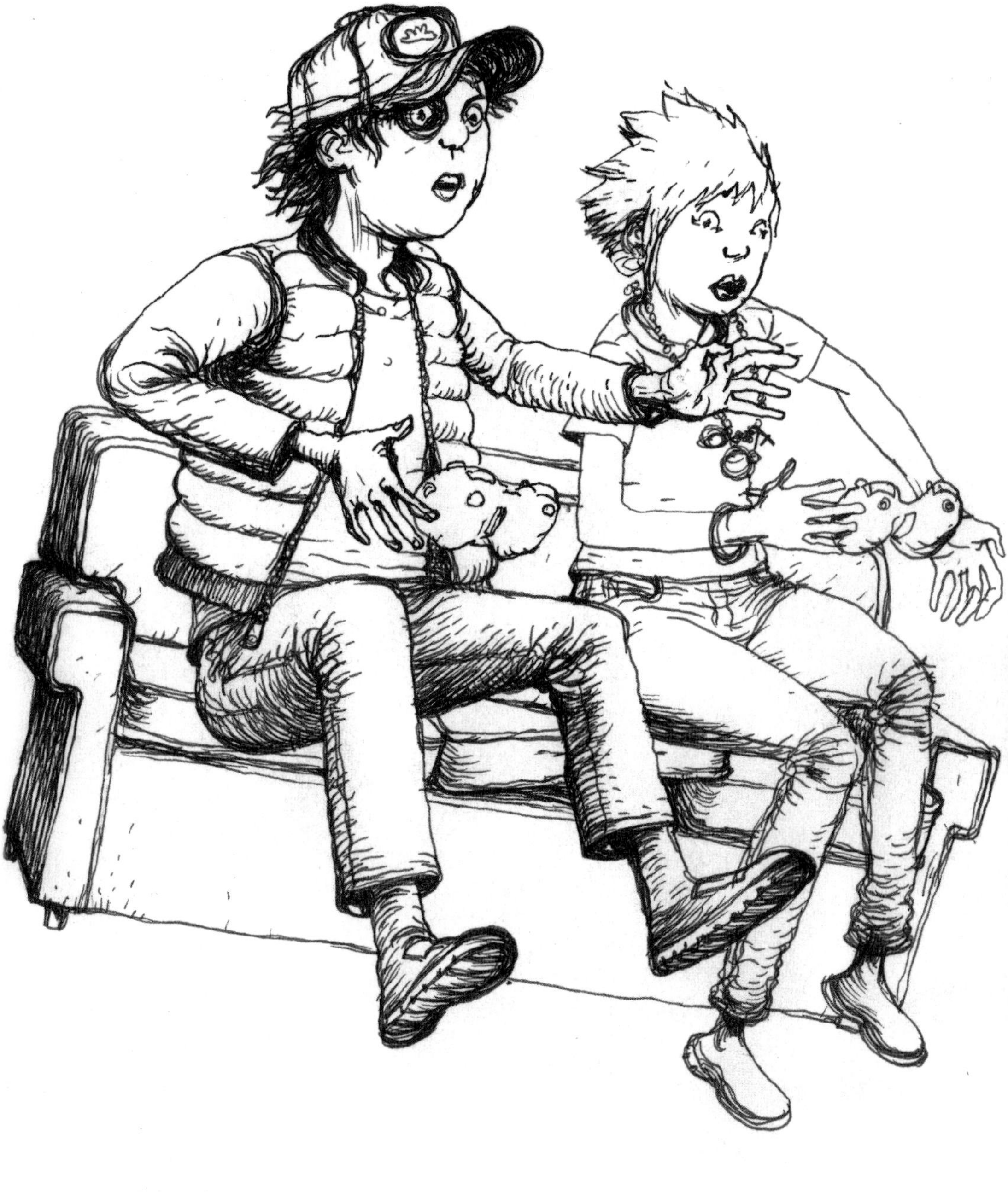

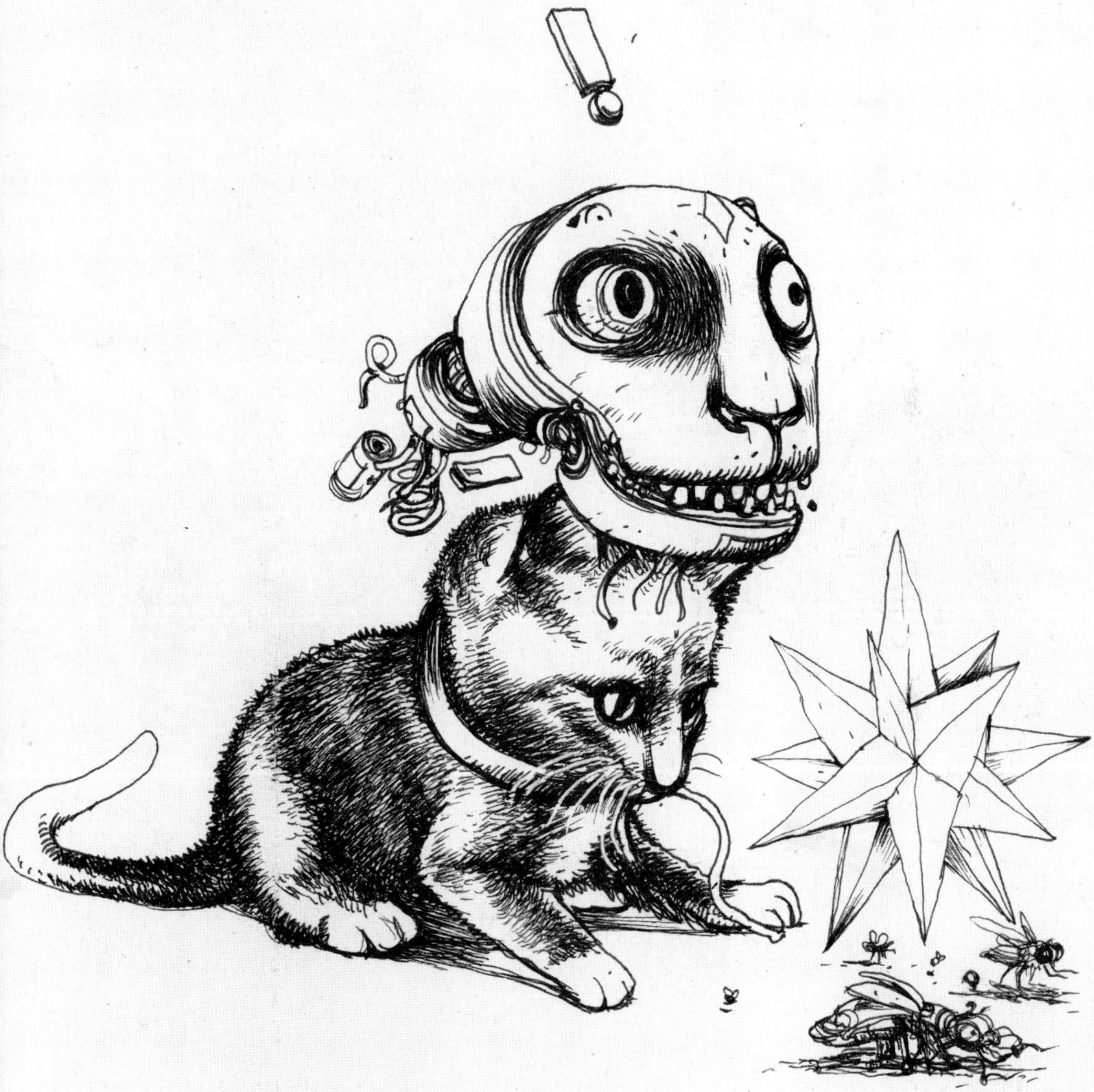

GREAT FALLS
A SENSE OF REST

Great Falls is an excellent band from Seattle, Washington.
A *SENSE OF REST* is available from Corpse Flower Records.

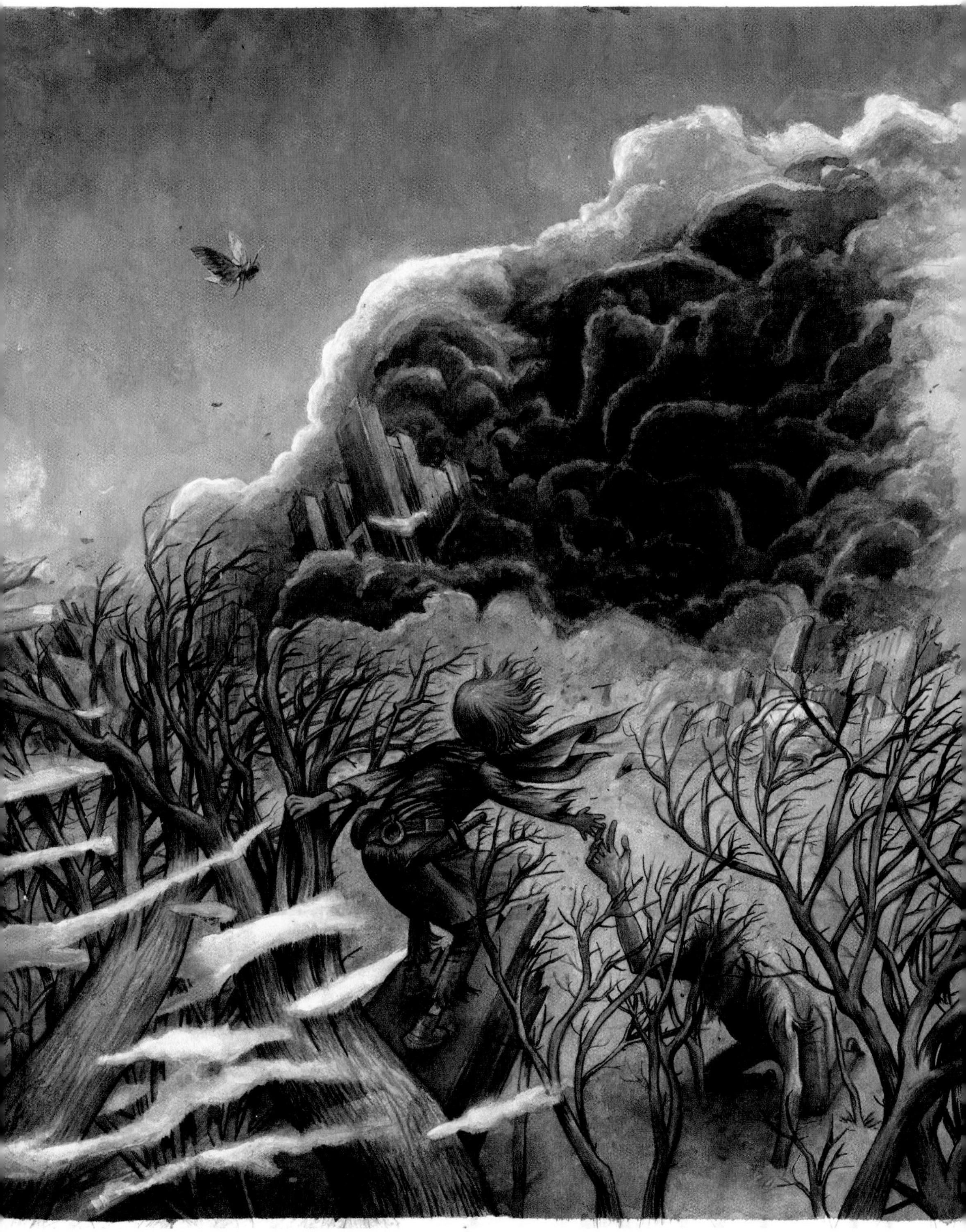

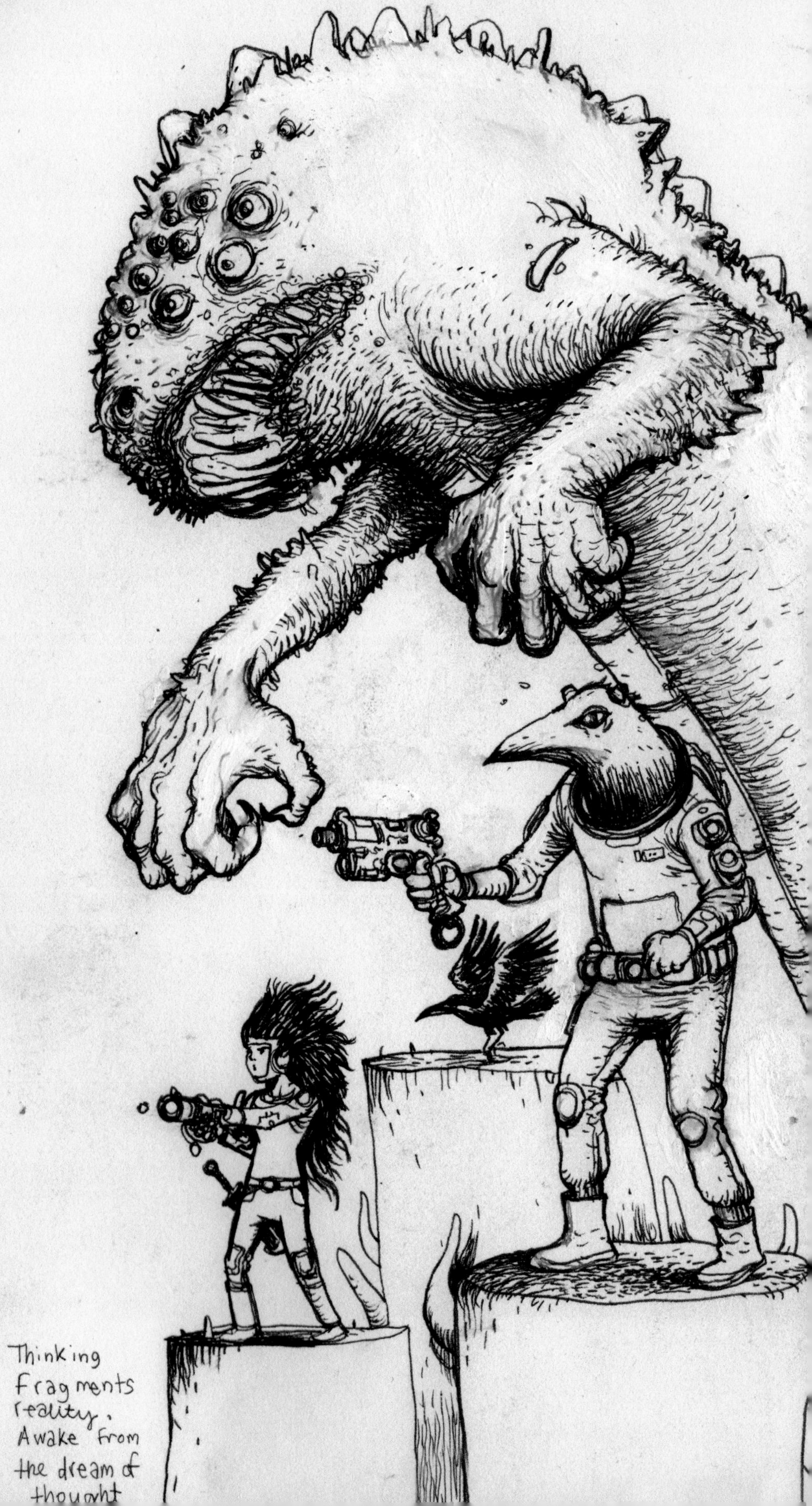
Thinking
fragments
reality.
Awake from
the dream of
thought

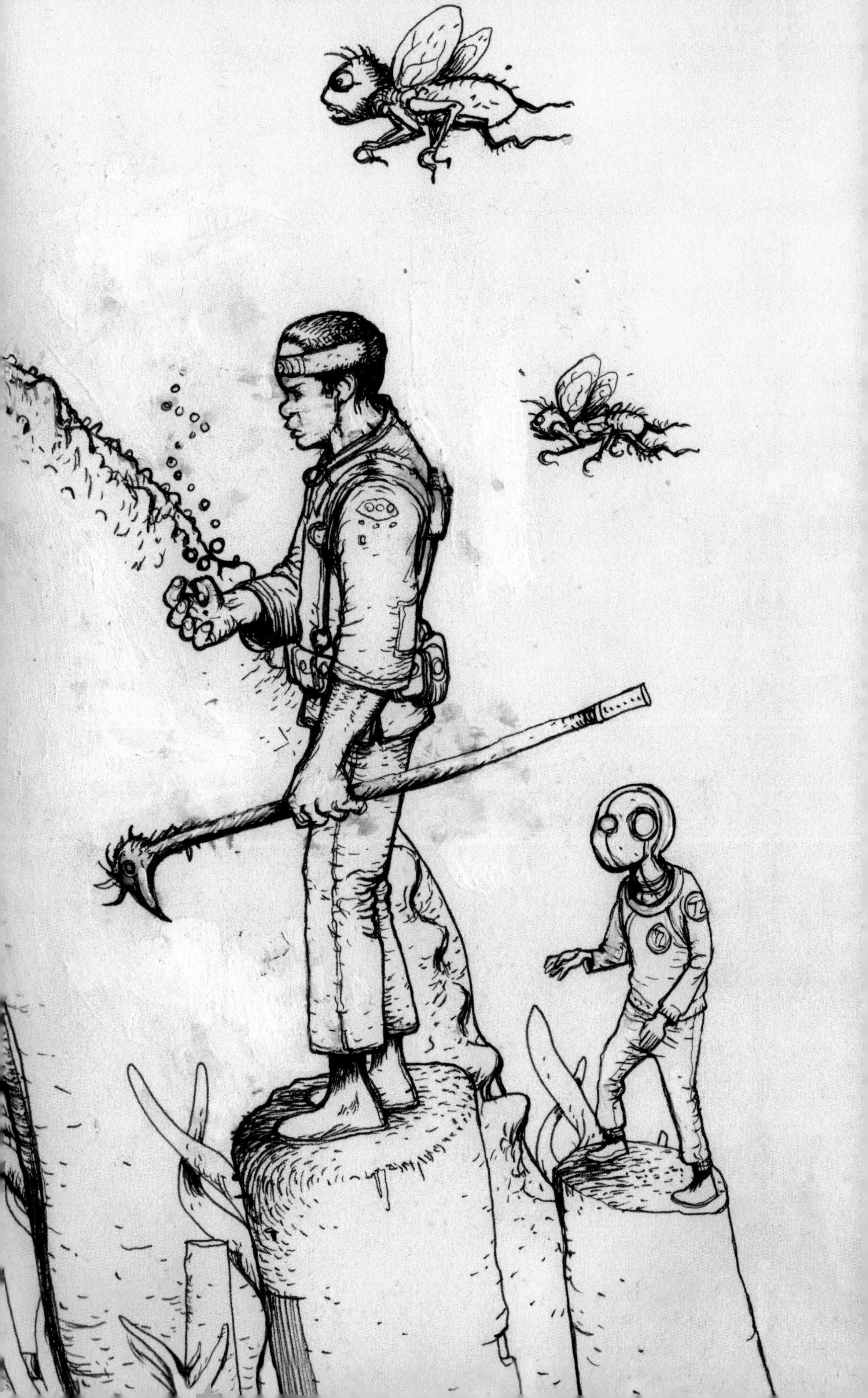

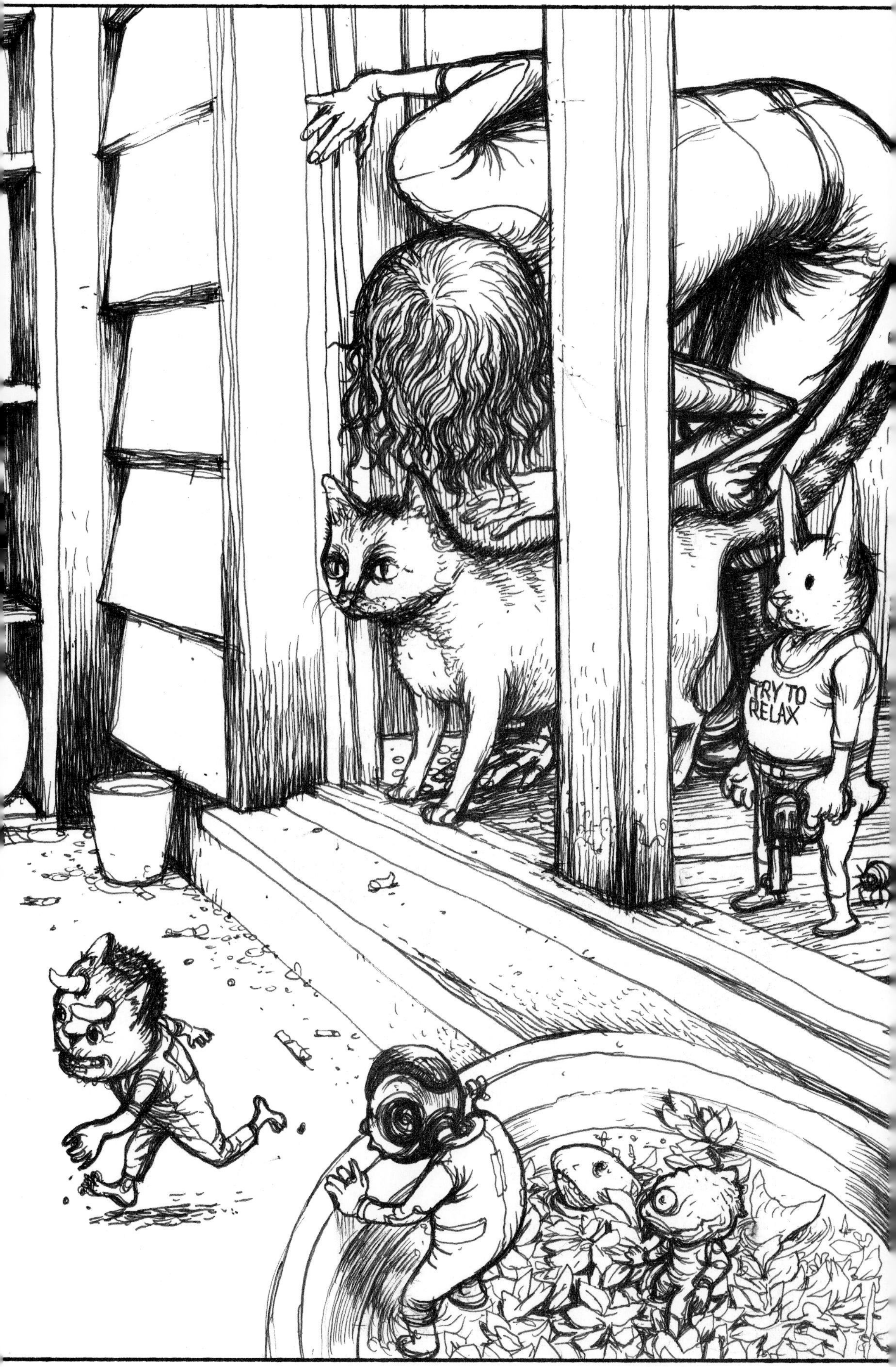
TRY TO RELAX

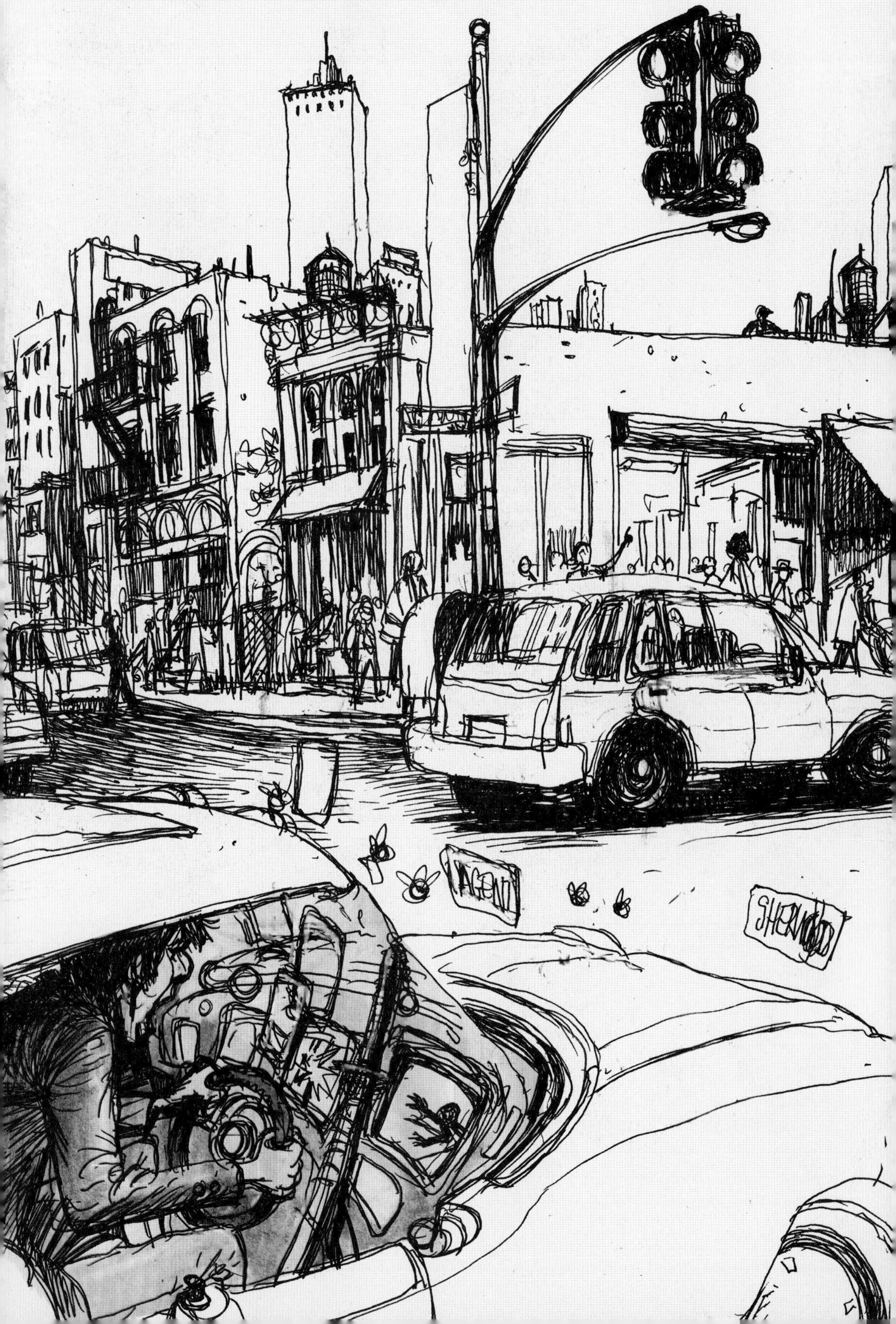
AGENT

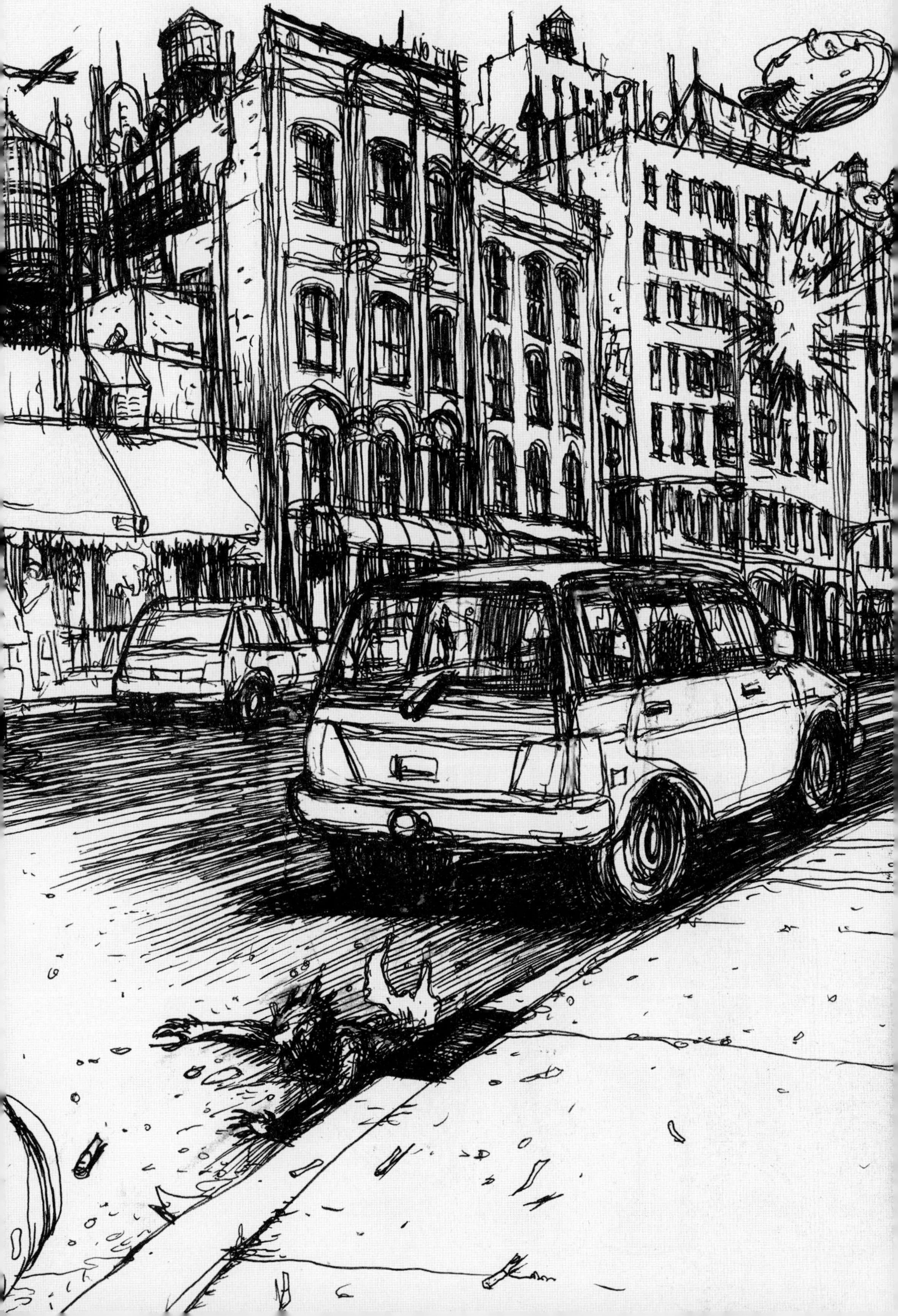
NO TIME

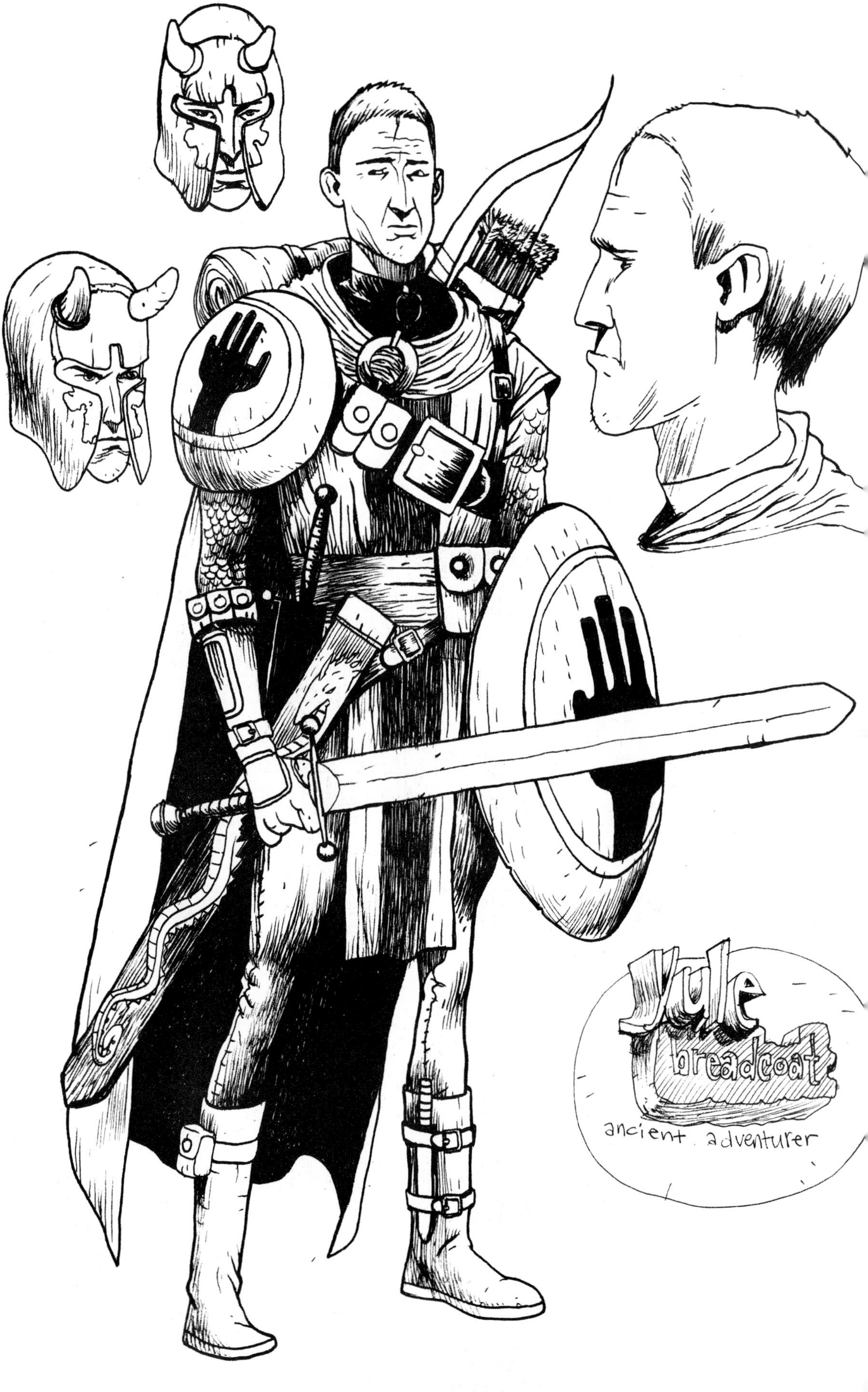
Yule
breadcoat
ancient adventurer

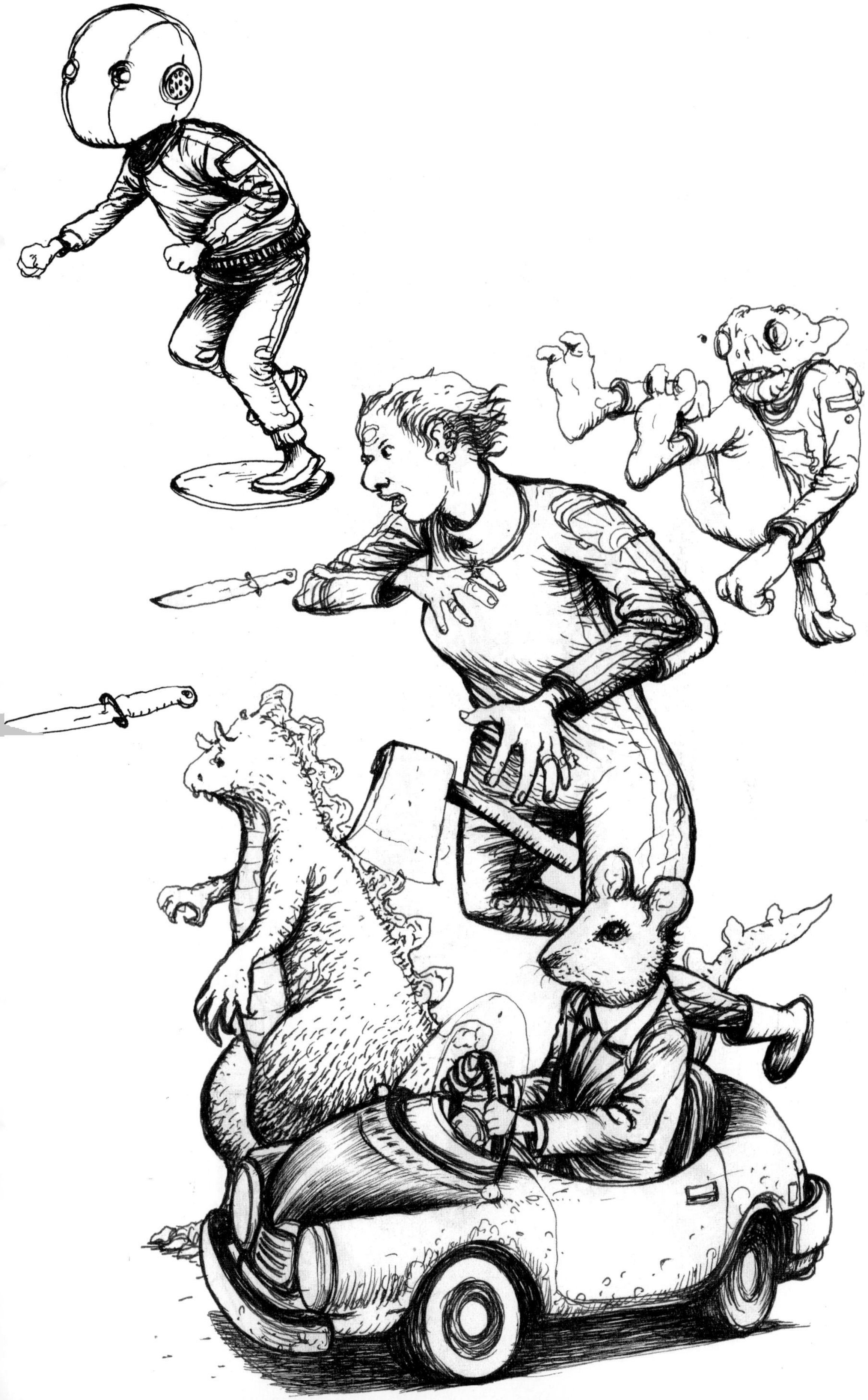

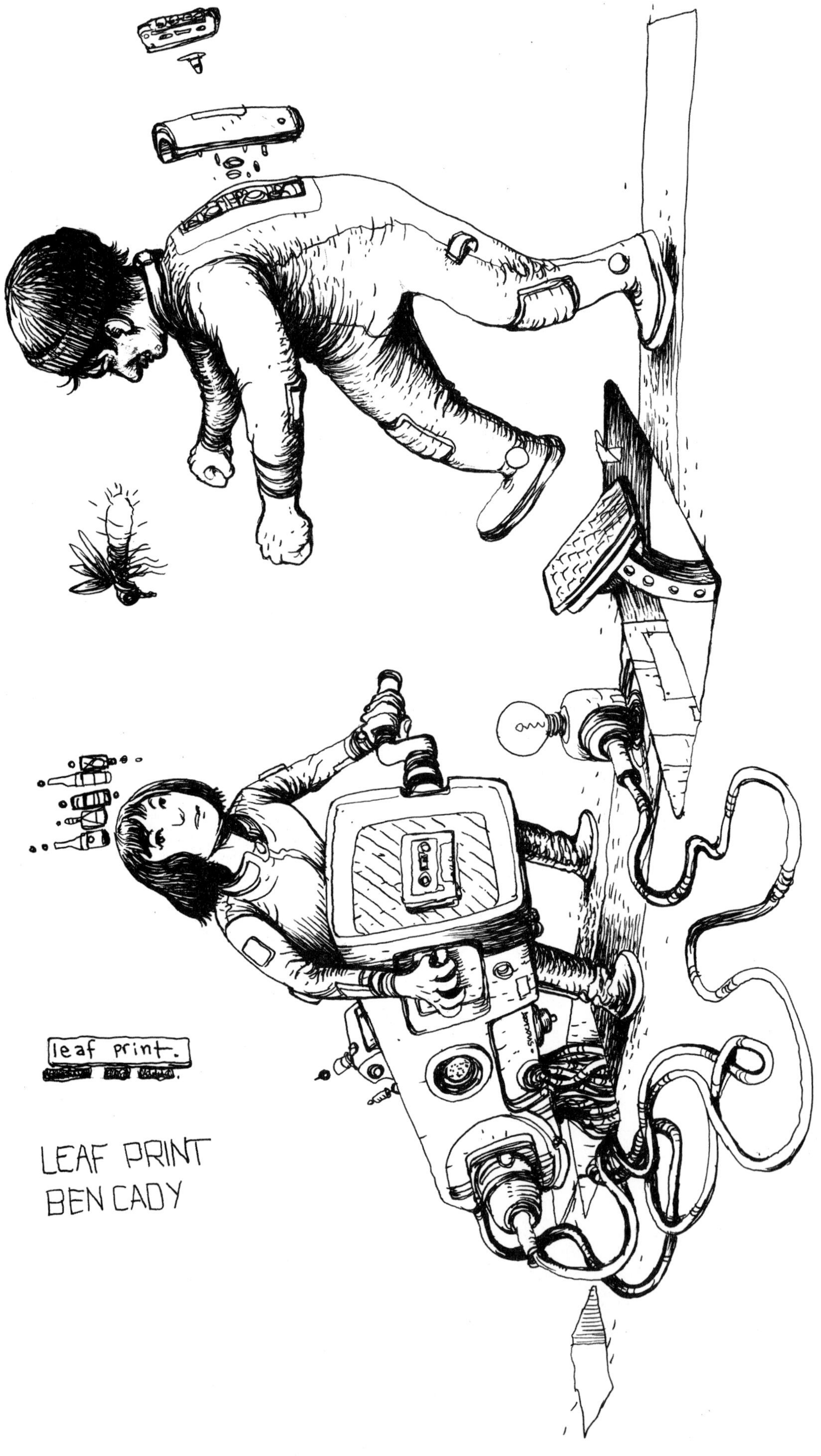
leaf print.

LEAF PRINT
BEN CADY

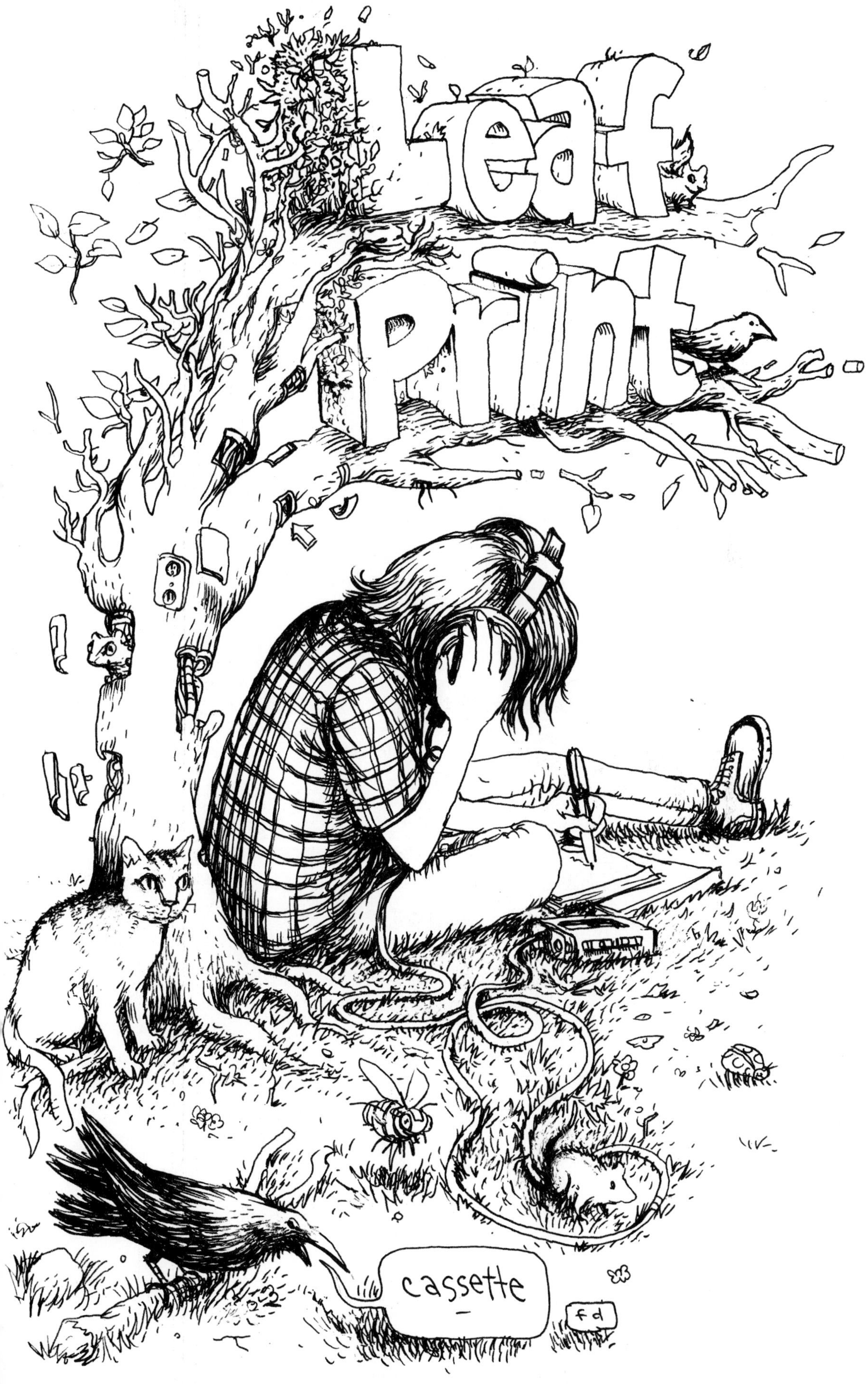
Leaf
Print
cassette
fd

Almendra Clementine is the main hero and leader in *IT WILL ALL HURT.*
Most of that book was drawn straight in pen without pencilling first. The story
started out as a stream of consciousness experiment, making it up as I went
along. The following tale was made in a similar way after i held a
contest online to name the alien astronaut character.

Leon Fireglove and Blam Dabbit

from the pages of

It Will All Hurt,

in: [redacted] Rugsby

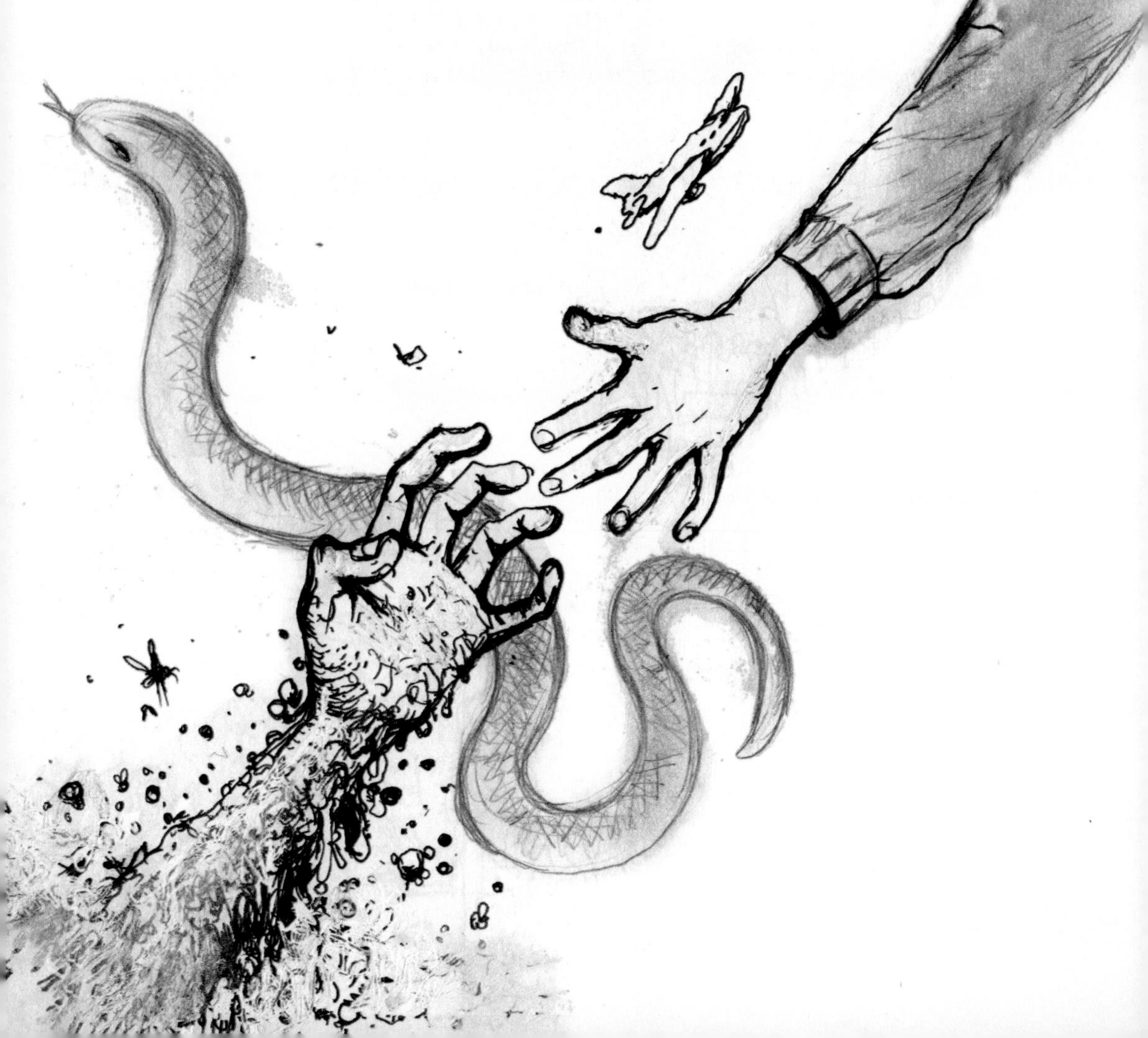

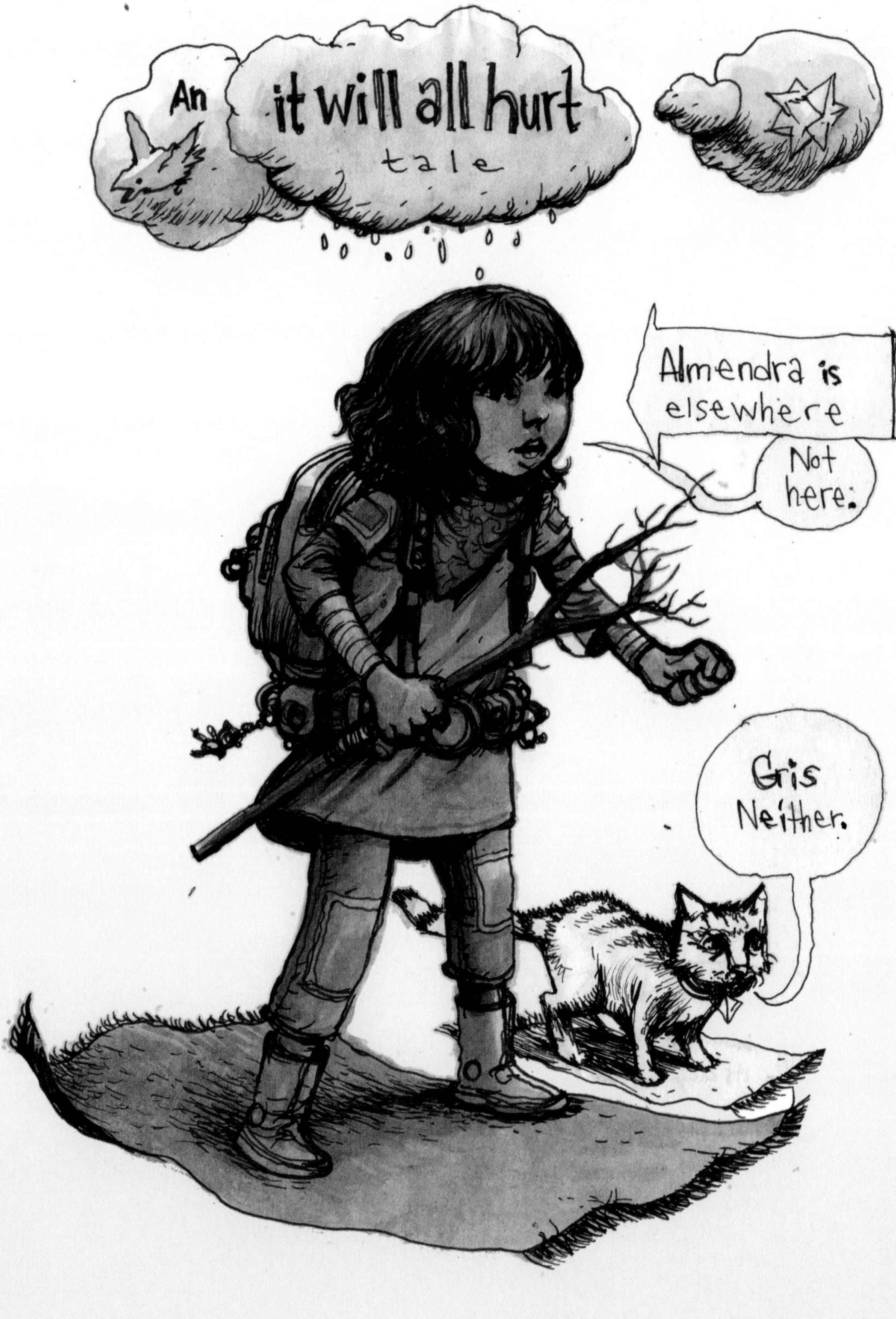
An it will all hurt tale
Almendra is elsewhere
Not here.
Gris Neither.

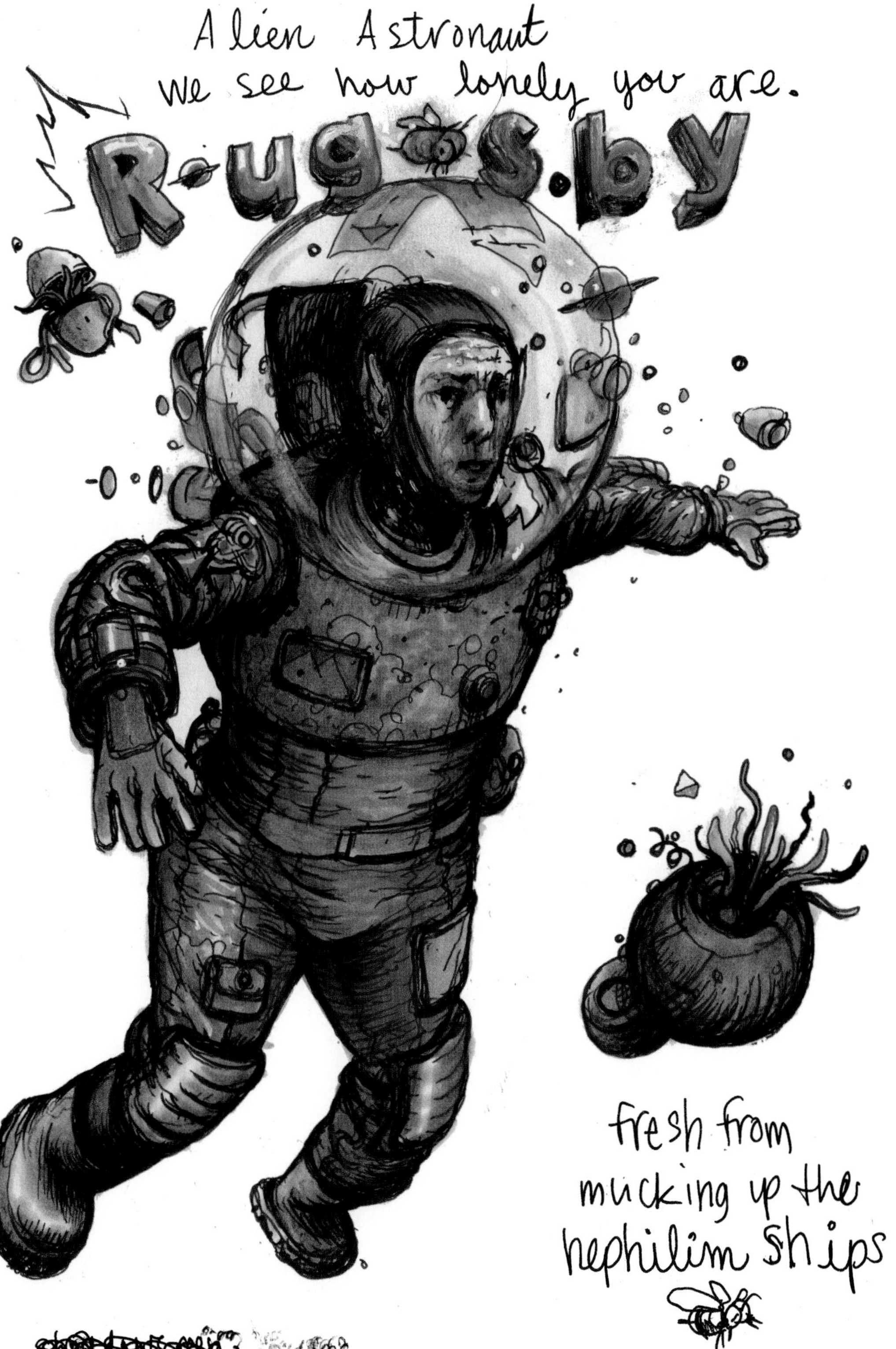
Alien Astronaut
we see how lonely you are.
Rugsby
fresh from
mucking up the
nephilim ships

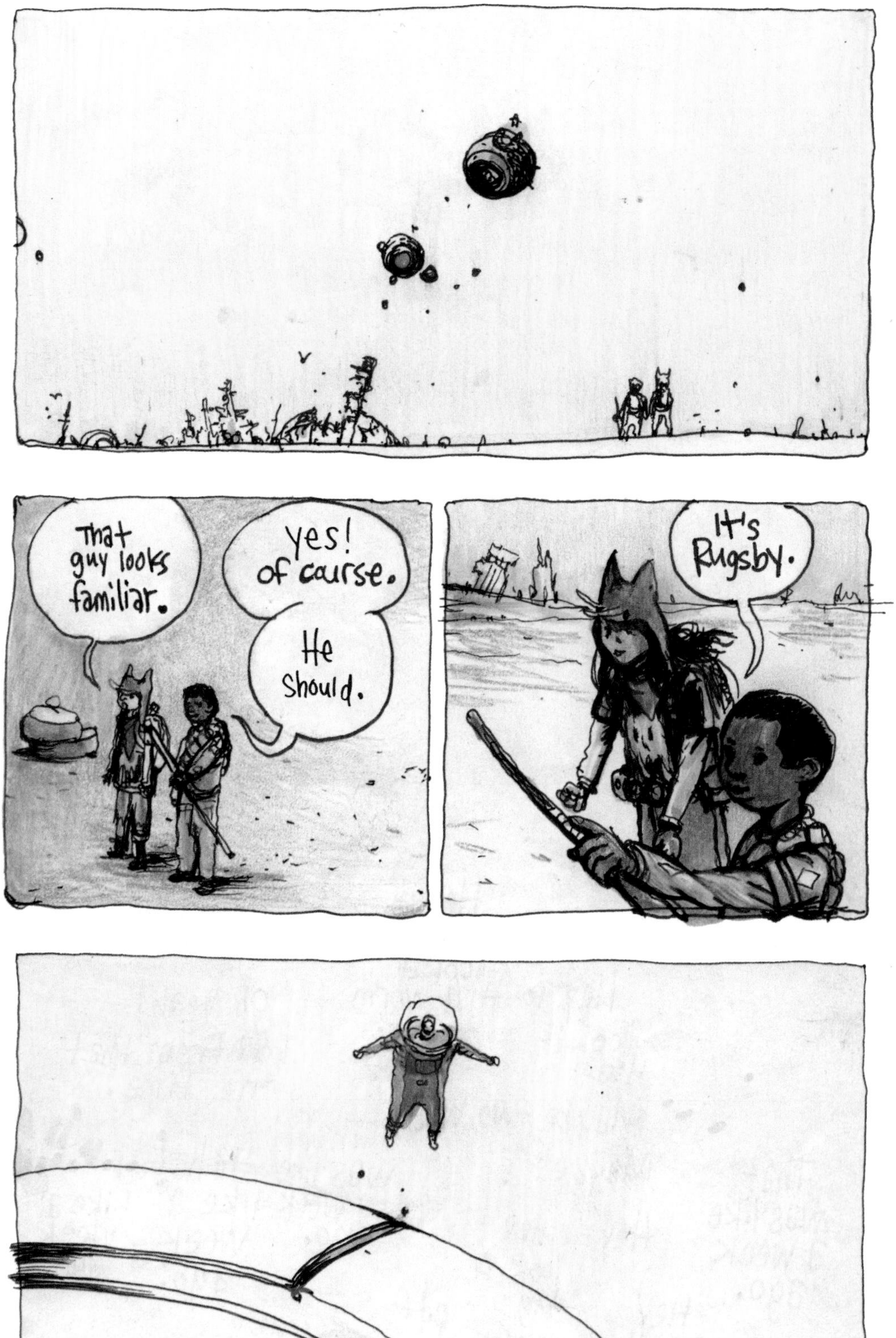
That guy looks familiar.
Yes! of course.
He should.
It's Rugsby.

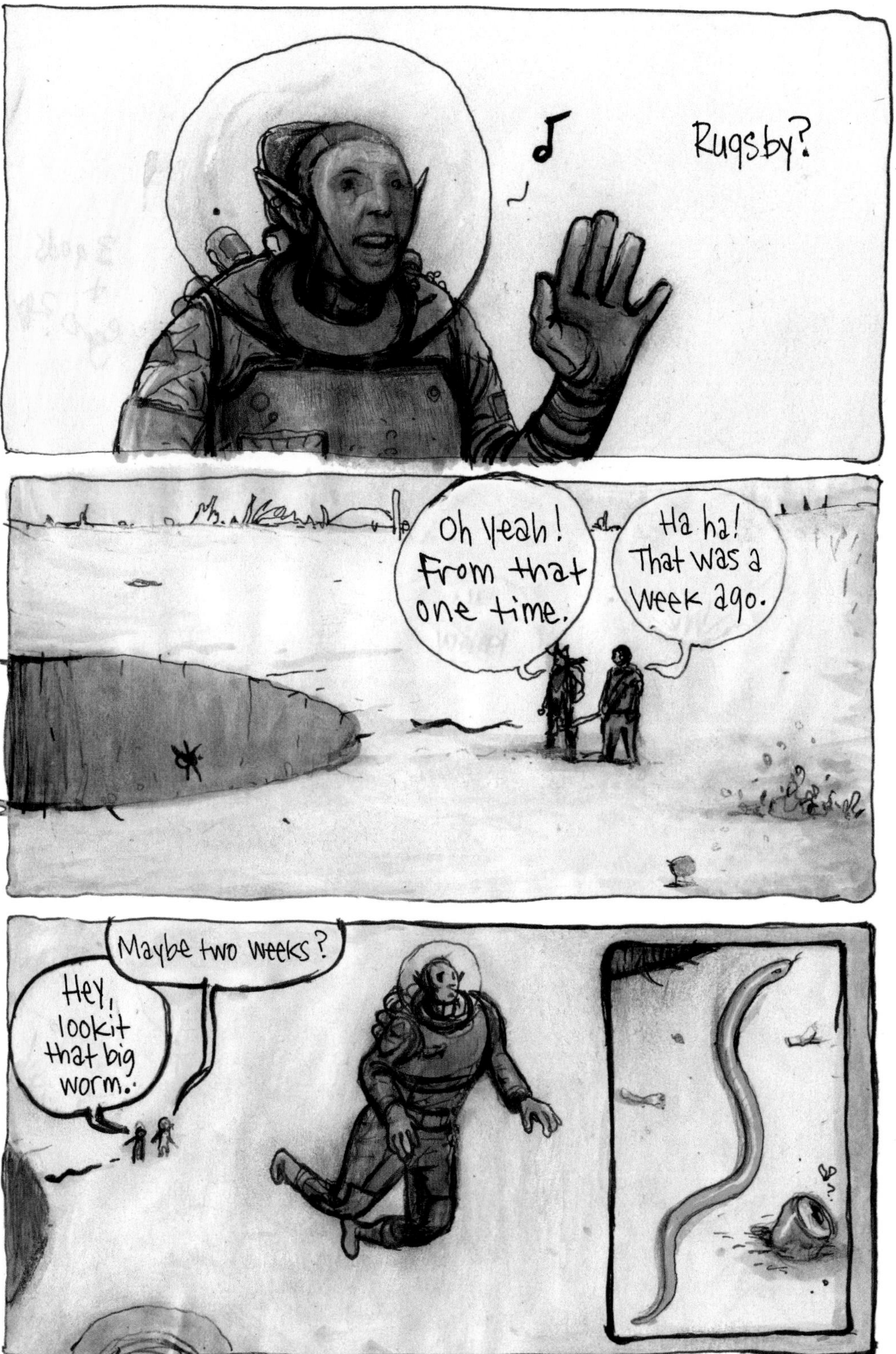
Rugsby?
Oh yeah! From that one time.
Ha ha! That was a week ago.
Maybe two weeks?
Hey, lookit that big worm.

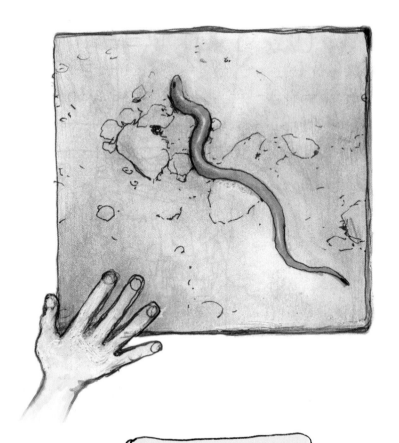

Caution, boy.

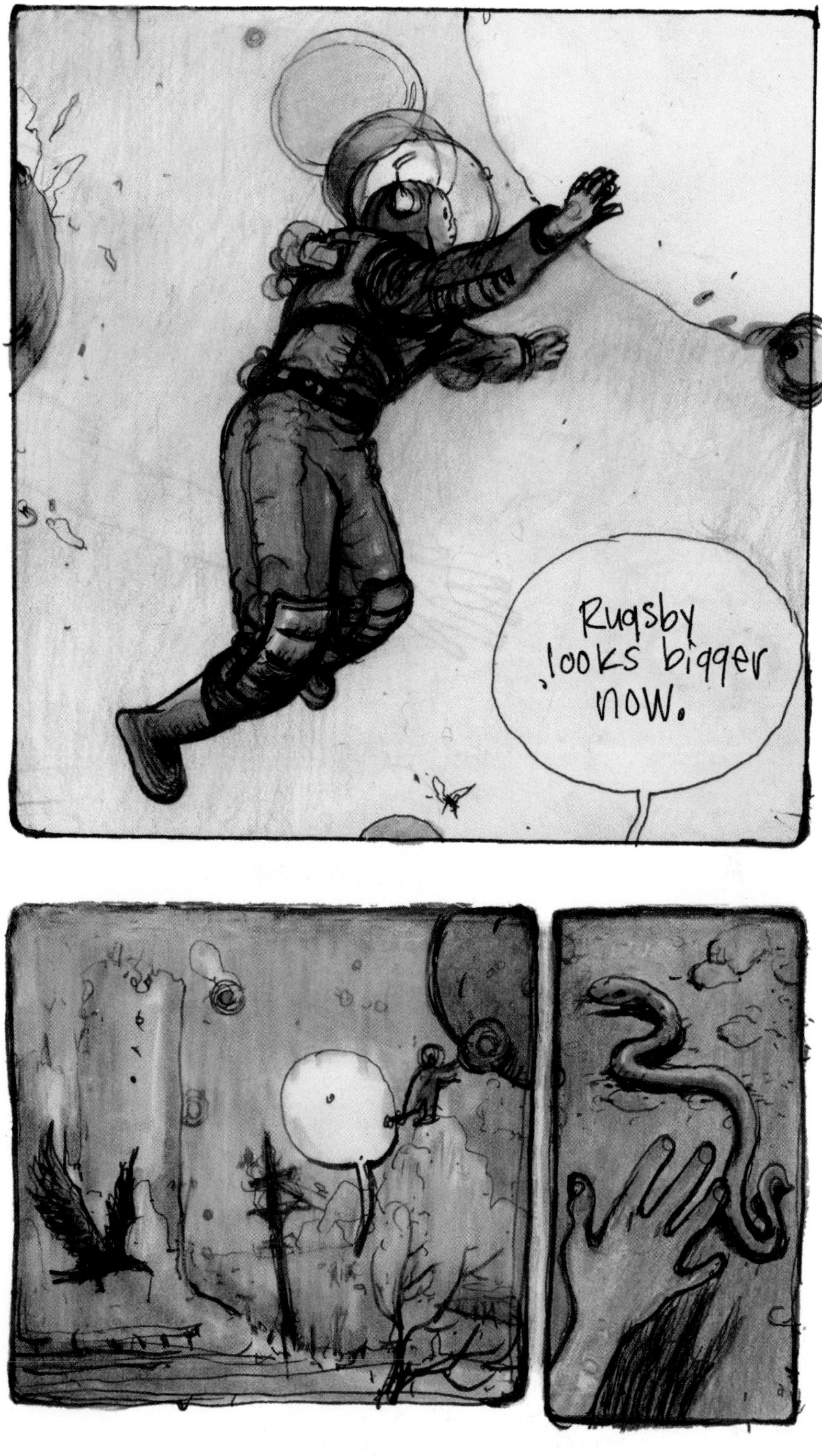
Rugsby looks bigger now.

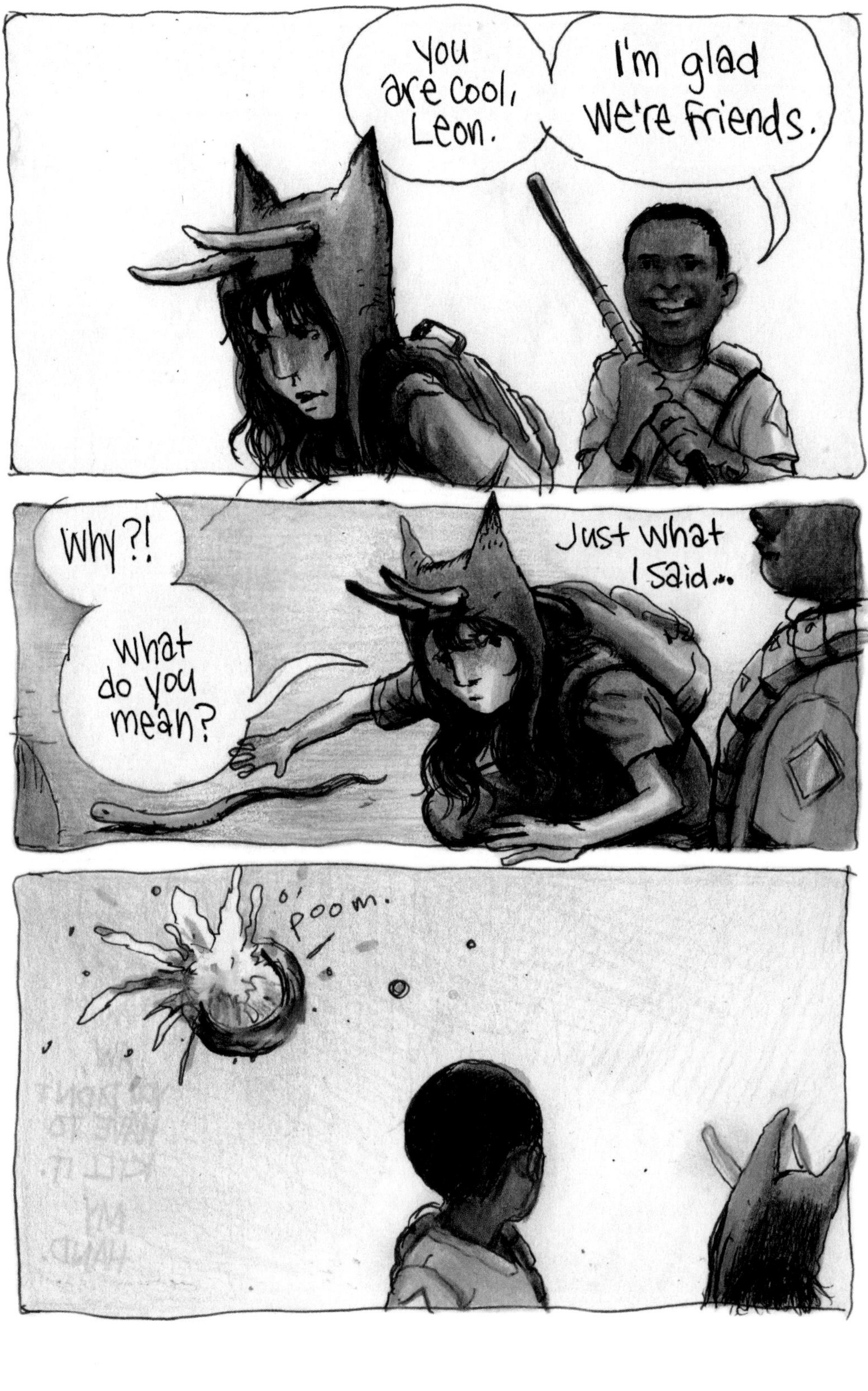
You are cool, Leon.
I'm glad we're friends.
Why?!
what do you mean?
Just what I said...
poom.

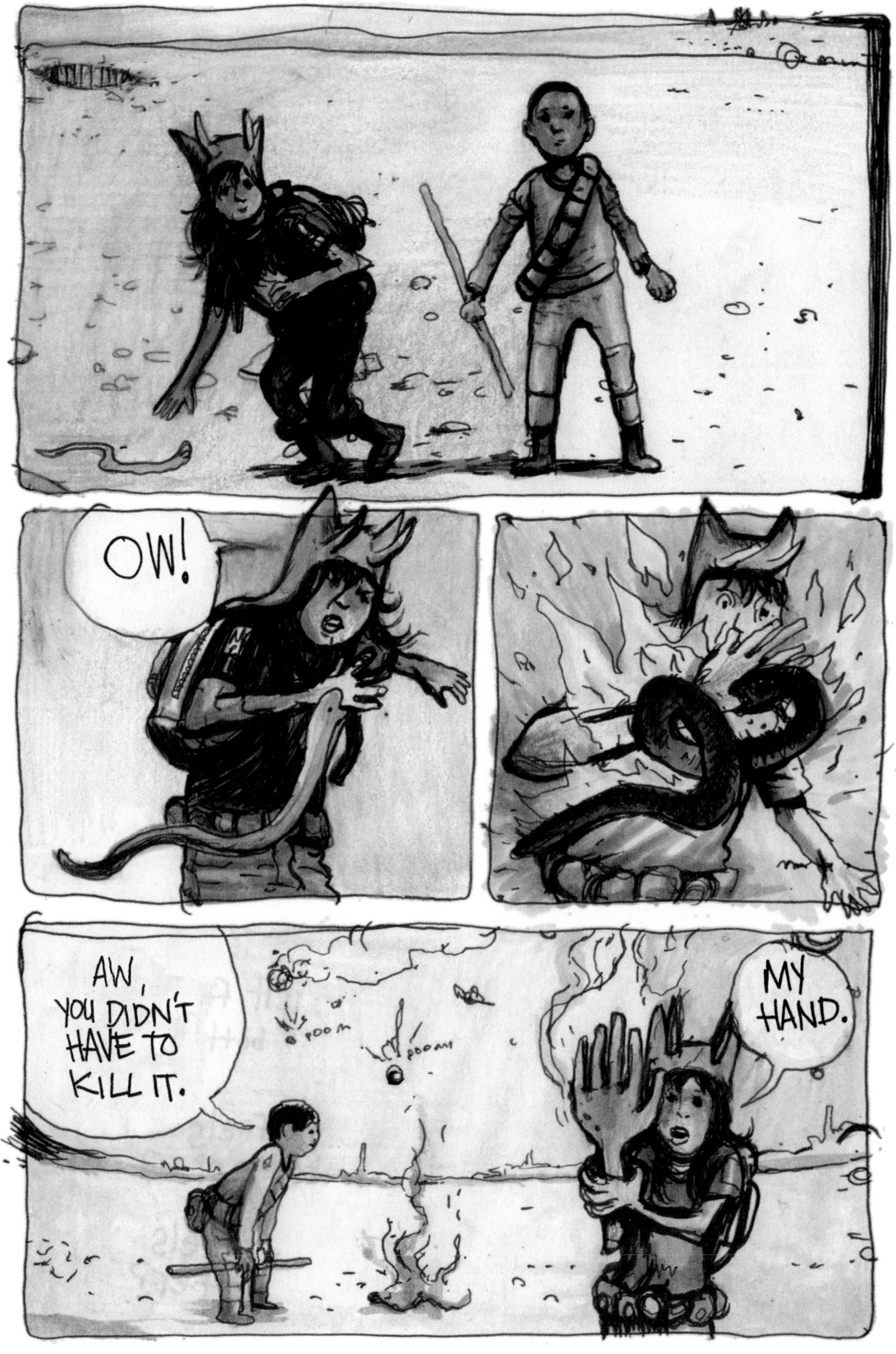
OW!
AW, YOU DIDN'T HAVE TO KILL IT.
POOM
POOM
MY HAND.

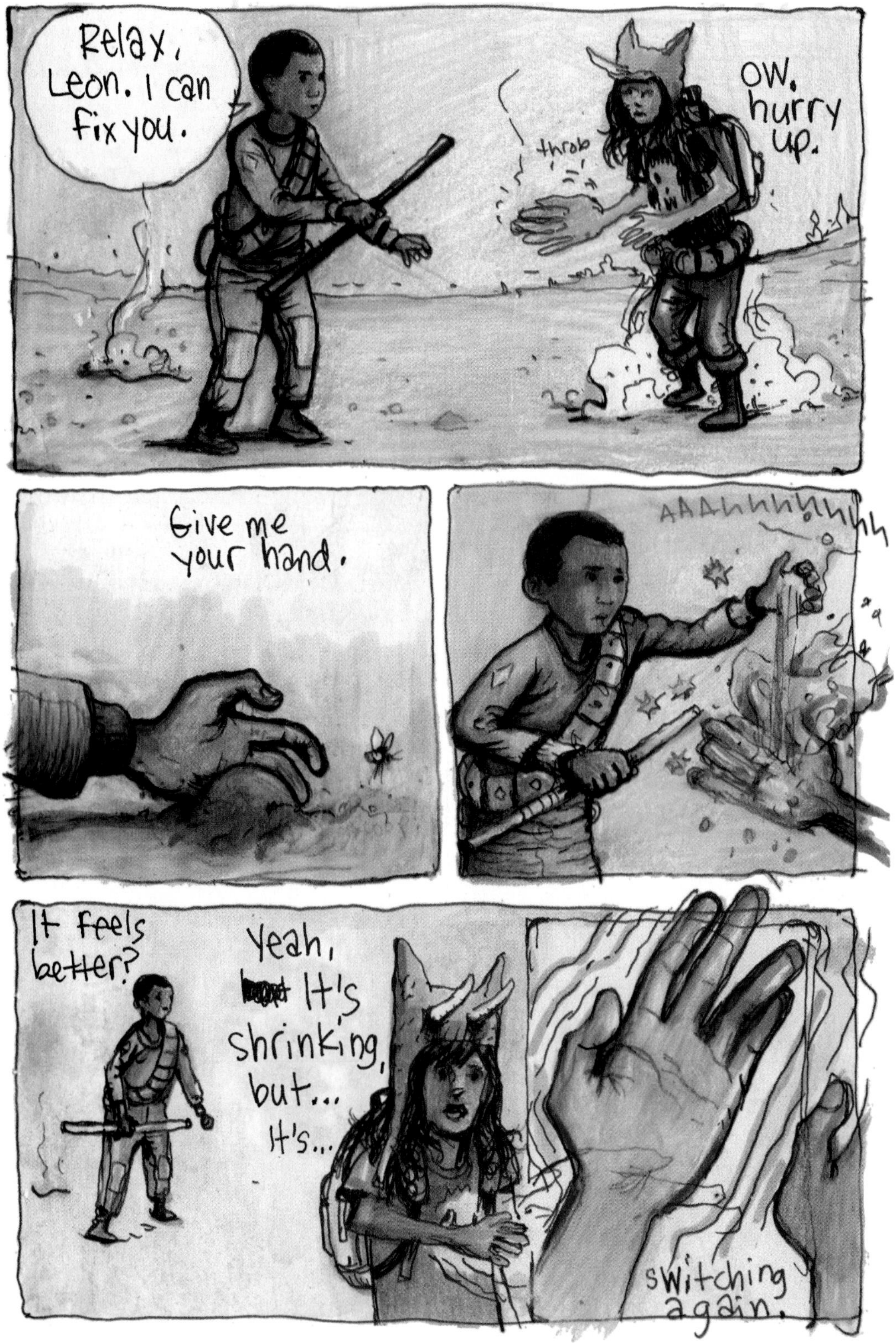
Relax, Leon. I can fix you.
throb
OW. hurry up.
Give me your hand.
AAAhhhhhhhhh
It feels better?
Yeah, It's shrinking, but...
It's...
switching again.

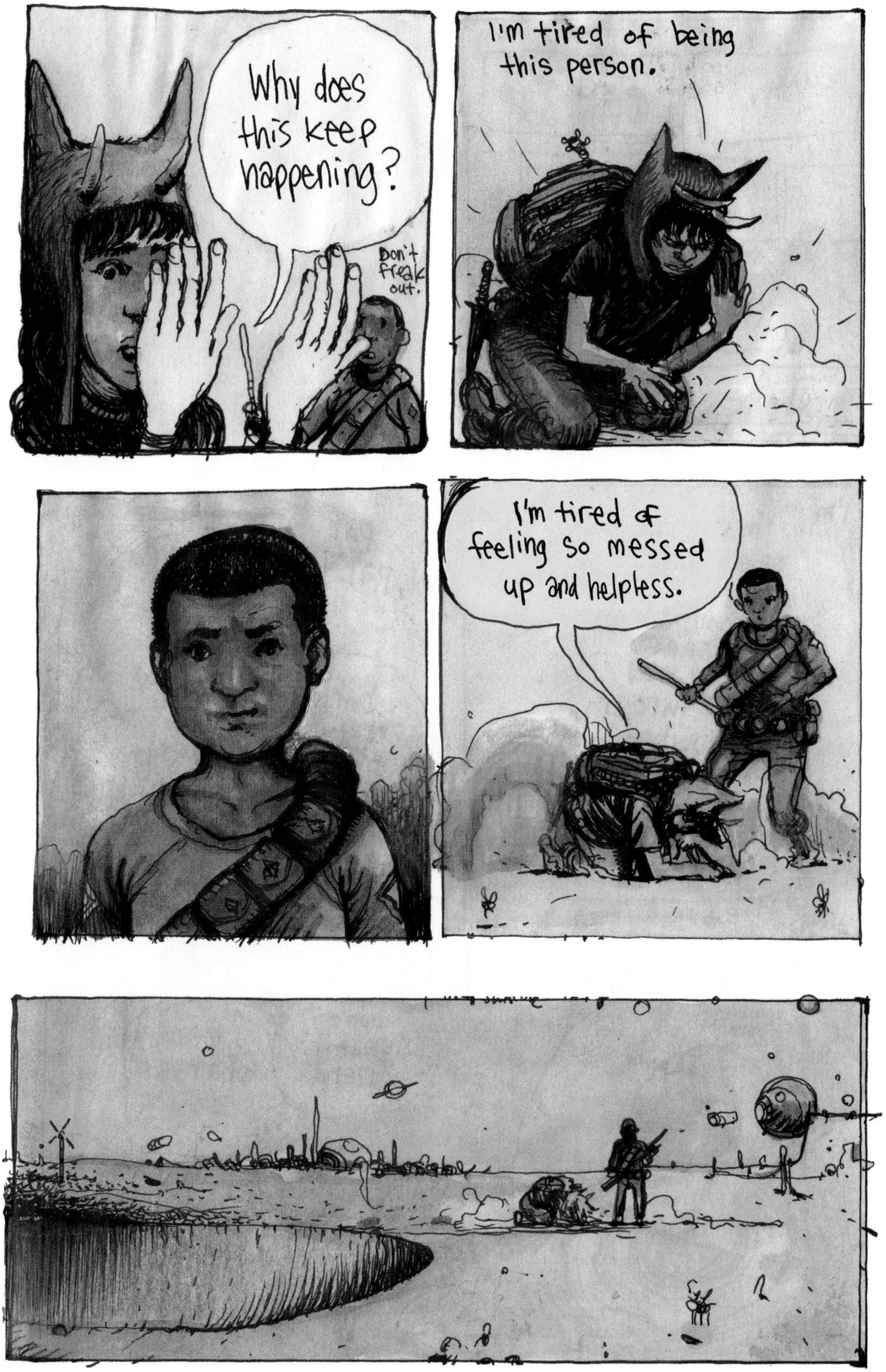

Why does this keep happening?
Don't freak out.
I'm tired of being this person.
I'm tired of feeling so messed up and helpless.

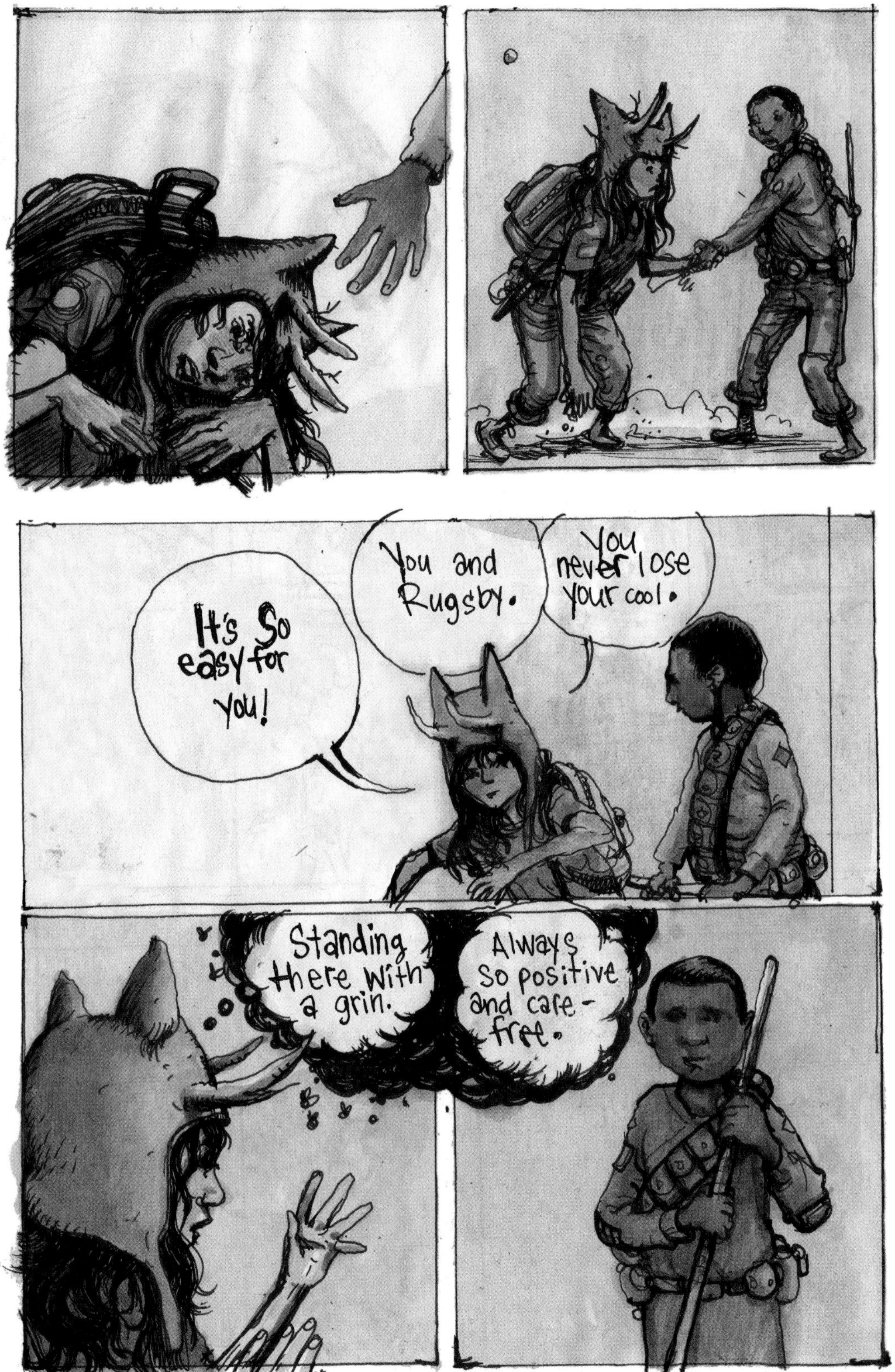
It's So easy for you!
You and Rugsby.
You never lose your cool.
Standing there with a grin.
Always so positive and care-free.

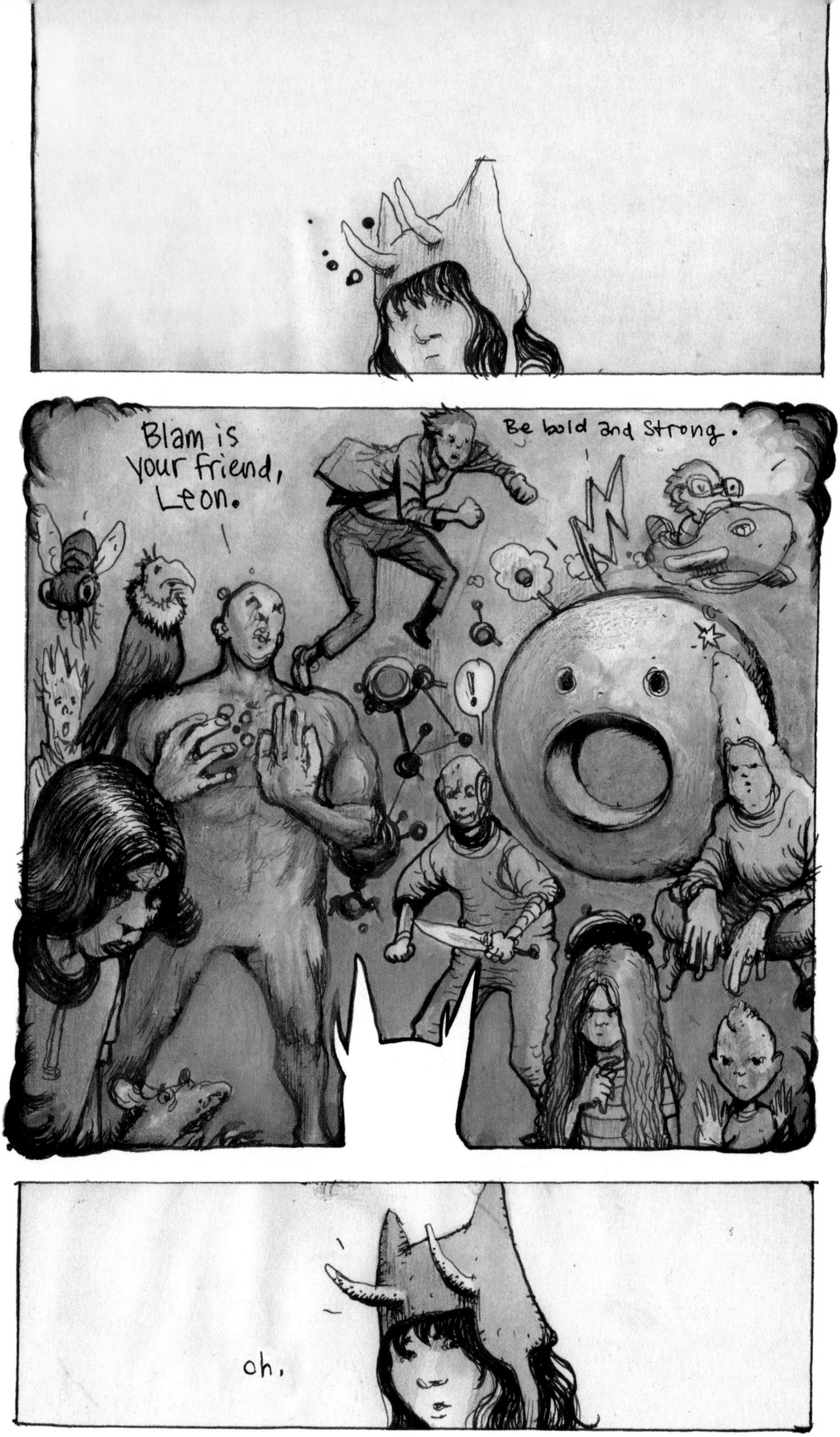
Blam is your friend, Leon.
Be bold and Strong.
!
oh.

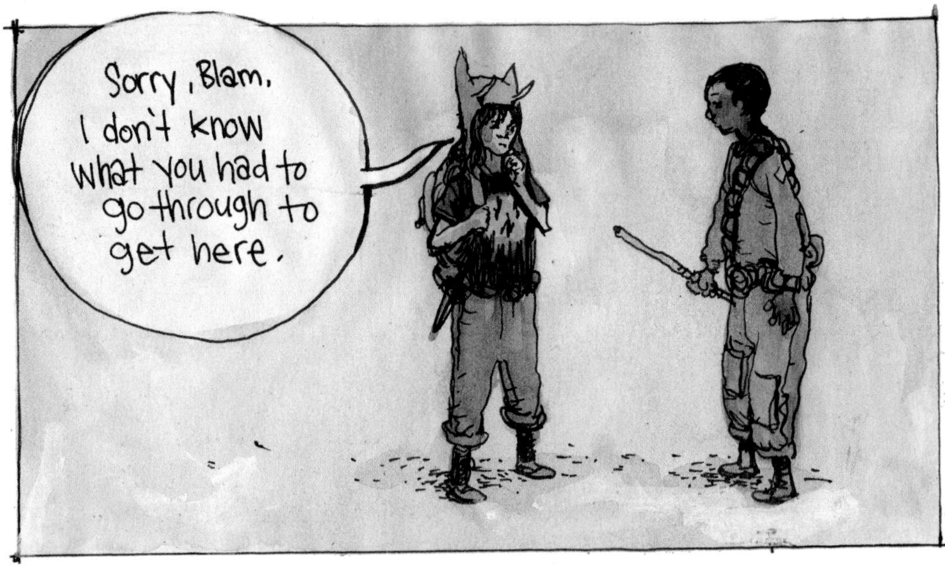
Sorry, Blam. I don't know what you had to go through to get here.

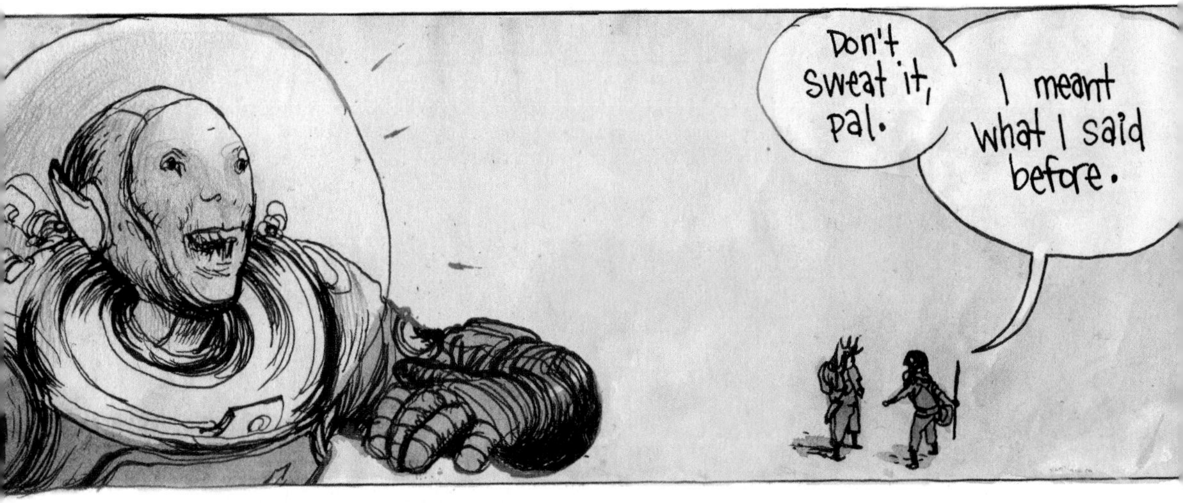
Don't sweat it, pal.
I meant what I said before.

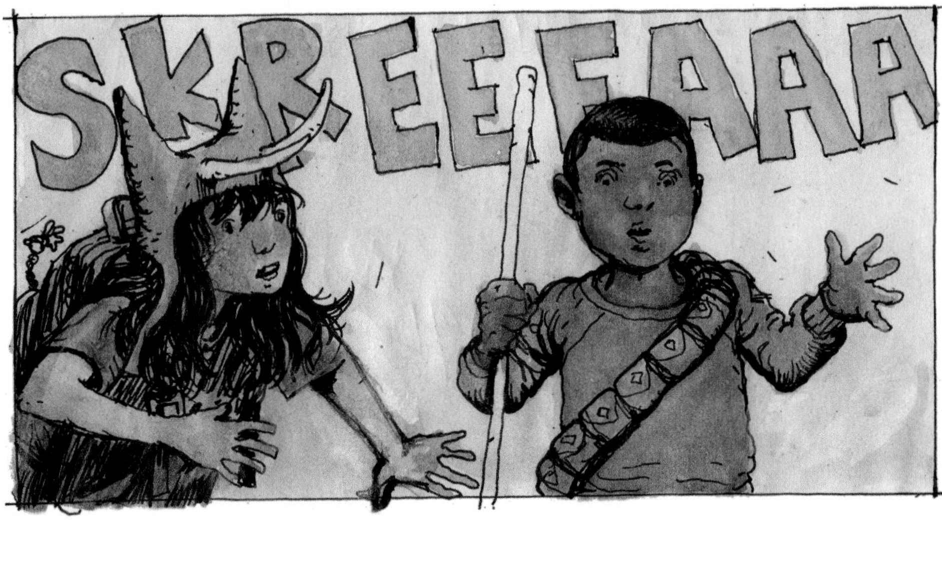
SKREEEAAA

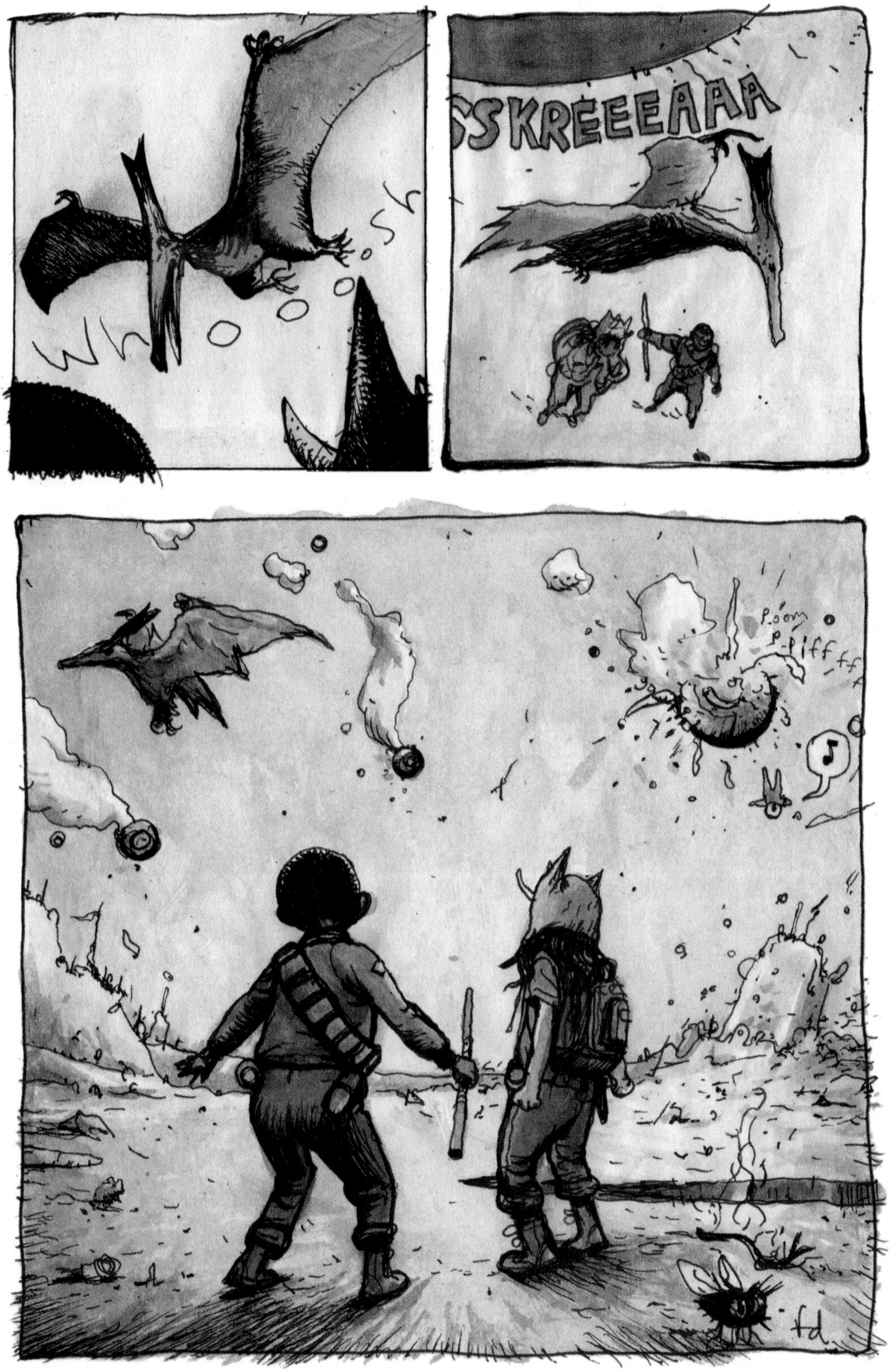
Whooosh
SSKREEEAAA
P-oom
P-piffff

teenage scum burners

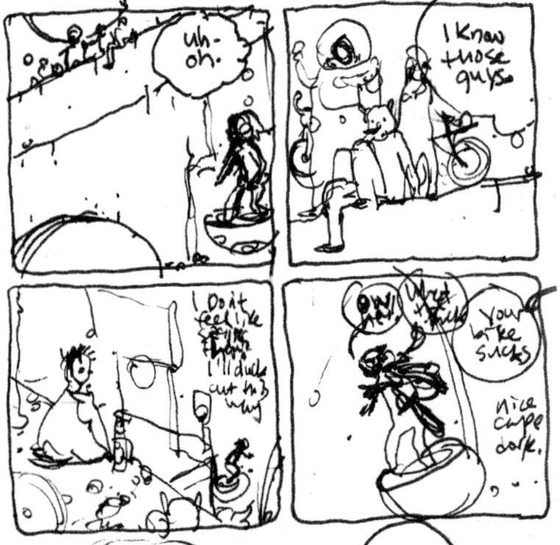
uh-oh.
I know those guys.
I'll duck out this way
Your bike sucks
nice cape dork.

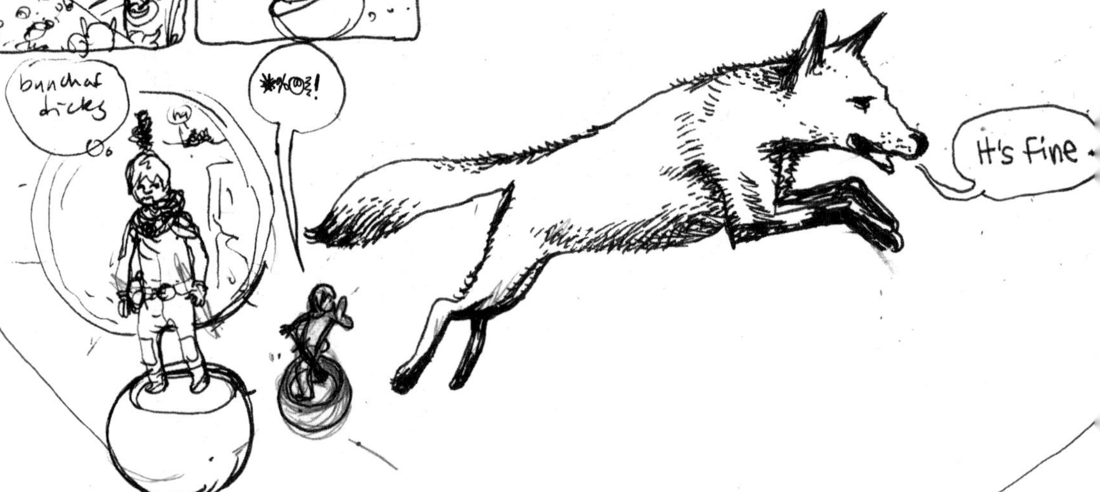
bunch of dicks
*%@≠!
It's fine

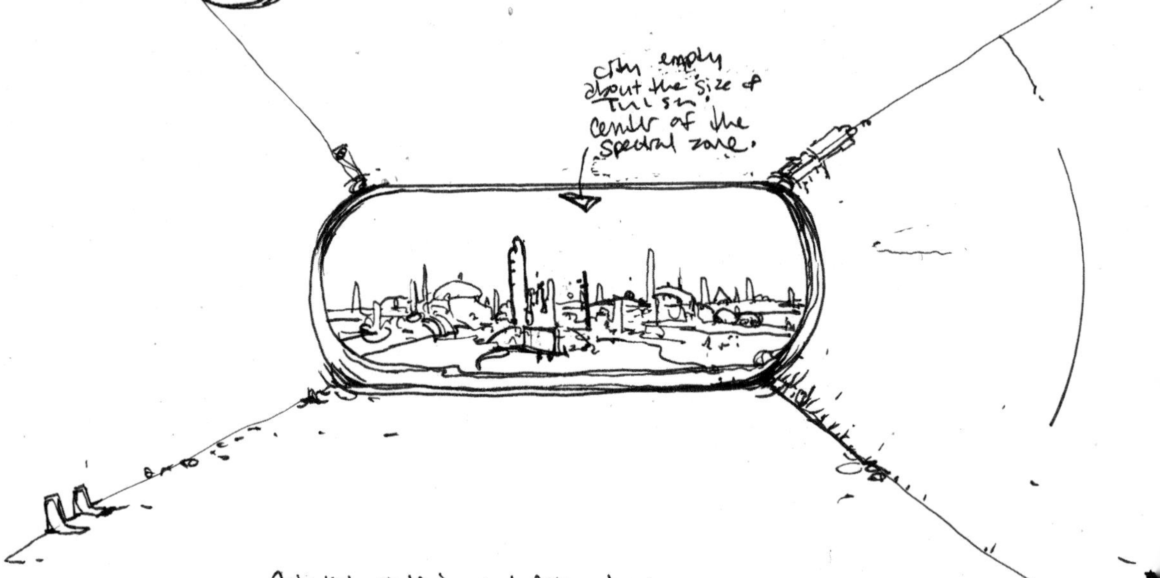
city empty about the size of Tulsa. center of the spectral zone.

Scientist ship is kind of like tardis
It has rats + bugs and a lot of stuff is
broken but Scientist is so focused
on building his robot body he
doesn't fix anything.
~~They took it~~ over
empty derelict ship. refurbished
some stuff added shields.
Sherwood – "Why don't you make little cleaner helper bots to fix all the stuff. Maybe you could do it or
Scientist – "A good idea. I have been meaning to but theres only so much time. help me with it" And
– Sherwood: I'm not smart enough to make stuff
but I'll help you you tell me what to do.

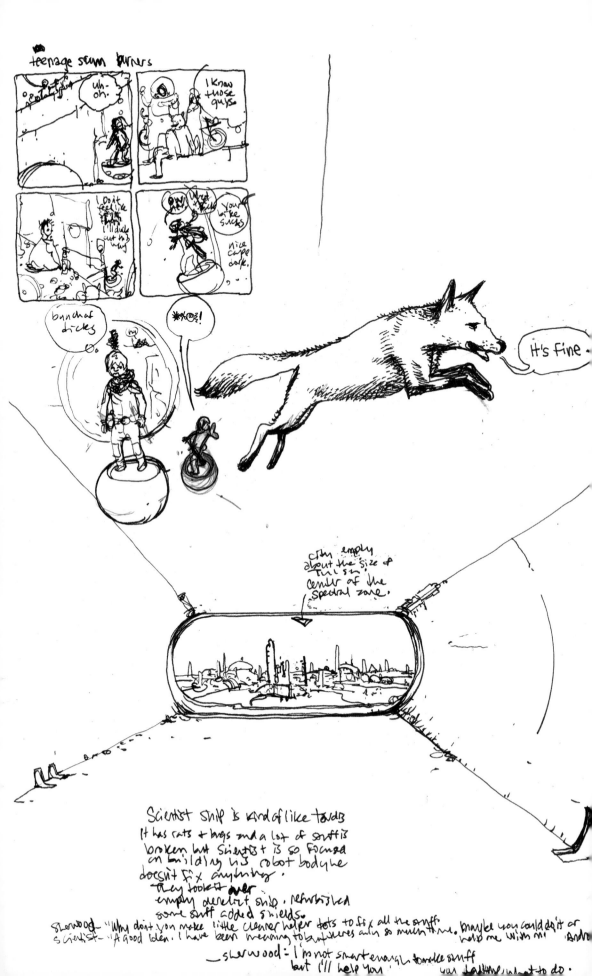

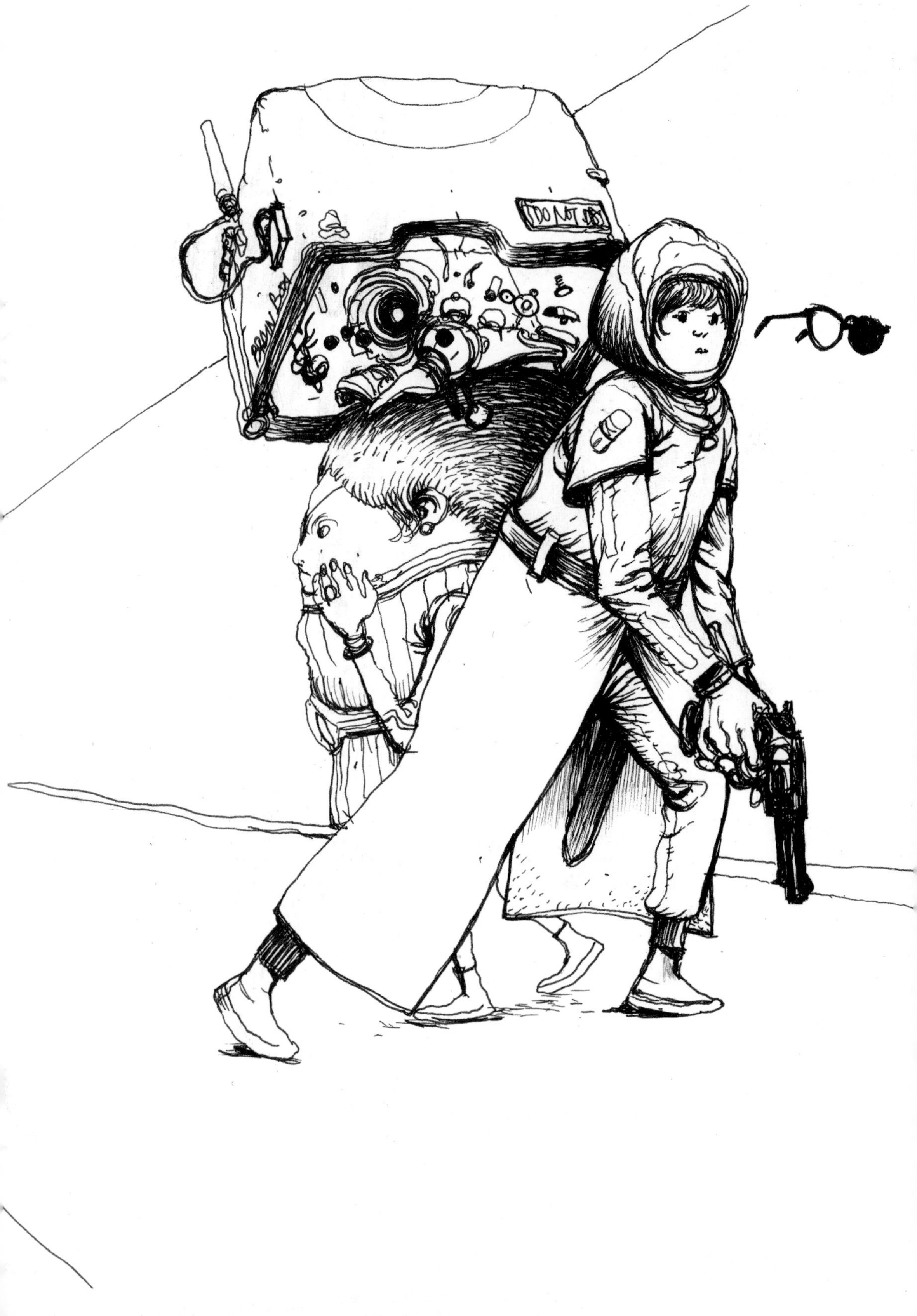
DO NOT
BRAIN BOX

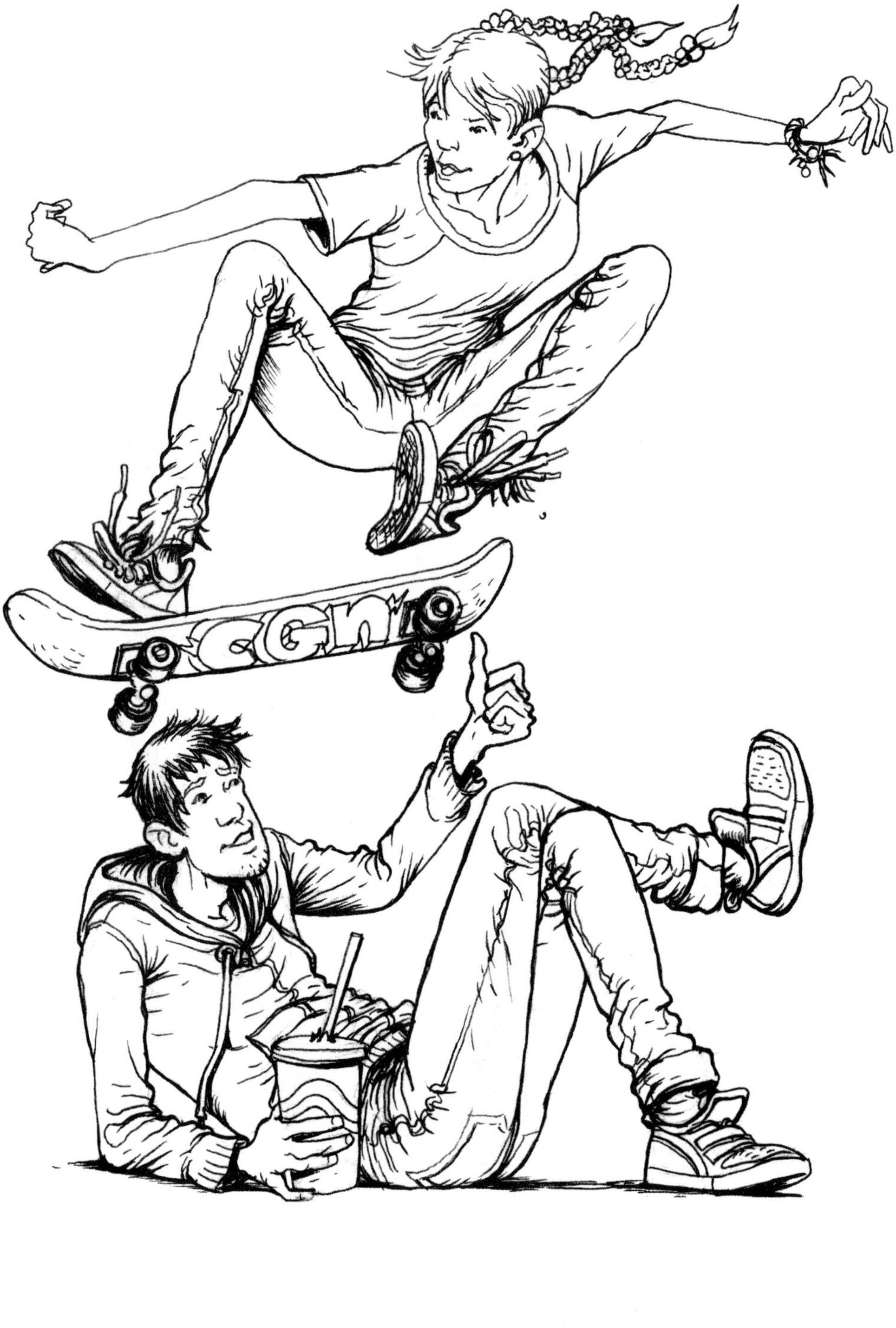
CGN

Pin-up for *THE CUTE GIRL NETWORK* by MK Reed, Greg Means, and Joe Flood.

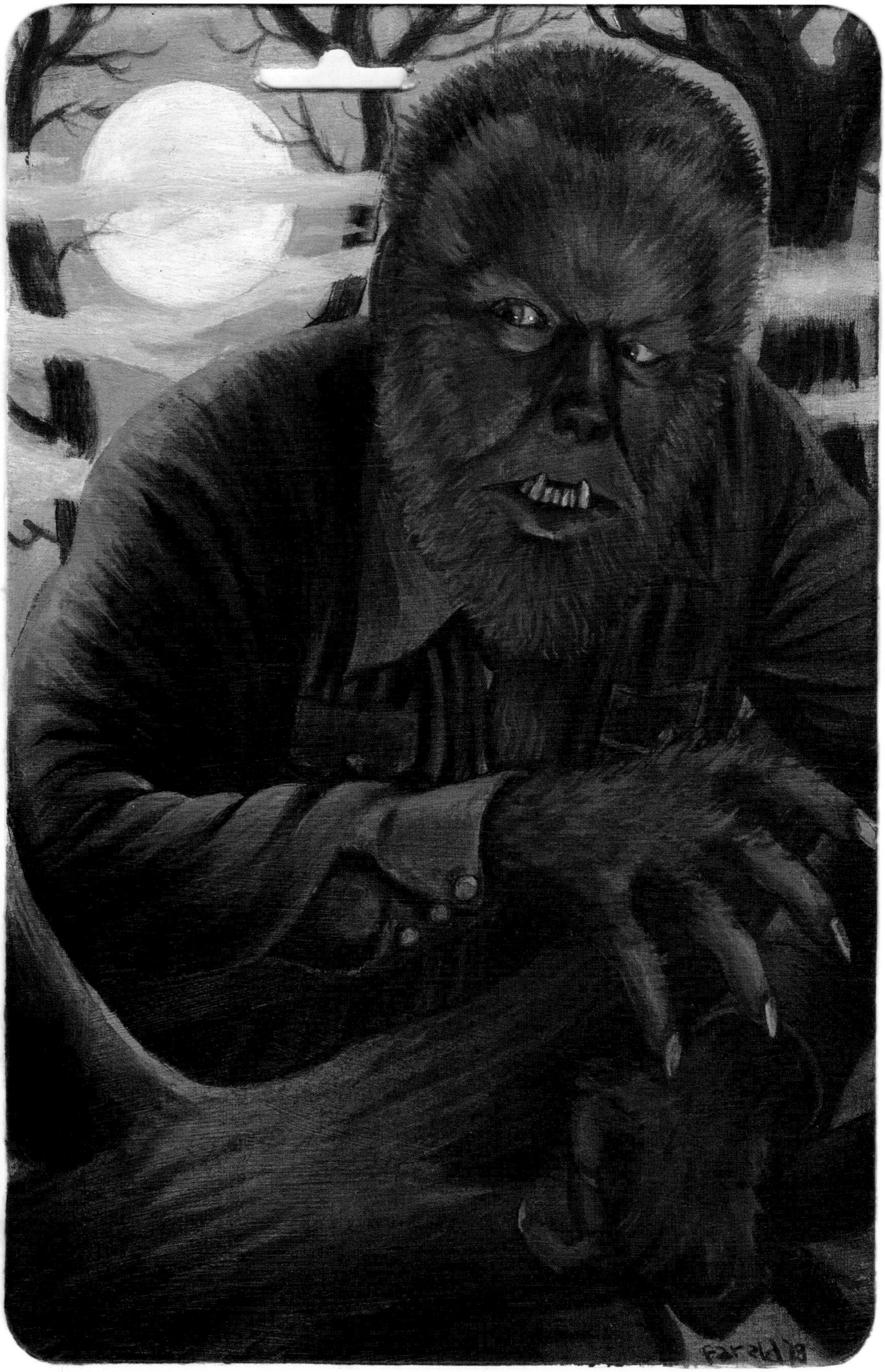

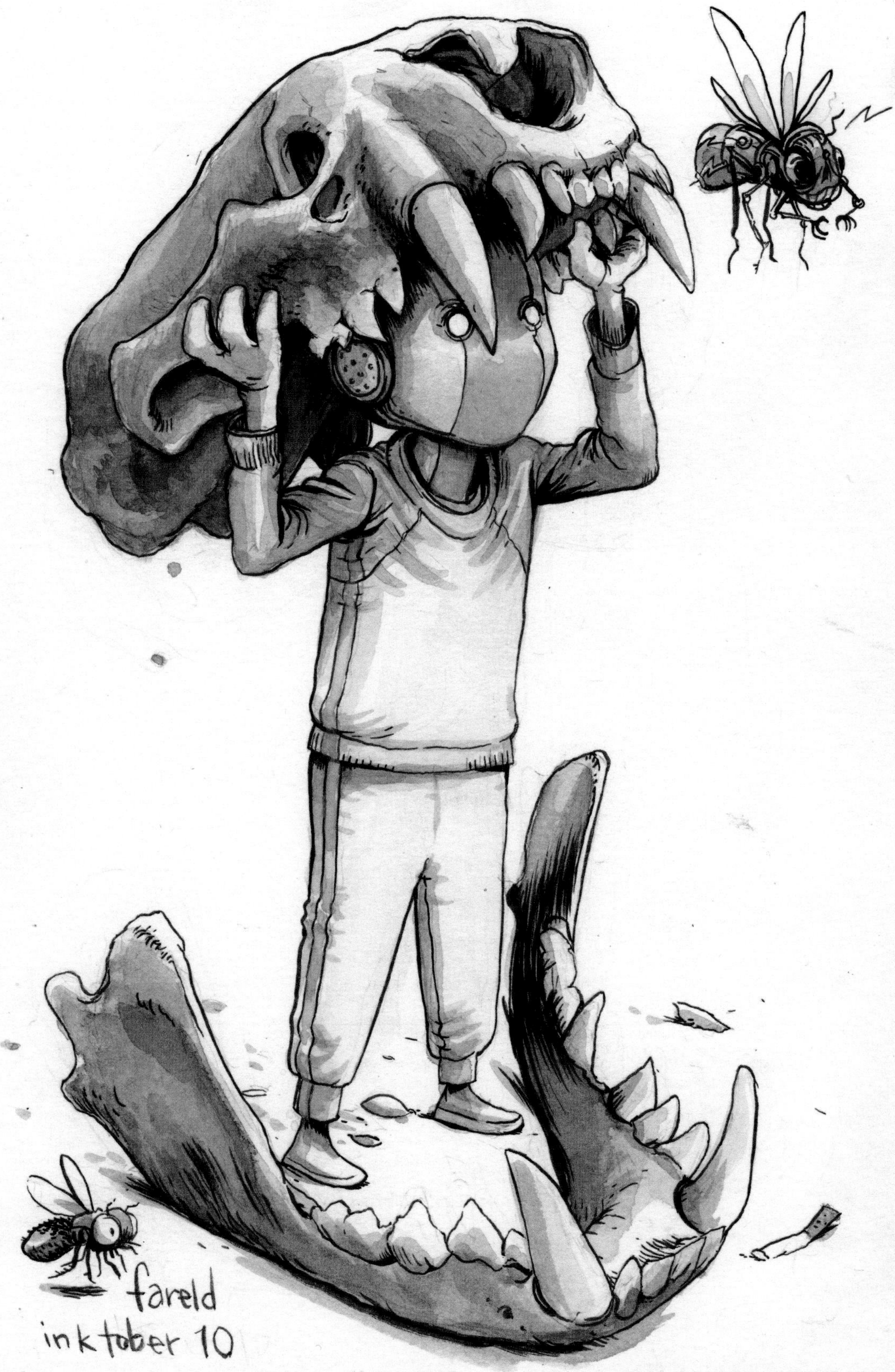
fareld
inktober 10

January 1 farld
2018

Robot Tod doesn't say much, but he's got heart.

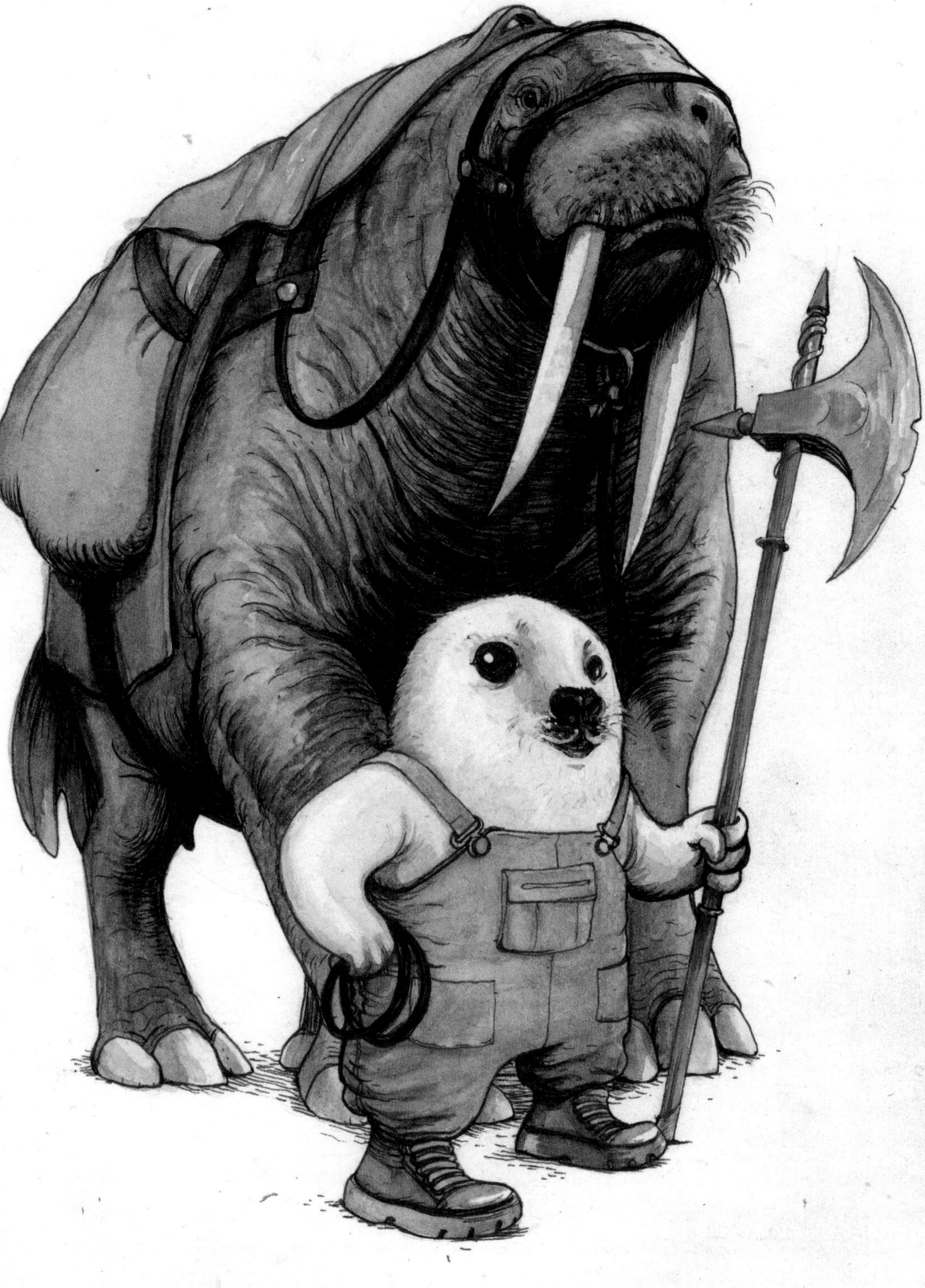

Ghus and Friendo from Brian K. Vaughan and Fiona Staples' *SAGA*.

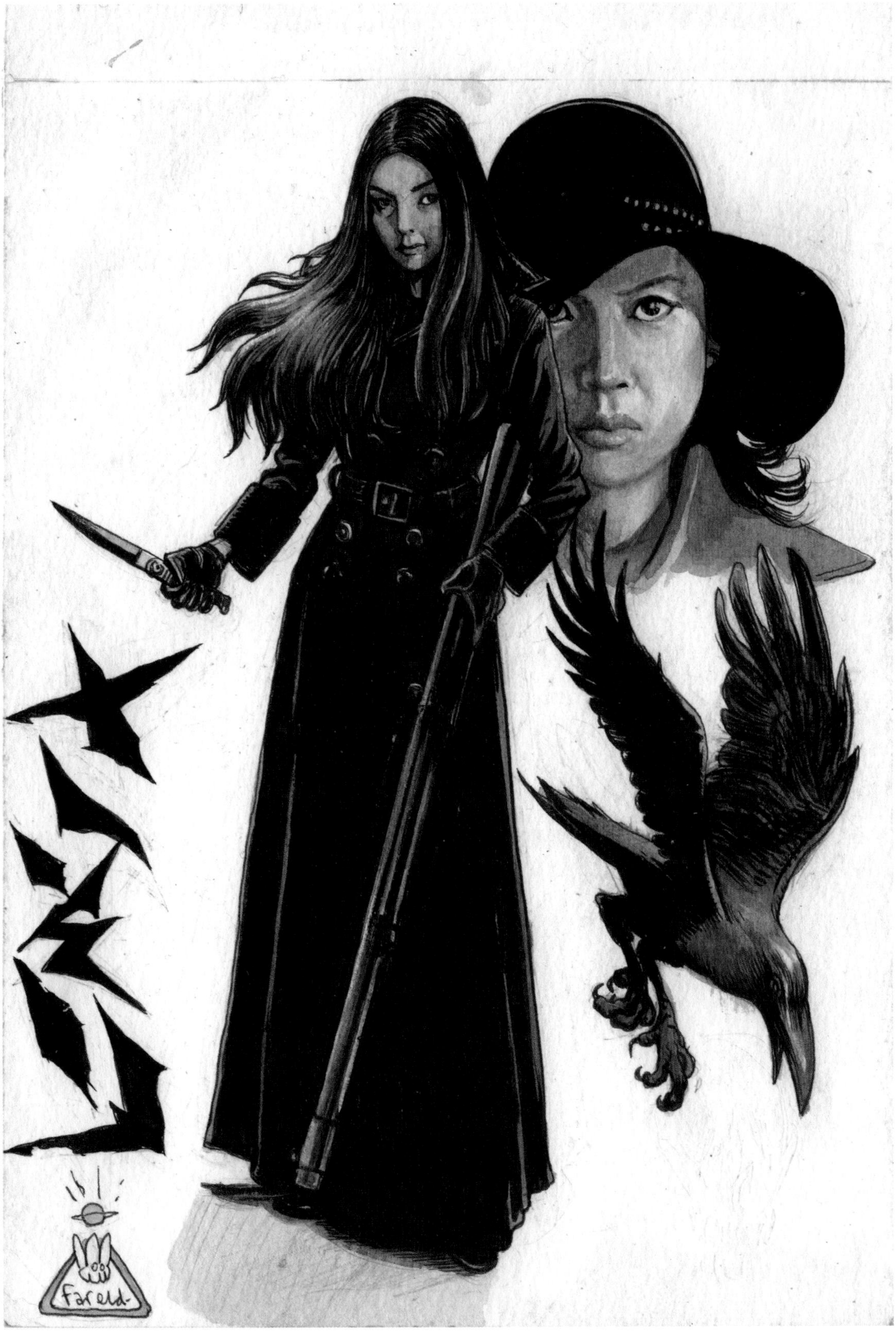
Fareld-

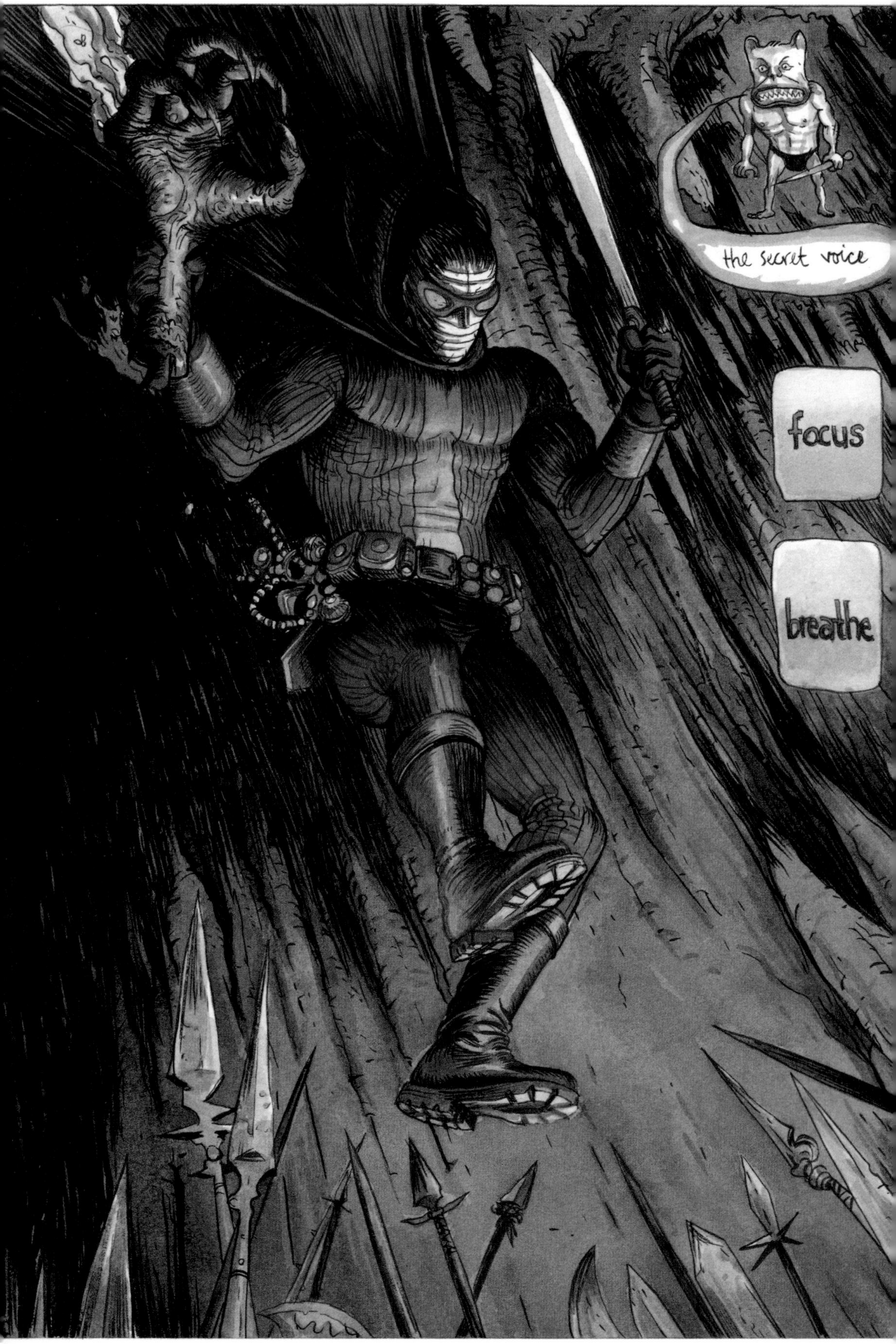
the secret voice
focus
breathe

Zack Soto's *THE SECRET VOICE.*

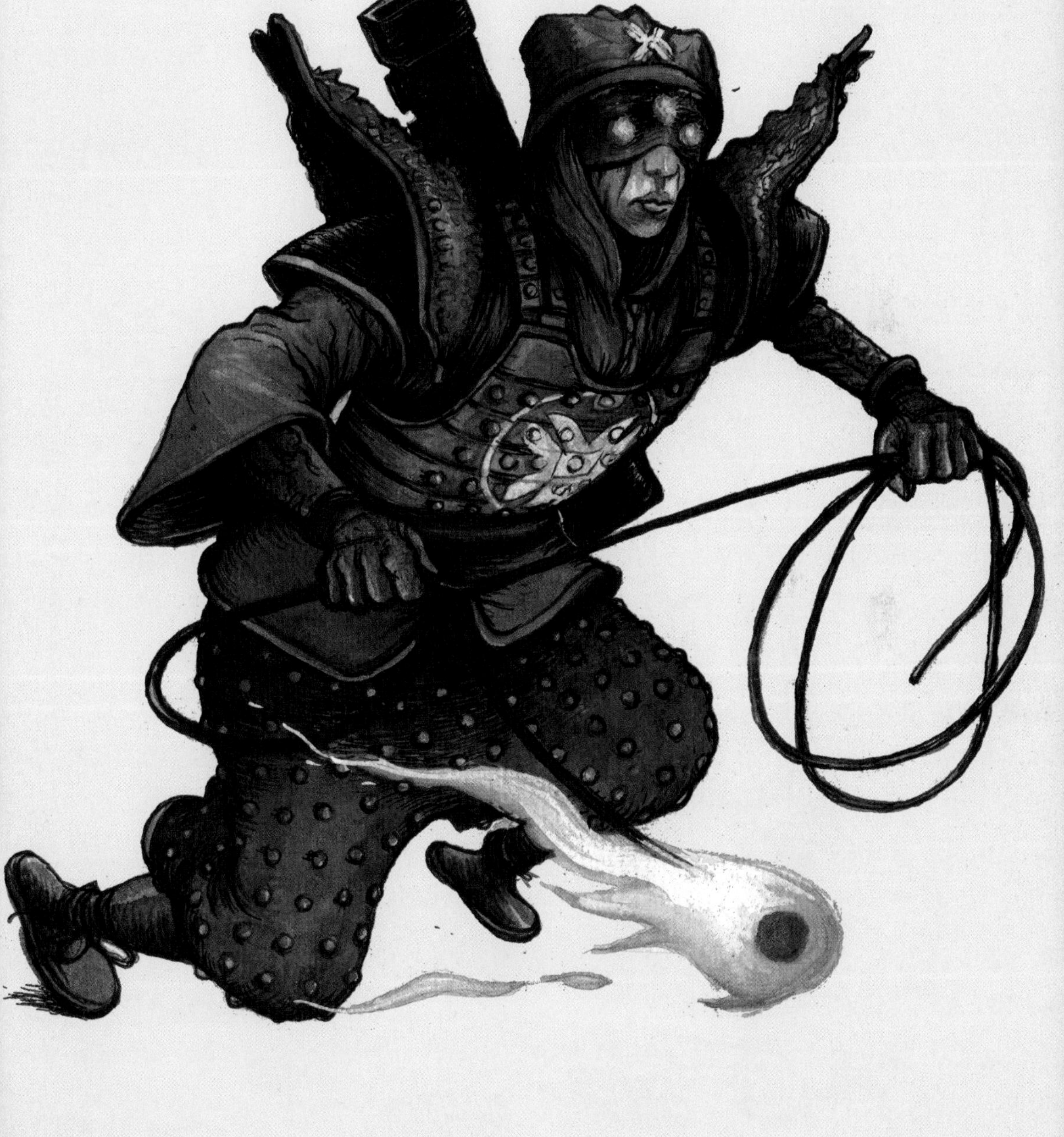

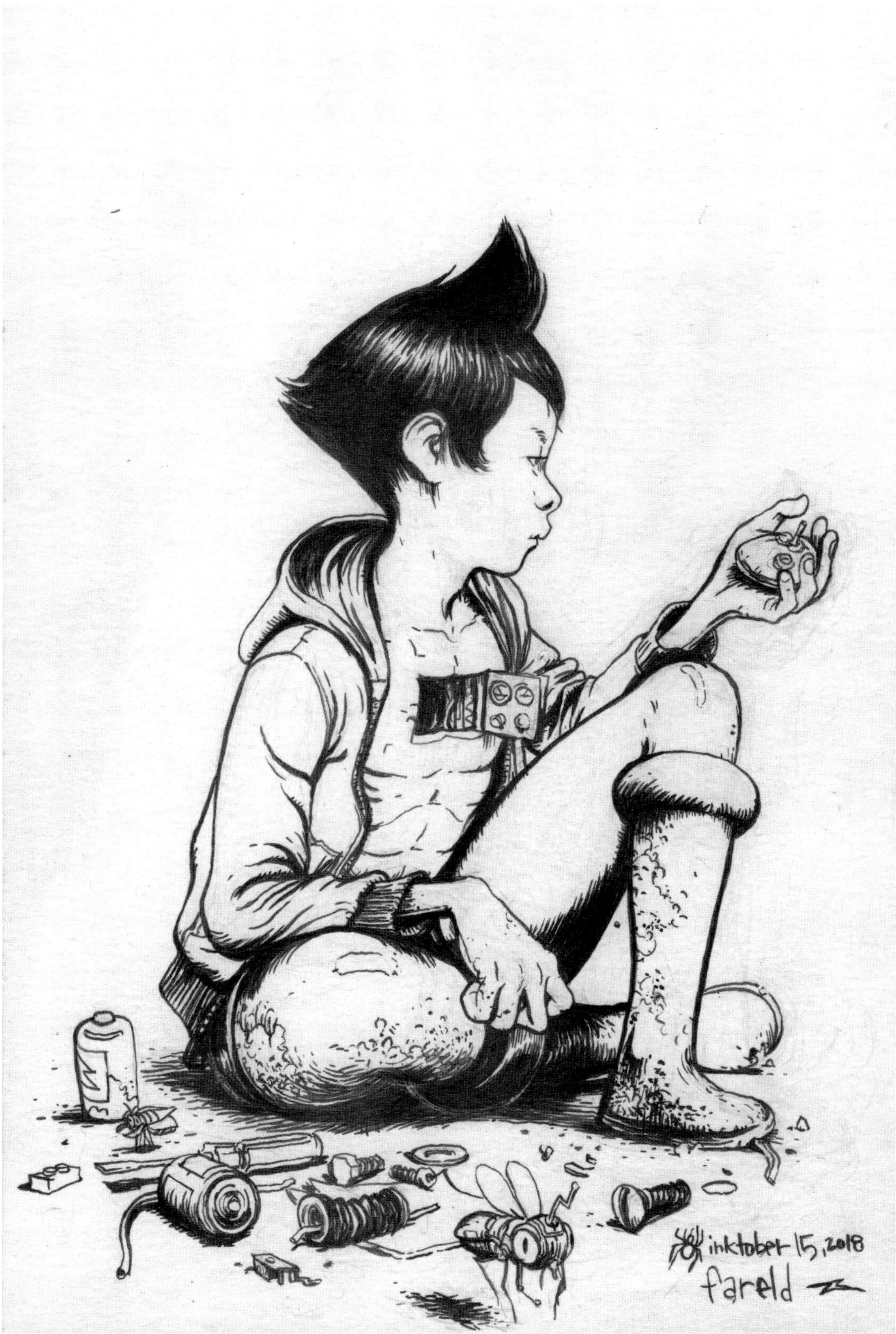
inktober 15, 2018
fareld

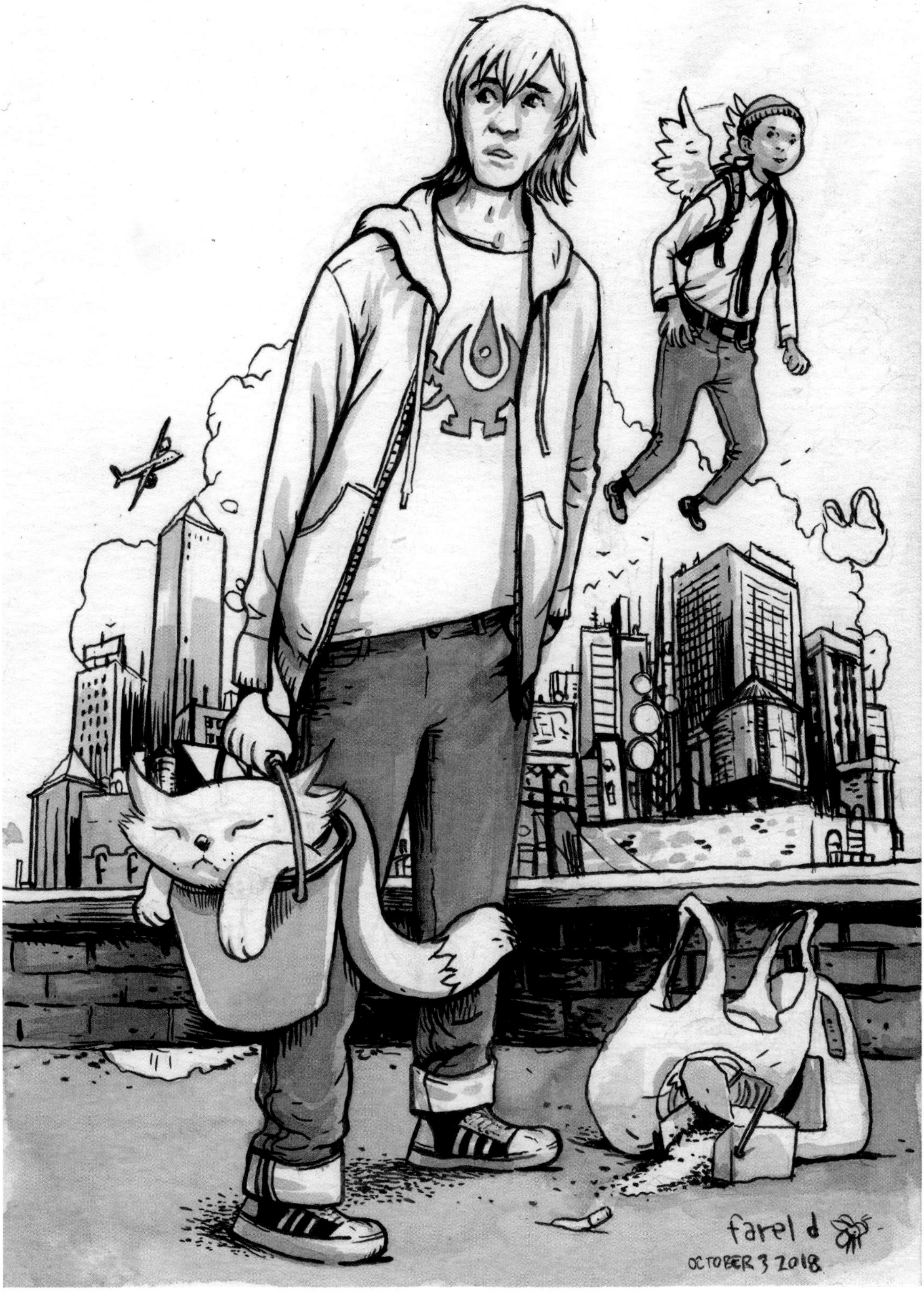
farel d
OCTOBER 3 2018

Brandon Graham's extraordinary *KING CITY* with Sinclair from *POP GUN WAR.*

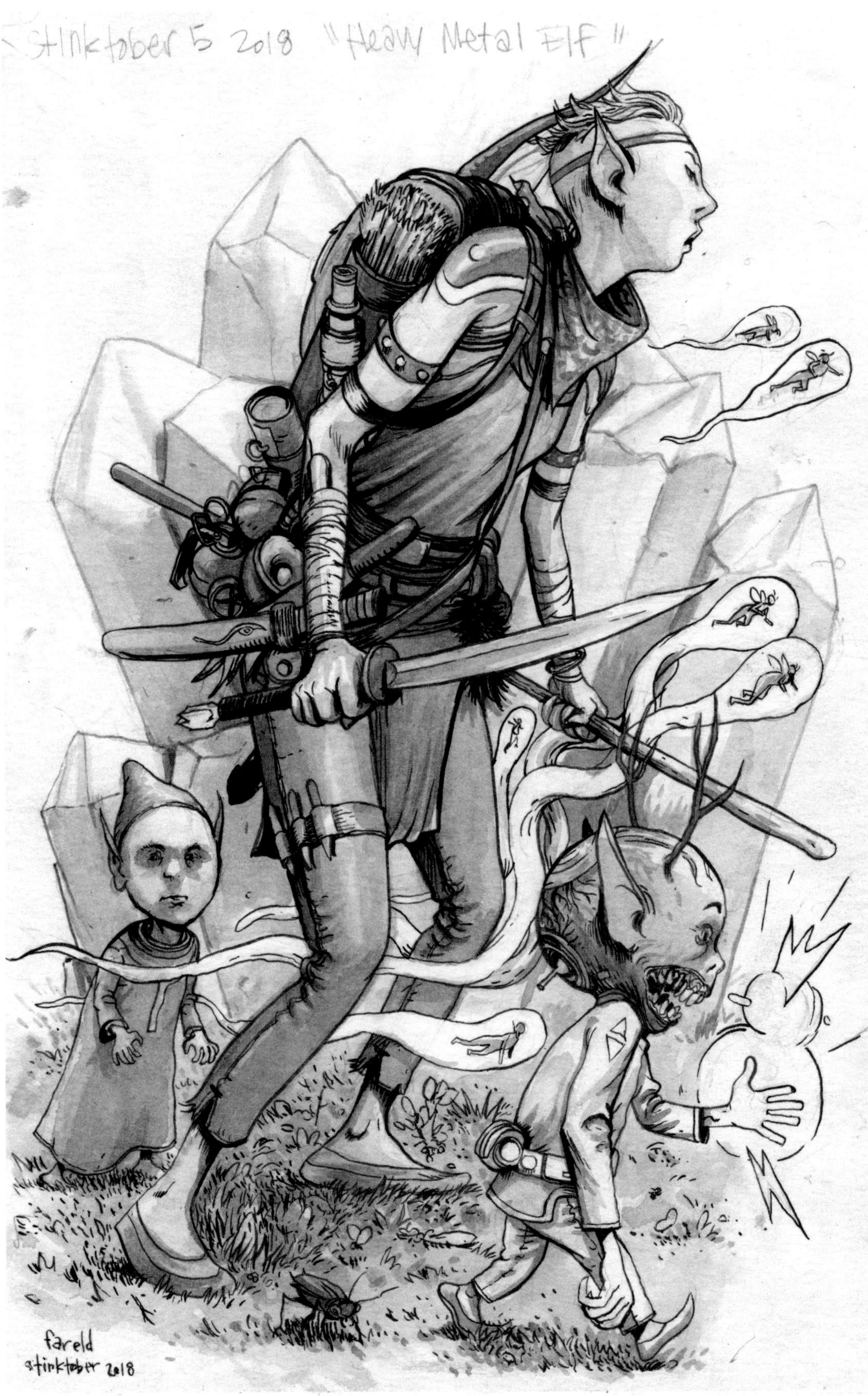
Stinktober 5 2018 "Heavy Metal Elf"
fareld
stinktober 2018

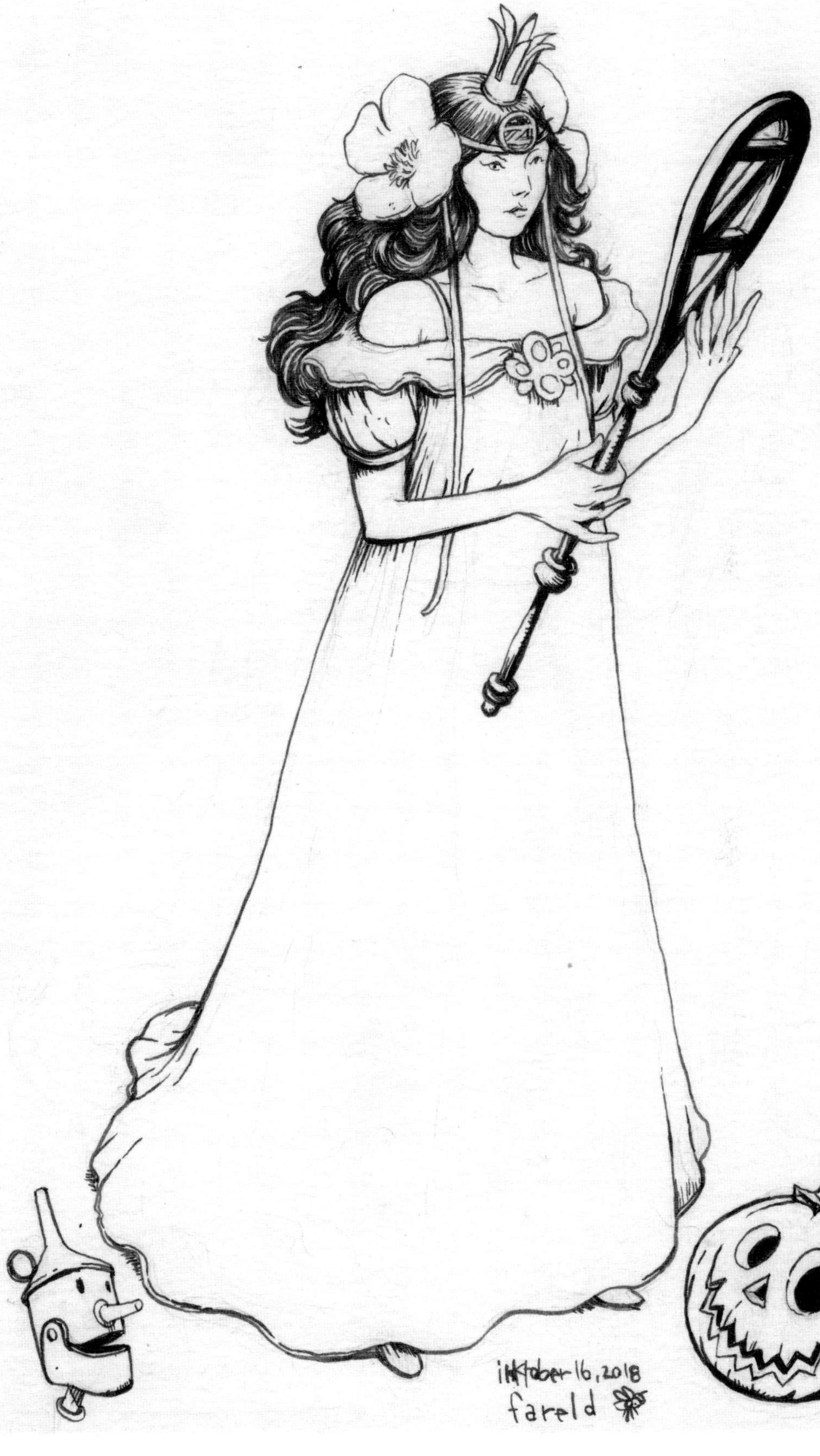
inktober 16, 2018
fareld

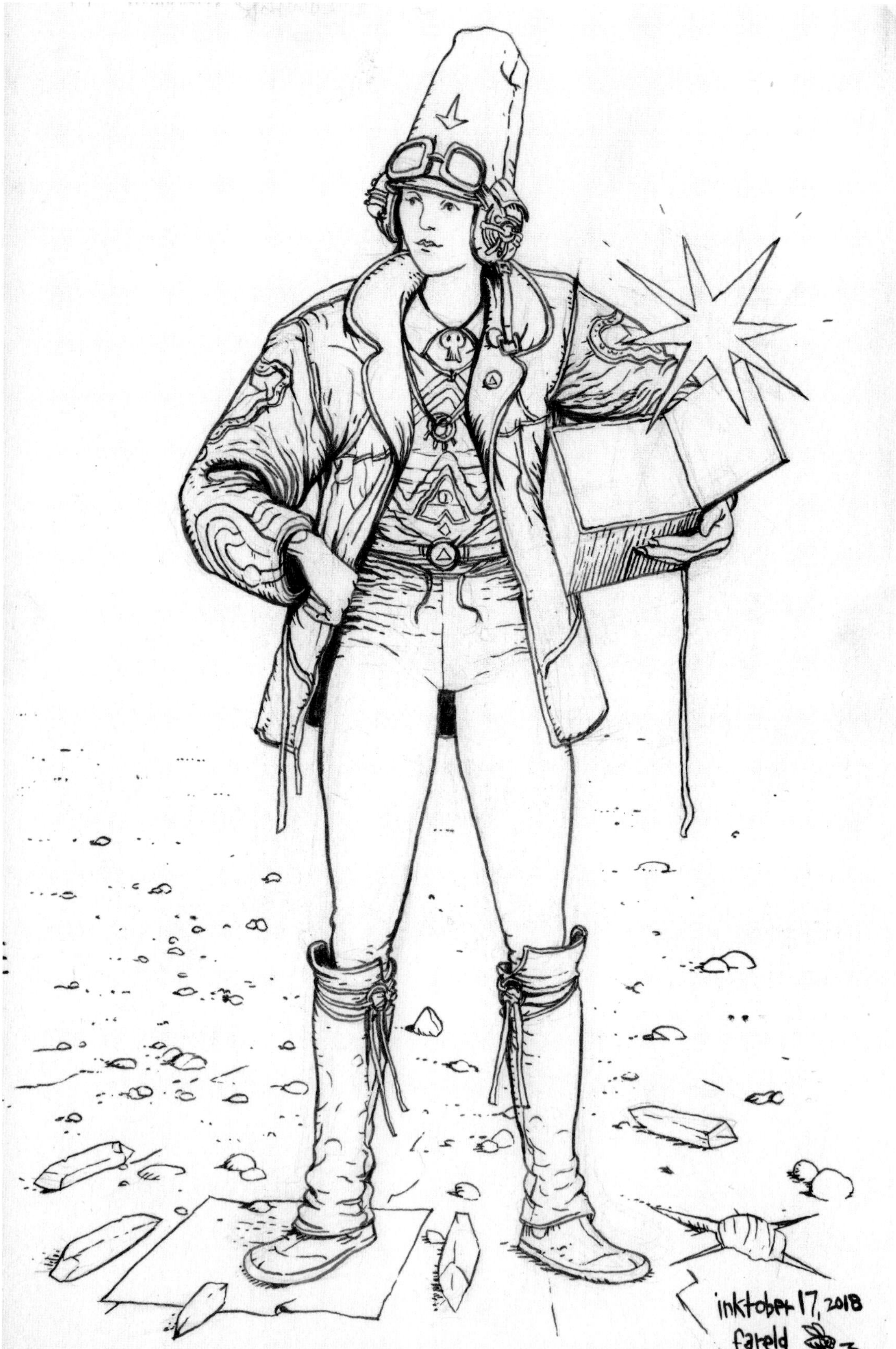
inktober 17, 2018
fareld

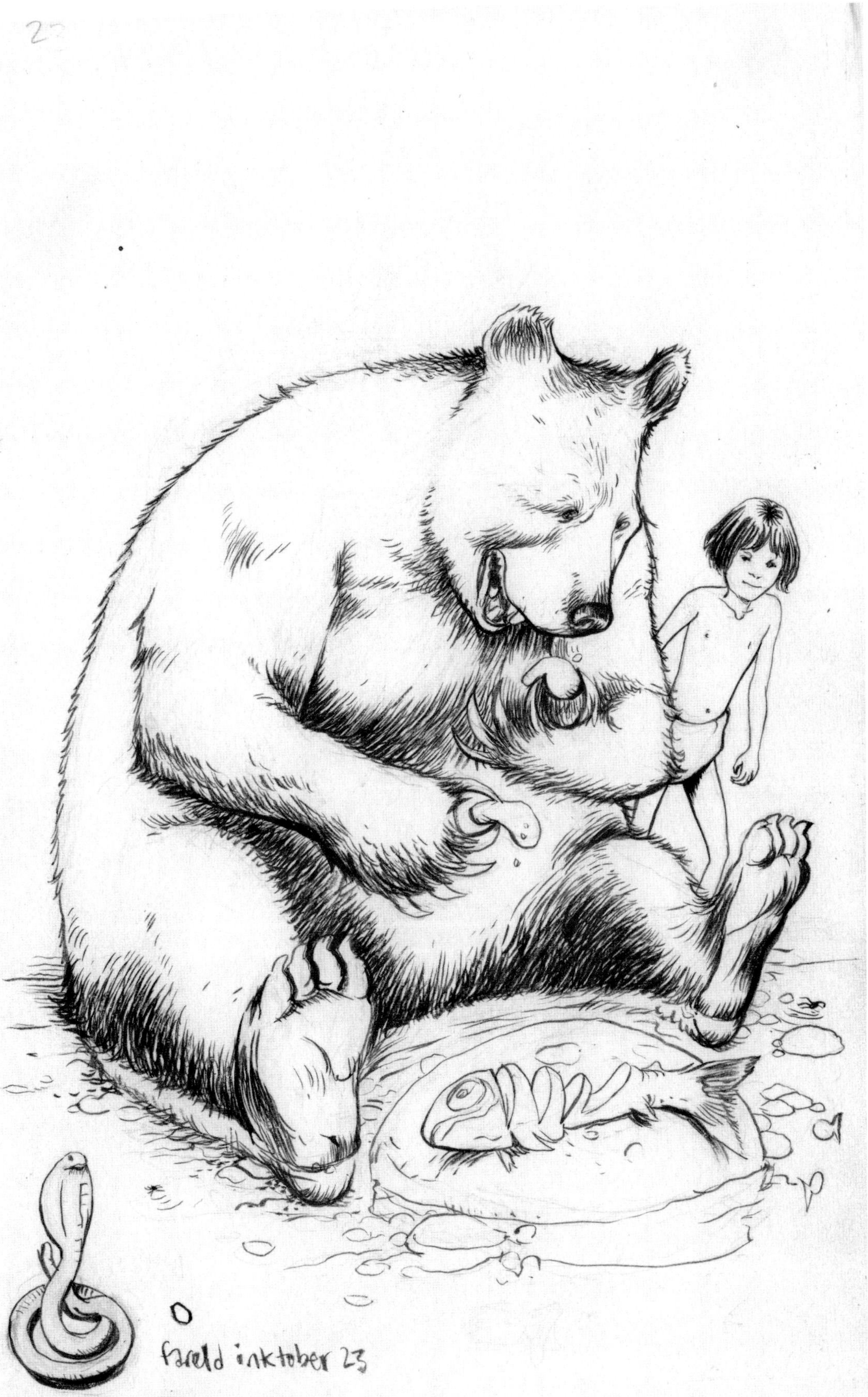
fareld inktober 23

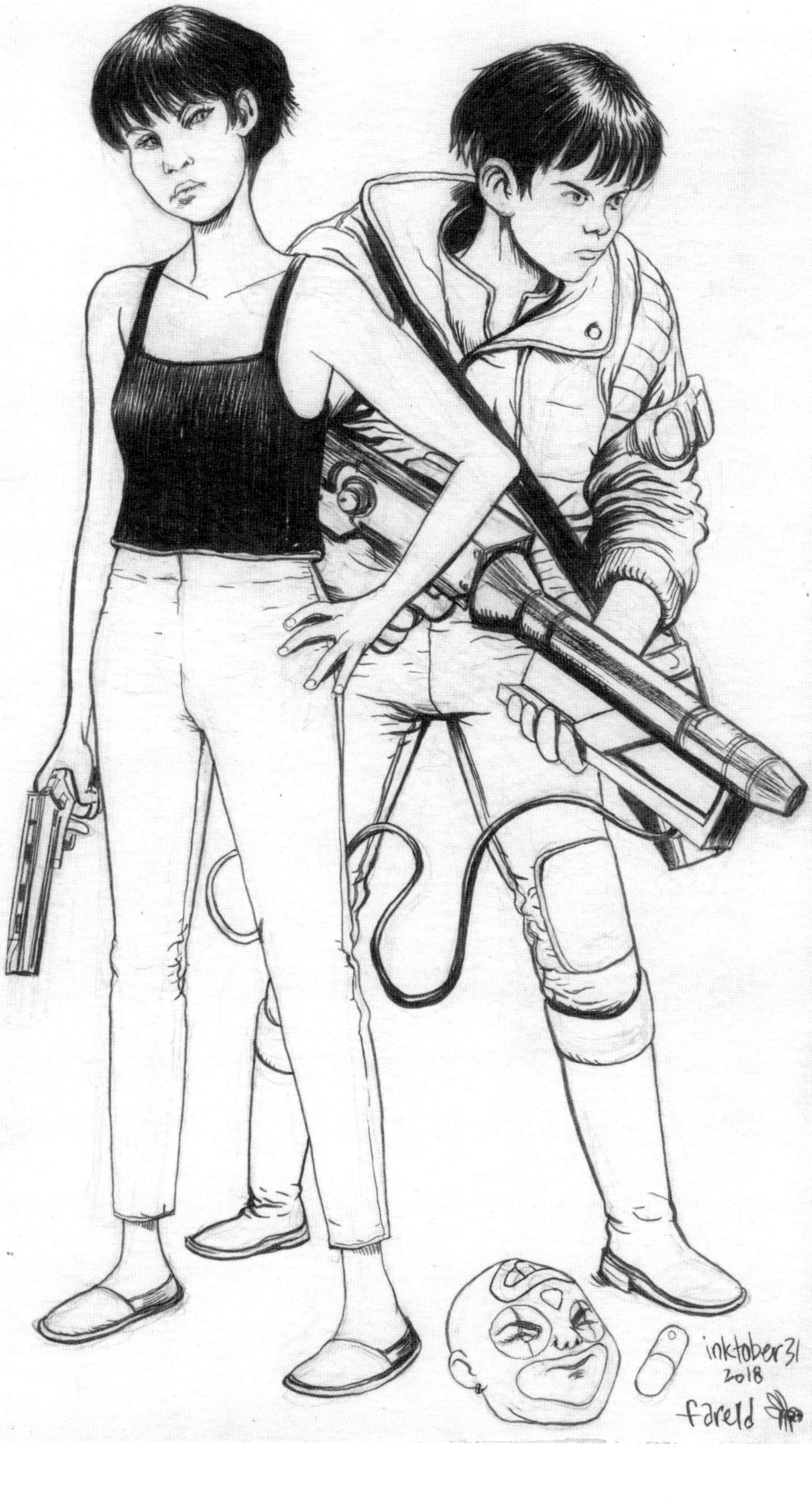
inktober31
2018
fareld

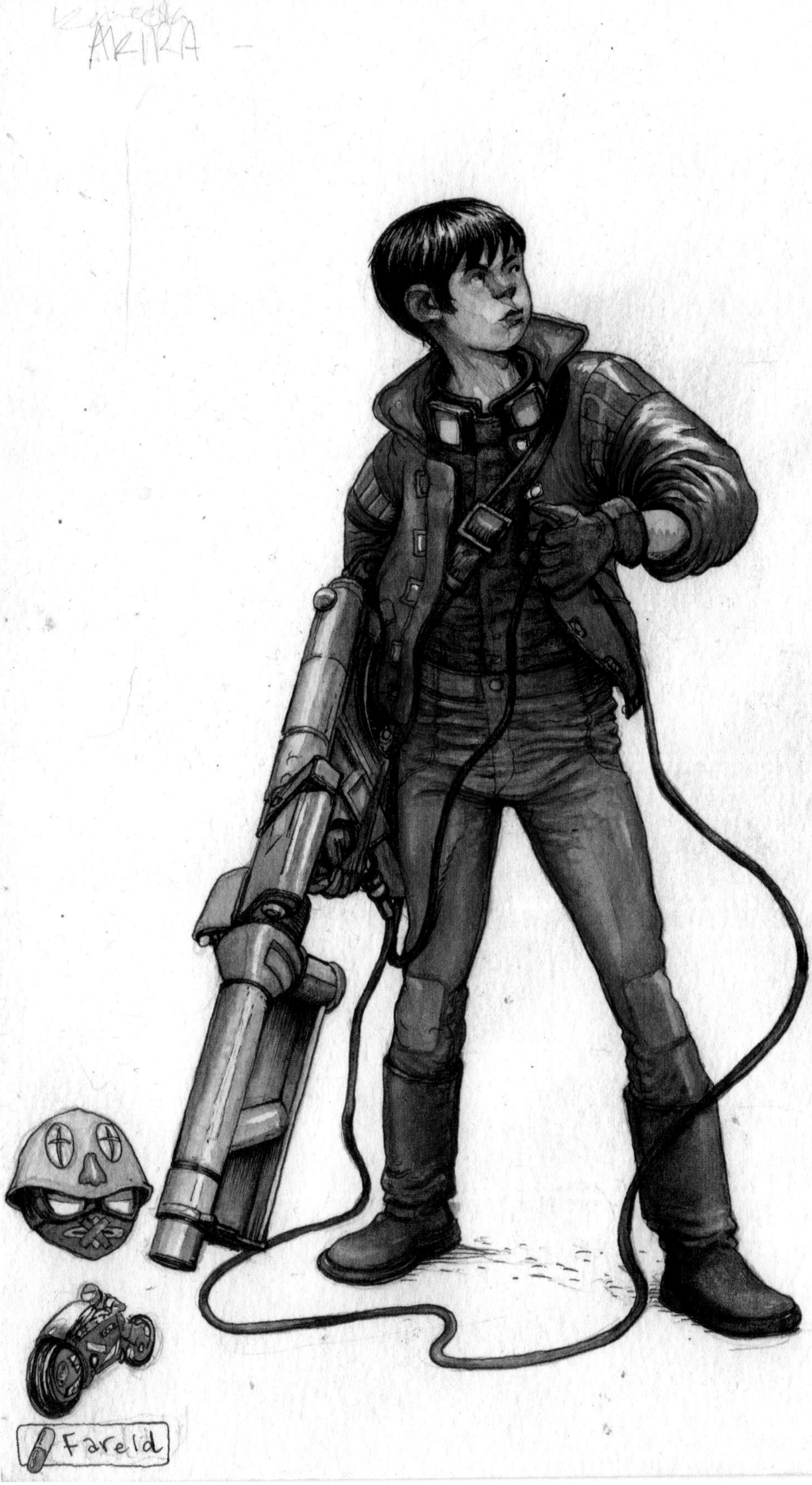
AKIRA
Fareld

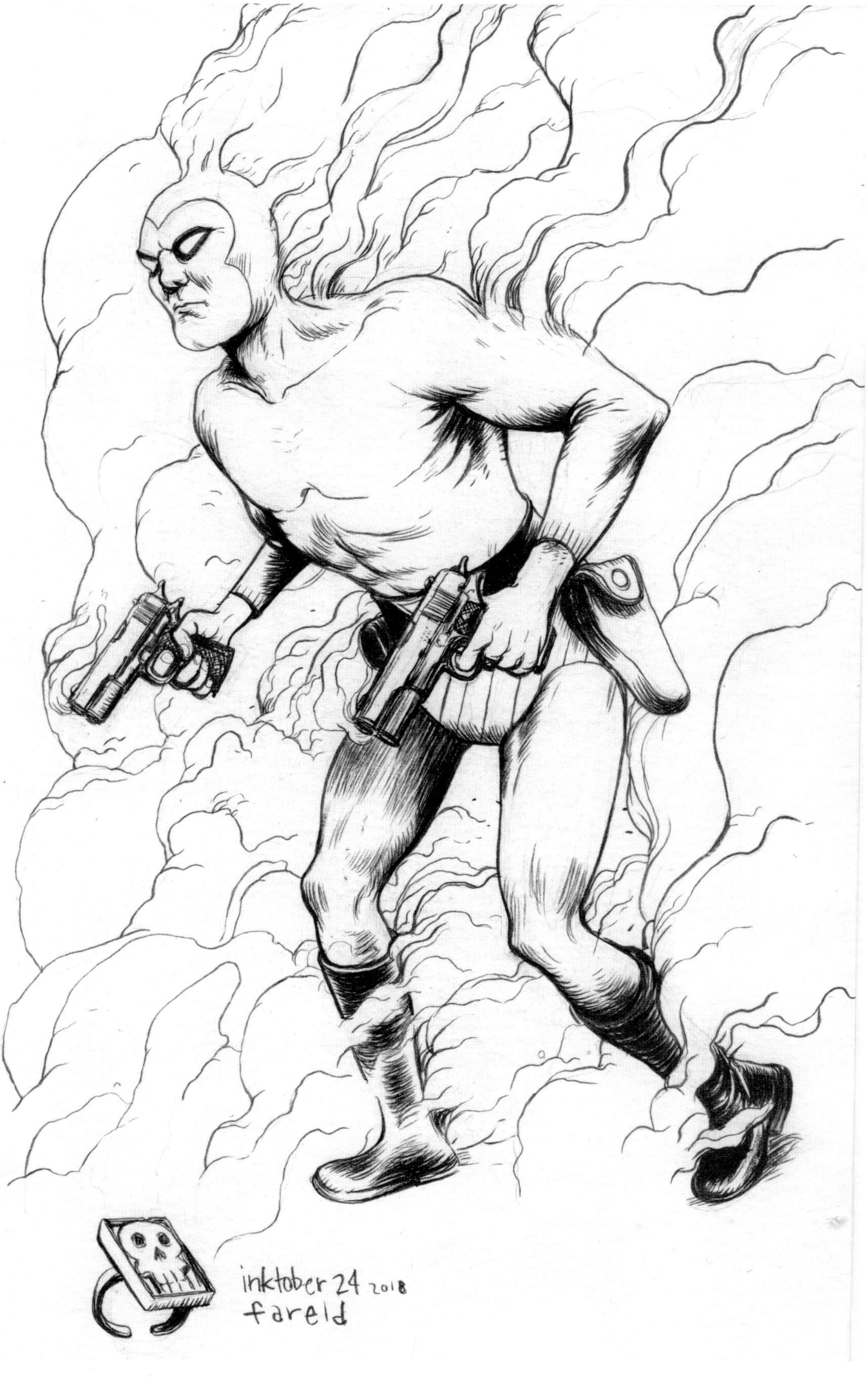
inktober 24 2018
fareld

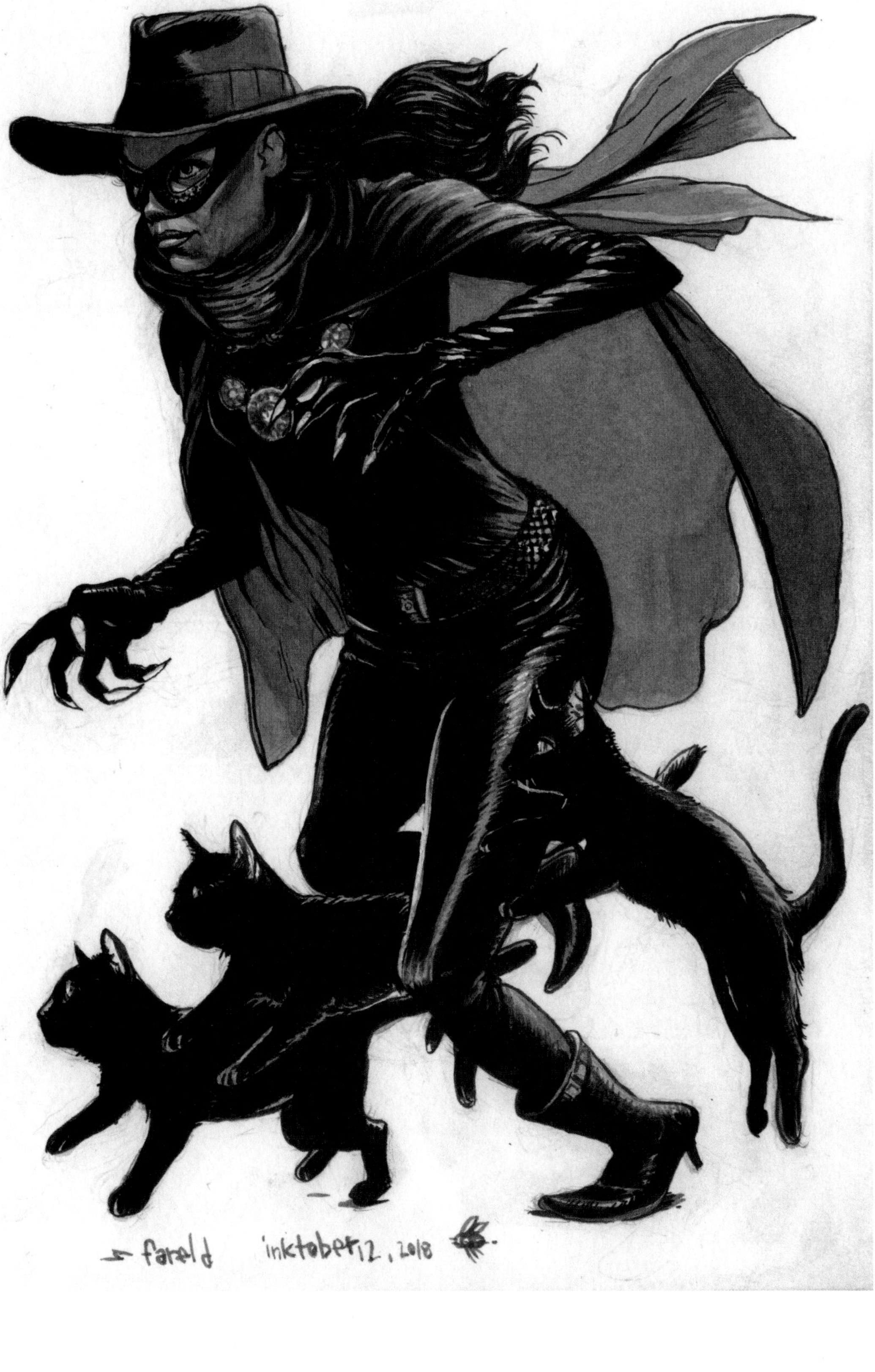
farel d
inktober 12, 2018

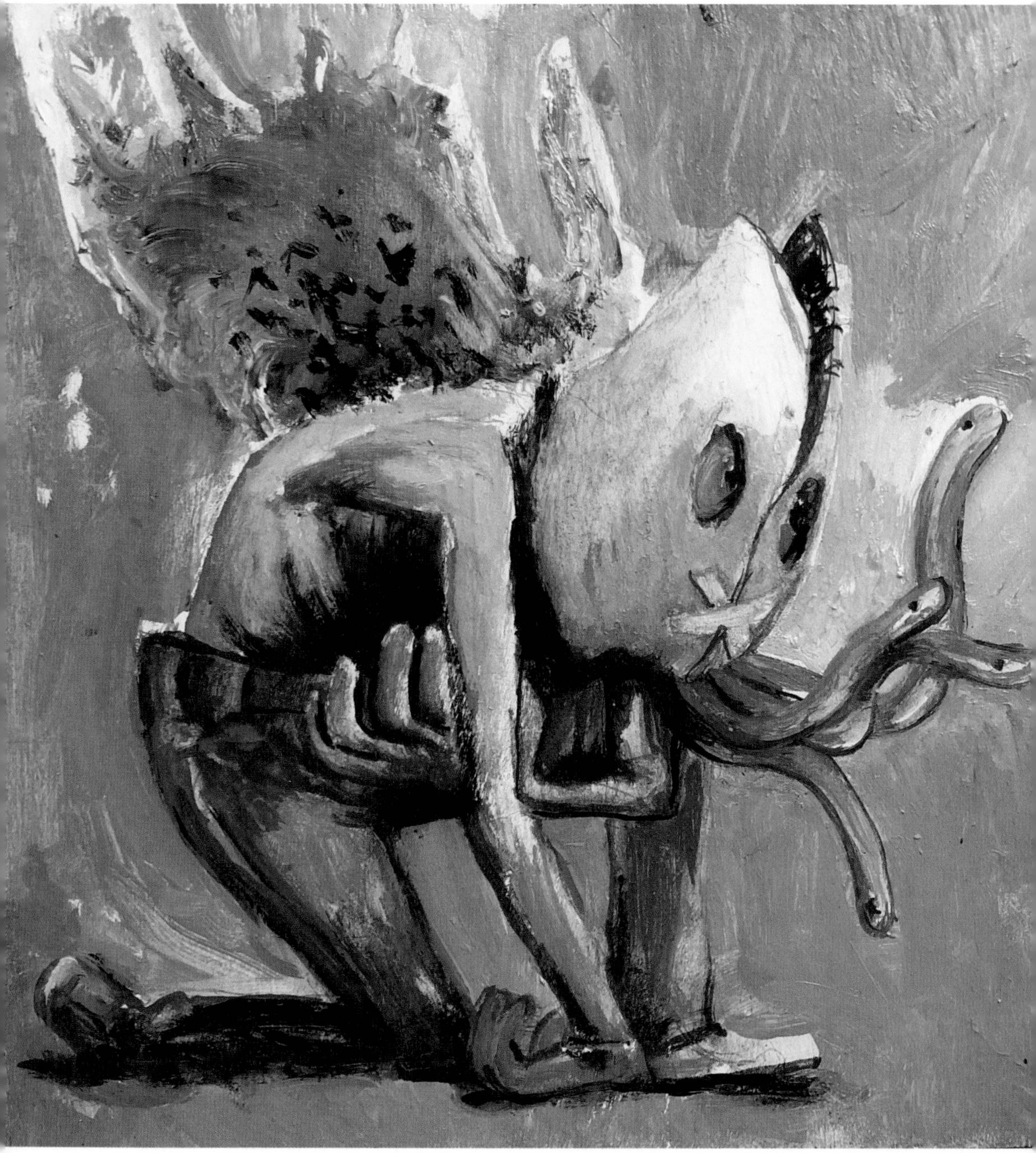

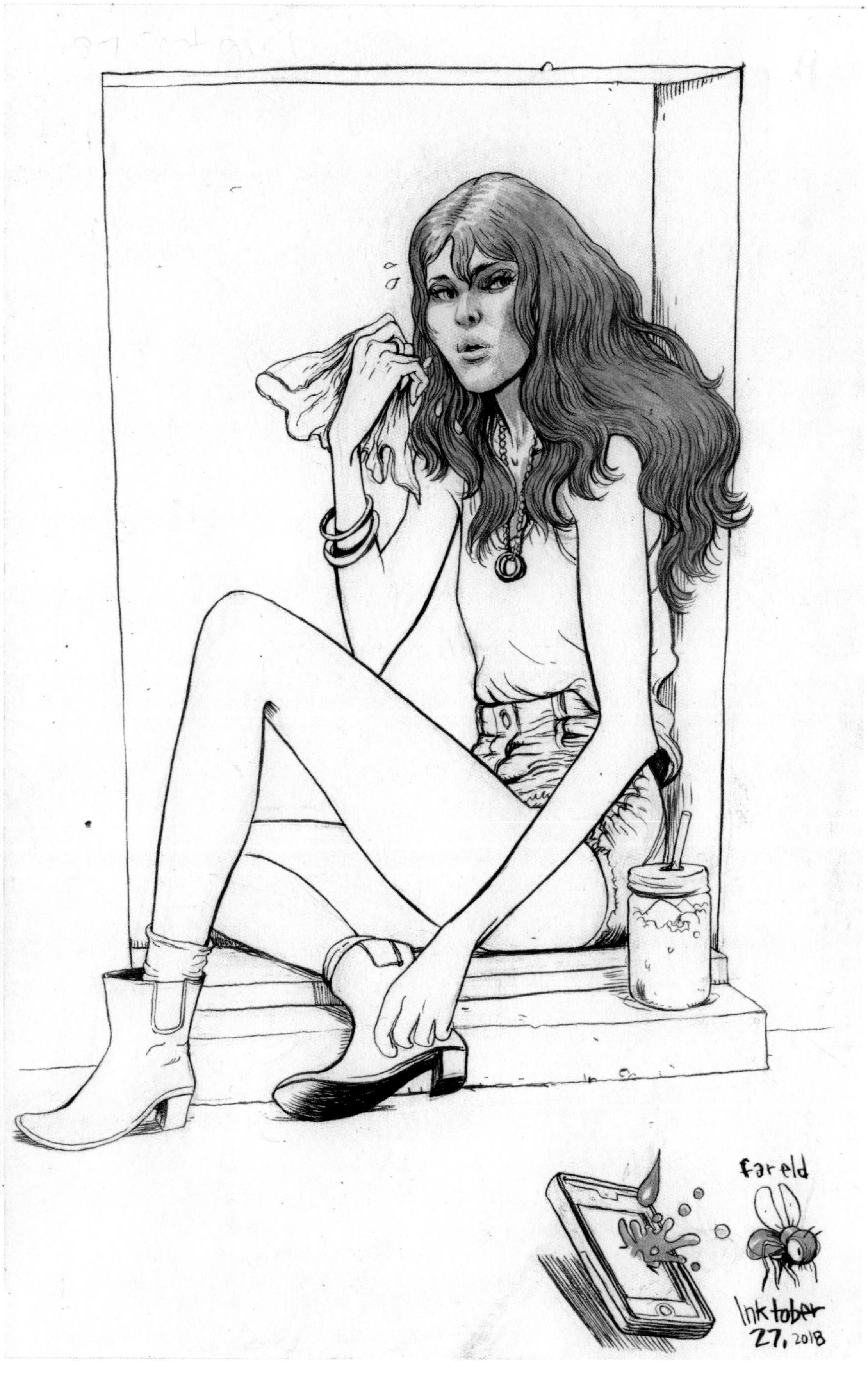
fareld
Inktober
27, 2018

SNOTGIRL, created by Bryan Lee O'Malley and Leslie Hung.

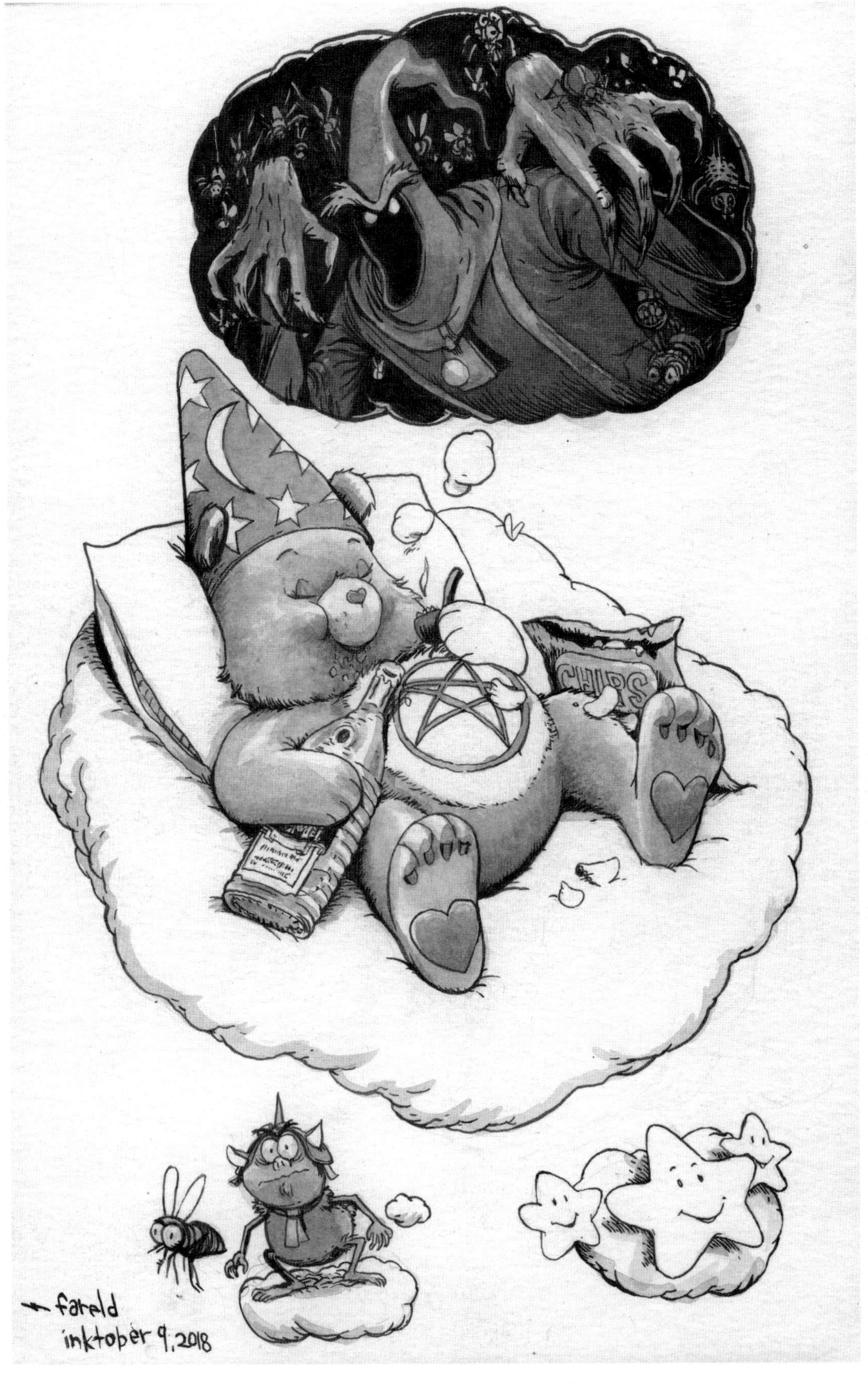
CHIPS
fareld
inktober 9, 2018

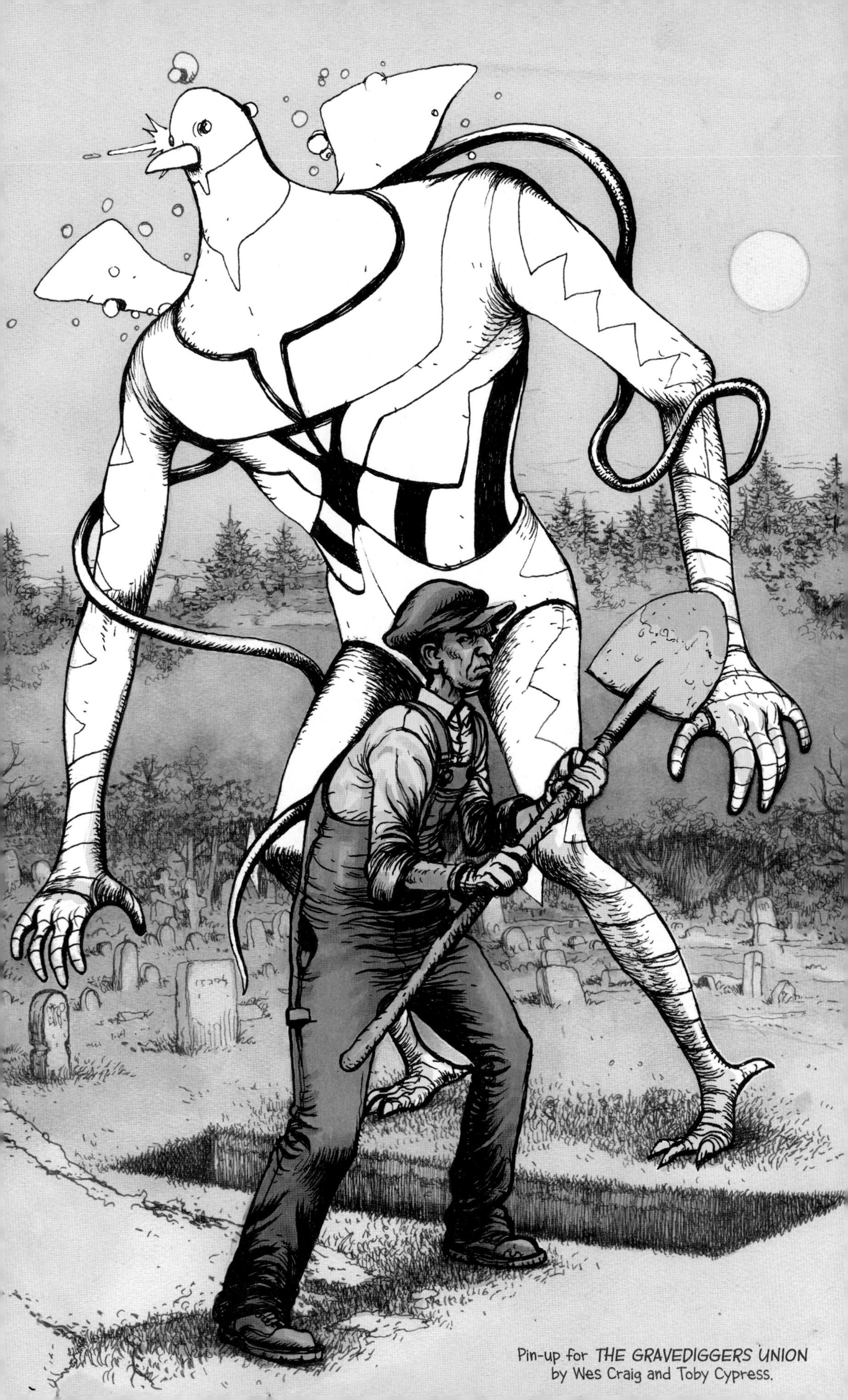

Pin-up for *THE GRAVEDIGGERS UNION*
by Wes Craig and Toby Cypress.

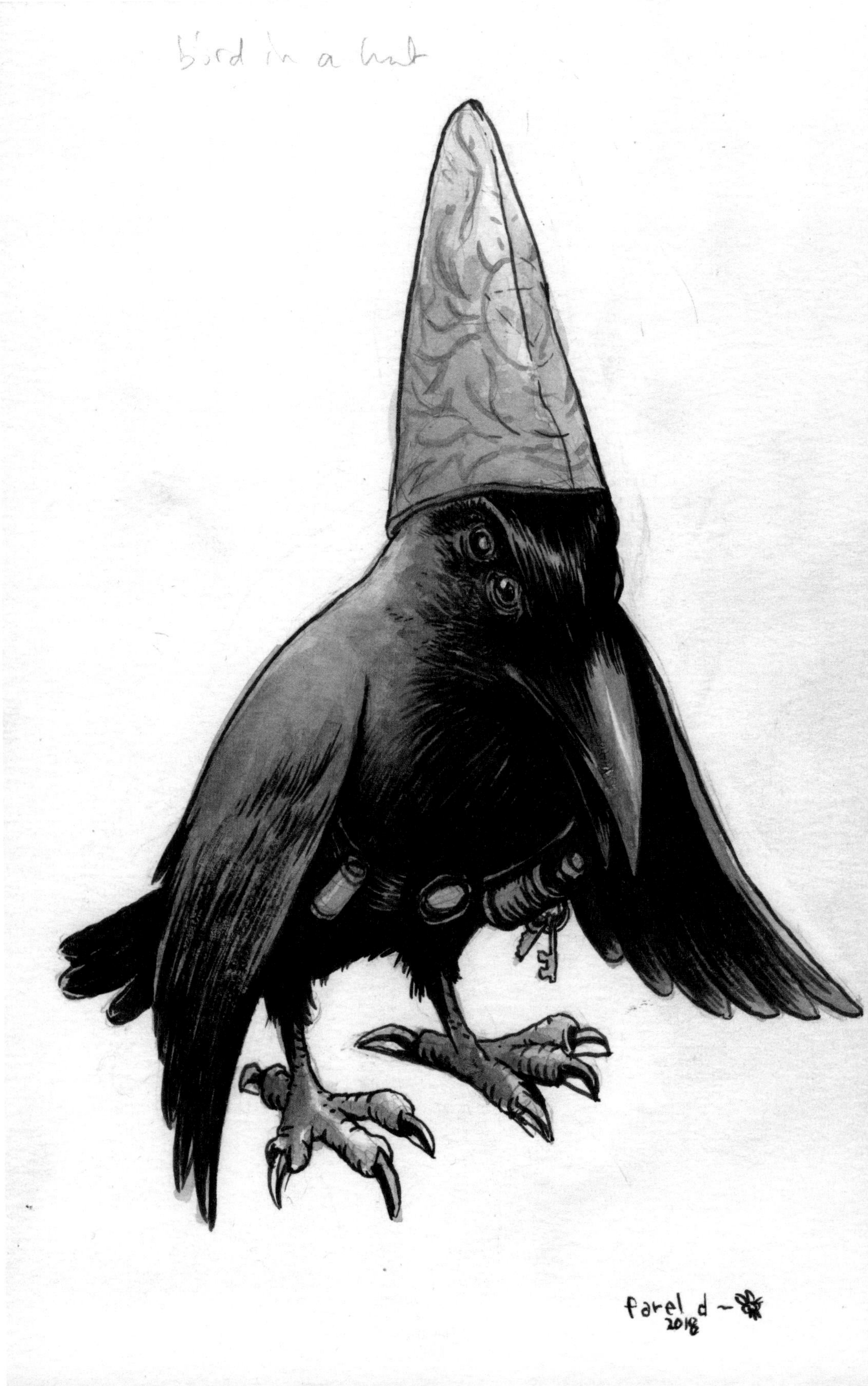
bird in a hat
farel d
2018

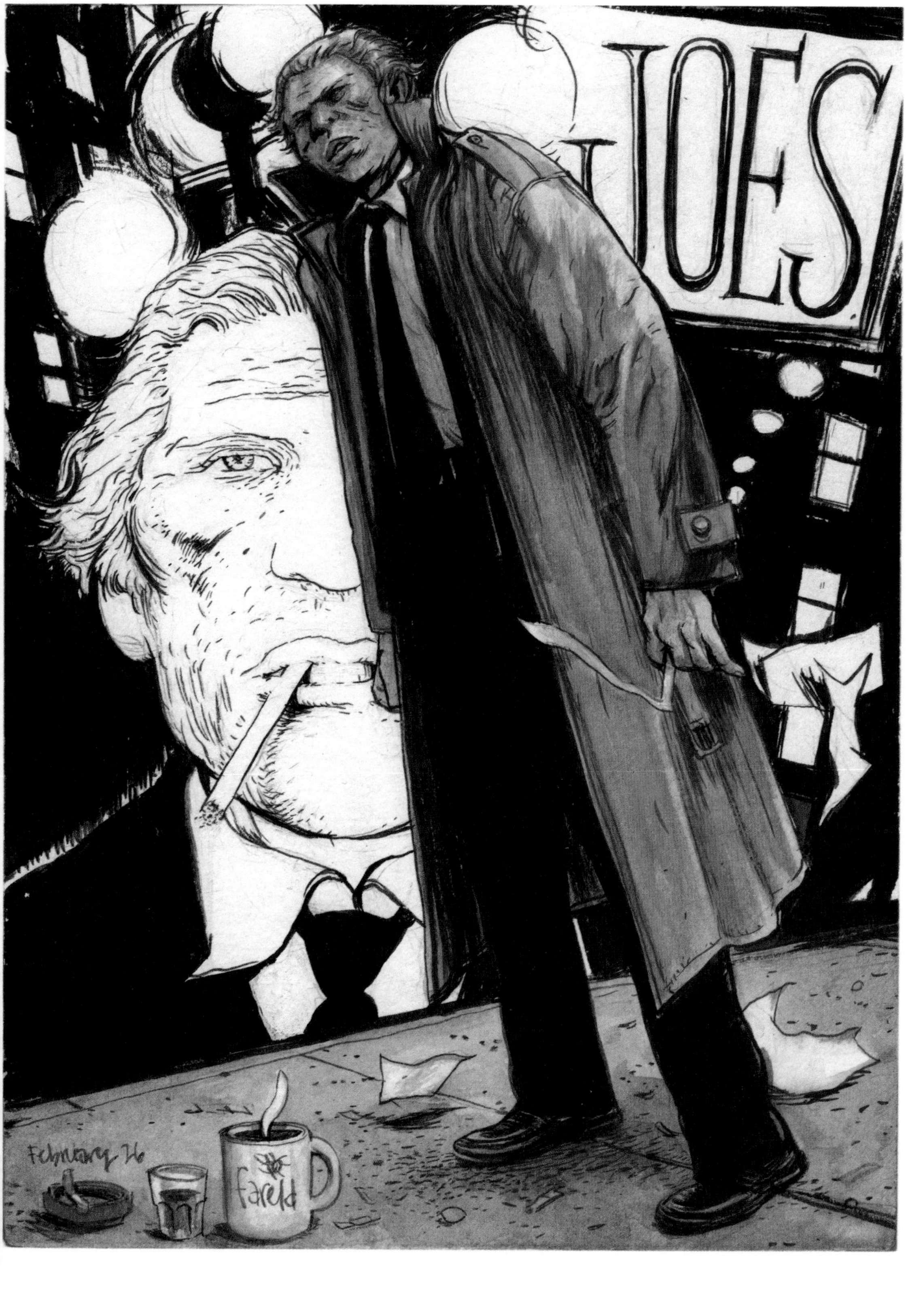
JOES
February 26

José Muñoz and Carlos Sampayo's hardboiled New York City investigator Alack Sinner.

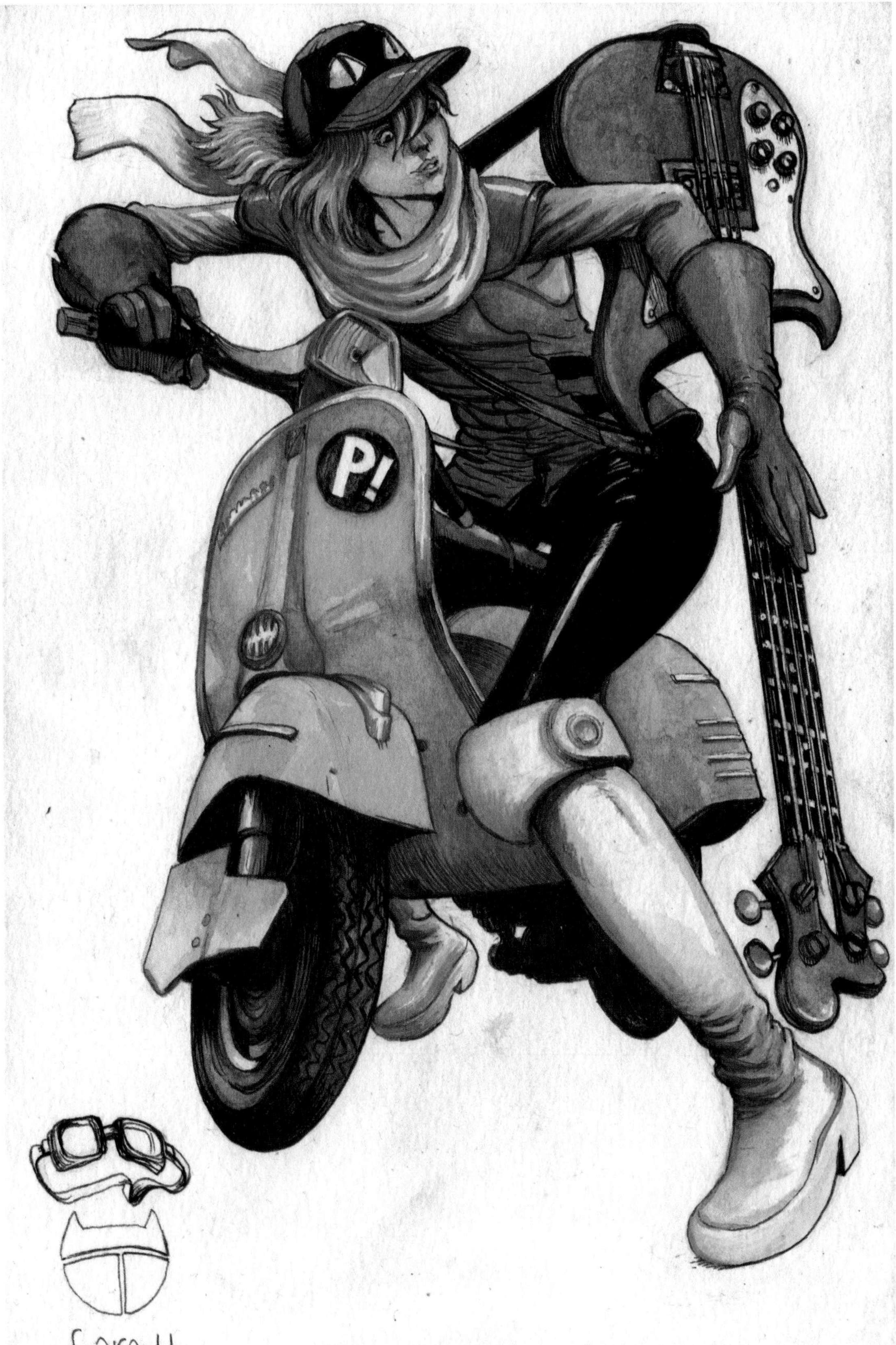
P!
farelld

 fareld   inktober 30 2018

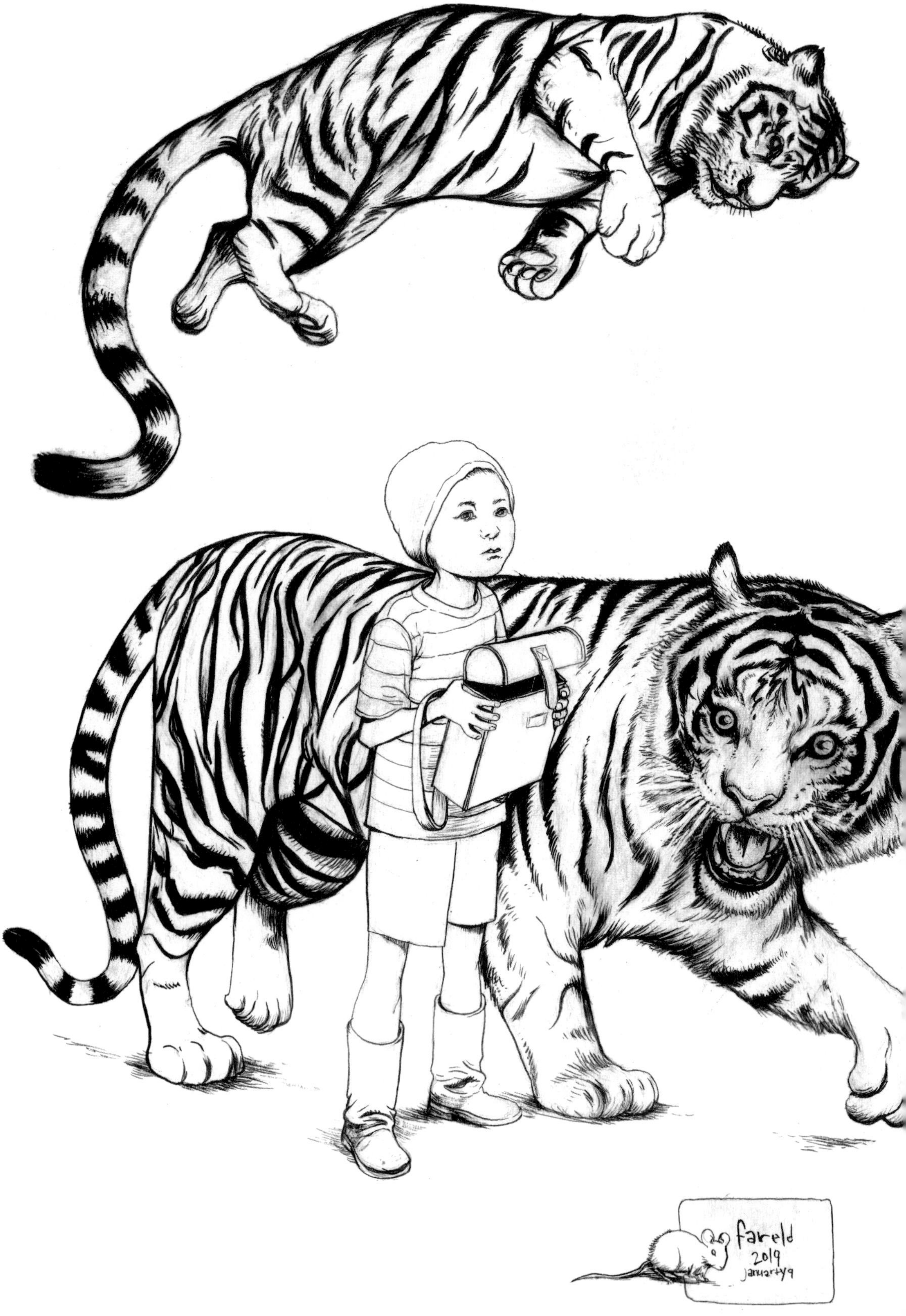
fareld
2019
january9

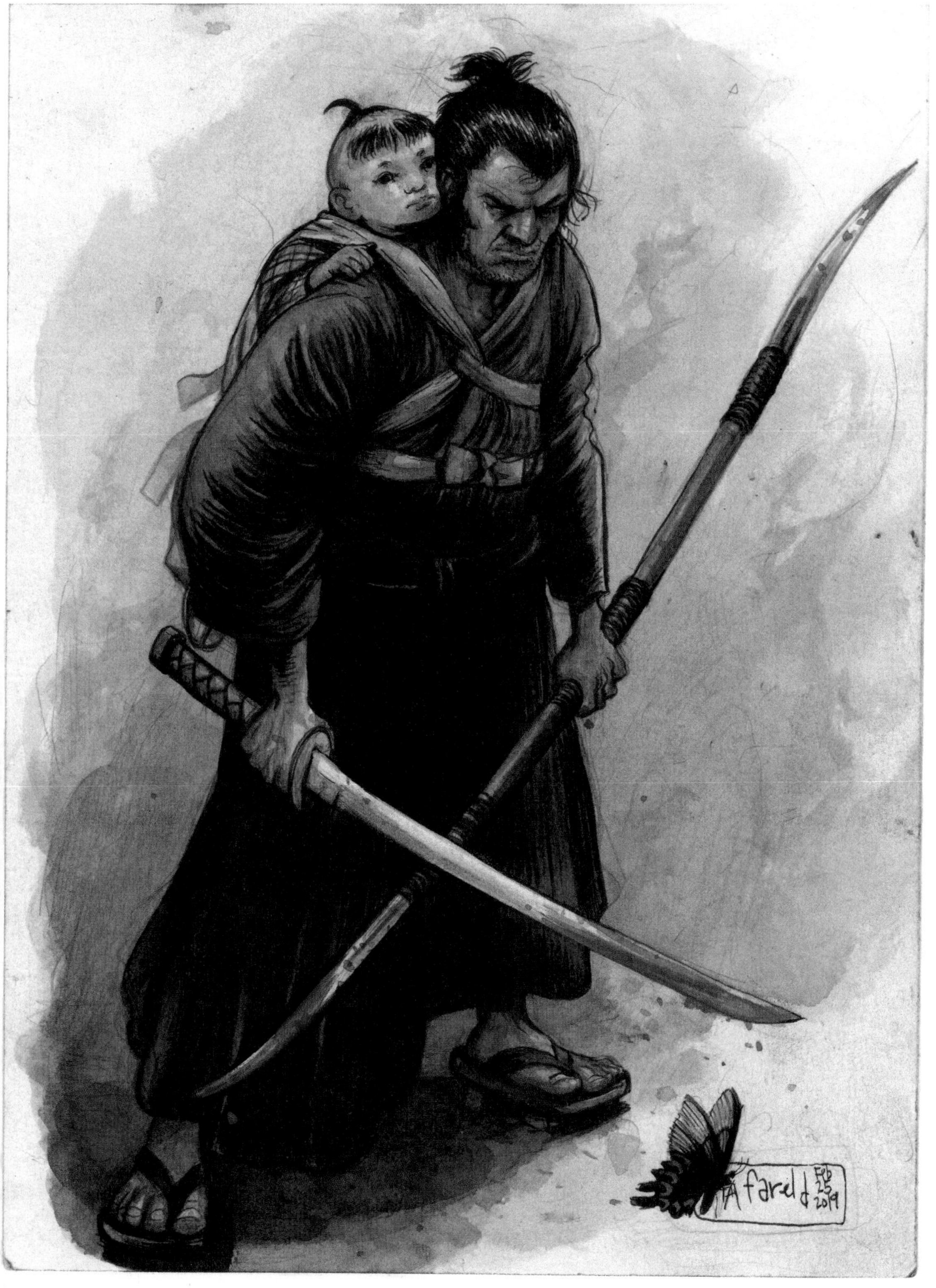

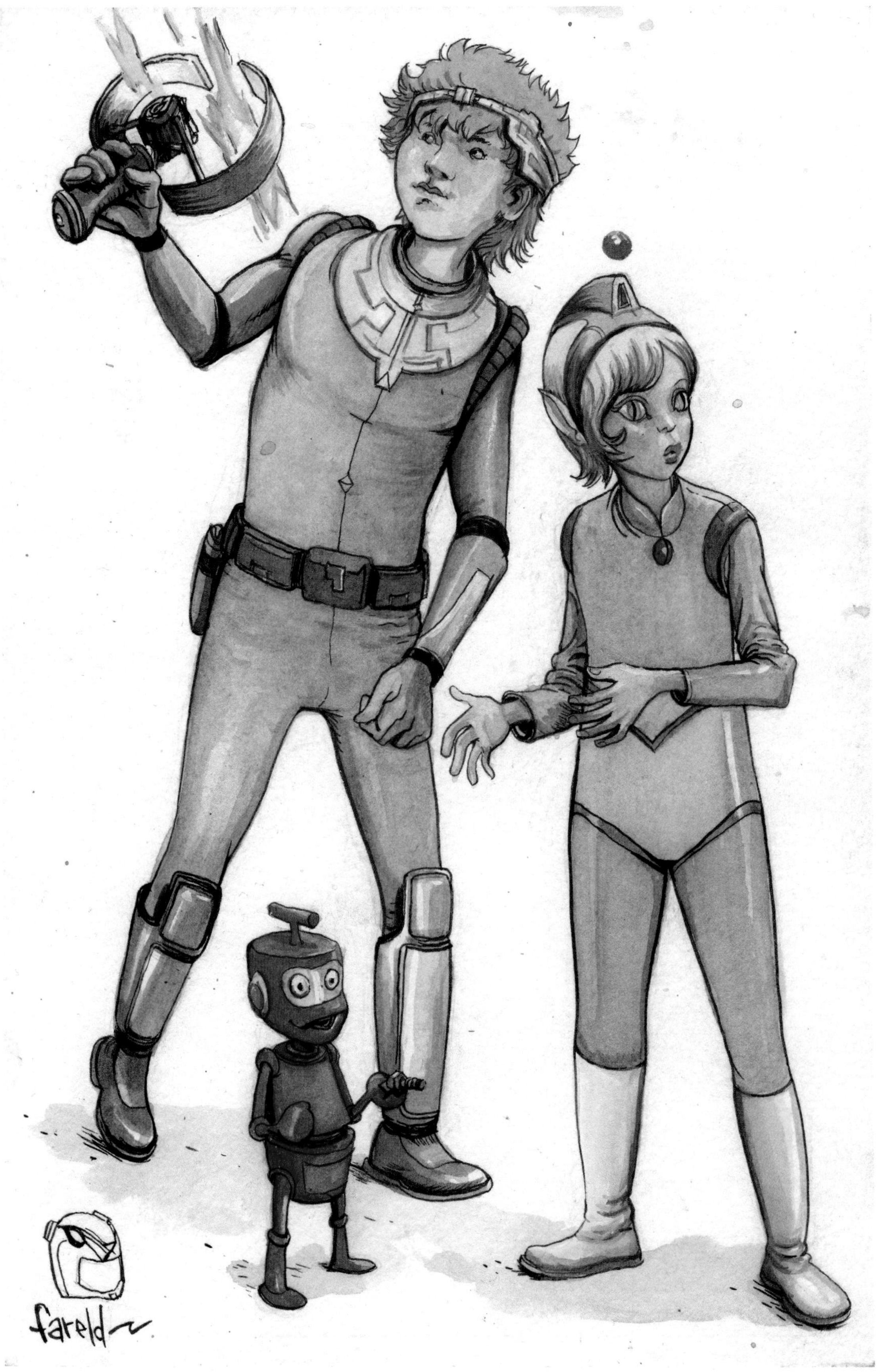
fareld

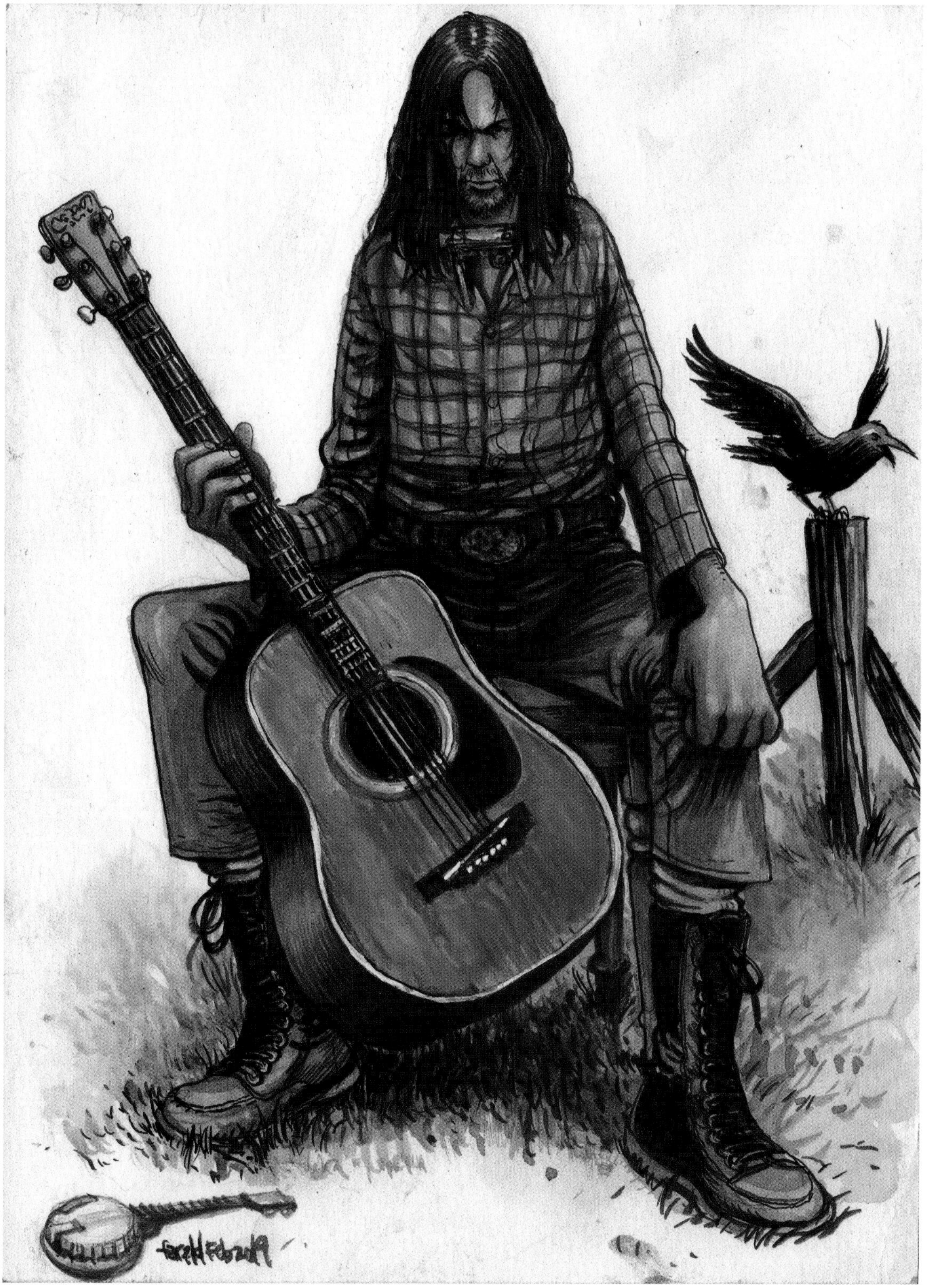

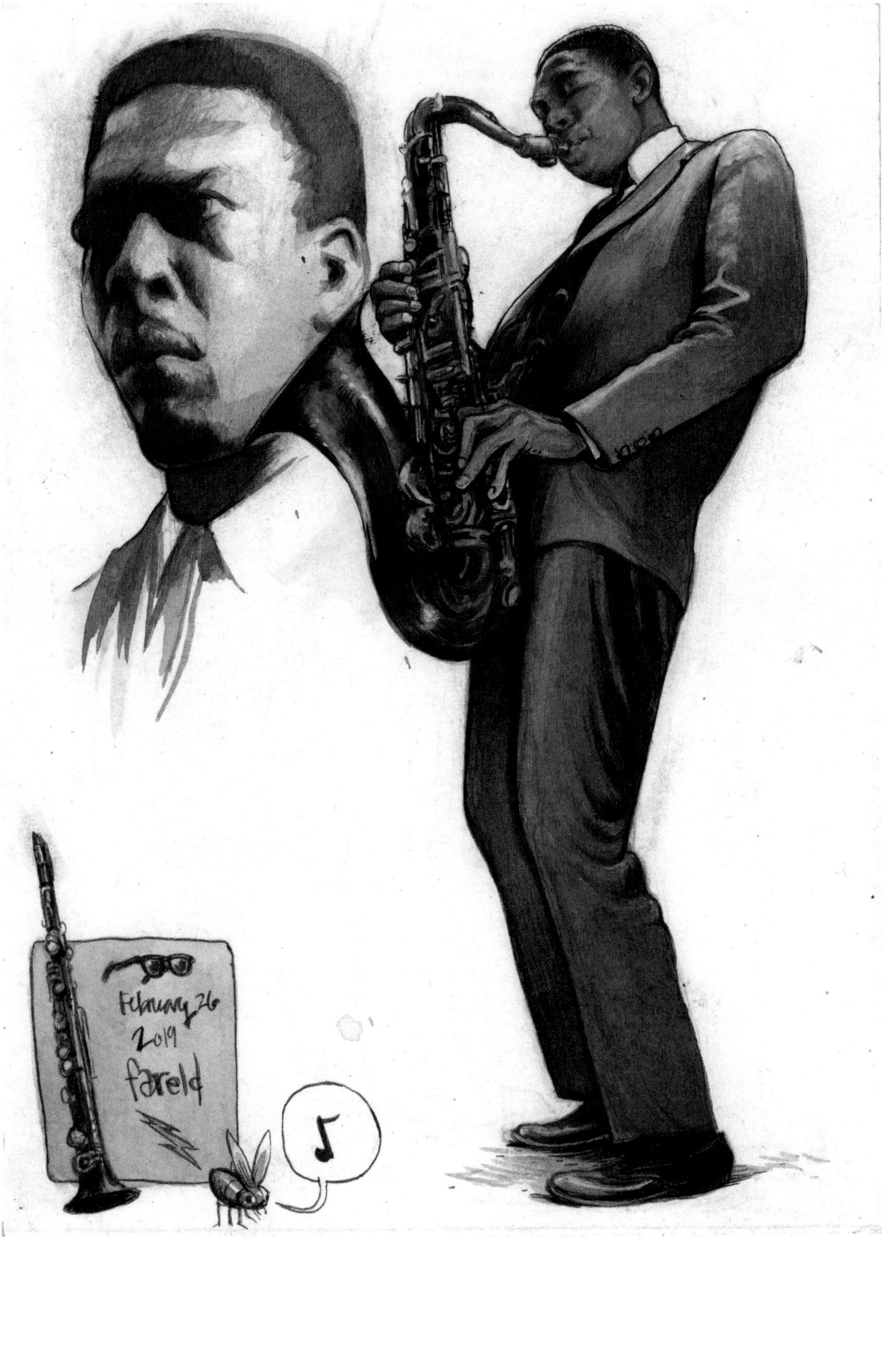
February 26
2019
fareld

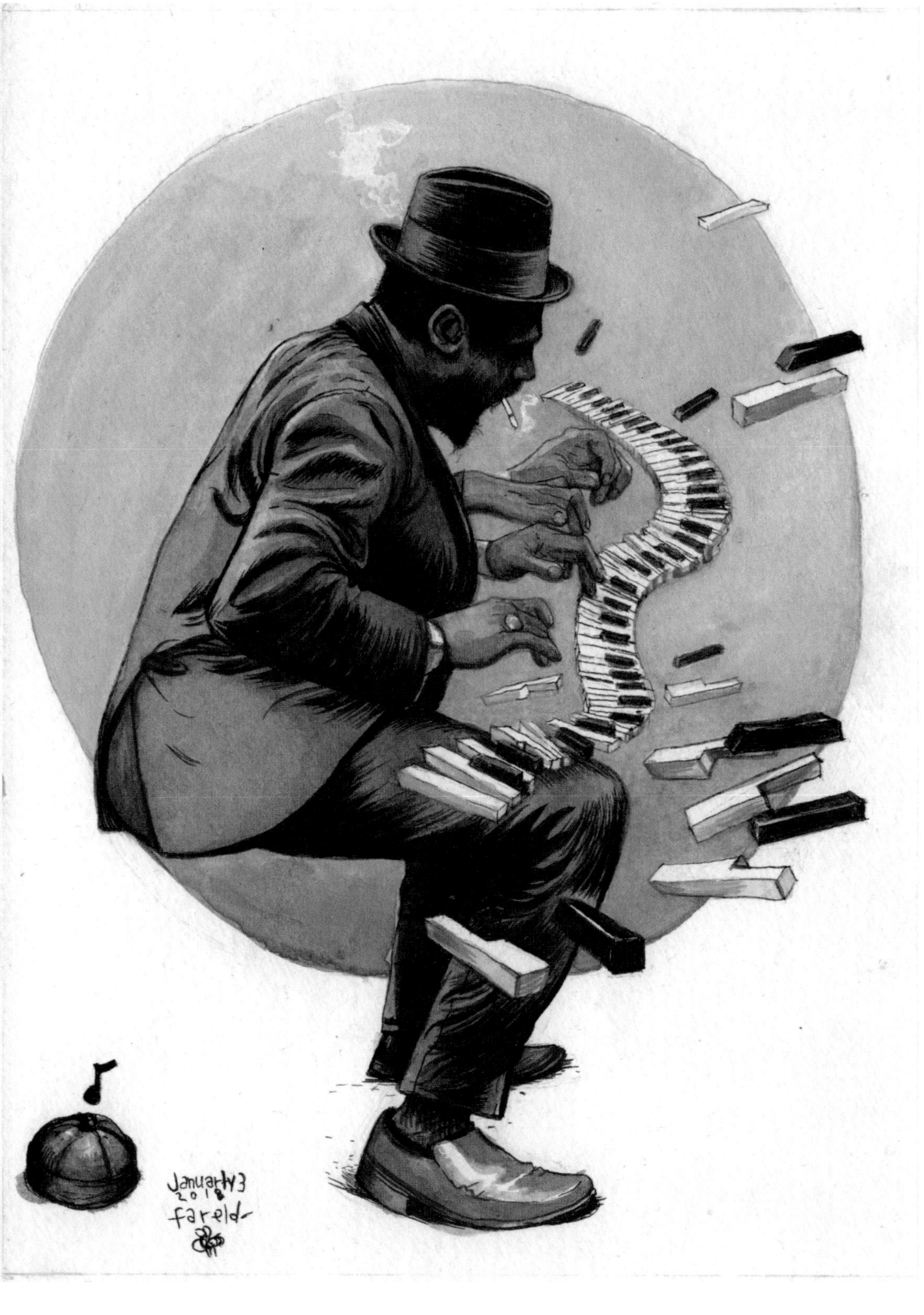
January 3
2018
fareld-

Fåreld

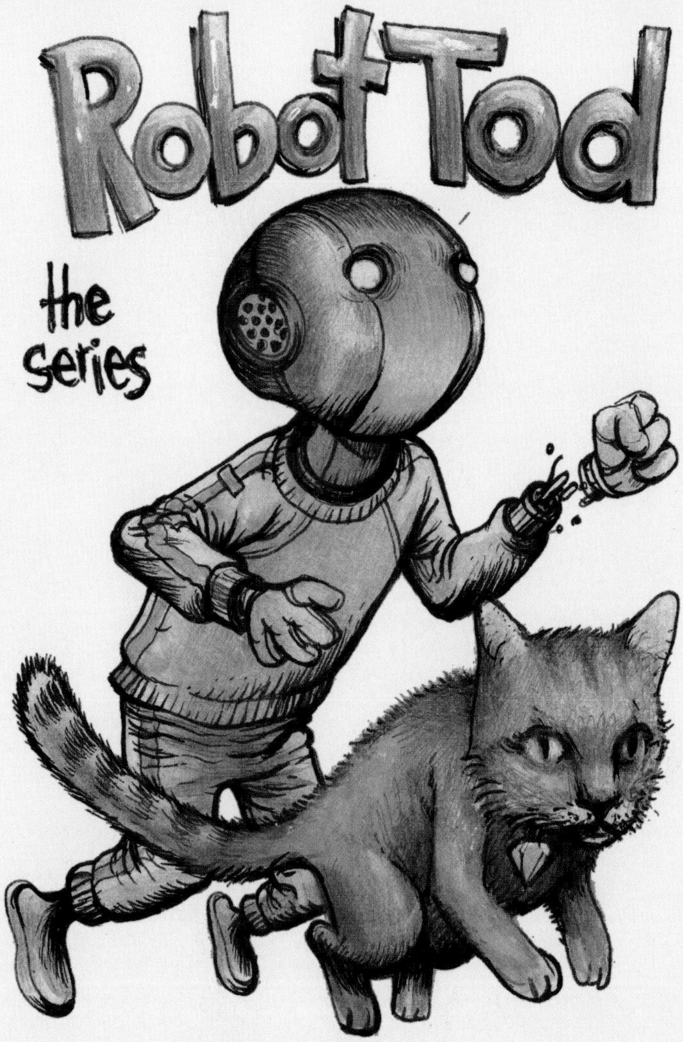
Robot Tod
the series

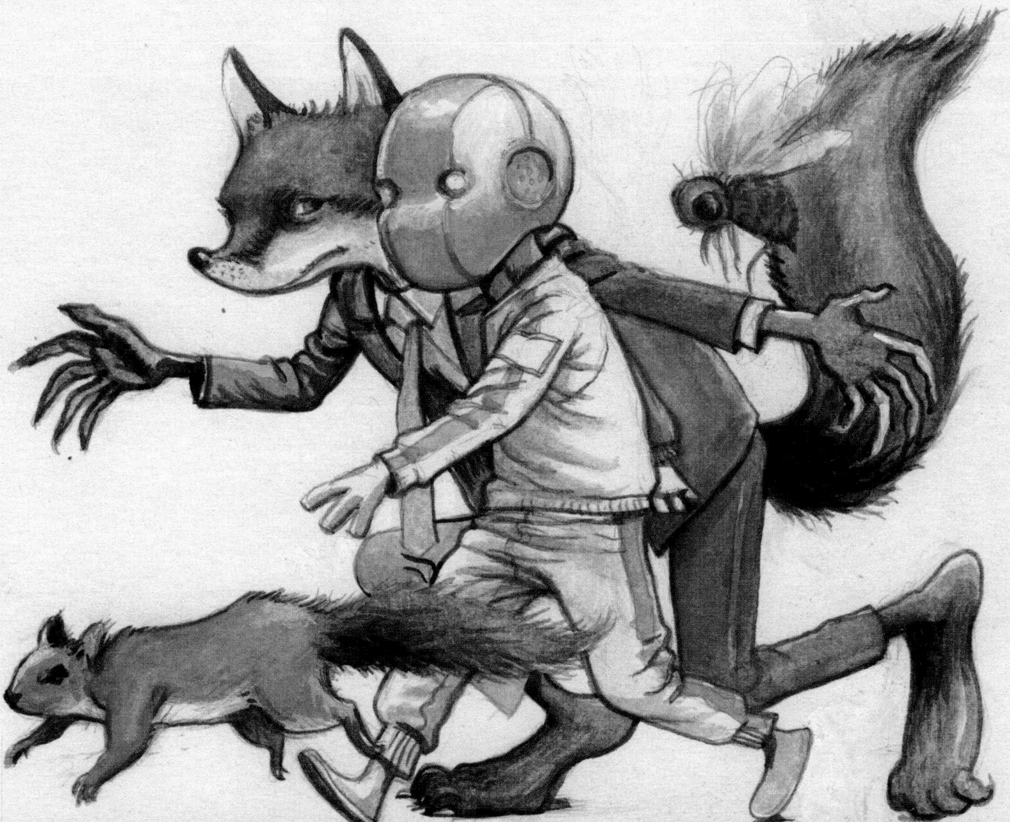

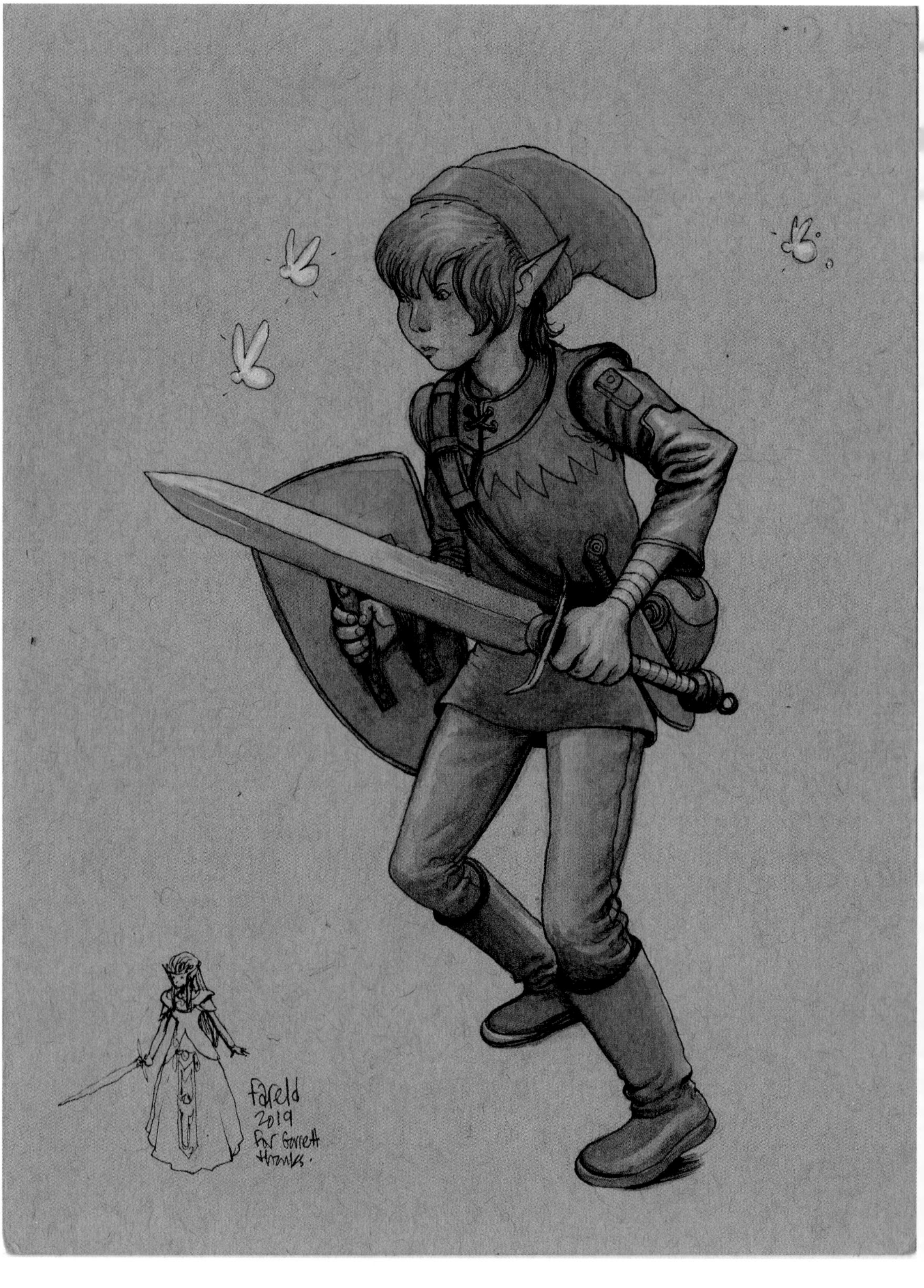

Fareld
2019
For Garrett
thanks.

Farald Drawcember 8 2018

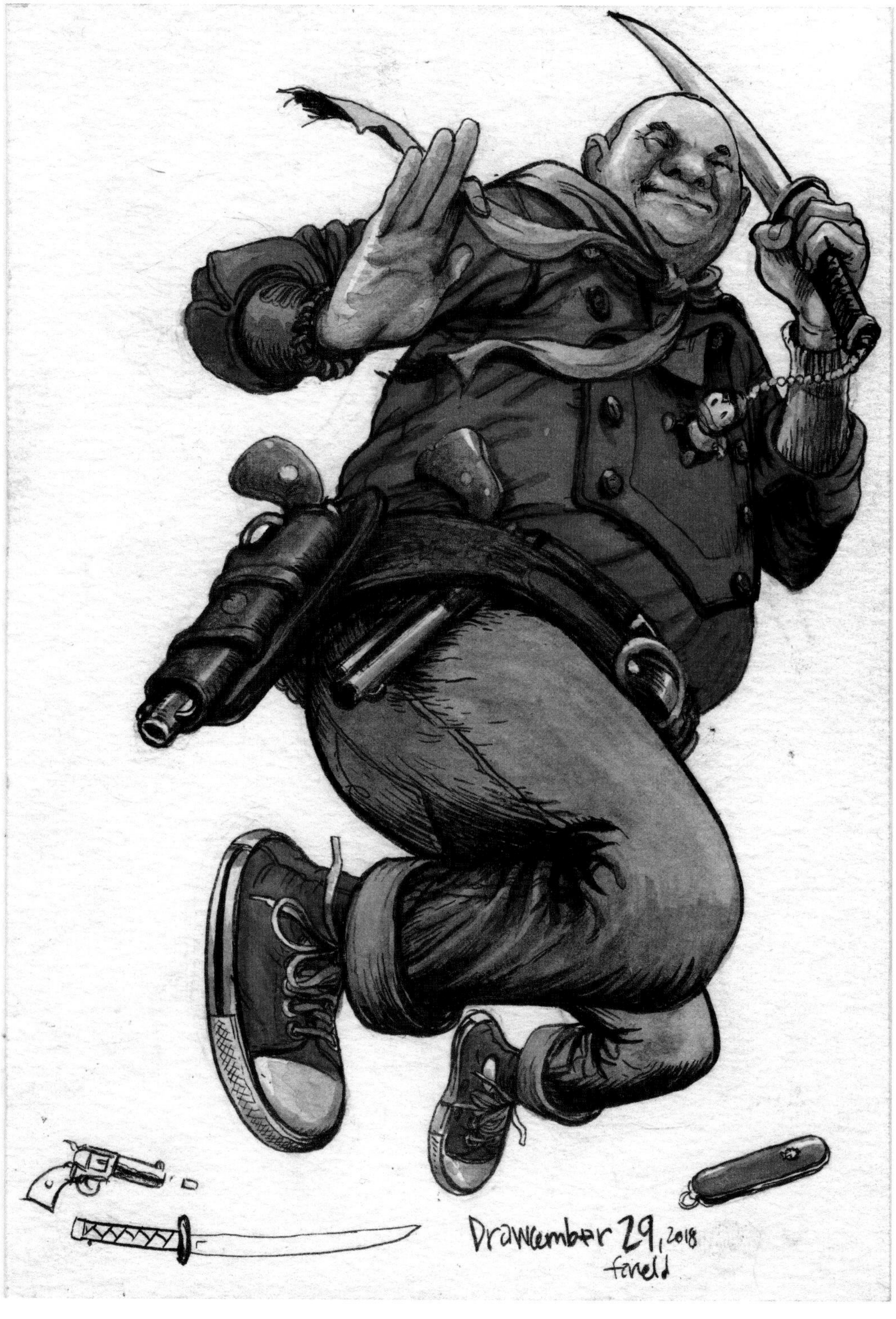
Drawcember 29, 2018
farell

SHAOLIN COWBOY is an excellent comic book series by Geof Darrow.

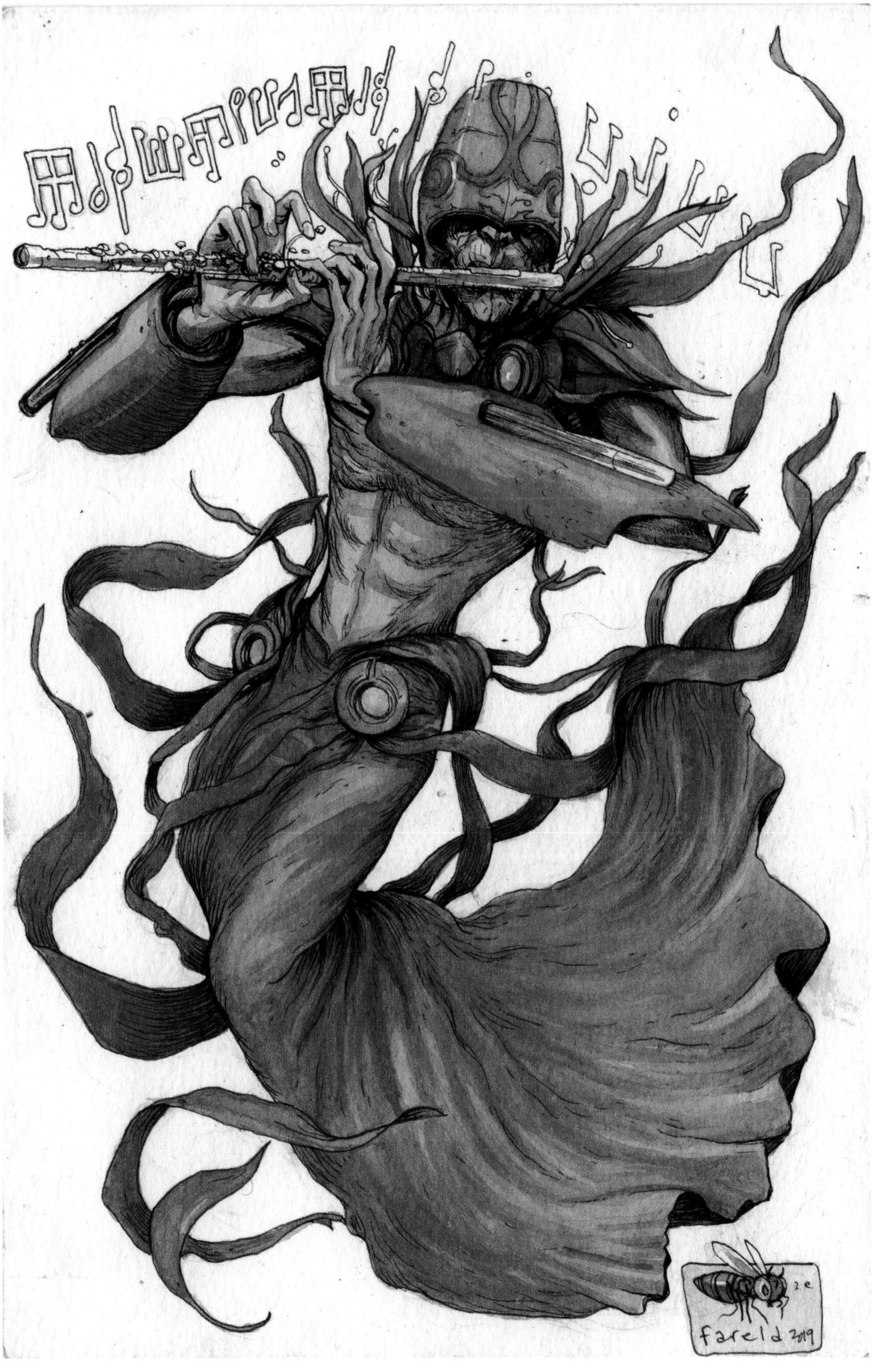
fareld 2019

Piper from one my favorite comics *SEVEN TO ETERNITY*,
by Rick Remender, Jerome Opeña, and Matt Hollingsworth

farkld Drawcember 9, 2018.

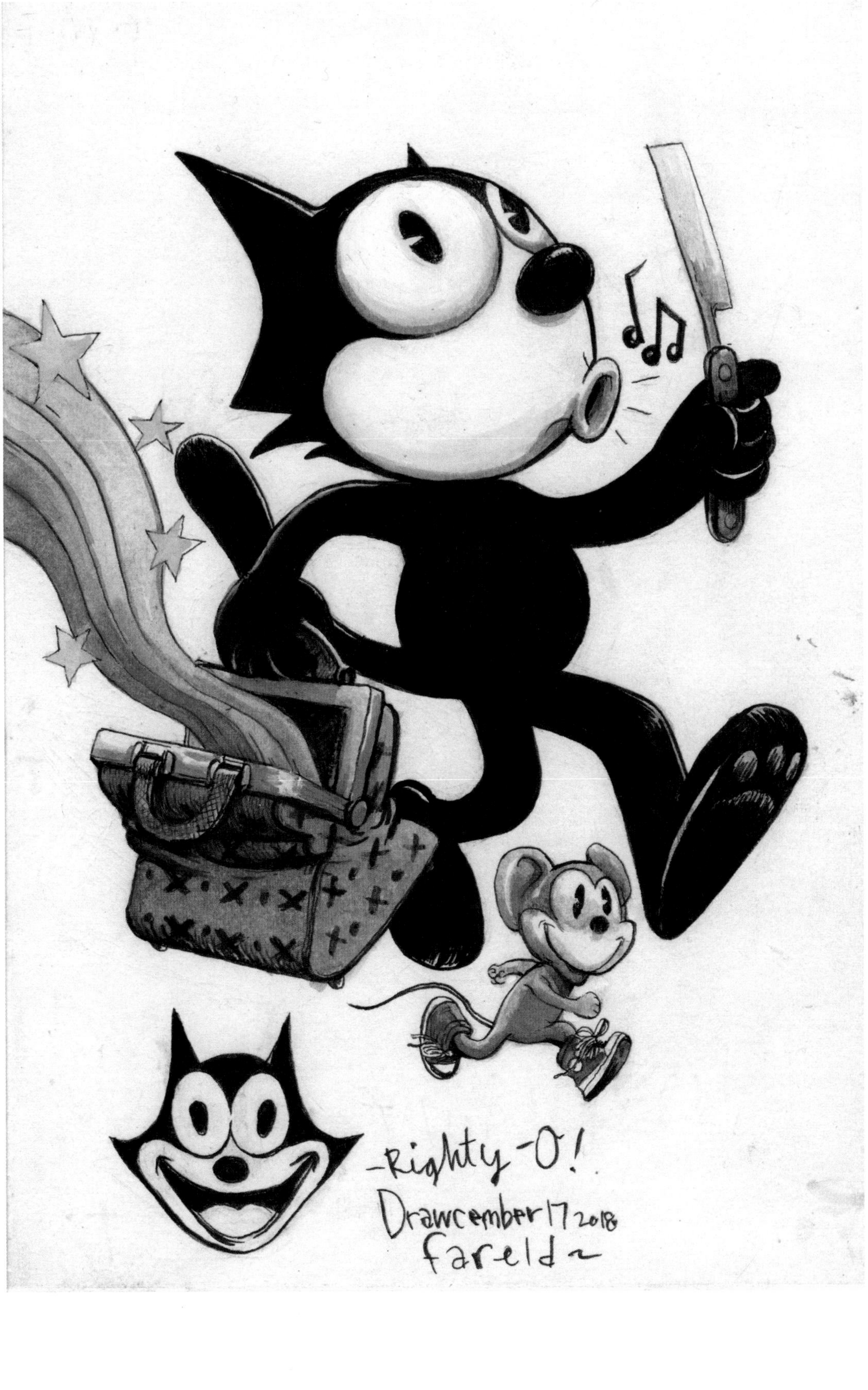
-Righty-O!
Drawcember 17 2018
fareld~

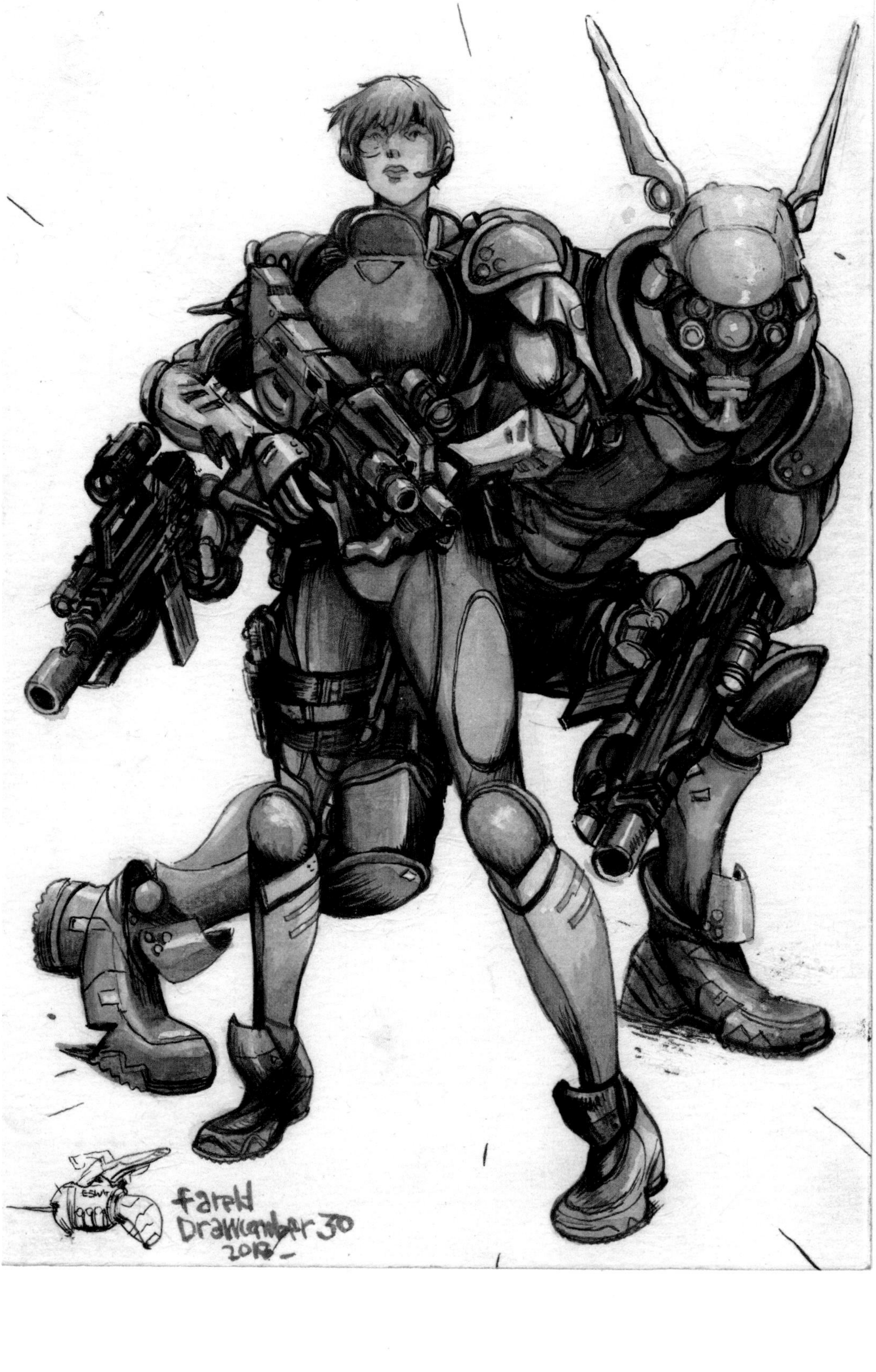
ESWAT
fareld
Drawcember 30
2013

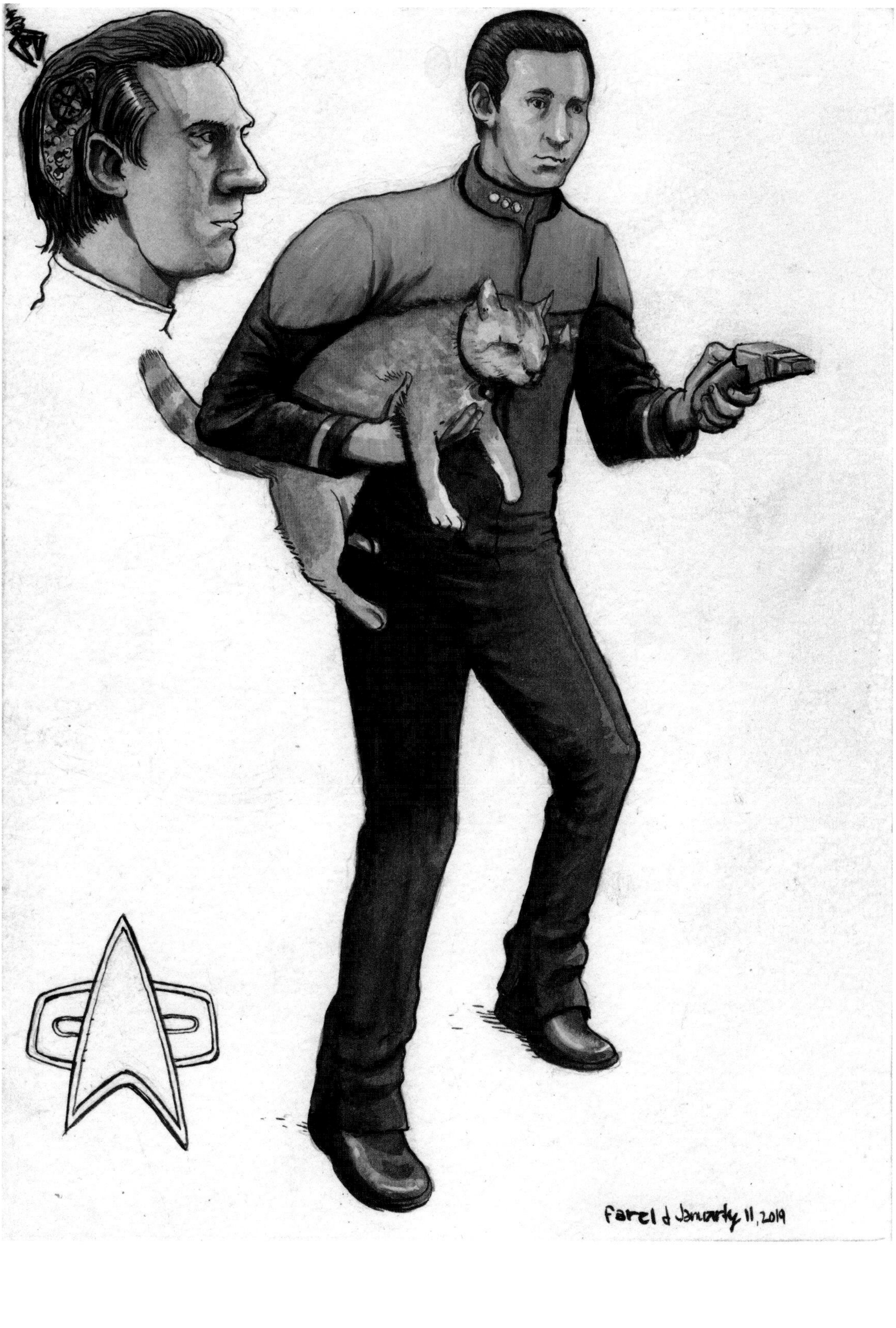
Farel d January 11, 2019

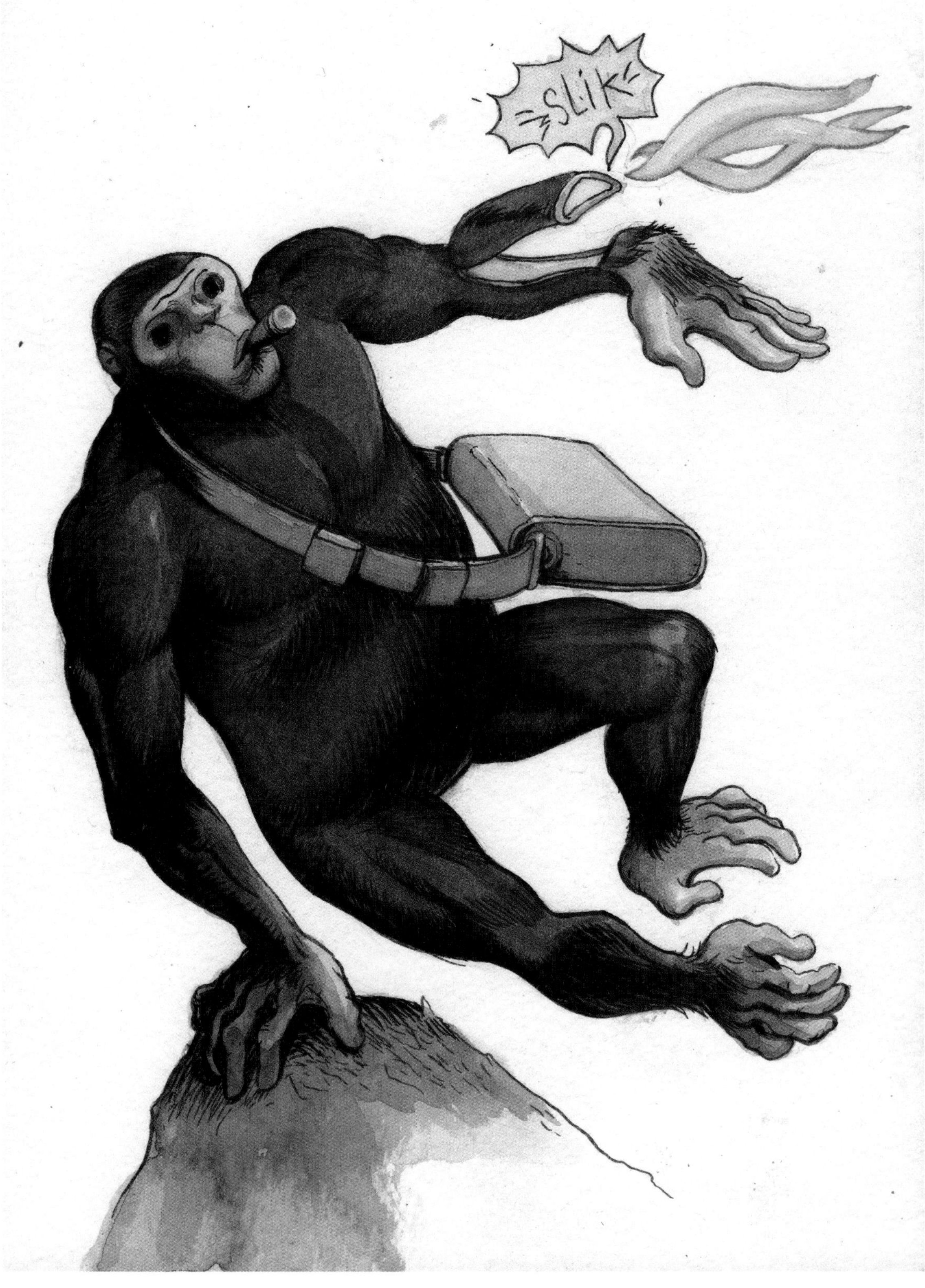
SLIK

The android Churchill from the brilliant science fiction epic *AAMA* by Frederik Peeters.

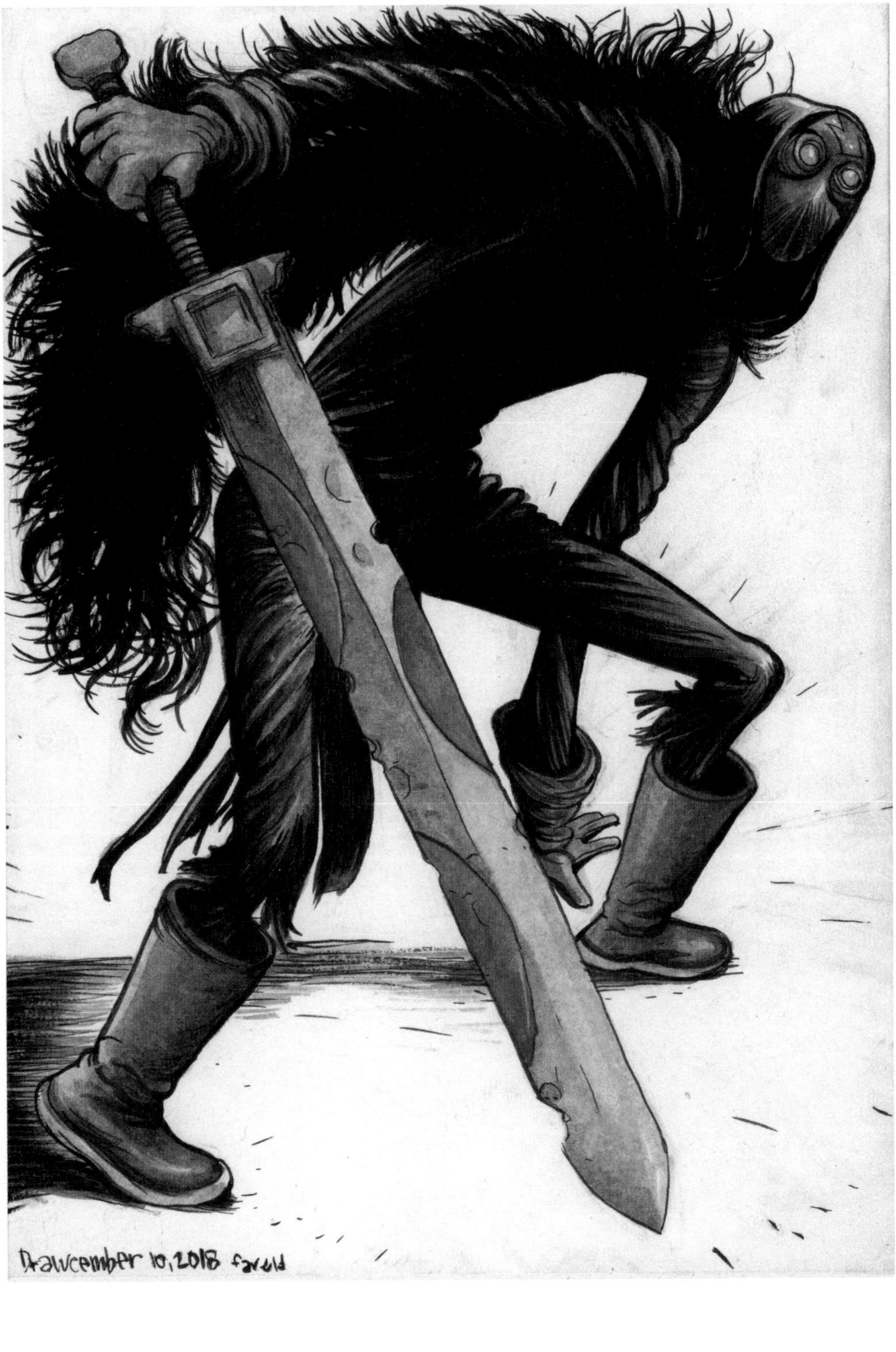
Drawcember 10, 2018

Rathraq, Scarecrow Warrior God from the pages of
RUMBLE by John Arcudi, James Harren, and David Rubin.

Drawcember 23, 2018   fareld

Drawcember 14, 2018 faceld

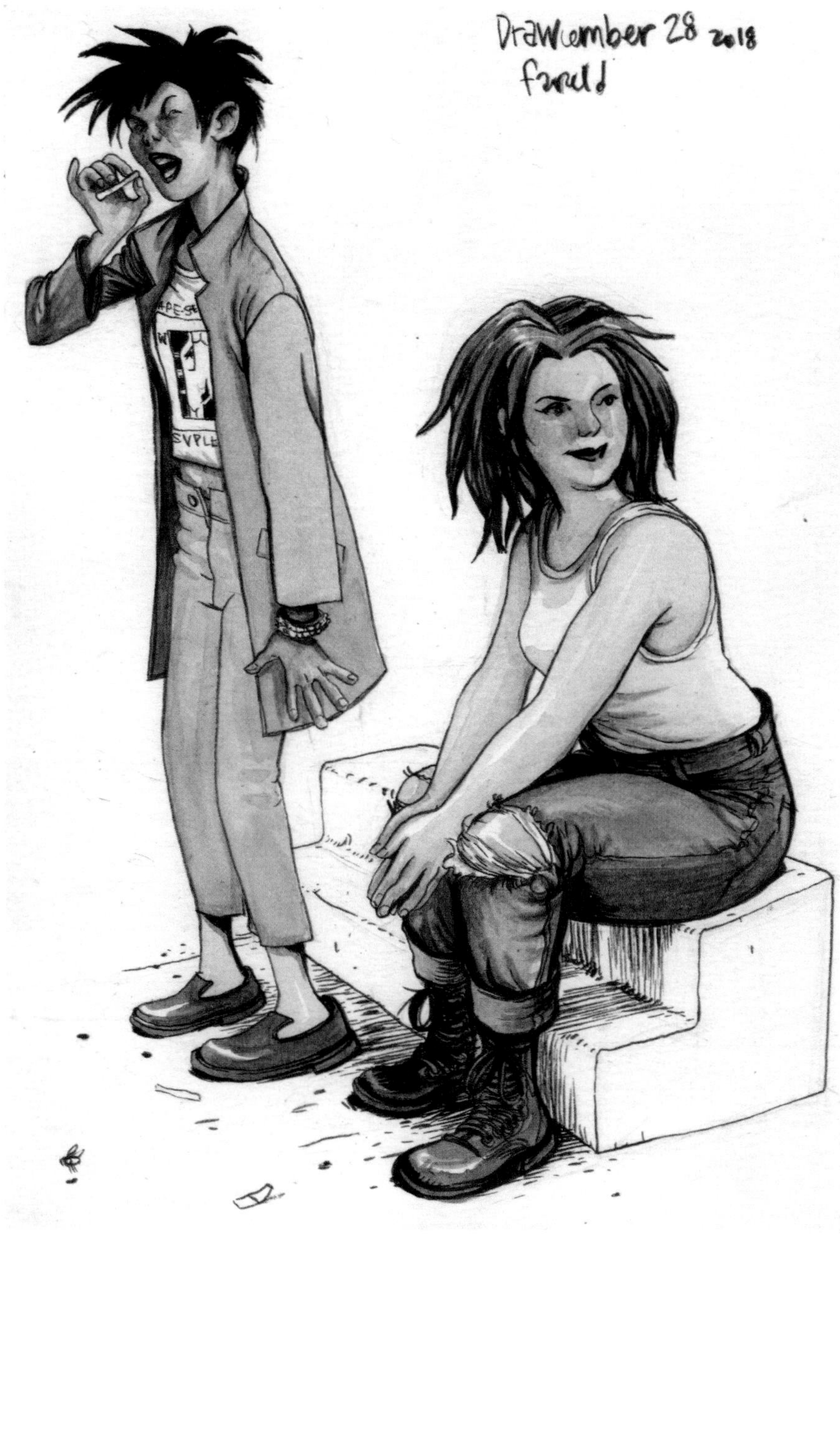
Drawcember 28 2018

Maggie and Hopey from Jamie Hernandez's *LOVE & ROCKETS*.

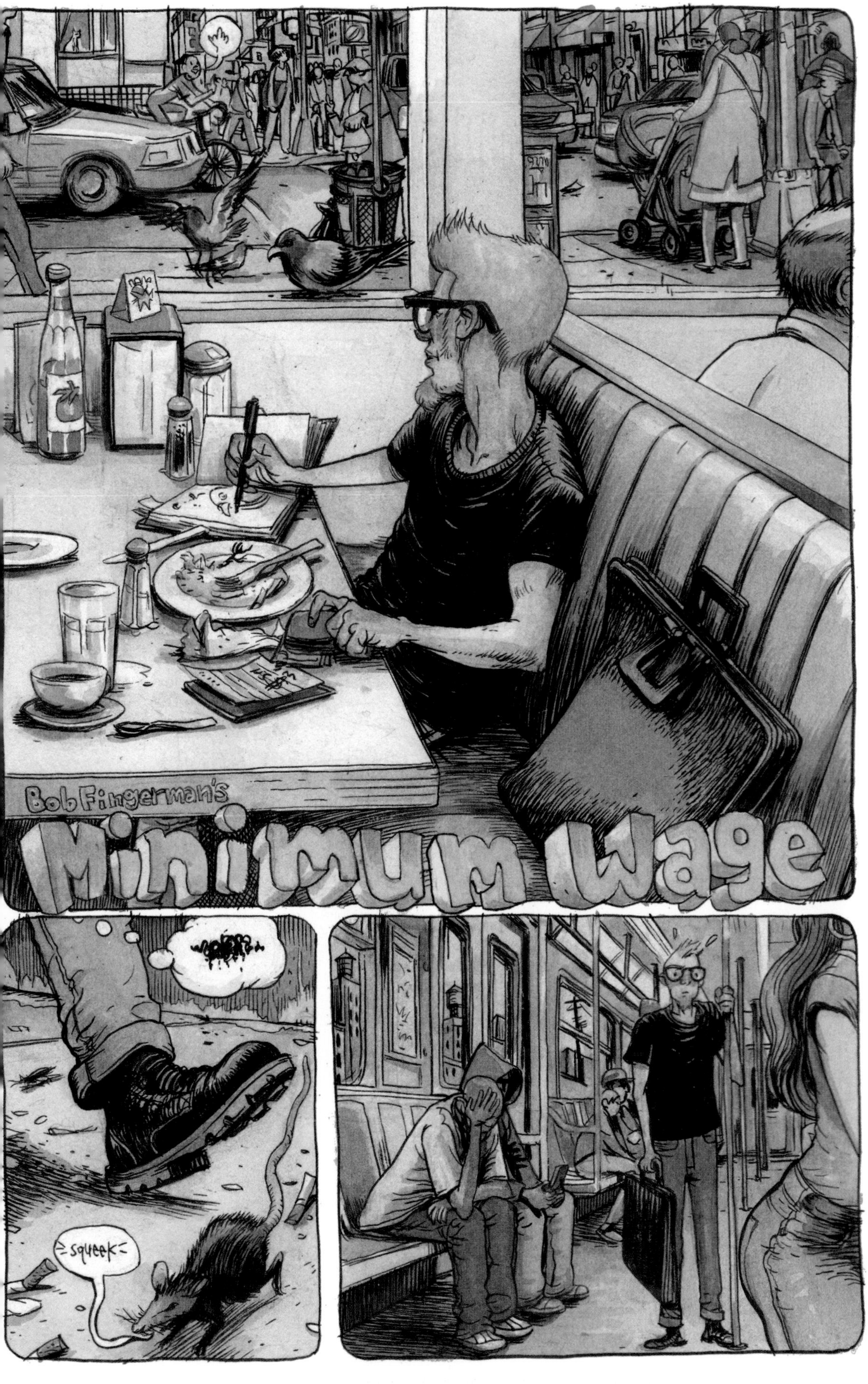

Bob Fingerman's
Minimum Wage
squeek

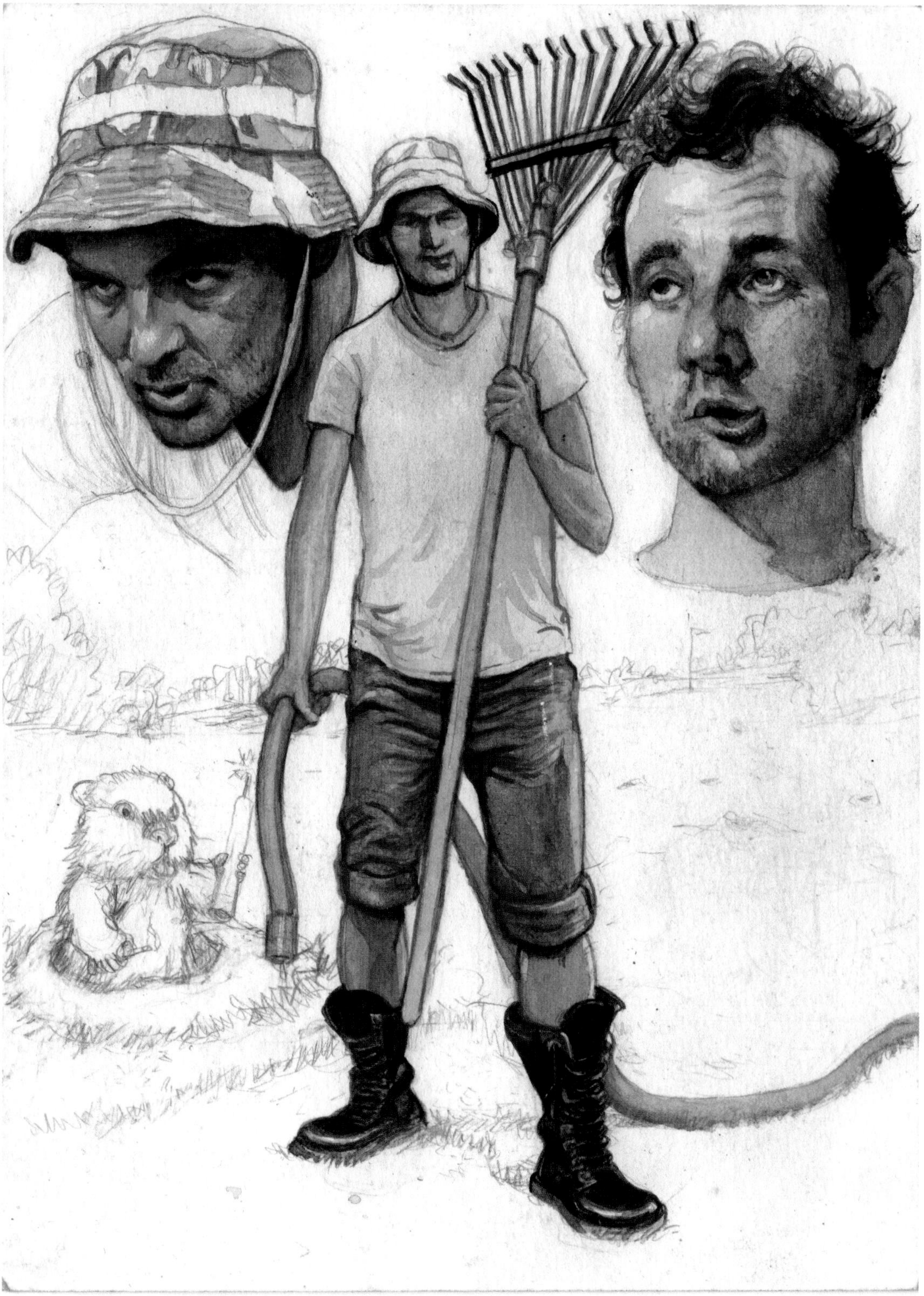

Drawcember 24, 2018 farold -

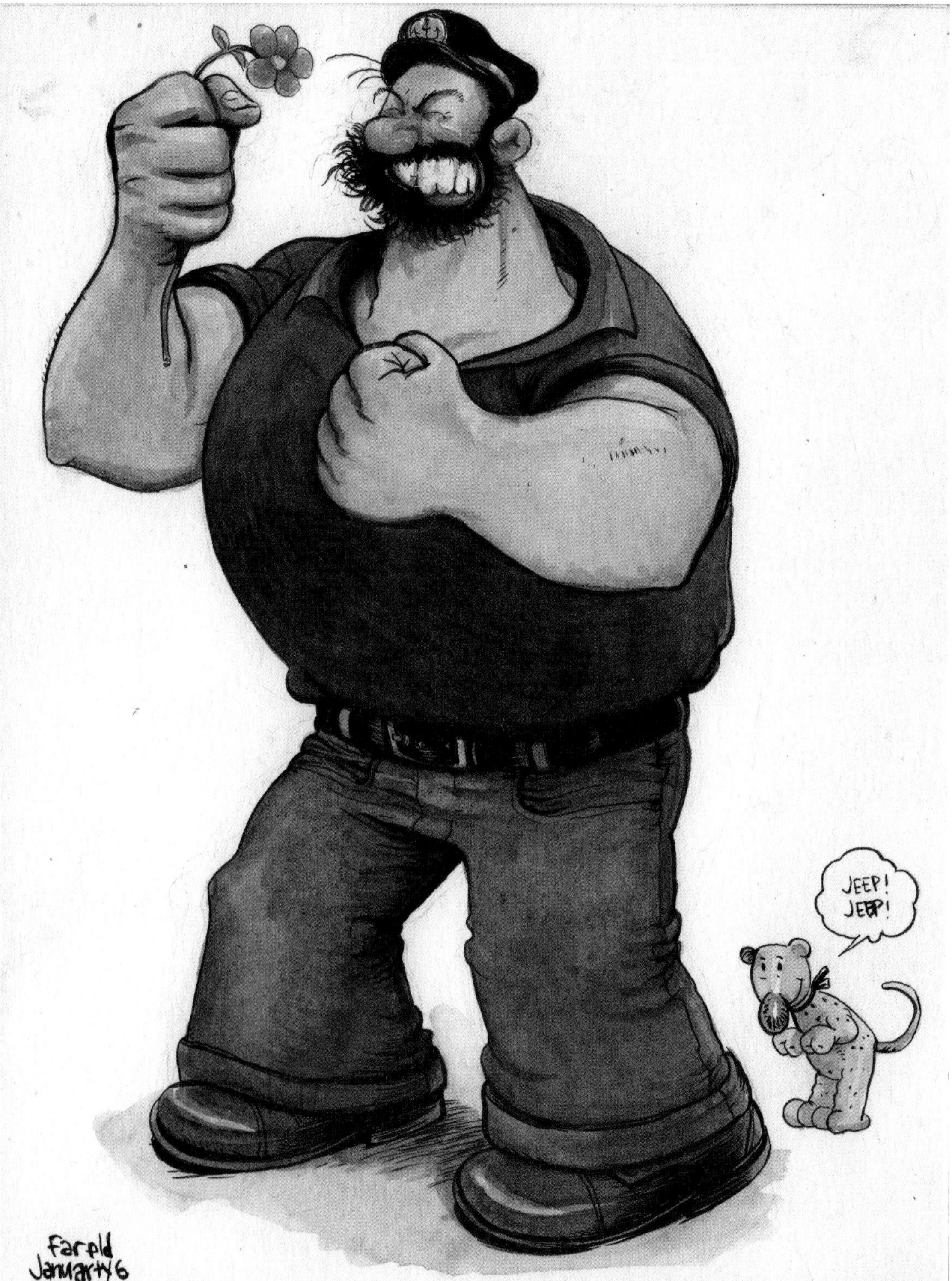
JEEP!
JEEP!
January 6
2019

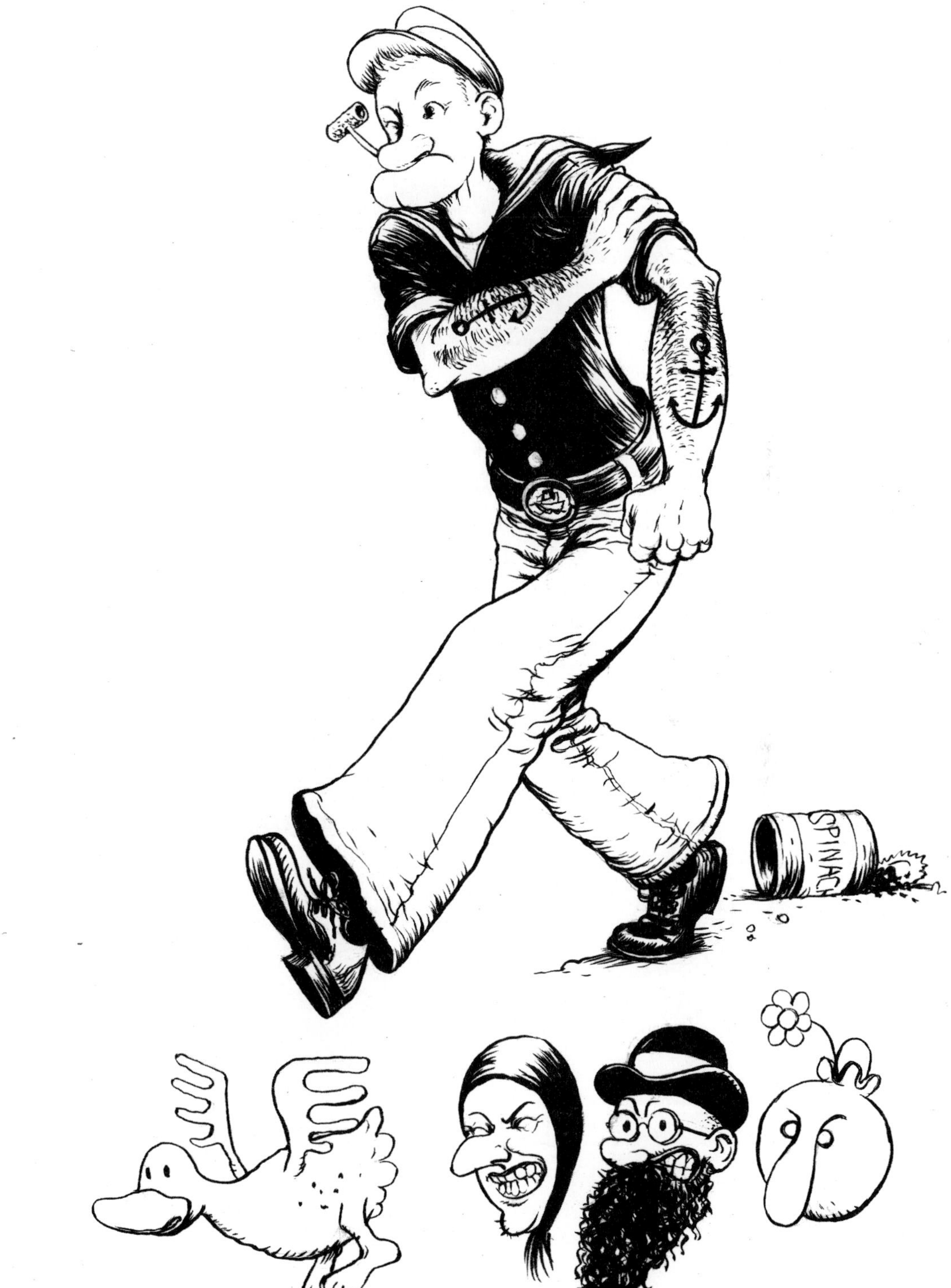
SPINAC
fareld inktober 20 2018
apologies to E.C.

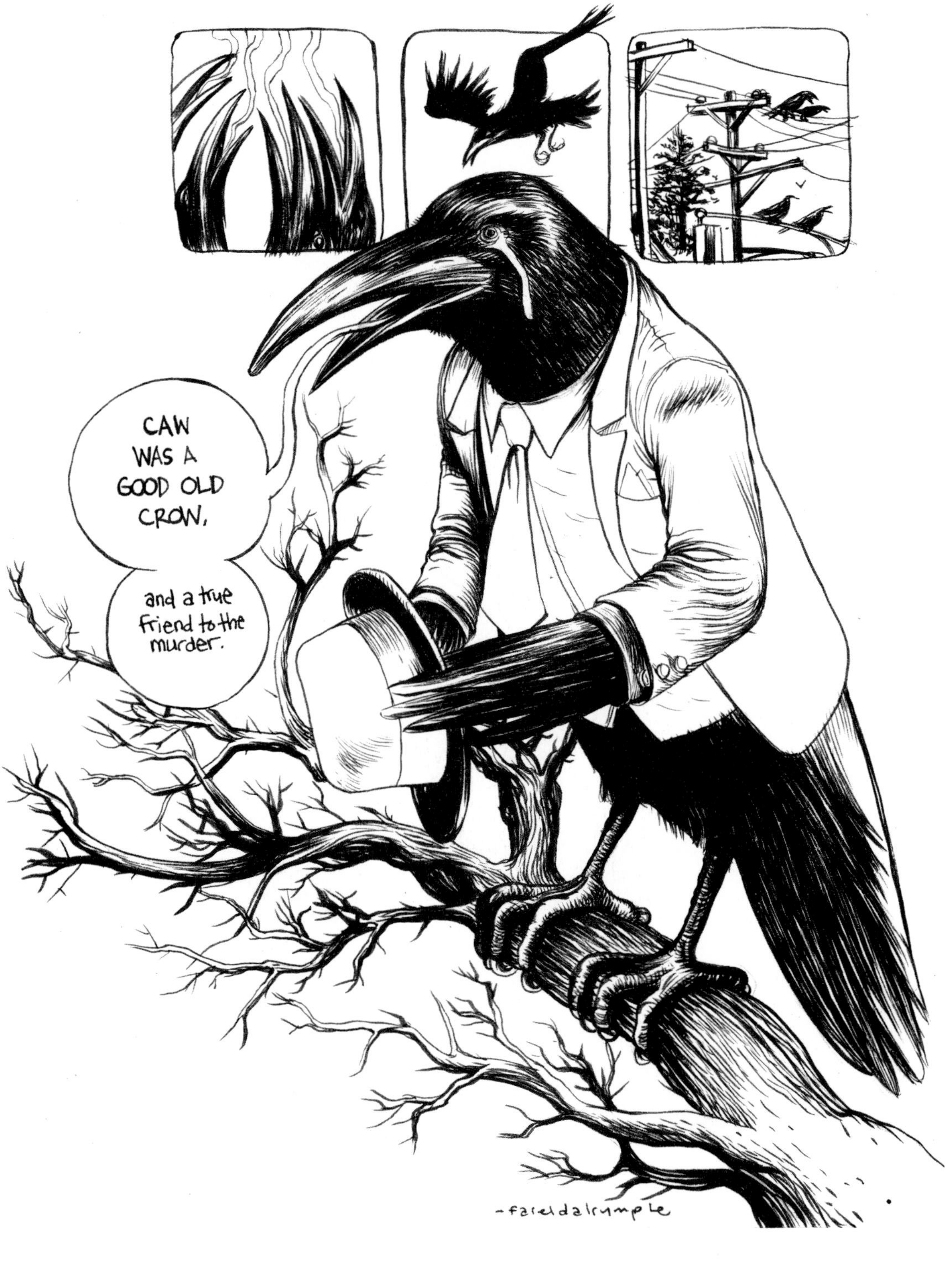
CAW WAS A GOOD OLD CROW,
and a true friend to the murder.
-fareldalrumple

Pin-up for *MISNOMER* #1 by Reid Psaltis.

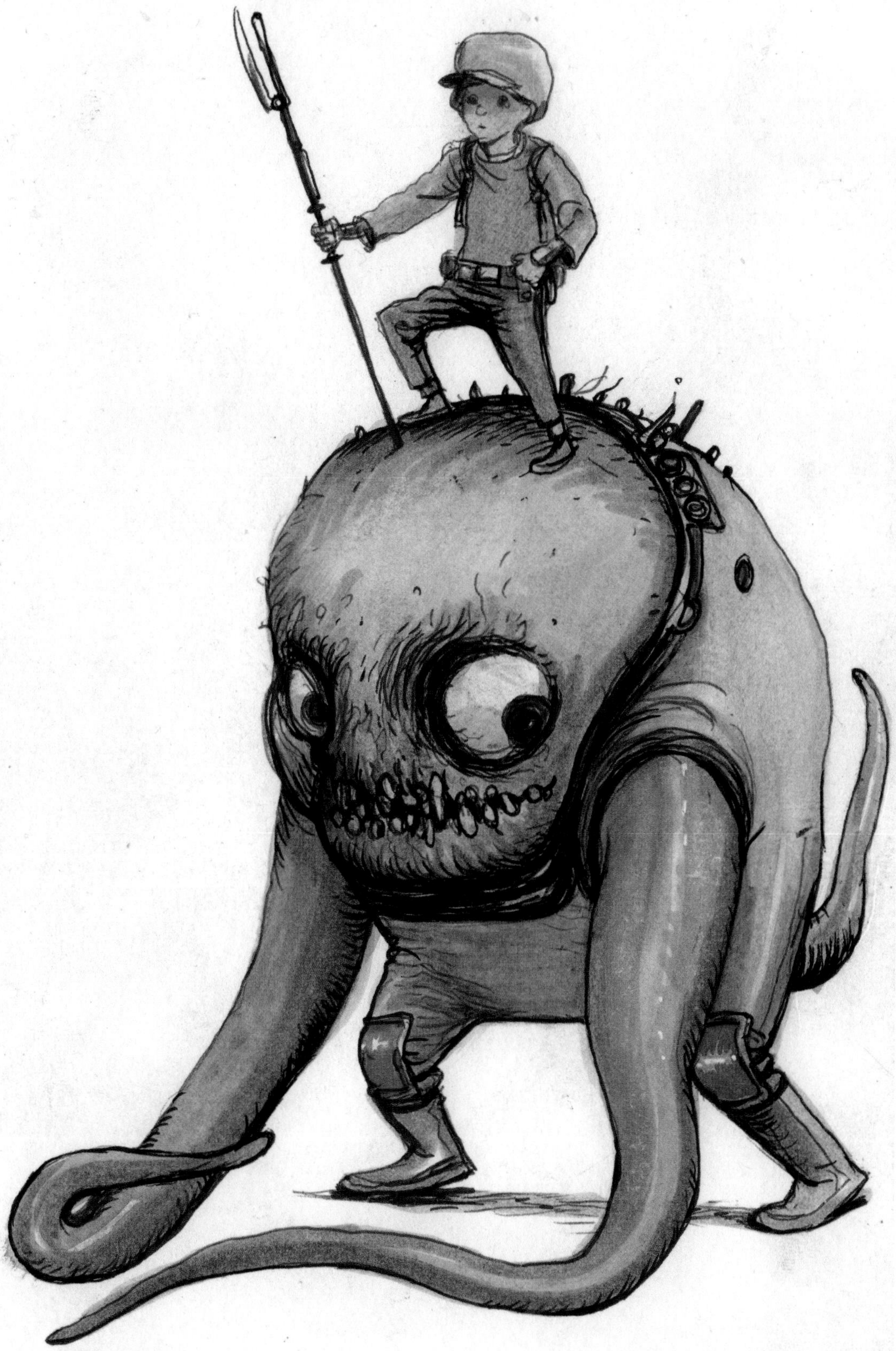

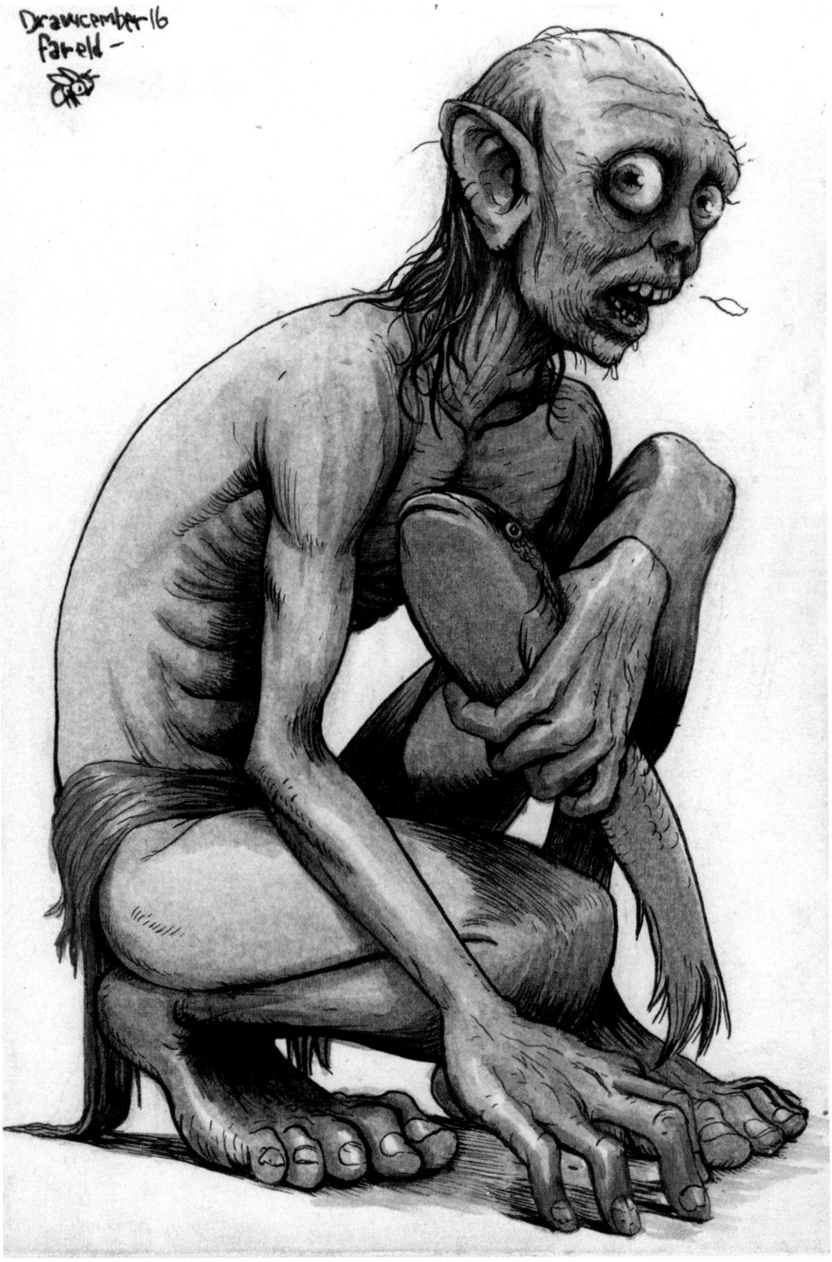
Drawcember 16
fareld -

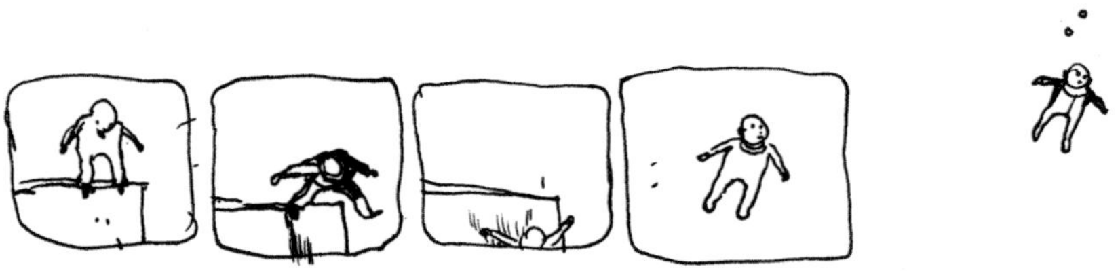

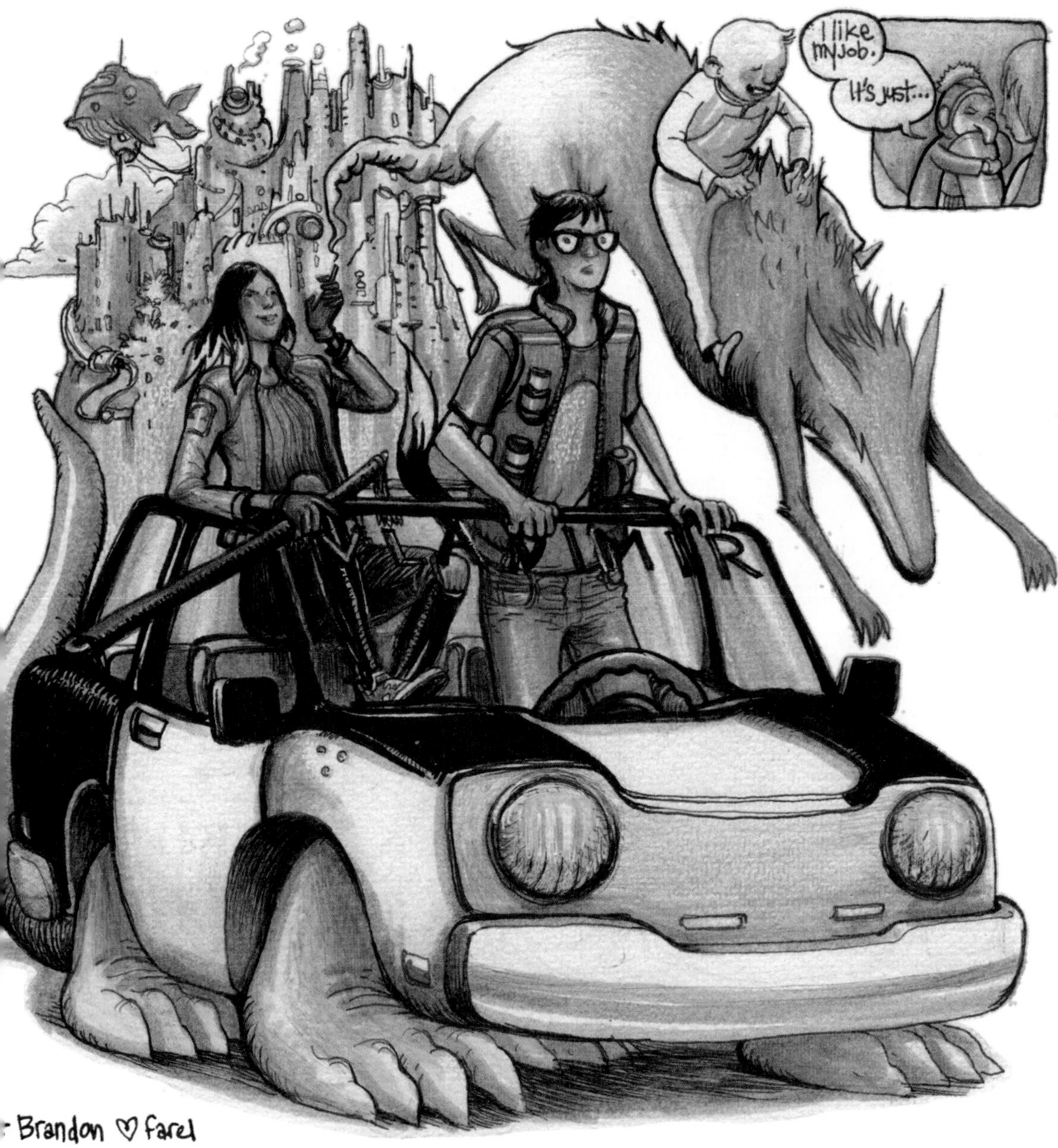

I like my job.
It's just...
Brandon ♡ farel

Brandon Graham's terrific **MULTIPLE WARHEADS.**

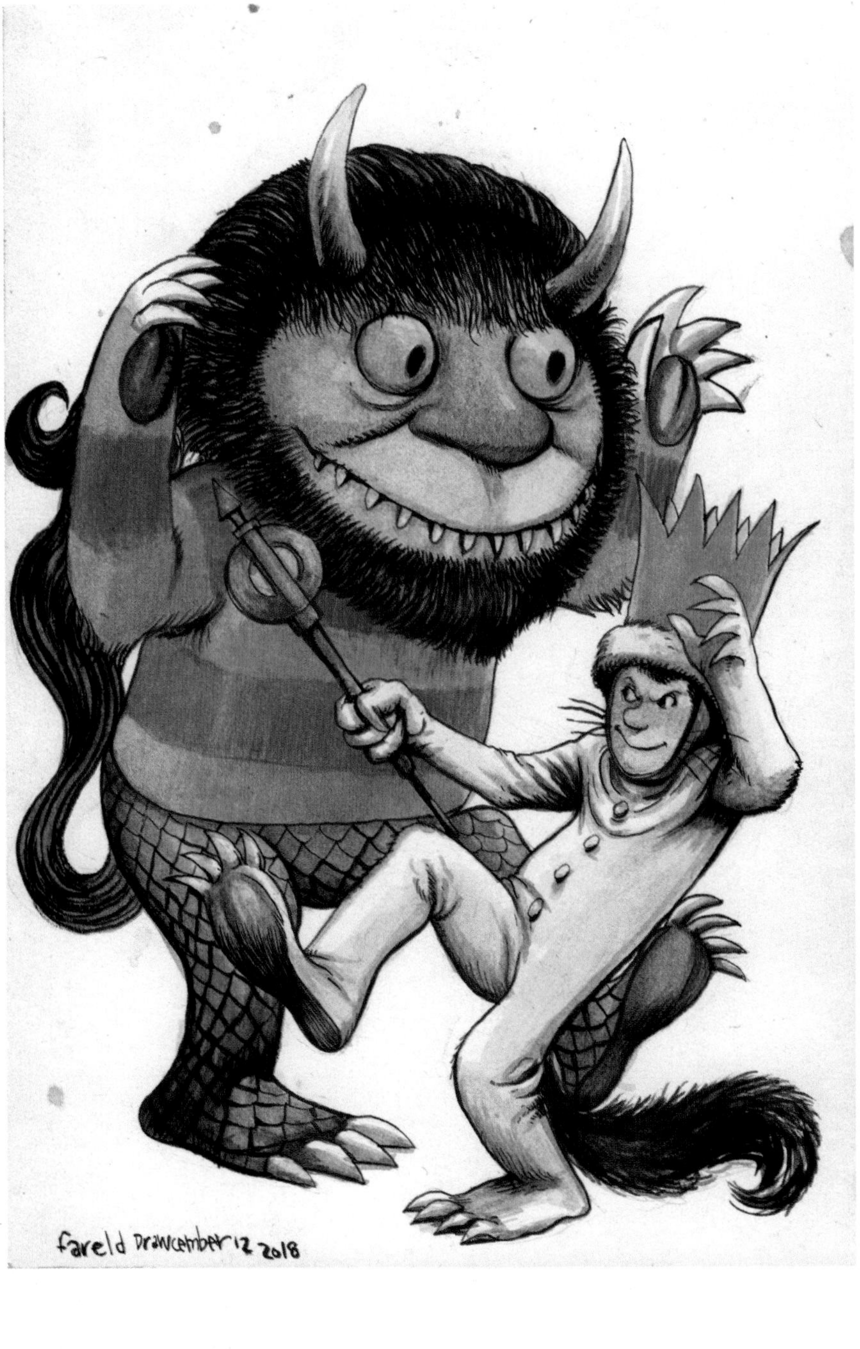
fareld Drawcember 12 2018

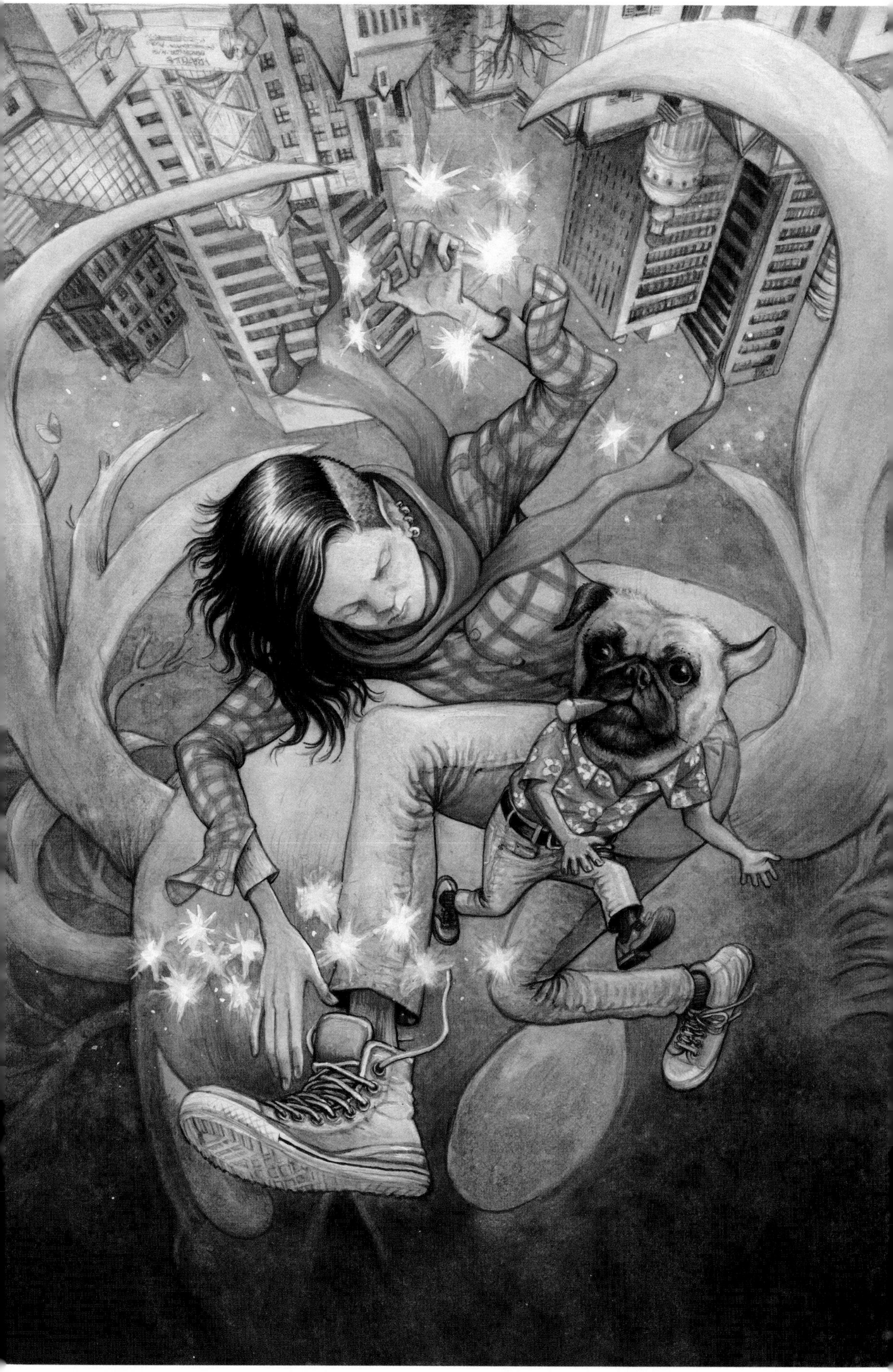

Variant cover for *GRUMBLE* by Rafer Roberts, Mike Norton, and Marissa Louise.

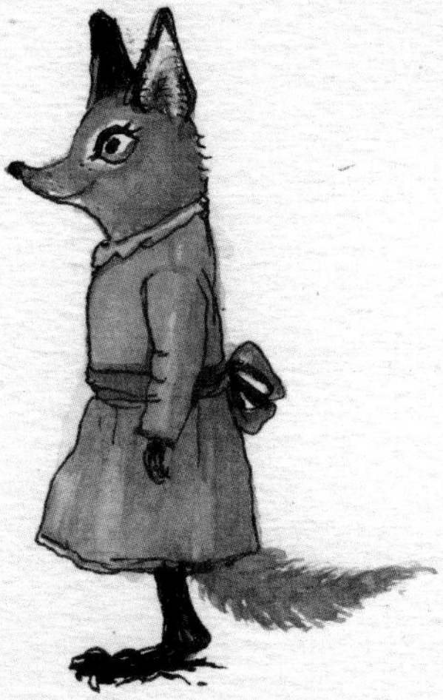

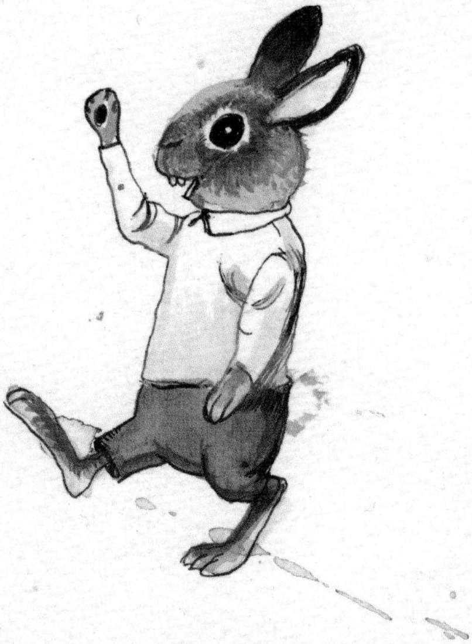

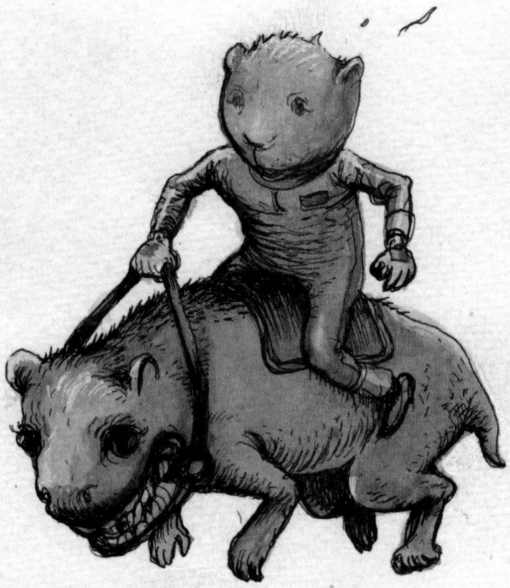

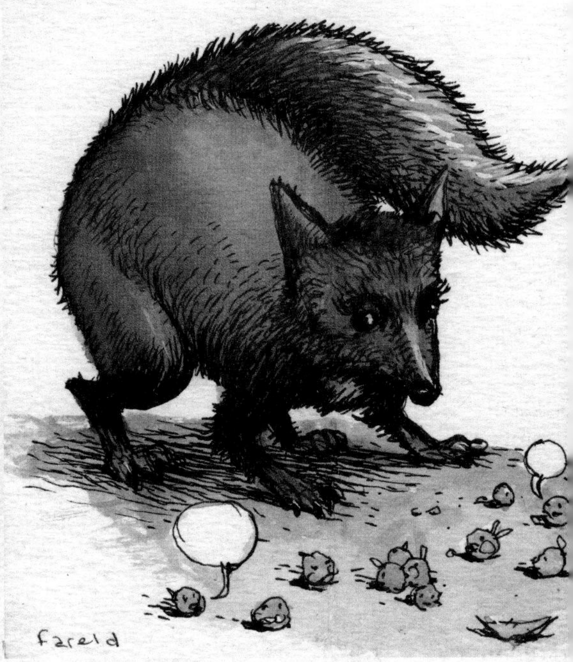
fareld

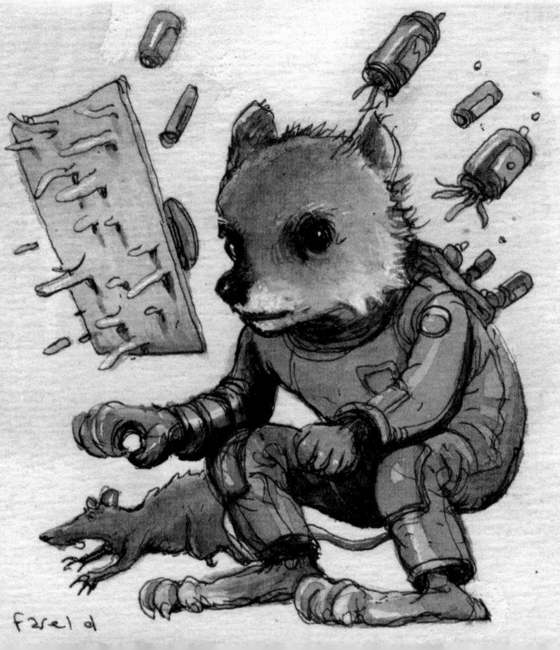
fareld

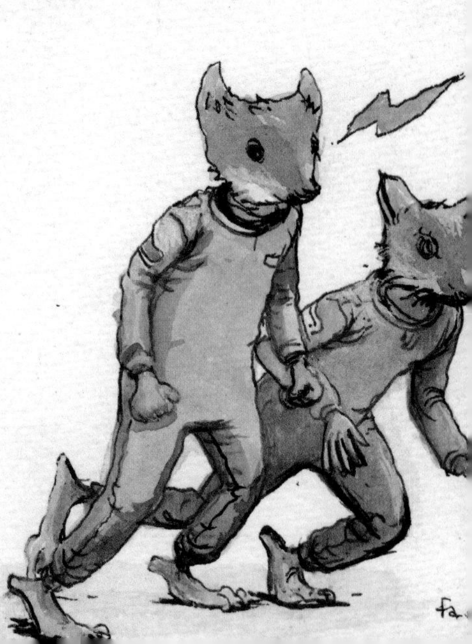

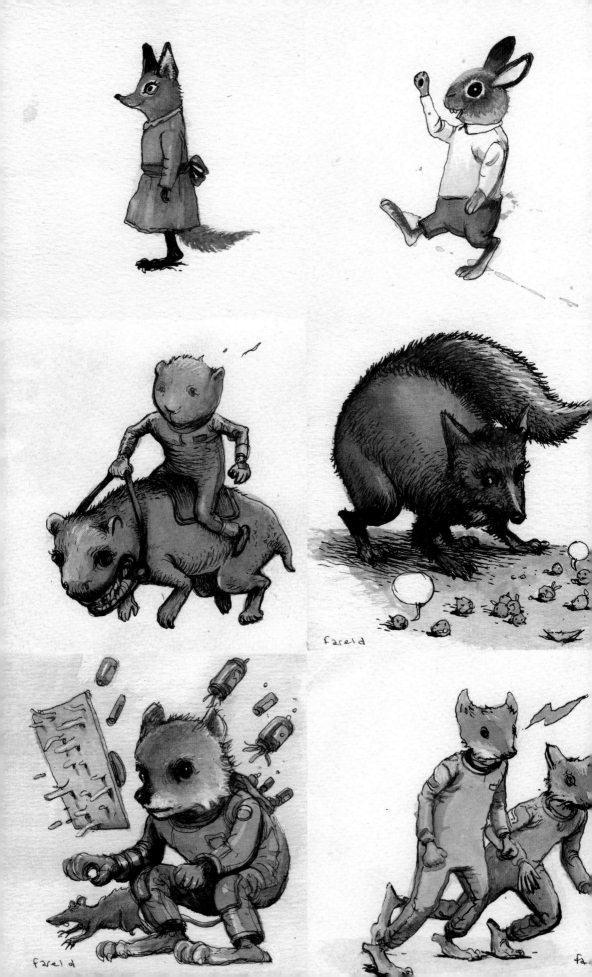

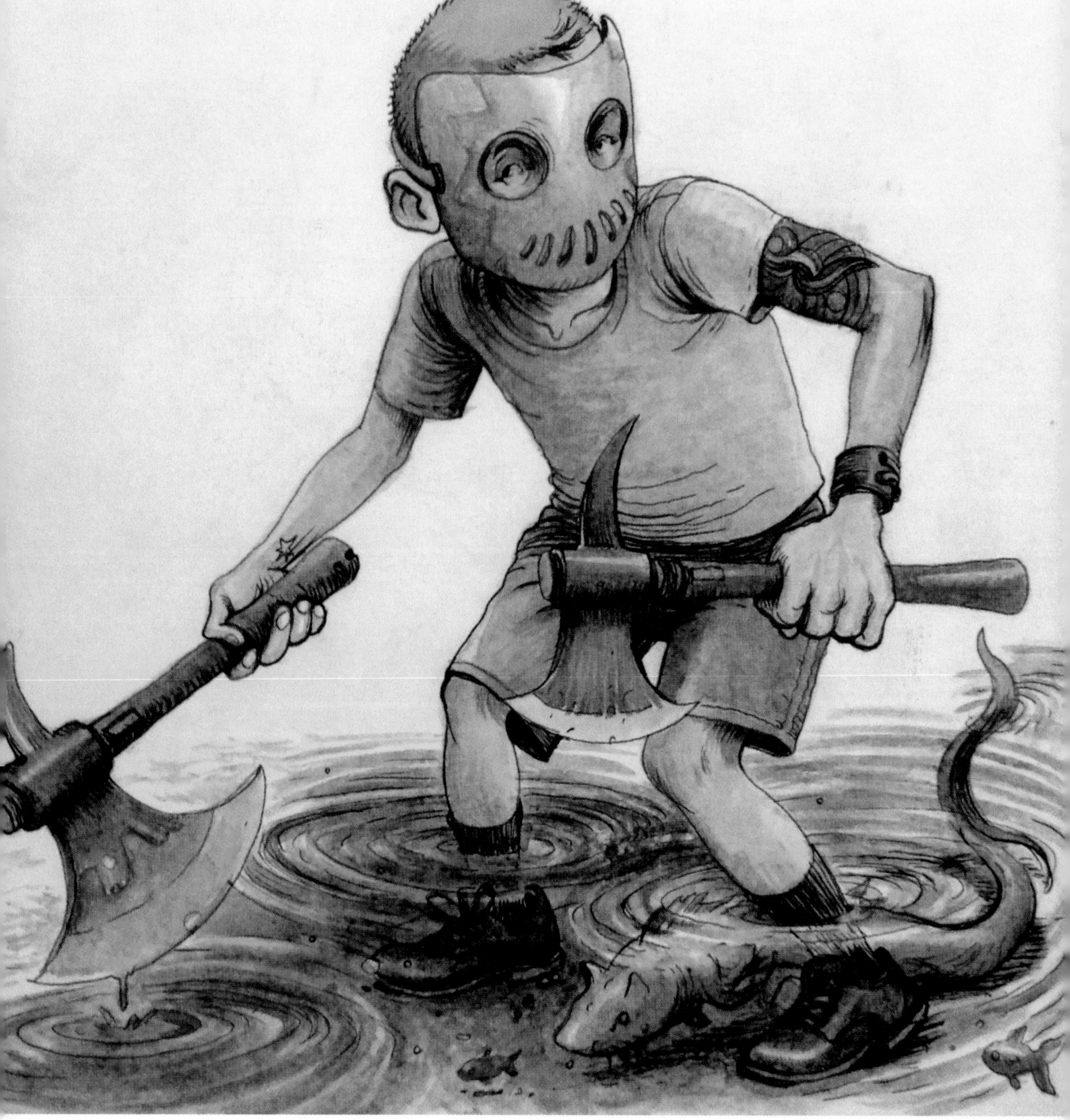

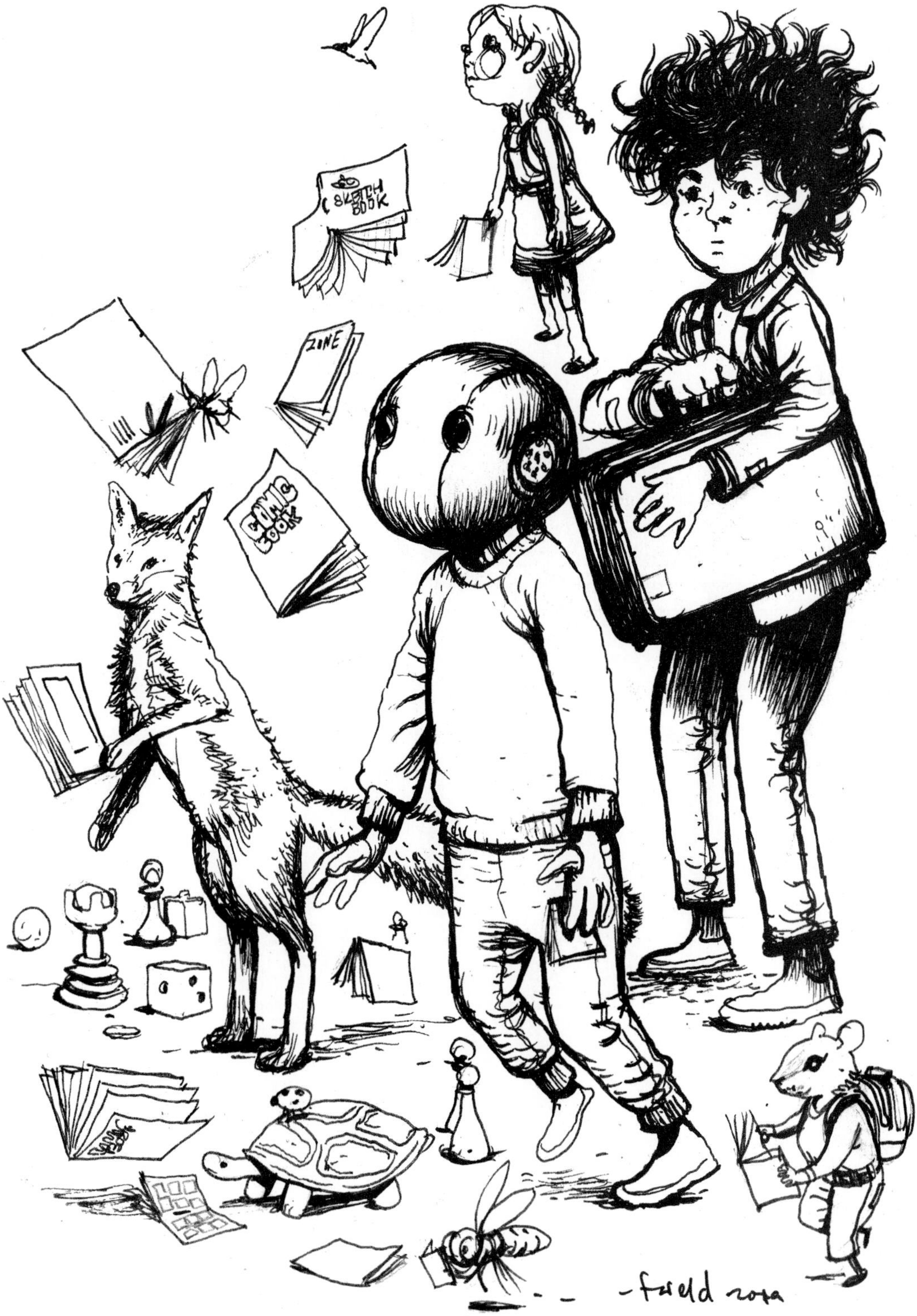
SKETCH BOOK
ZINE
COMIC BOOK

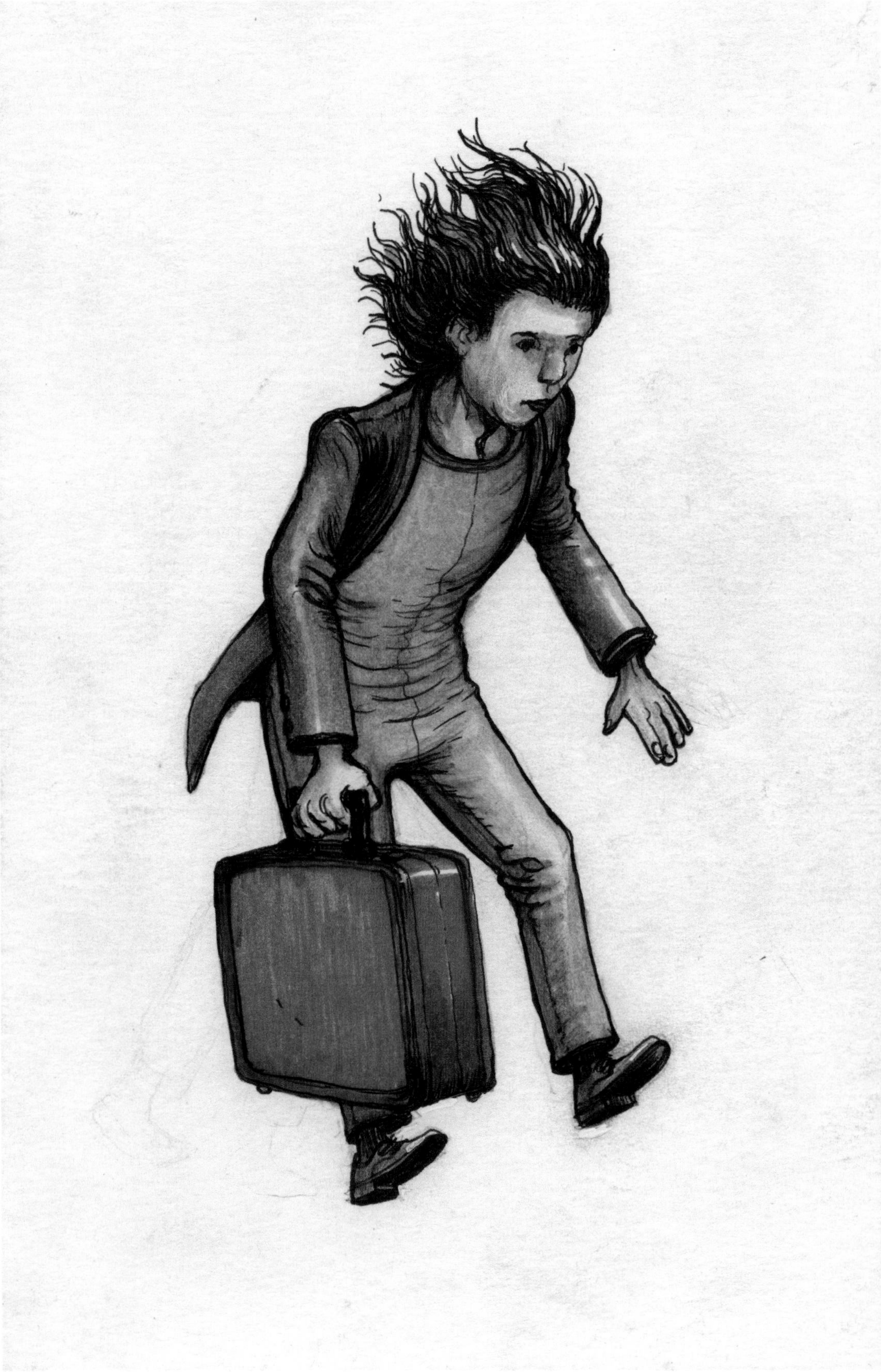

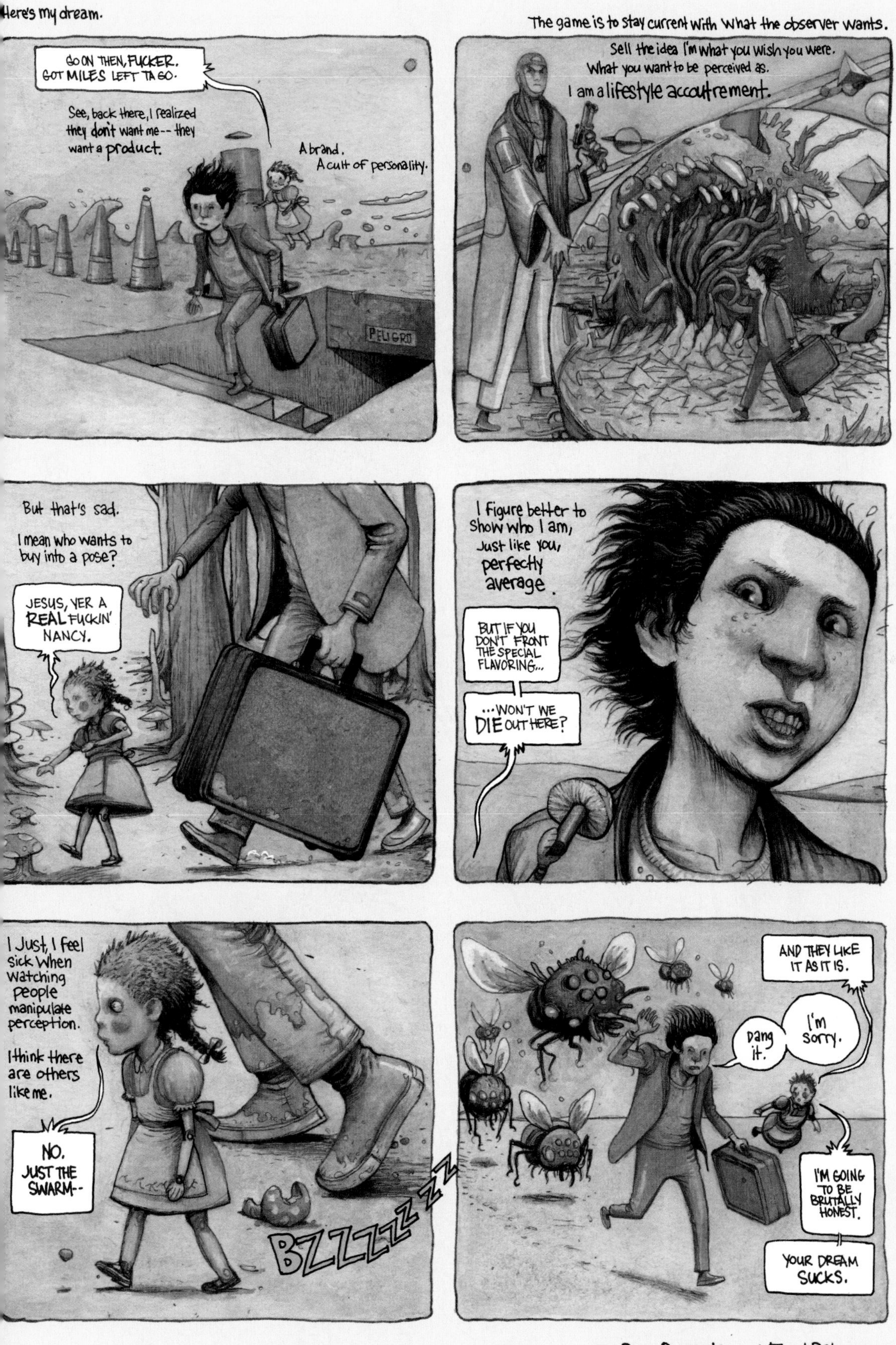
Here's my dream.
GO ON THEN, FUCKER. GOT MILES LEFT TA GO.
See, back there, I realized they don't want me-- they want a product.
A brand. A cult of personality.
PELIGRO
The game is to stay current with what the observer wants.
Sell the idea I'm what you wish you were. What you want to be perceived as. I am a lifestyle accoutrement.
But that's sad.
I mean who wants to buy into a pose?
JESUS, YER A REAL FUCKIN' NANCY.
I figure better to show who I am, just like you, perfectly average.
BUT IF YOU DON'T FRONT THE SPECIAL FLAVORING...
...WON'T WE DIE OUT HERE?
I just, I feel sick when watching people manipulate perception.
I think there are others like me.
NO. JUST THE SWARM--
BZZZZZZ
AND THEY LIKE IT AS IT IS.
I'm sorry.
Dang it.
I'M GOING TO BE BRUTALLY HONEST.
YOUR DREAM SUCKS.

By Rick Remender and Farel Dalrymple

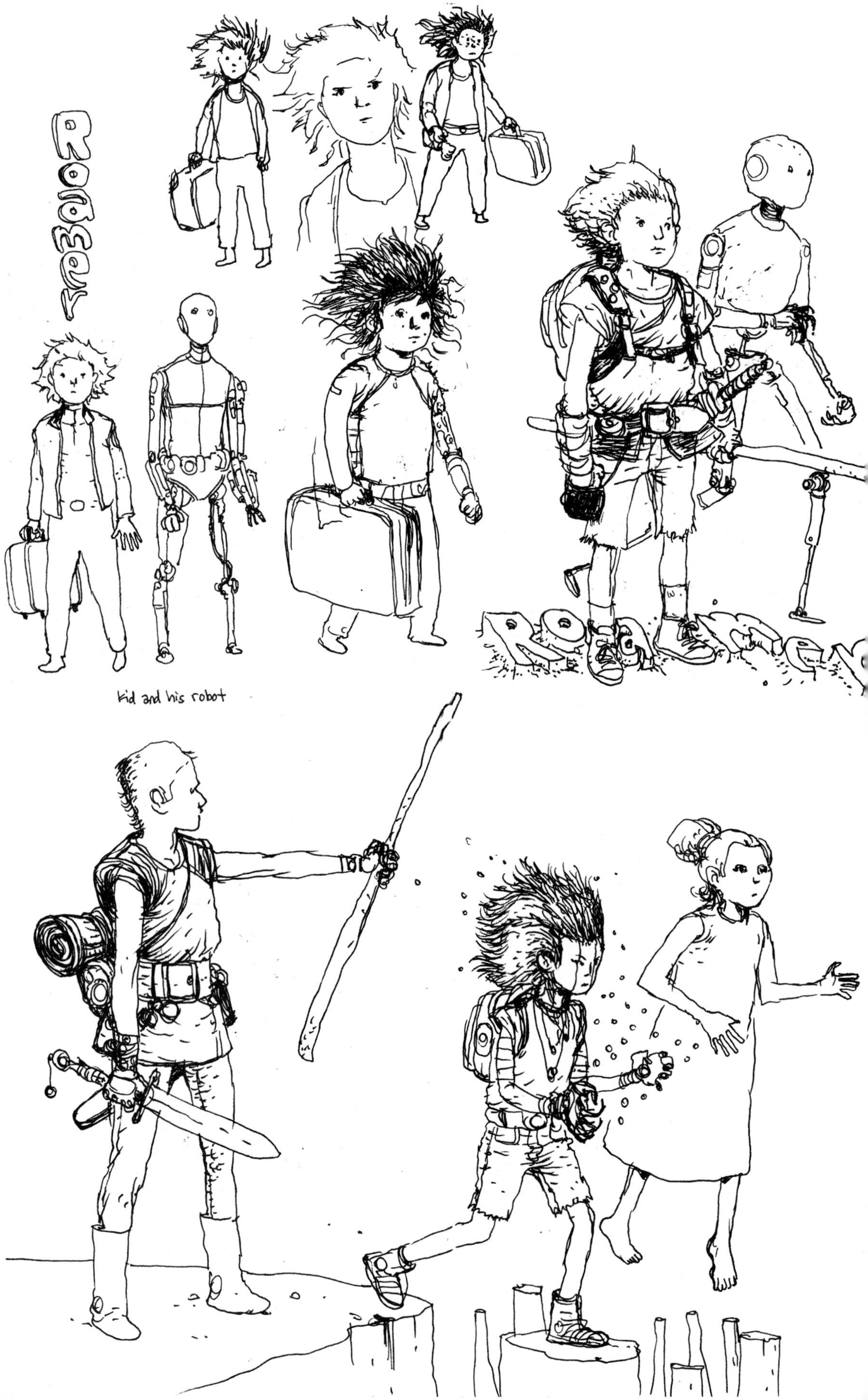
Roamer
kid and his robot

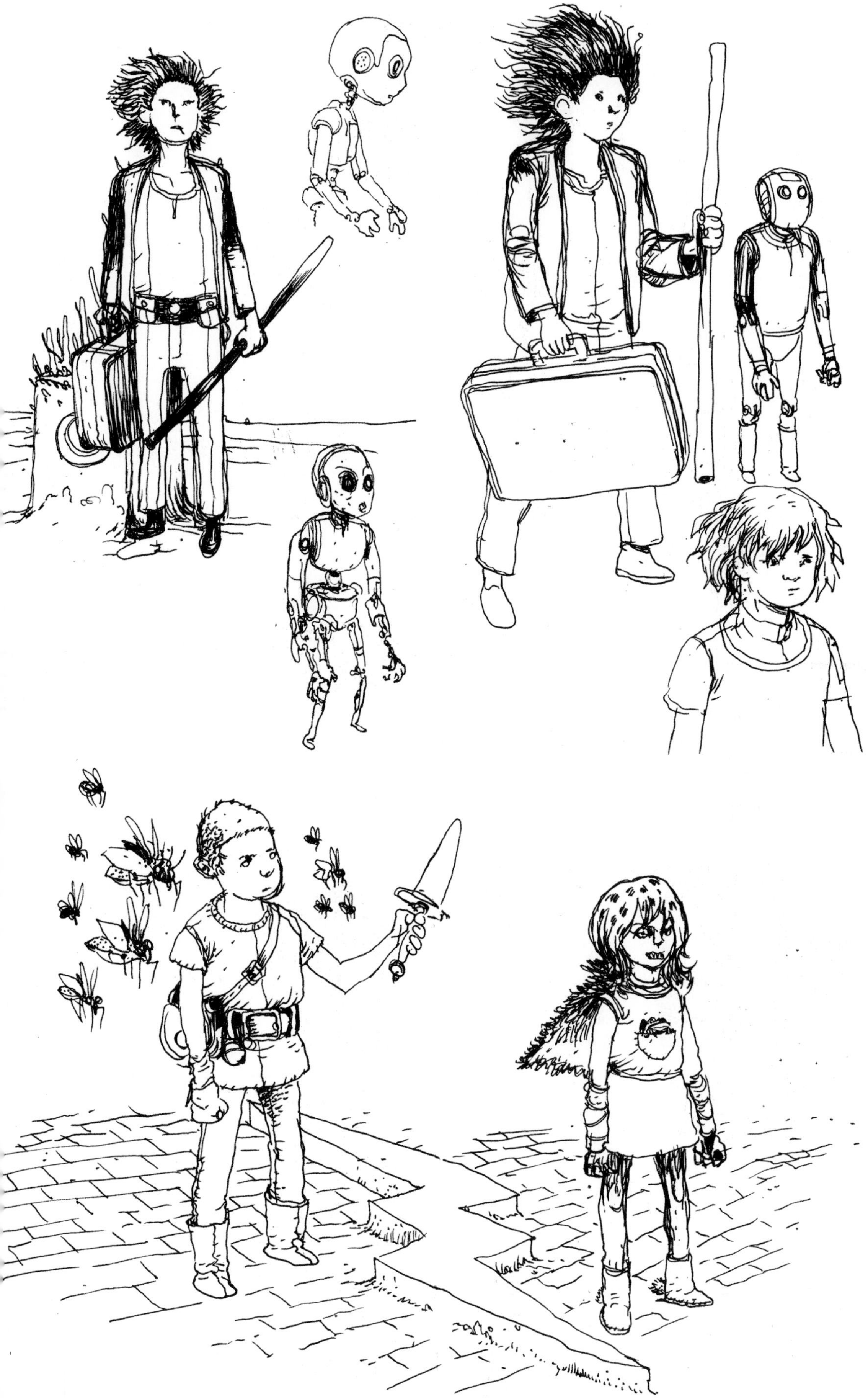

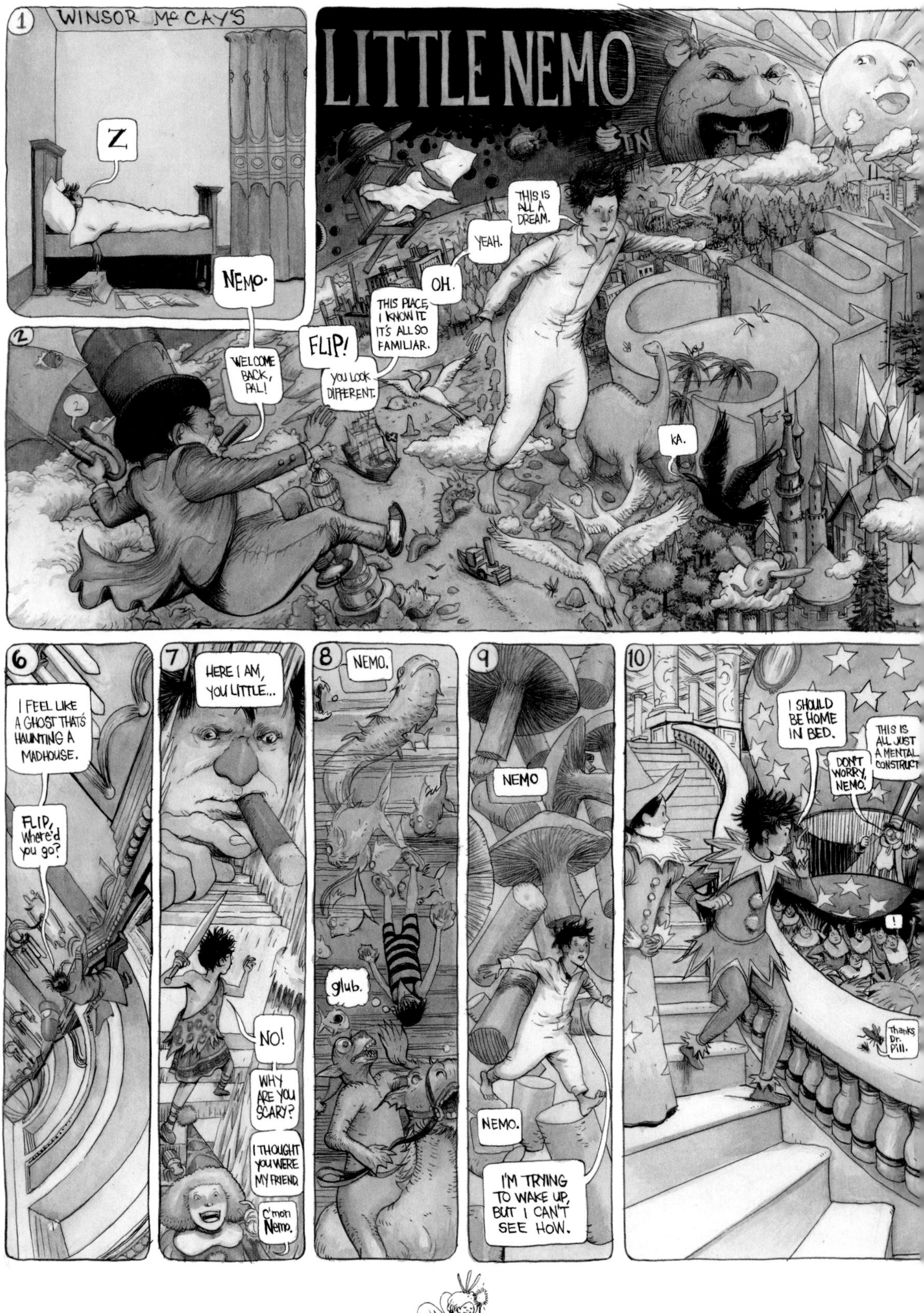
WINSOR McCAY'S
Z
LITTLE NEMO
IN
NEMO.
WELCOME BACK, PAL!
FLIP!
YOU LOOK DIFFERENT.
THIS PLACE, I KNOW IT. IT'S ALL SO FAMILIAR.
OH.
YEAH.
THIS IS ALL A DREAM.
KA.
I FEEL LIKE A GHOST THAT'S HAUNTING A MADHOUSE.
FLIP, Where'd you go?
HERE I AM, YOU LITTLE...
NO!
WHY ARE YOU SCARY?
I THOUGHT YOU WERE MY FRIEND.
C'mon Nemo.
NEMO.
glub.
NEMO
NEMO.
I'M TRYING TO WAKE UP, BUT I CAN'T SEE HOW.
I SHOULD BE HOME IN BED.
THIS IS ALL JUST A MENTAL CONSTRUCT
DON'T WORRY, NEMO.
!
Thanks Dr. Pill.

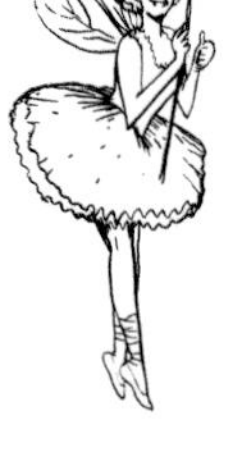

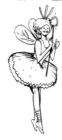

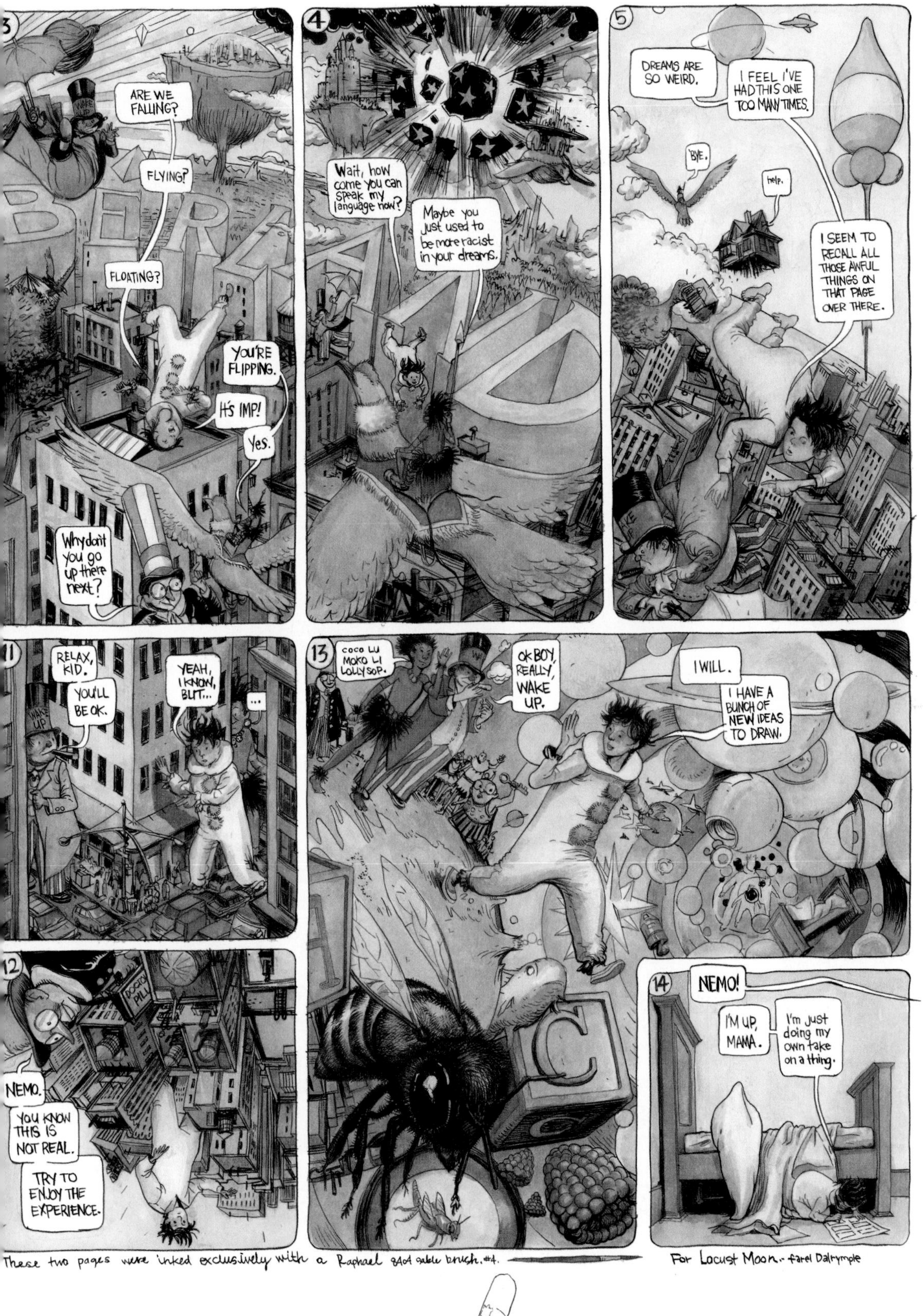
ARE WE FALLING?
FLYING?
FLOATING?
YOU'RE FLIPPING.
It's IMP!
Yes.
Why don't you go up there next?
Wait, how come you can speak my language now?
Maybe you just used to be more racist in your dreams.
DREAMS ARE SO WEIRD.
I FEEL I'VE HAD THIS ONE TOO MANY TIMES.
BYE.
help.
I SEEM TO RECALL ALL THOSE AWFUL THINGS ON THAT PAGE OVER THERE.
RELAX, KID.
YOU'LL BE OK.
YEAH, I KNOW, BUT...
...
NEMO.
YOU KNOW THIS IS NOT REAL.
TRY TO ENJOY THE EXPERIENCE.
COCO LU MOKO LI LOLLYSOP.
OK BOY, REALLY, WAKE UP.
I WILL.
I HAVE A BUNCH OF NEW IDEAS TO DRAW.
NEMO!
I'M UP, MAMA.
I'm just doing my own take on a thing.

These two pages were inked exclusively with a Raphael 8404 sable brush. #4.

For Locust Moon. - Farel Dalrymple

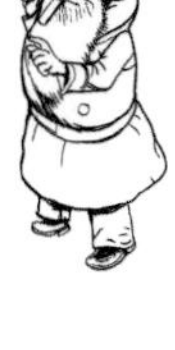

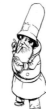

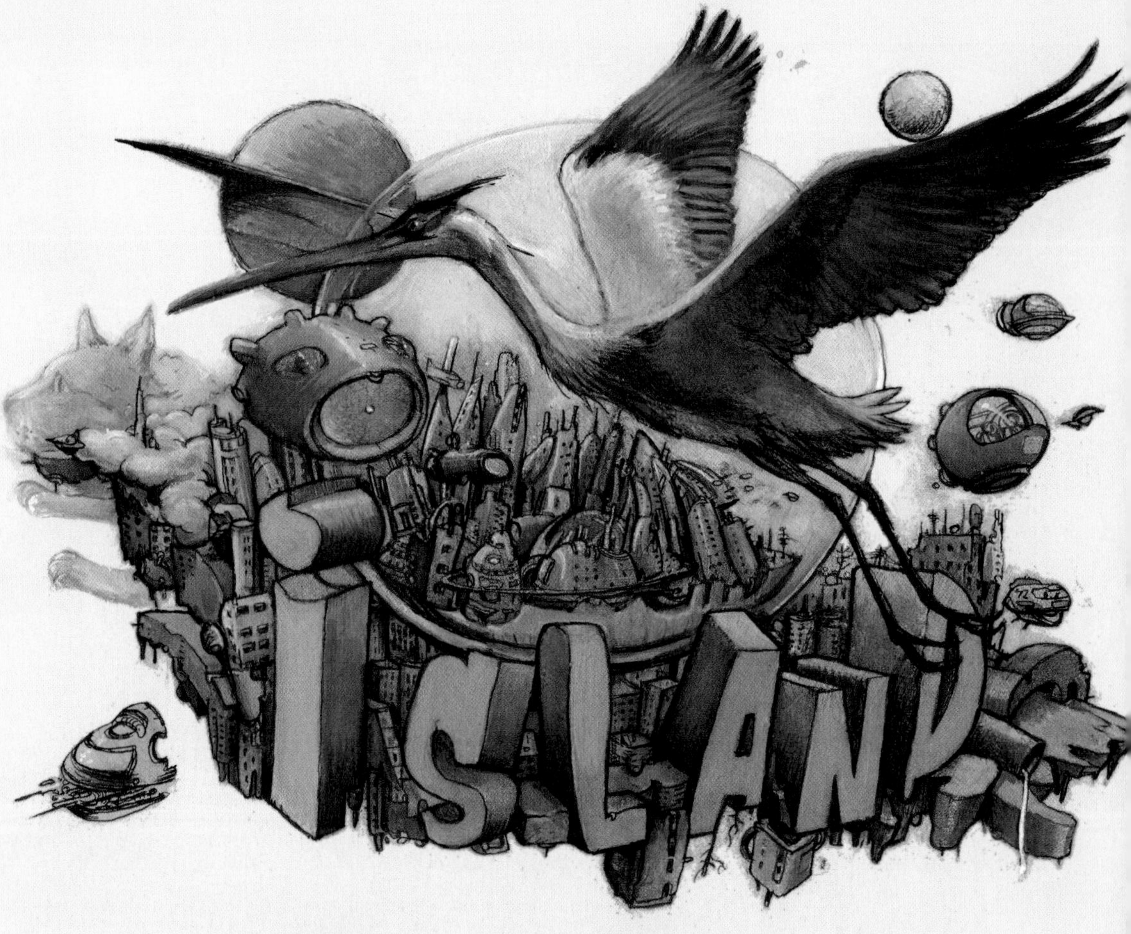
ISLAND

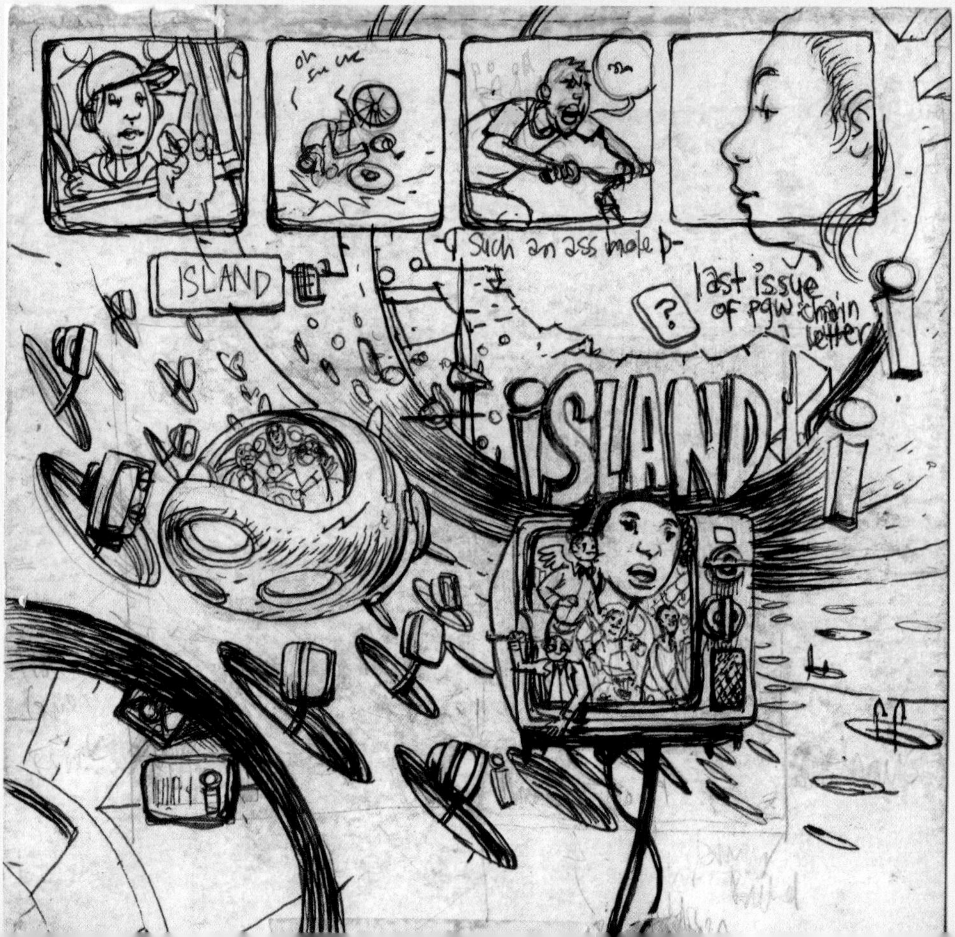
ISLAND
Such an ass hole
last issue of pgw chain letter
ISLAND

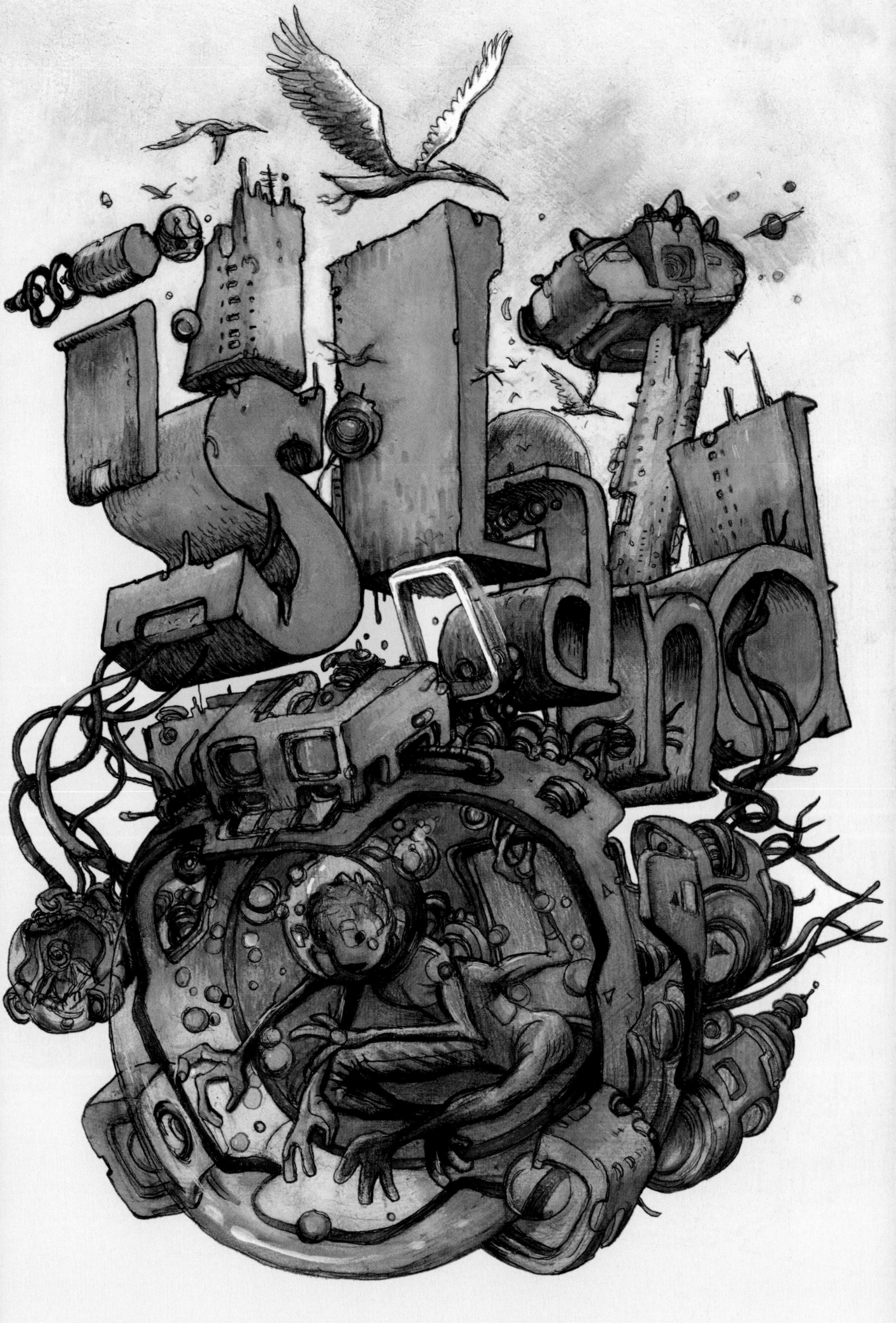
island

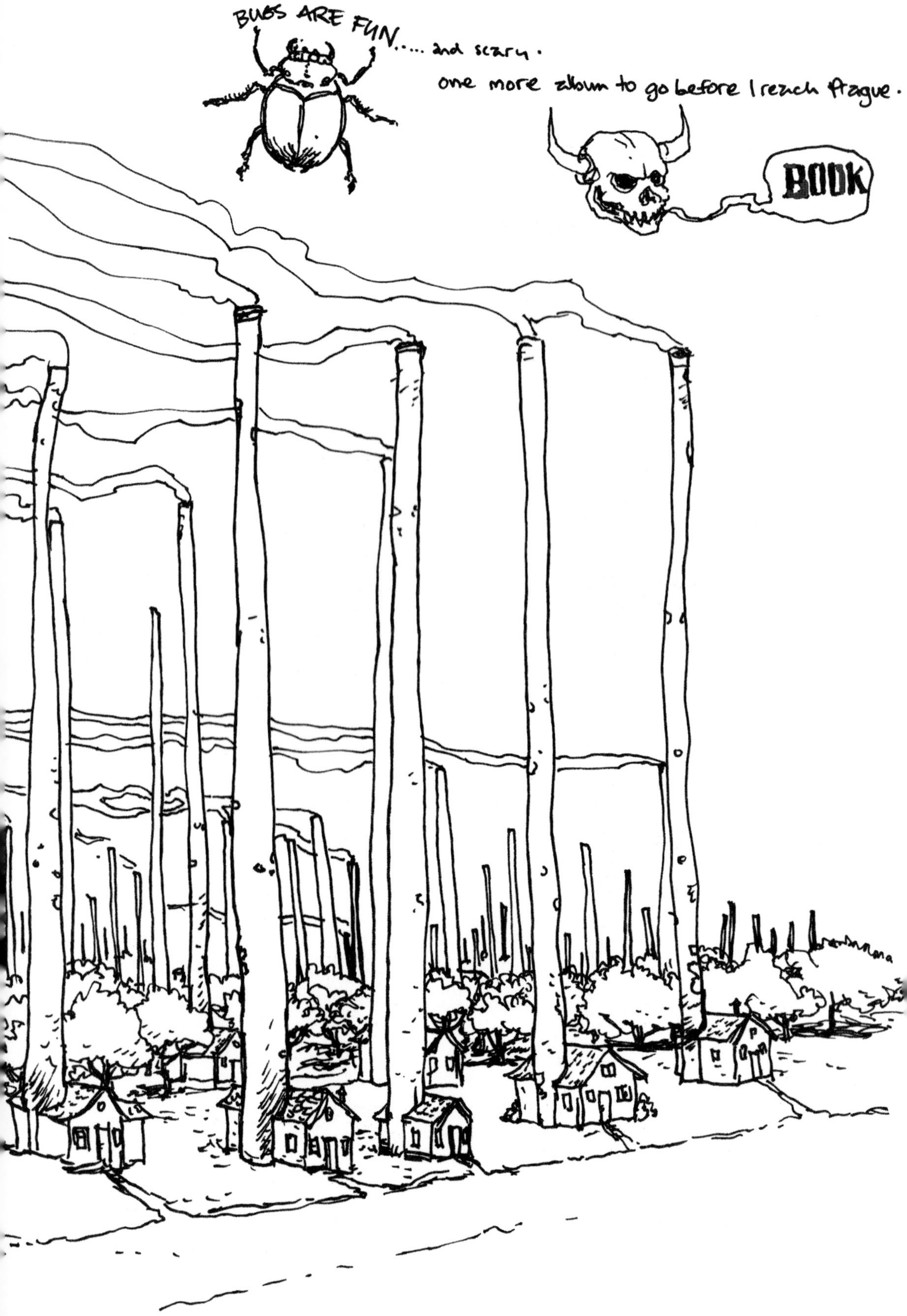
BUGS ARE FUN..... and scary.
one more album to go before I reach Prague.
BOOK

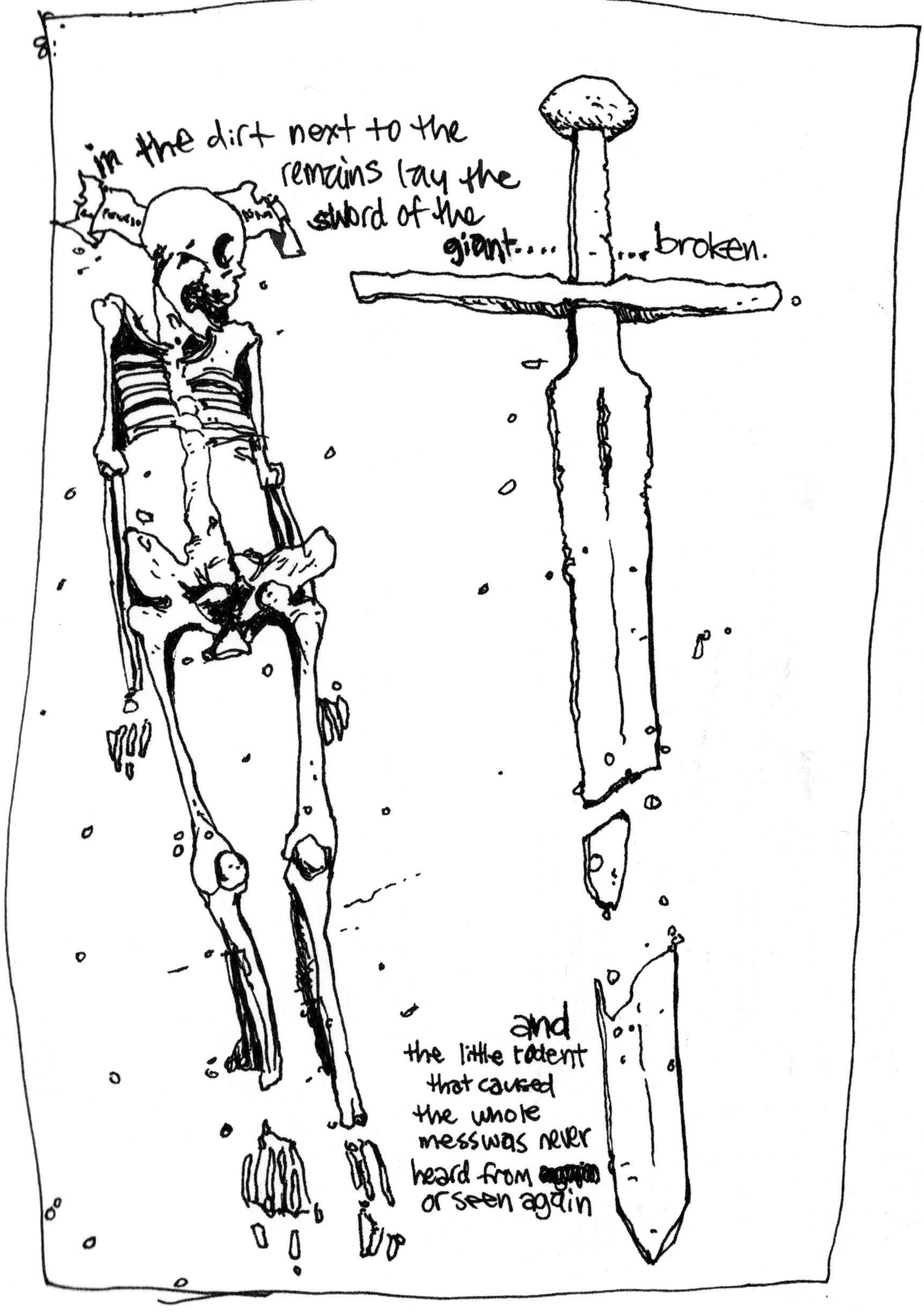
8:
in the dirt next to the
remains lay the
sword of the
giant.... ...broken.
and
the little rodent
that caused
the whole
mess was never
heard from [redacted]
or seen again

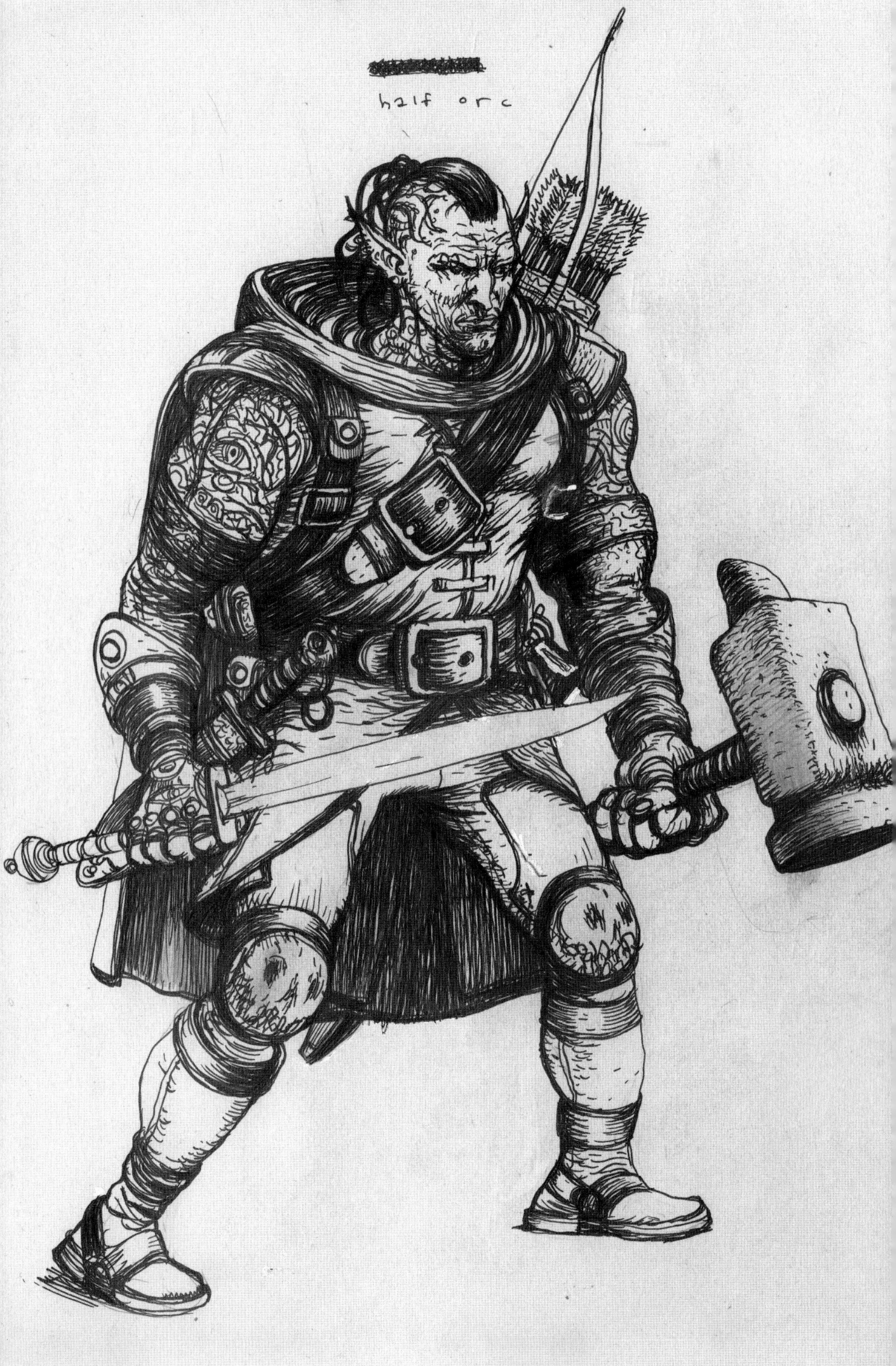
[redacted]
half orc

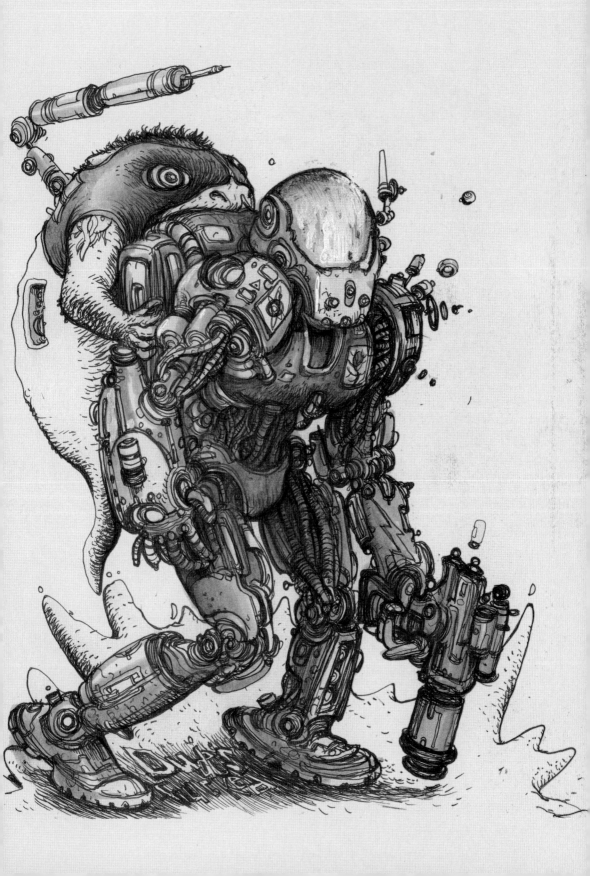

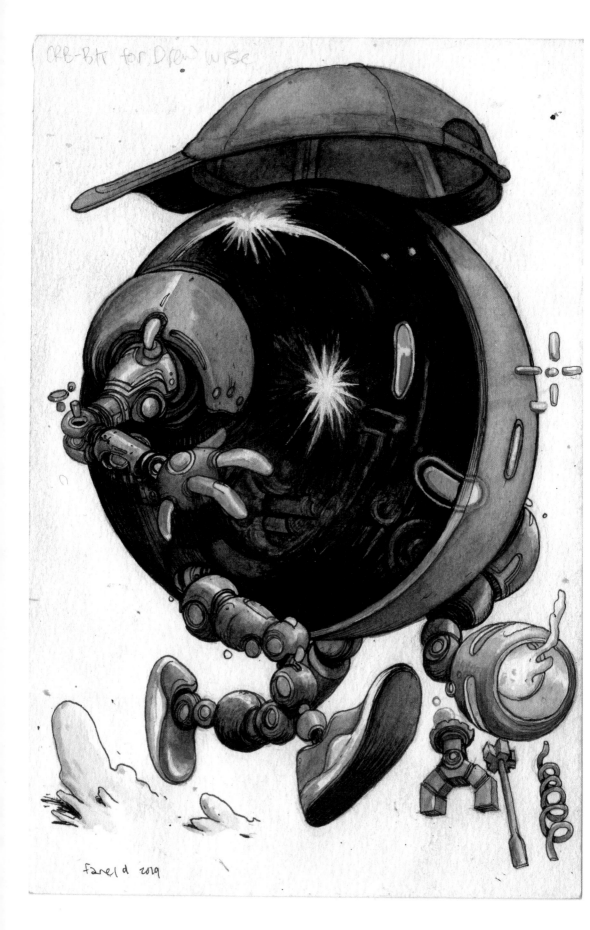

ORB-BIT for Drew Wise

farel d 2019

Concept art for *ORB-BIT*, a retro game in development.

pints

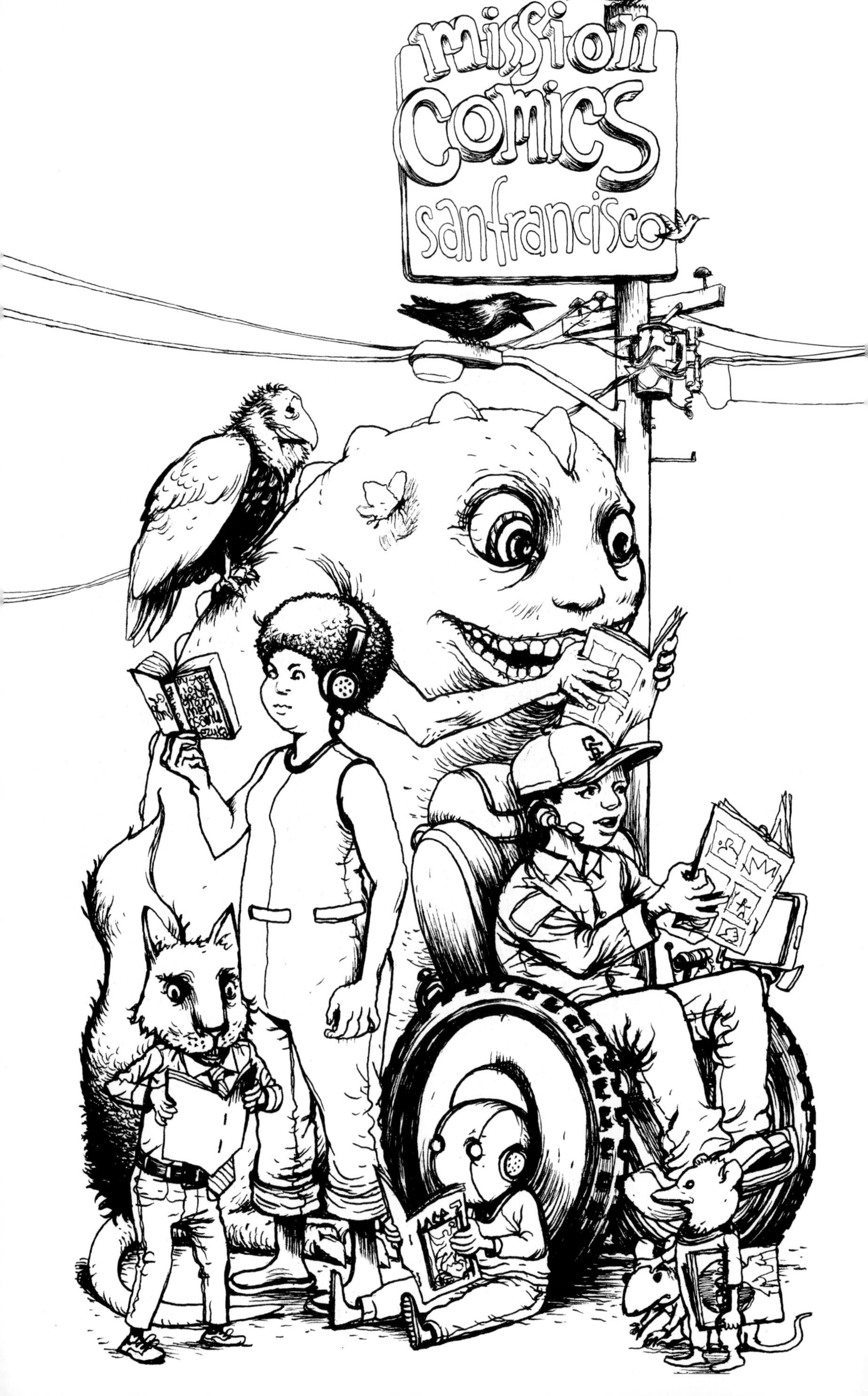
mission
Comics
sanfrancisco

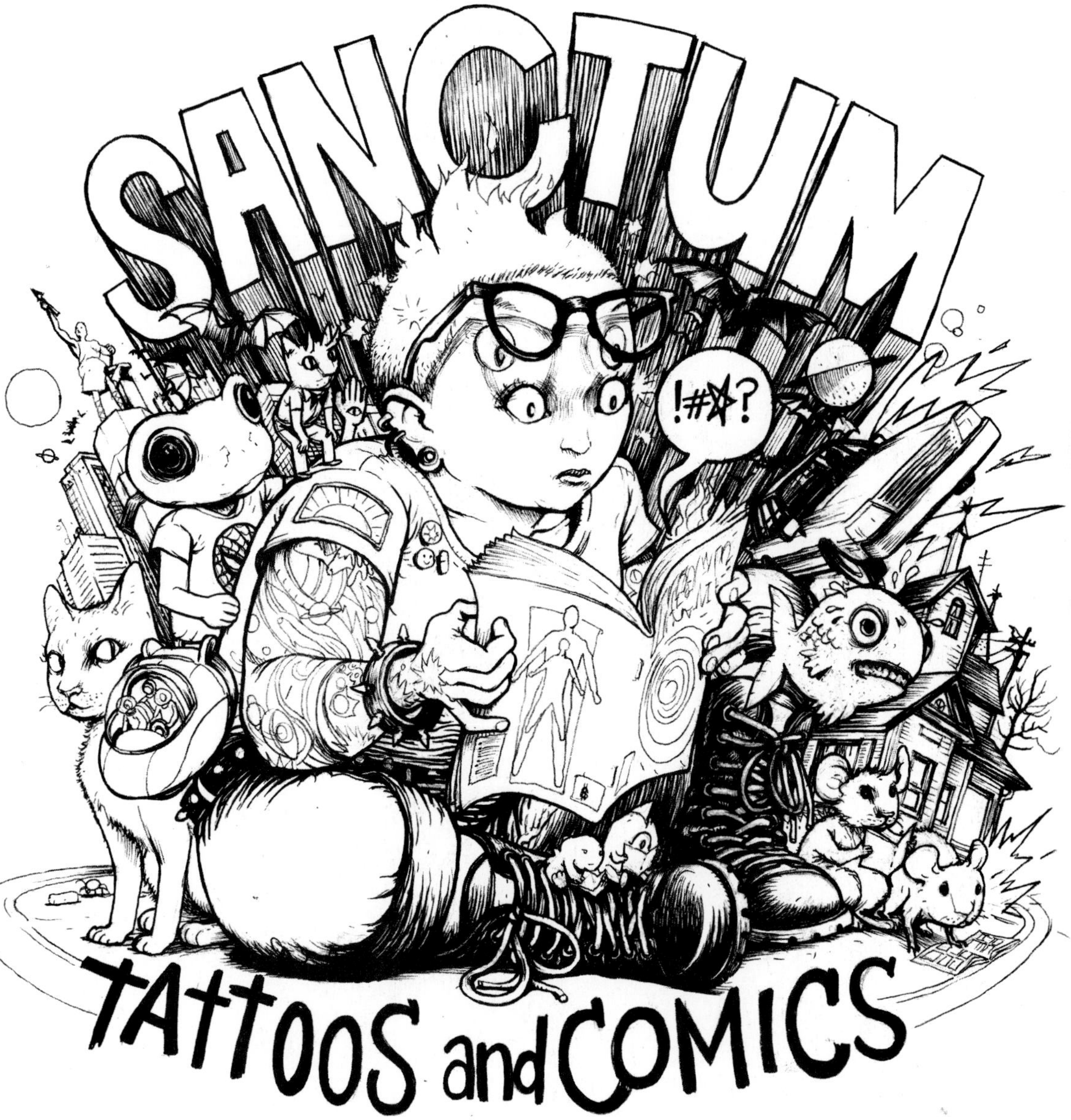
SANCTUM
!#✡?
TATTOOS and COMICS

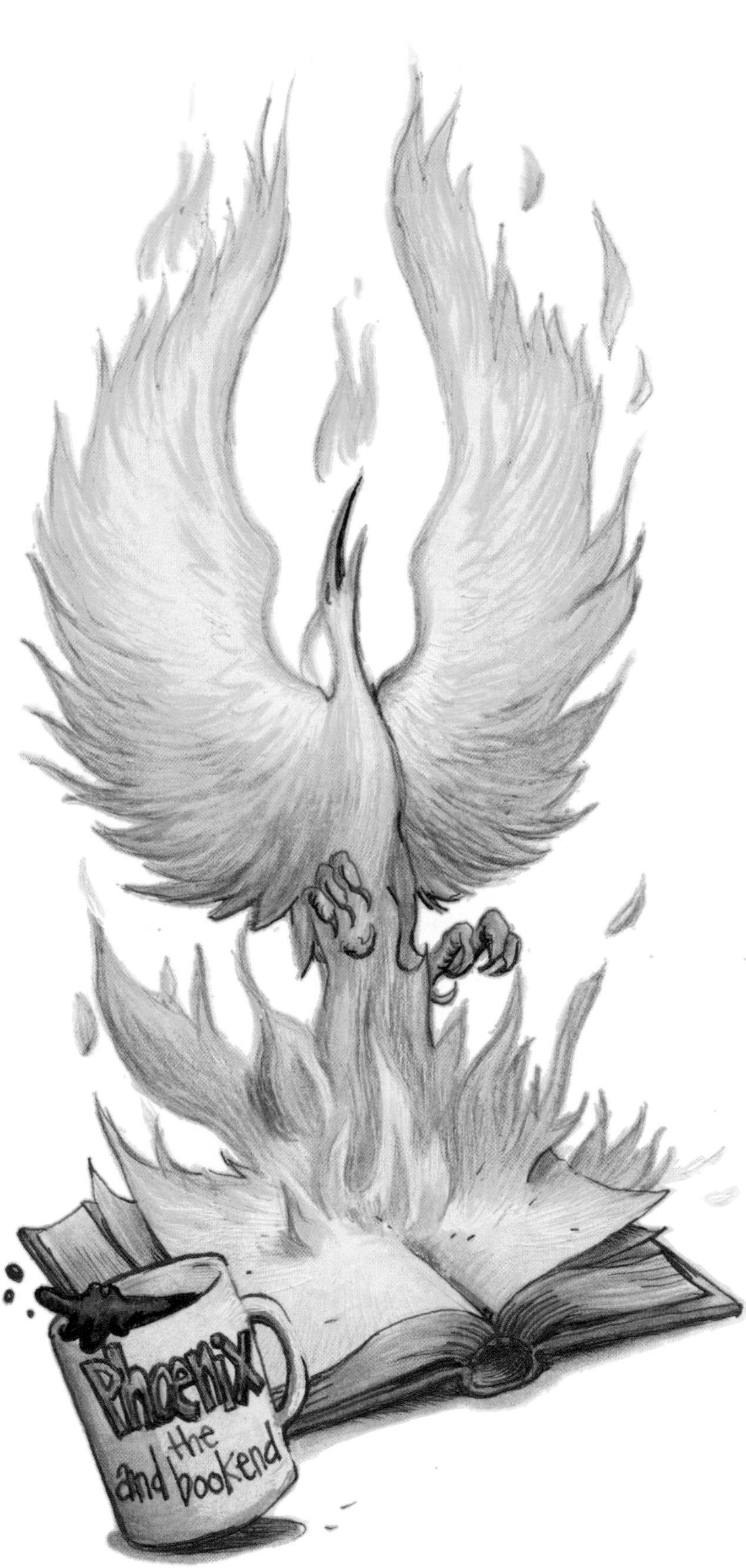
Phoenix
the
and bookend

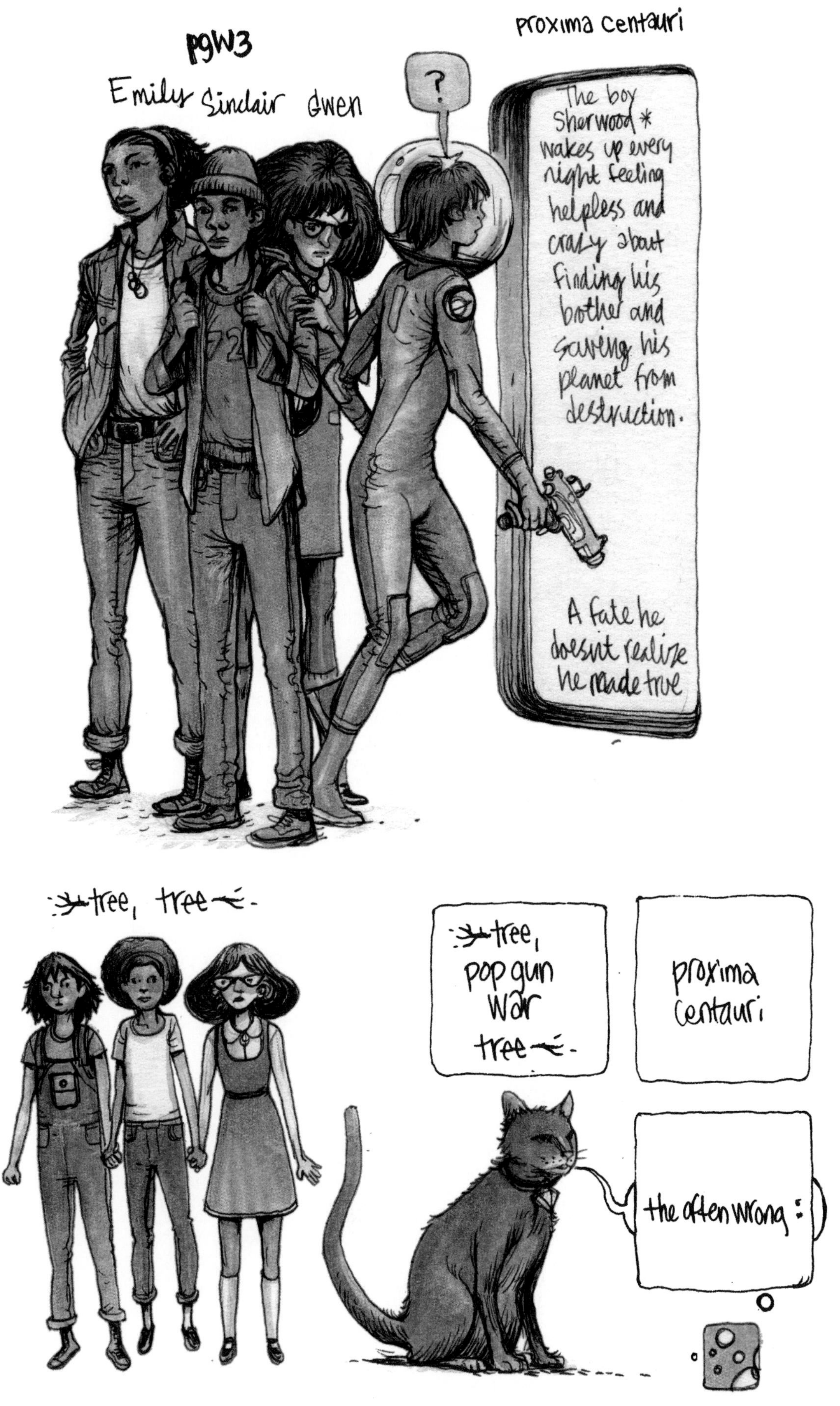
pgw3
proxima centauri
Emily Sinclair Gwen
?
The boy Sherwood * wakes up every night feeling helpless and crazy about finding his brother and saving his planet from destruction.
A fate he doesnt realize he made true
tree, tree
tree, pop gun war tree
proxima centauri
the often wrong :

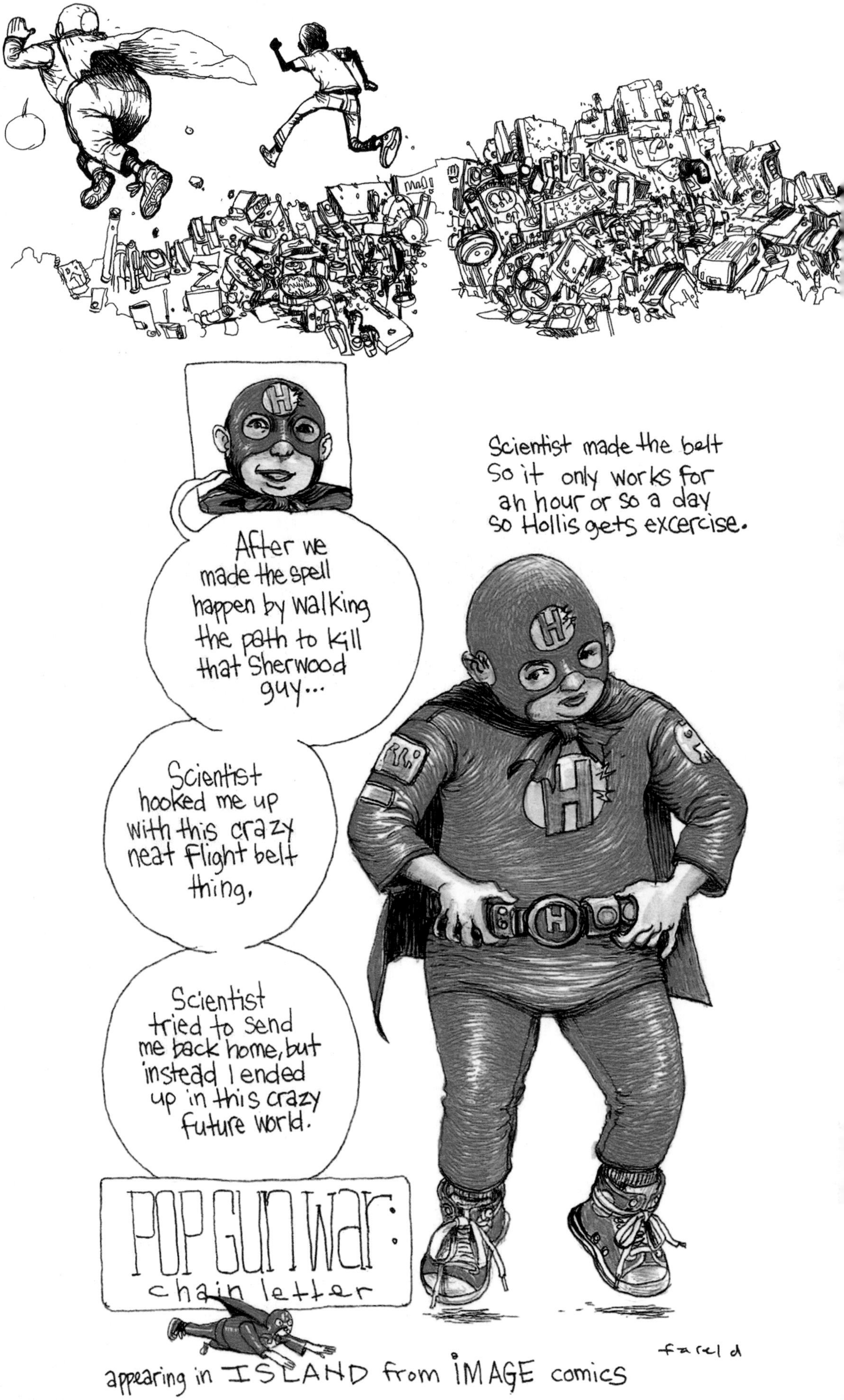
After we made the spell happen by walking the path to kill that Sherwood guy...
Scientist hooked me up with this crazy neat flight belt thing.
Scientist tried to send me back home, but instead I ended up in this crazy future world.
Scientist made the belt So it only works for an hour or so a day so Hollis gets excercise.
POP GUN WAR:
chain letter
farel d
appearing in ISLAND from IMAGE comics

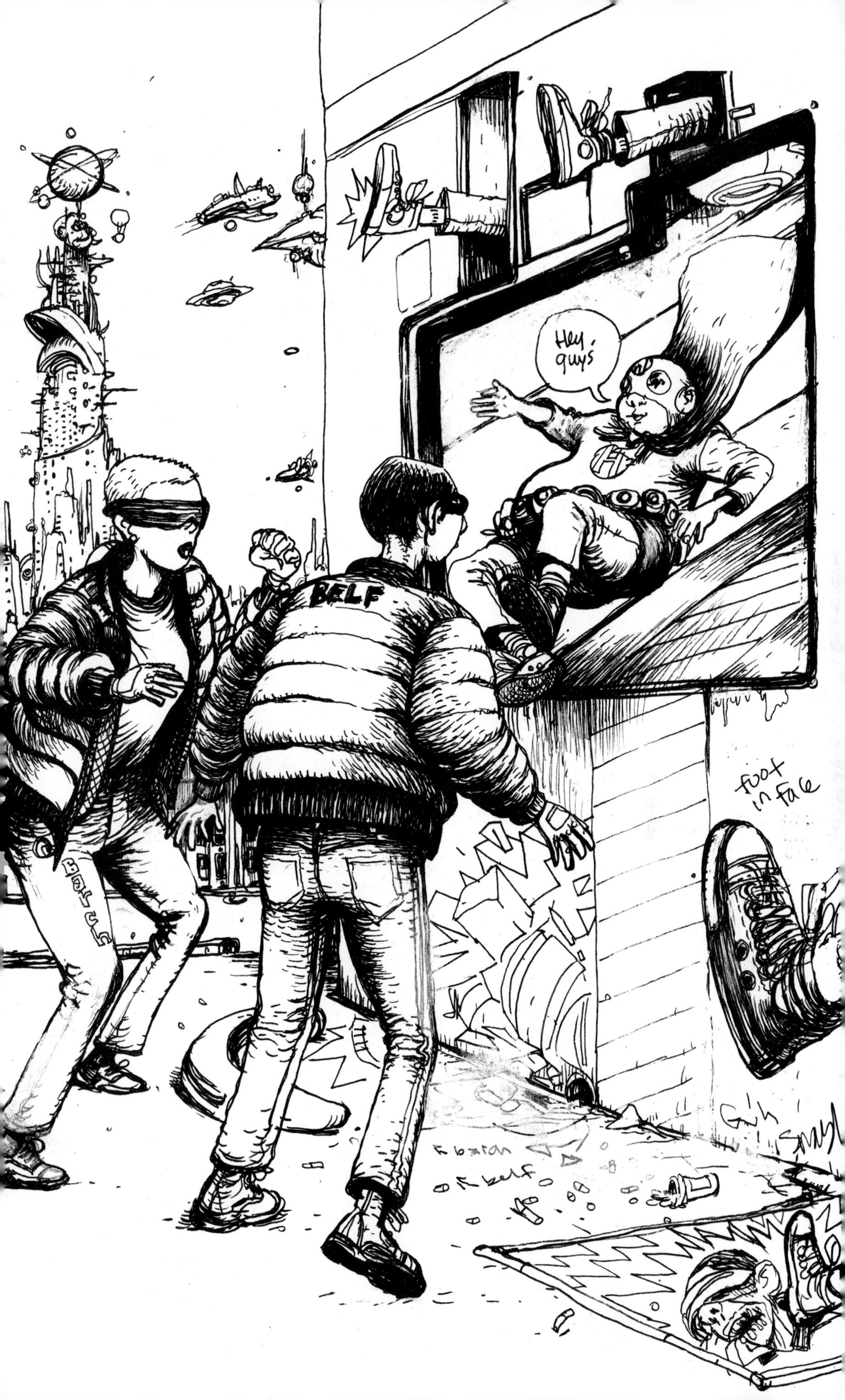
Hey, guys
BELF
foot in face

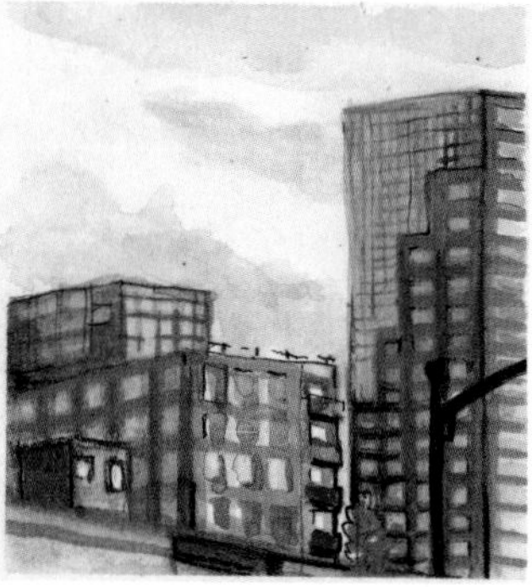
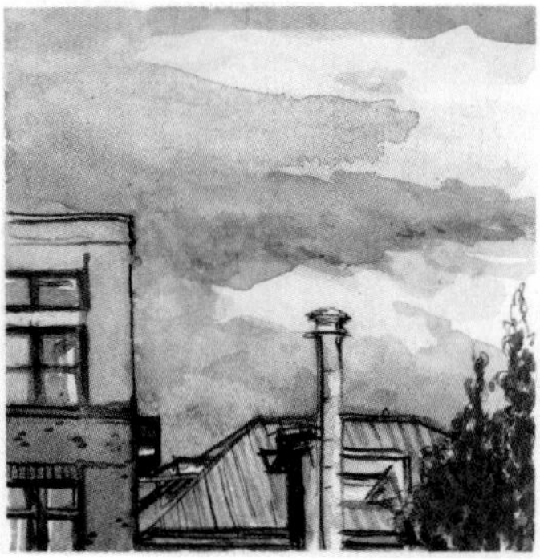
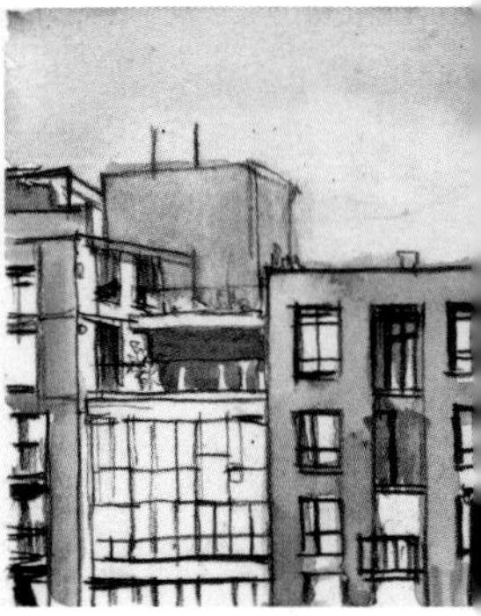
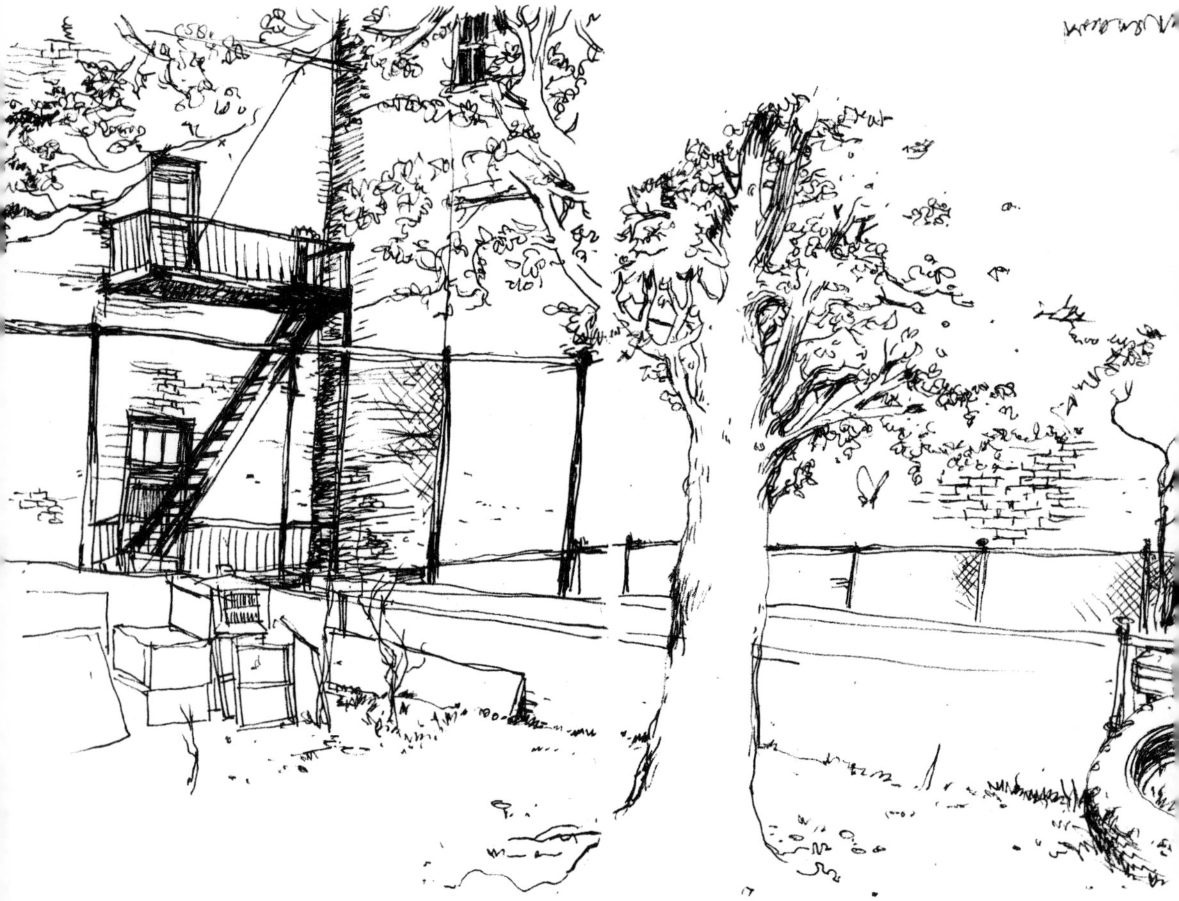

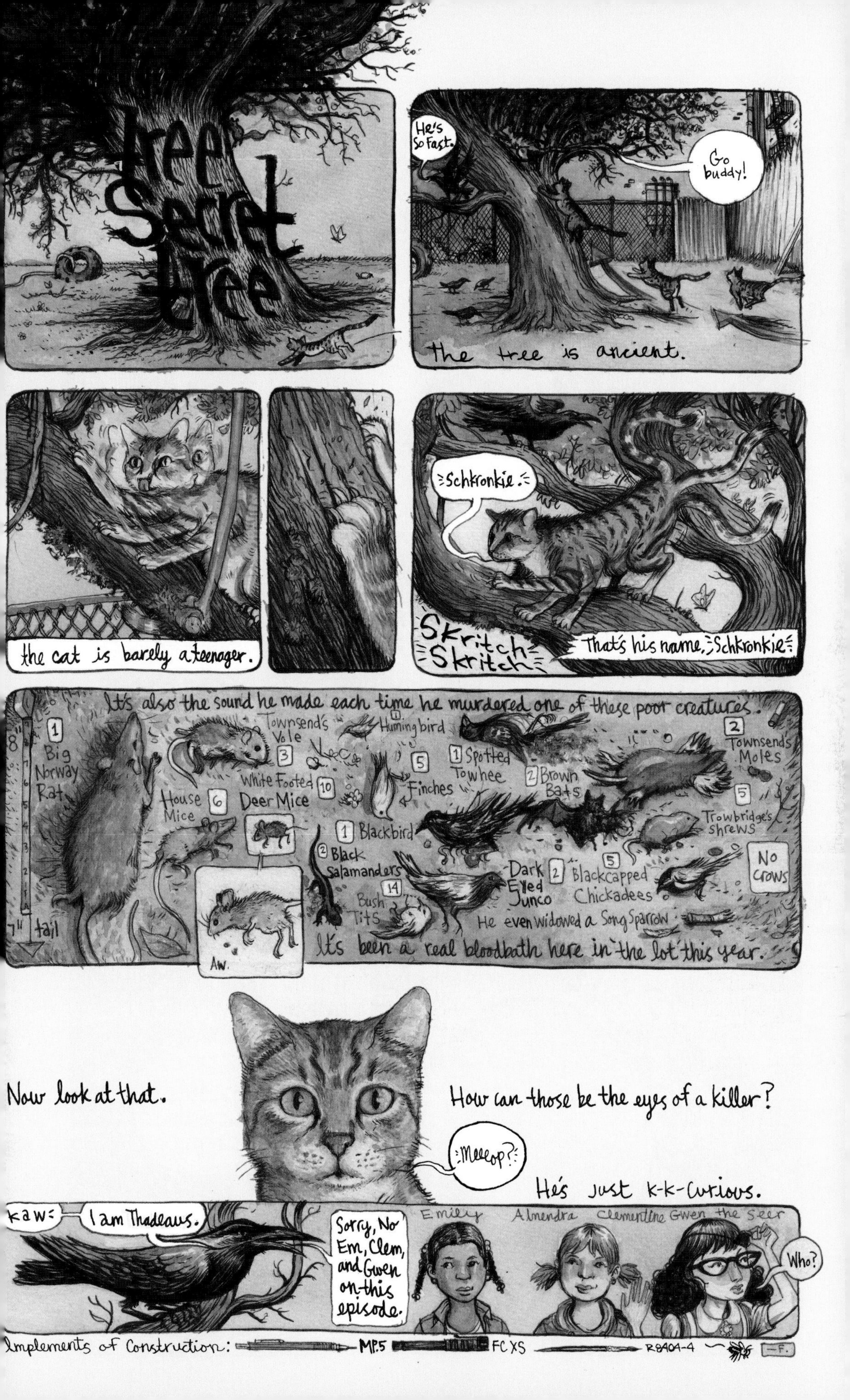
Tree Secret Tree
He's So Fast.
Go buddy!
the tree is ancient.
the cat is barely a teenager.
Schkronkie.
Skritch Skritch
That's his name, Schkronkie
It's also the sound he made each time he murdered one of these poor creatures.
1 Big Norway Rat
8"
7" tail
Townsend's Vole 3
1 Huming bird
1 Spotted Towhee
2 Townsend's Moles
White Footed Deer Mice 10
House Mice 6
5 Finches
2 Brown Bats
5 Trowbridge's shrews
1 Blackbird
2 Black Salamanders
14 Bush Tits
Dark Eyed Junco 2
5 Blackcapped Chickadees
No crows
He even widowed a Song Sparrow
Aw.
It's been a real bloodbath here in the lot this year.
Now look at that.
How can those be the eyes of a killer?
Meeop?
He's just k-k-curious.
kaw
I am Thadeaus.
Sorry, No Em, Clem, and Gwen on this episode.
Emily
Almendra
Clementine
Gwen the Seer
Who?
Implements of Construction: MP.5 FC XS R8404-4 —F.

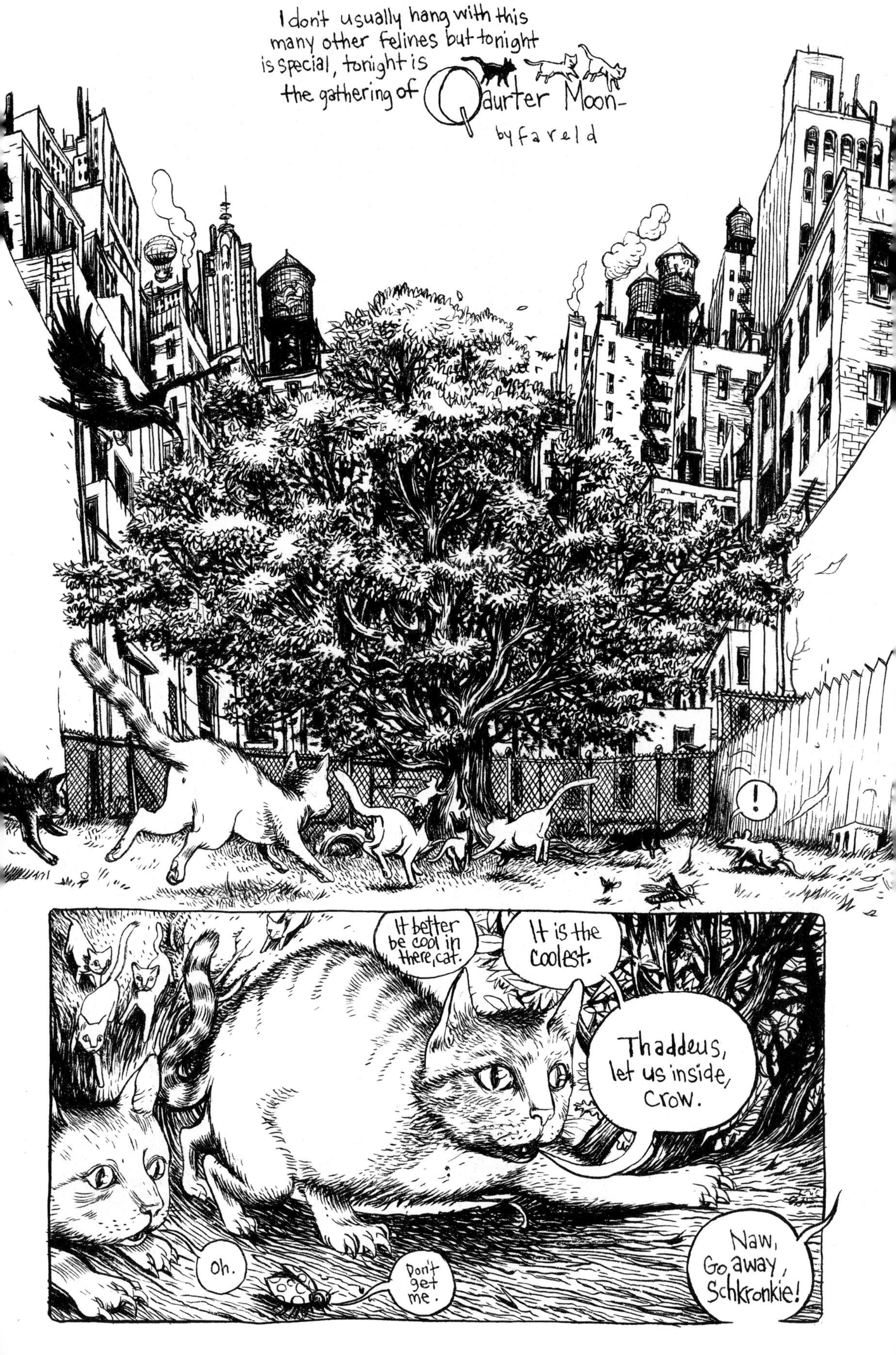
I don't usually hang with this many other felines but tonight is special, tonight is the gathering of Qaurter Moon-
by fareld
!
It better be cool in there, cat.
It is the coolest.
Thaddeus, let us inside, crow.
Oh.
Don't get me.
Naw, Go away, Schkronkie!

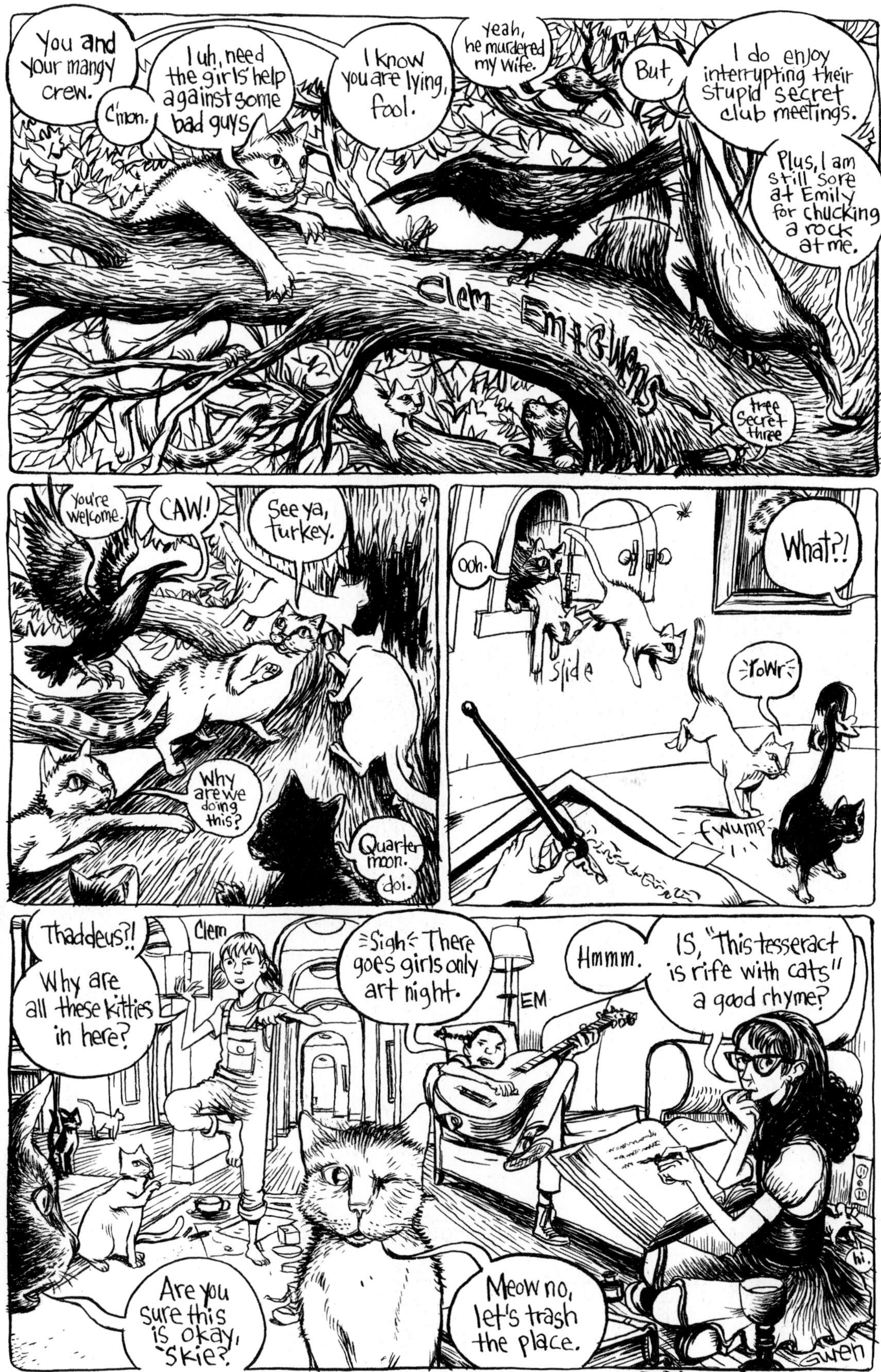
You and your mangy crew.
C'mon.
I uh, need the girls' help against some bad guys
I know you are lying, fool.
Yeah, he murdered my wife.
But,
I do enjoy interrupting their stupid secret club meetings.
Plus, I am still sore at Emily for chucking a rock at me.
Clem Em + Gwen
tree Secret three
You're welcome.
CAW!
See ya, turkey.
Why are we doing this?
Quarter moon. doi.
Ooh.
What?!
slide
rowr
fwump
Thaddeus?!
Why are all these kitties in here?
Clem
Sigh There goes girls only art night.
EM
Hmmm.
IS, "This tesseract is rife with cats" a good rhyme?
hi.
Are you sure this is okay, 'Skie?
Meow no, let's trash the place.
Gwen

Make some magic. ~ Make some art.

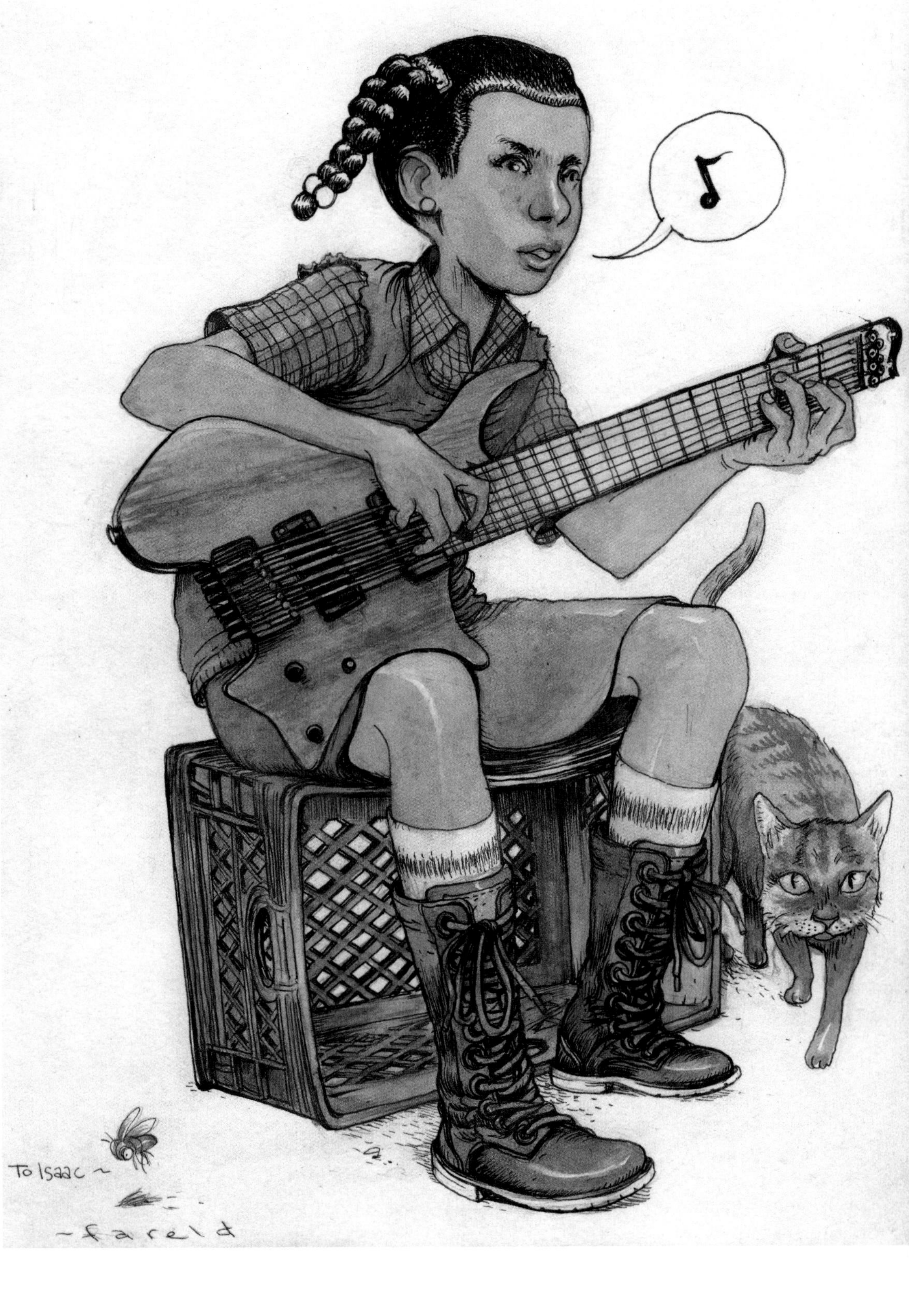
To Isaac ~
~fareid

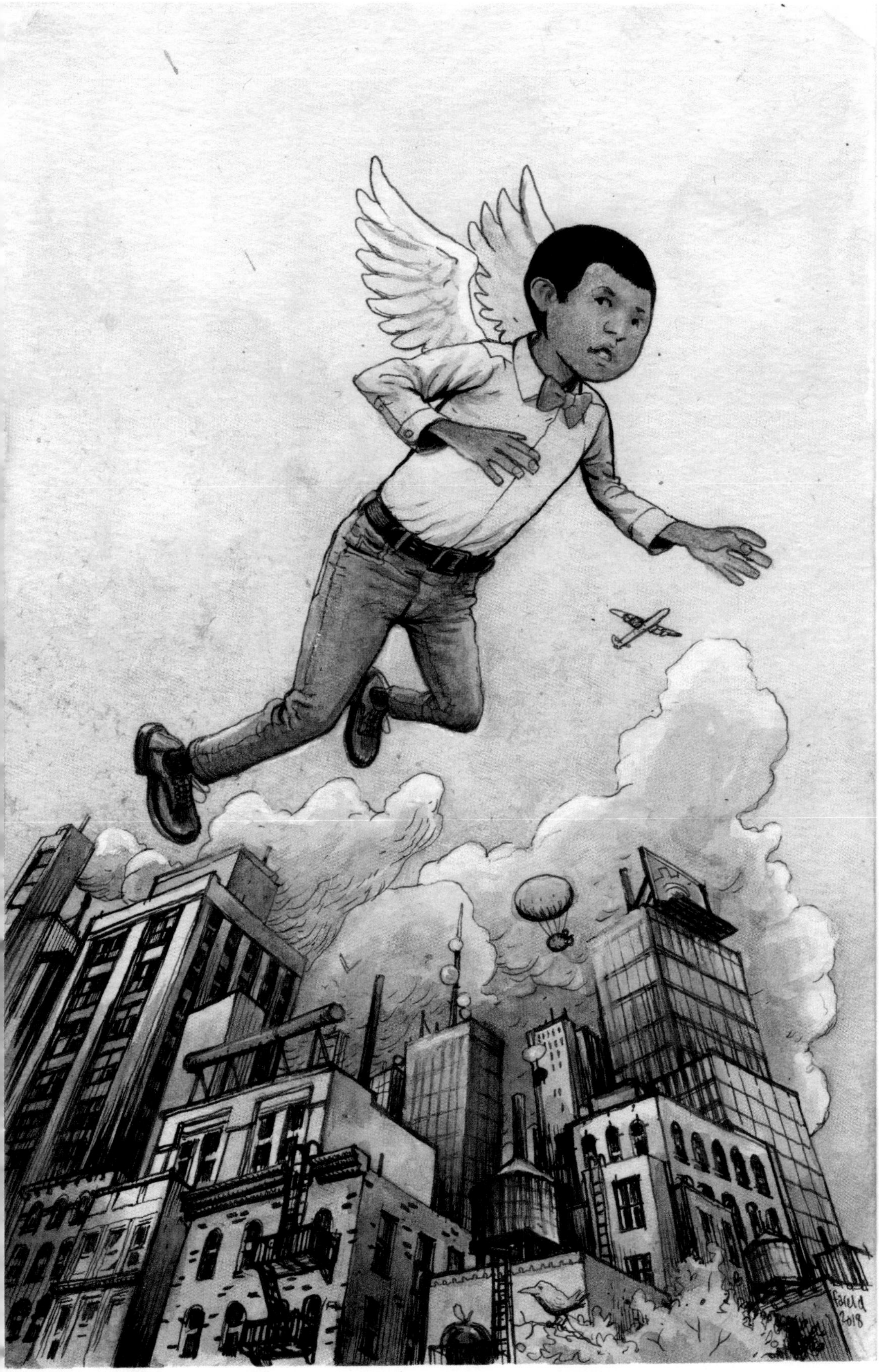

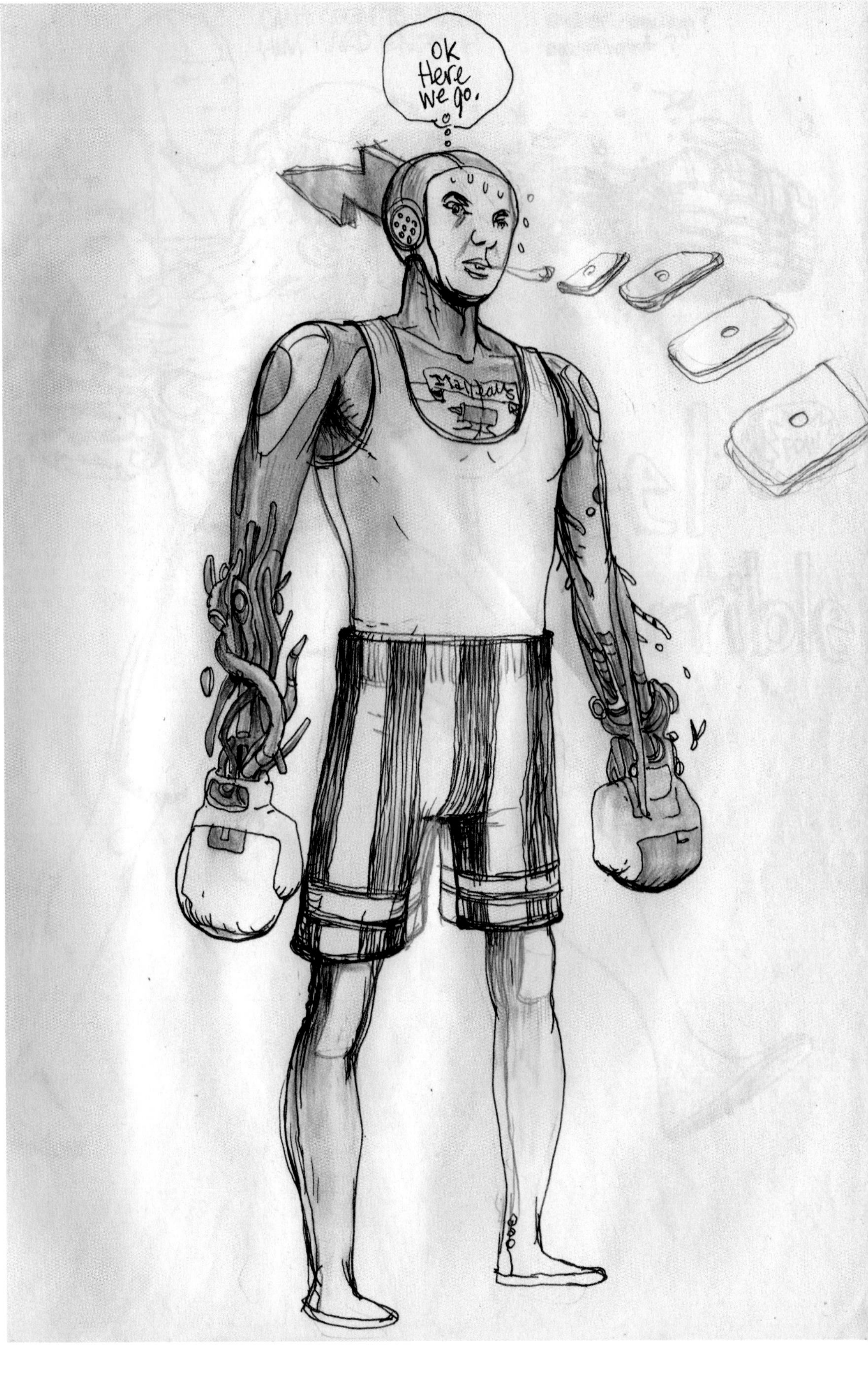
OK Here we go.

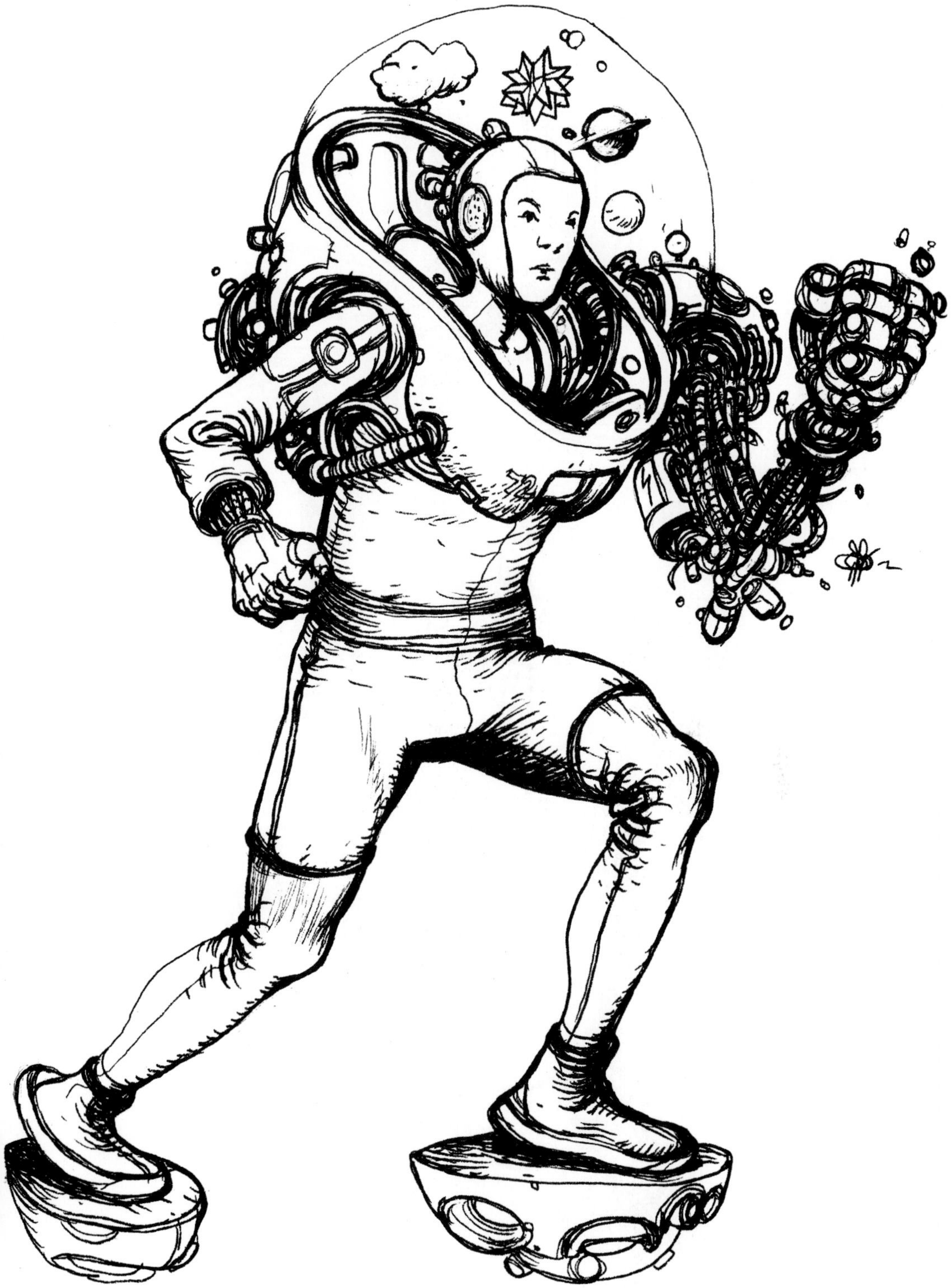

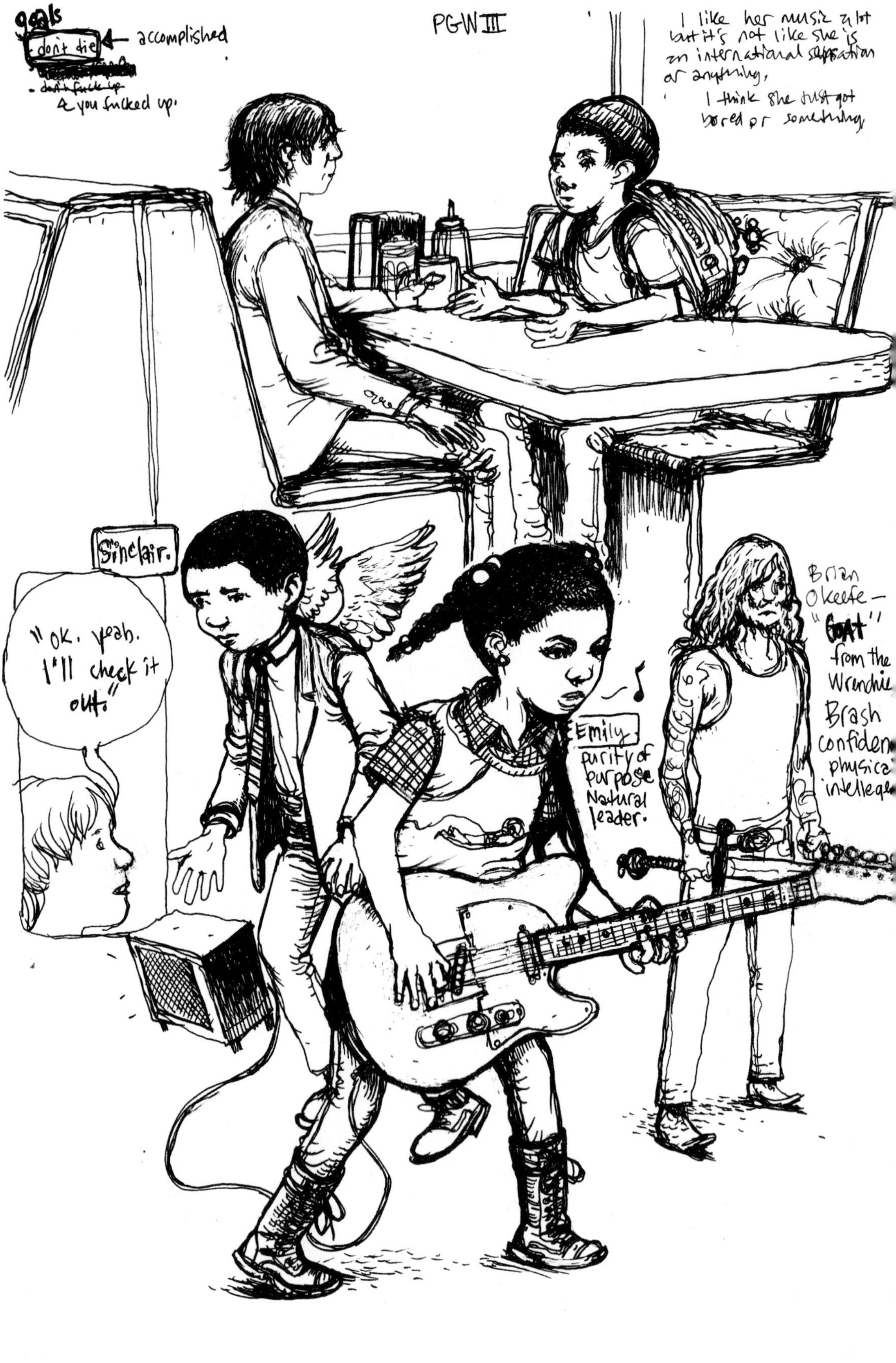

goals
- don't die ← accomplished
[redacted]
- don't fuck up
↳ you fucked up.
PGW III
I like her music a lot but it's not like she is an international sensation or anything,
I think she just got bored or something,
Sinclair.
"ok. yeah. I'll check it out."
Emily
purity of purpose Natural leader.
Brian Okeefe – "GOAT" from the Wrenchie
Brash confiden physica intelleg

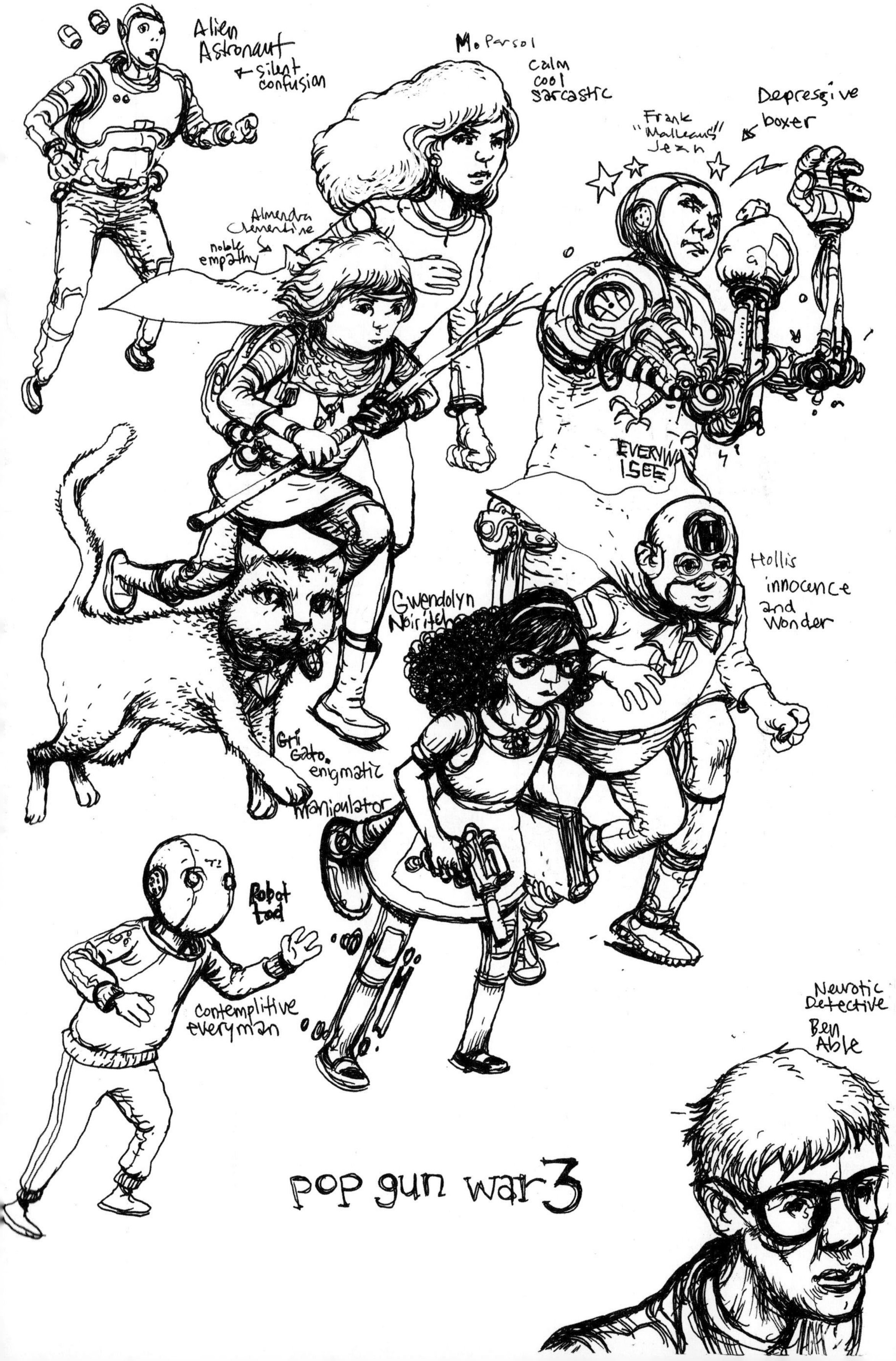
Alien Astronaut
silent confusion
M. Parsol
calm cool sarcastic
Depressive boxer
Frank "Malleaus" Jean
Almendra Clementine
noble empathy
EVERYWA I SEE
Hollis innocence and Wonder
Gwendolyn Noiriteh
Gri Gato. enigmatic
manipulator
Robot Tod
contemplitive everyman
Neurotic Detective
Ben Able
pop gun war 3

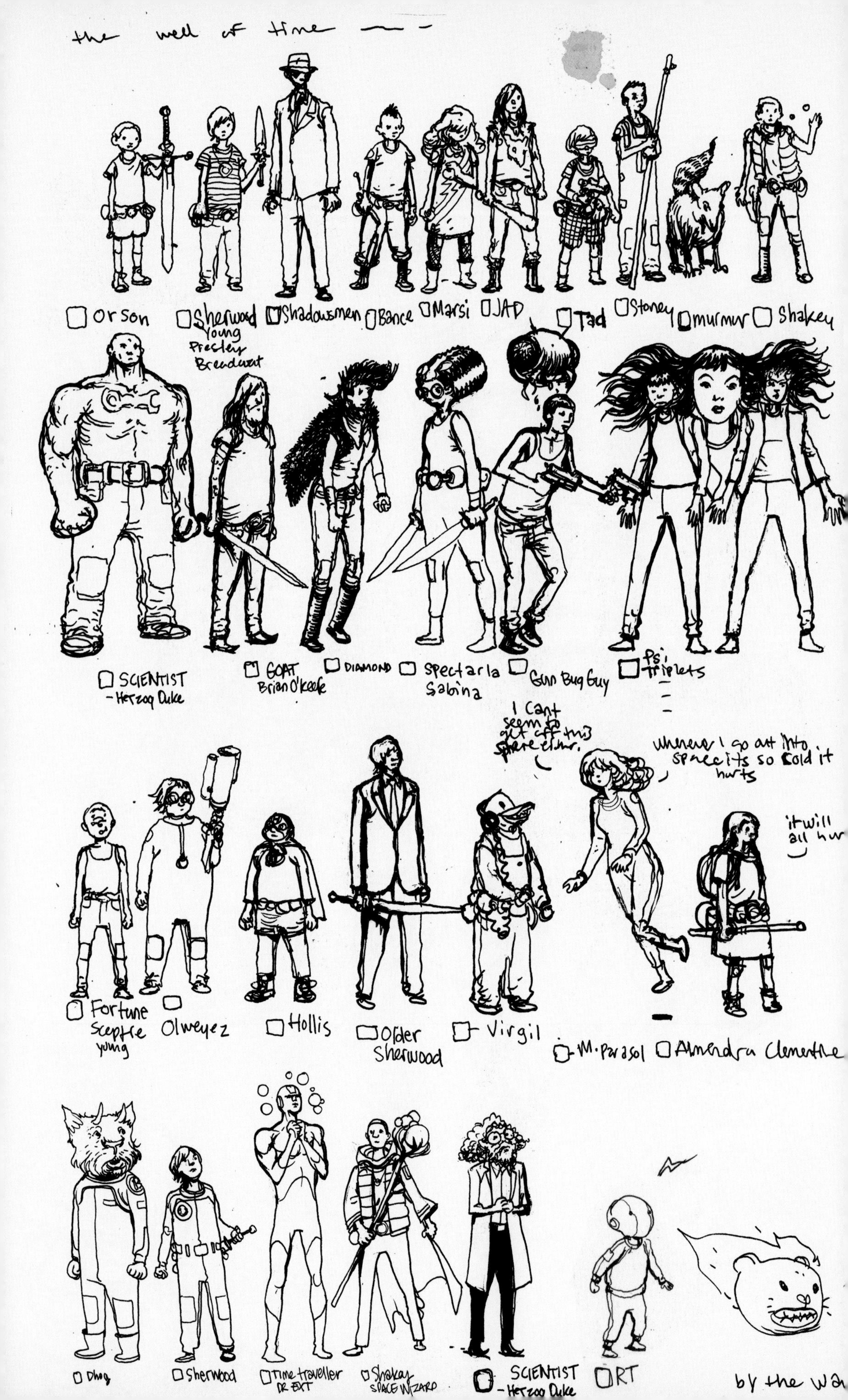

the well of time
Orson
Sherwood
Young
Presley
Breadwat
Shadowsmen
Bance
Marsi
JAD
Tad
Stoney
murmur
Shakey
SCIENTIST
- Herzog Duke
GOAT
Brian O'Keefe
DIAMOND
Spectarla
Sabina
Gun Bug Guy
Psi
triplets
I Cant seem to get off this sphere elder.
whenever I go out into space its so cold it hurts
it will all hur
Fortune
Sceptre
young
Olweyez
Hollis
Older
Sherwood
Virgil
M. Parasol
Almendra Clementine
Dhog
Sherwood
Time traveller
DR EXT
Shakey
SPACE WIZARD
SCIENTIST
- Herzog Duke
RT
by the wa

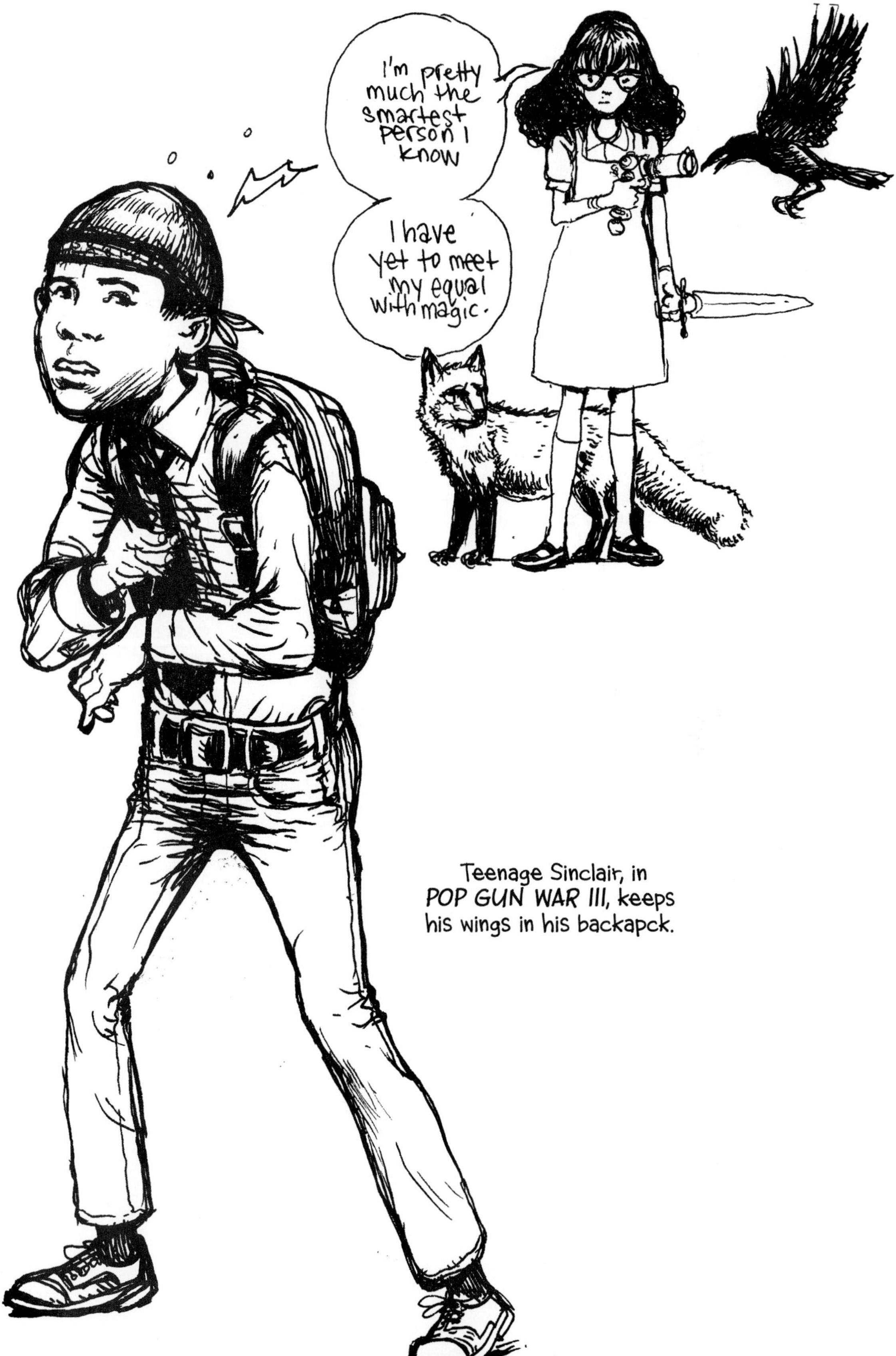
I'm pretty much the smartest person I know
I have yet to meet my equal with magic.

Teenage Sinclair, in *POP GUN WAR III*, keeps his wings in his backapck.

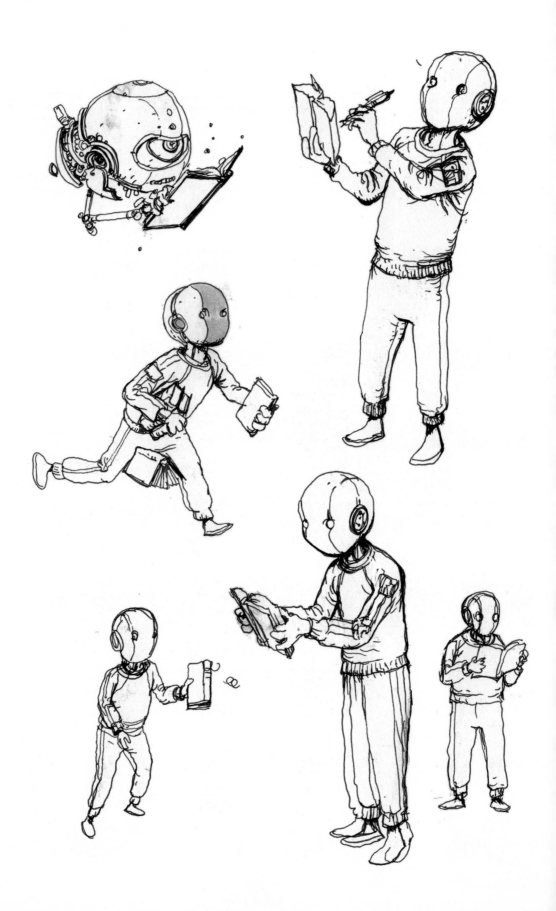

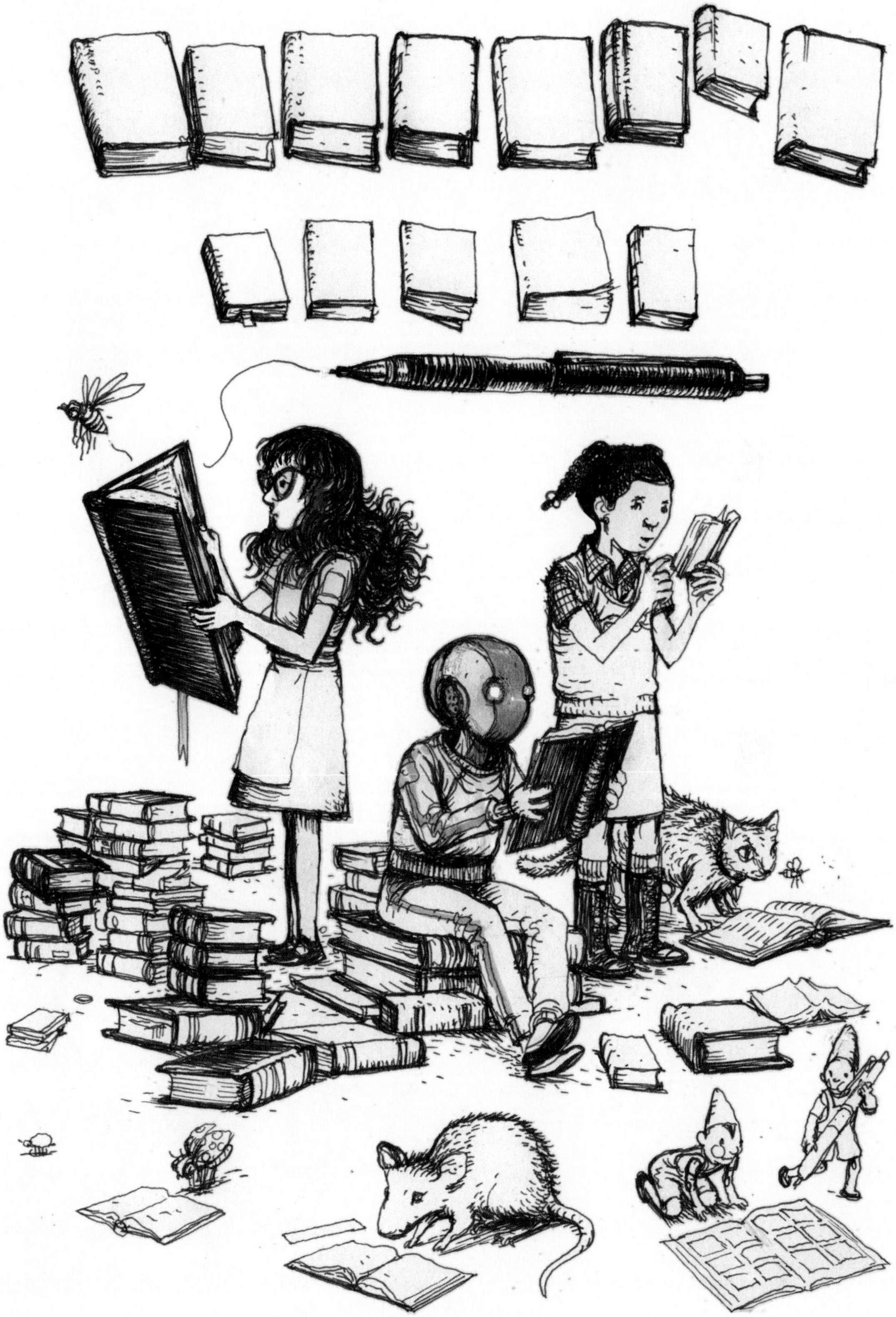

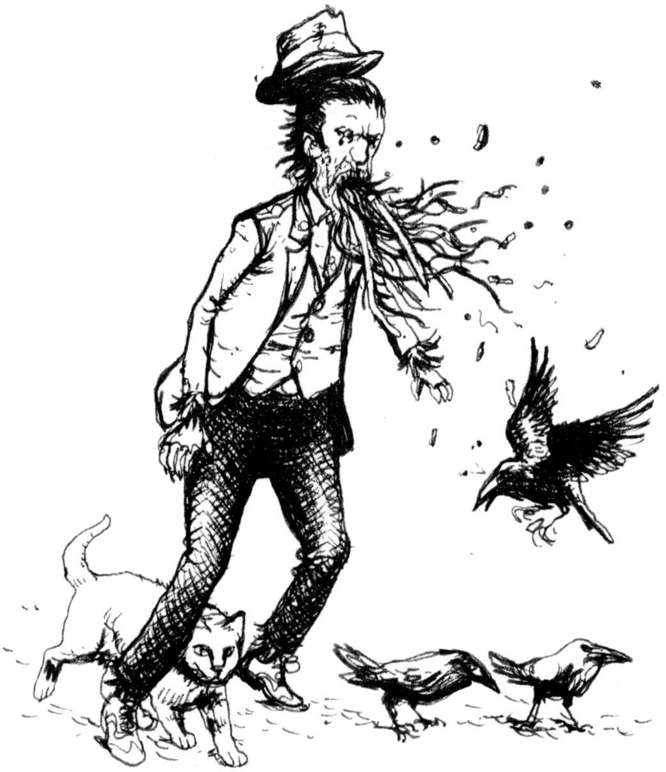

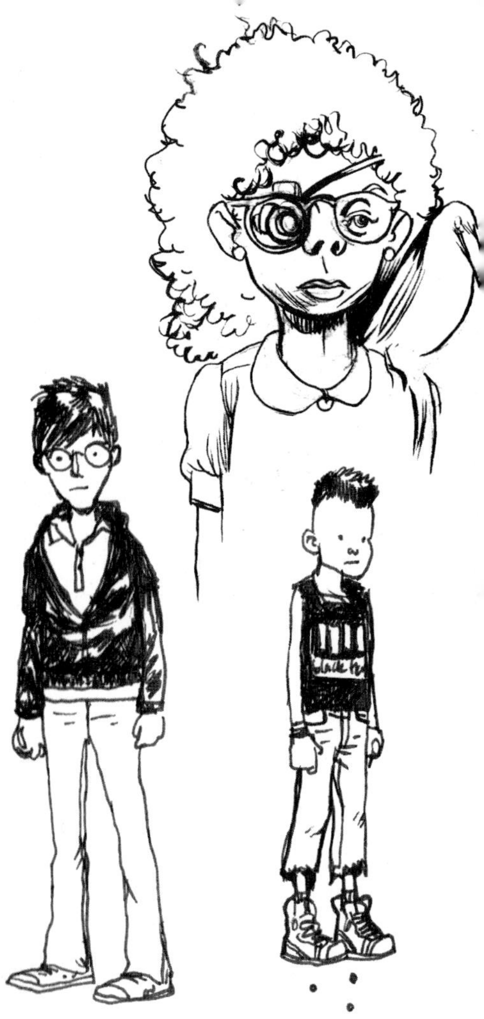

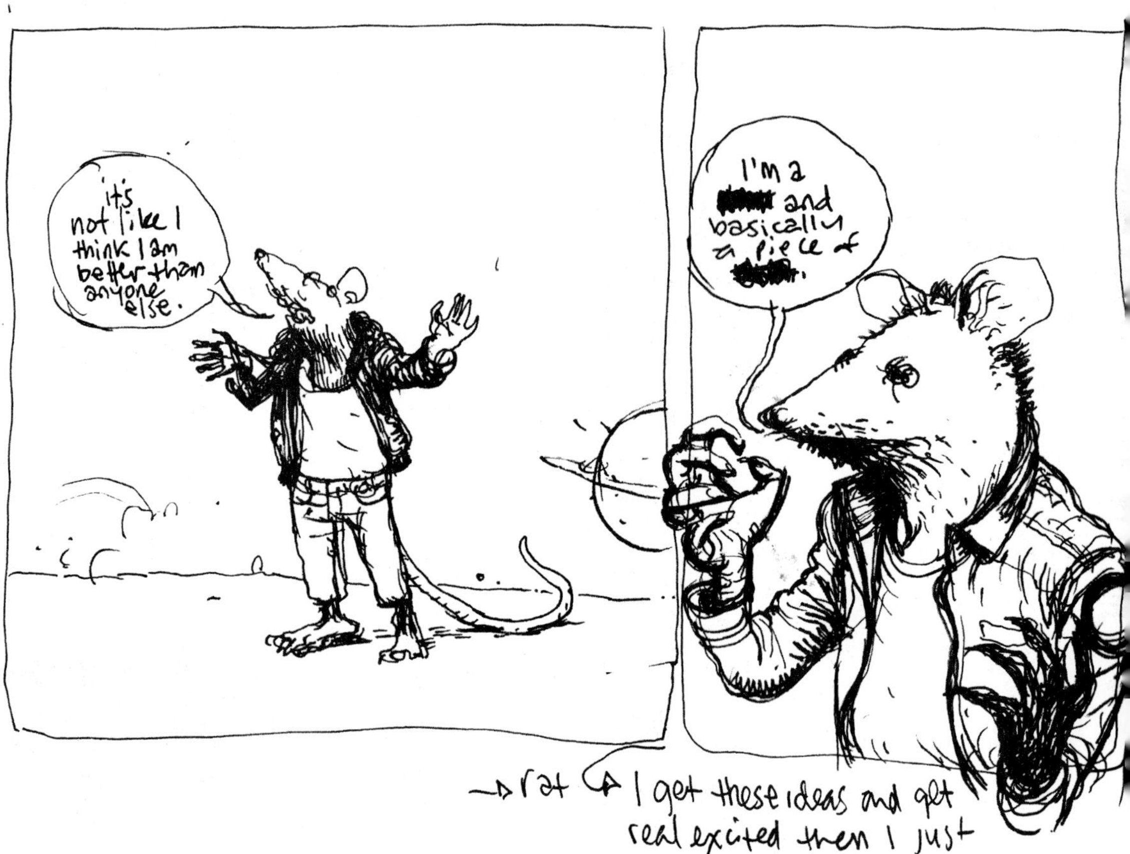
it's not like I think I am better than anyone else.
I'm a [redacted] and basically a piece of [redacted].

→ rat ← I get these ideas and get real excited then I just ~~start~~ thinking about what a creepy [redacted] I am.

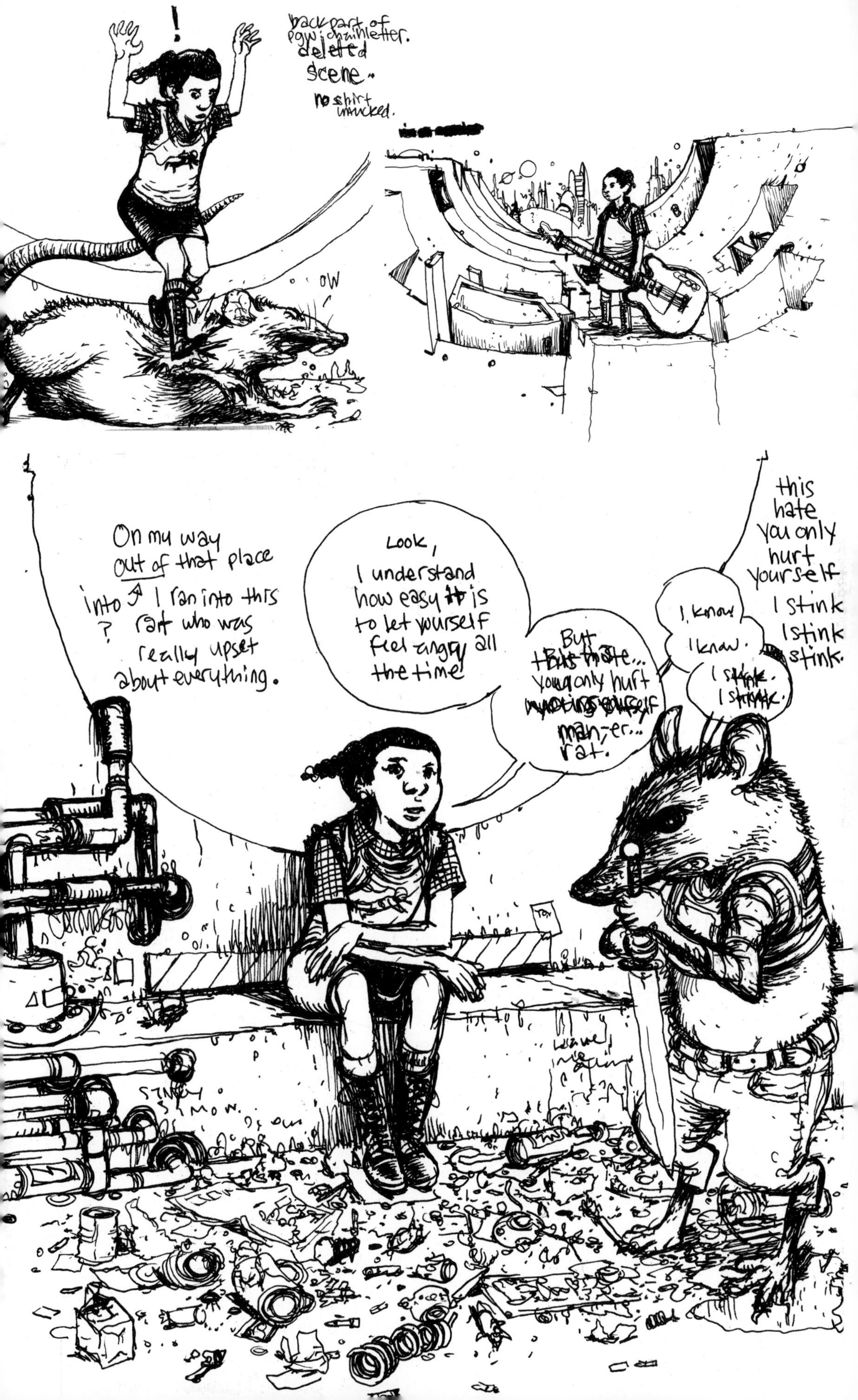
!
back part of pgw chainletter. deleted scene..
no shirt untucked.
OW
On my way out of that place into ? I ran into this rat who was really upset about everything.
Look, I understand how easy is to let yourself feel angry all the time!
But ... you only hurt yourself man, er... rat.
this hate you only hurt yourself
I stink I stink stink.
I know!
I know.
I stink.
I stink.
STINKY SIMON.
leave me alone

x

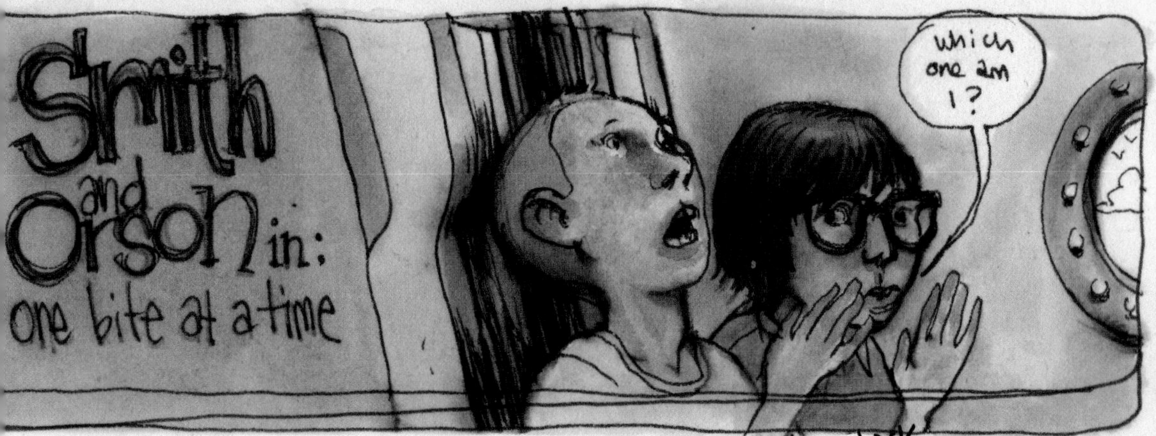
Smith and Orson in:
one bite at a time
which one am I?

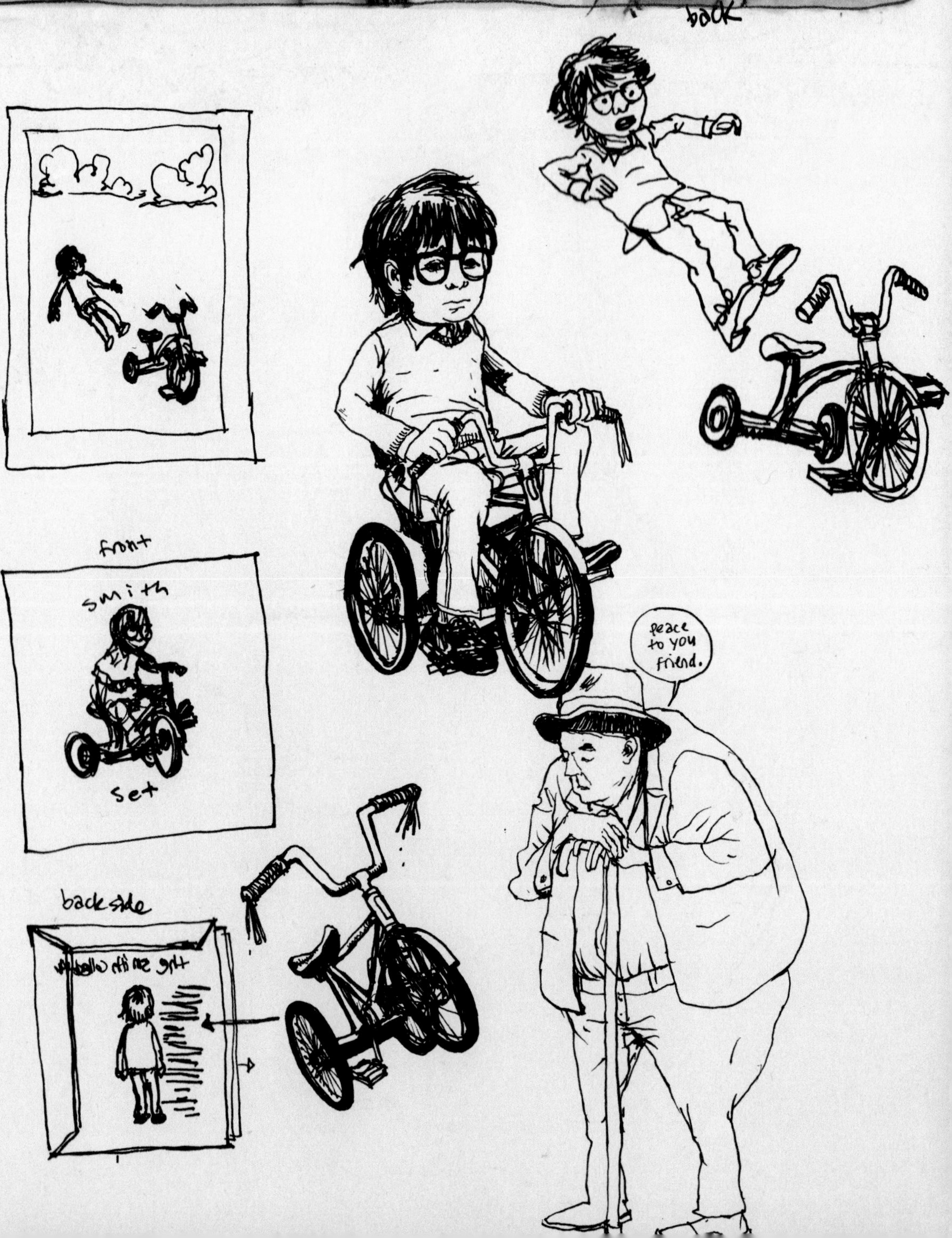
back
front
smith
set
backside
peace to you friend.

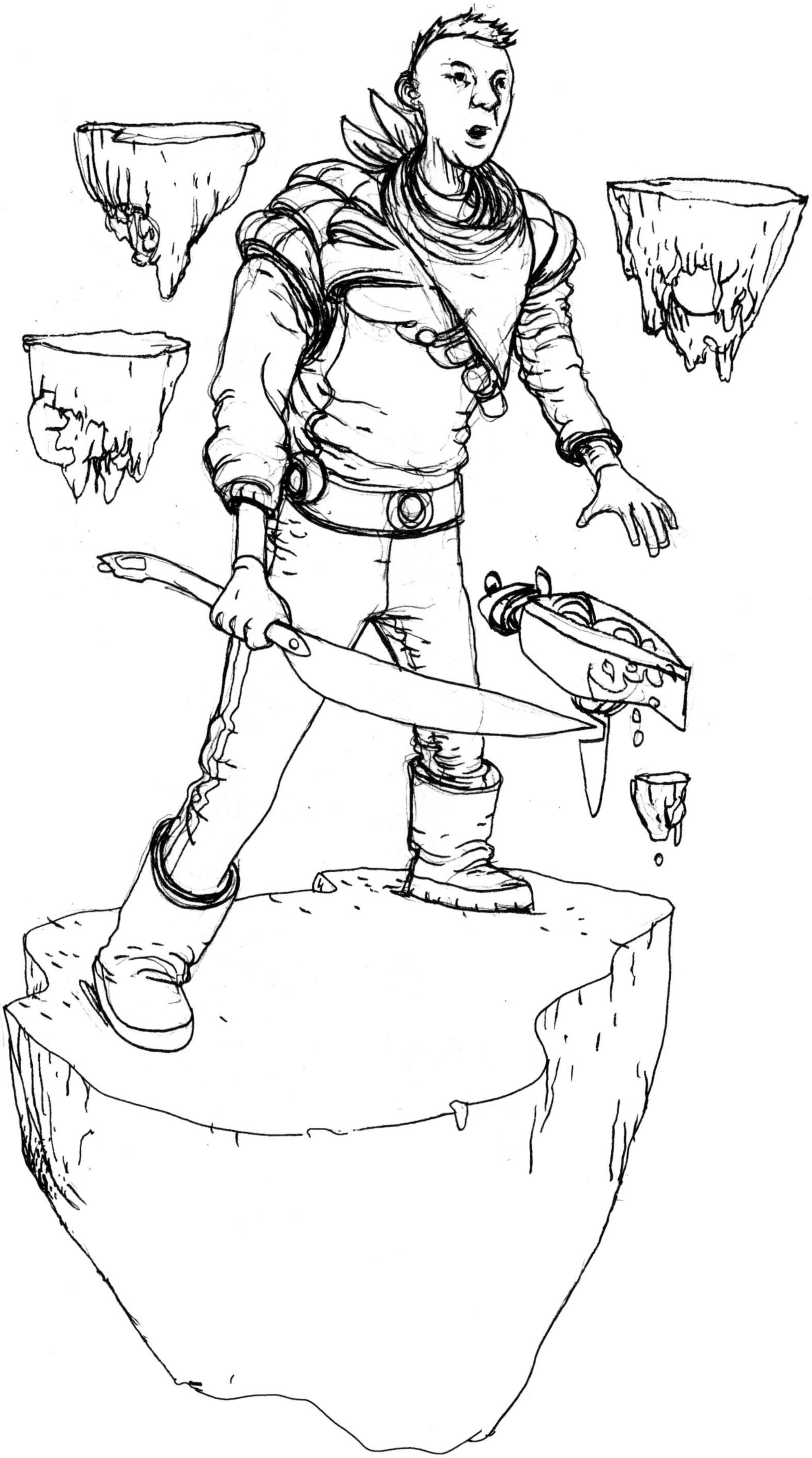

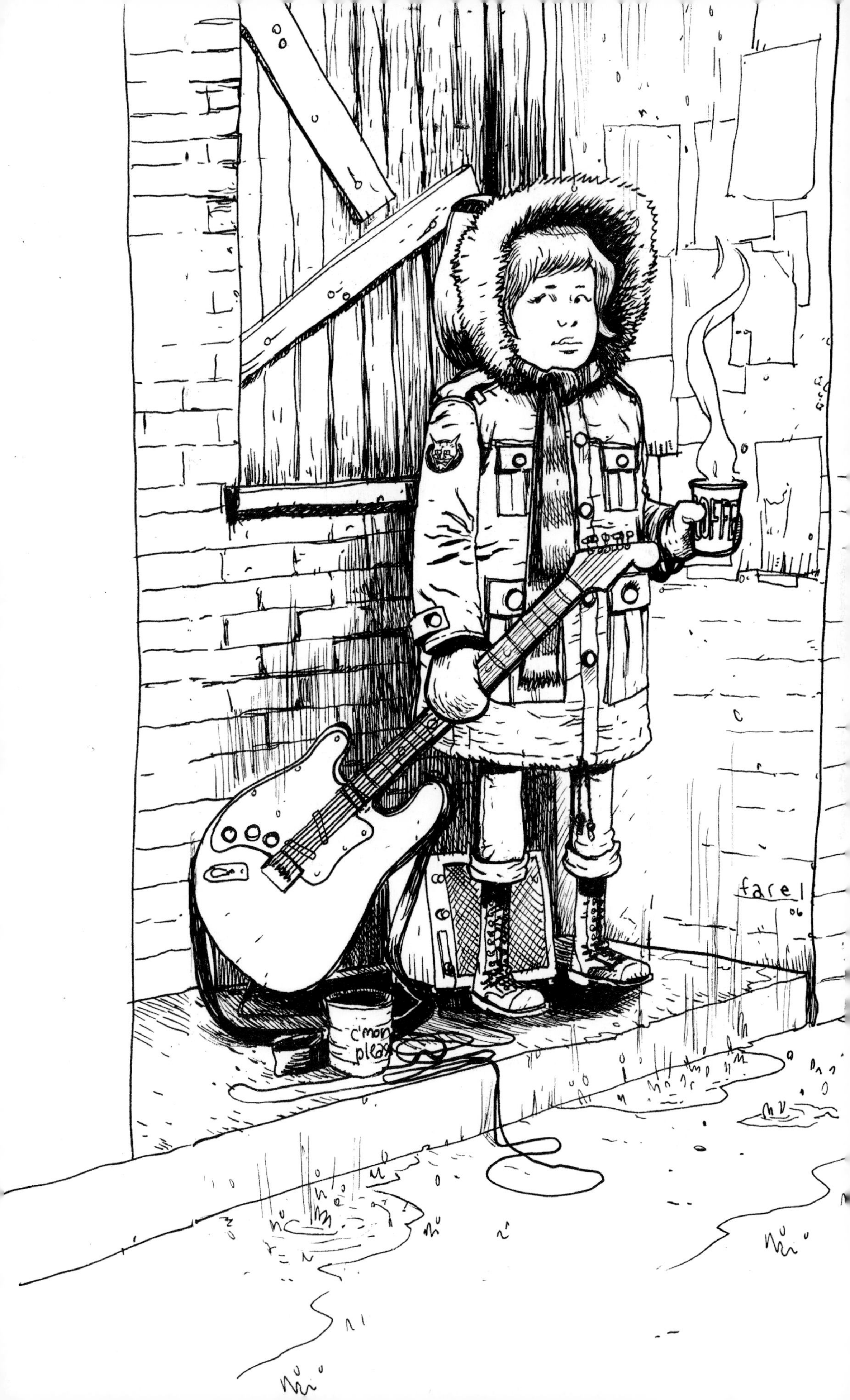
c'mon
pleas
farel
06

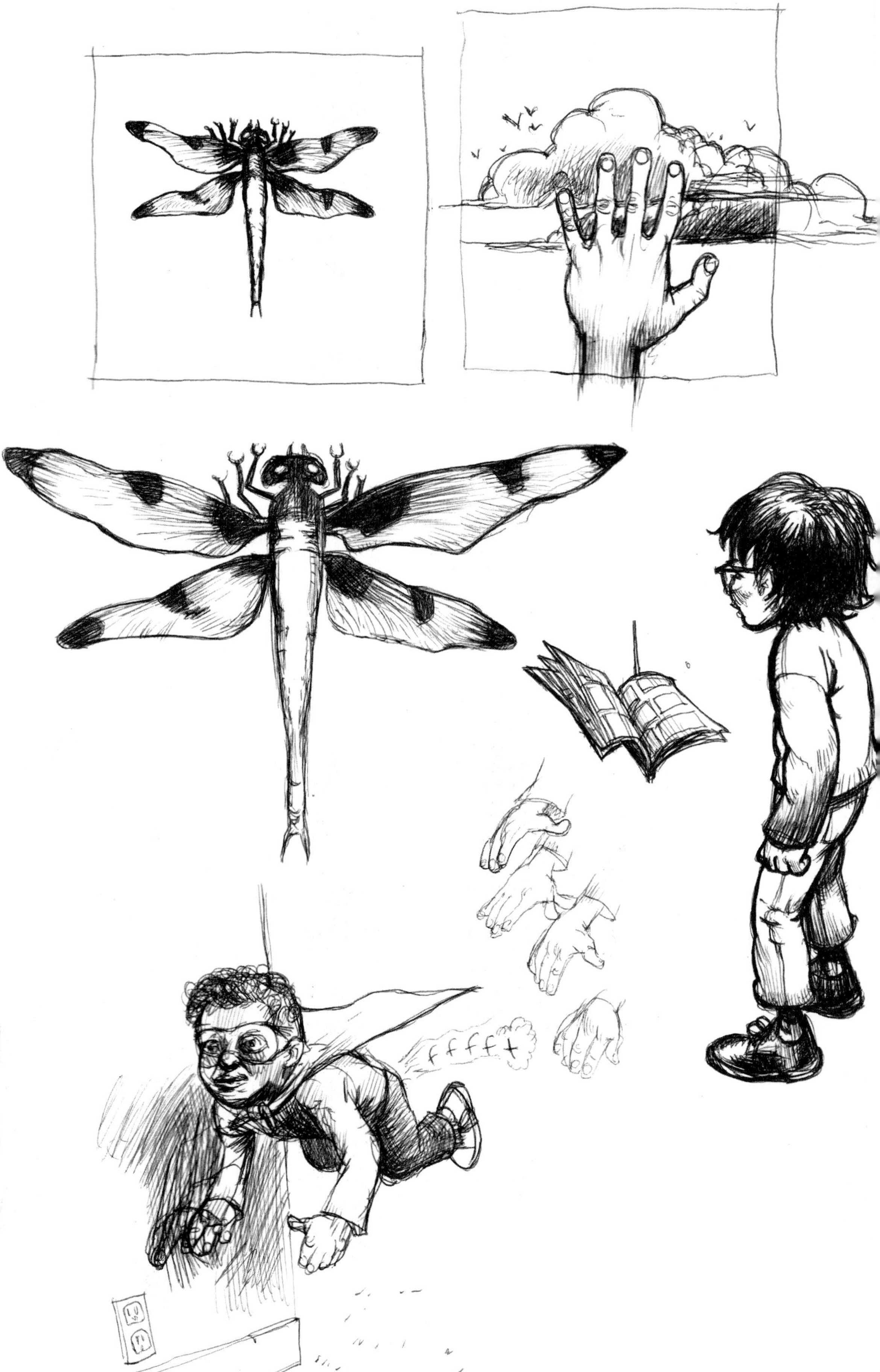
fffft

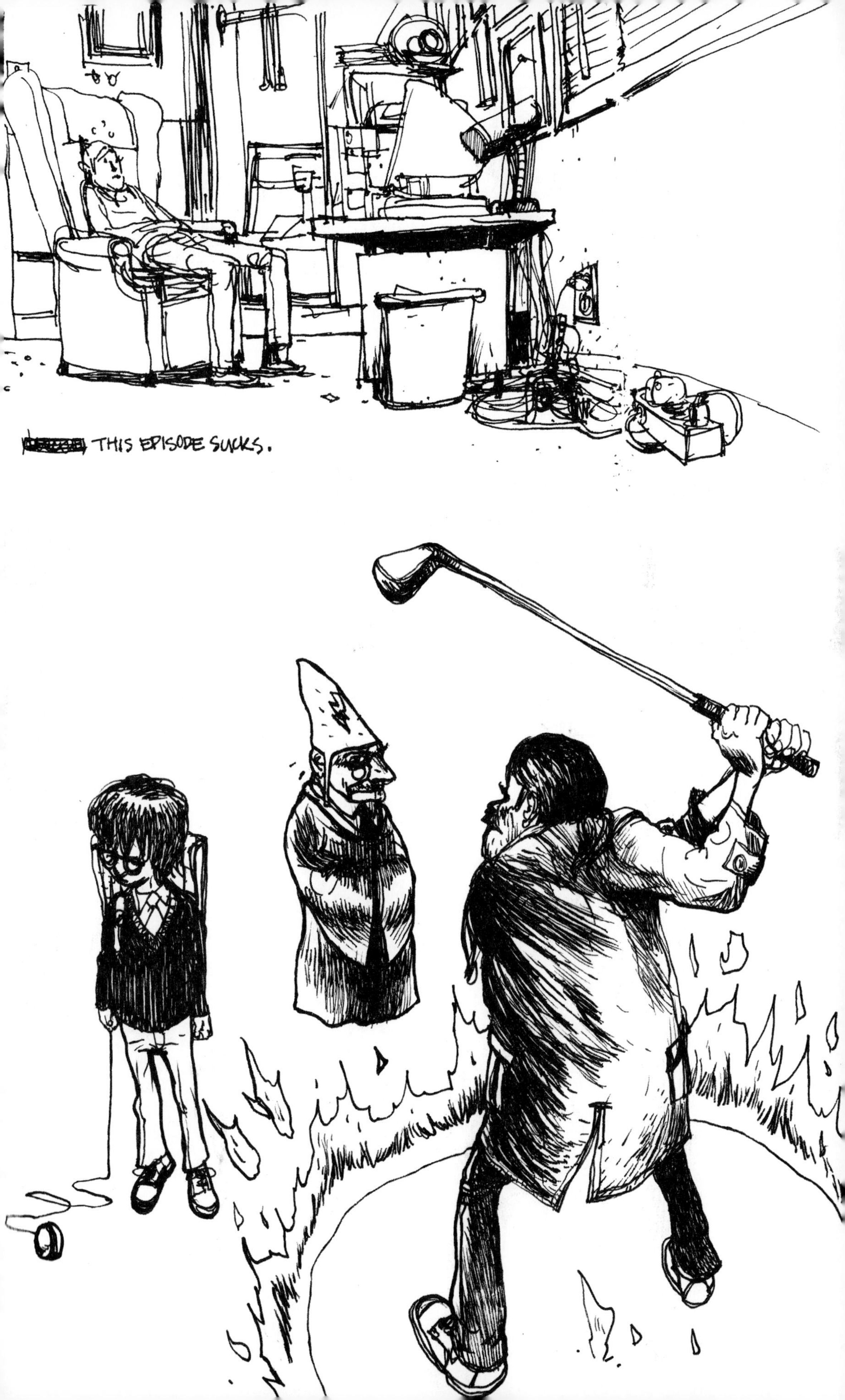
[redacted] THIS EPISODE SUCKS.

3/14/03   on the bike.

slept all day then
Friday night- worked with Rick at Att. til 2am
Zac and Roger showed up
shot a movie. I made a walkon
on with my shirt off. got home w/gill at 4am
tried to sleep. couldit. stayed up then
went to alt at 10:00am to pick up
stuff I left there. went to Brooklyn to
pick up page to sell.

crowded alt
but I didit mind

fell asleep at noon. woke up at 5:15 went
Kinkos then work. a lot of cameos that
night: Celia Bullwinkle, Lane Twitchell,
Teller... Esao made a rare
appearance. Met sarah the squirrel and her
boy friend. Of course the regulars Zac
and Keith were there. John Mejias came
by and showed us the awesome new page

covers. Ended up hanging
out with Mark drinking 40's. and Zac
Zac left early. Mark taught me some
boxing tips and told me some stories.
I think I will be better person as a result.
got home around 5:00 am. I accidentally
woke up gill. She was pissed. probably
one of times she has been the most angry.
I tried to apologize but she wasn't having
it. Tried to sleep but it took me a while.
~~~~~ She was obviously pissed at me for
staying out but wont tell me.

you're a
natural

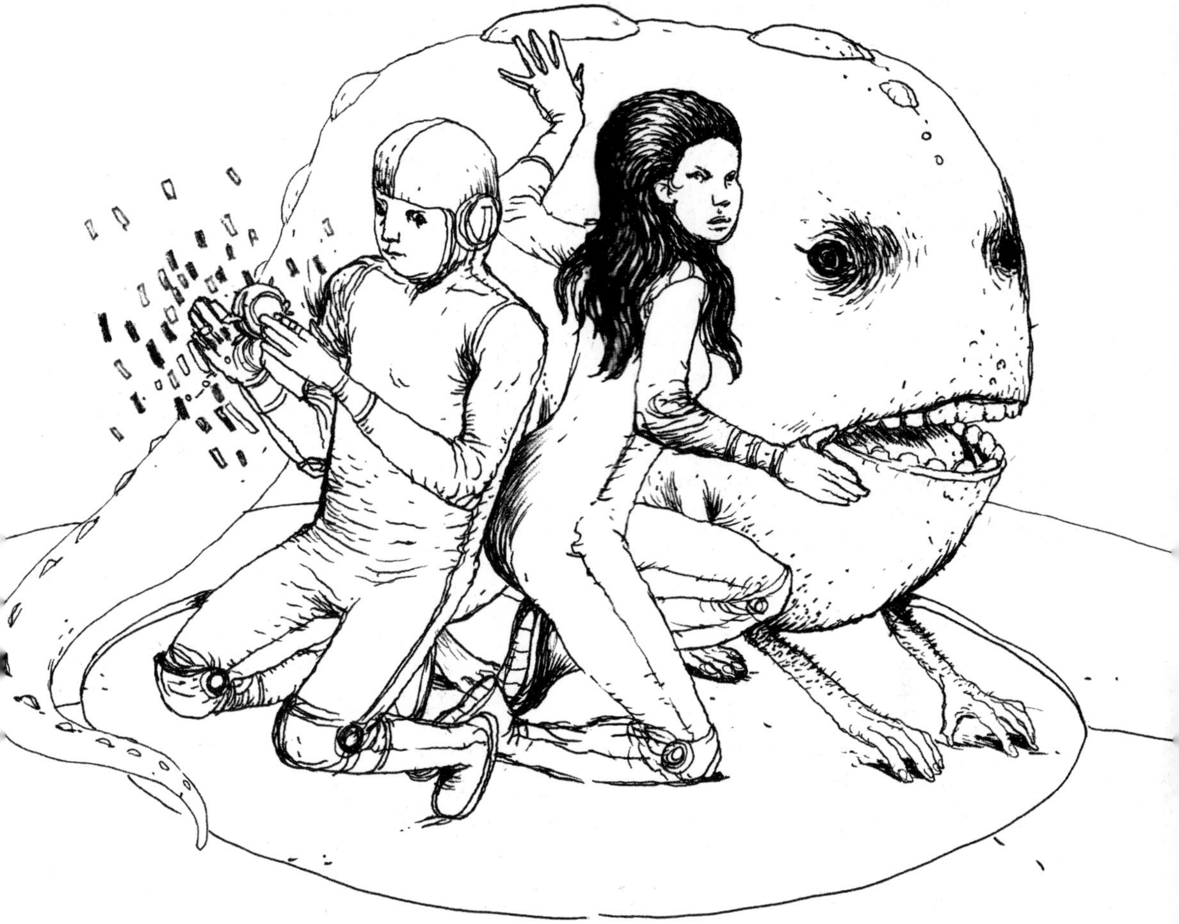

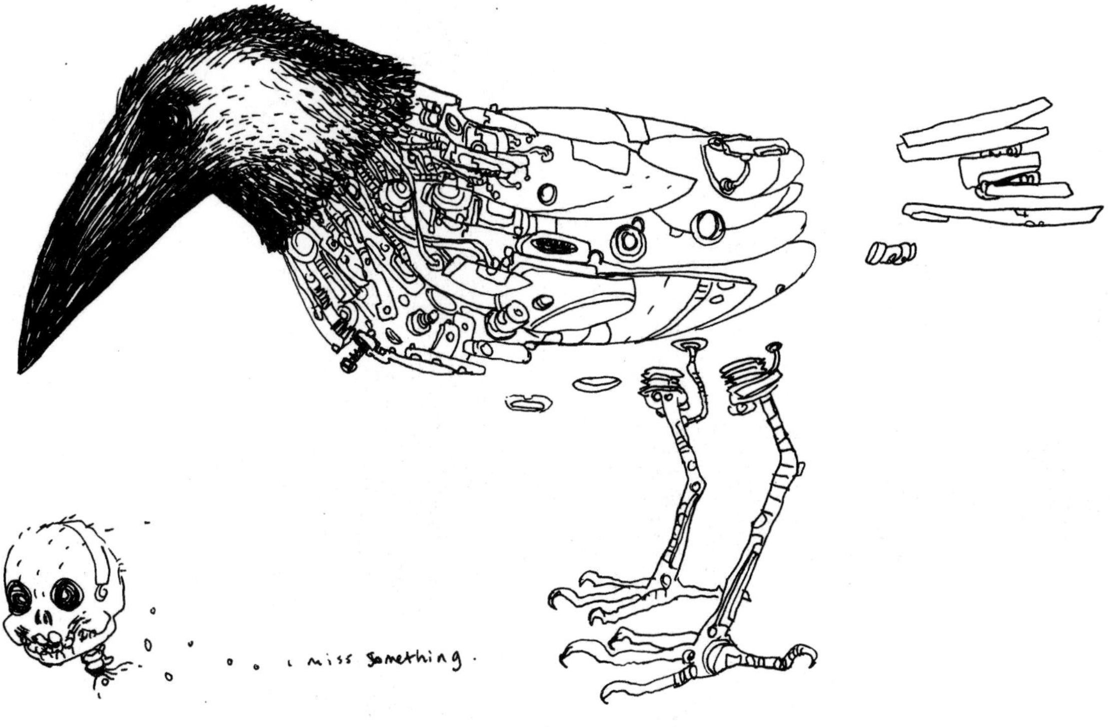
i miss something.

[redacted]

ICELAND
2016

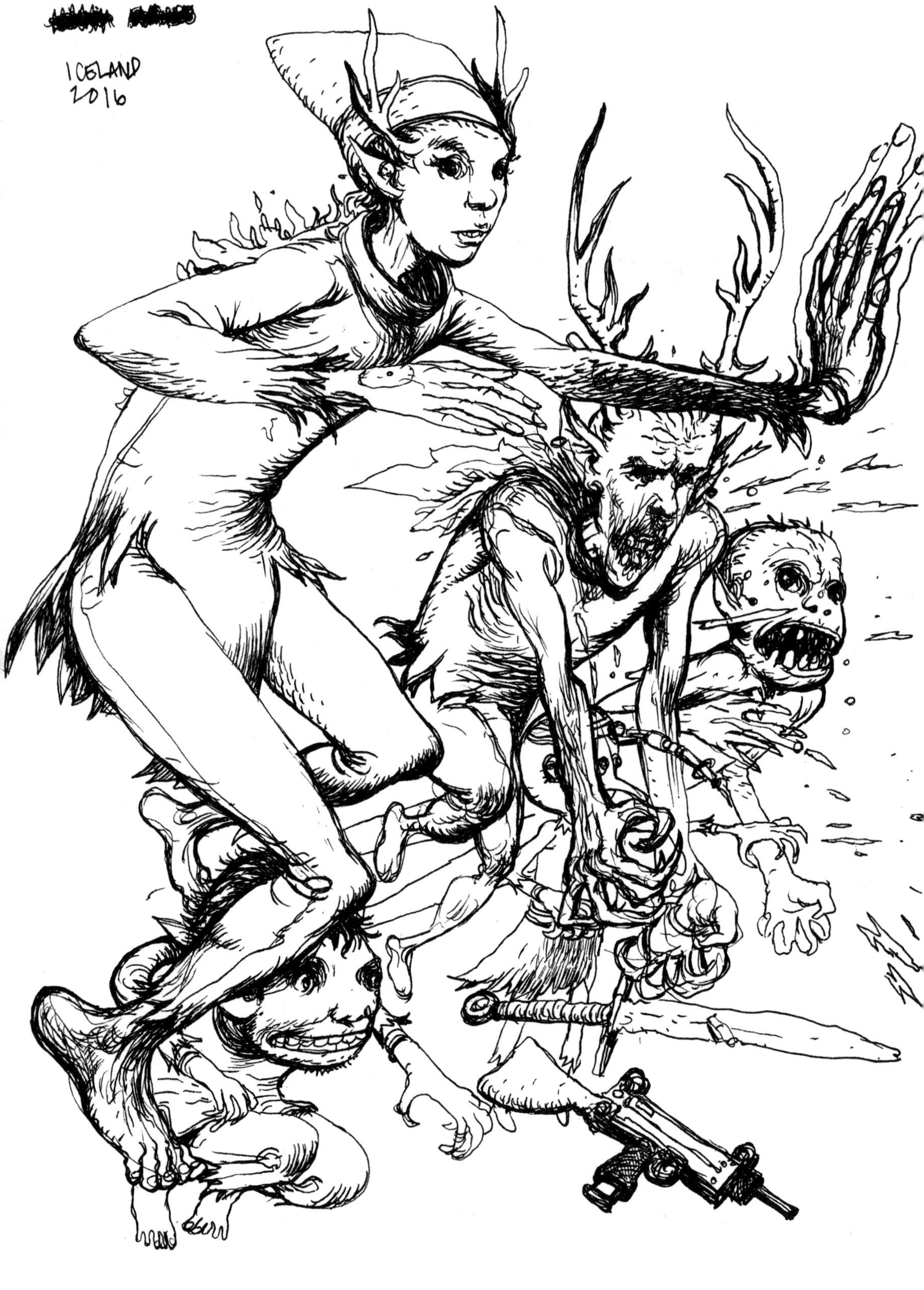

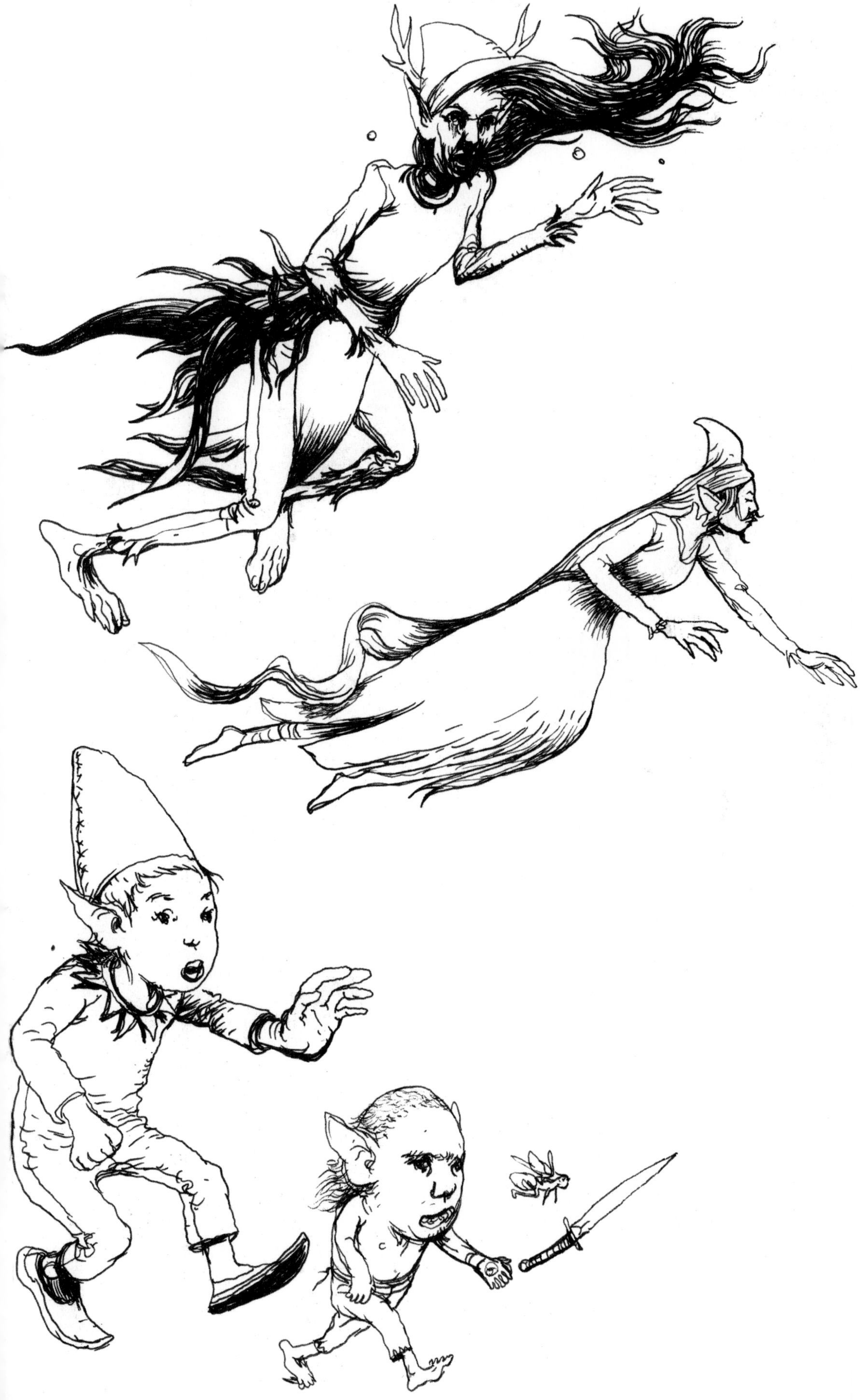

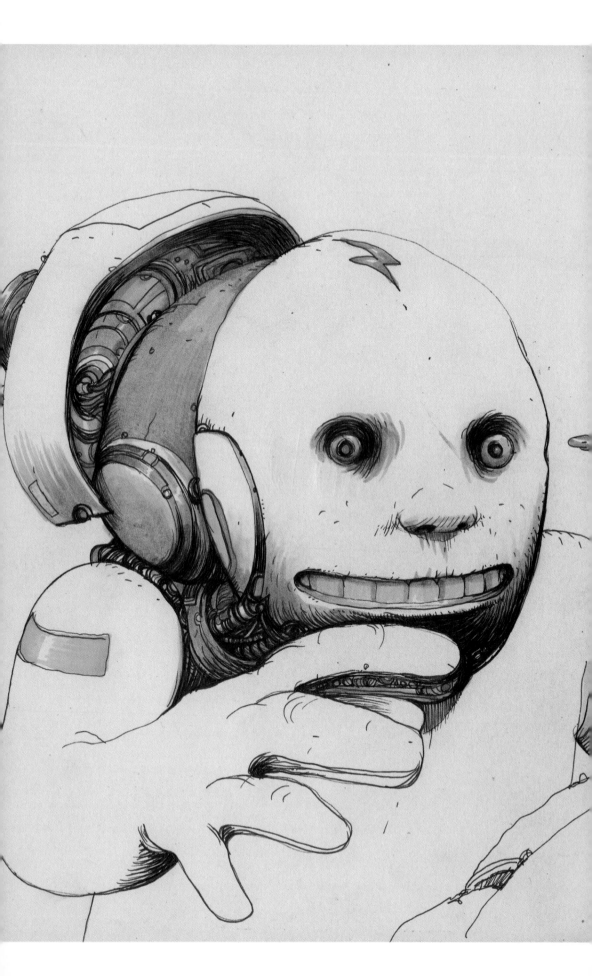

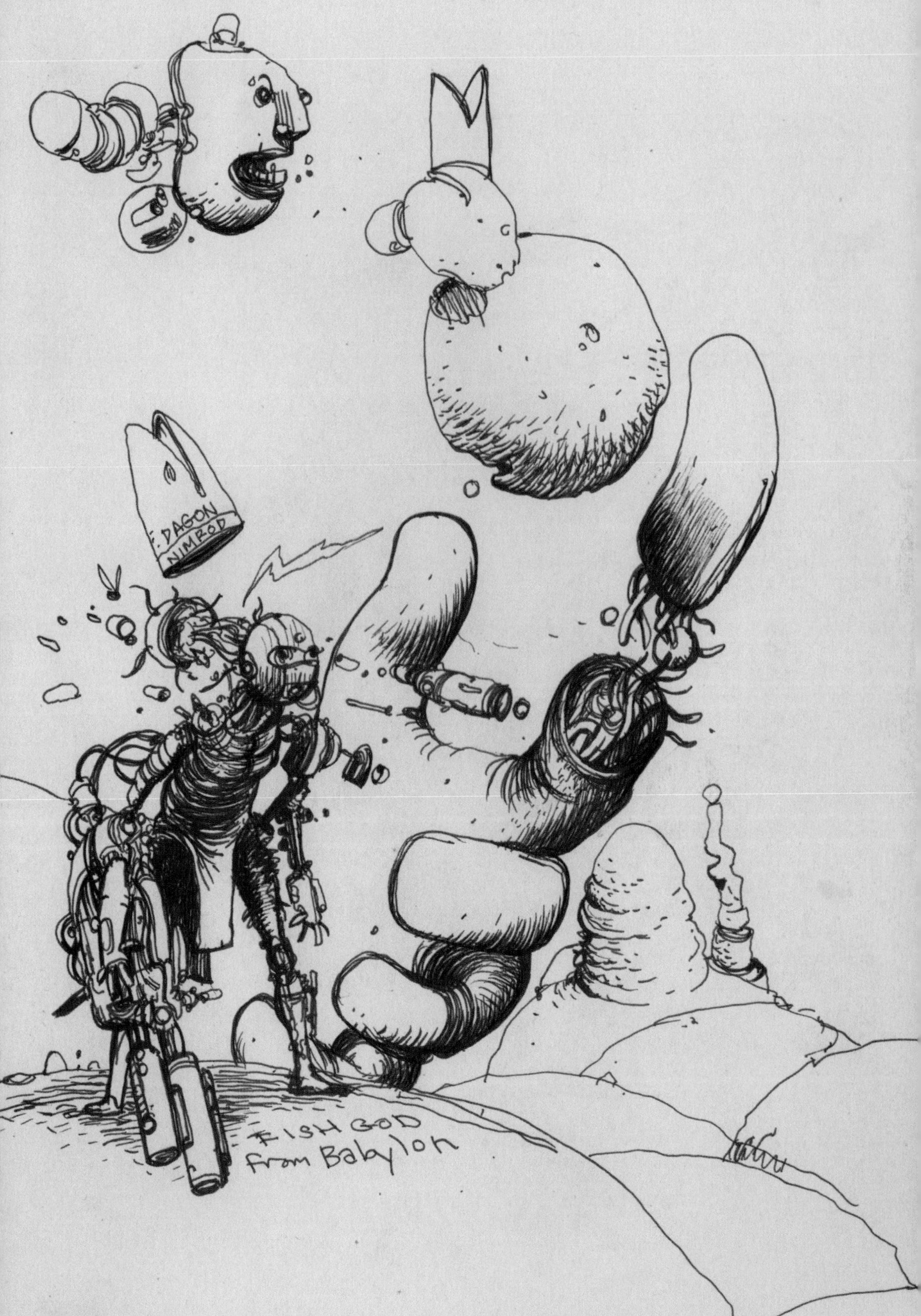
DAGON
NIMROD
FISH GOD
from Babylon

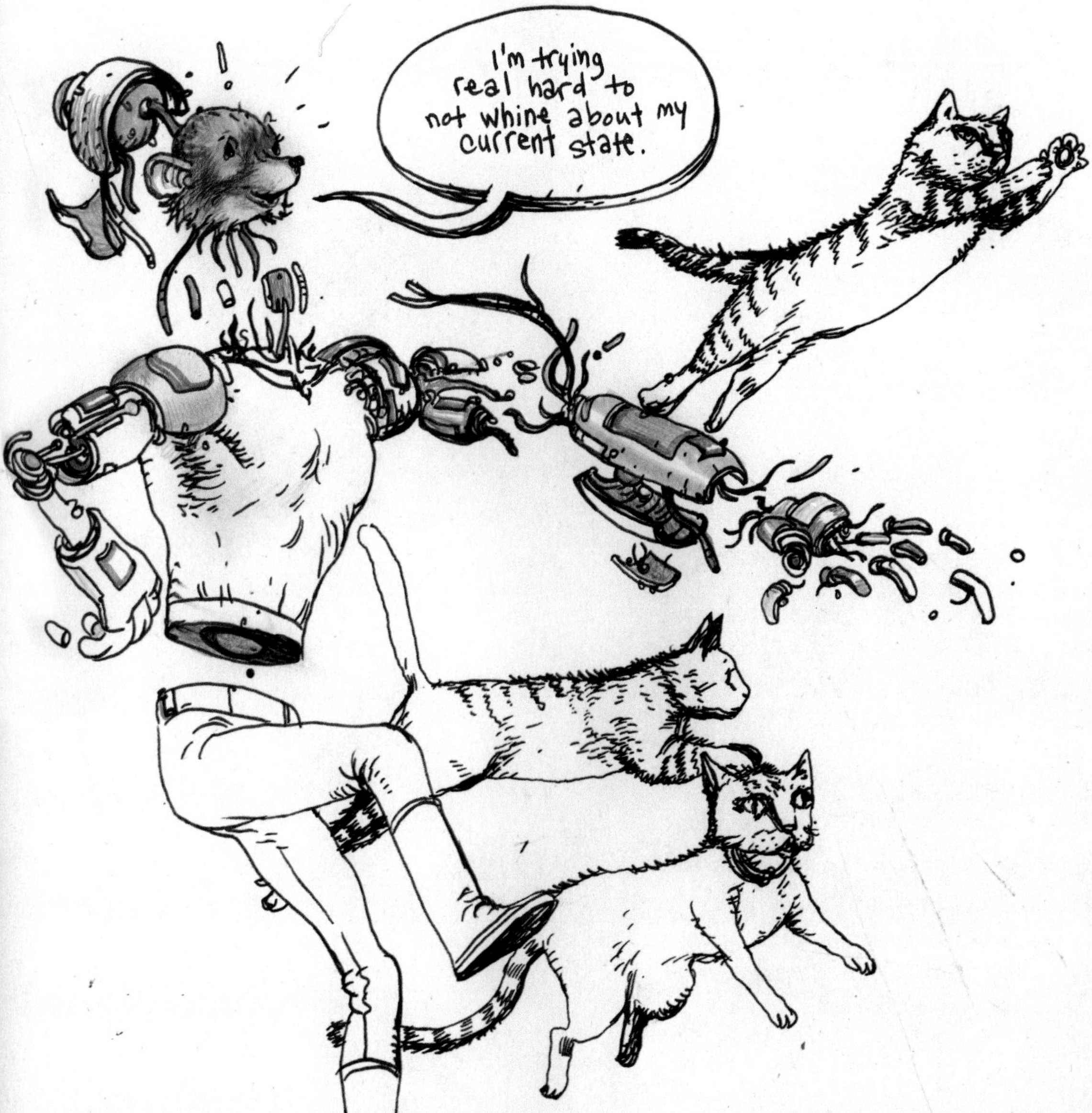
!
I'm trying real hard to not whine about my current state.

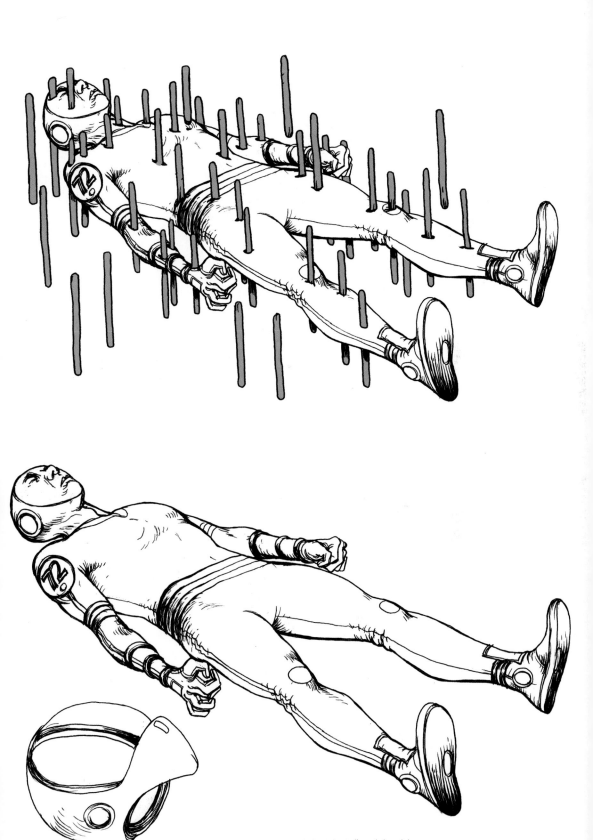

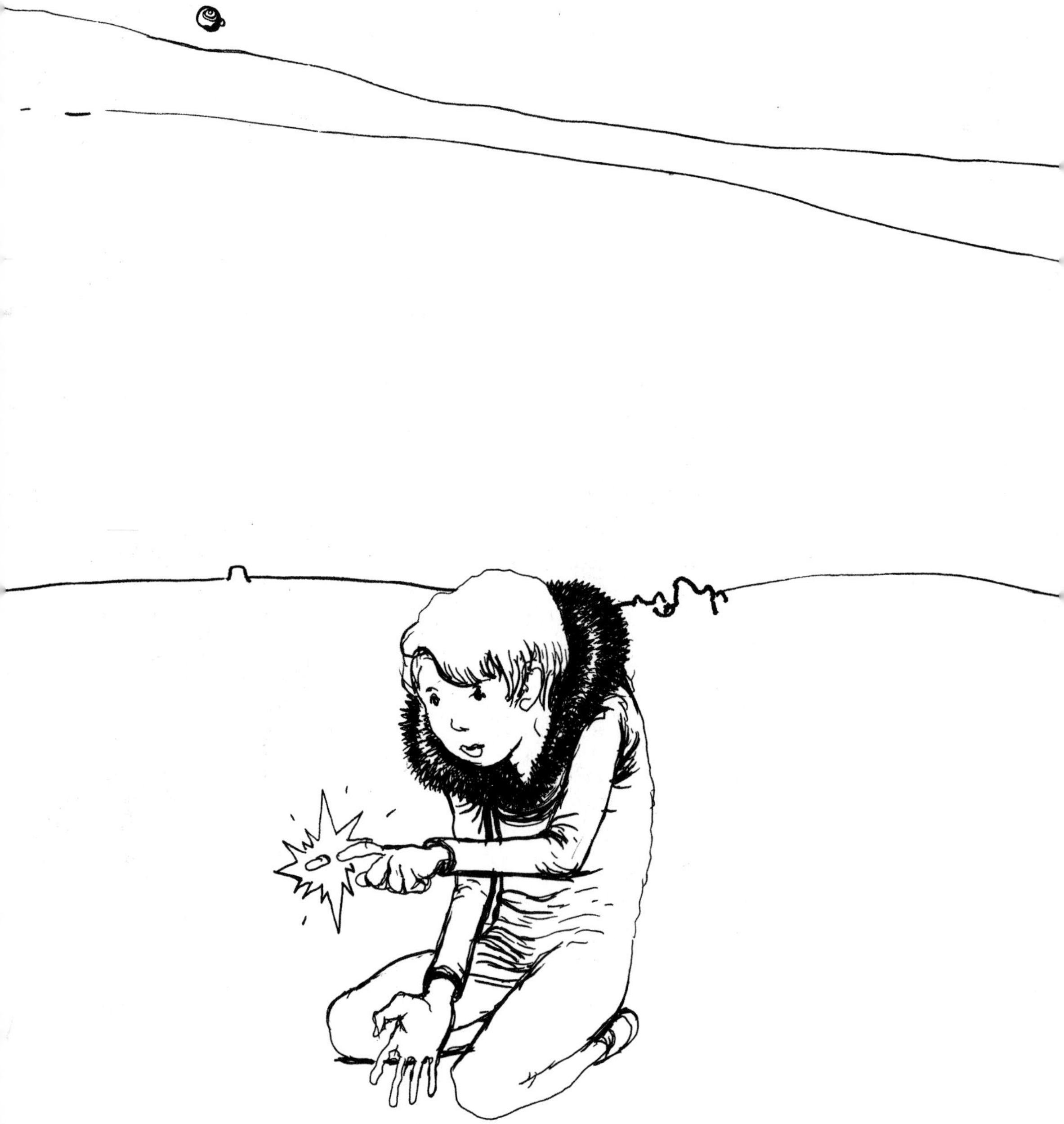

wisdom comes with the ability to be still.
just look and
just listen
no more is needed
to be still, look and listen
activates the non-conceptual intelligence
within you
let stillness direct your words and
actions.

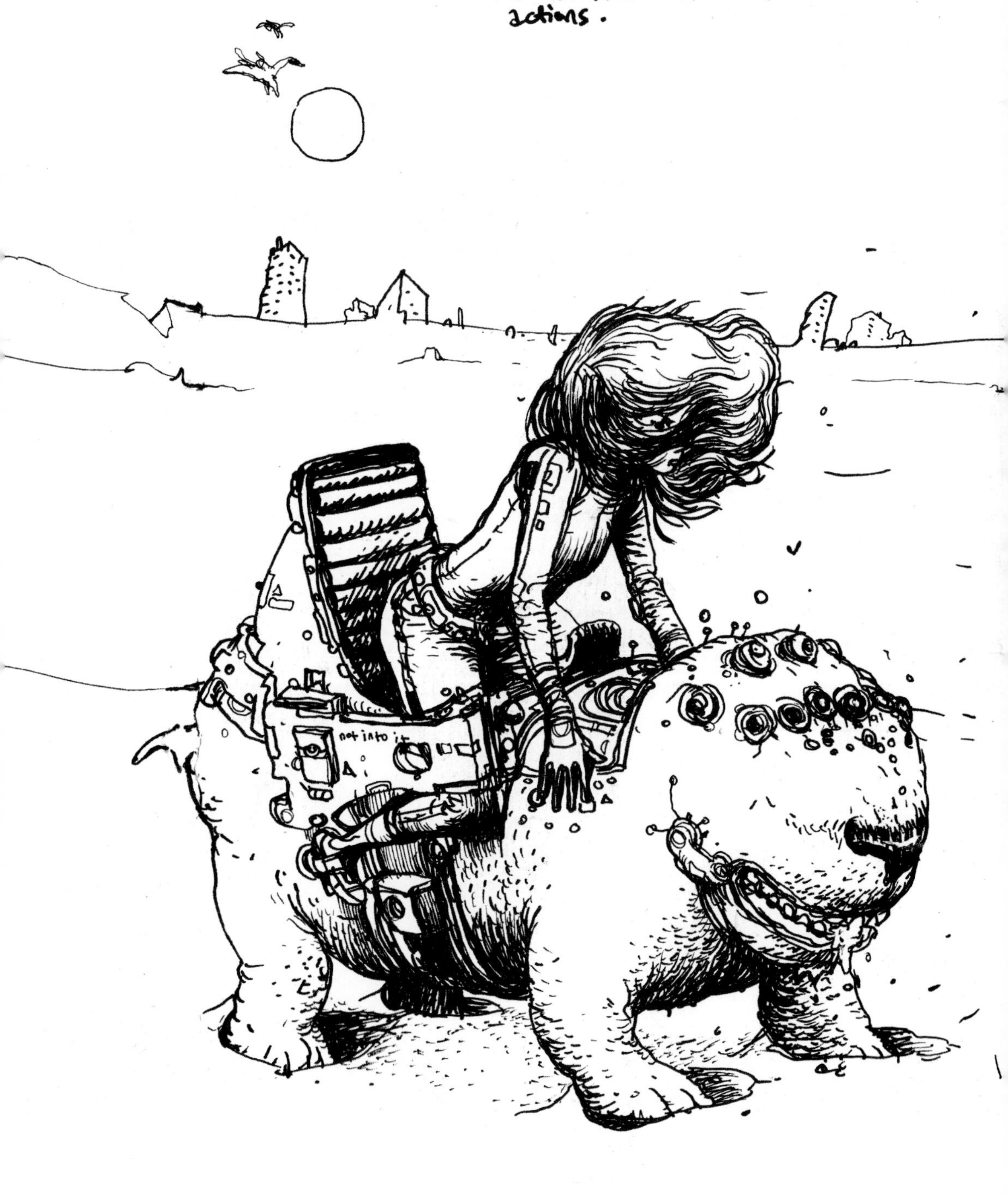
not into it

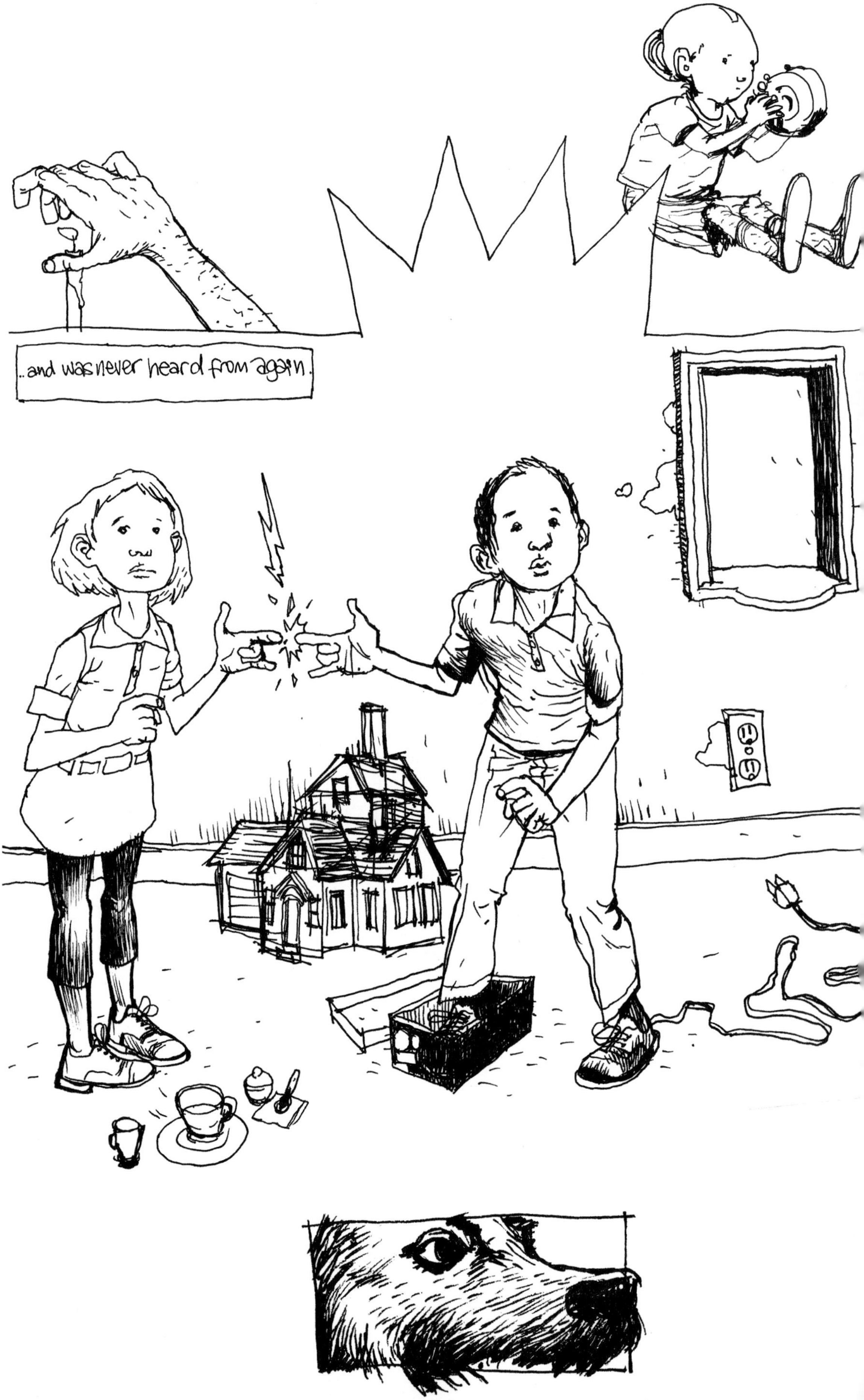
..and was never heard from again.

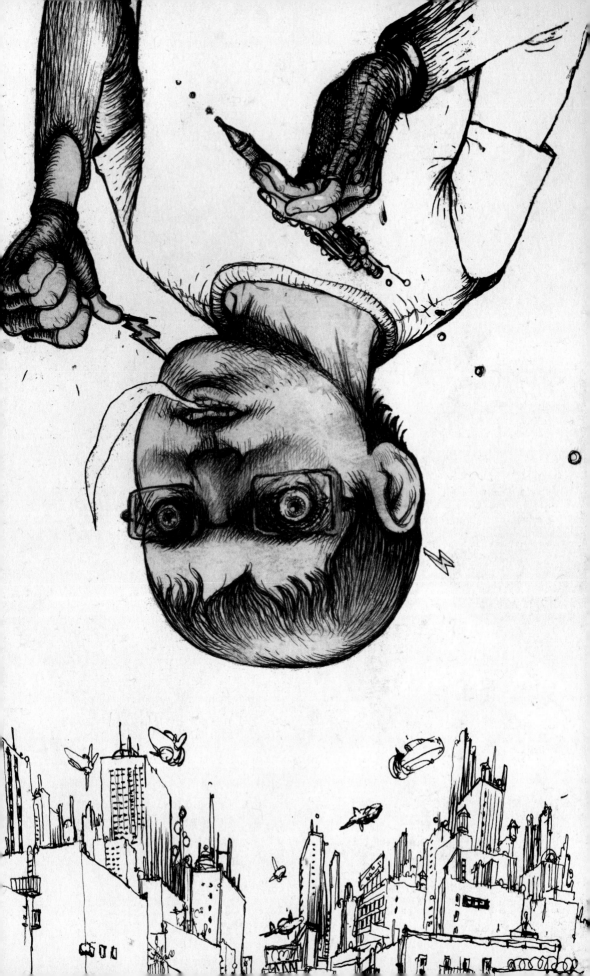

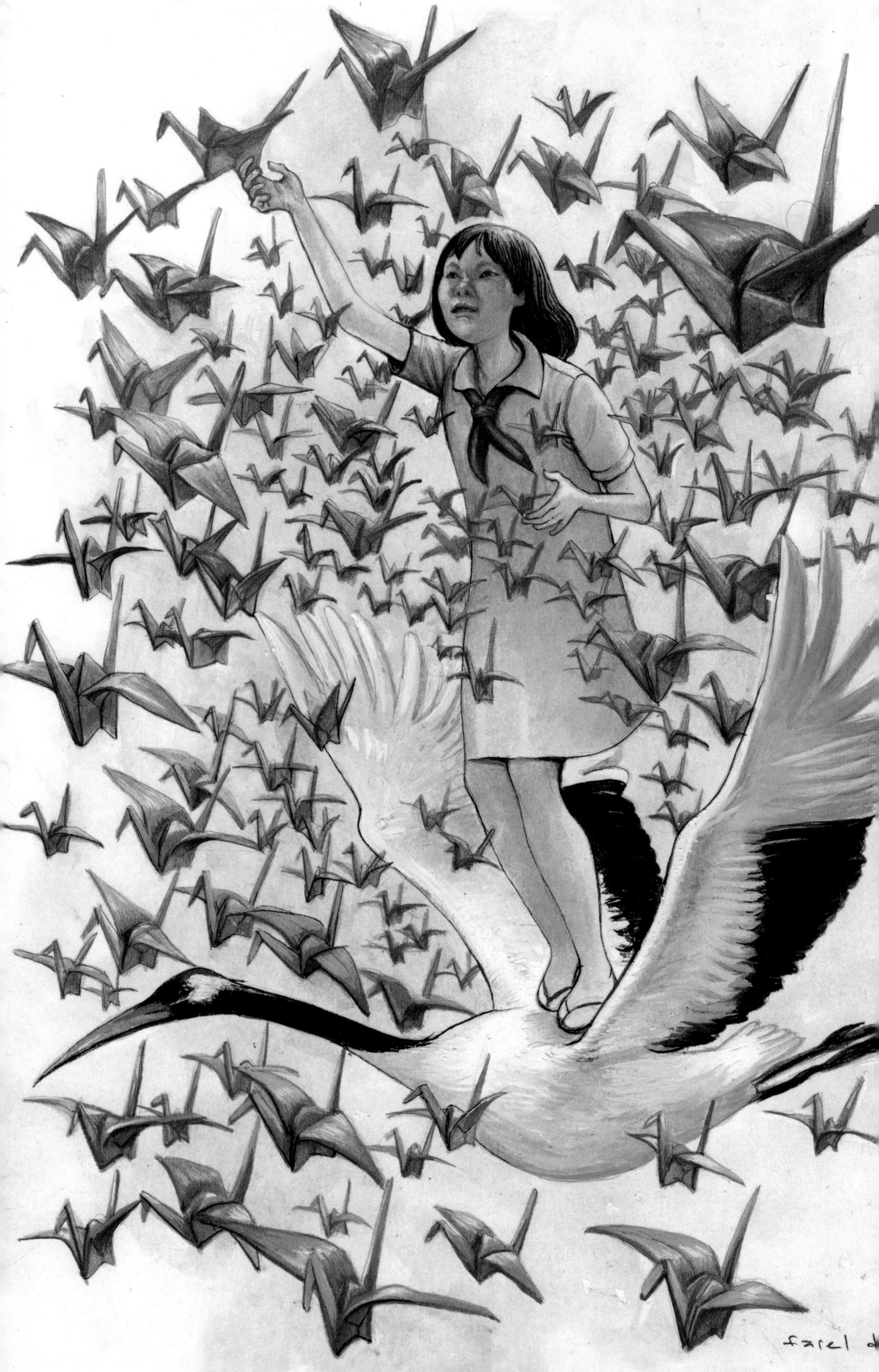

Sasaki Sadako folded one thousand origami cranes.

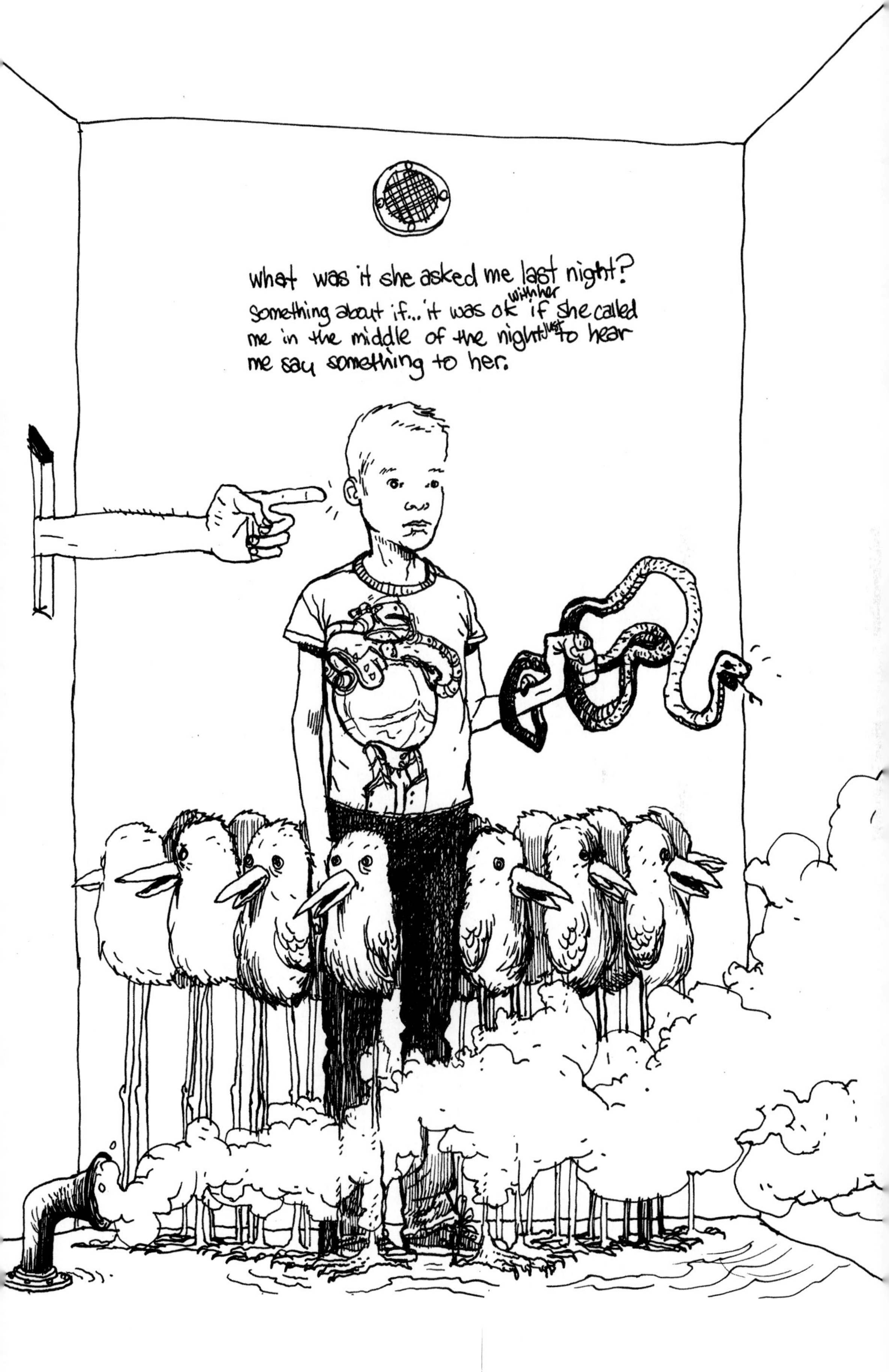
what was it she asked me last night? something about if... it was ok with her if she called me in the middle of the night just to hear me say something to her.

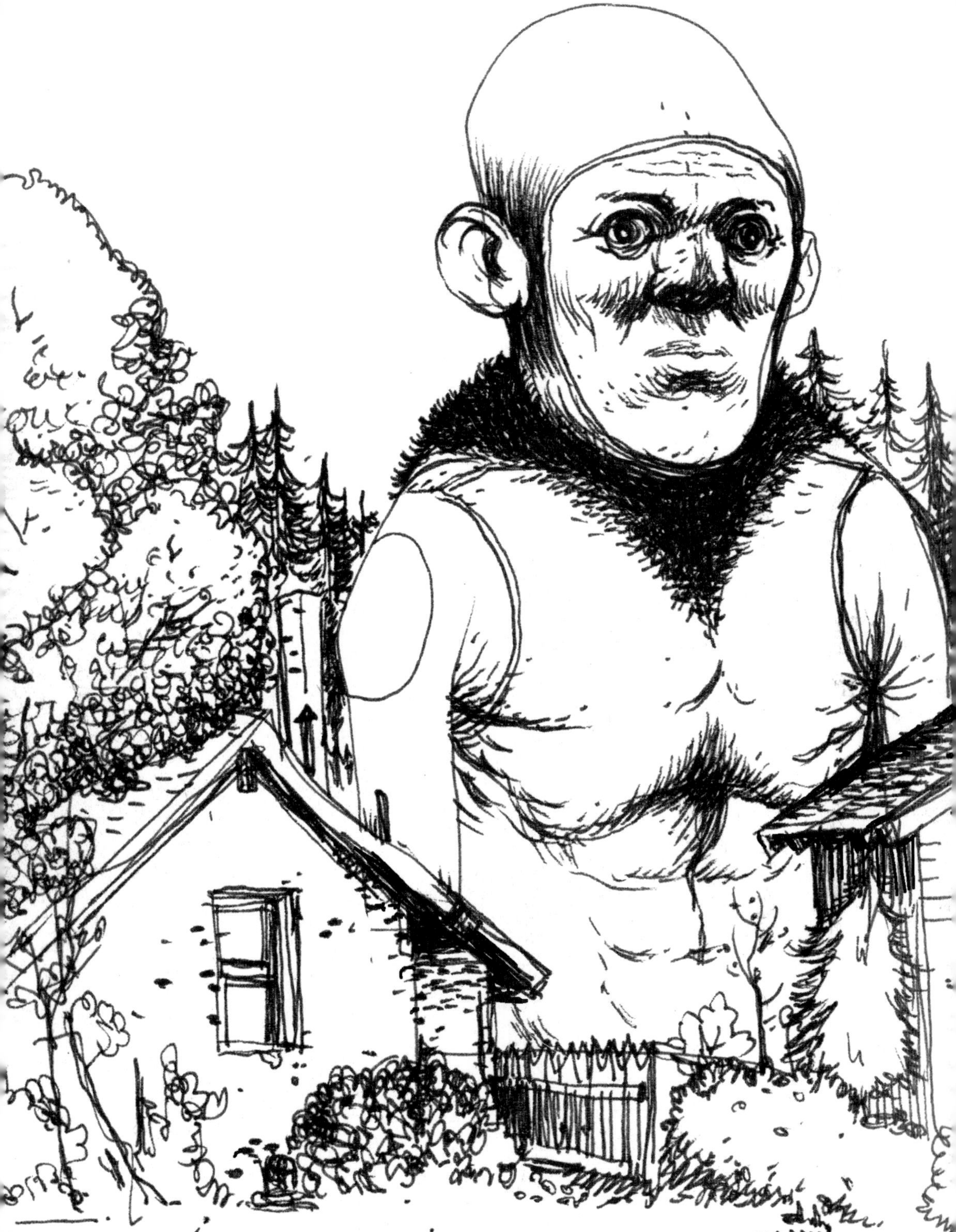

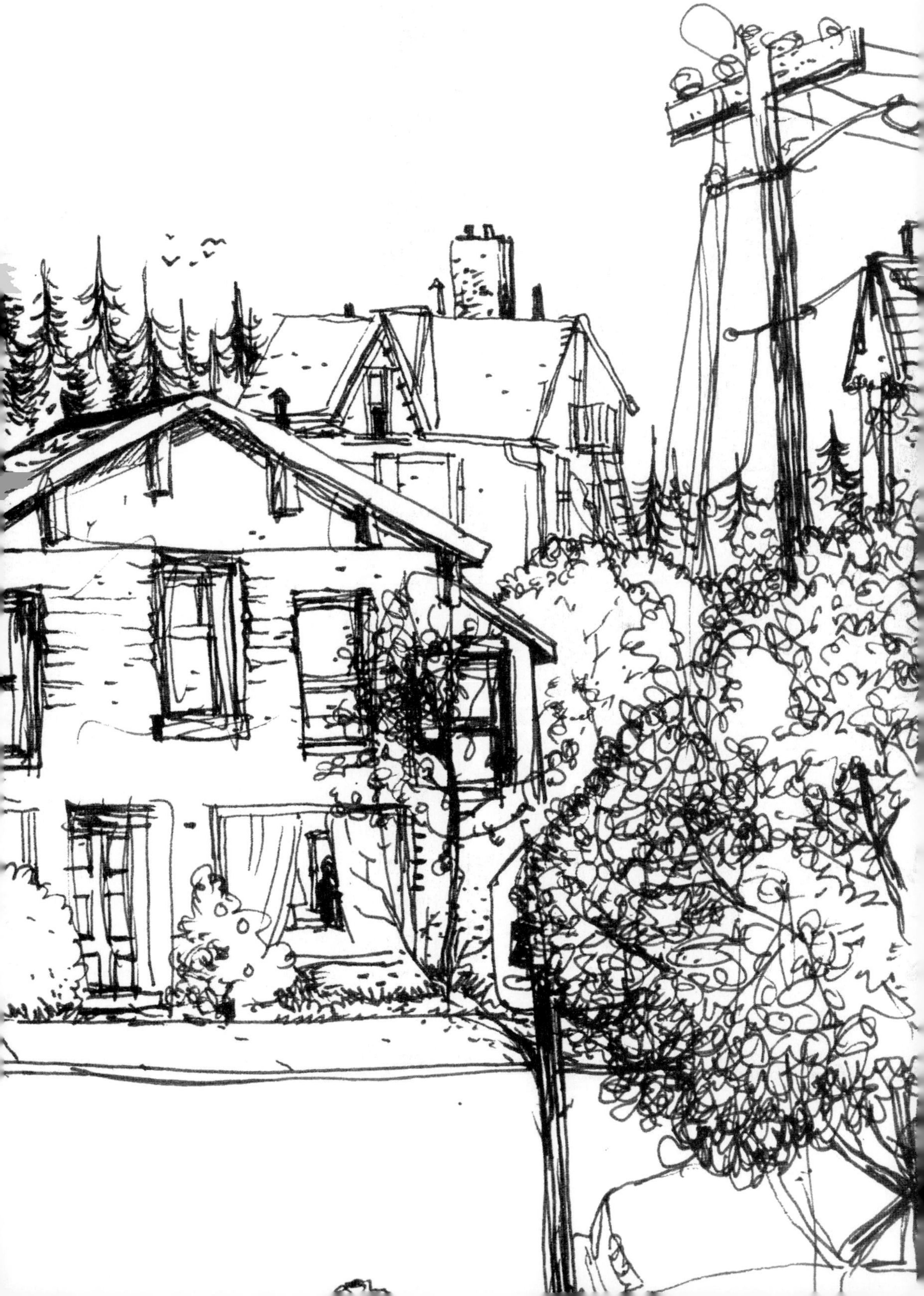

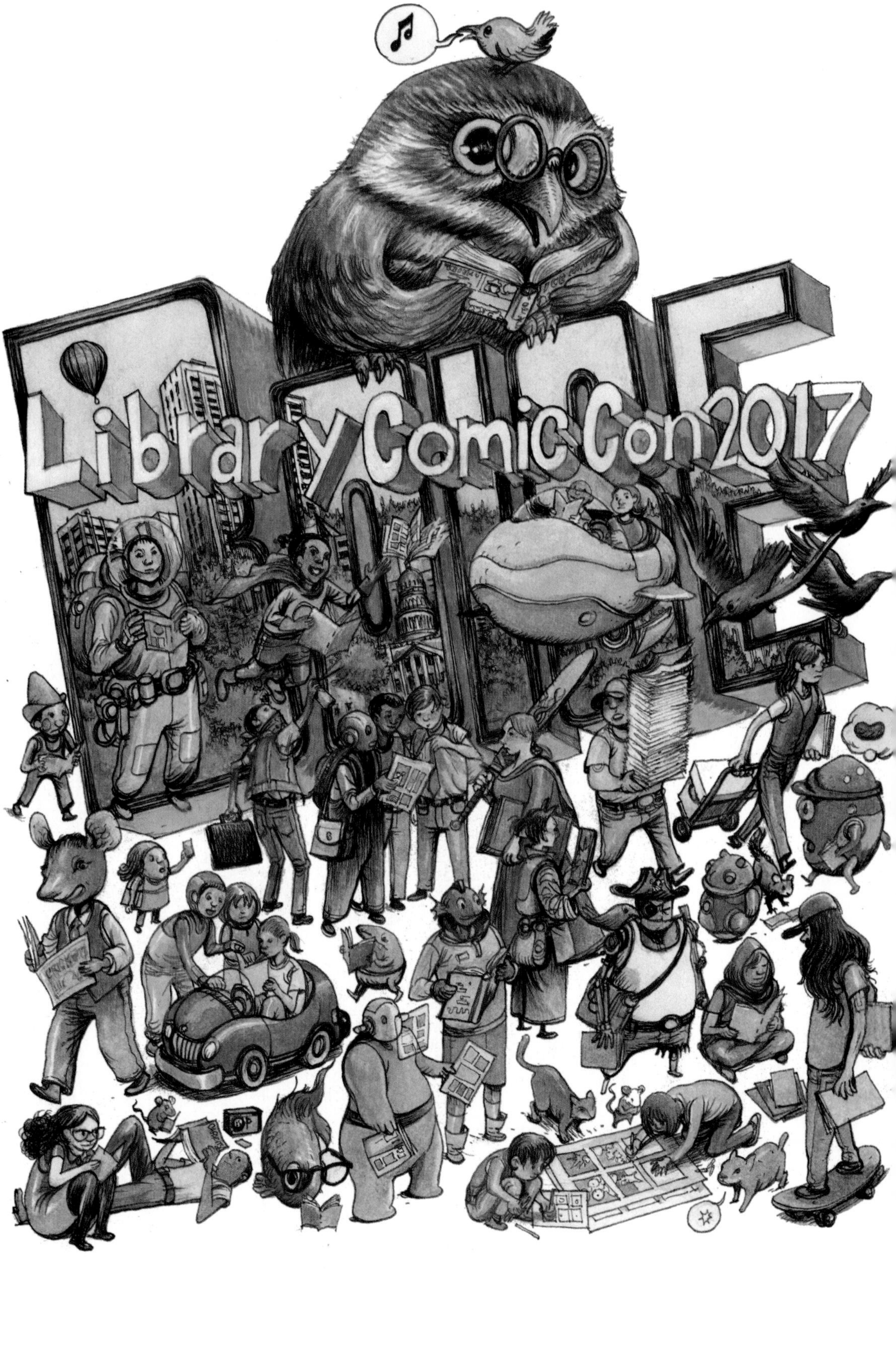
Library Comic Con 2017

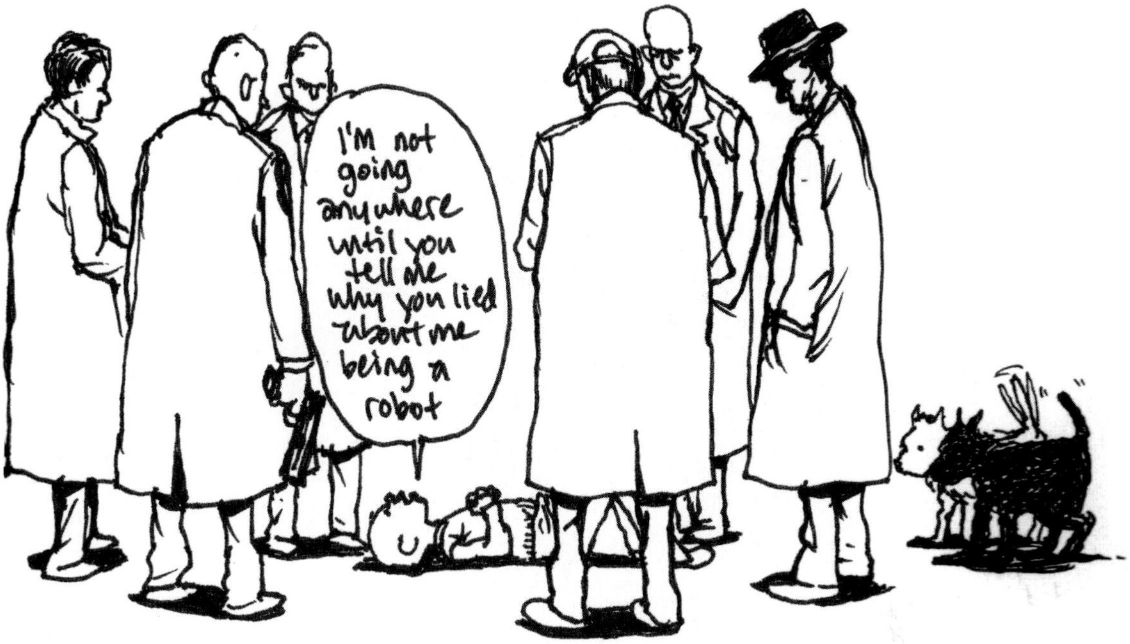
I'm not going anywhere until you tell me why you lied about me being a robot

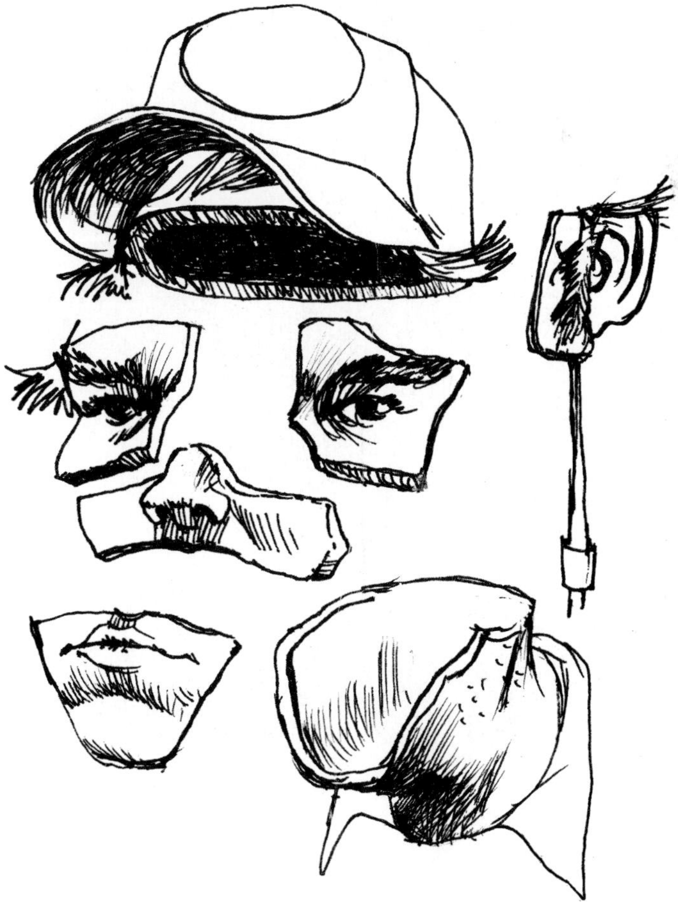

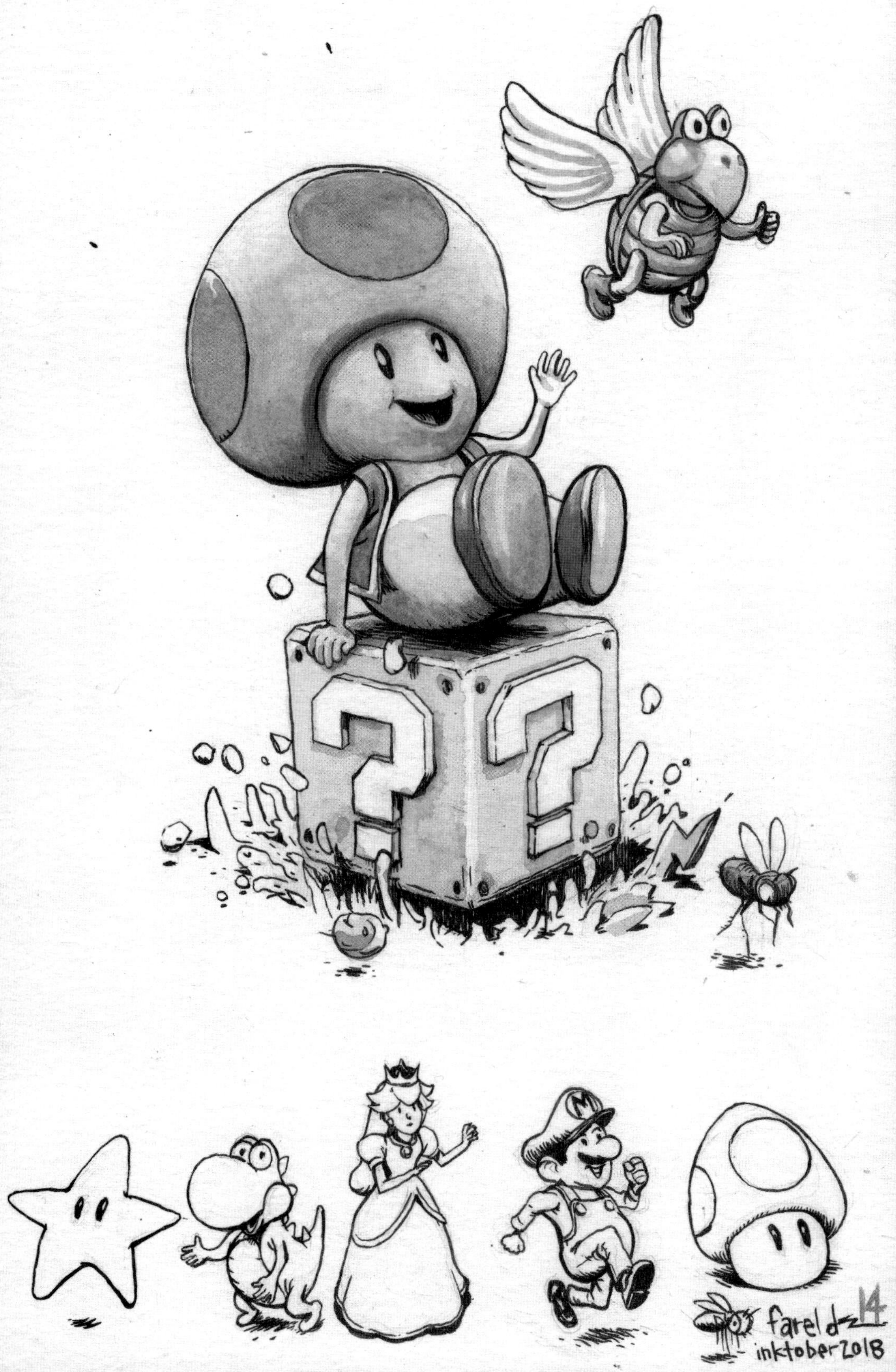

M
farel dz 14
inktober 2018

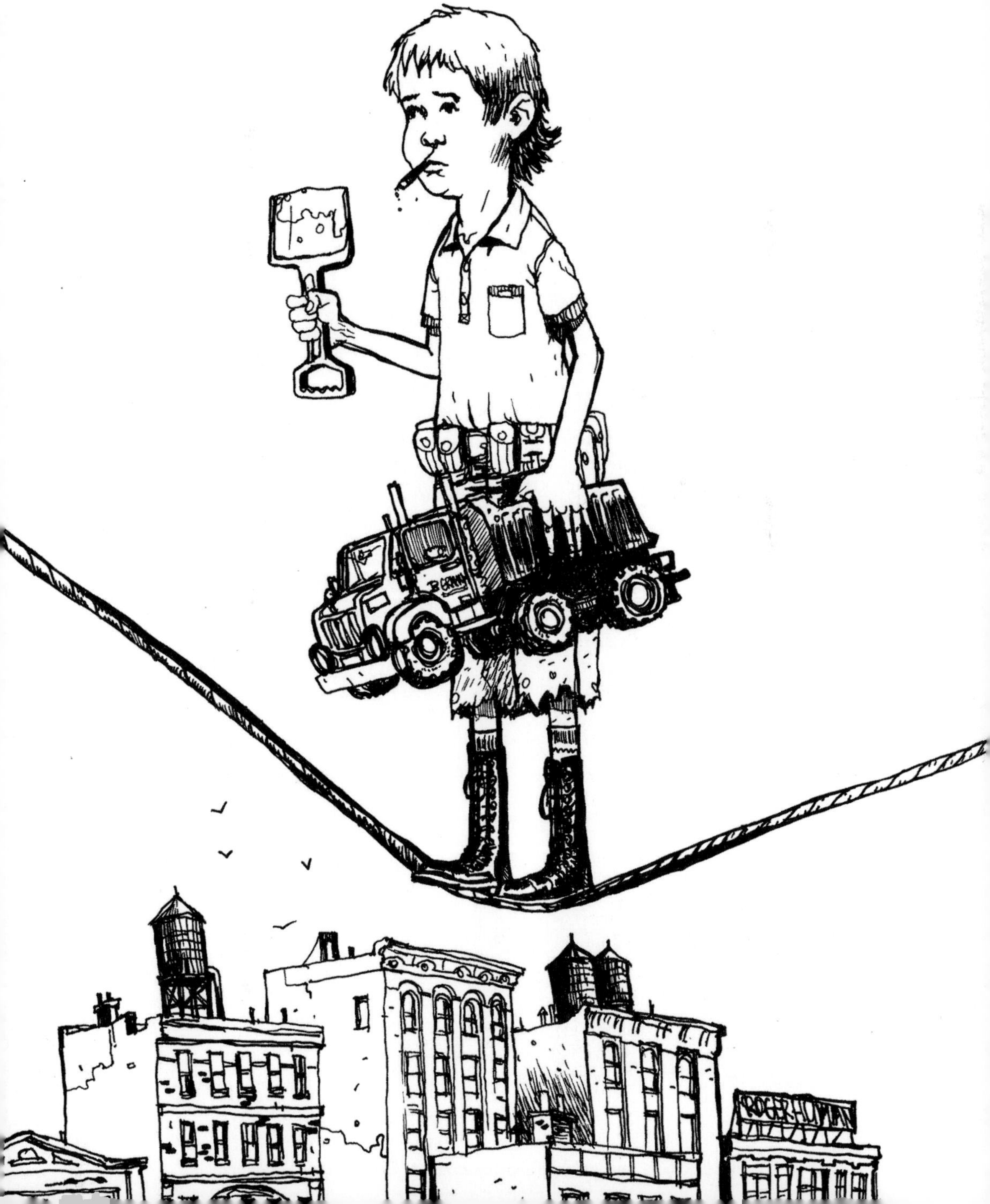

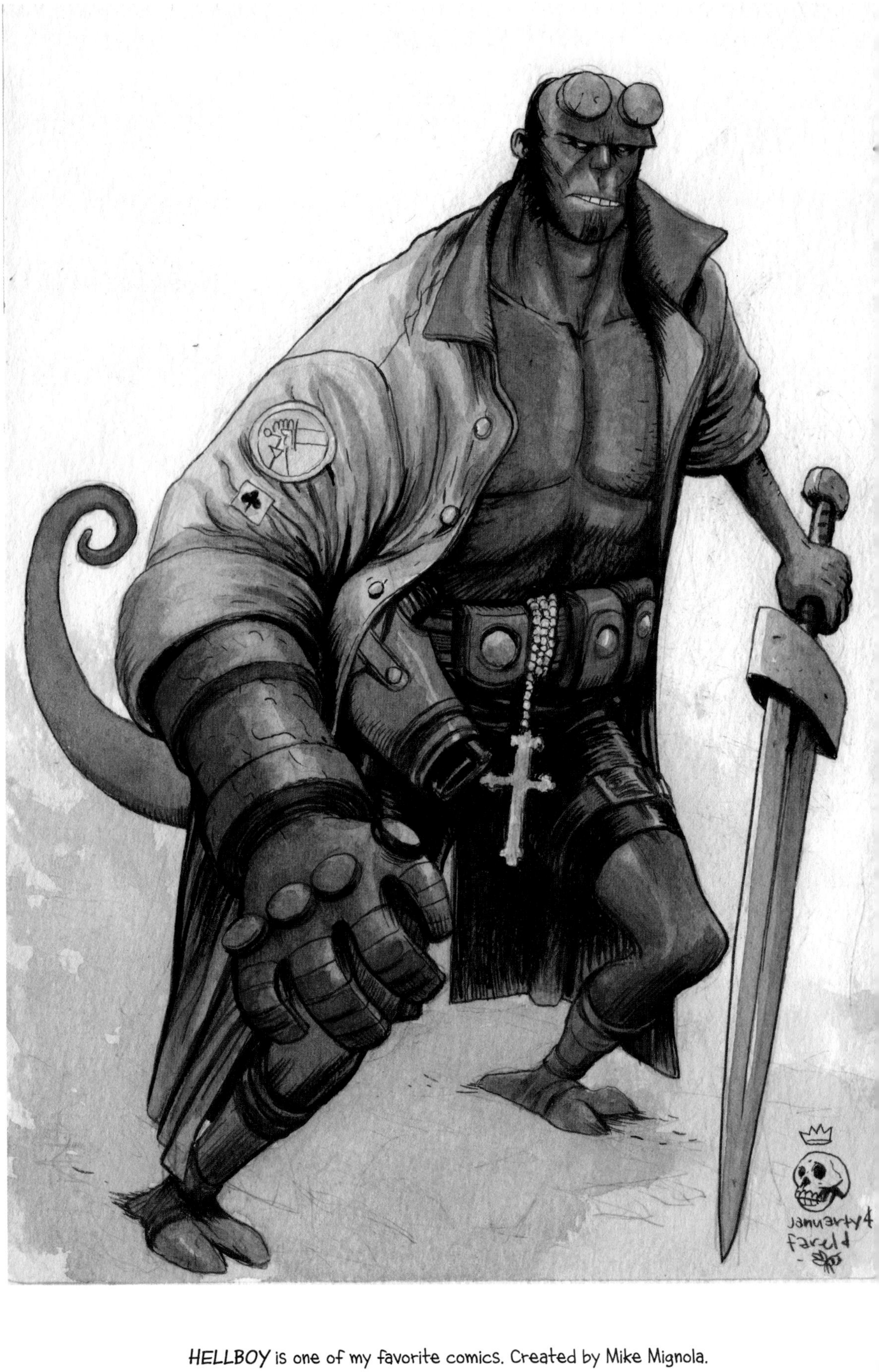

HELLBOY is one of my favorite comics. Created by Mike Mignola.

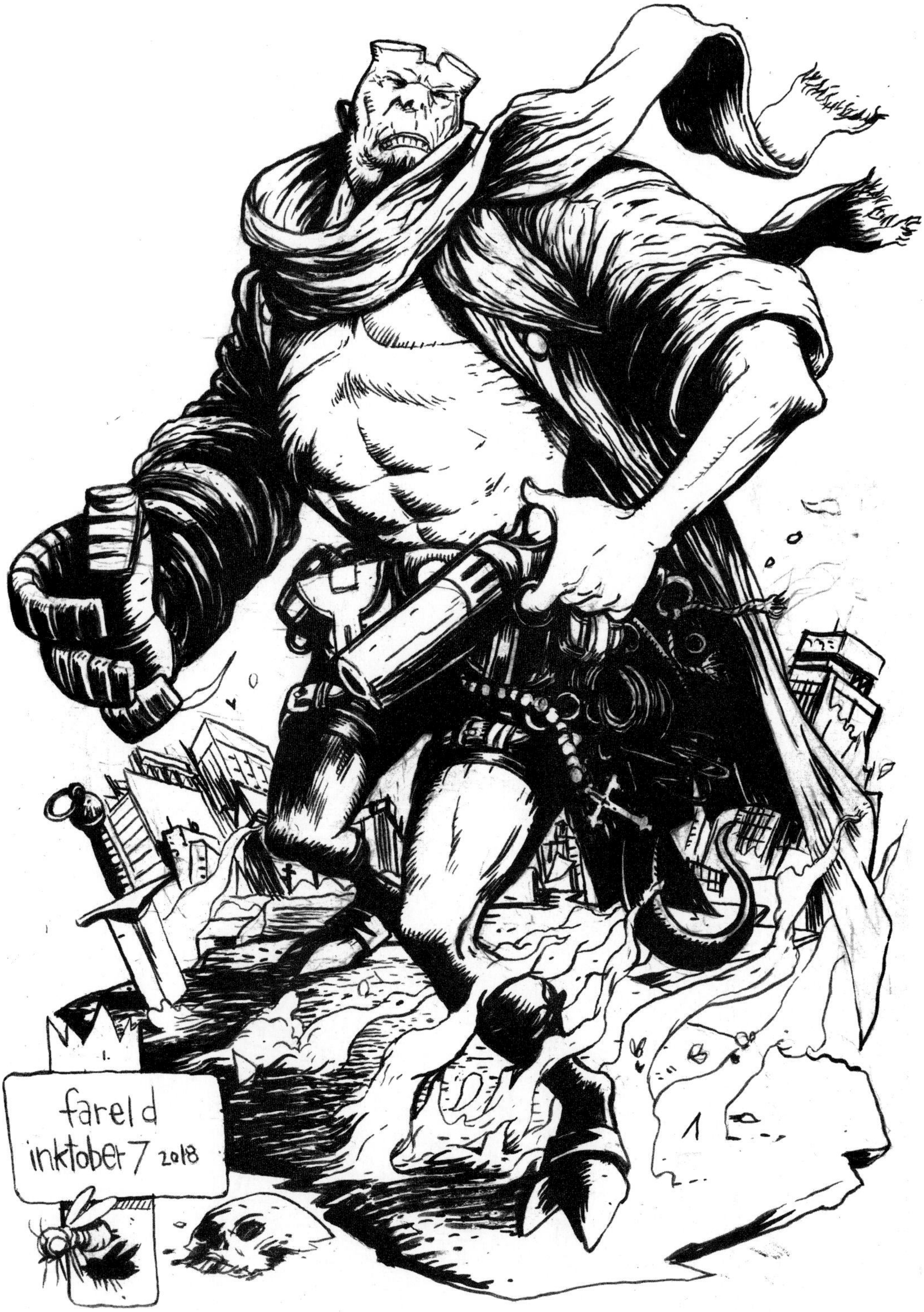
fareld
inktober 7 2018

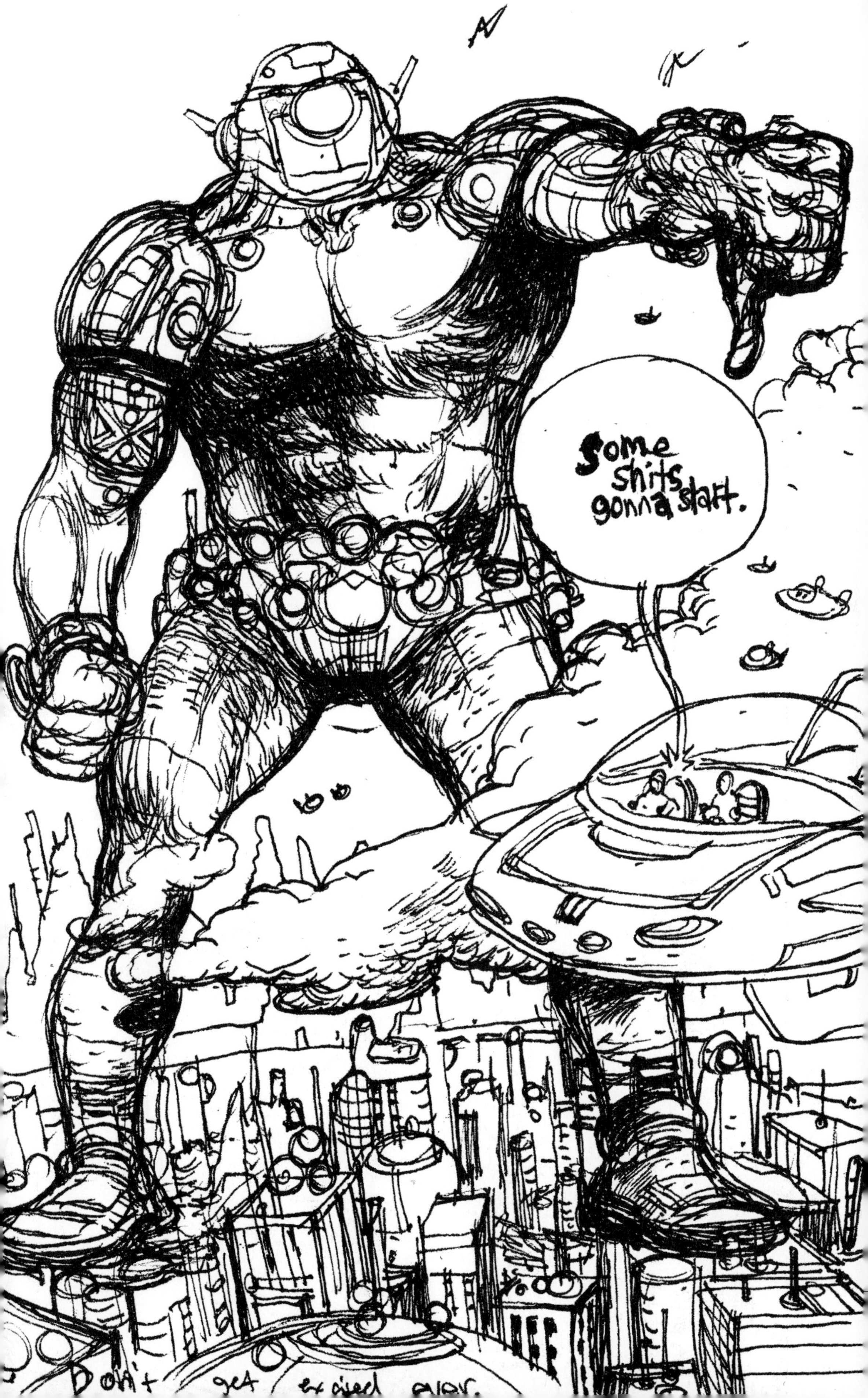
Some shits gonna start.
Don't get excited ever.

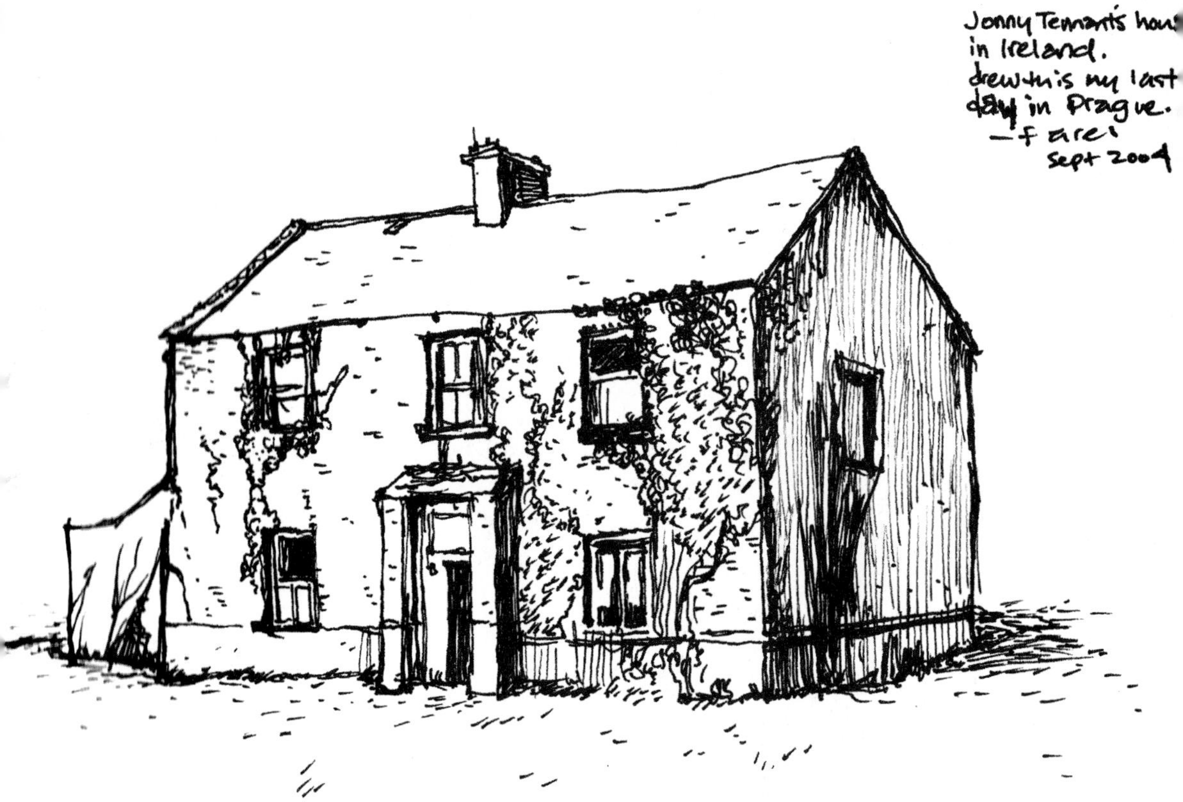
Jonny Tennant's hous
in Ireland.
drew this my last
day in Prague.
—Farel
Sept 2004

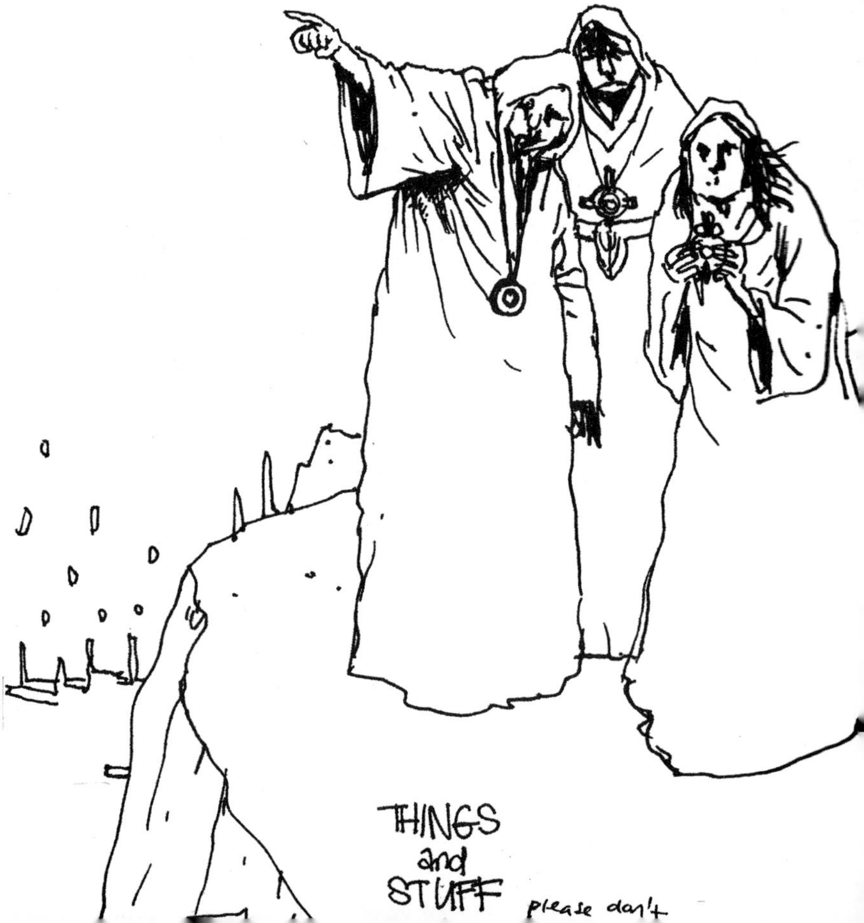
THINGS
and
STUFF
please don't

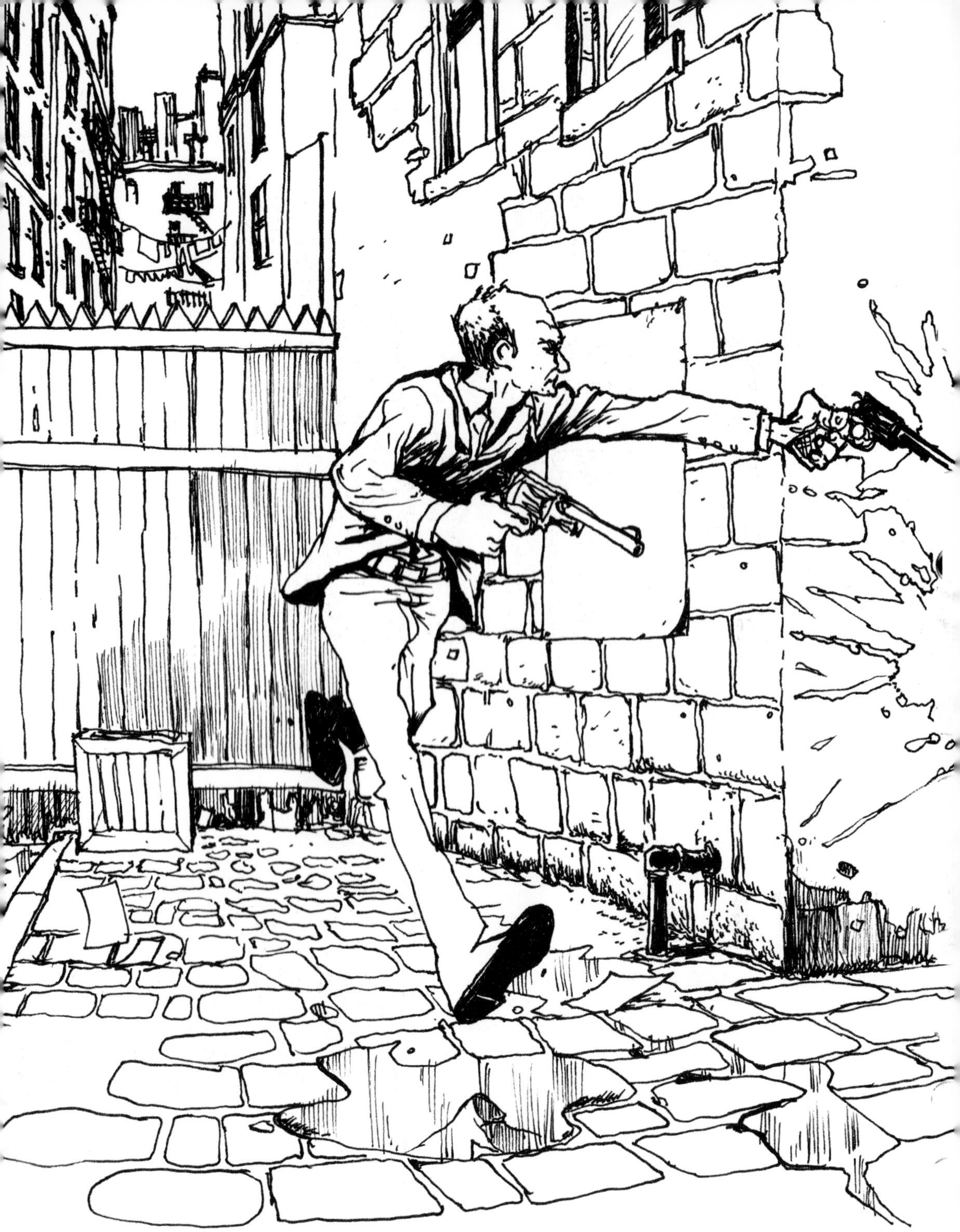

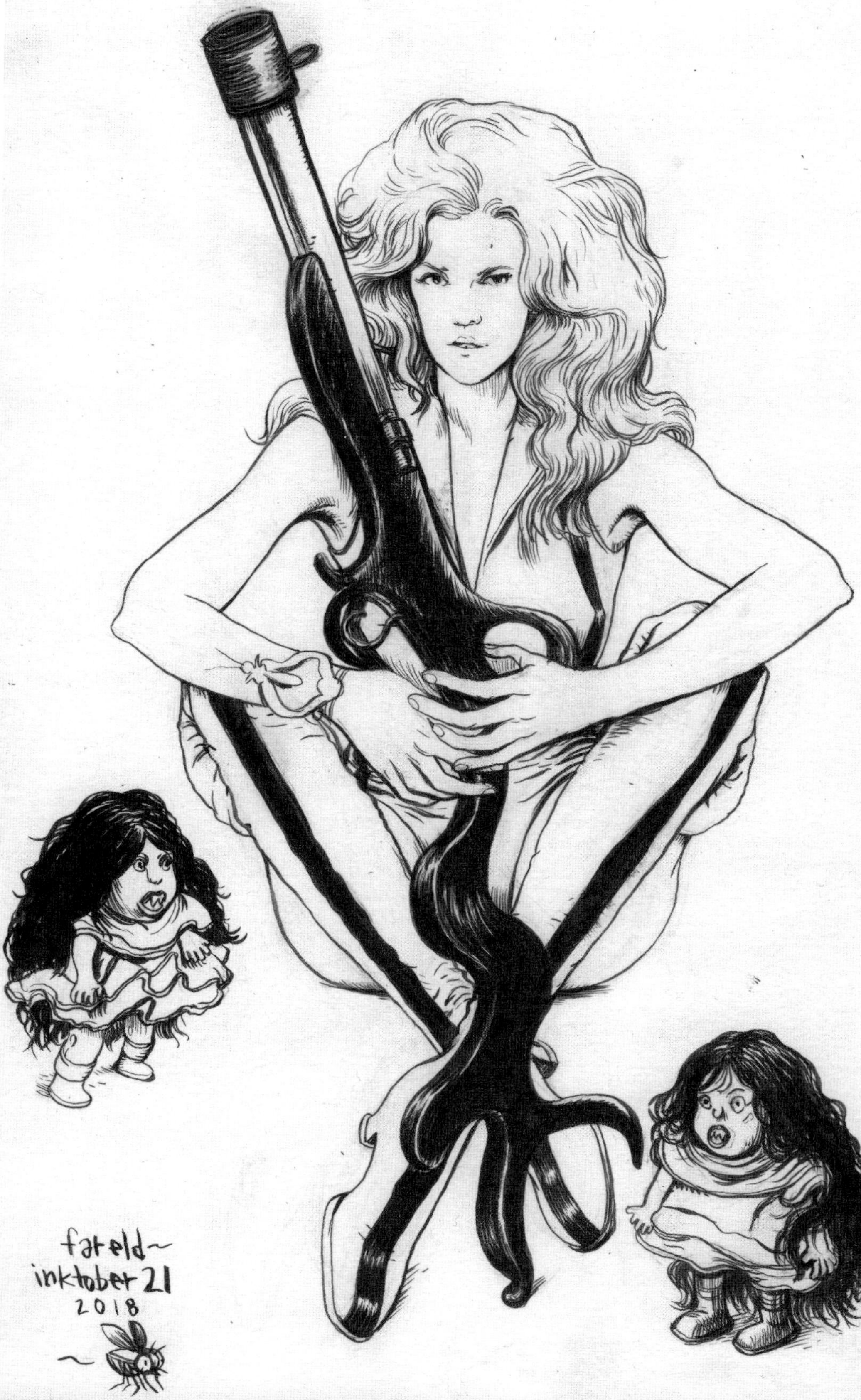
fareld~
inktober 21
2018

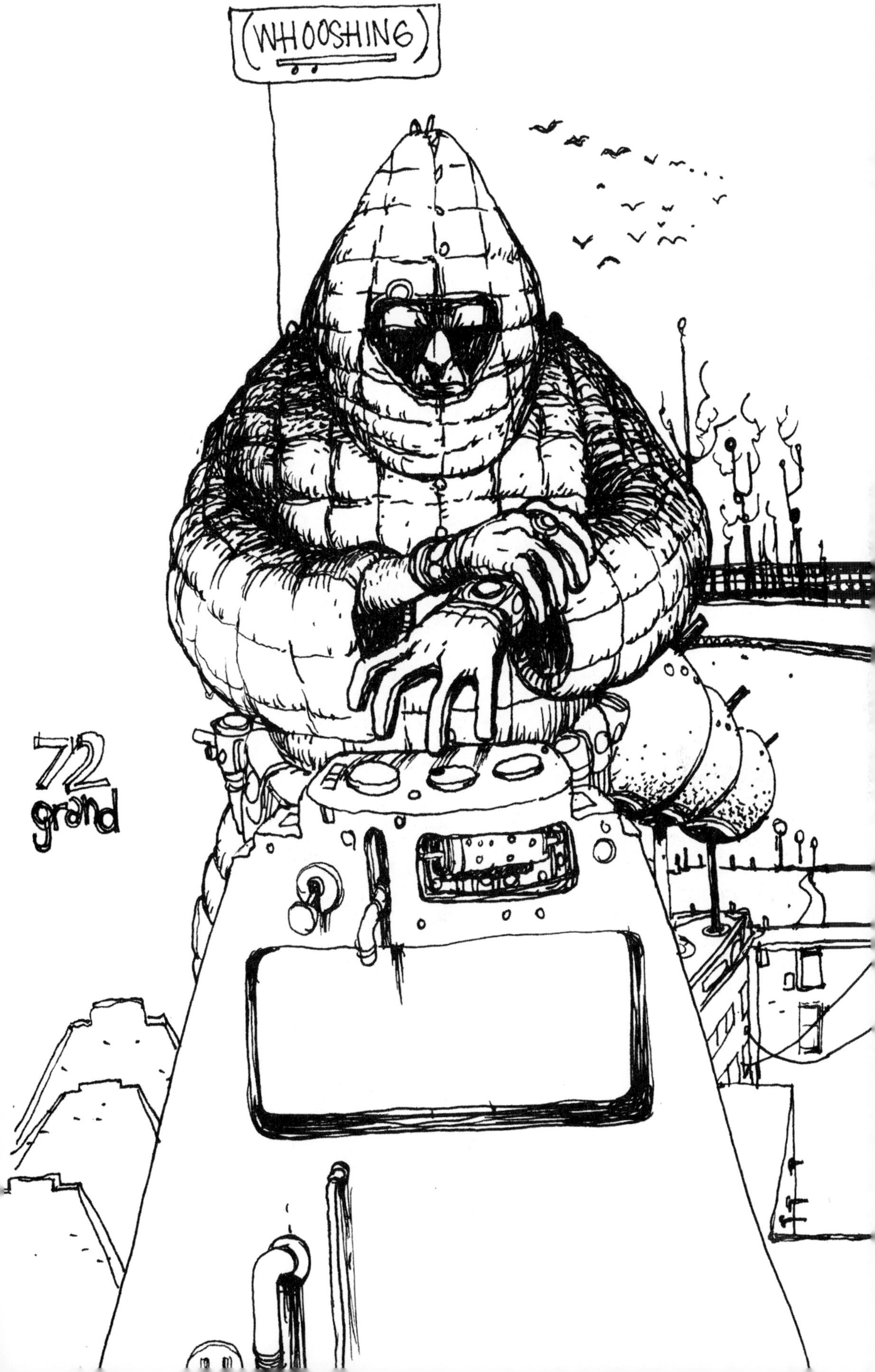

(WHOOSHING)
72
grand

Flawed Wetware

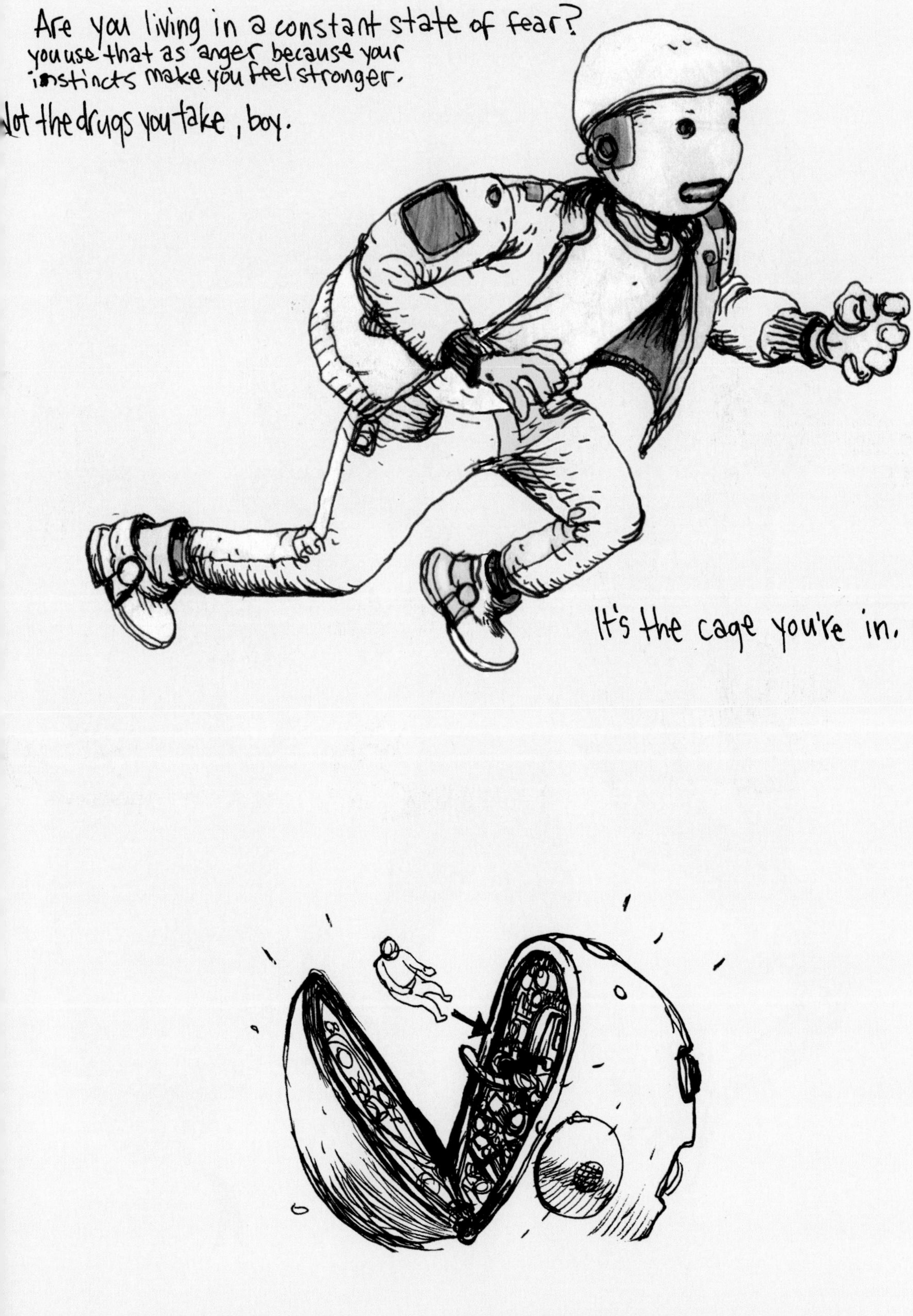
Are you living in a constant state of fear?
you use that as anger because your instincts make you feel stronger.
Not the drugs you take, boy.
It's the cage you're in.

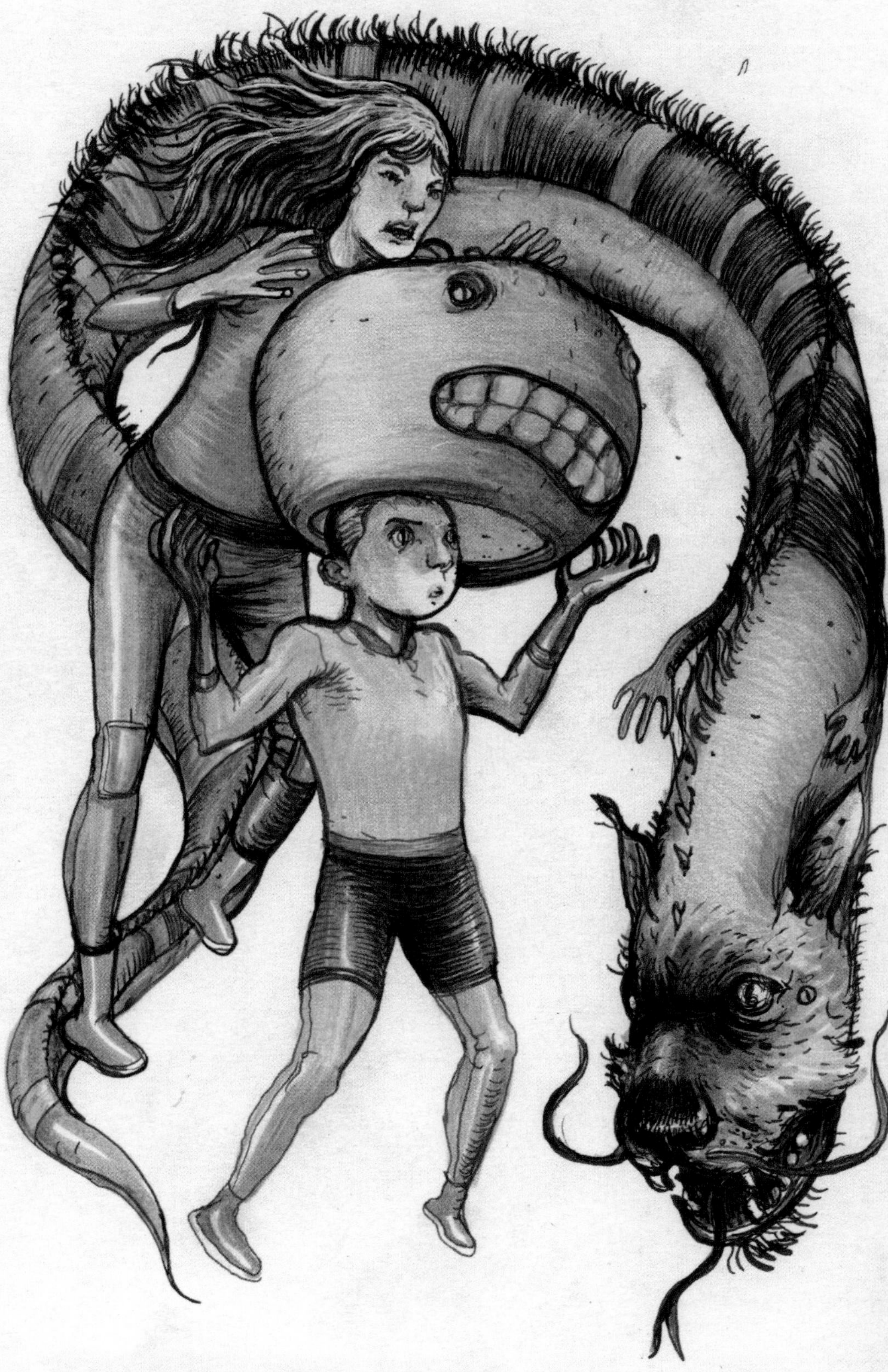

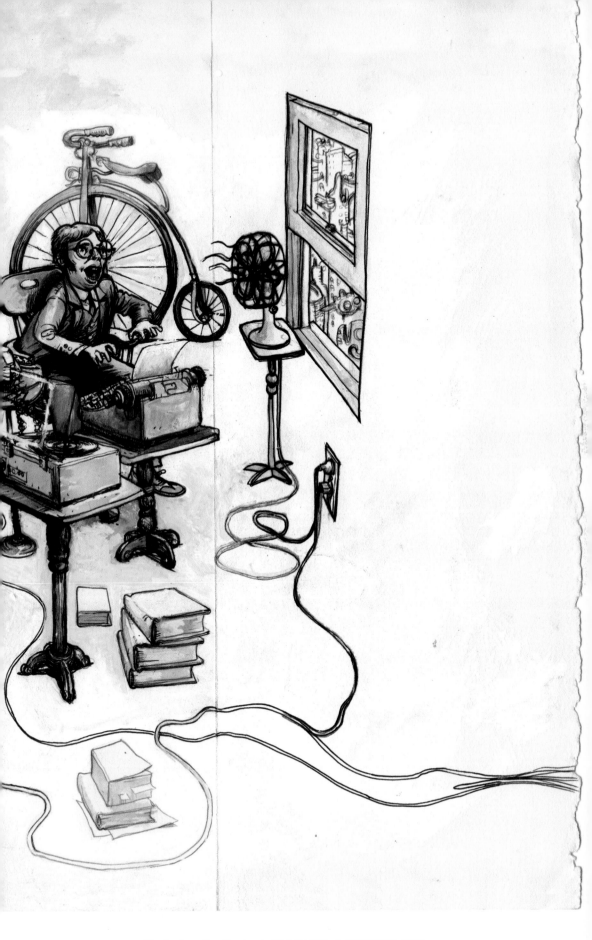

Illustration for the book *DIY MAGIC: A STRANGE AND WHIMSICAL GUIDE TO CREATIVITY* by Anthony Alvarado.

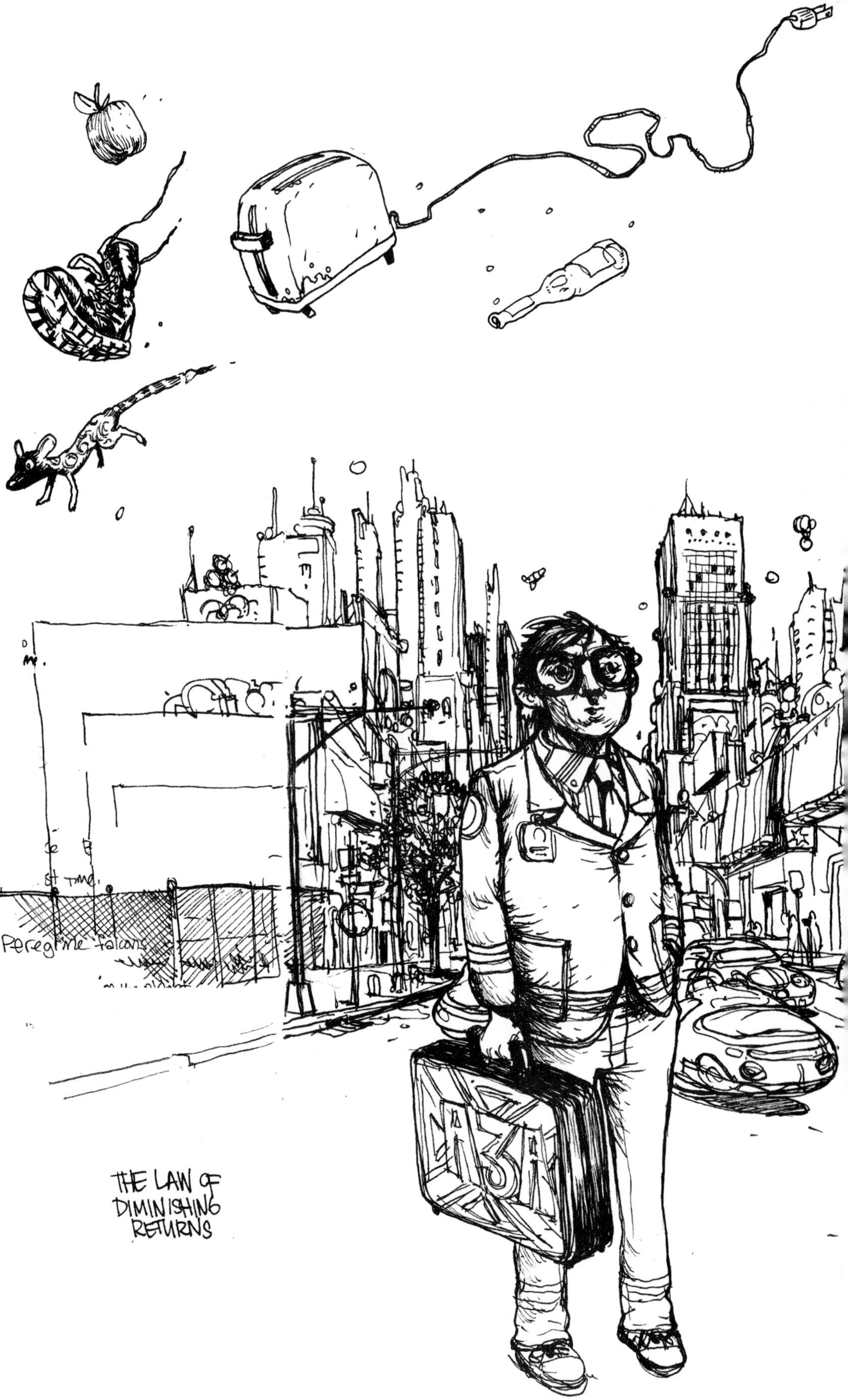
out Peregrine falcons
THE LAW OF
DIMINISHING
RETURNS

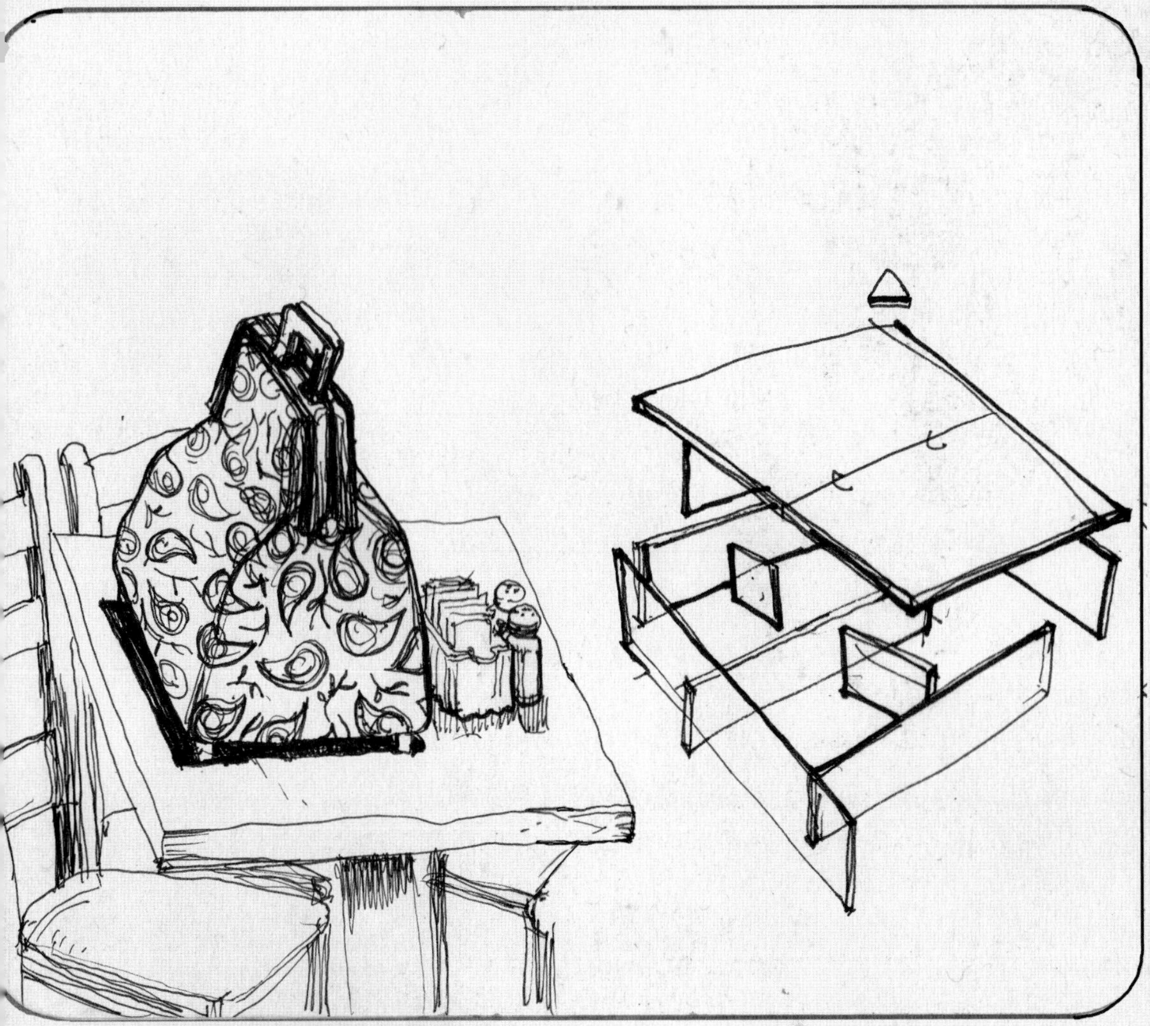

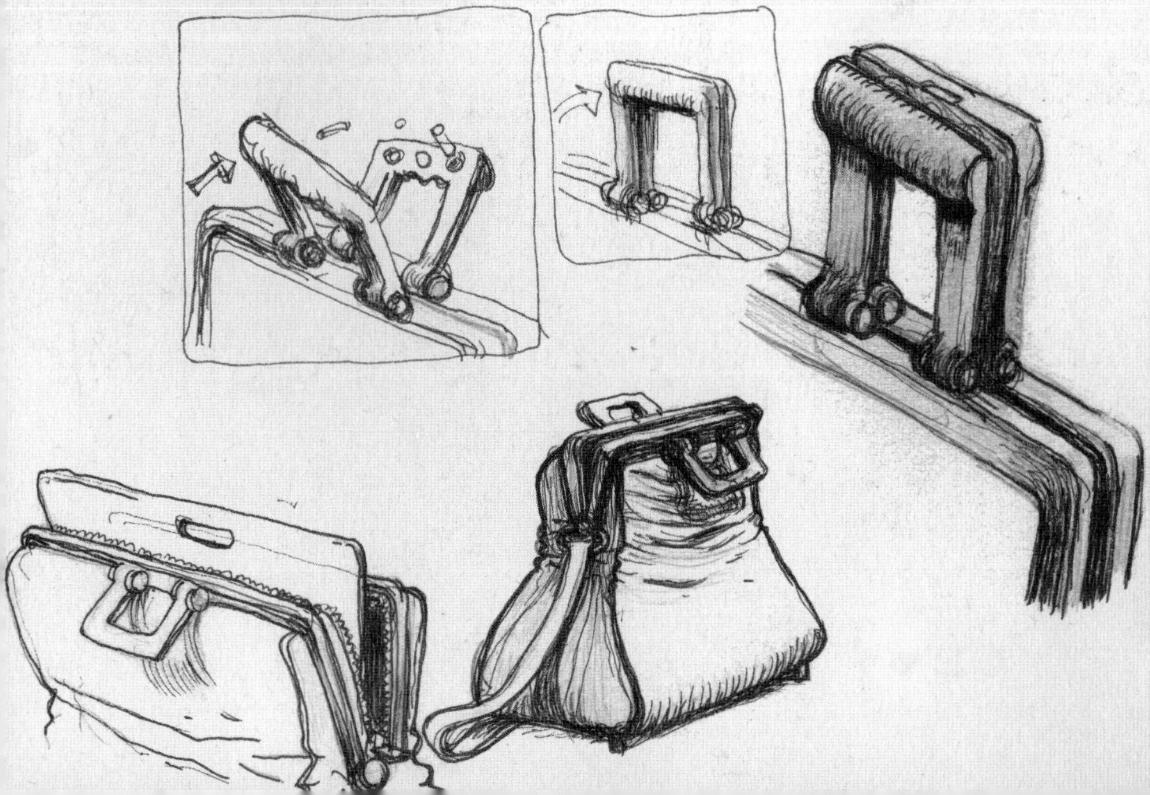

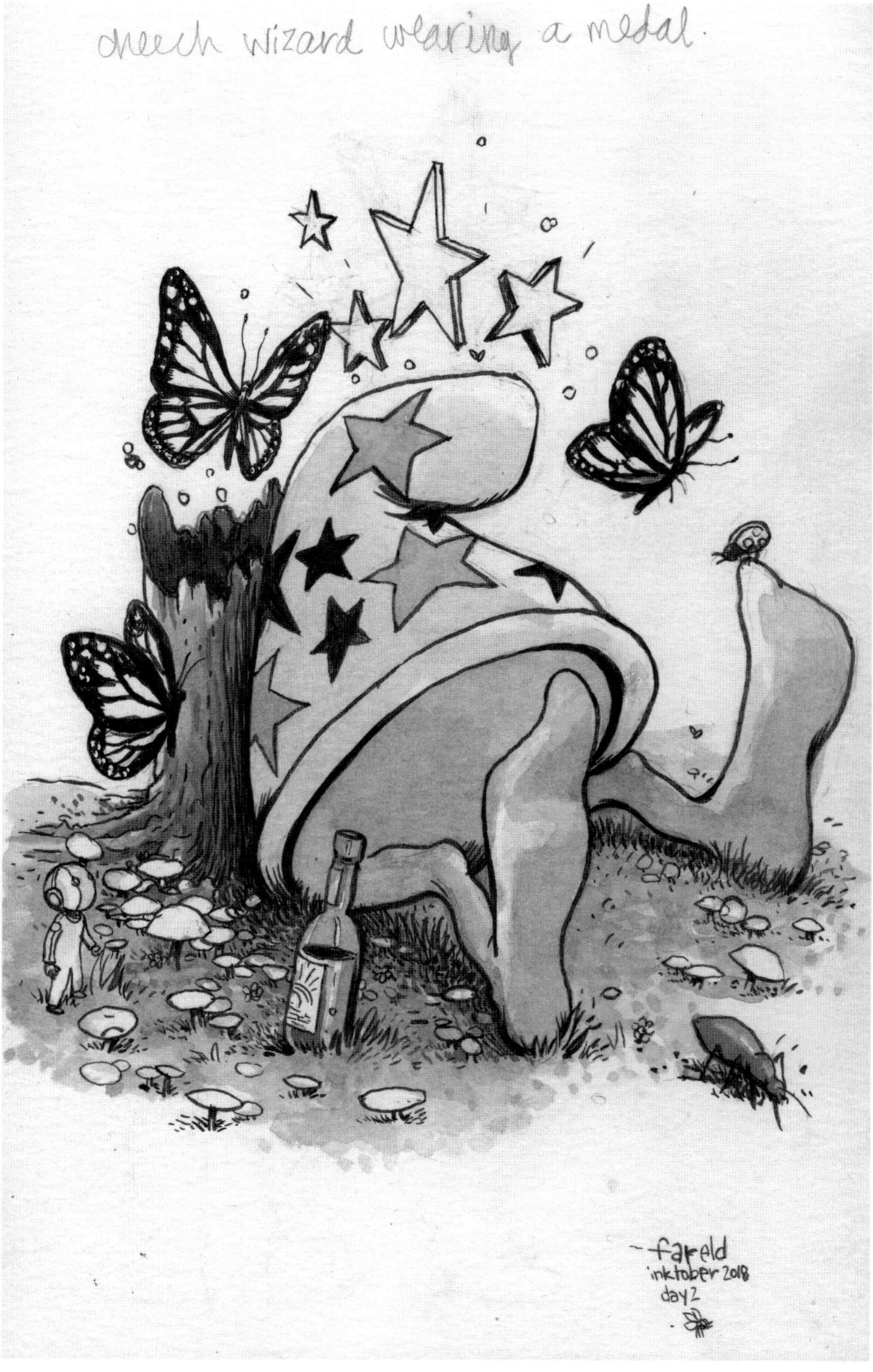
cheech wizard wearing a medal.
~fareld
inktober 2018
day 2

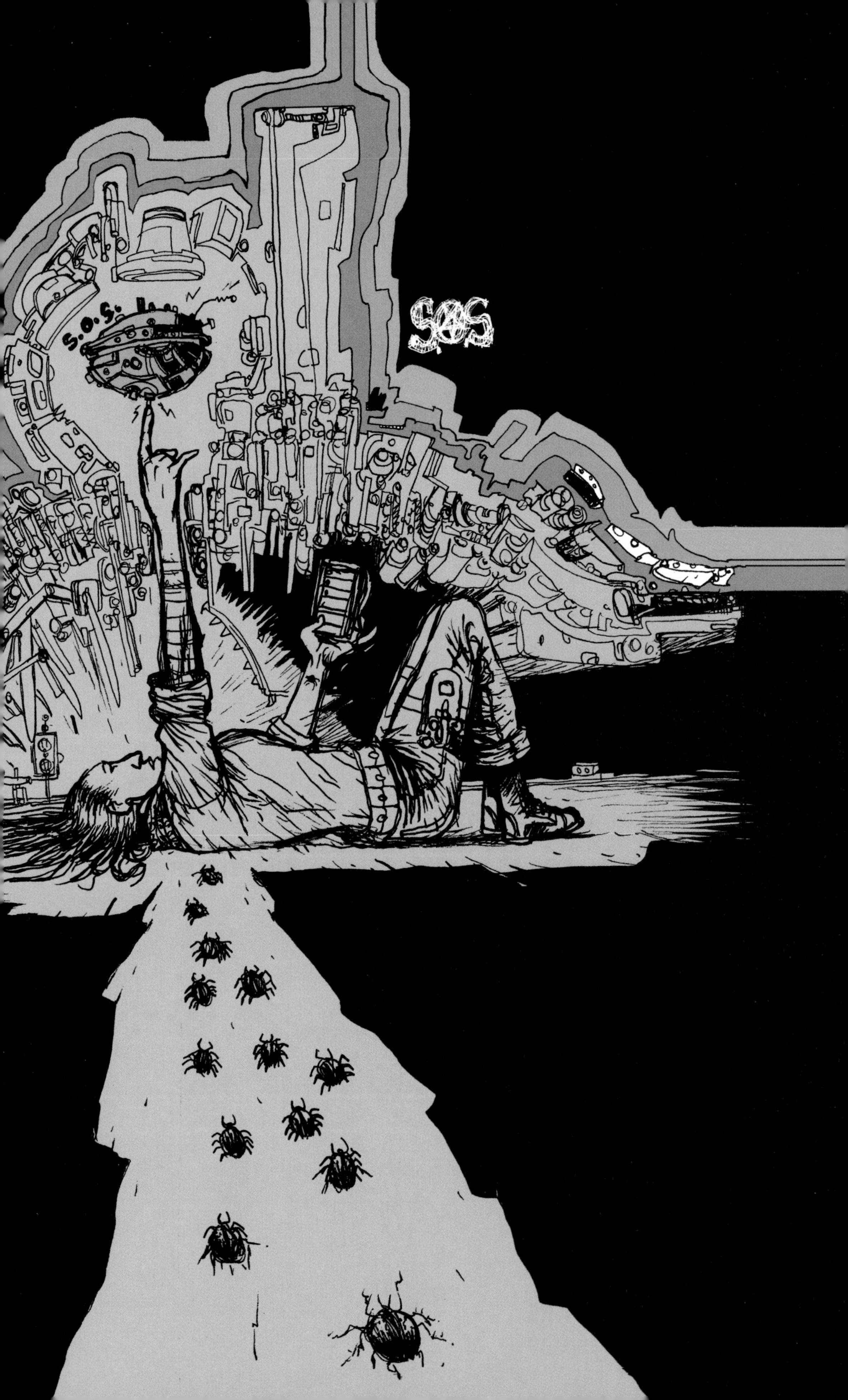
S.O.S.
SOS

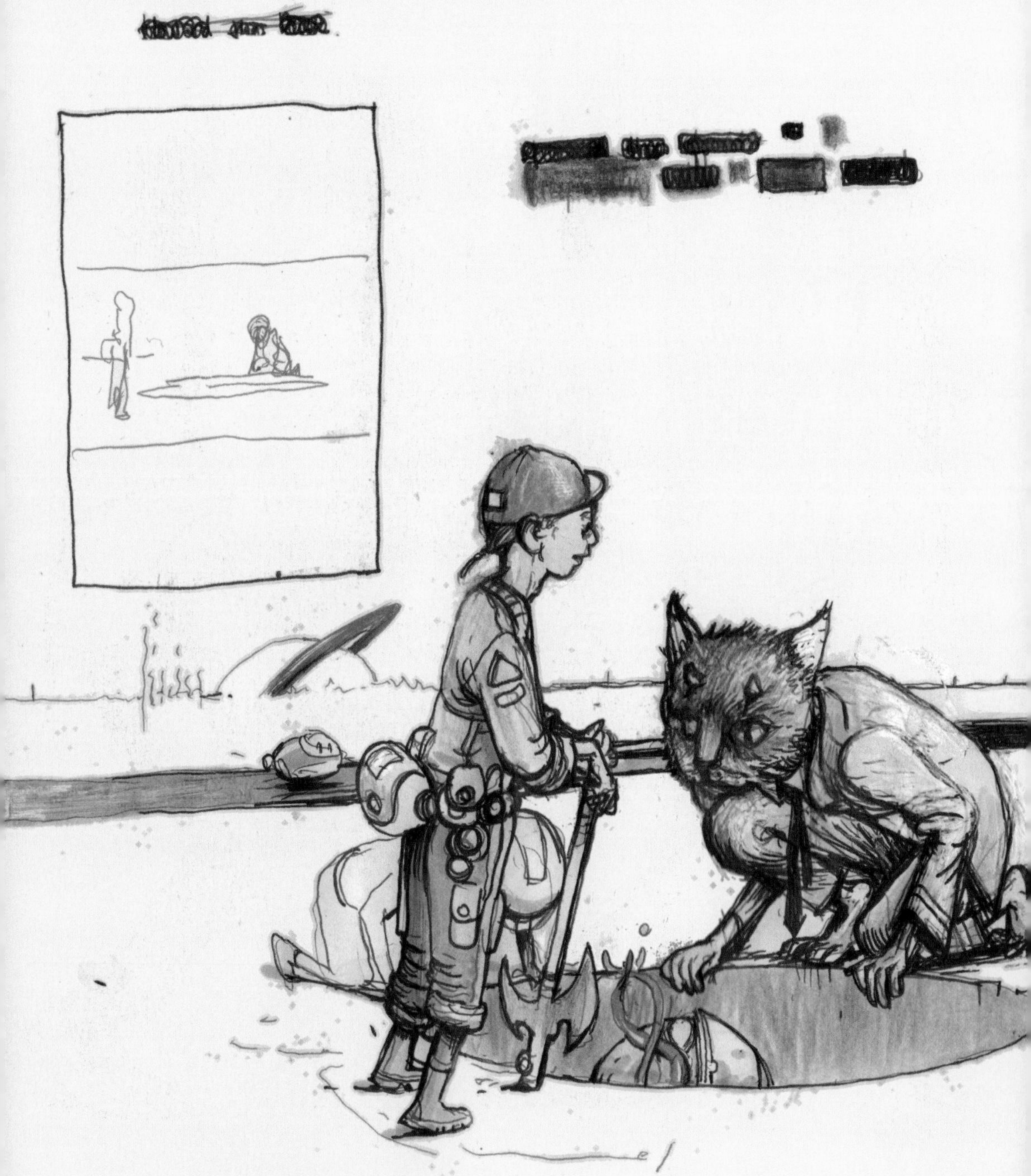

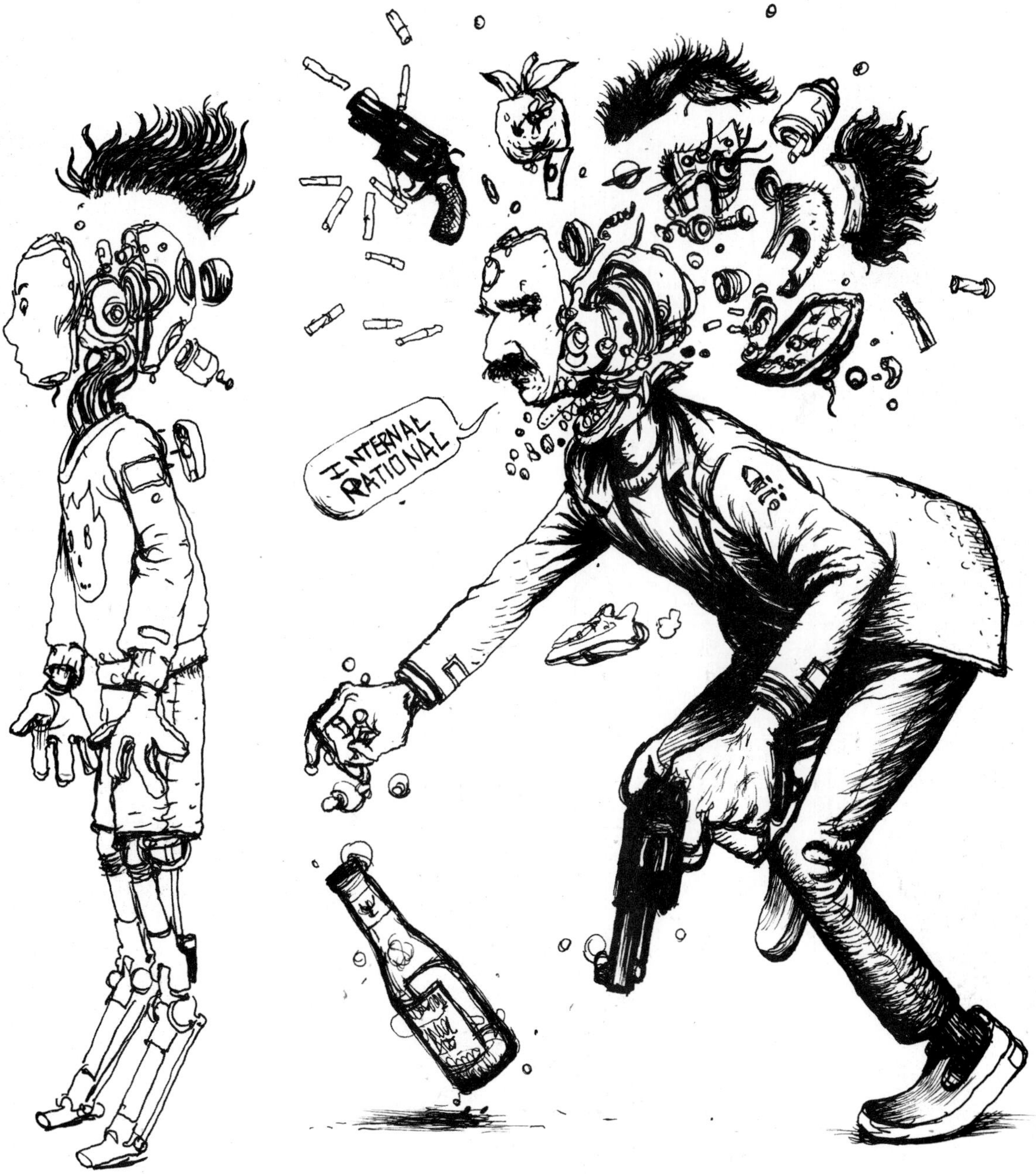
INTERNAL RATIONAL

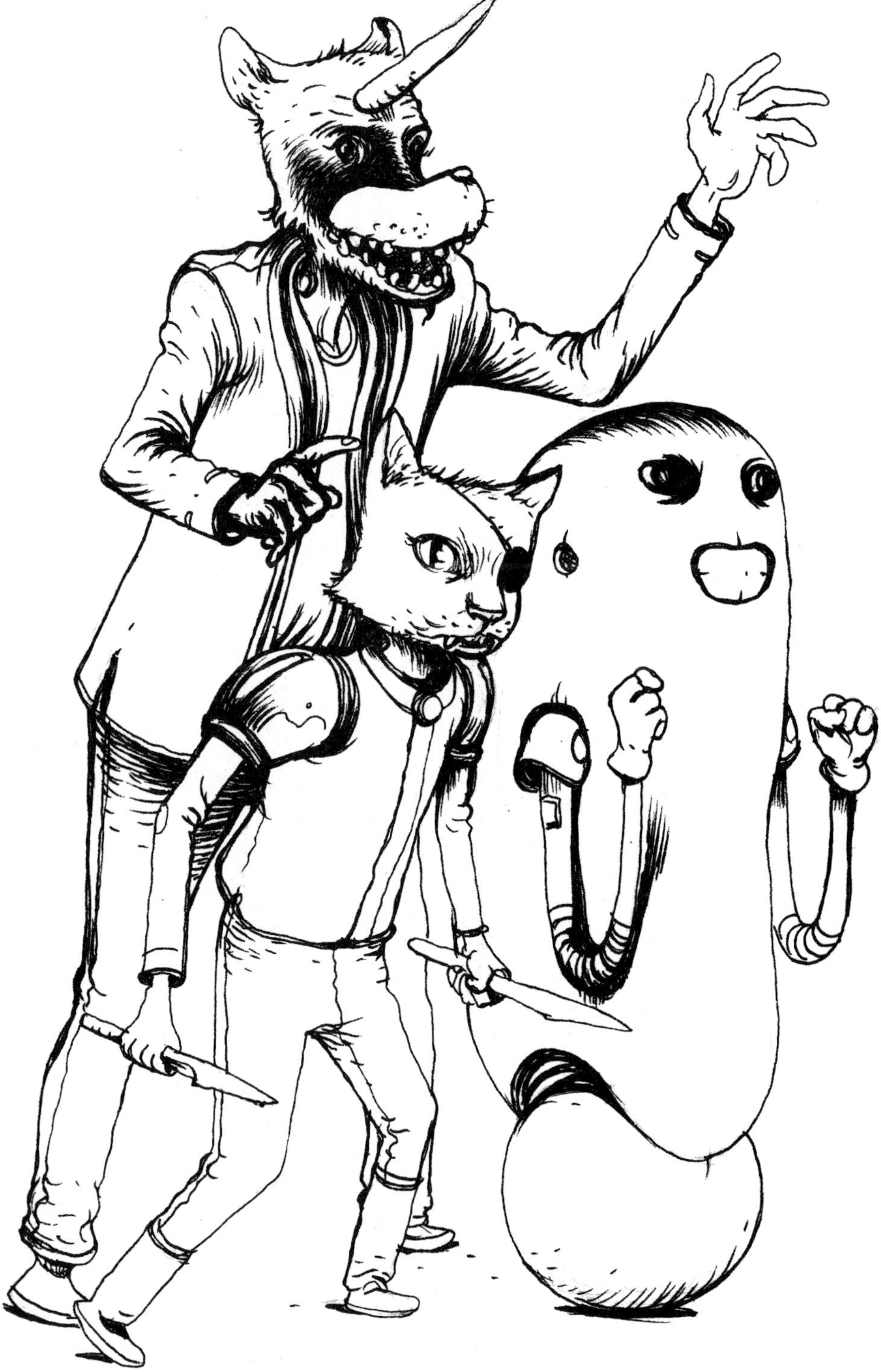

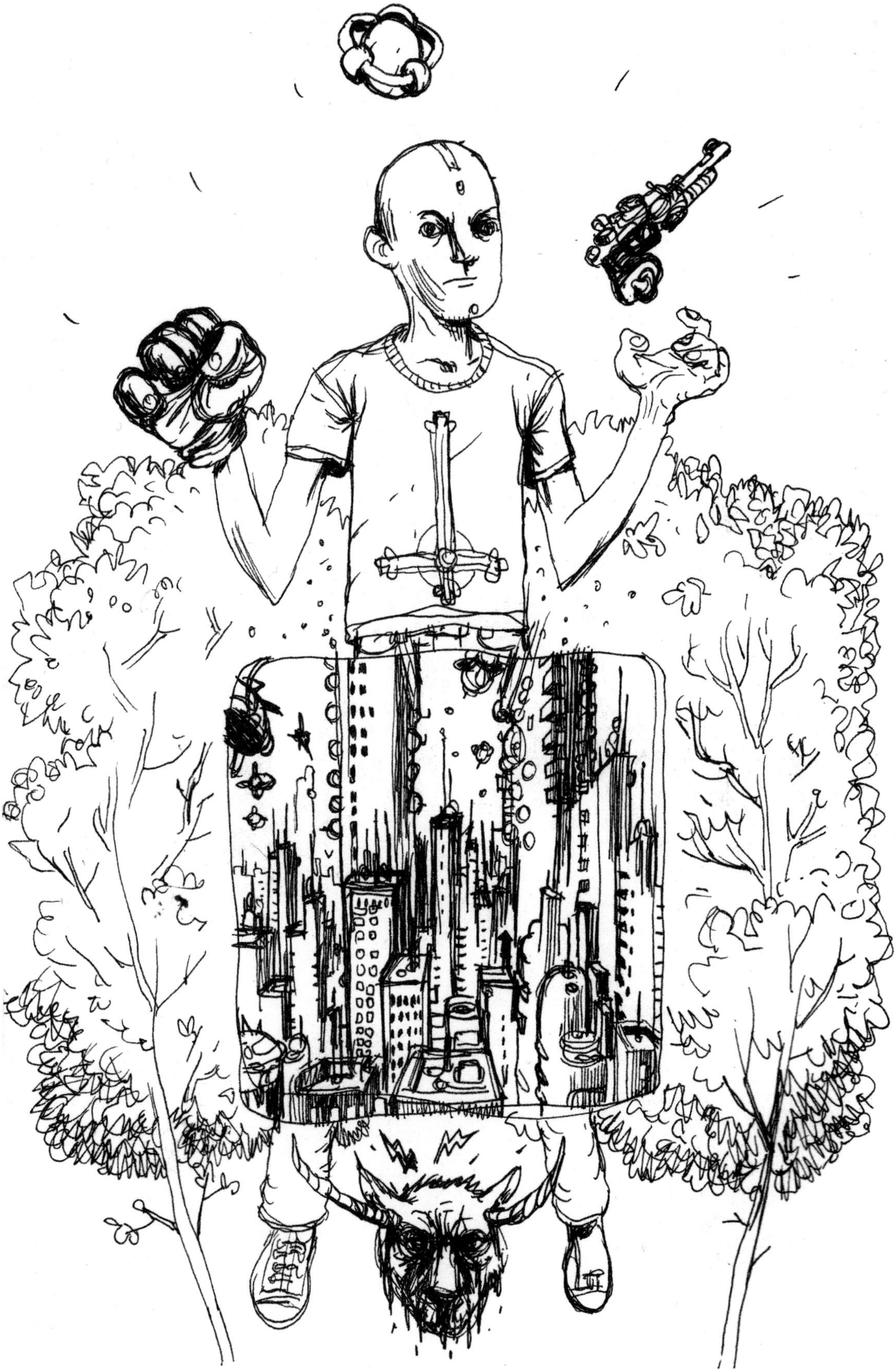

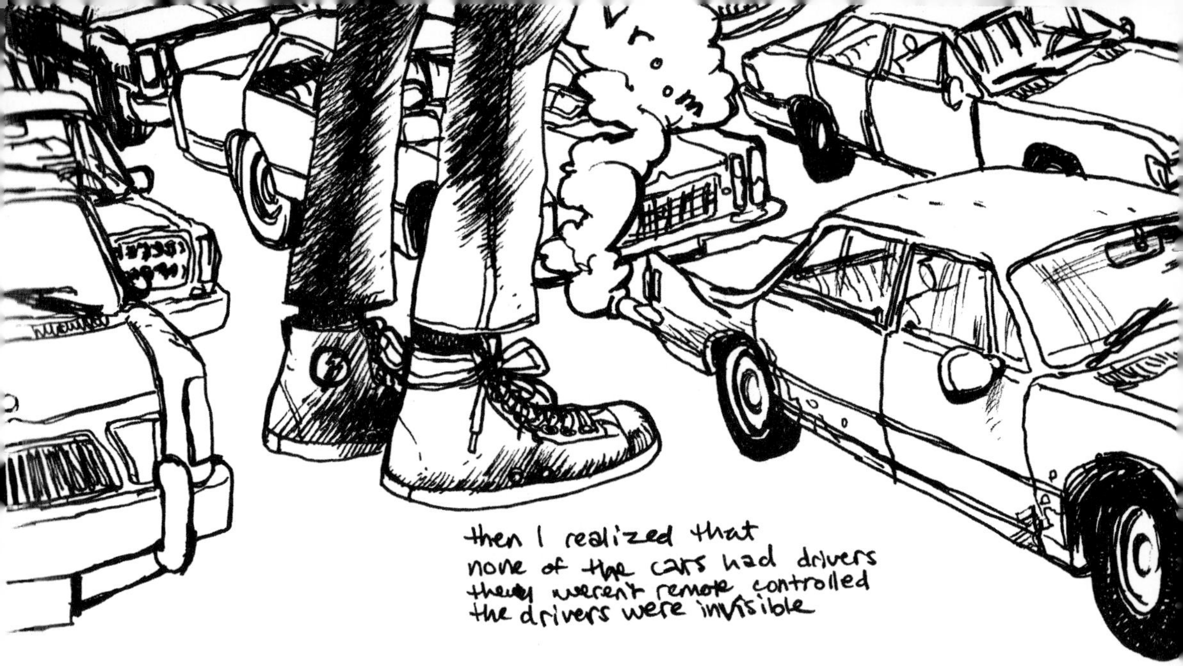
vroom
then I realized that
none of the cars had drivers
they weren't remote controlled
the drivers were invisible

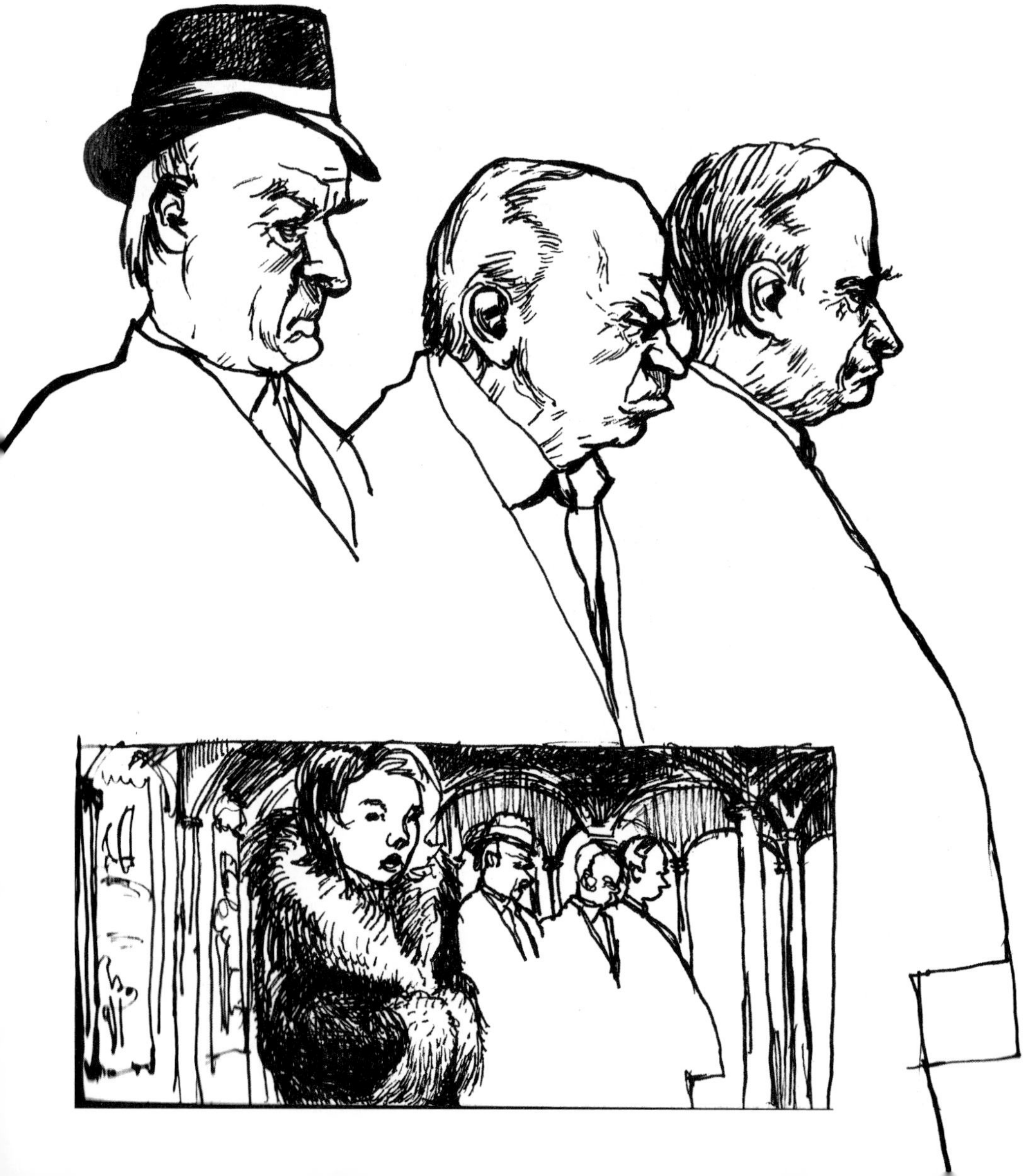

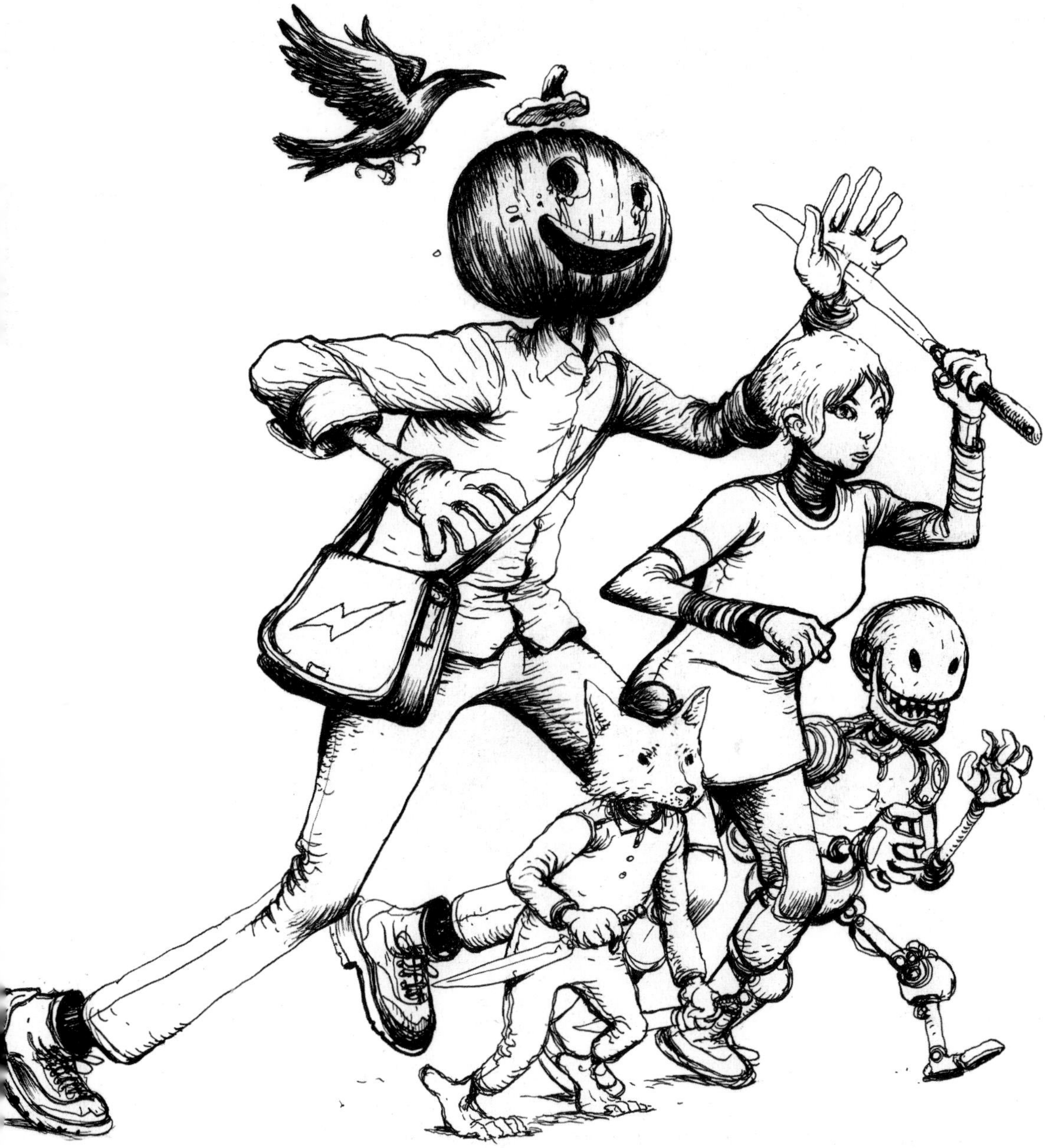

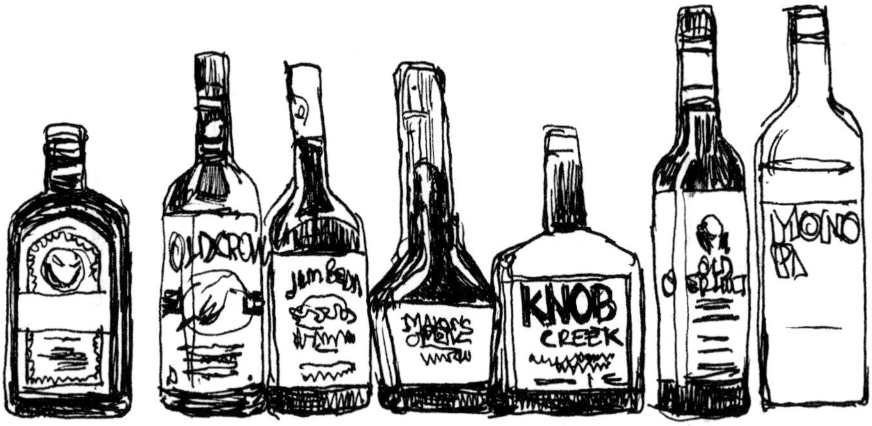
OLD CROW
KNOB
CREEK

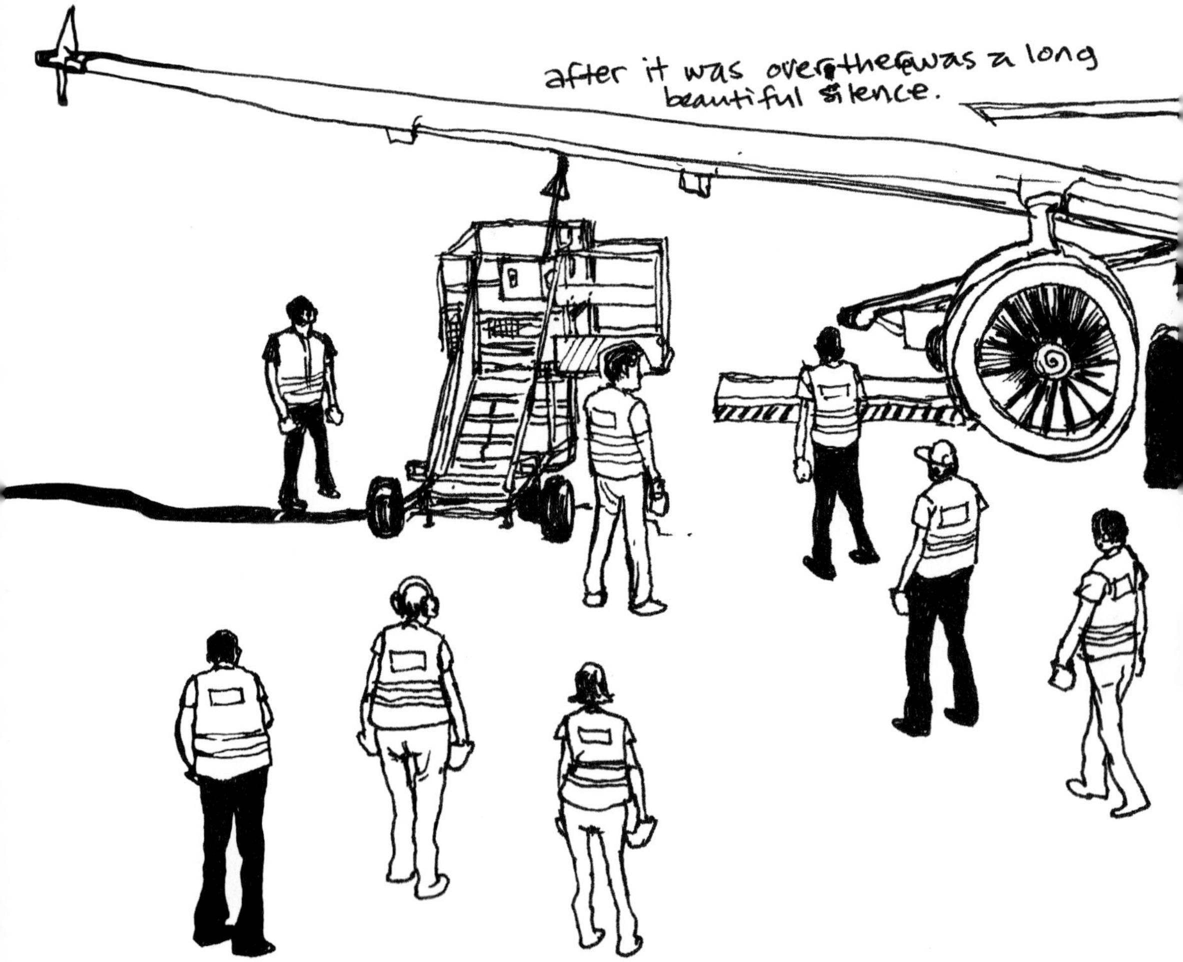
after it was over there was a long beautiful silence.

ome ugust 19 2004

I walked around the outside of the Colosem today. This old woman who may have had leaprosy or maybe was just pretending. I am a sucker of satan's cock for wanting to draw her so I had to do this out of my head. I saw some evil bastard take her picture. she just kept walking back and forth clanging her cup.

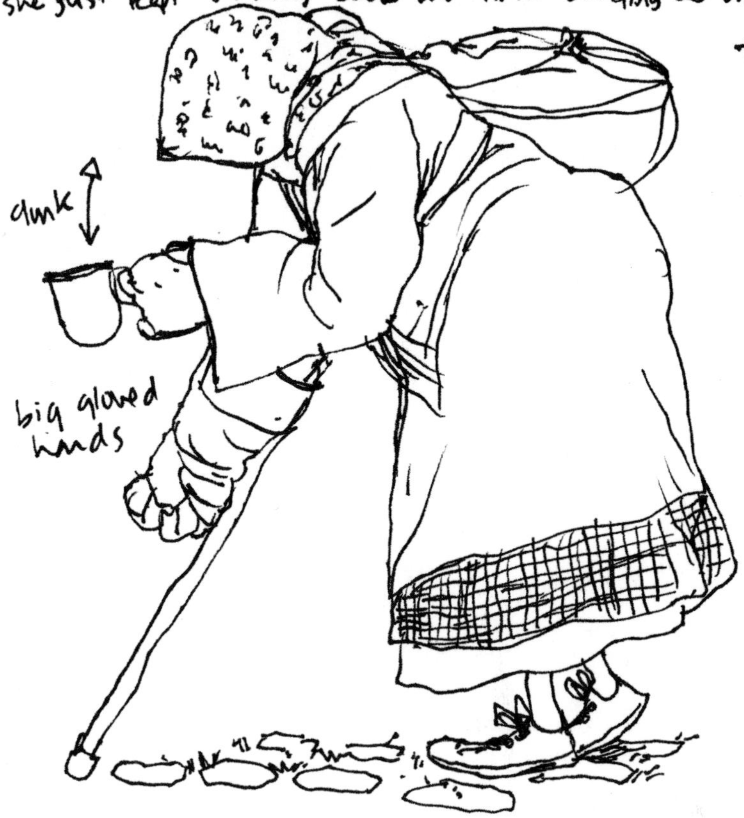

clunk
big gloved hands

Then an hour later I saw another lady who looked just like her. Rome has an entire army of these beggers

I also dug the nuns on bicycles.

Sitting at the vatican. I'm not even religious. this place is huge I think I got sun burned the pigeons here attack people

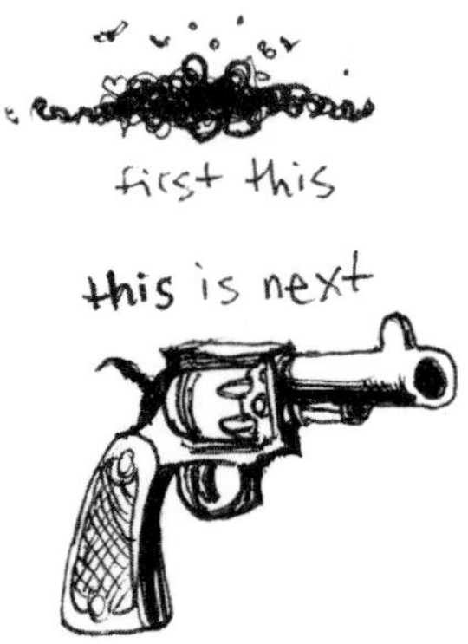

first this
this is next

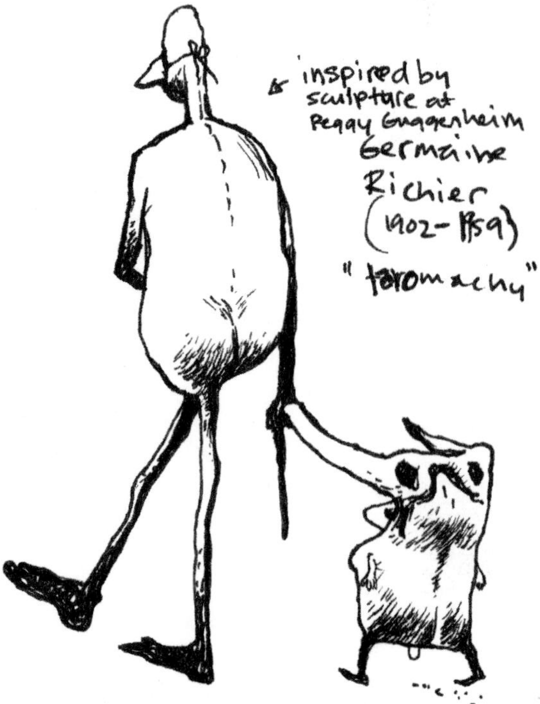

inspired by sculpture at Peggy Guggenheim Germaine Richier (1902-1959) "Tauromachy"

"I just wanted to be sure of you."

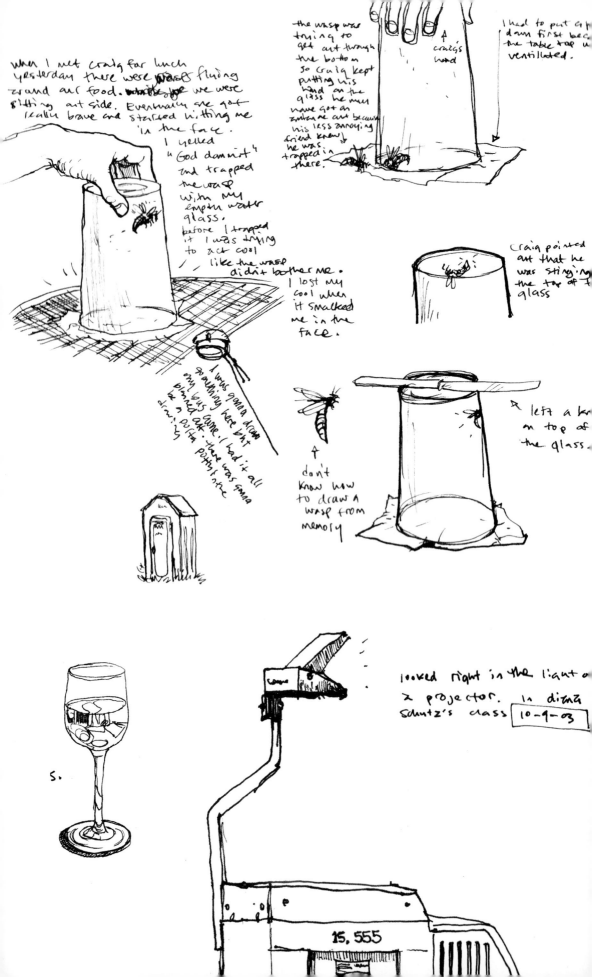

when I met craig for lunch yesterday there were wasps flying around our food. we were sitting outside. Eventually one got really brave and started hitting me in the face.

I yelled "God dammit" and trapped the wasp with my empty water glass. before I trapped it I was trying to act cool like the wasp didn't bother me. I lost my cool when it smacked me in the face.

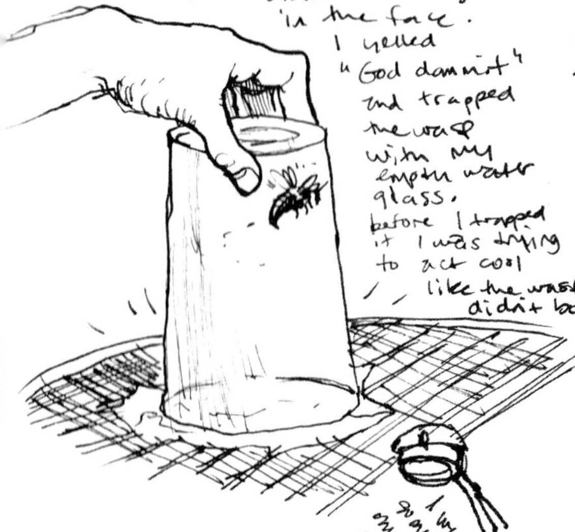

the wasp was trying to get out through the bottom so craig kept putting his hand on the glass. he may have got an entrance out because his less annoying friend knew he was trapped in there.

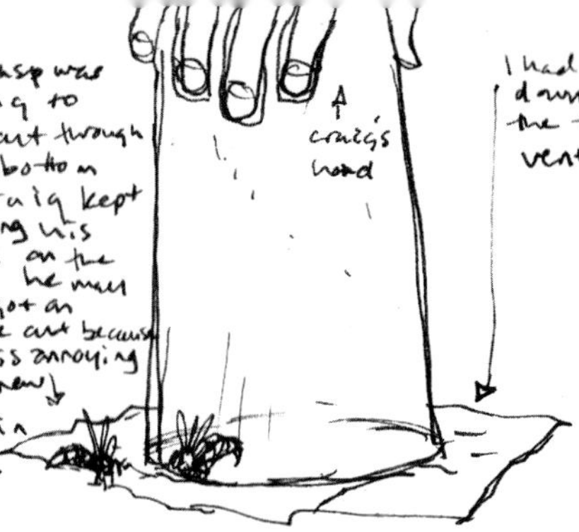
craig's hand

I had to put a p down first bec the table top w ventillated.

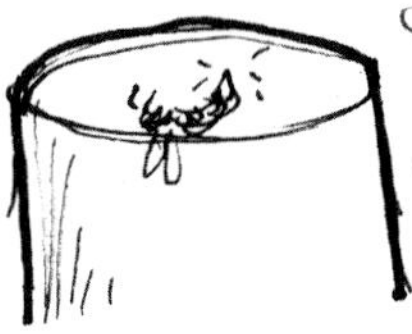

craig pointed out that he was stinging the top of t glass

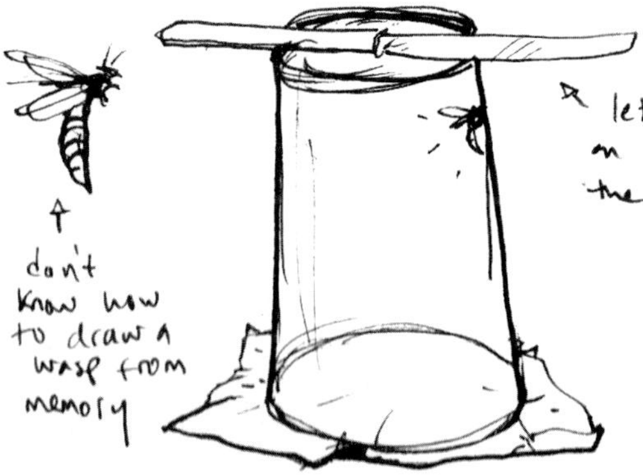

left a kn on top of the glass.

don't know how to draw a wasp from memory

I was gonna draw something here but my bus came. I had it all planned out. there was gonna be a potta potty in the drawing

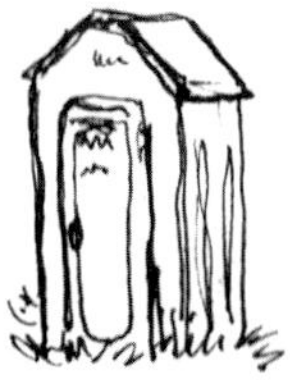

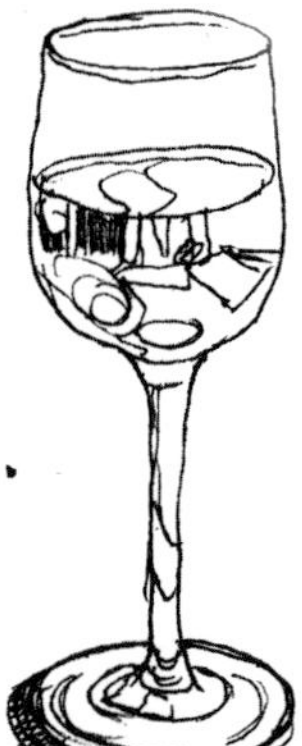

5.

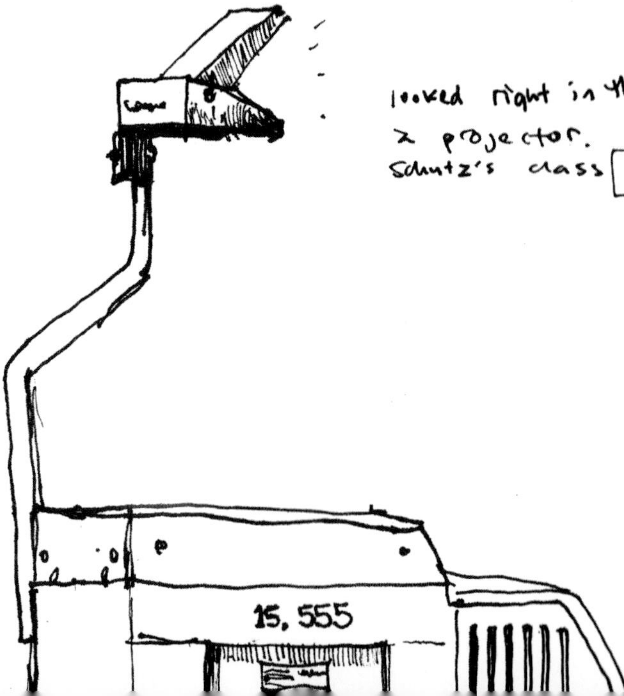
15,555

looked right in the light o a projector. In diana schutz's class 10-9-03

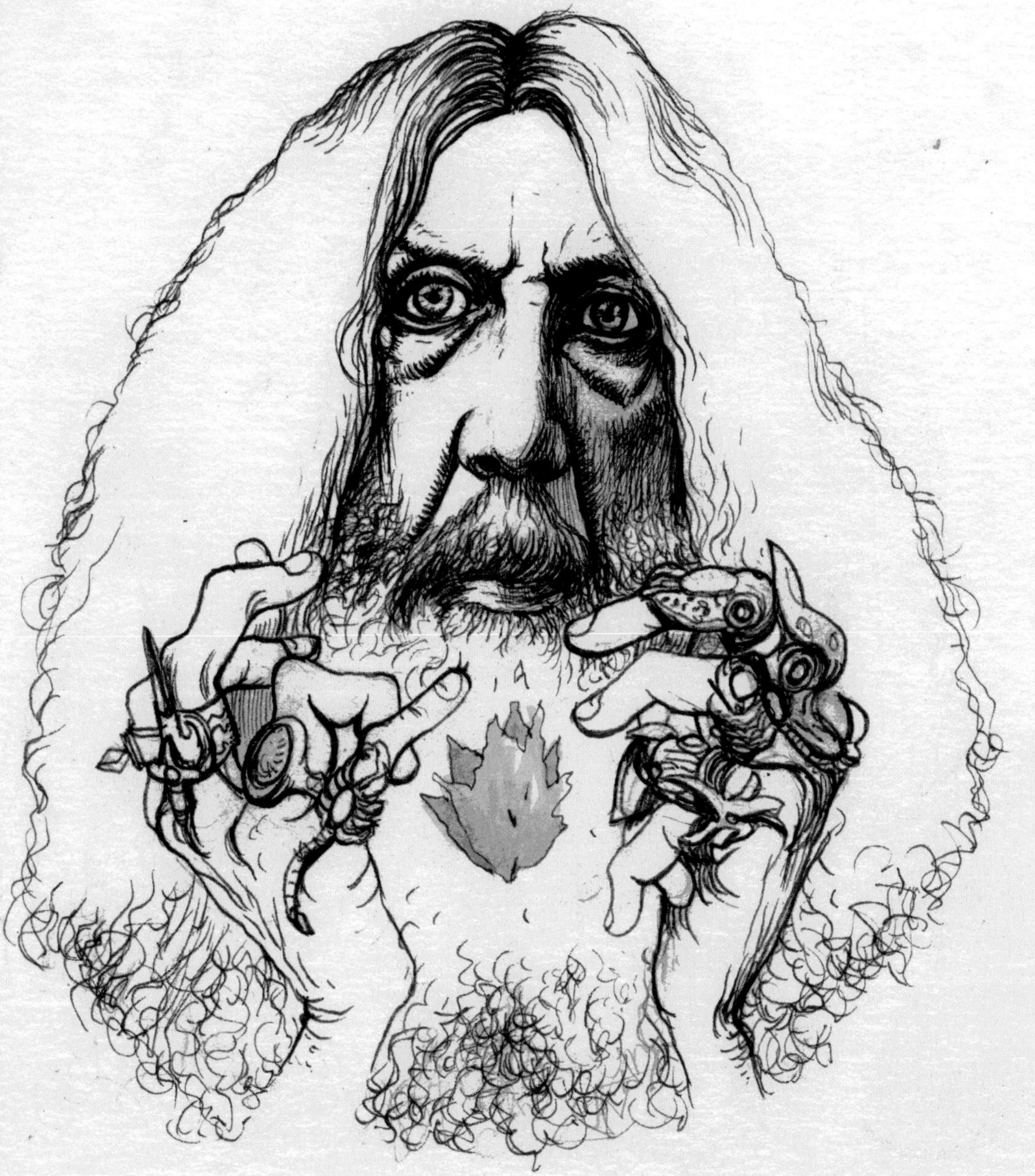

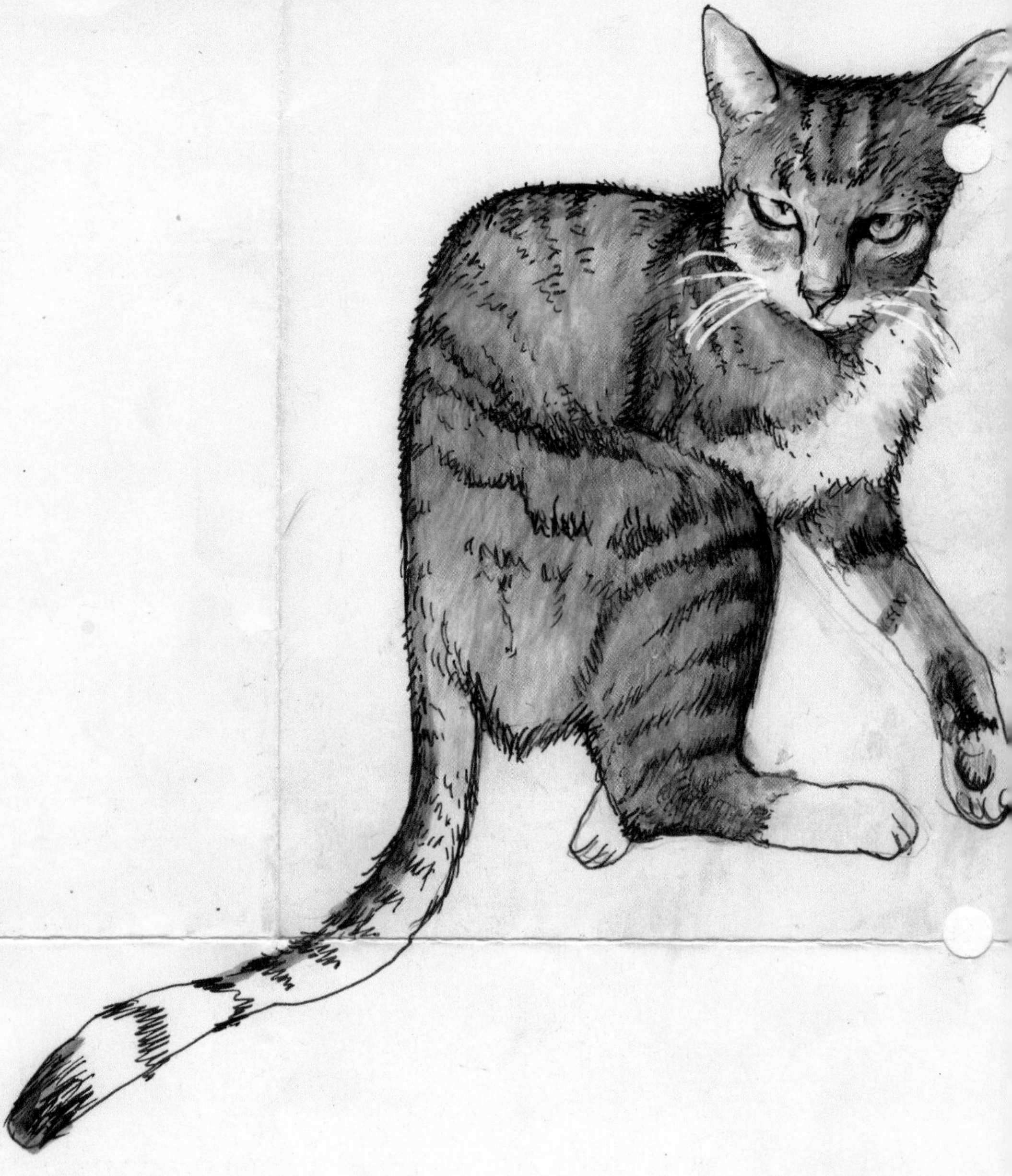

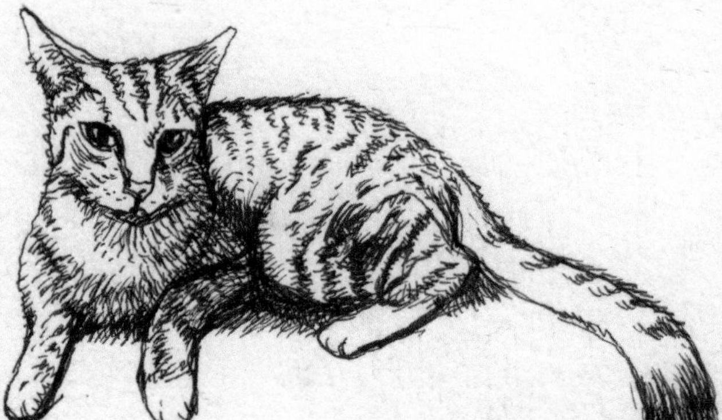

My heart breaks whenever I think about you.

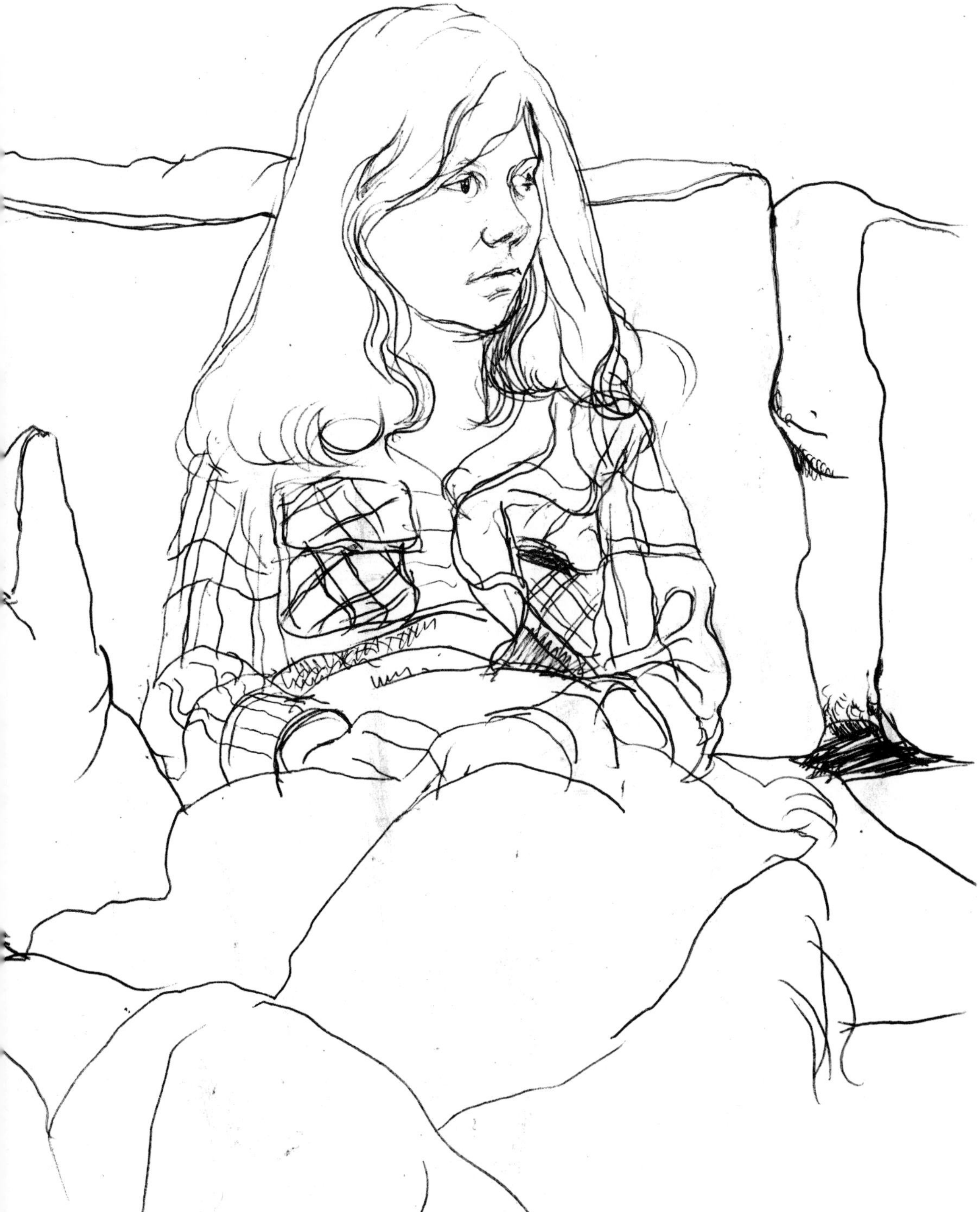

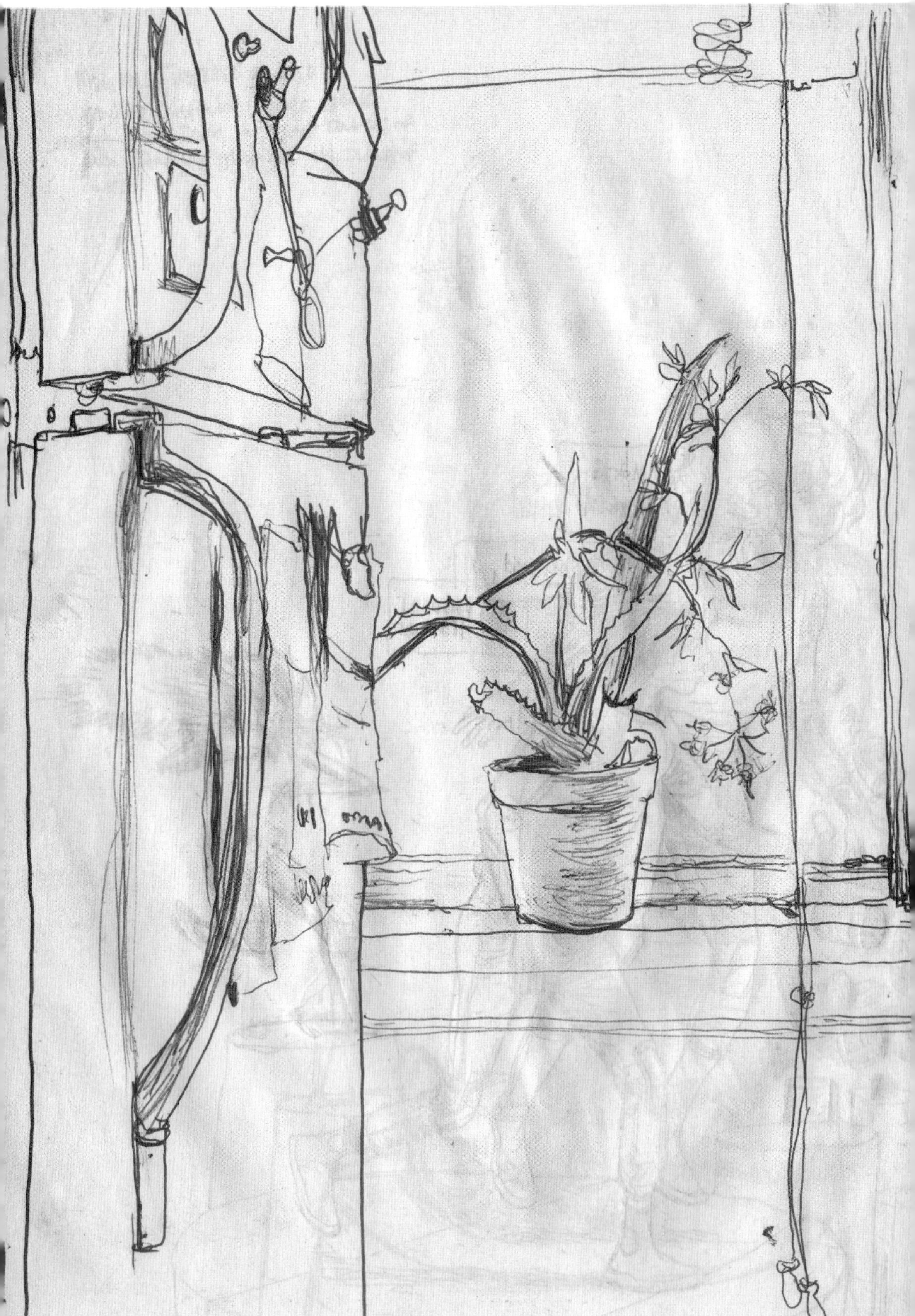

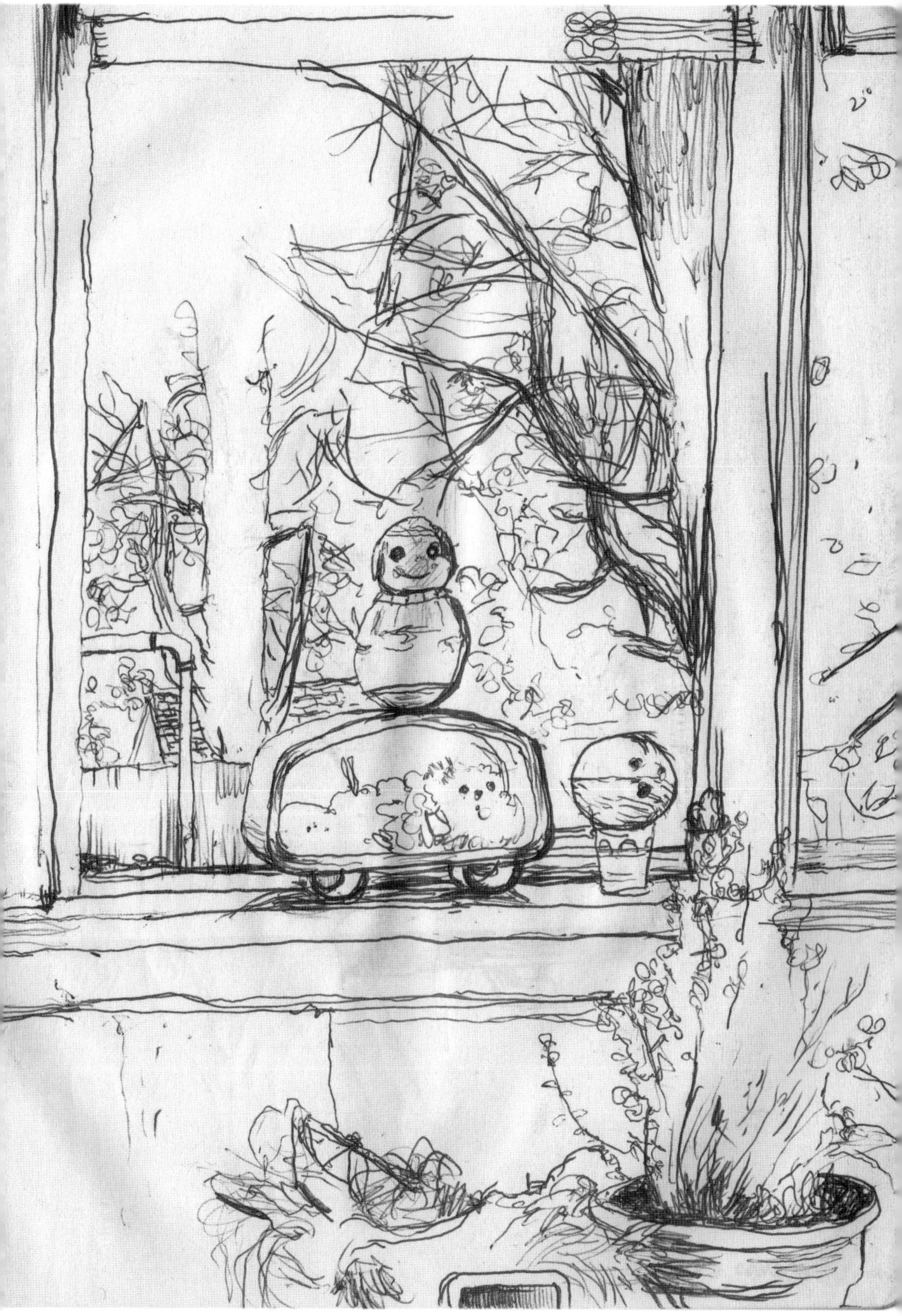

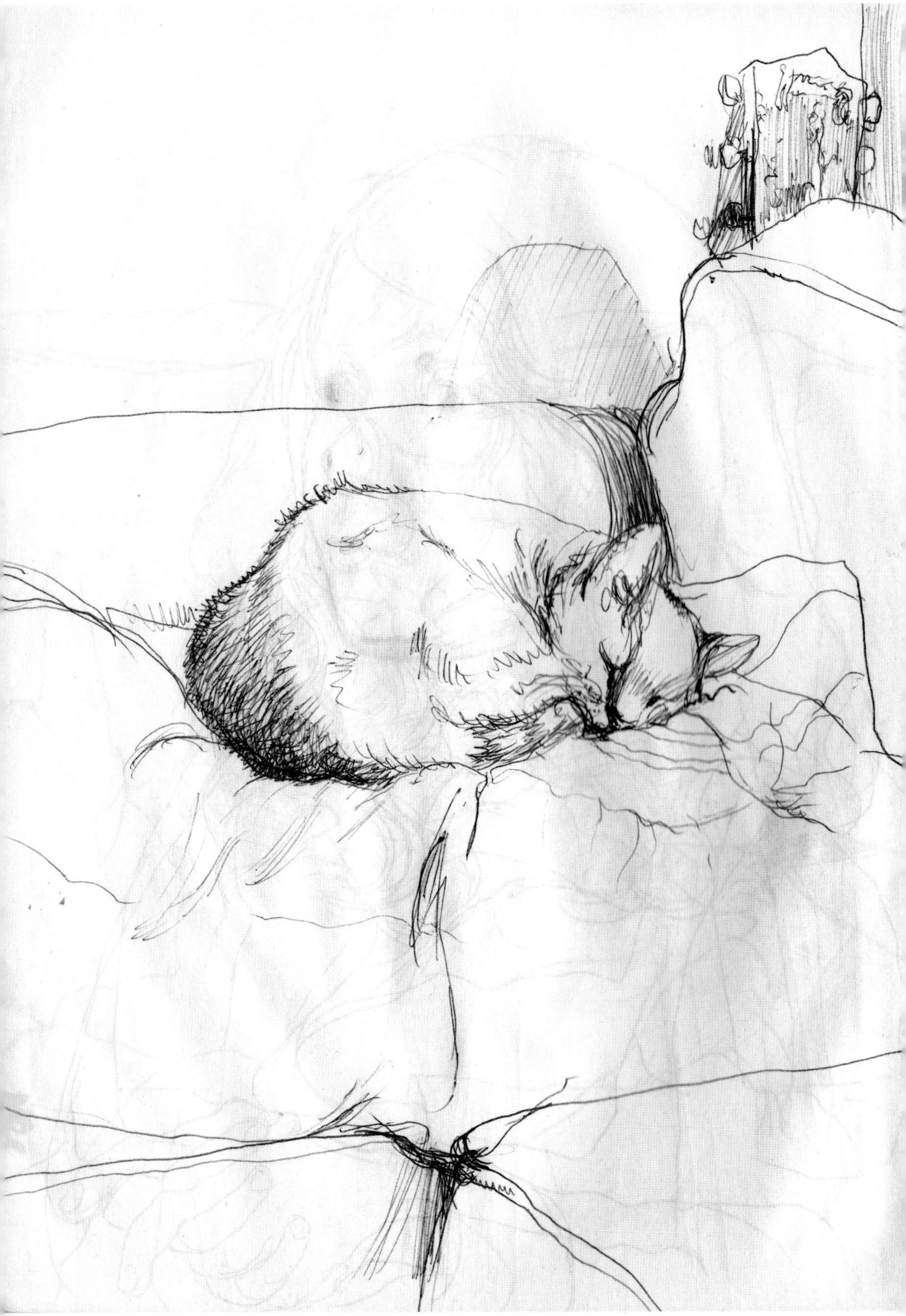

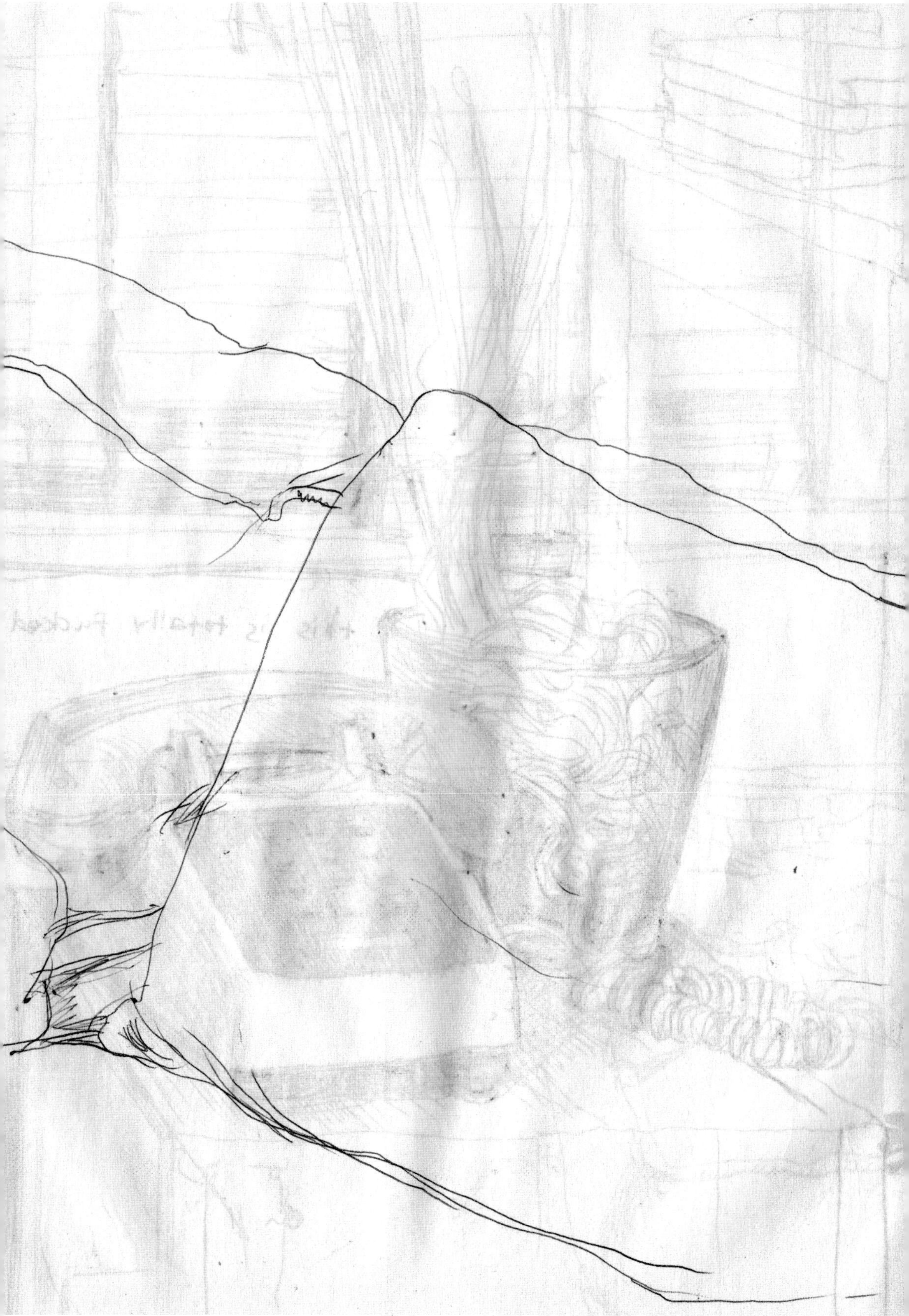

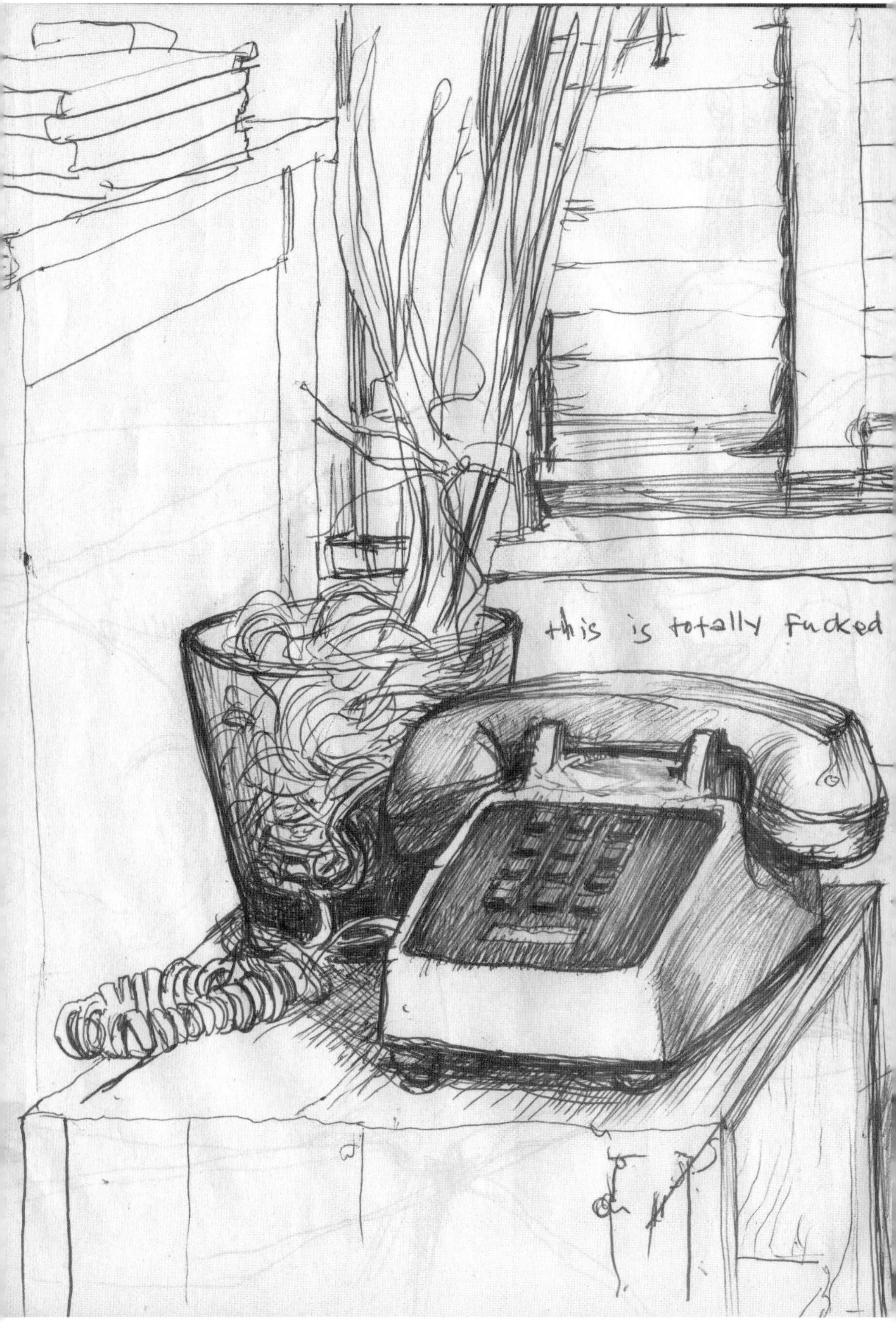
this is totally fucked

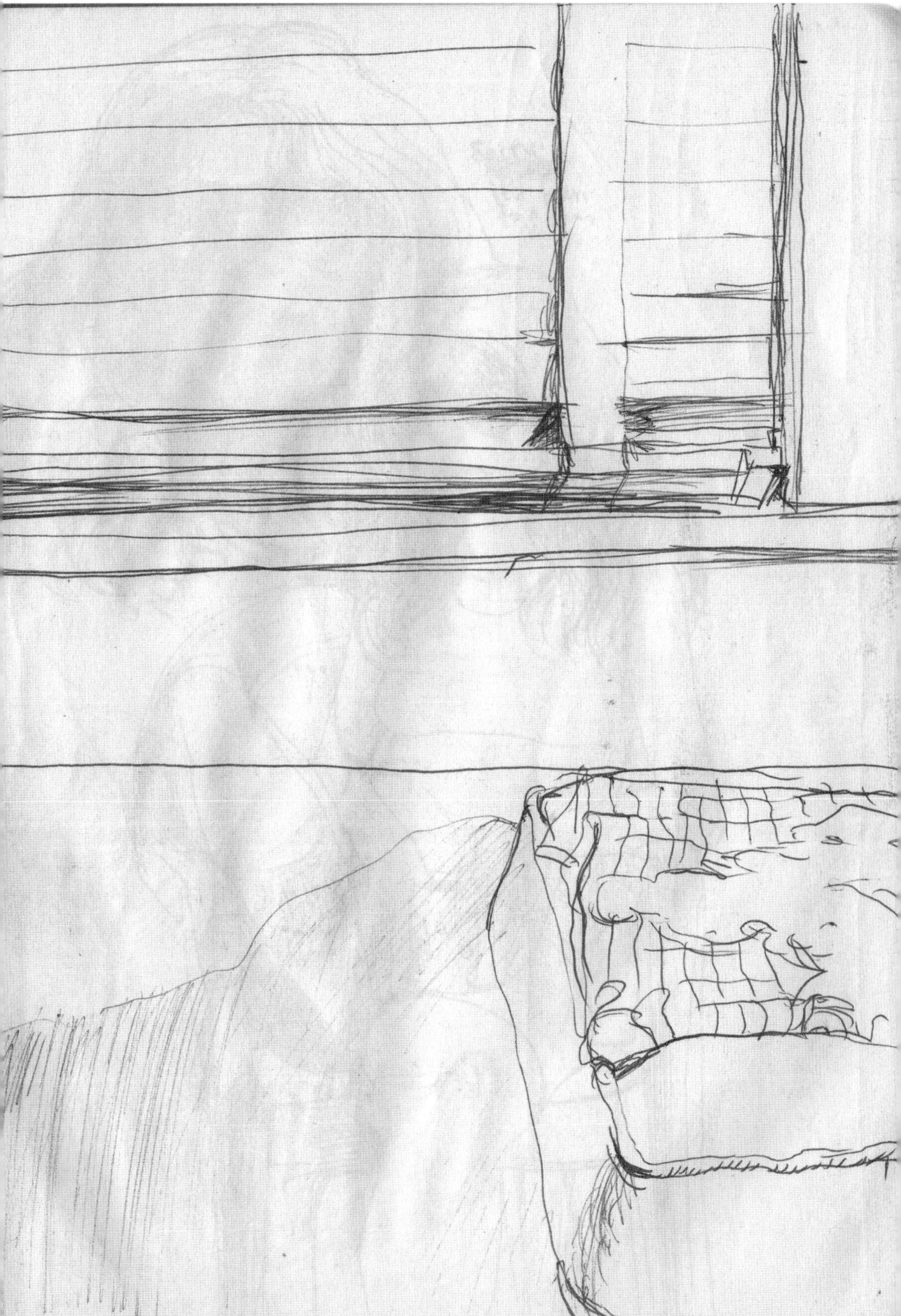

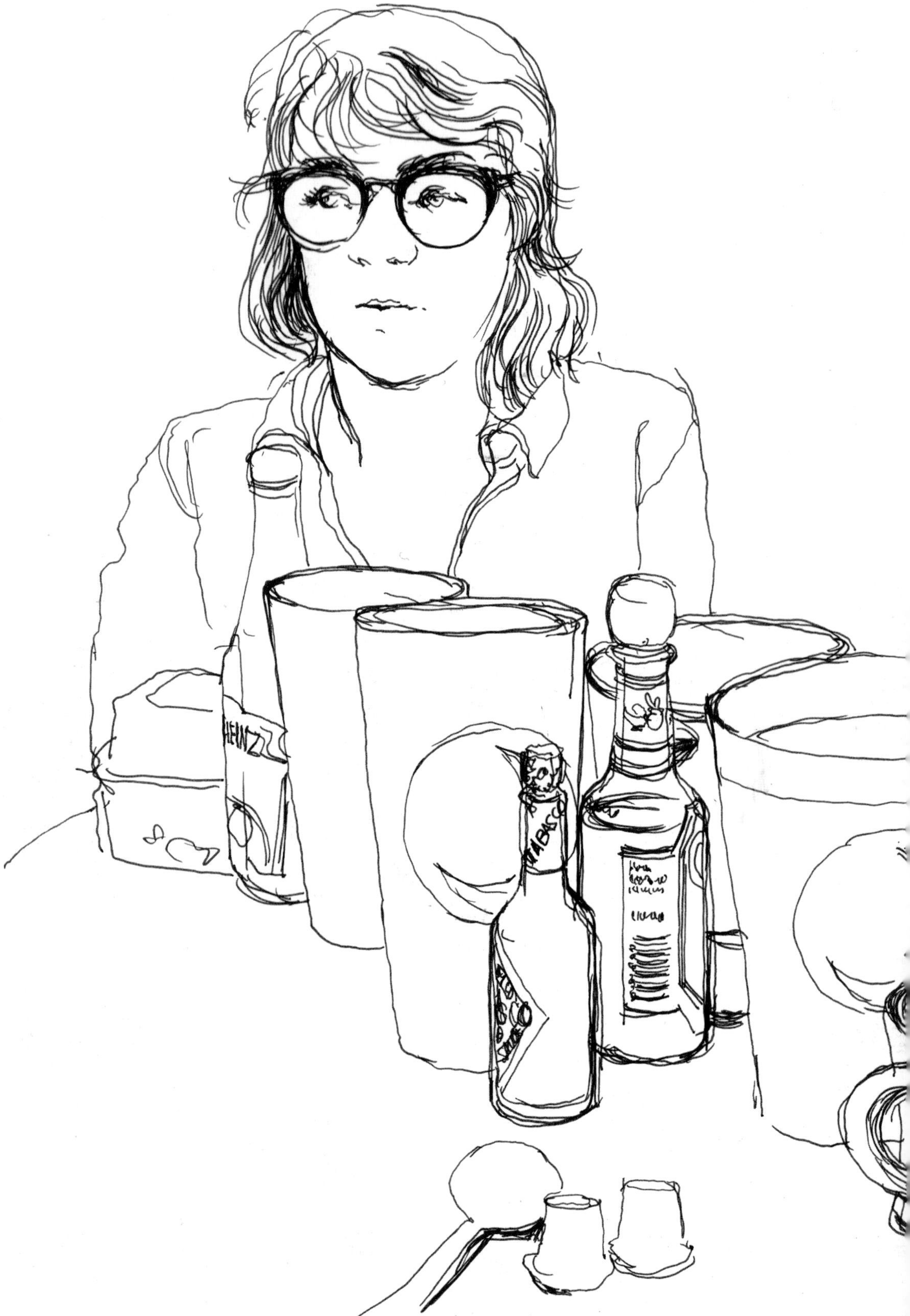
HEINZ
TABASCO

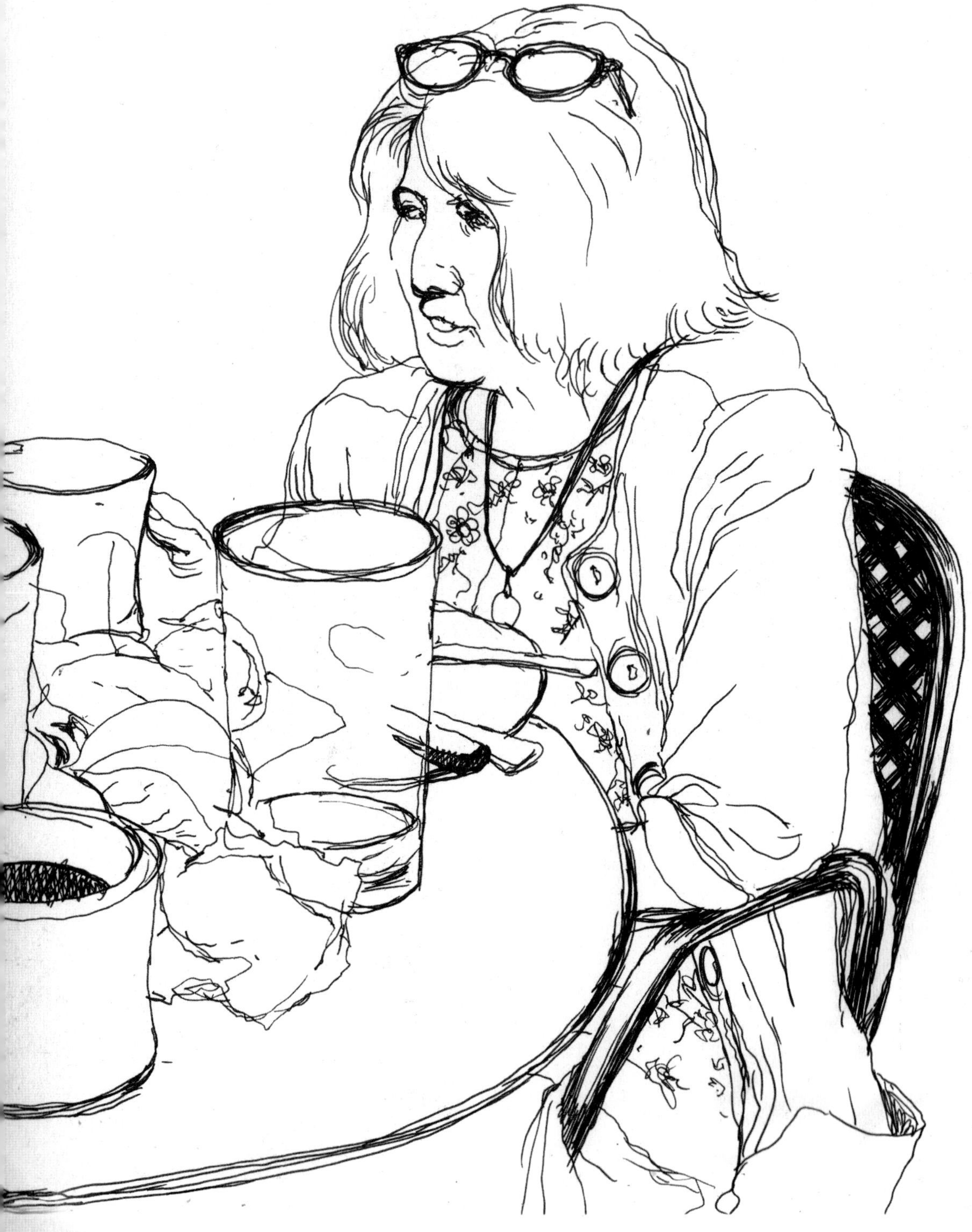

Lombard and Leavitt
Wednesday Jan 13, '10
Ladybug cafe

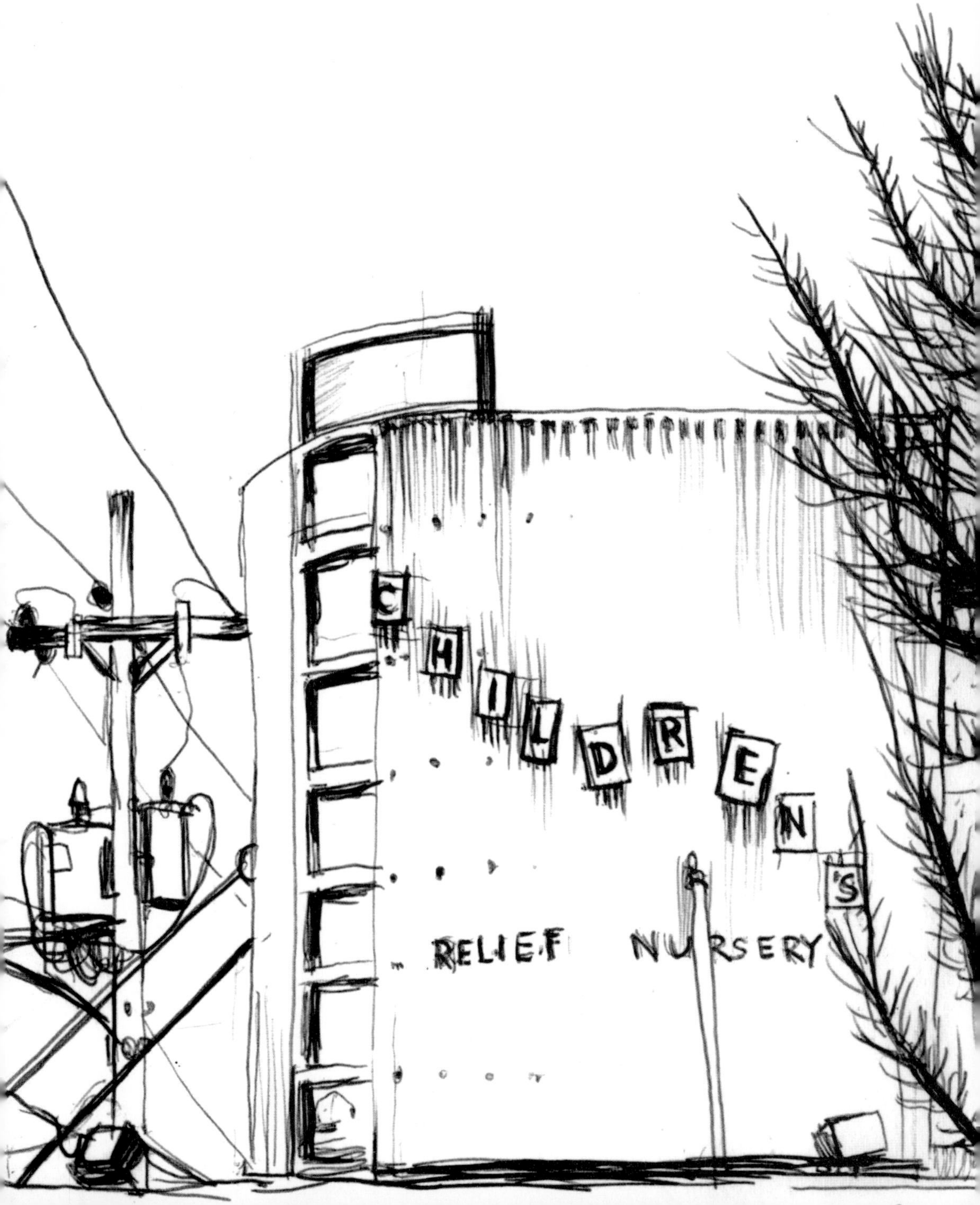
CHILDREN'S
RELIEF NURSERY

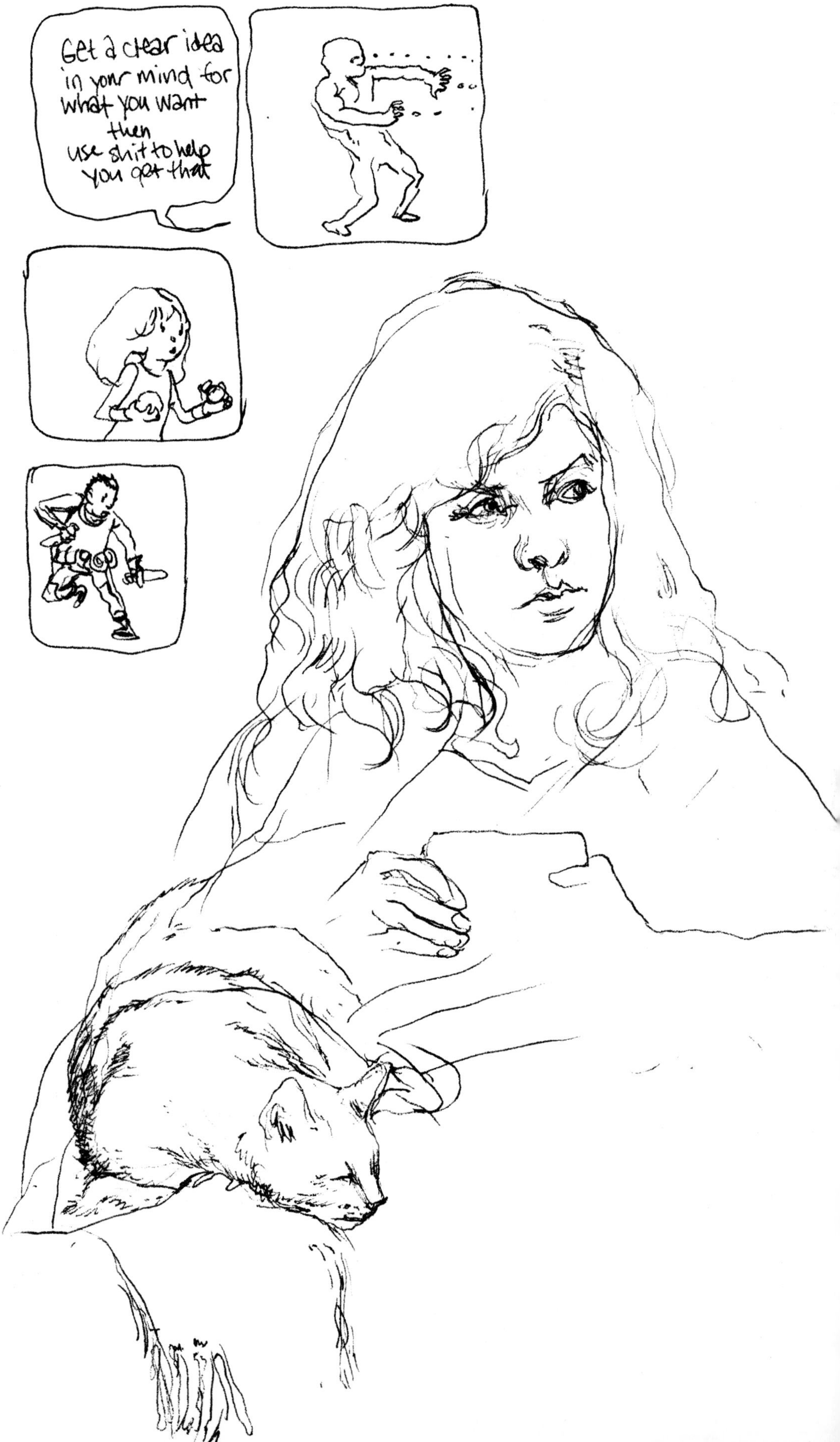
Get a clear idea in your mind for what you want then use shit to help you get that

At airport
Seen from far away off
through a frame of steel
through glass and plastic filter

Spots on the airport tarmac weree tiny on the tarmac
a man down to distraction at his work in his orange vest.
We are sitting at a bar. I think a football game is on ▪▪

noms
house
Nov

so this man was bouncing
his catching matching
orange traffic direction
light on the tarmac
and managing to catch
it on the up flip about
every third toss.
It was all in the throw, a
hard thing to aim

Sounds of the highway
next door
black helicopters

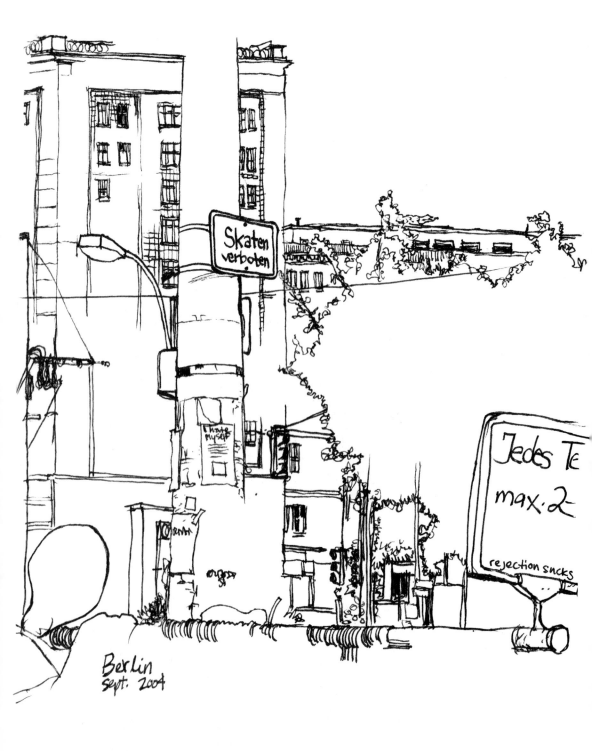

Skaten verboten

i hate myself

Jedes Te
max. 2

rejection sucks

Berlin
Sept. 2004

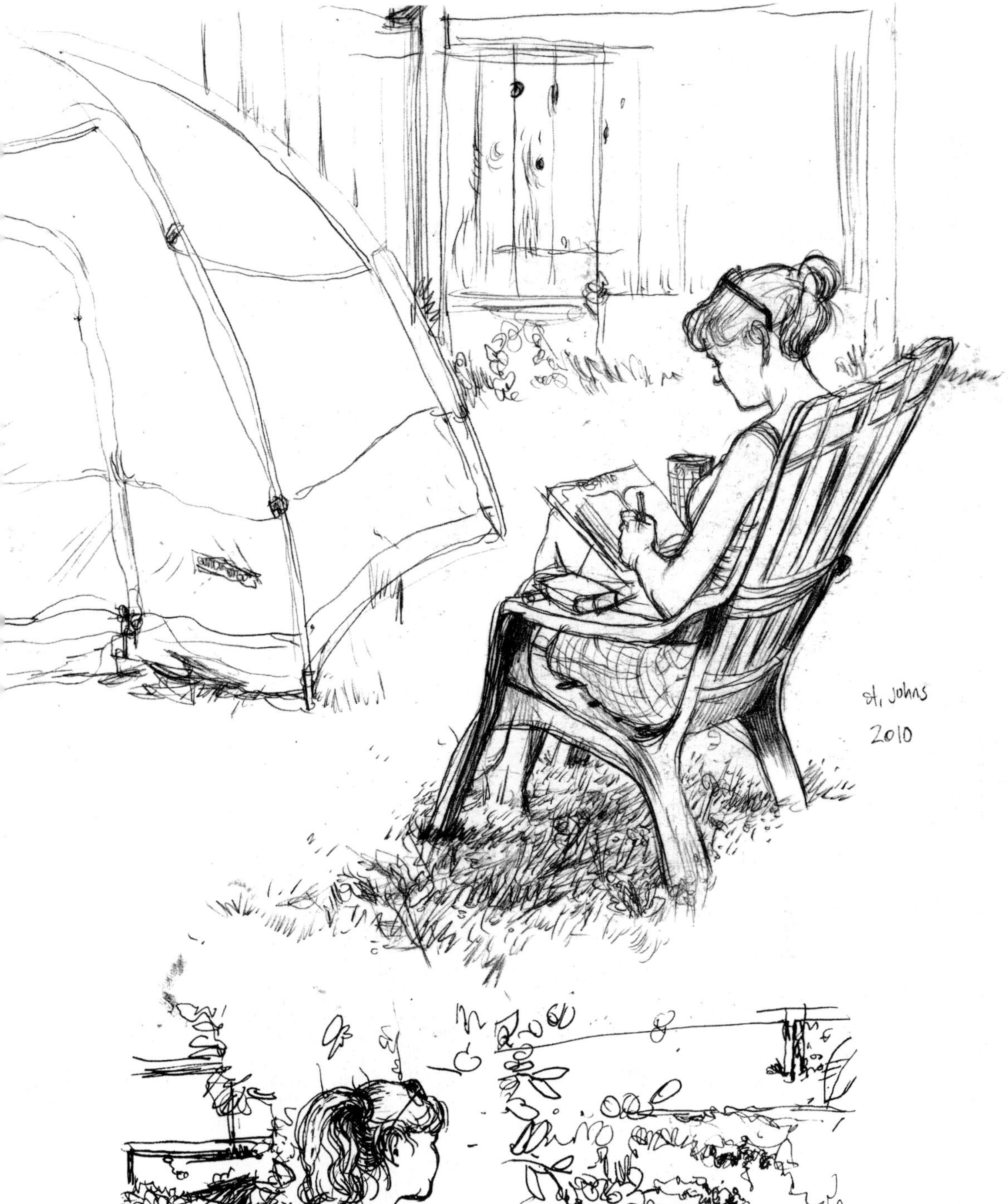
st. johns
2010

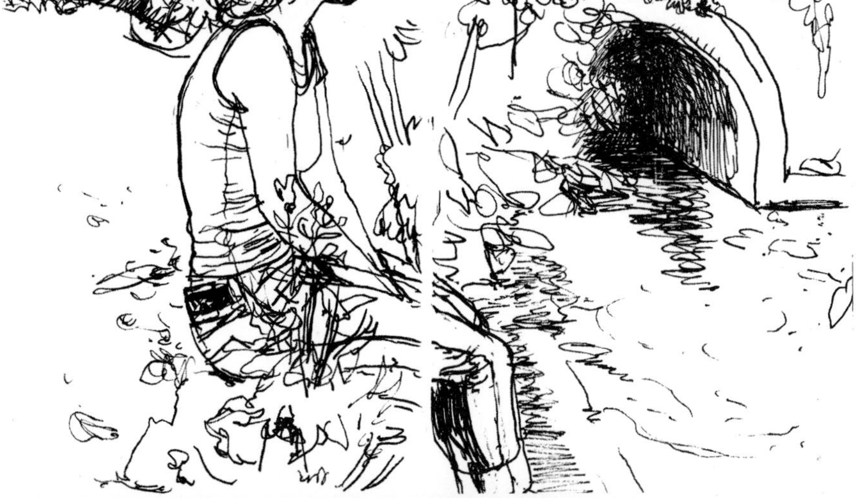

R.i.p.
Porangelos
miss you bubby

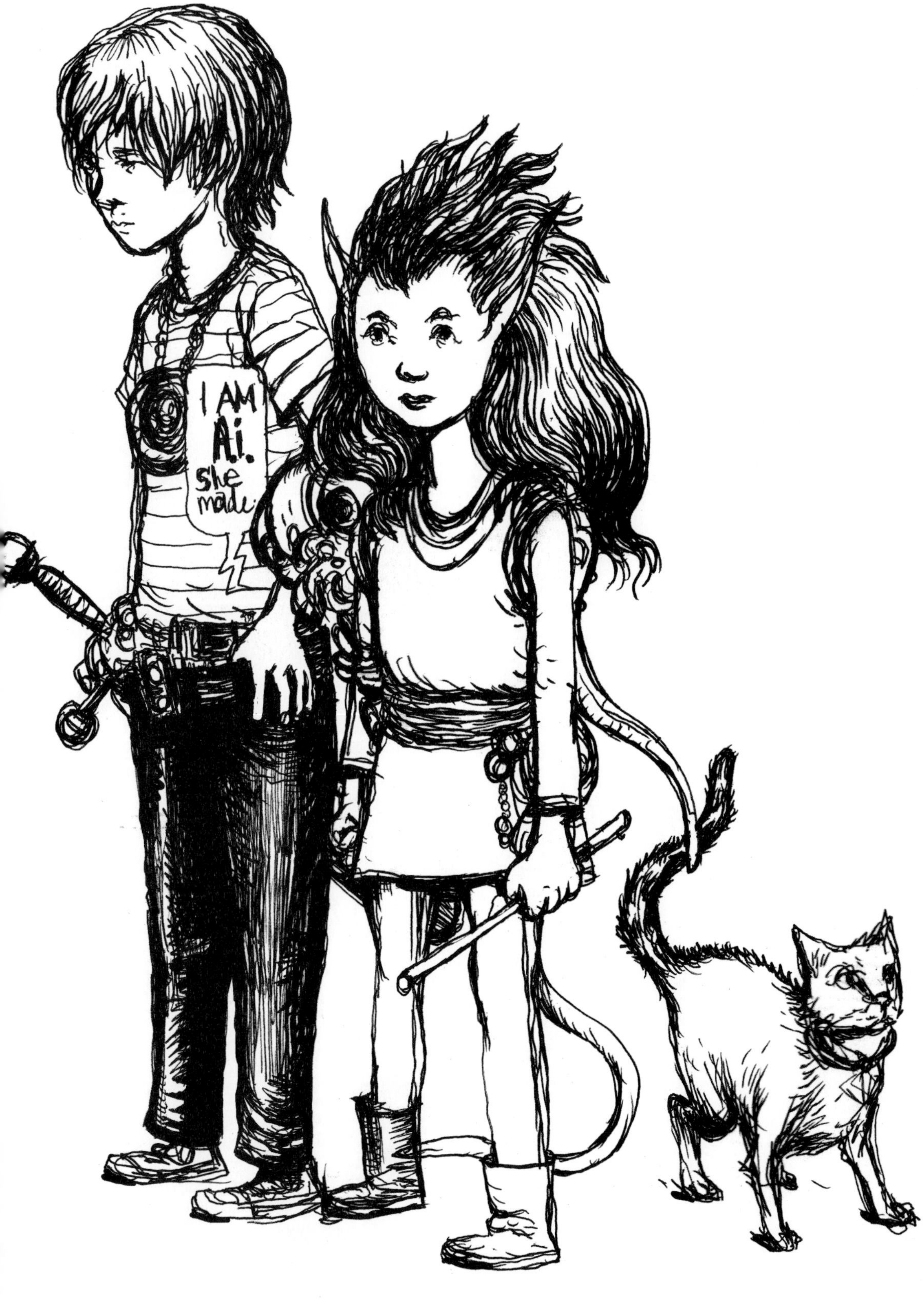
I AM
A.I.
she
made

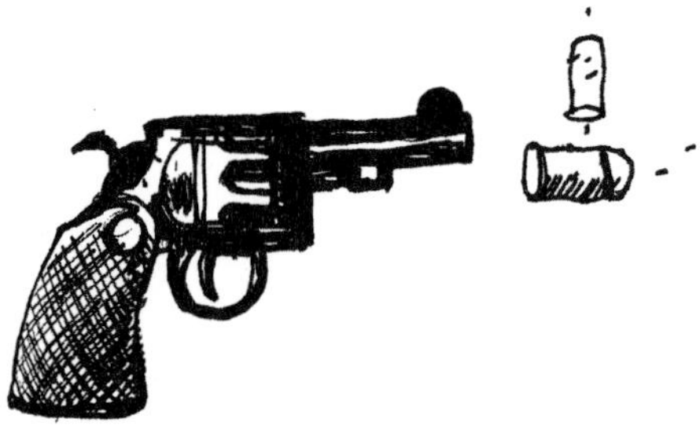

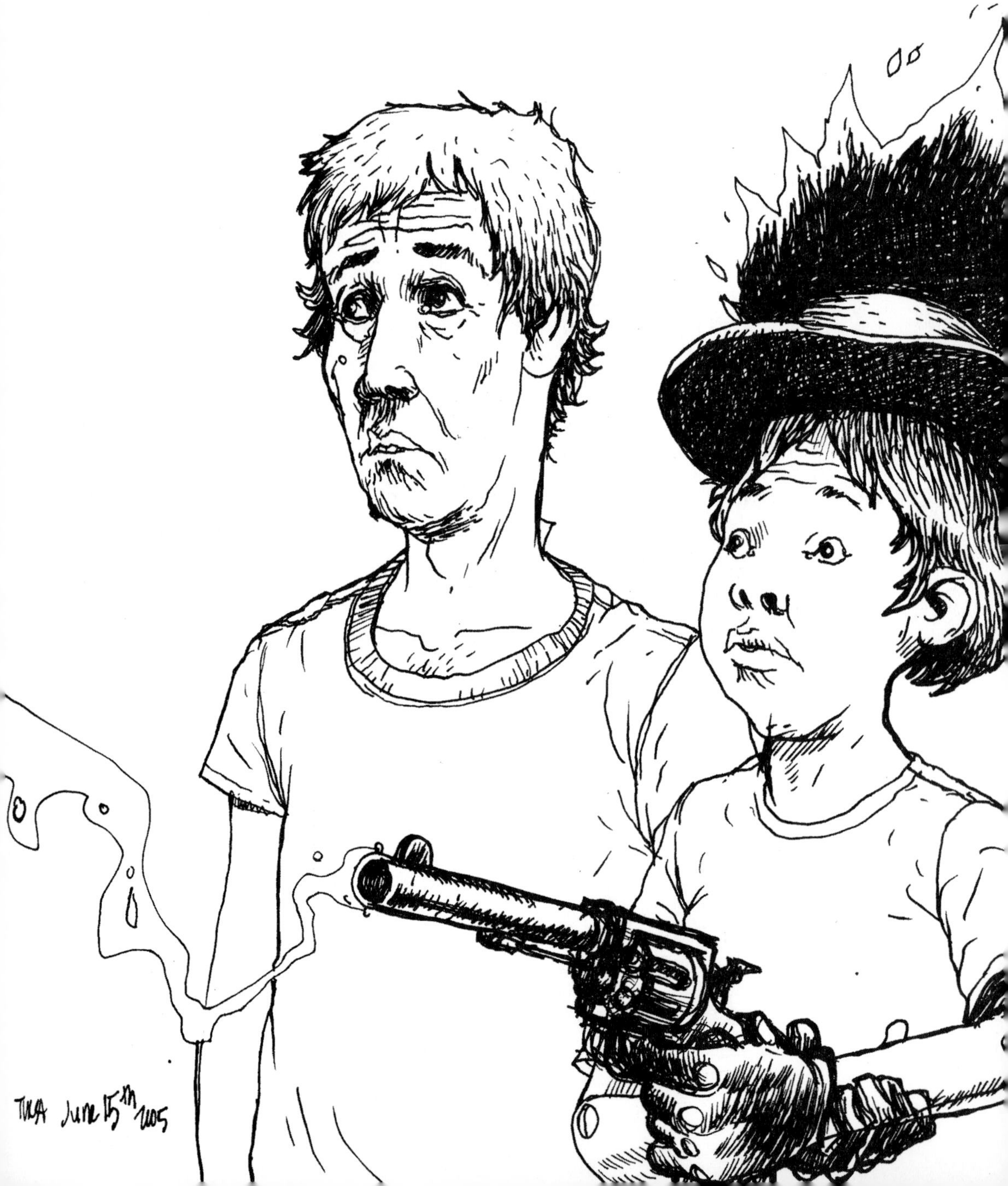
June 15th 2005

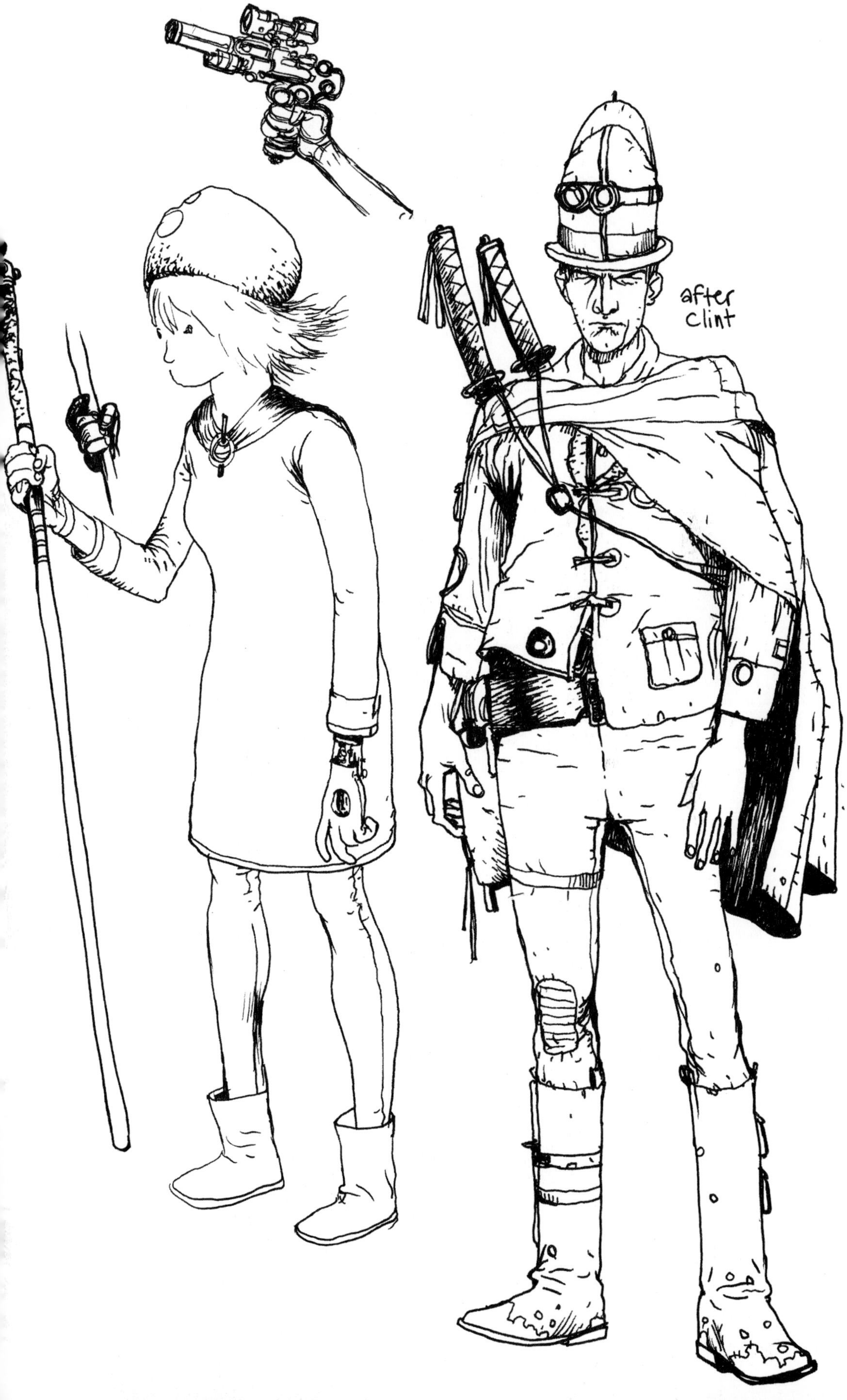
after
Clint

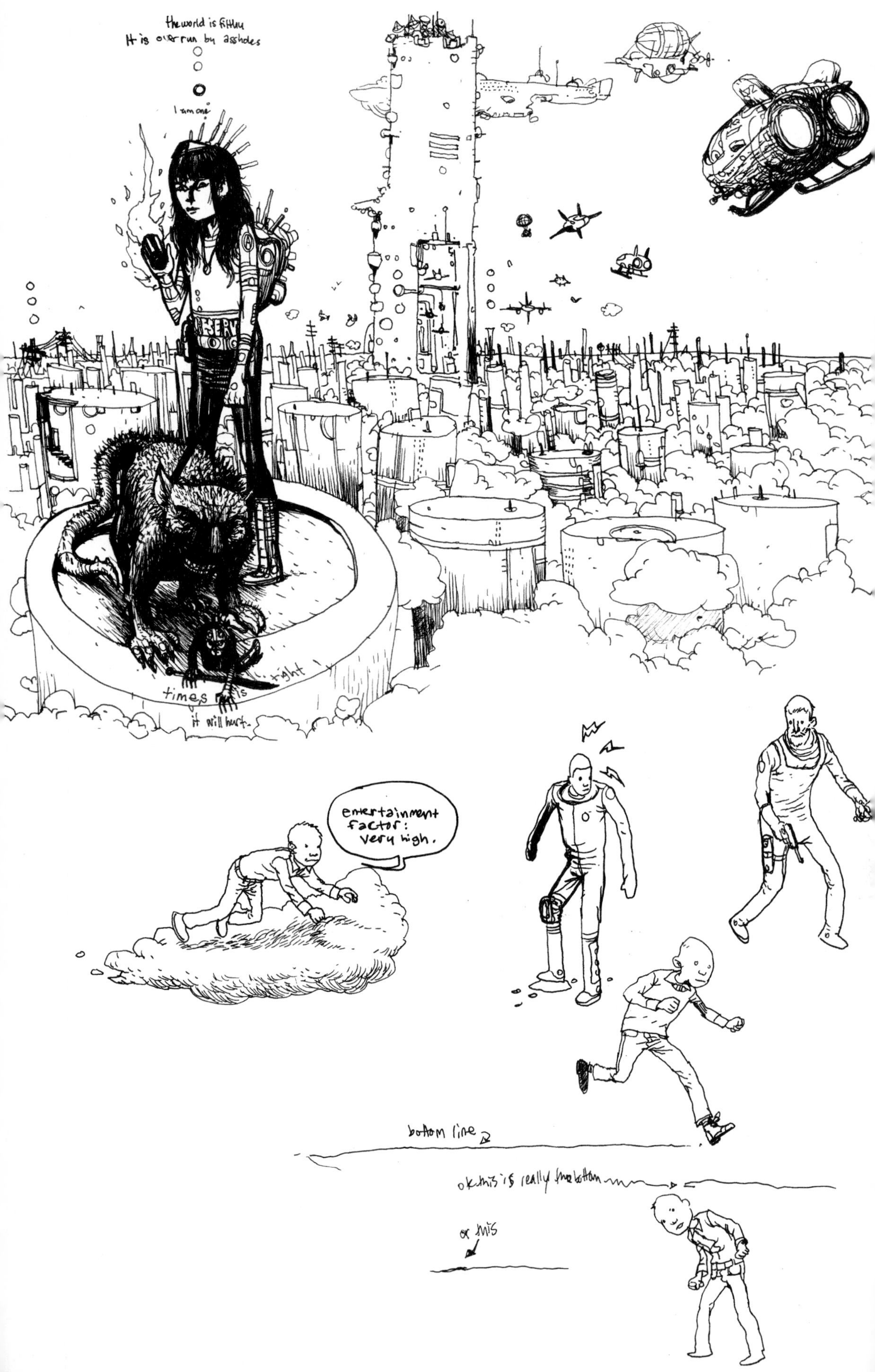
the world is filthy
It is overrun by assholes
I am one
times is right
it will hurt.
entertainment factor: very high.
bottom line
ok this is really the bottom
or this

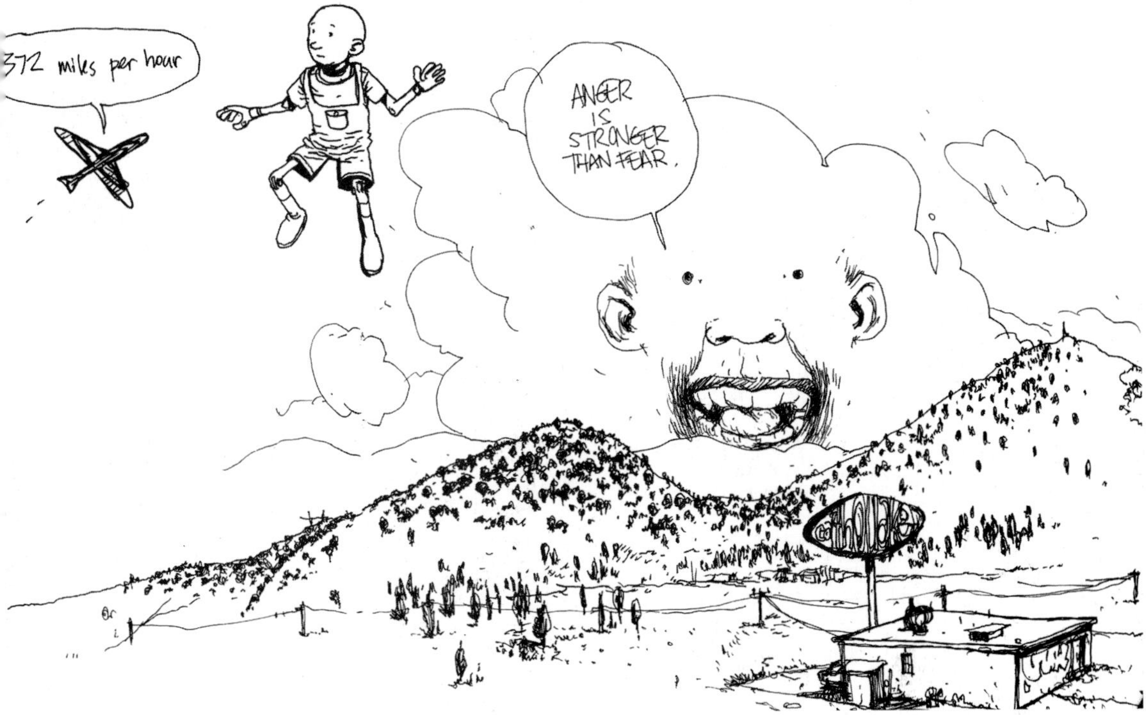
372 miles per hour
ANGER IS STRONGER THAN FEAR

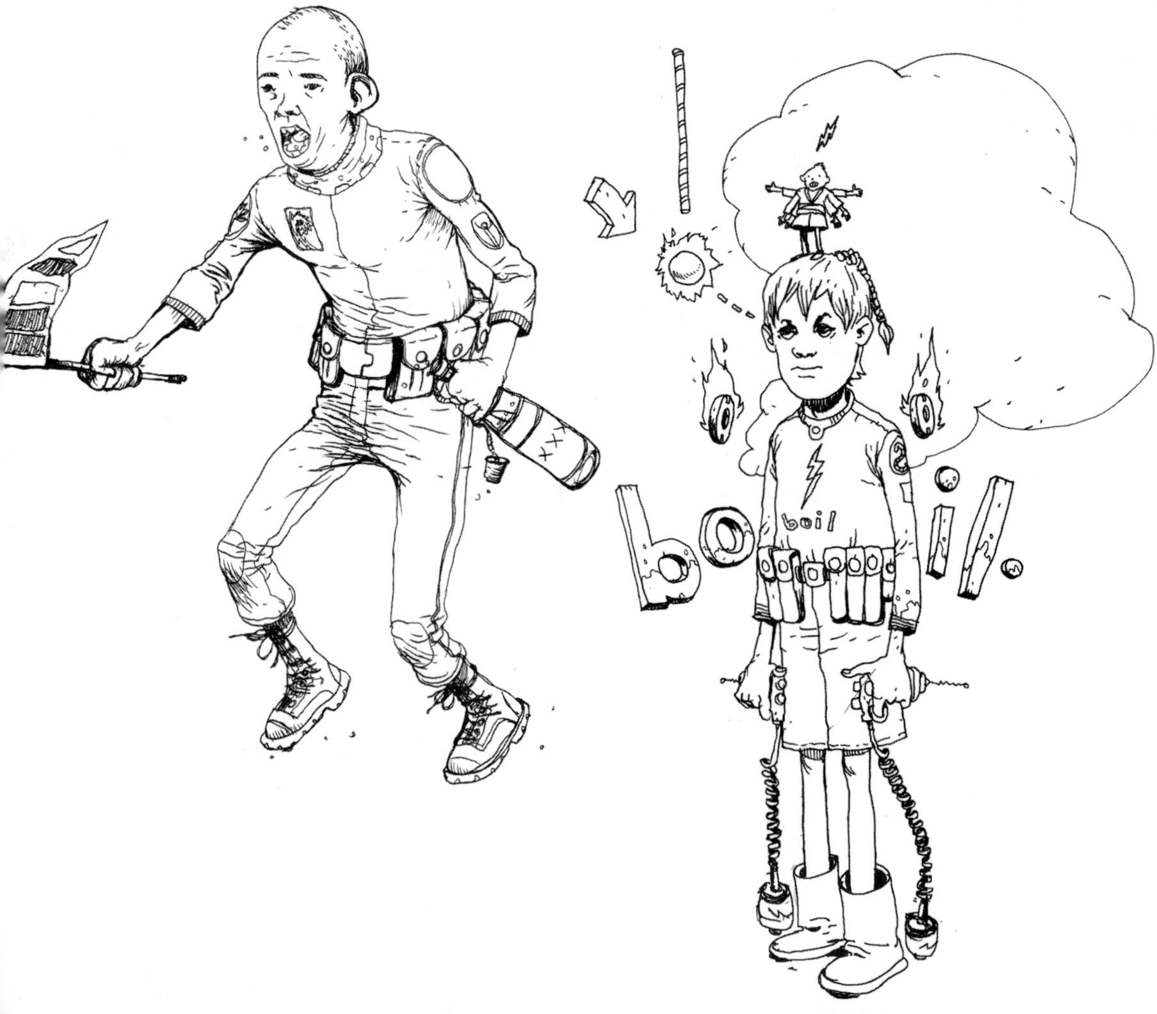
boil
boil

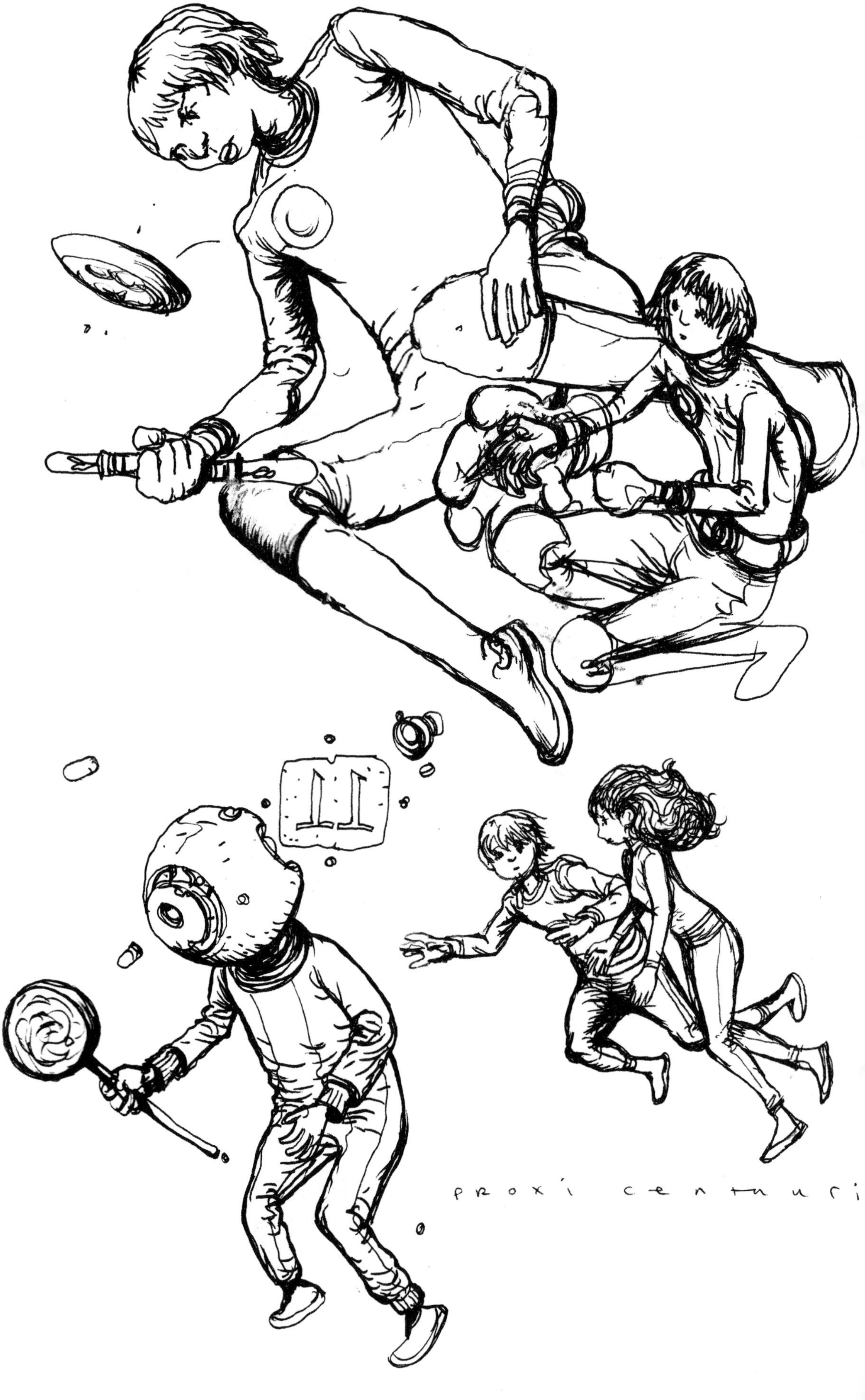
proxi centauri

PROXIMA
CENTAURI

a drift
forever

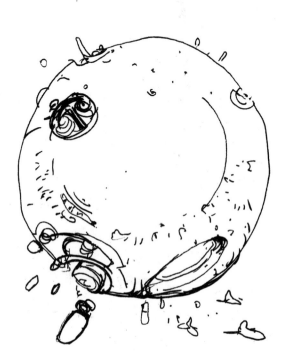

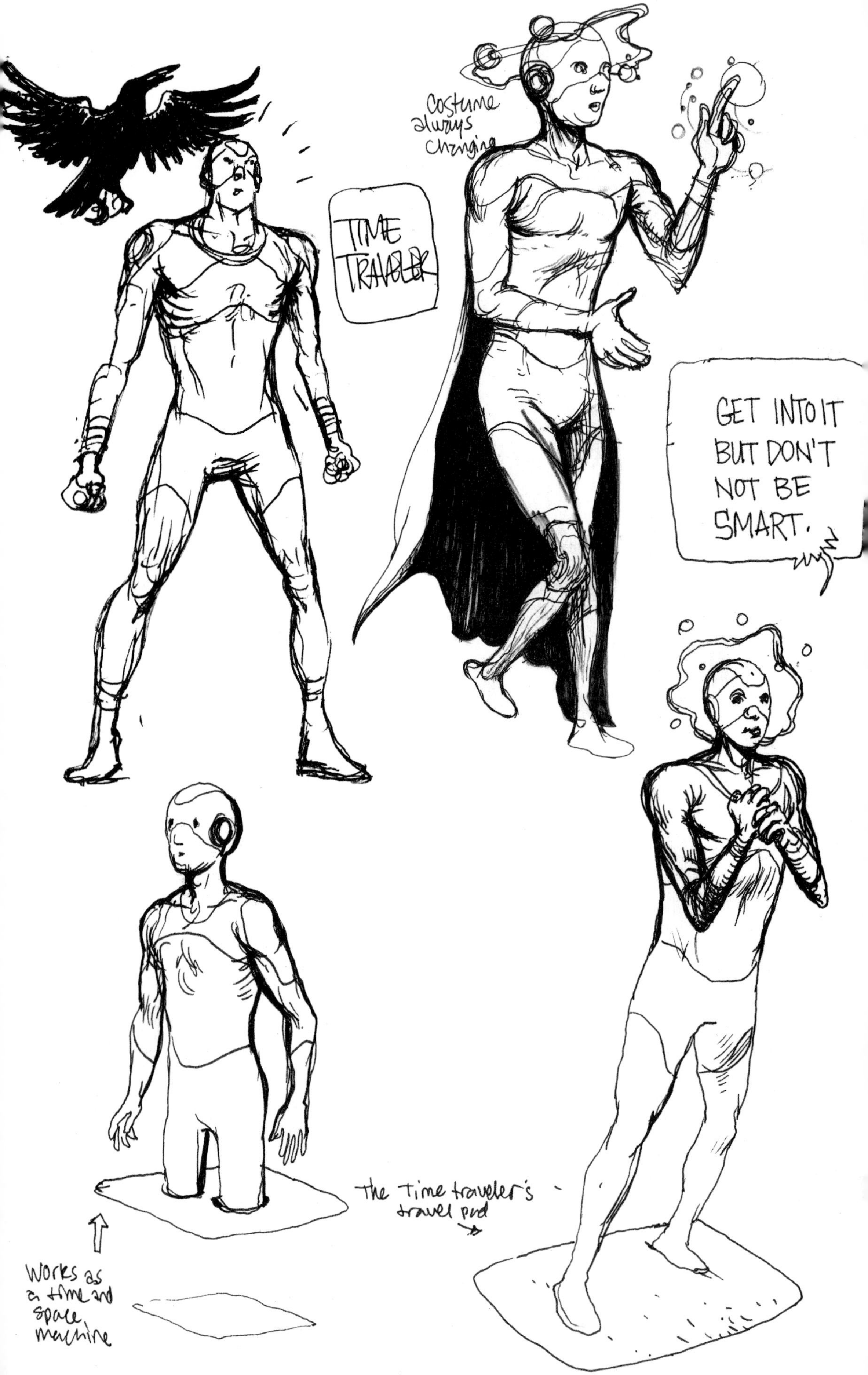
Costume always changing
TIME TRAVELER
GET INTO IT BUT DON'T NOT BE SMART.
The Time traveler's travel pad
Works as a time and space machine

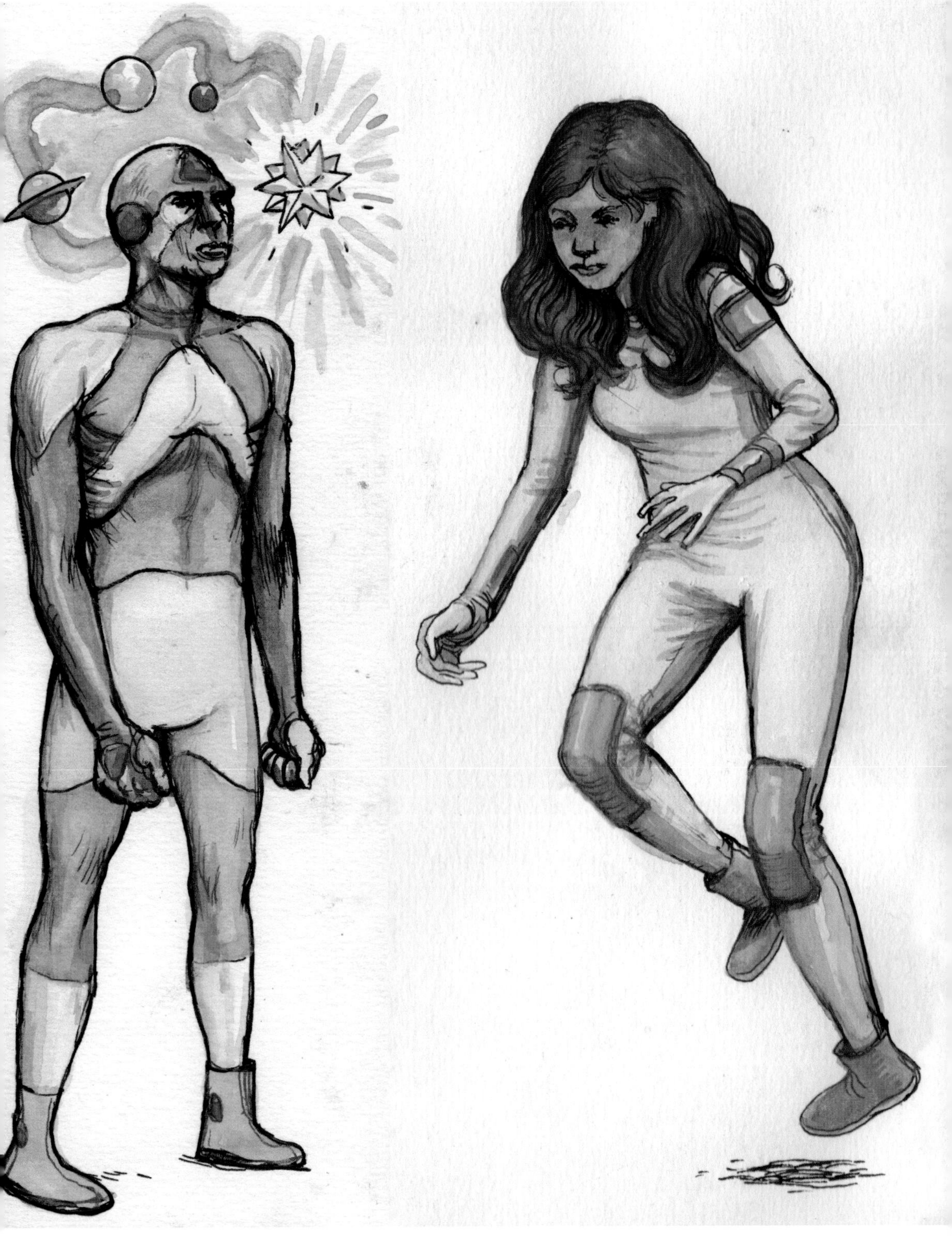

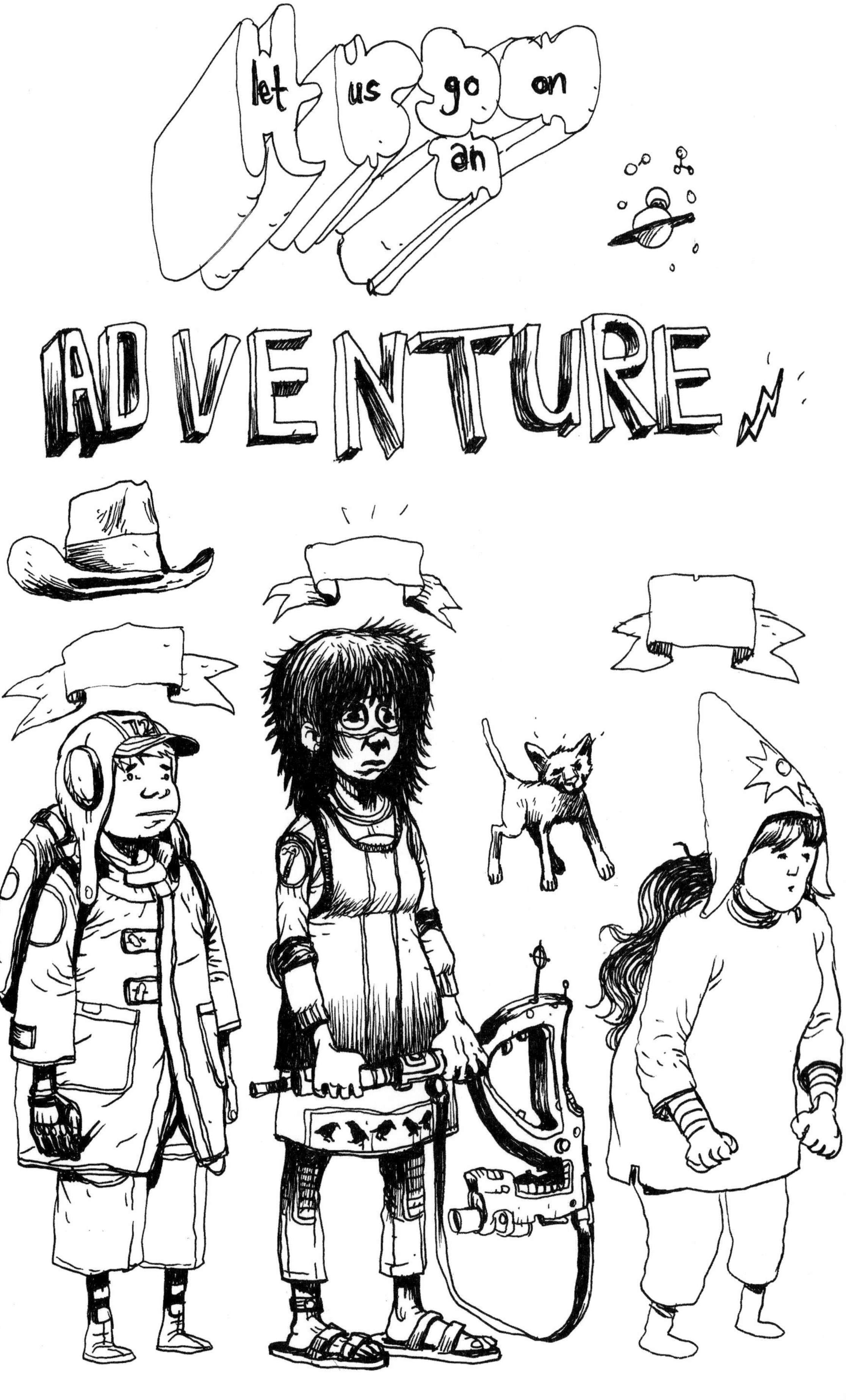
let us go on an
ADVENTURE

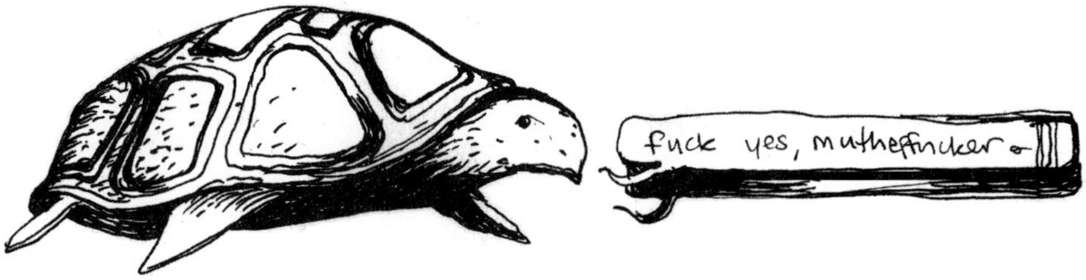
fuck yes, muthefucker.

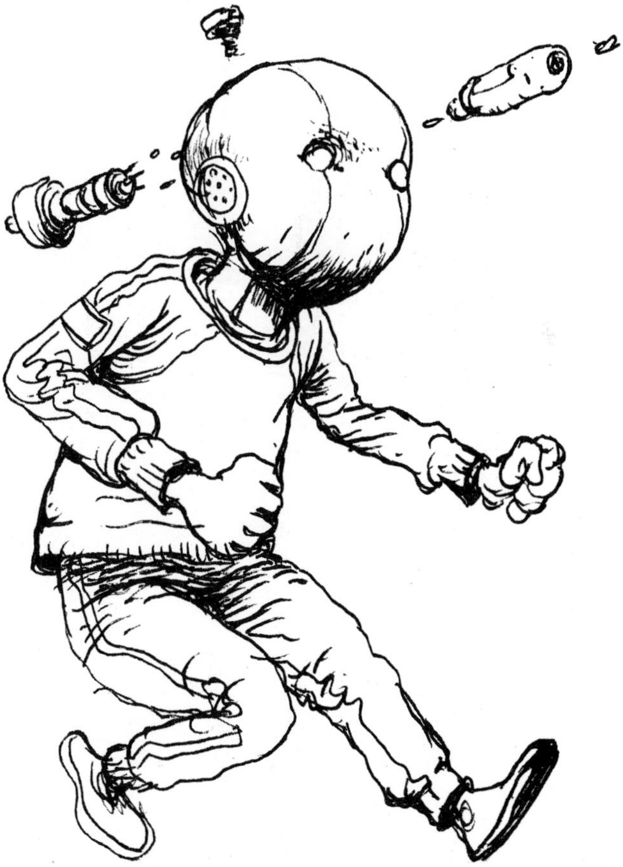

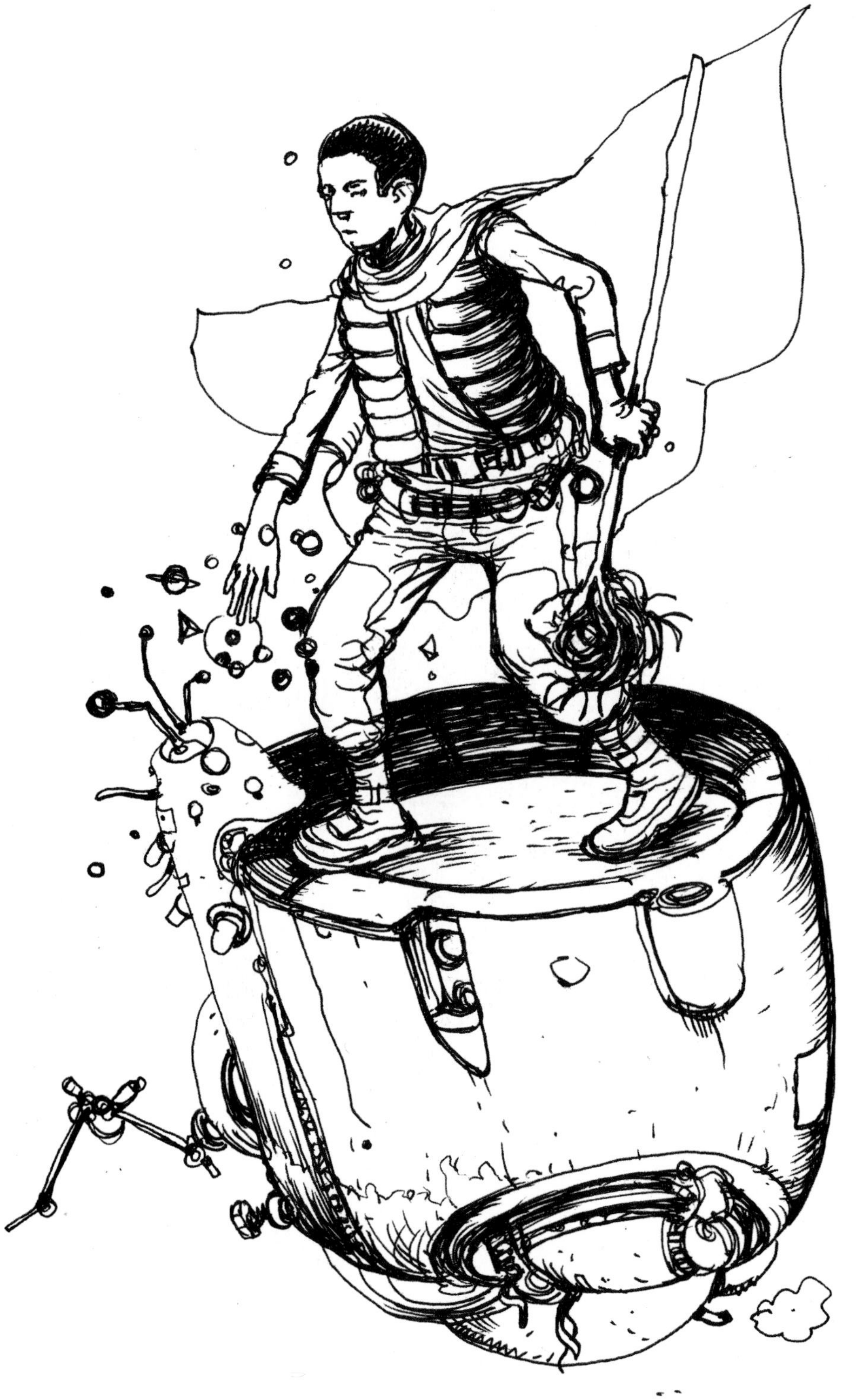

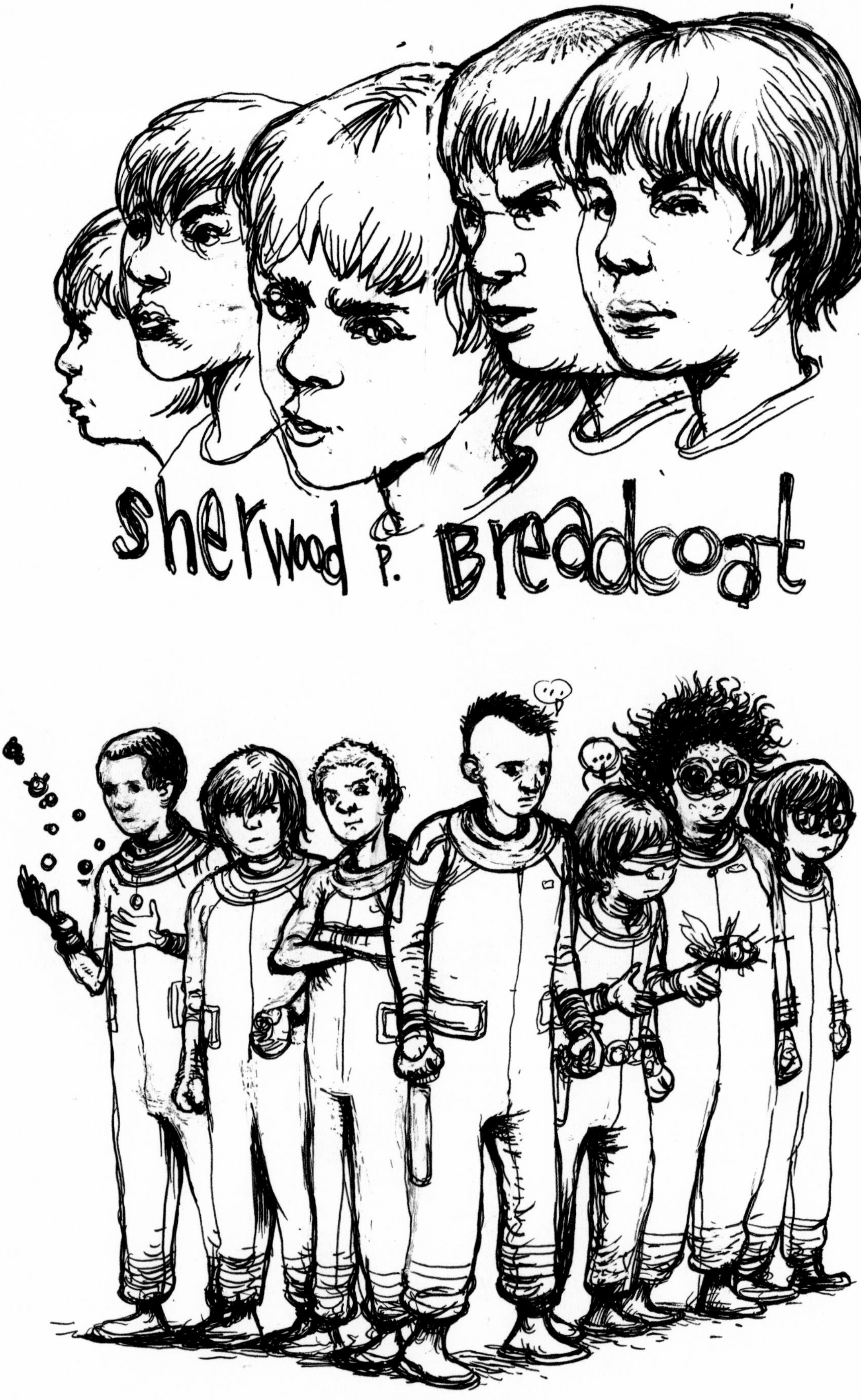
Sherwood P. Breadcoat

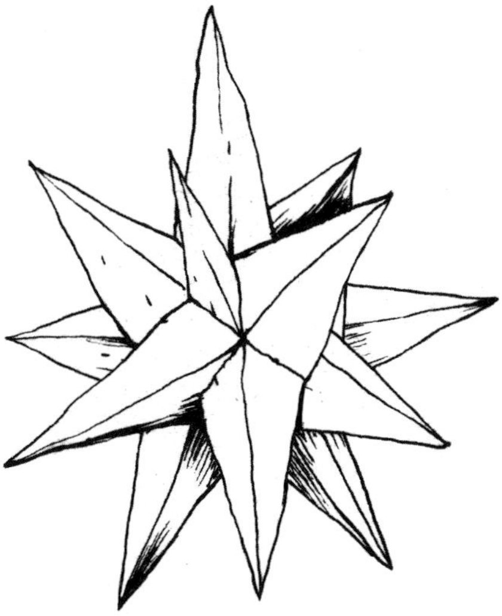

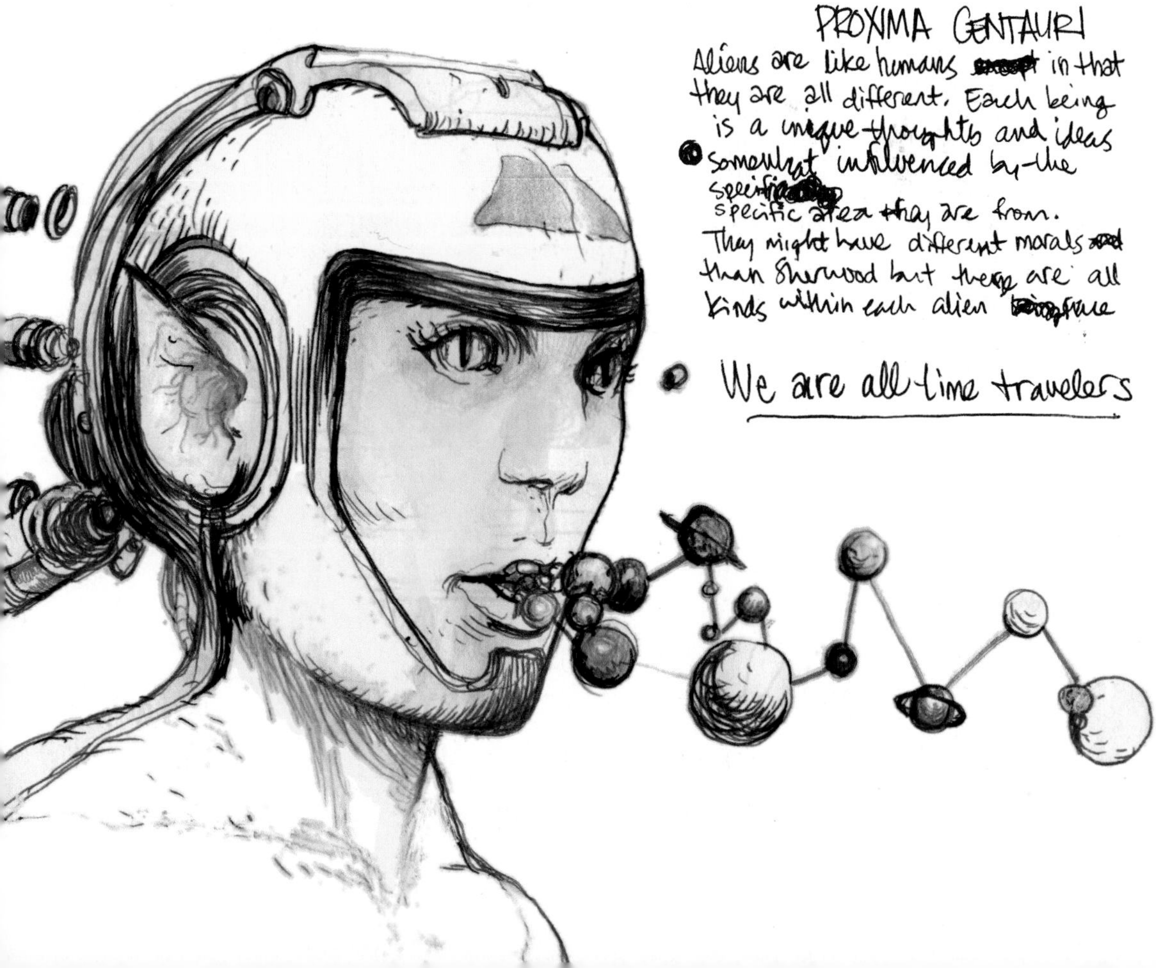
PROXIMA CENTAURI
Aliens are like humans in that
they are all different. Each being
is a unique thoughts and ideas
somewhat influenced by the
specific area they are from.
They might have different morals
than Sherwood but there are all
kinds within each alien race
We are all time travelers

Maintance workers on the proxima centauri never speak and came from a secret center of the station. they are all clones of course.

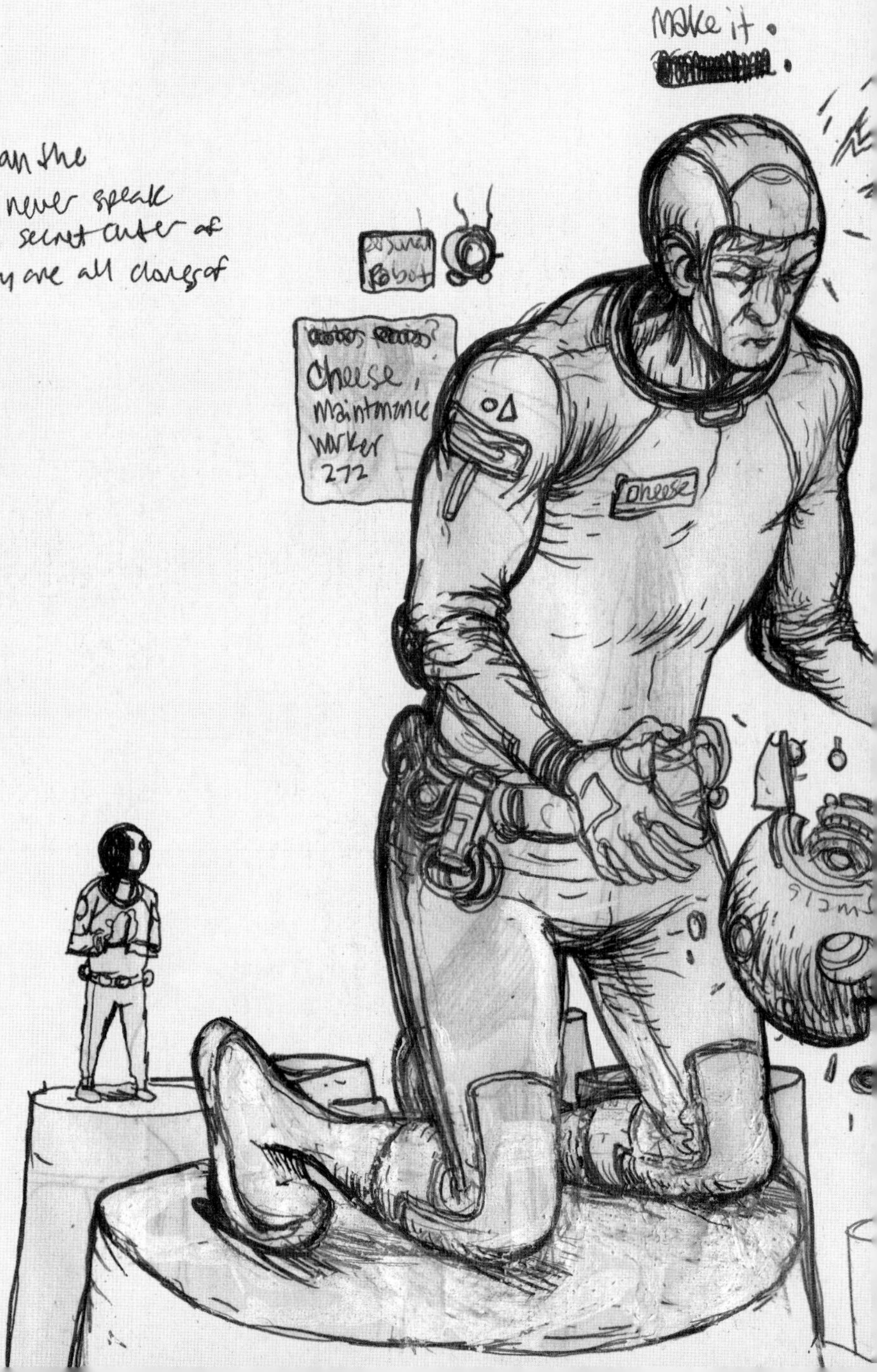
Make it.
Robot
Cheese,
Maintmance
worker
272
Cheese

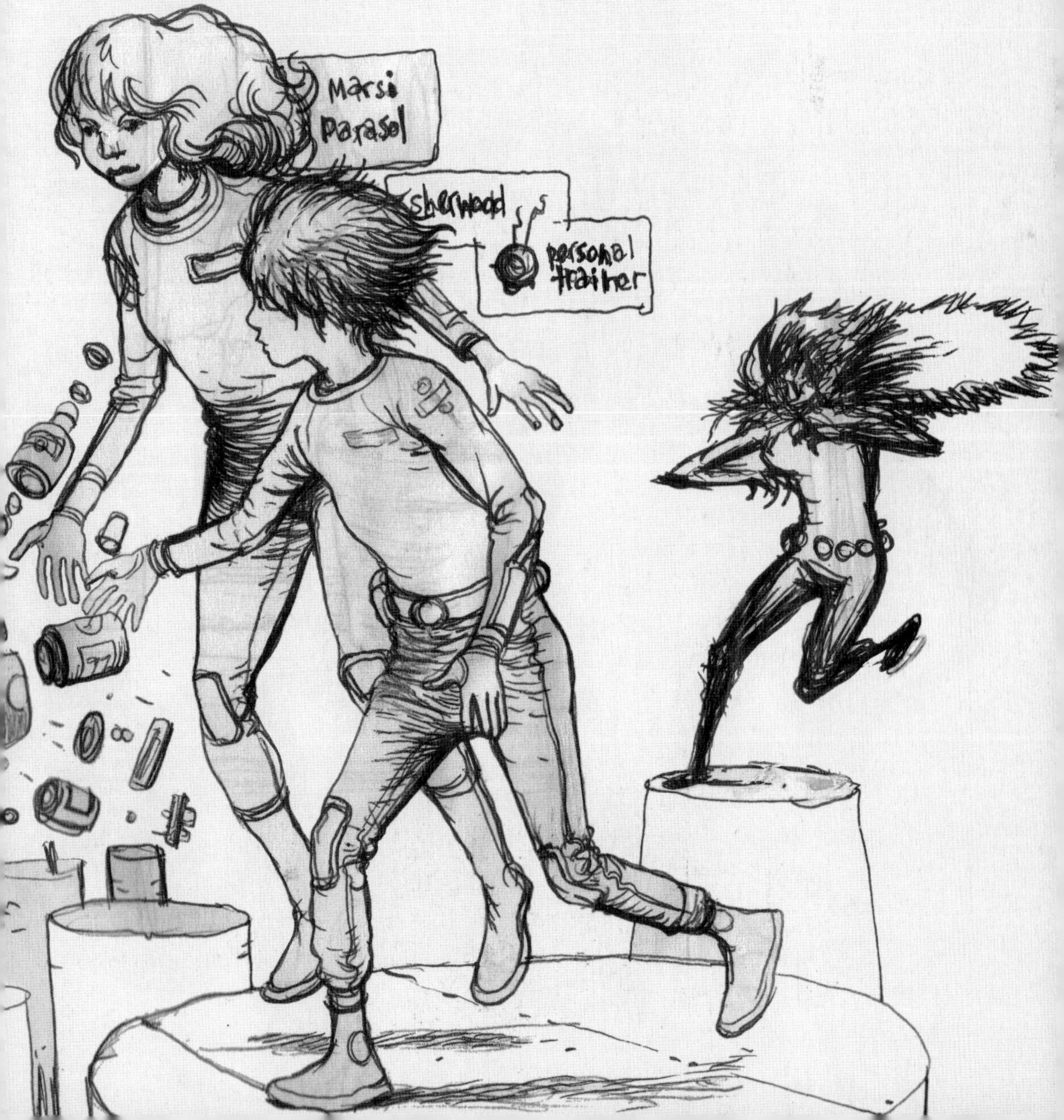
Marsi Parasol
sherwood
personal trainer

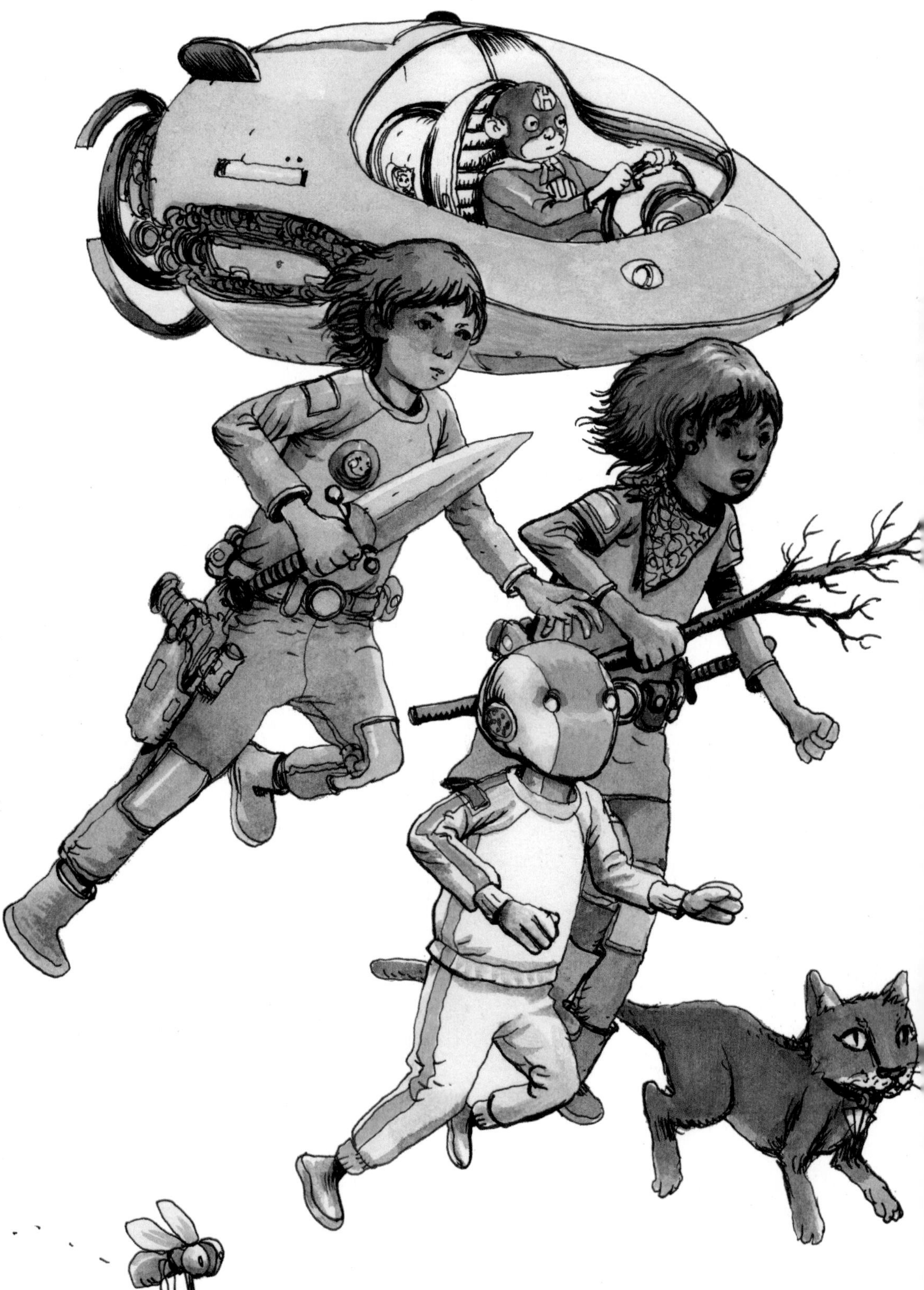

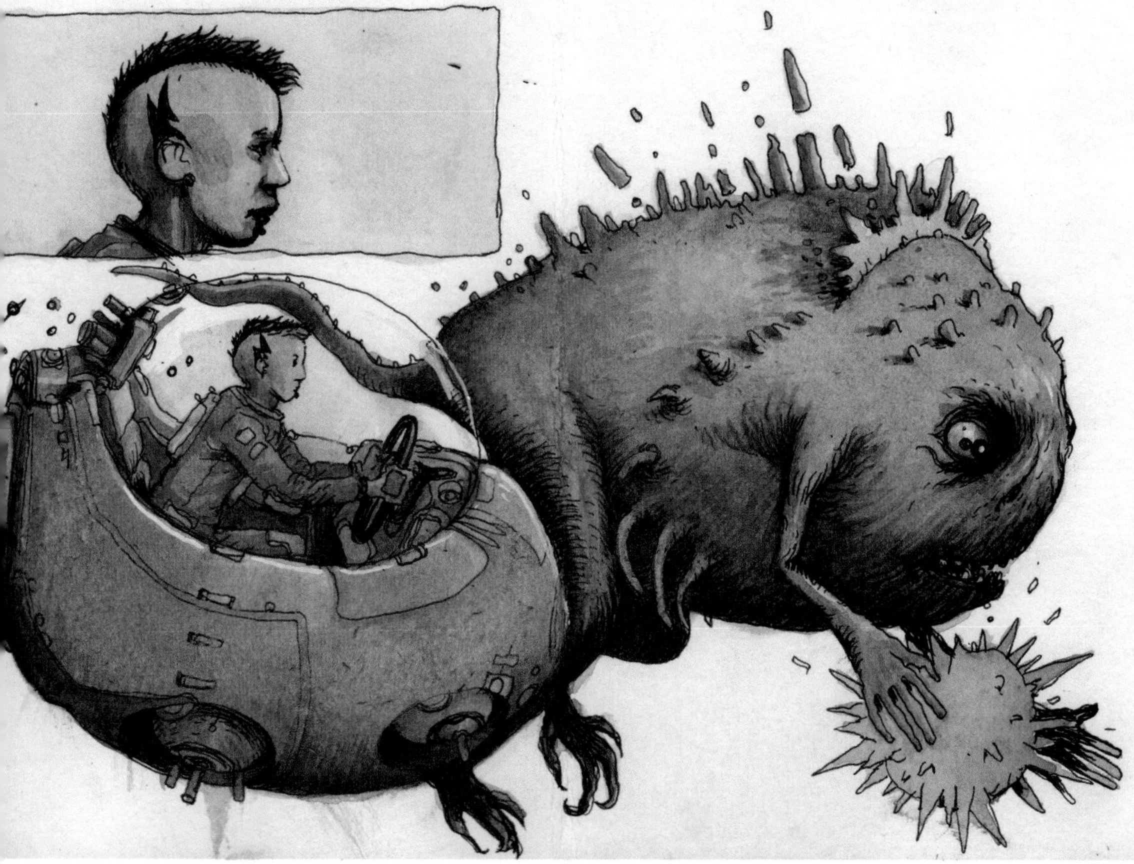

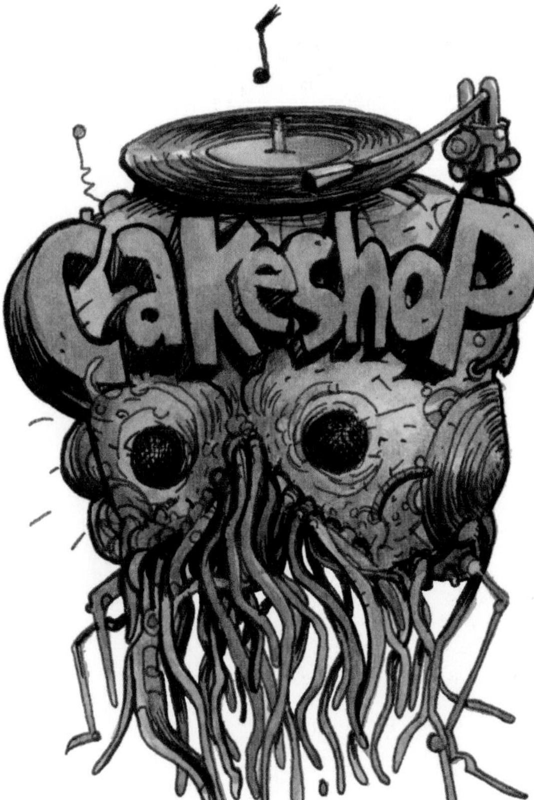
CAKESHOP

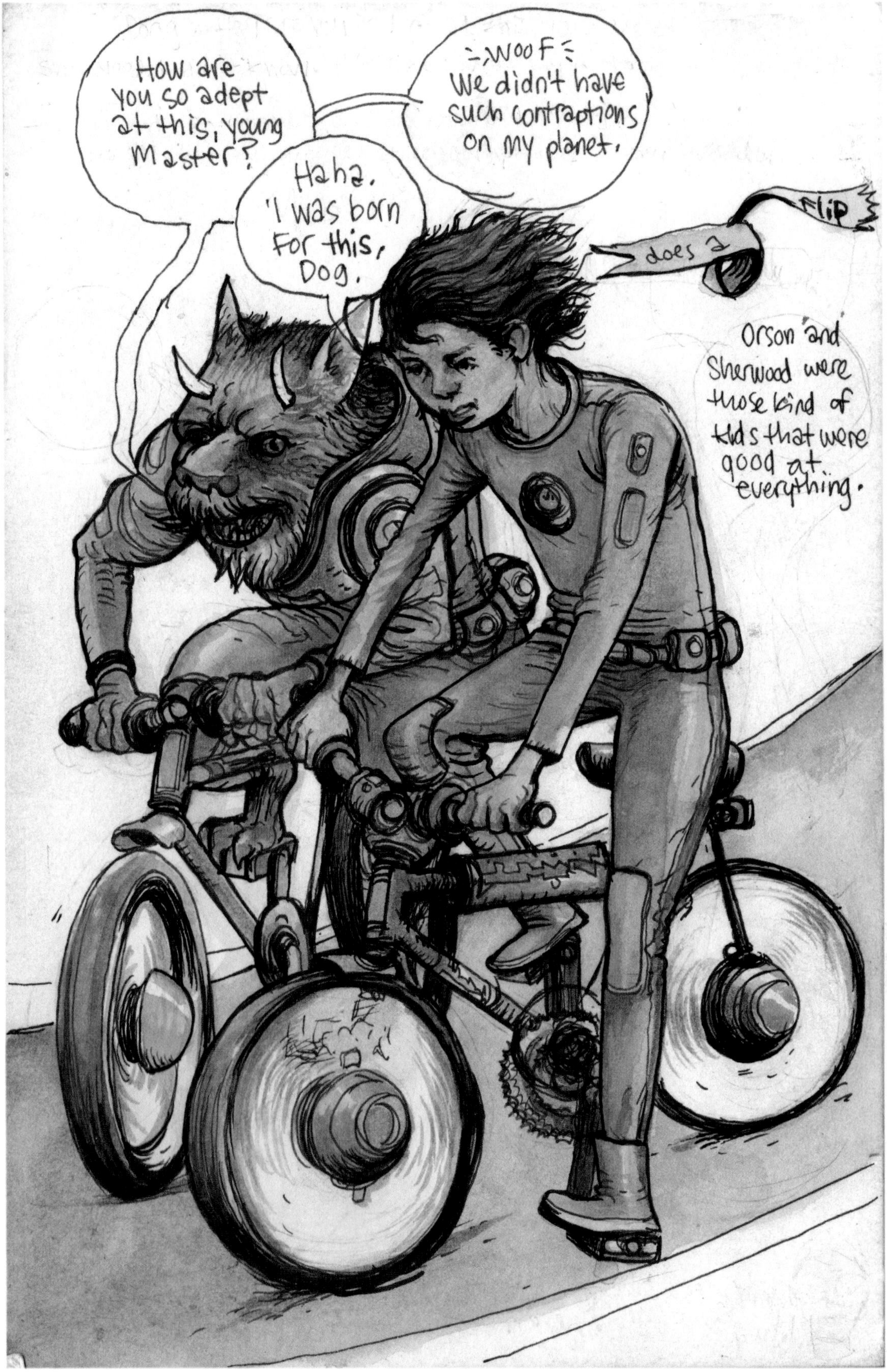
How are you so adept at this, young Master?
-WOOF-
We didn't have such contraptions on my planet.
Haha. I was born for this, Dog.
does a
FLIP
Orson and Sherwood were those kind of kids that were good at everything.

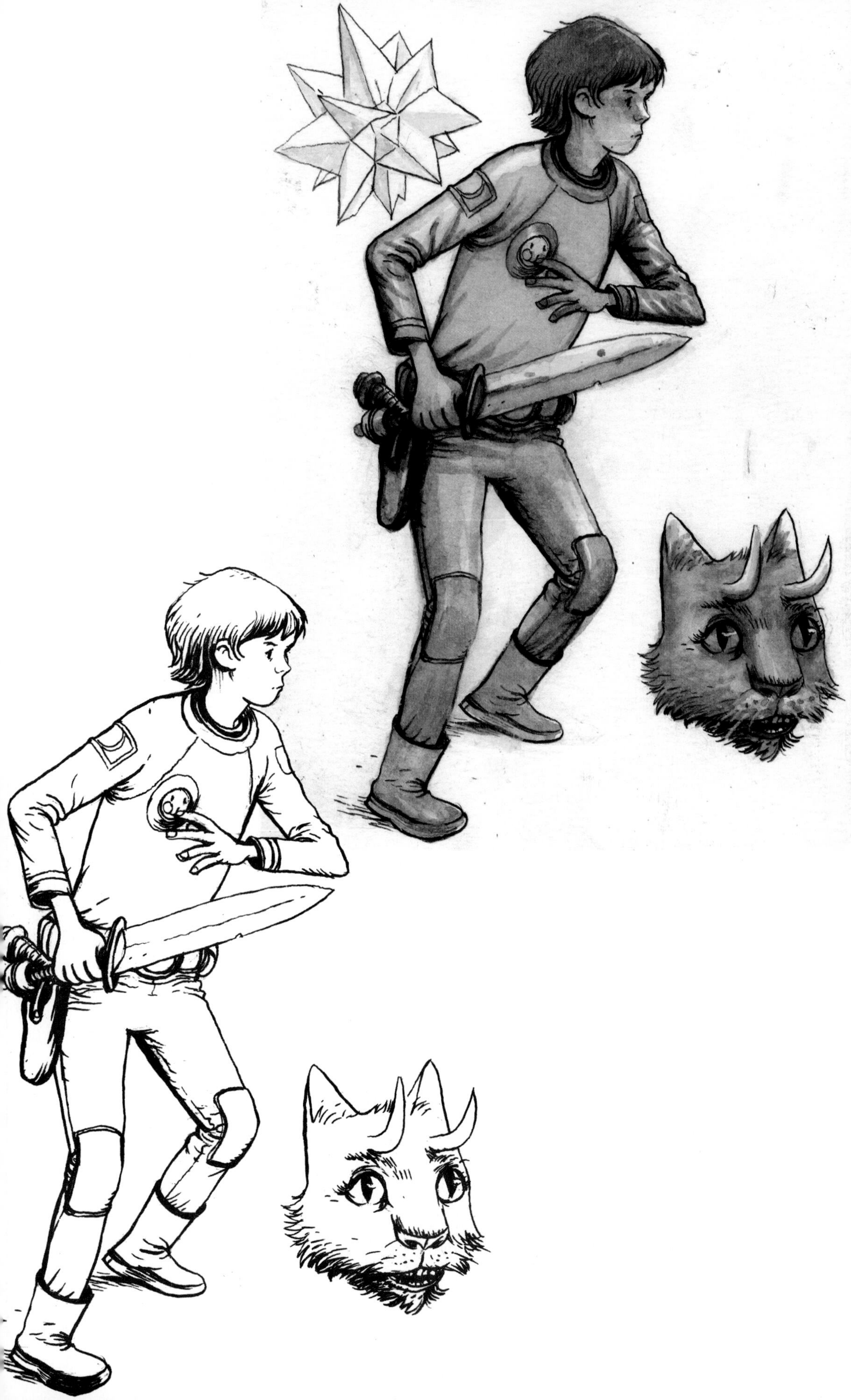

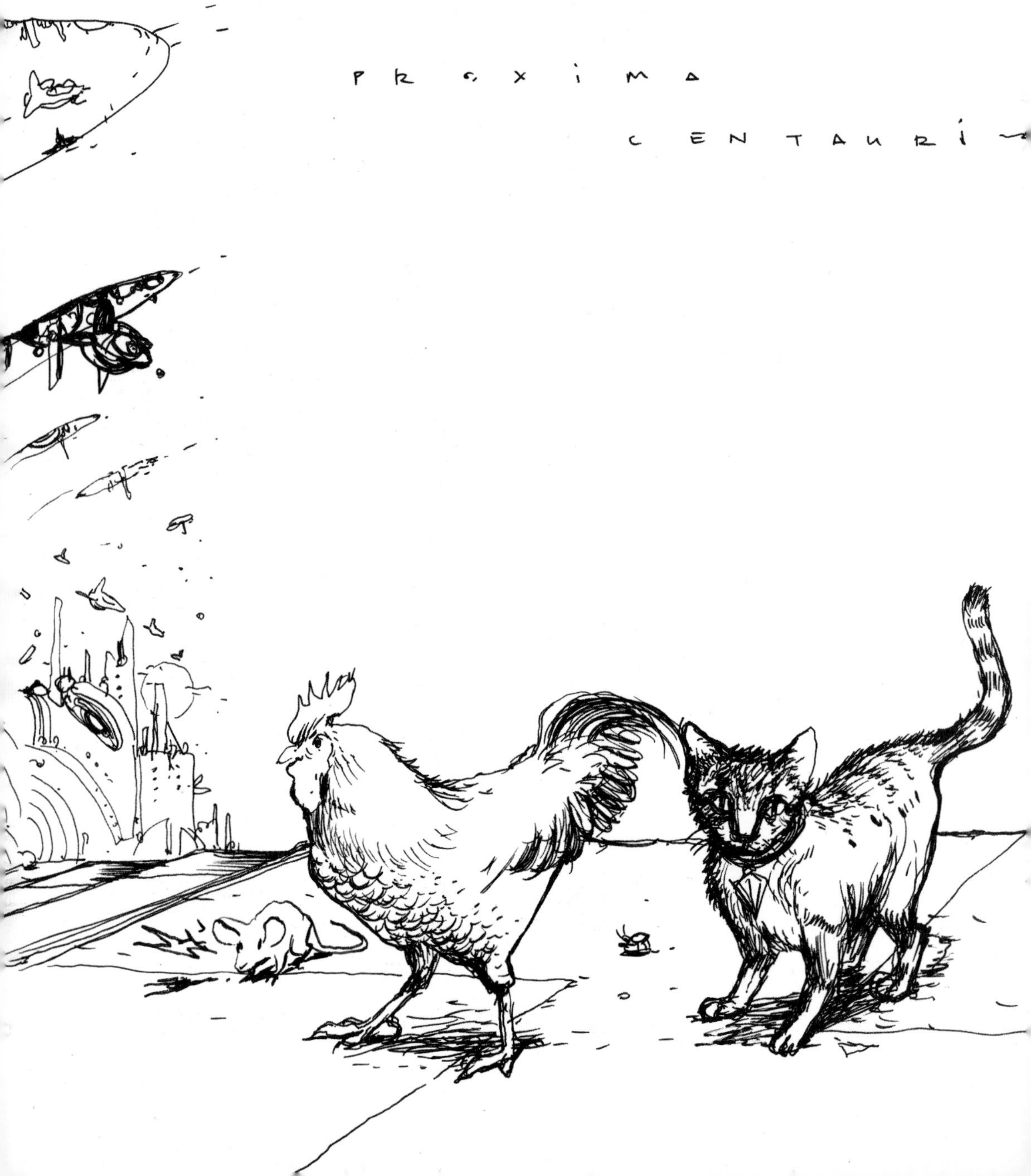
PROXIMA
CENTAURI

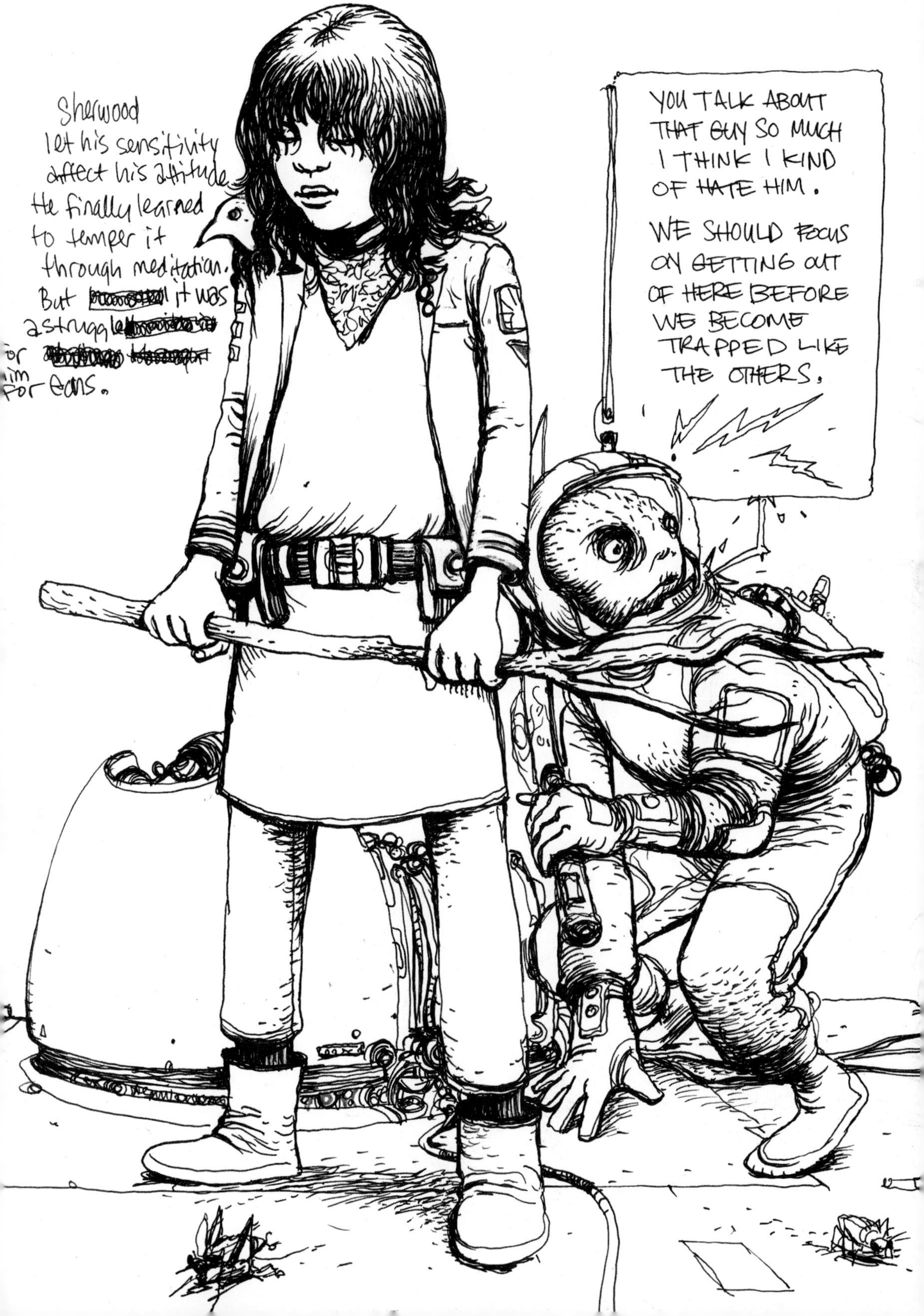
Sherwood
let his sensitivity
affect his attitude
He finally learned
to temper it
through meditation.
But it was
a struggle
or
im
for eons.
YOU TALK ABOUT THAT GUY SO MUCH I THINK I KIND OF HATE HIM.
WE SHOULD FOCUS ON GETTING OUT OF HERE BEFORE WE BECOME TRAPPED LIKE THE OTHERS.

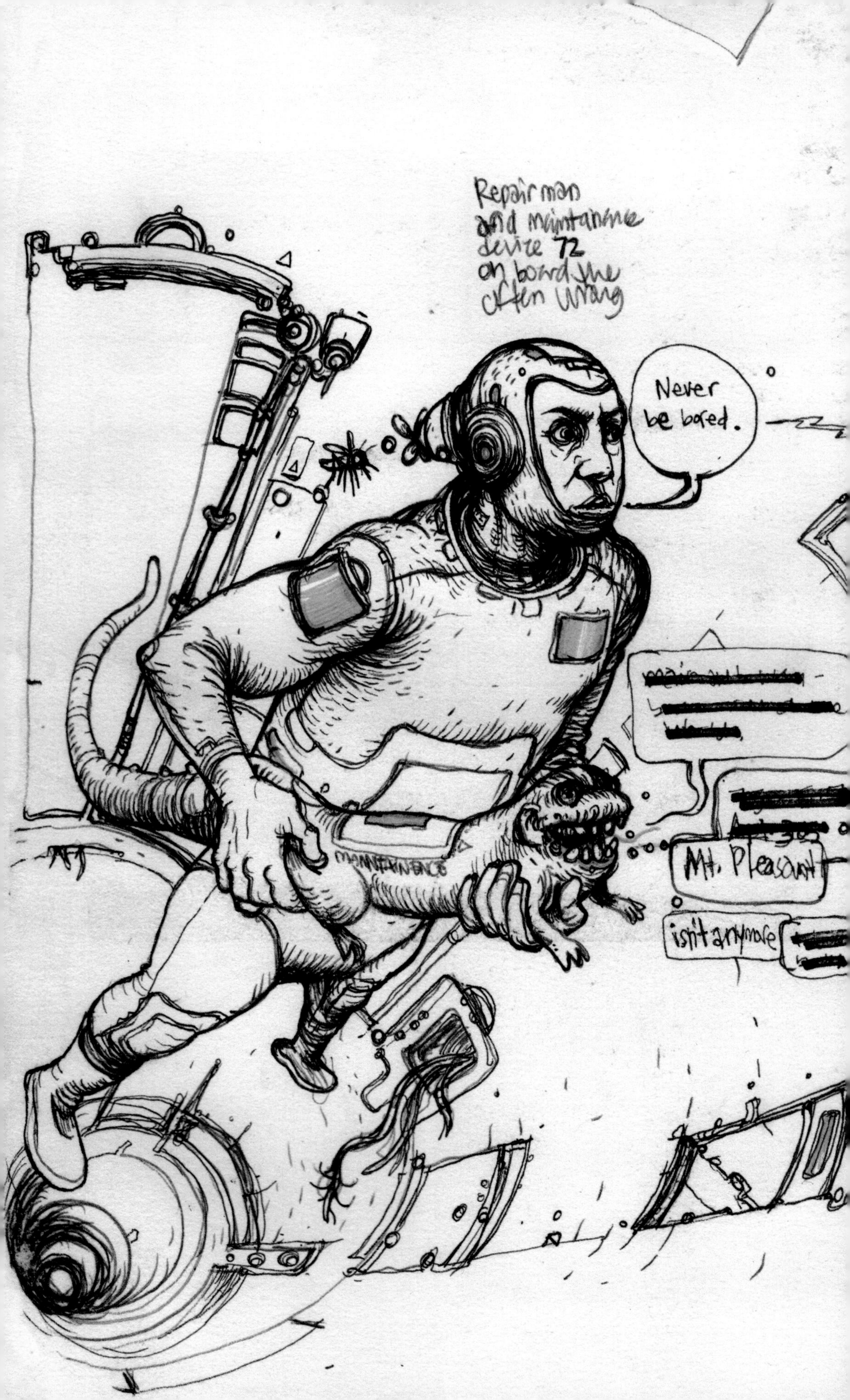
Repairman and maintainance device 72 on board the often wrong
Never be bored.
[redacted]
[redacted]
Mt. Pleasant
isn't anymore
[redacted]

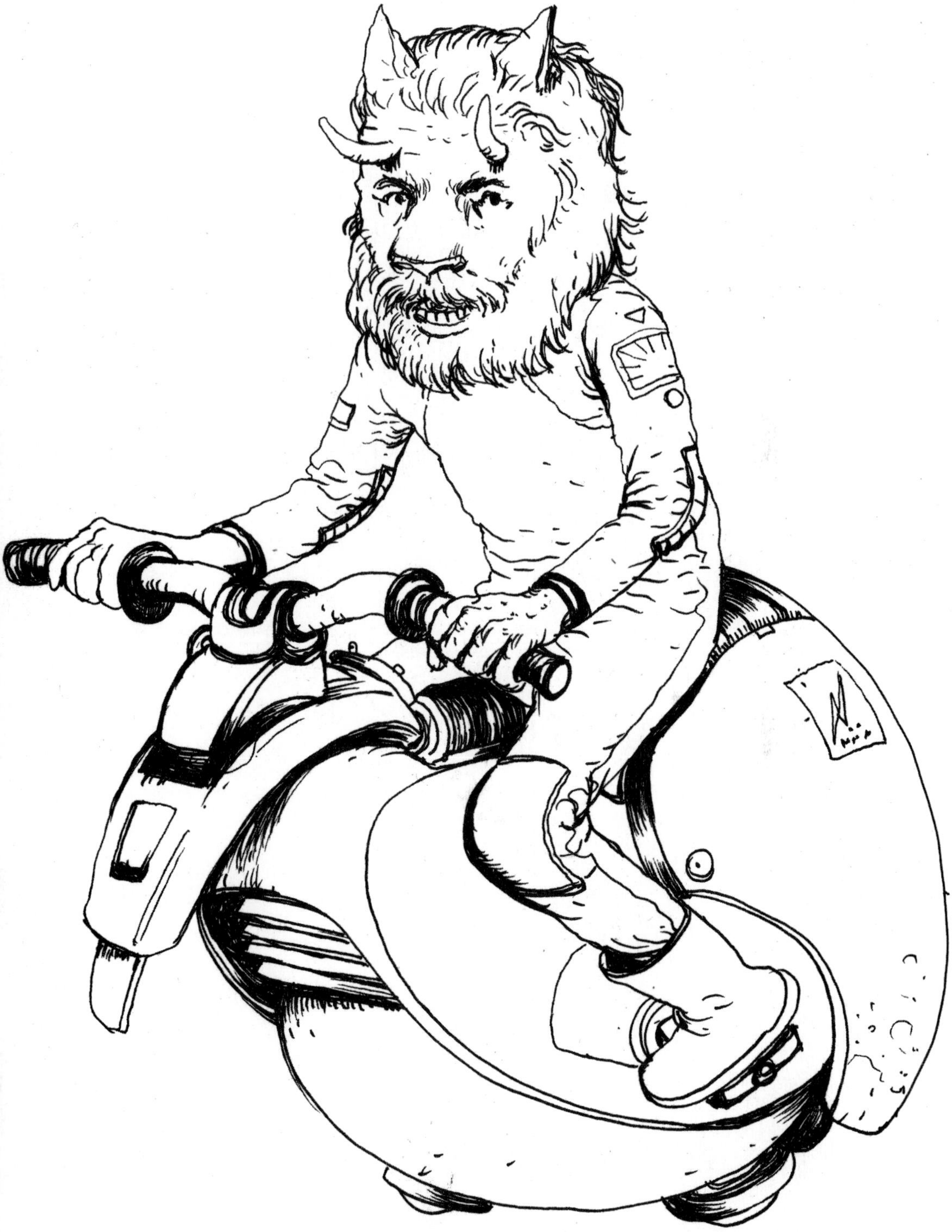

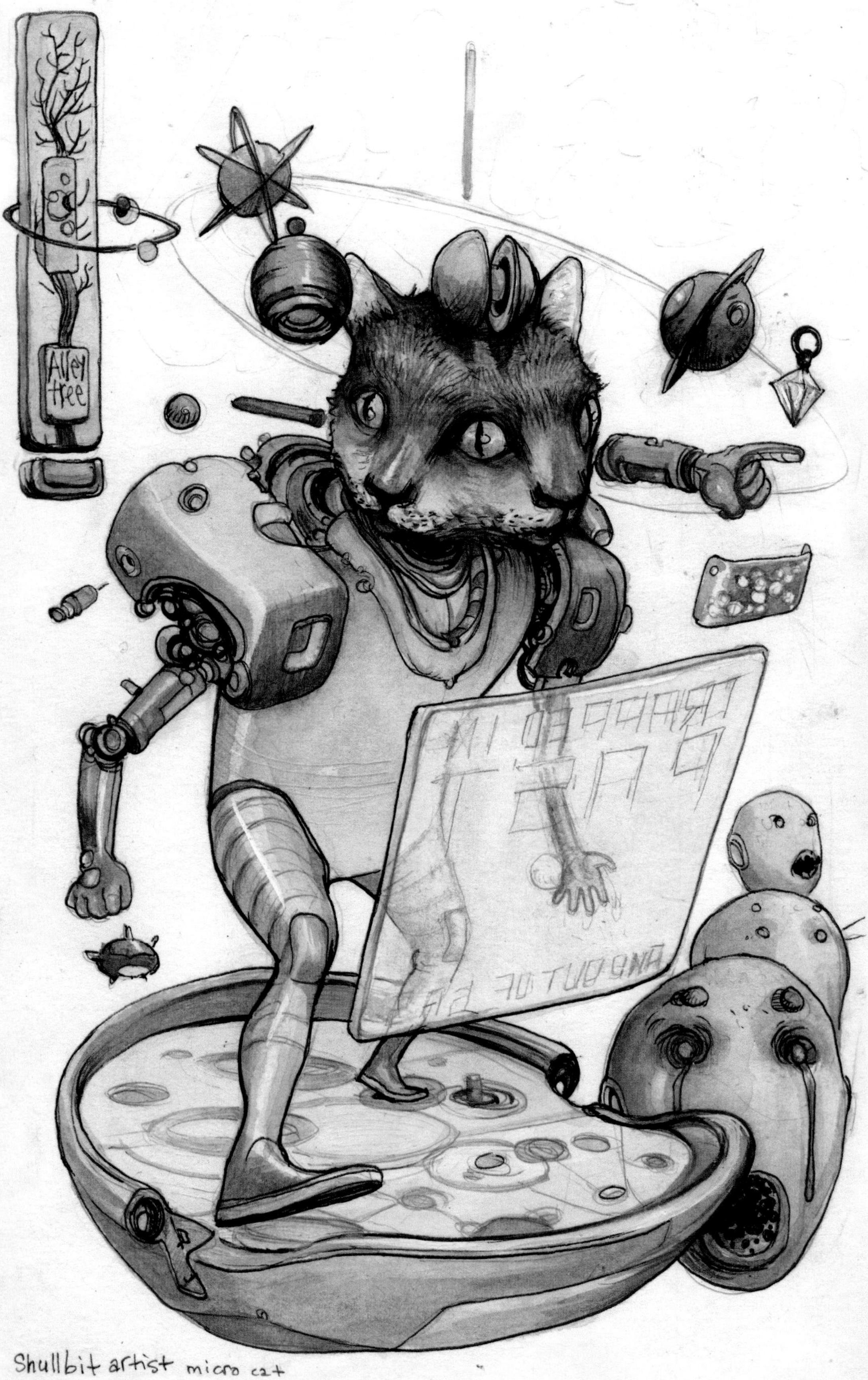
Alley tree

Shullbit artist micro cat

farel'd

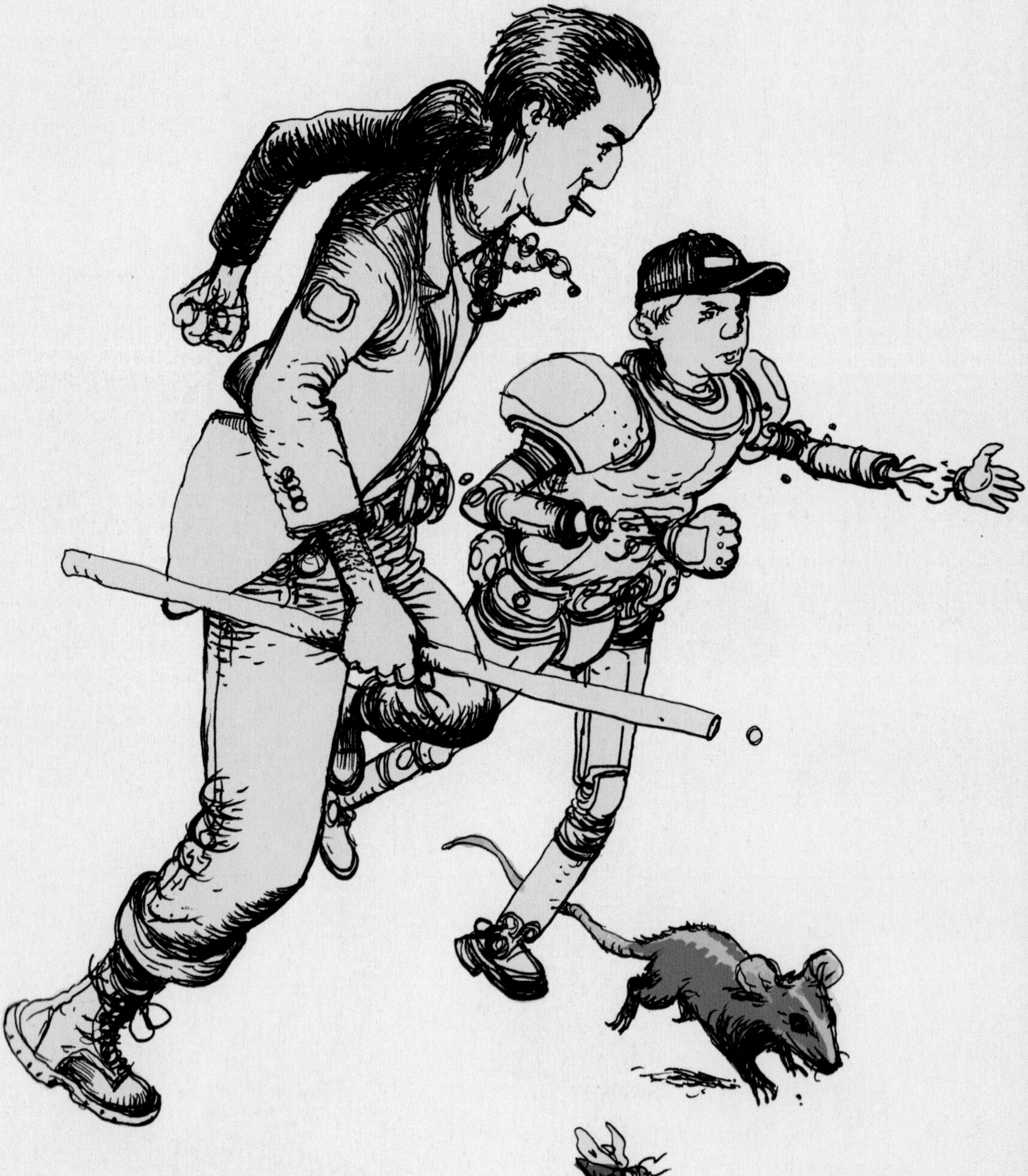

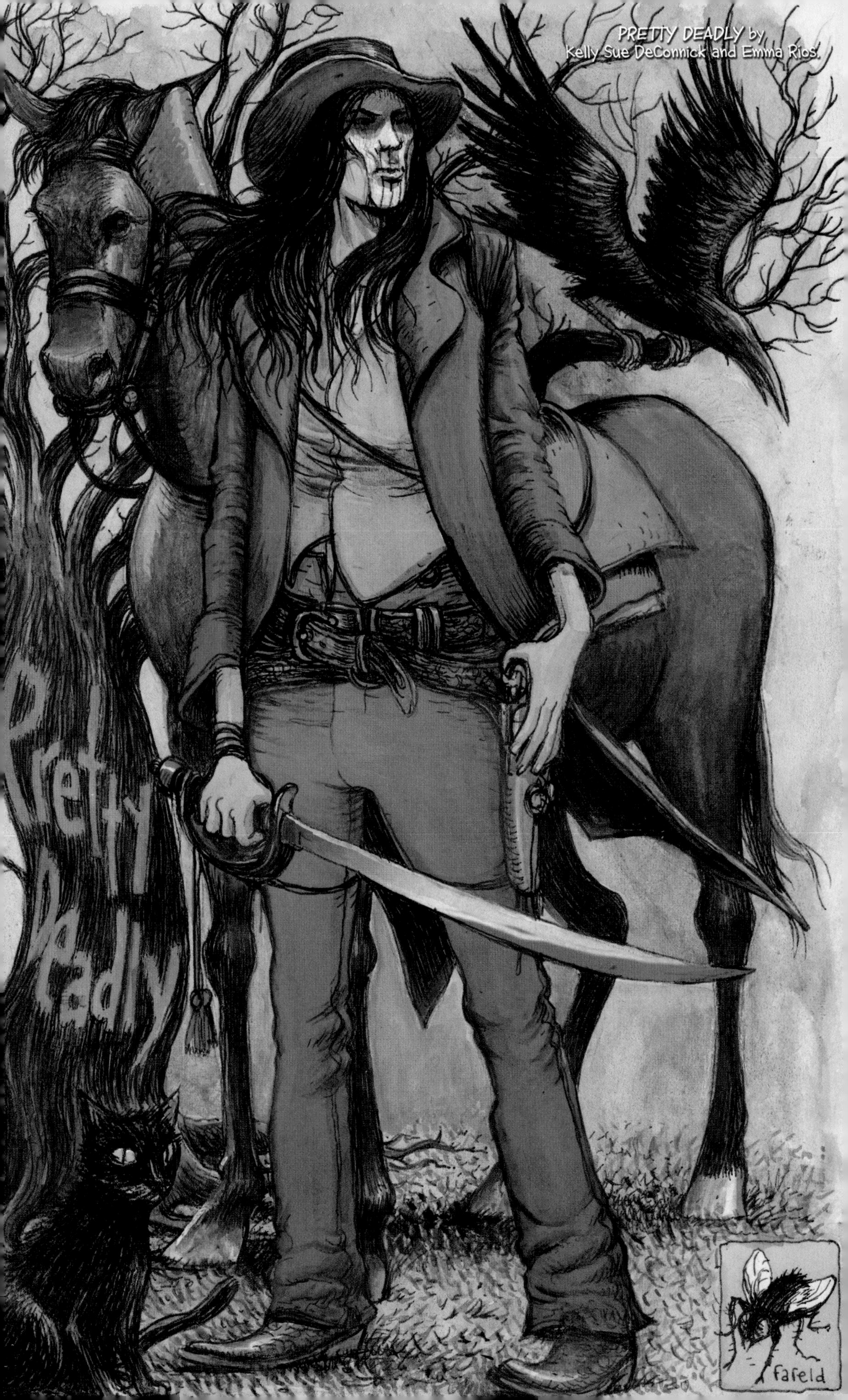
PRETTY DEADLY by
Kelly Sue DeConnick and Emma Rios.
Pretty Deadly
fafeld

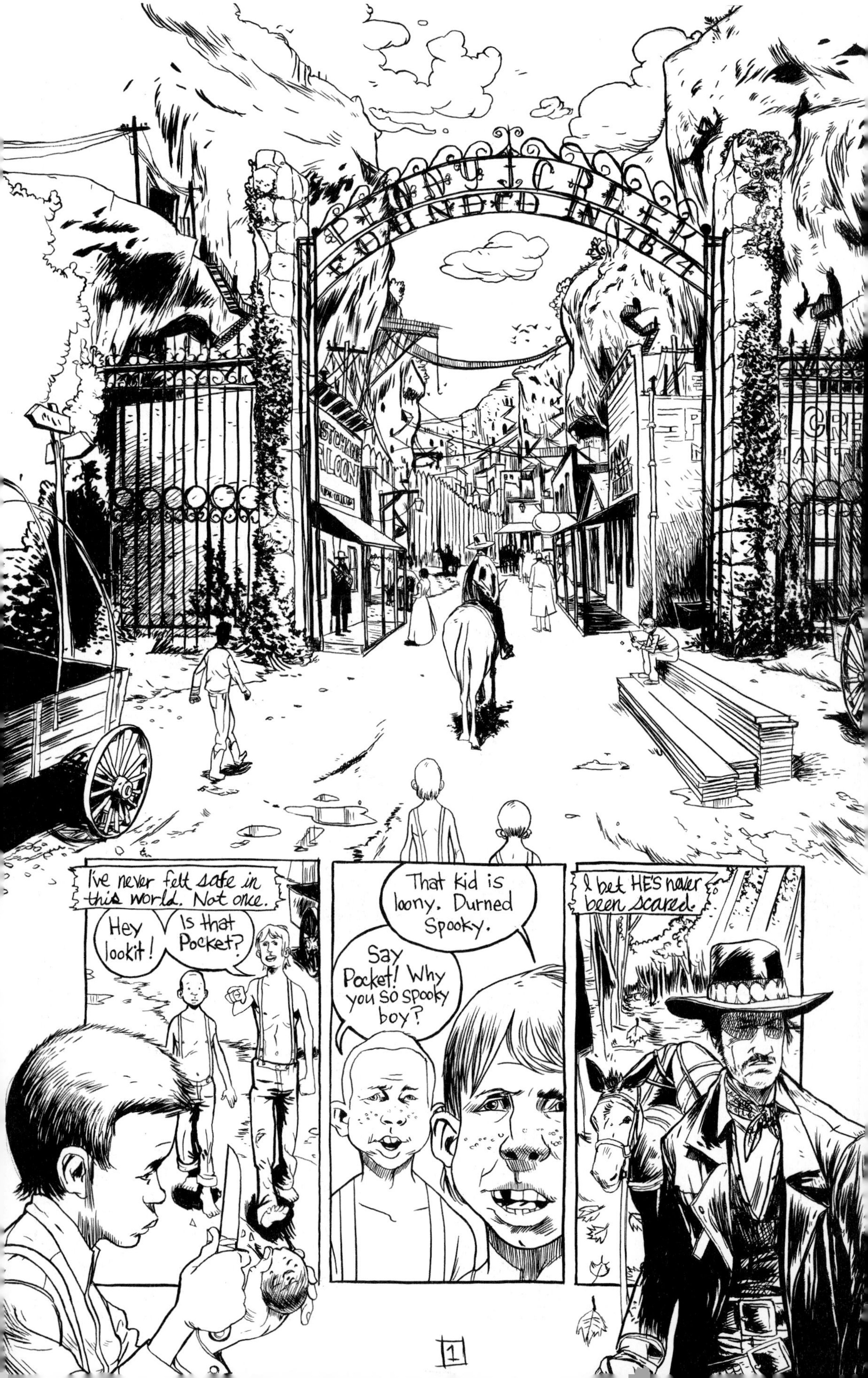
FOUNDED IN 1874
I've never felt safe in this world. Not once.
Hey lookit!
Is that Pocket?
That kid is loony. Durned Spooky.
Say Pocket! Why you so spooky boy?
I bet HE'S never been scared.

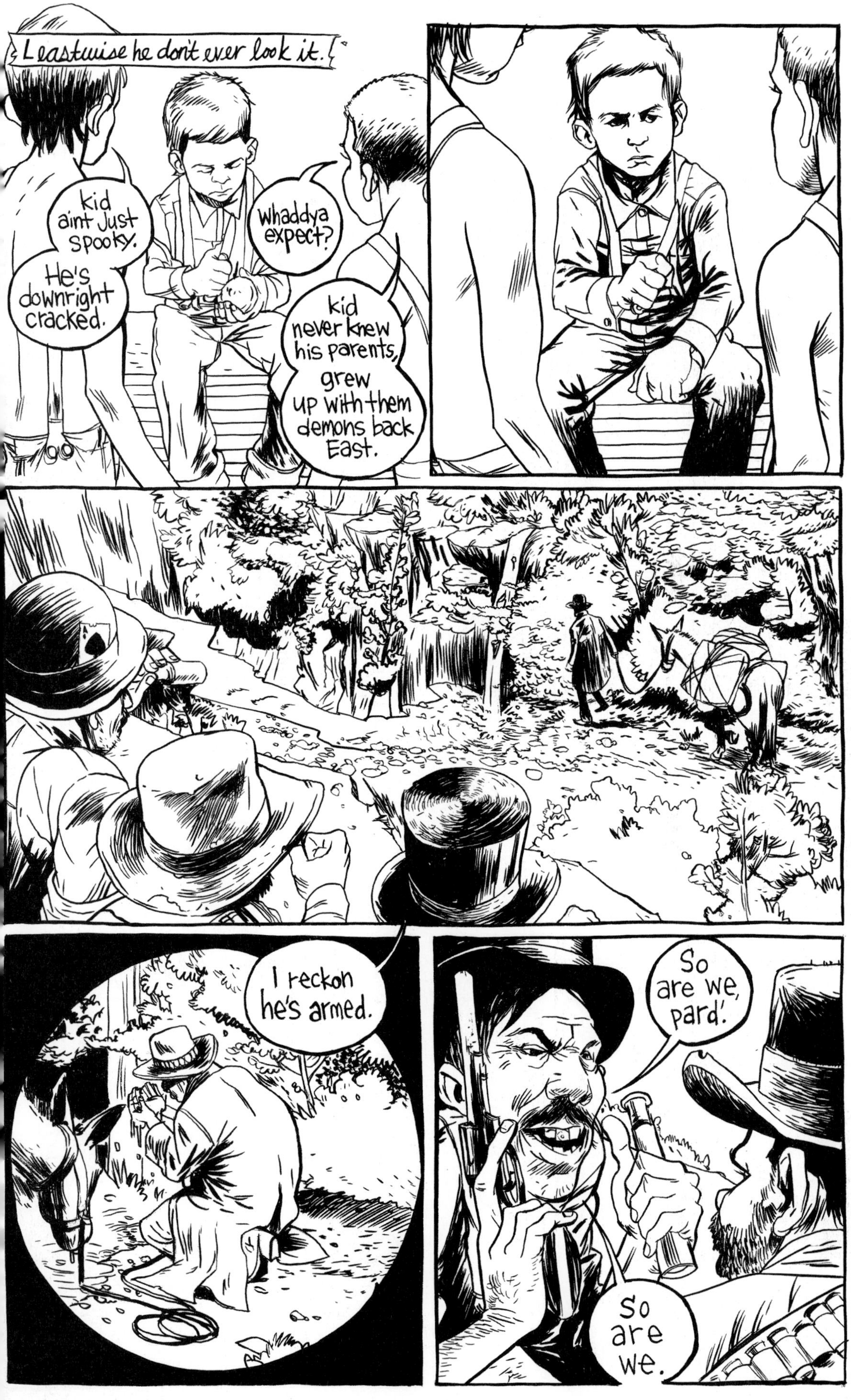
Leastwise he don't ever look it.
kid aint just spooky.
He's downright cracked.
Whaddya expect?
kid never knew his parents, grew up with them demons back East.
I reckon he's armed.
So are we, pard'.
So are we.

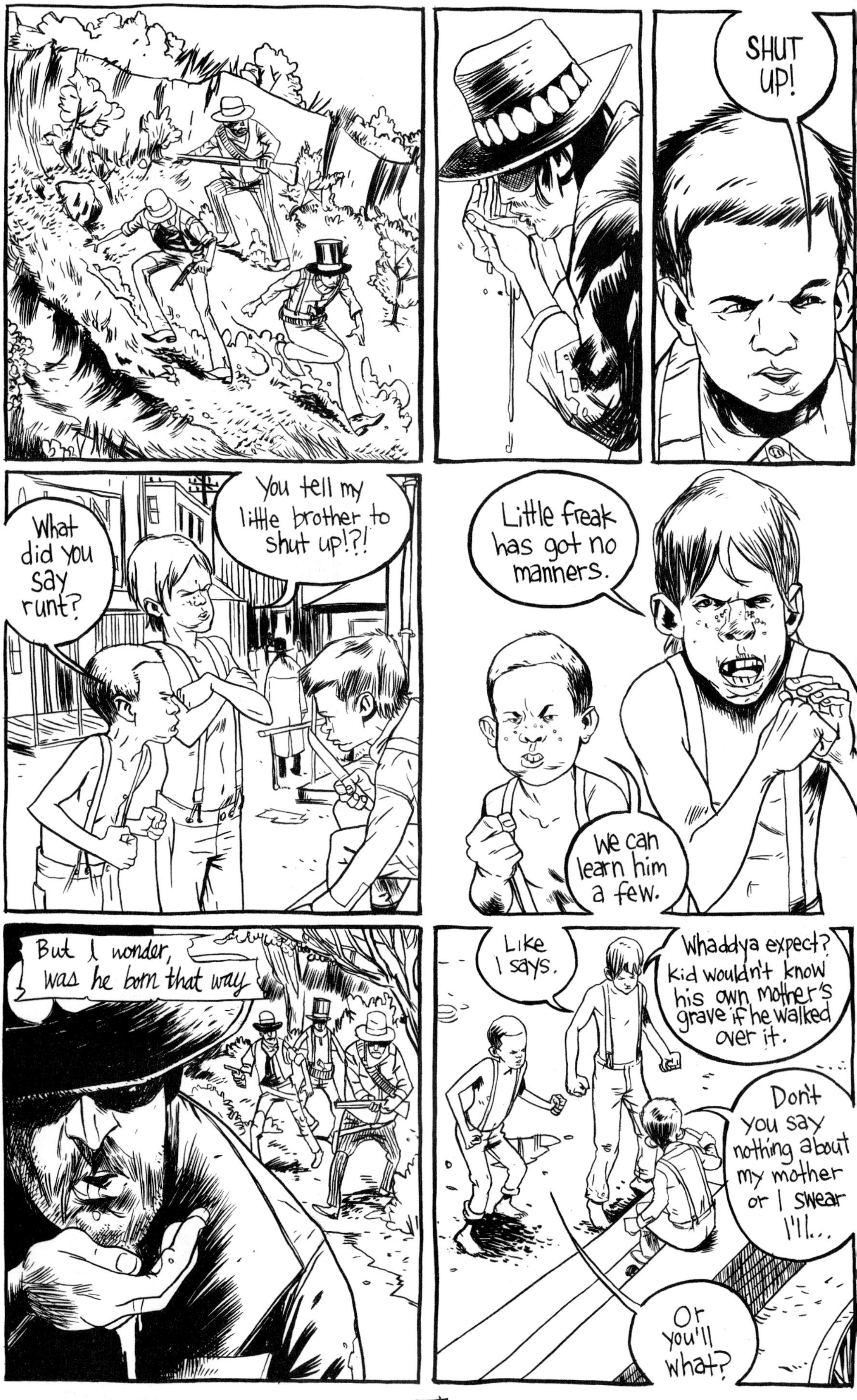
SHUT UP!
What did you say runt?
You tell my little brother to shut up!?!
Little freak has got no manners.
We can learn him a few.
But I wonder, was he born that way
Like I says.
Whaddya expect? Kid wouldn't know his own mother's grave if he walked over it.
Don't you say nothing about my mother or I swear I'll...
Or you'll what?

ne previous three pages were written by ason Sacher as a pitch for a sci-fi western nat sadly didn't catch the interest of any ublishers in like 2003 or whenever that was?

his page has a few of the many character esigns for the series and a little action equence I thought might still be fun o actually draw someday.

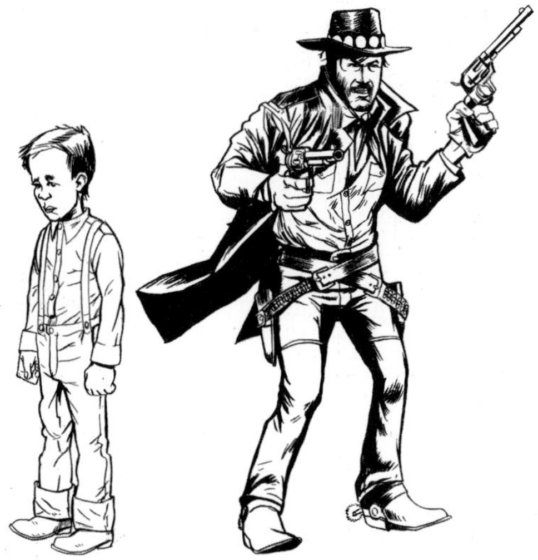

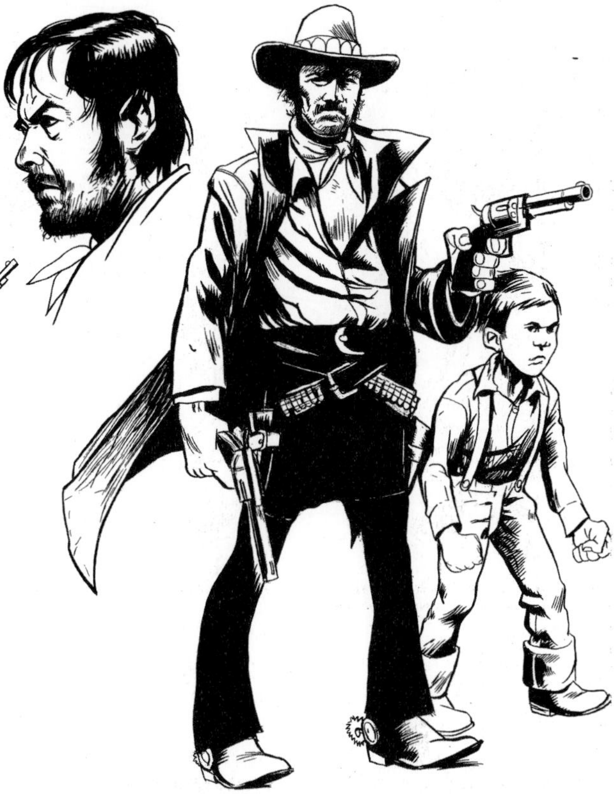

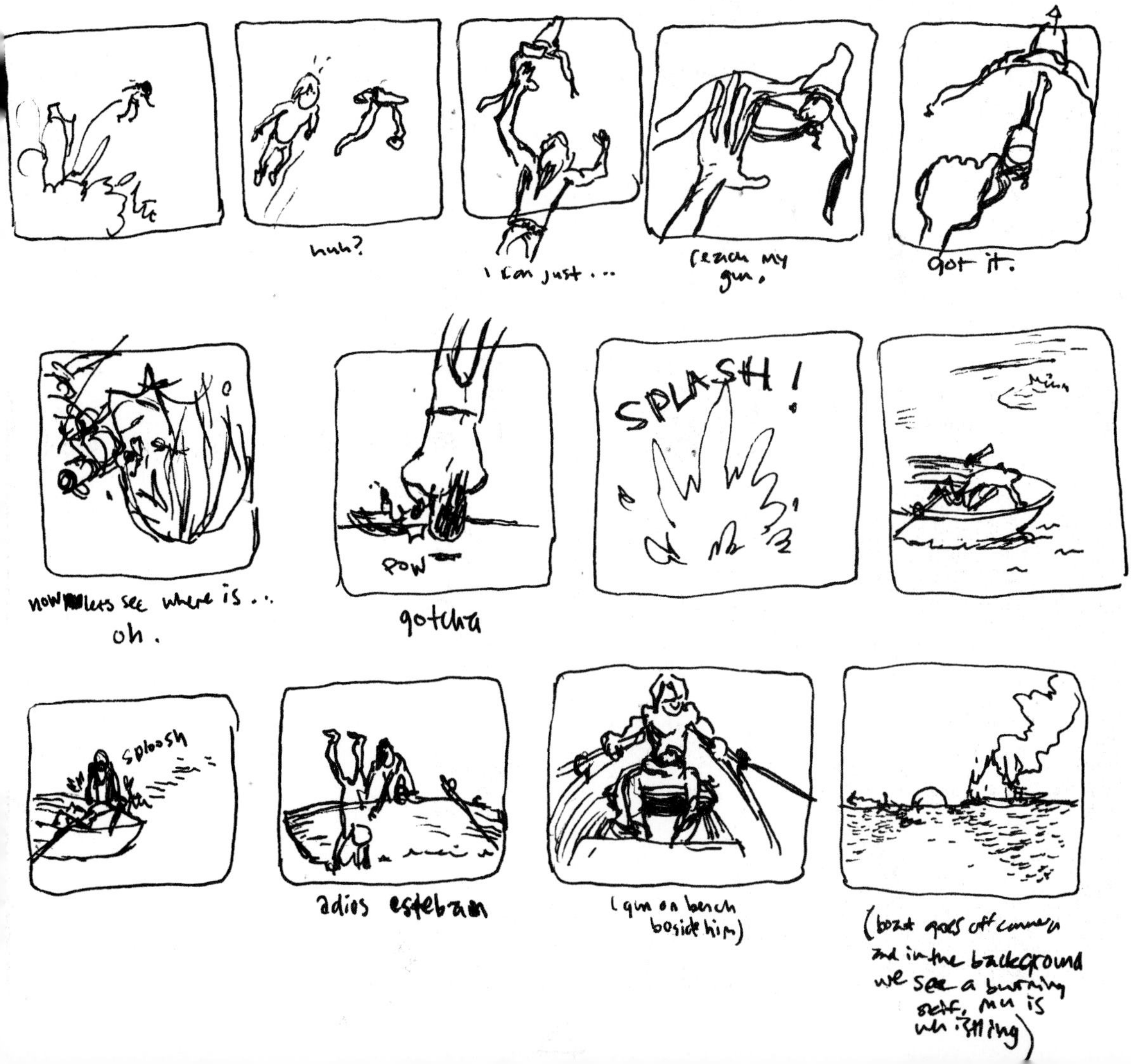

huh?
I can just...
reach my gun.
got it.
now lets see where is..
oh.
pow
gotcha
SPLASH!
sploosh
adios esteban
(gun on bench beside him)
(boat goes off camera and in the background we see a burning ship, Mu is whistling)

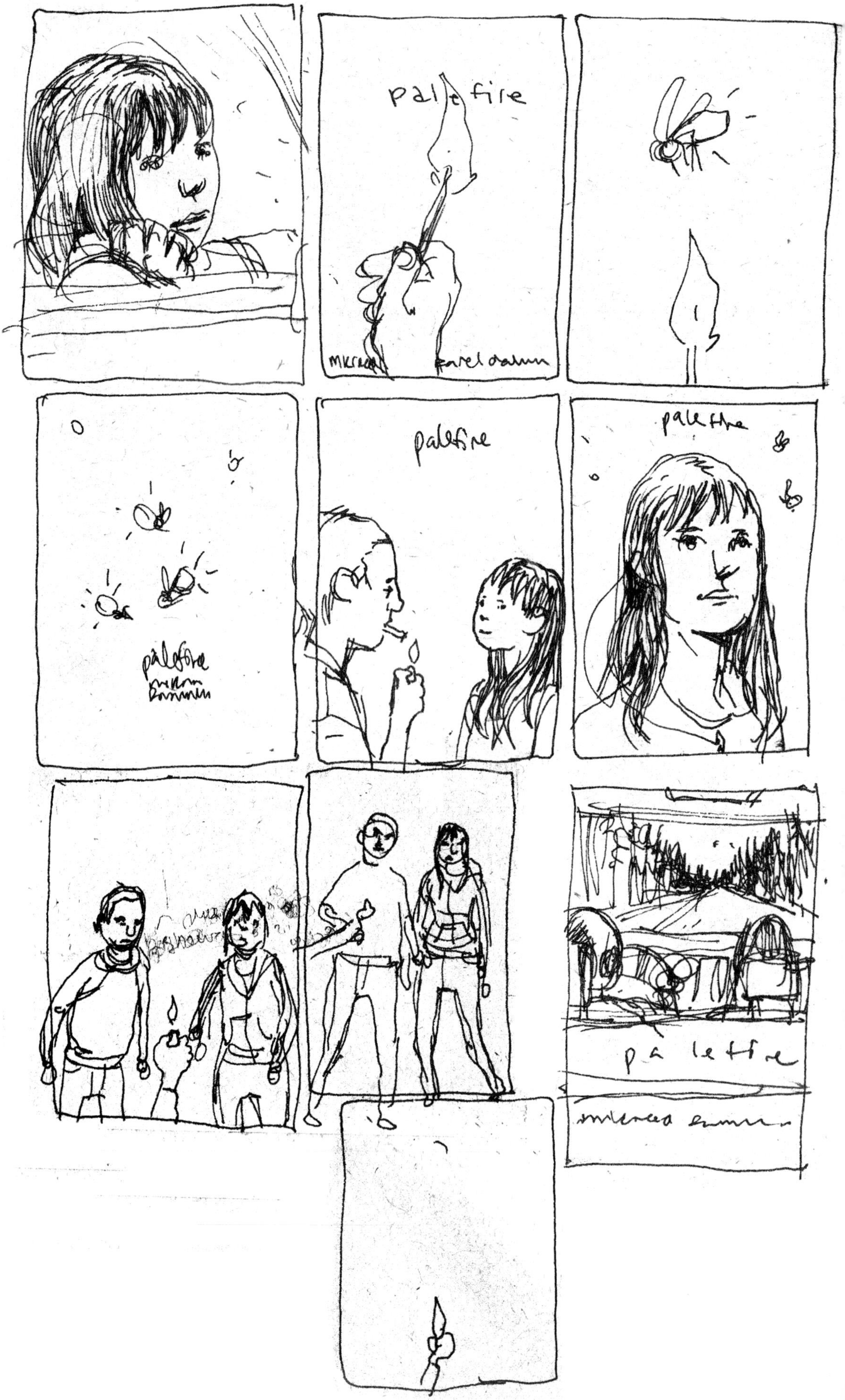
pale fire
palefire
palefire
pale fire
pa le fire

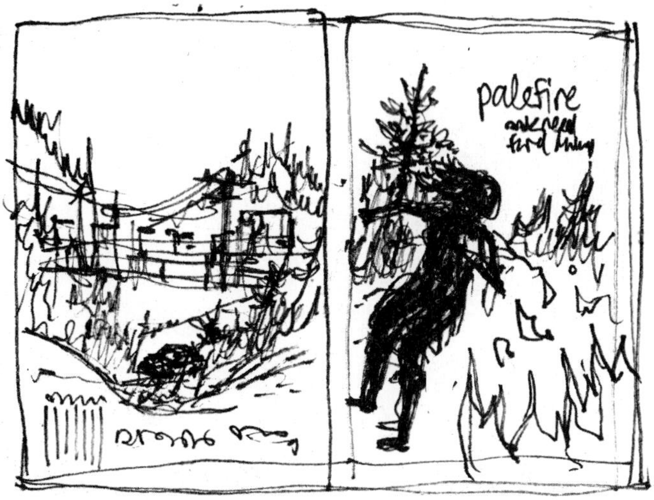
palefire

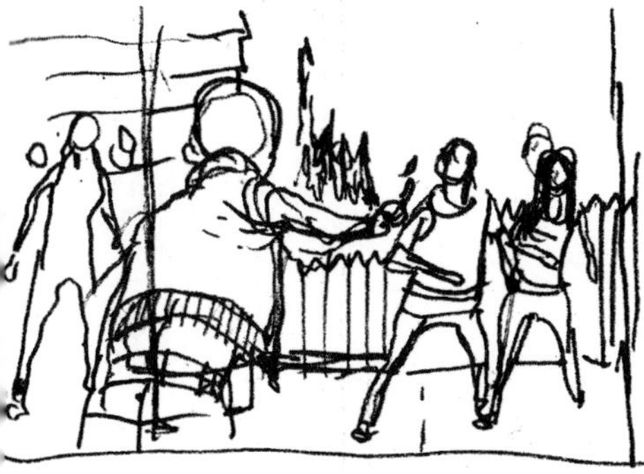

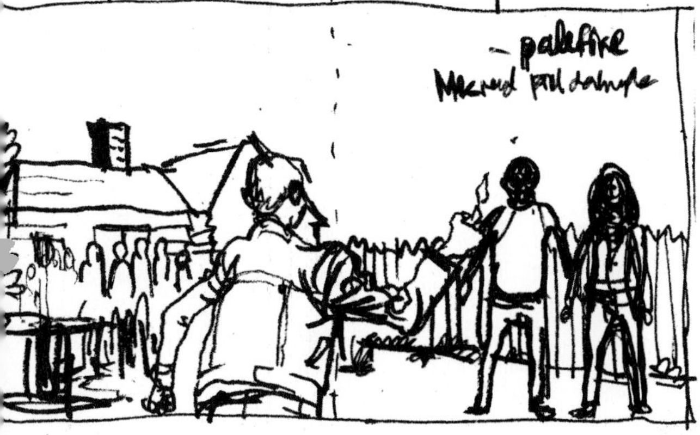
palefire

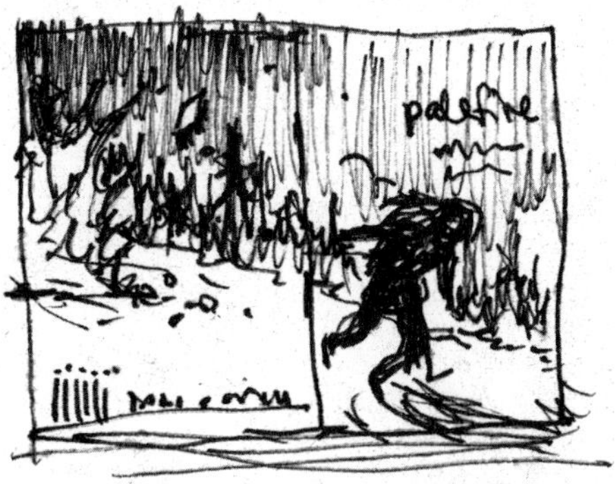
palefire

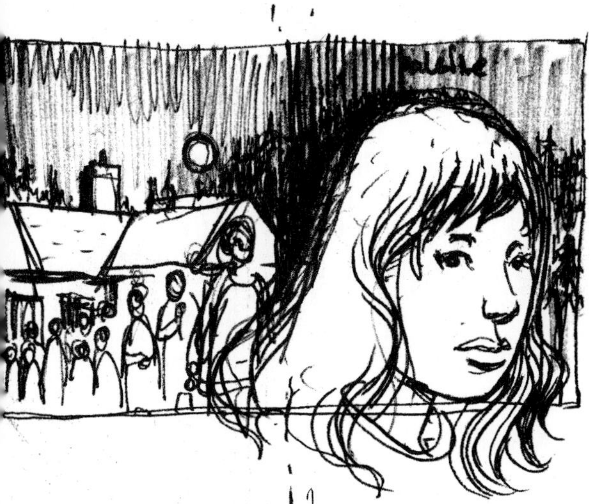
palefire

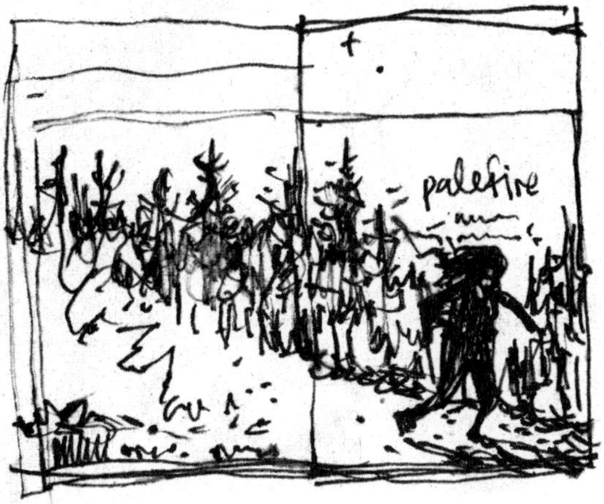
palefire

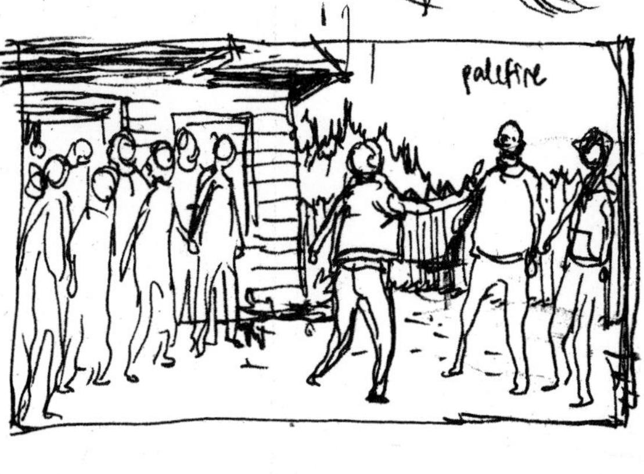
palefire

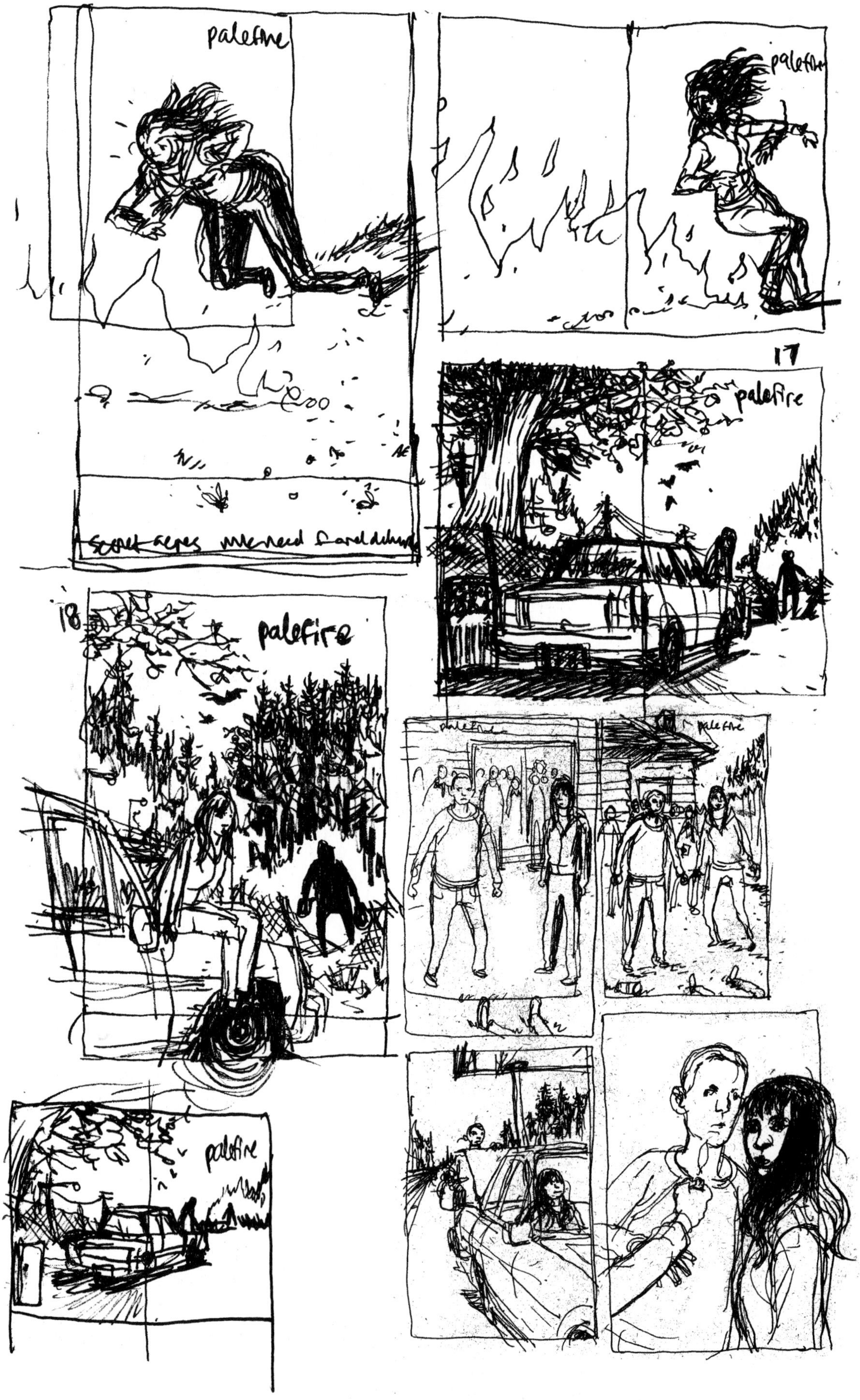
palefire
palefire
17
palefire
18
palefire
palefire
palefire
palefire

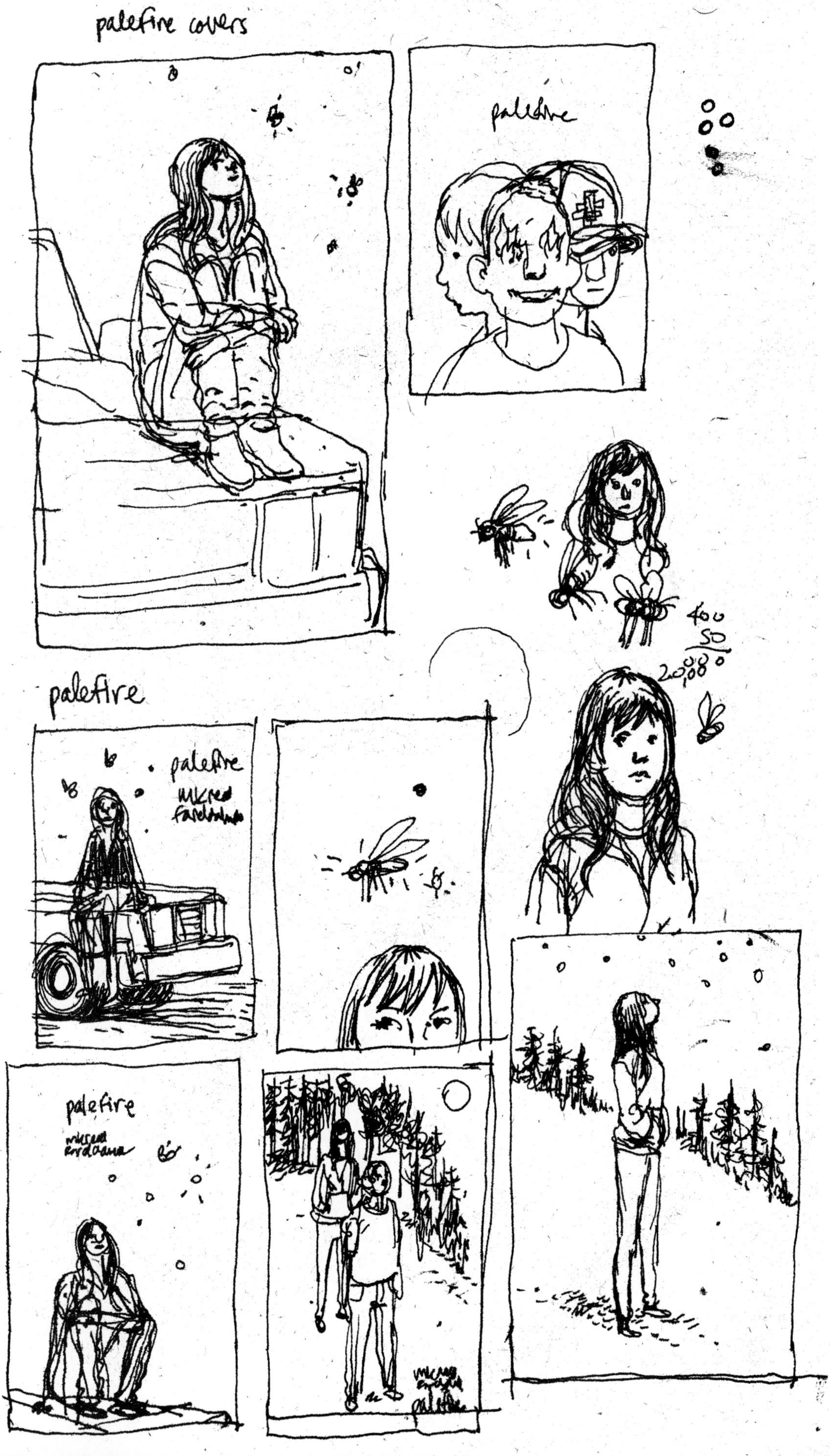
palefire covers
palefire
palefire
palefire
palefire

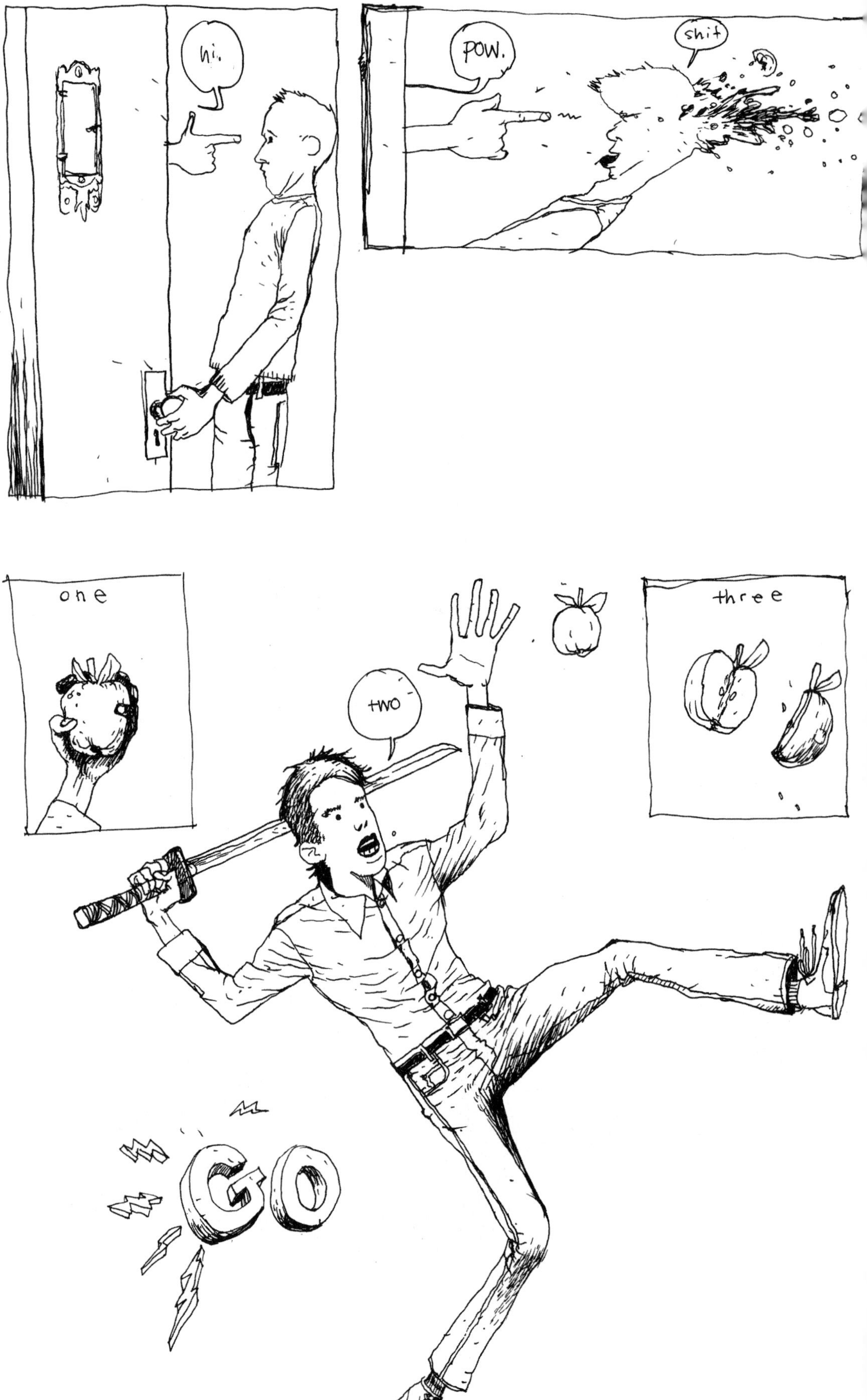
hi.
POW.
shit
one
two
three
GO

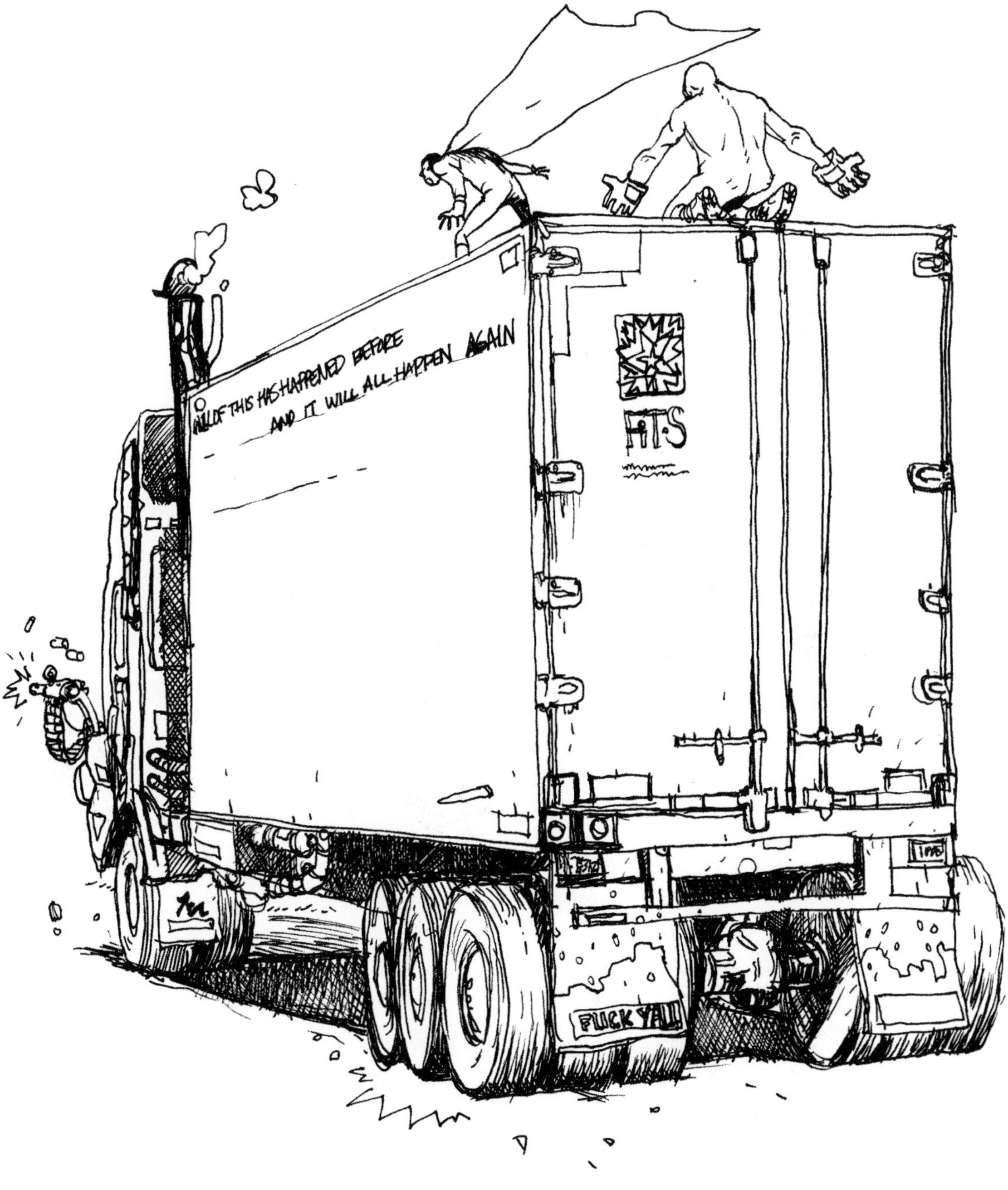
ALL OF THIS HAS HAPPENED BEFORE
AND IT WILL ALL HAPPEN AGAIN
FUCK YALL

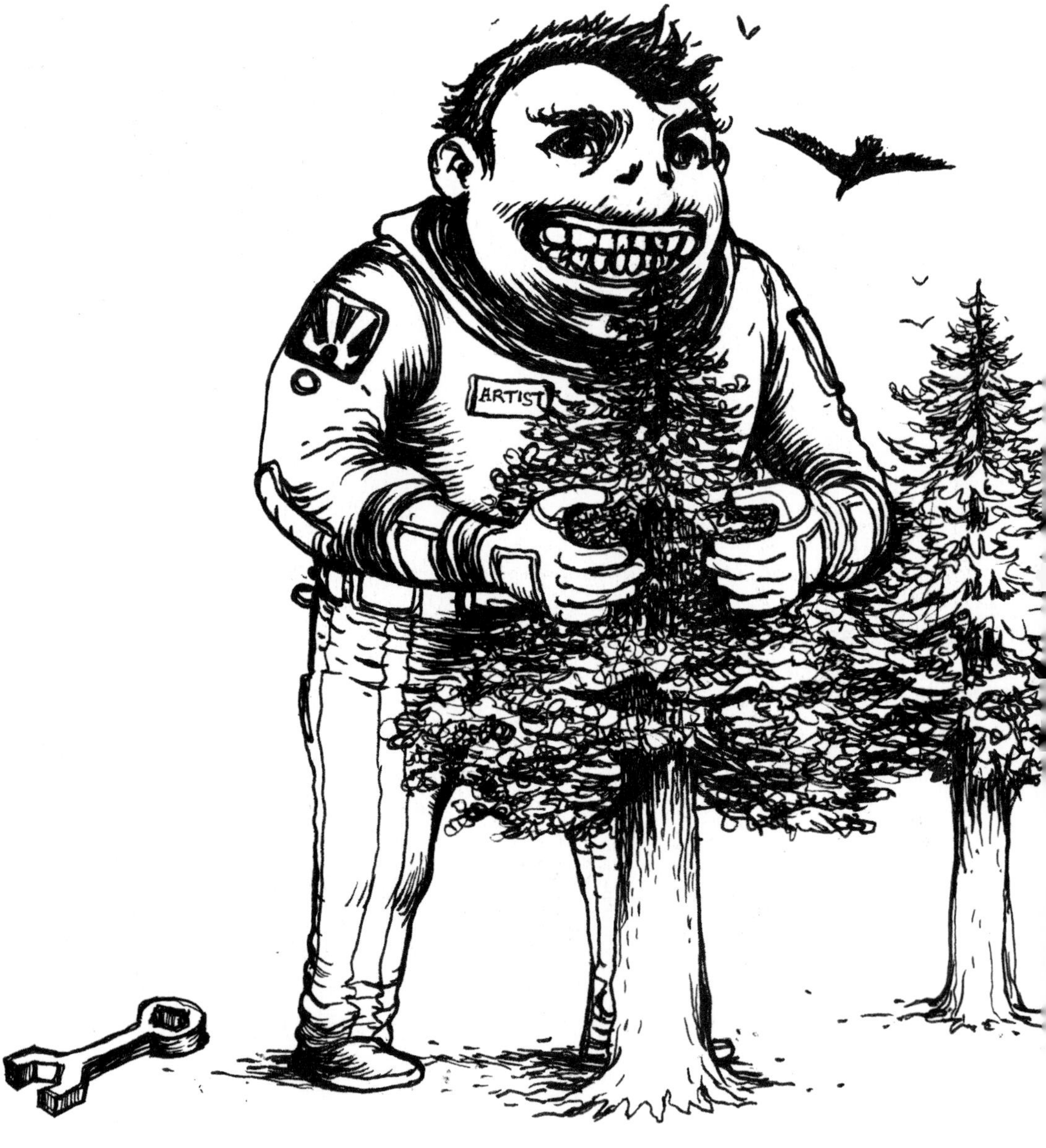
ARTIST

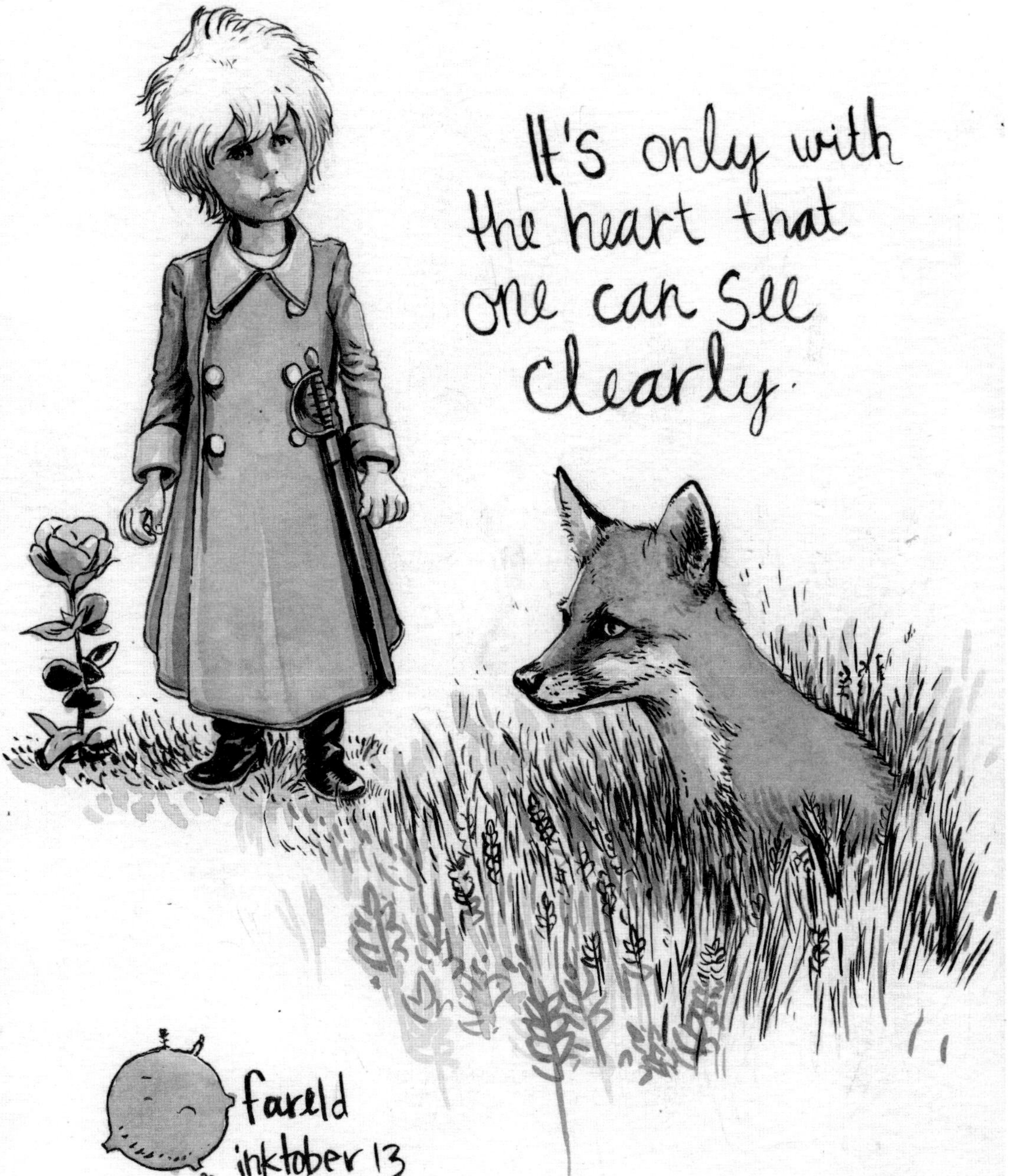
It's only with
the heart that
one can see
clearly.
fareld
inktober 13
2018

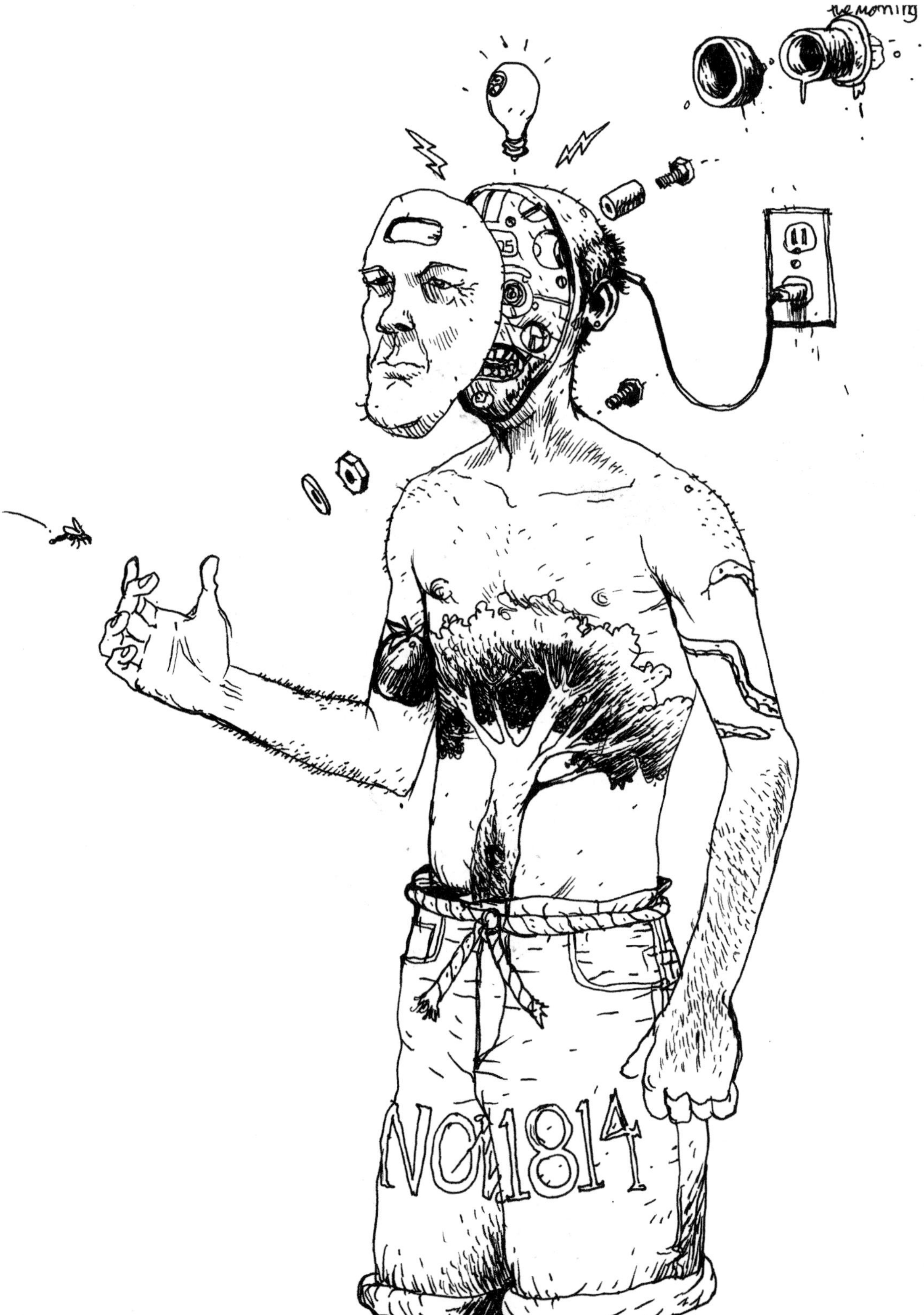
NO1814

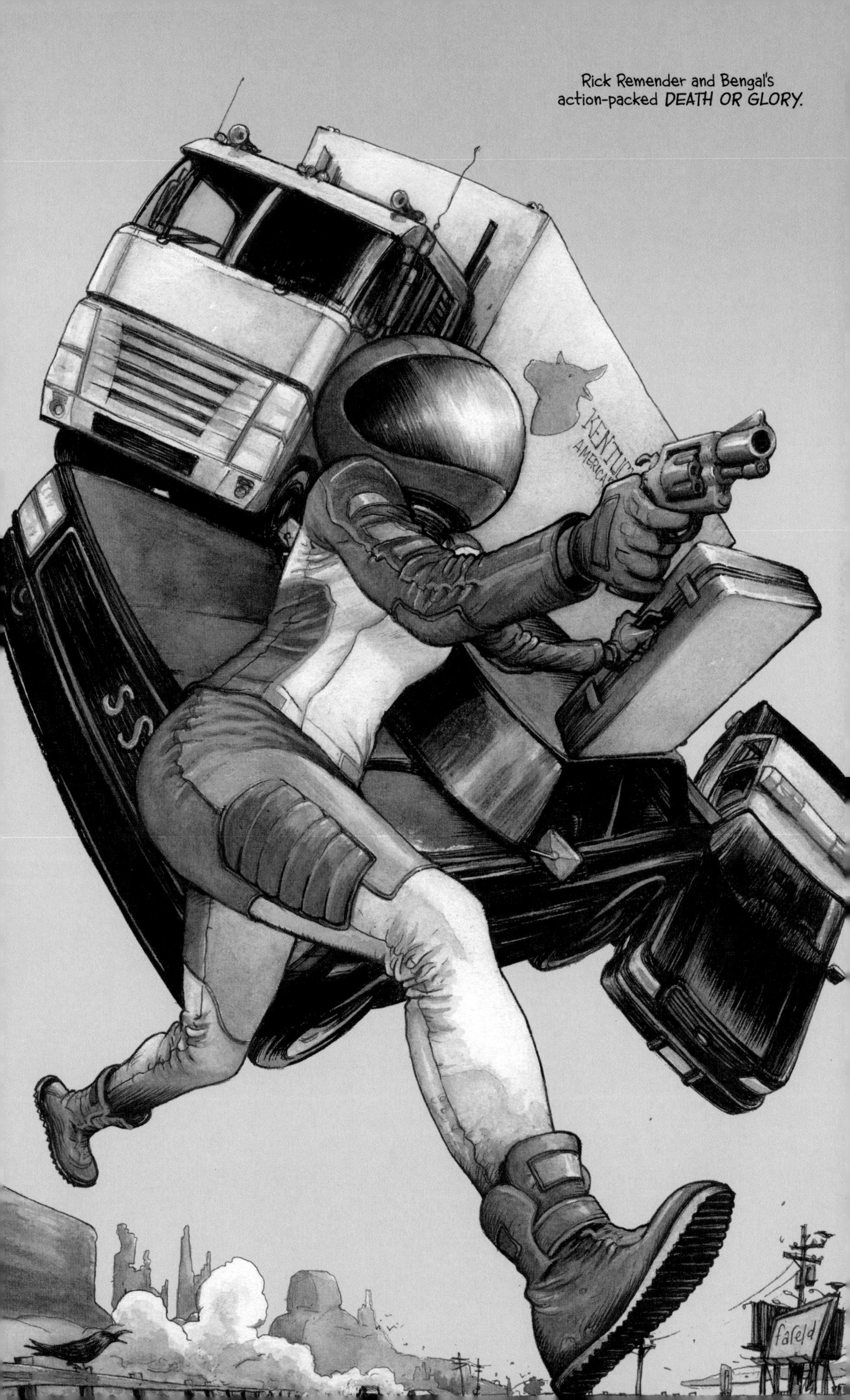

Rick Remender and Bengal's
action-packed *DEATH OR GLORY.*

Cover for the sterling supernatural superhero thriller, *SHAMAN* by Ben Kahn and Bruno Hidalgo.

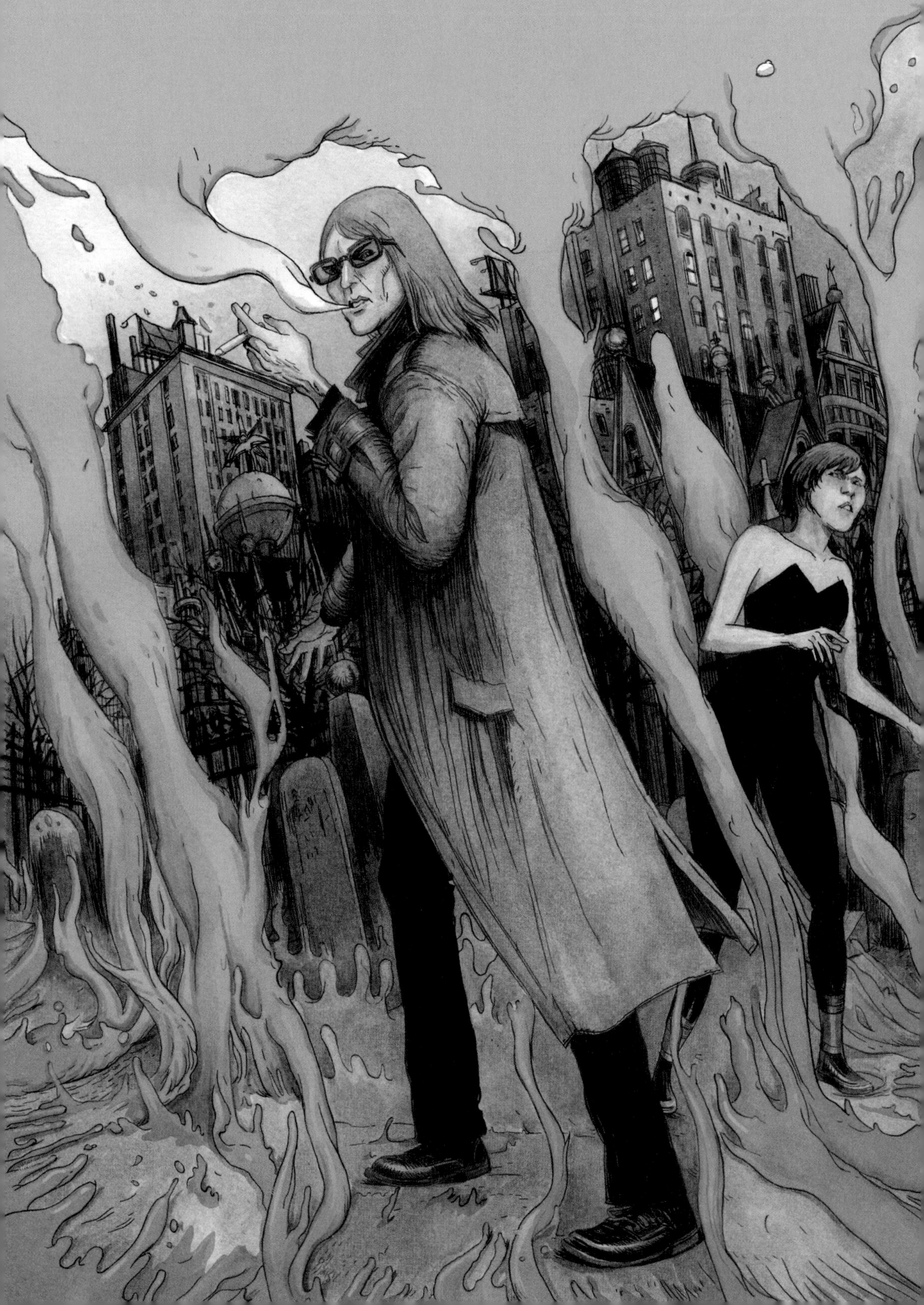

rejection

by farel dalrymple

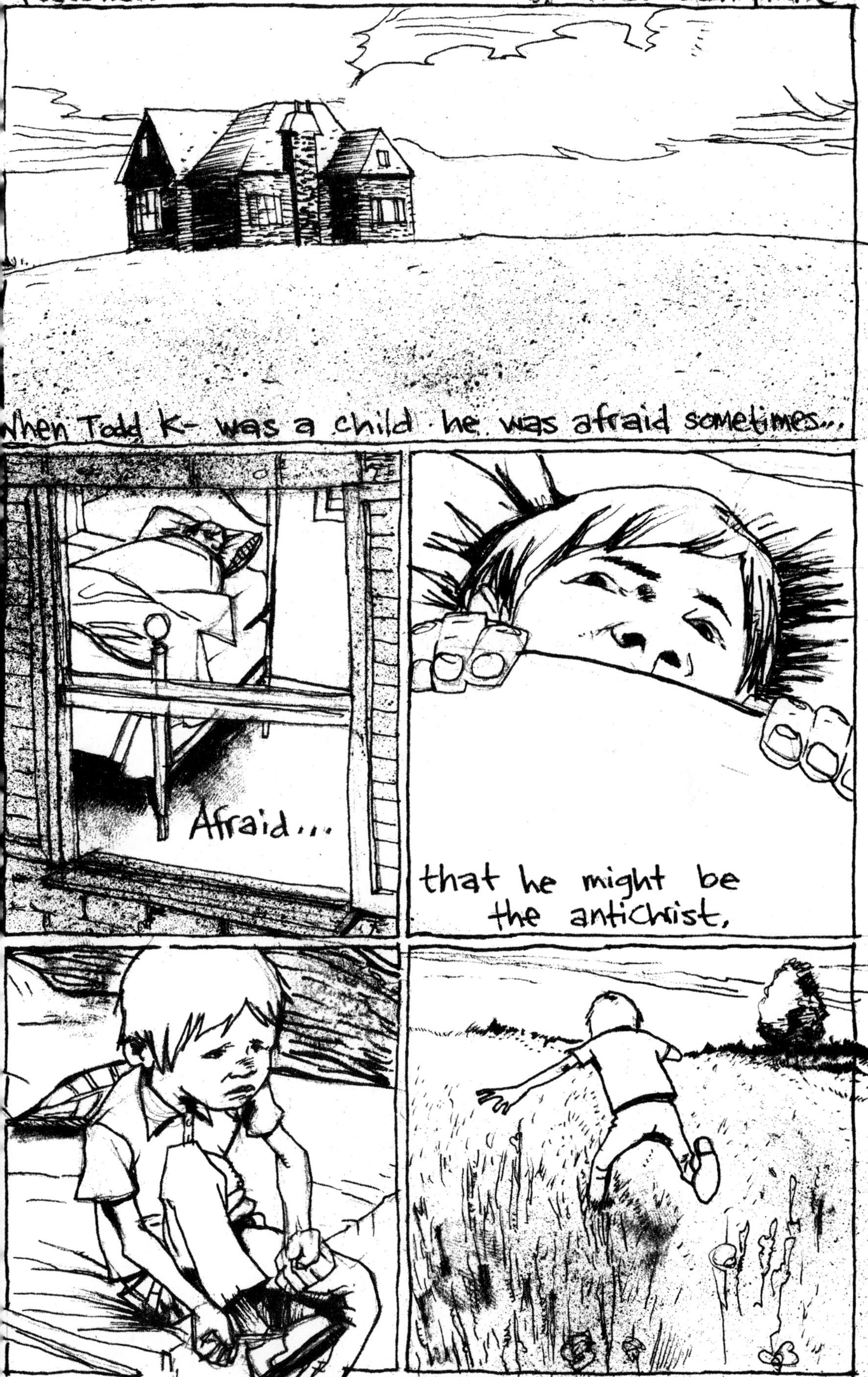
When Todd K- was a child he was afraid sometimes...
Afraid...
that he might be the antichrist,

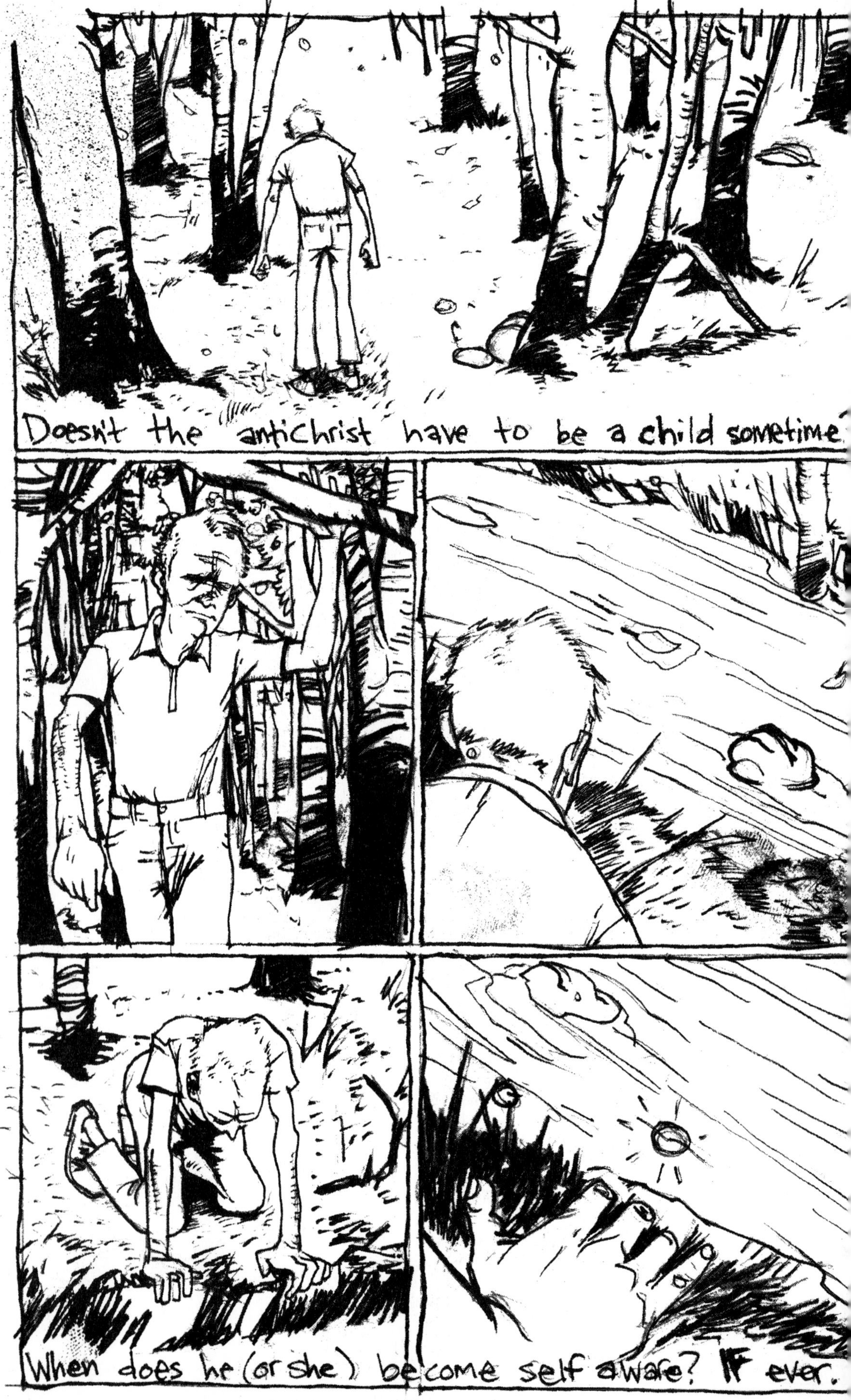

Doesn't the antichrist have to be a child sometime?
When does he (or she) become self aware? IF ever.

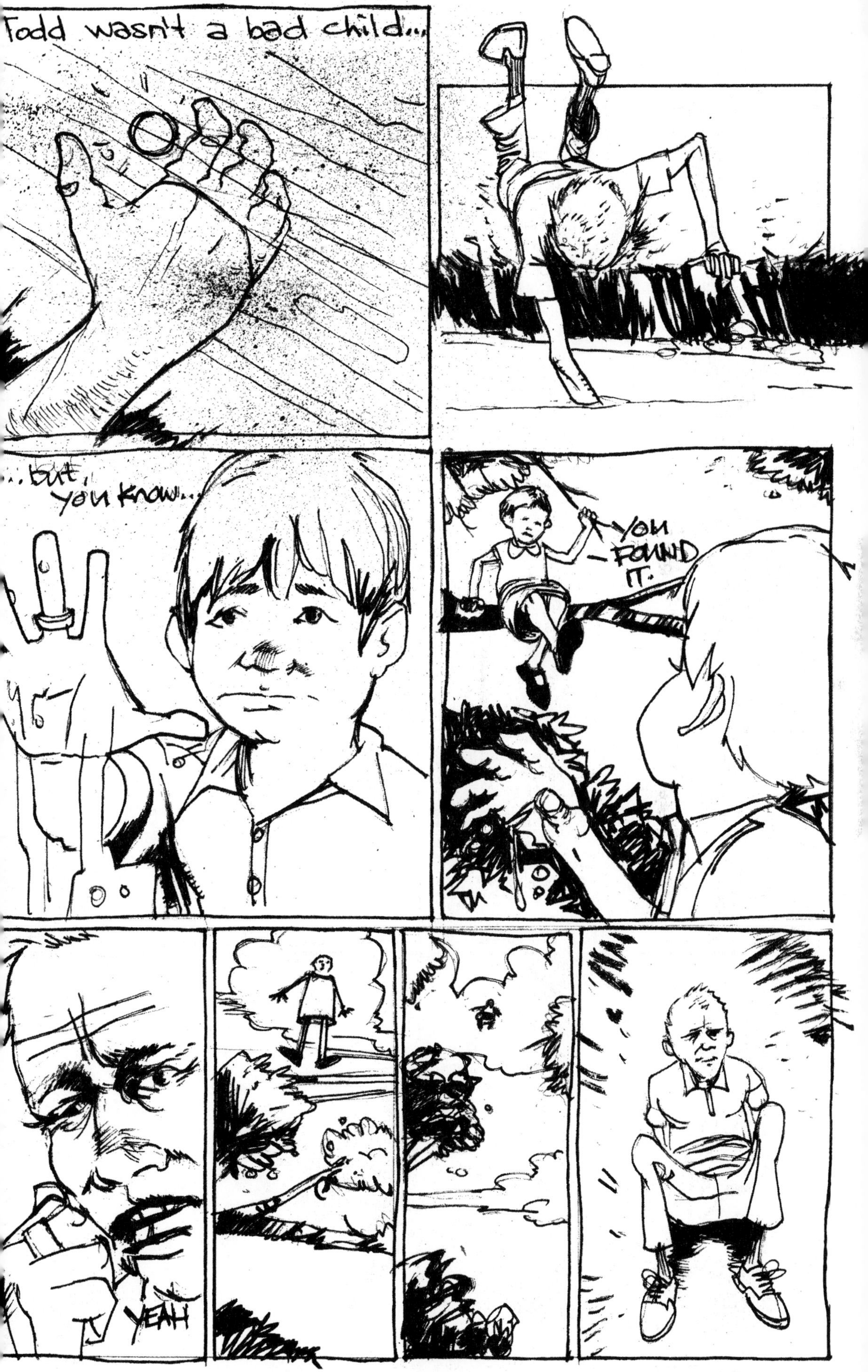
Todd wasn't a bad child...
...but, you know...
YOU FOUND IT.
YEAH

Originally published in MEATAHUS issue 2.

[redacted]

Variant cover for Wesley Craig and Rick Remender's *DEADLY CLASS*.

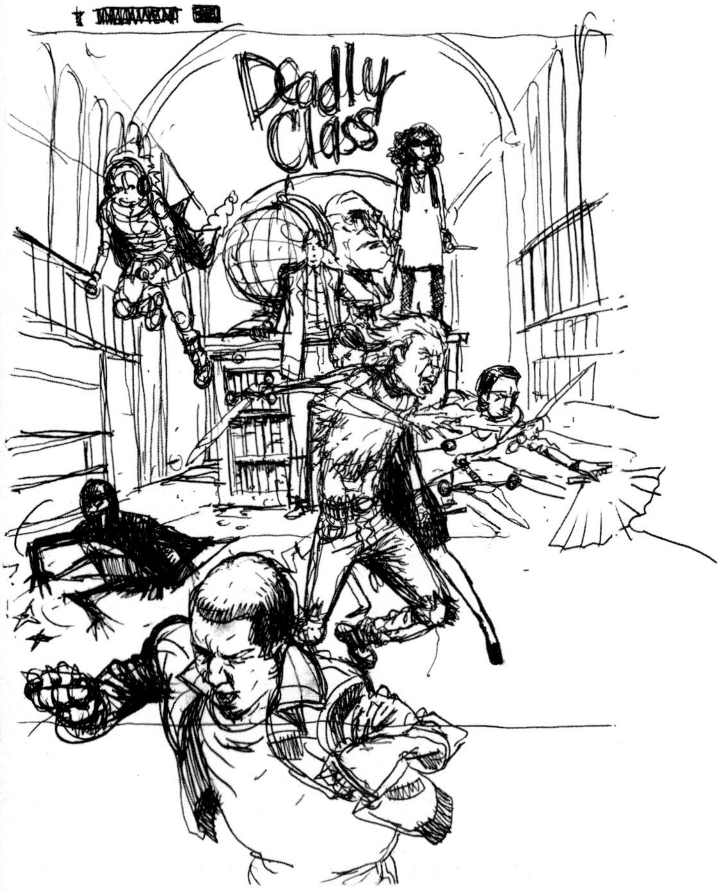
Deadly Class

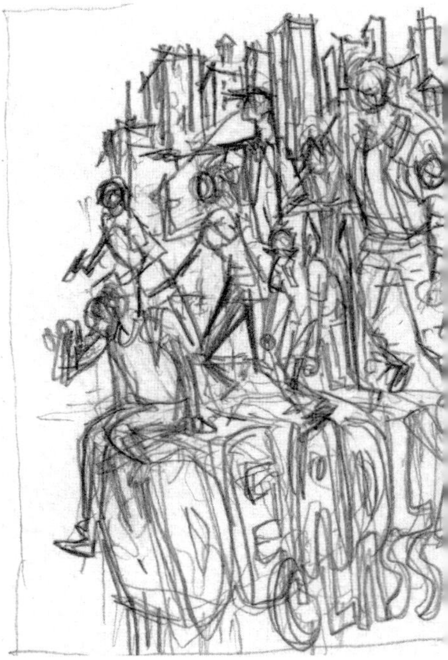

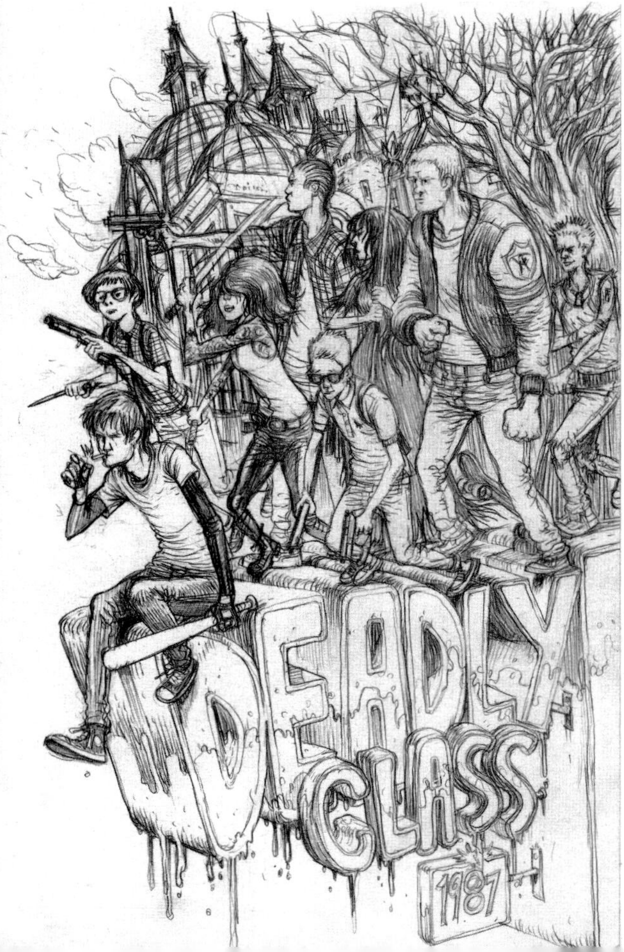
DEADLY
CLASS
1987

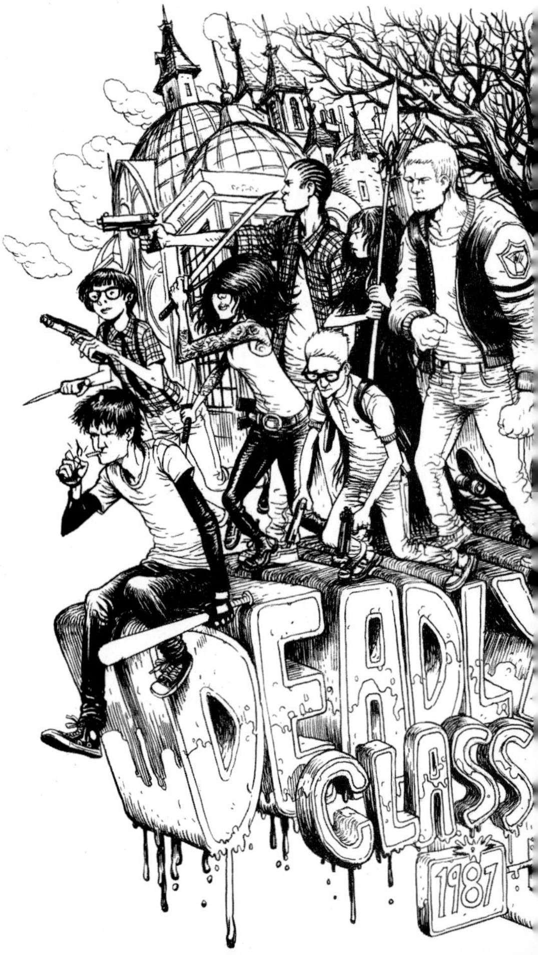
DEADLY
CLASS
1987

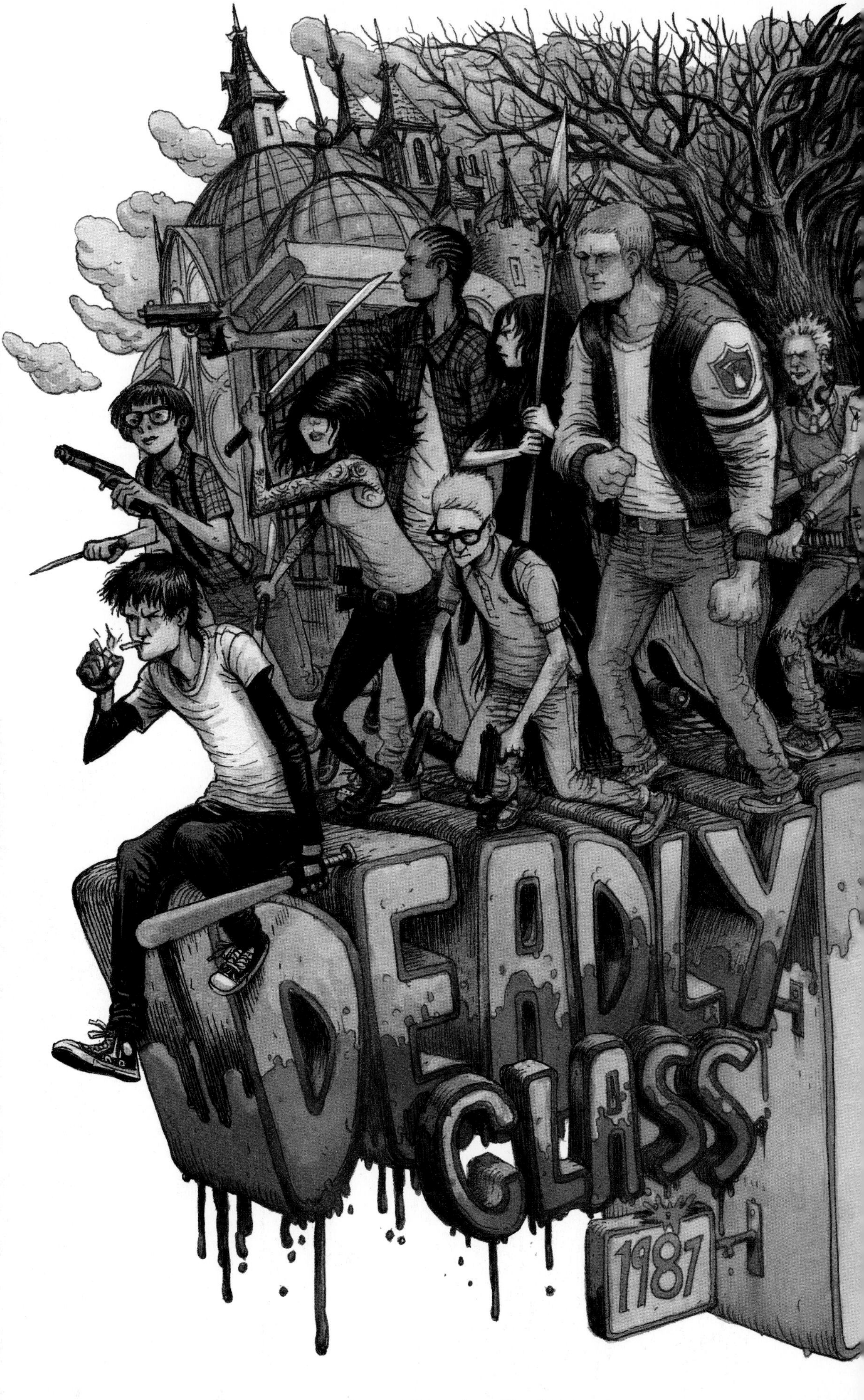
DEADLY
CLASS
1987

Variant cover for Matt Kindt and David Rubin's magnificent comic book, *ETHER*.

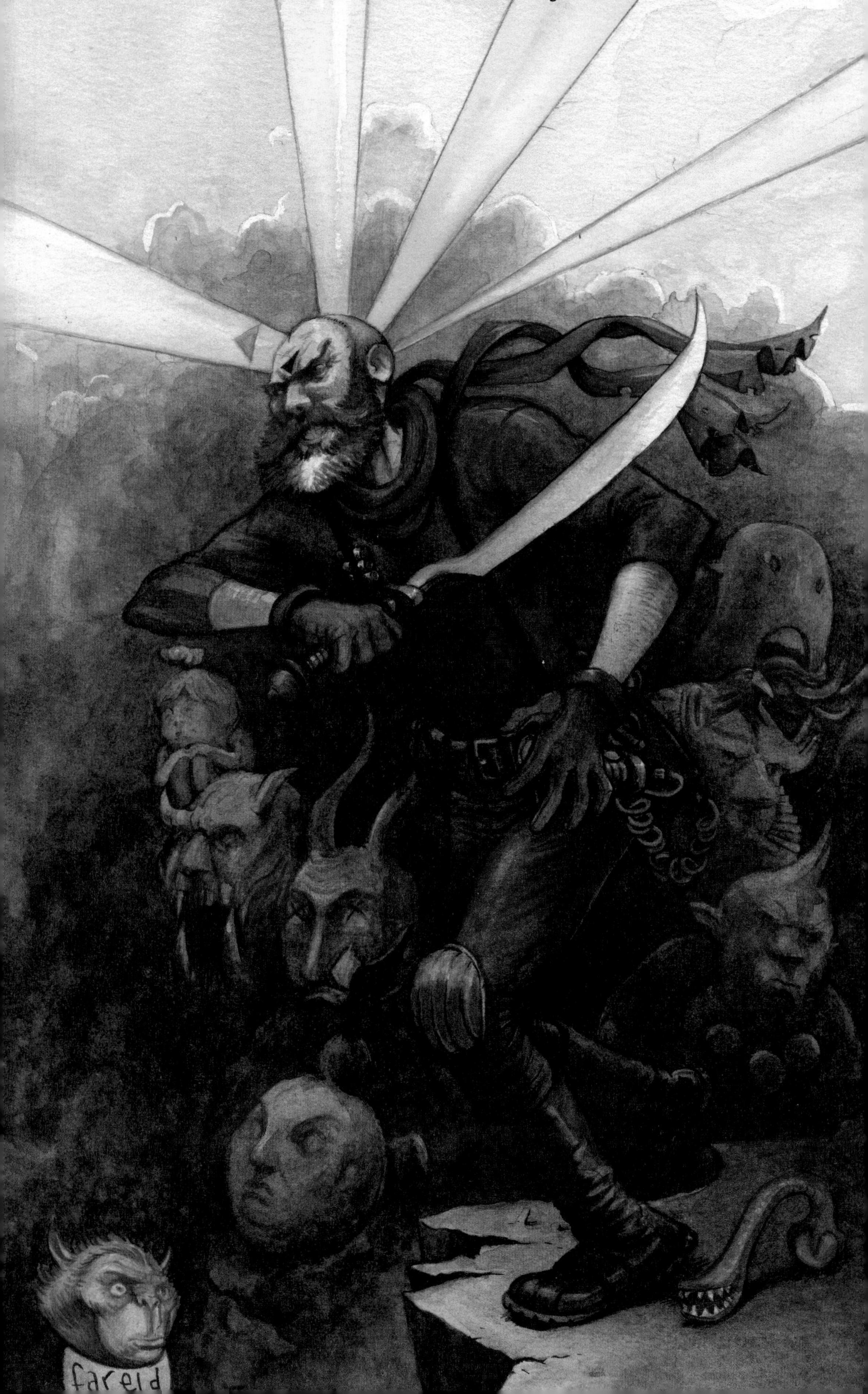

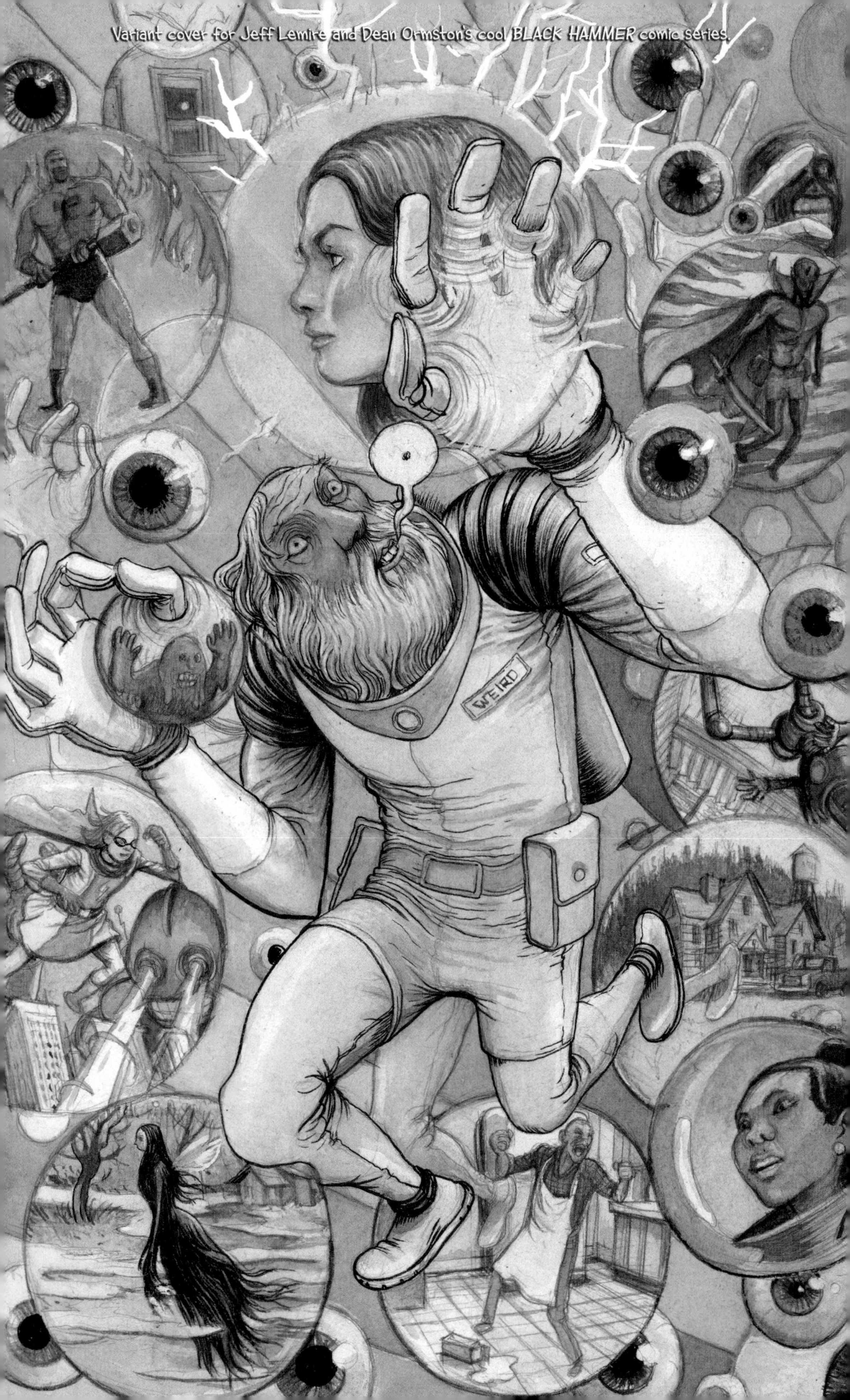
WEIRD

Variant cover for Jeff Lemire and Dean Ormston's cool *BLACK HAMMER* comic series.

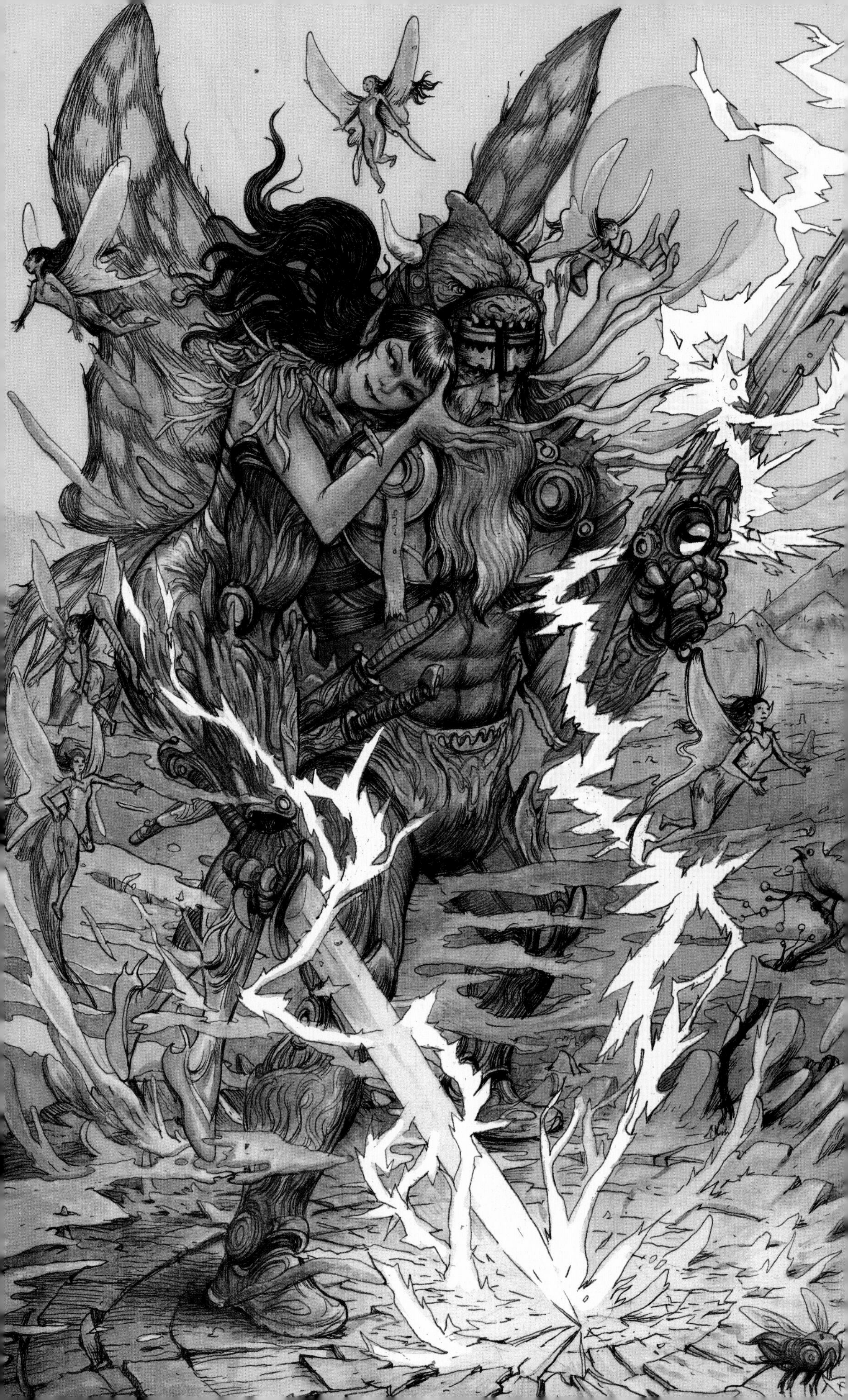

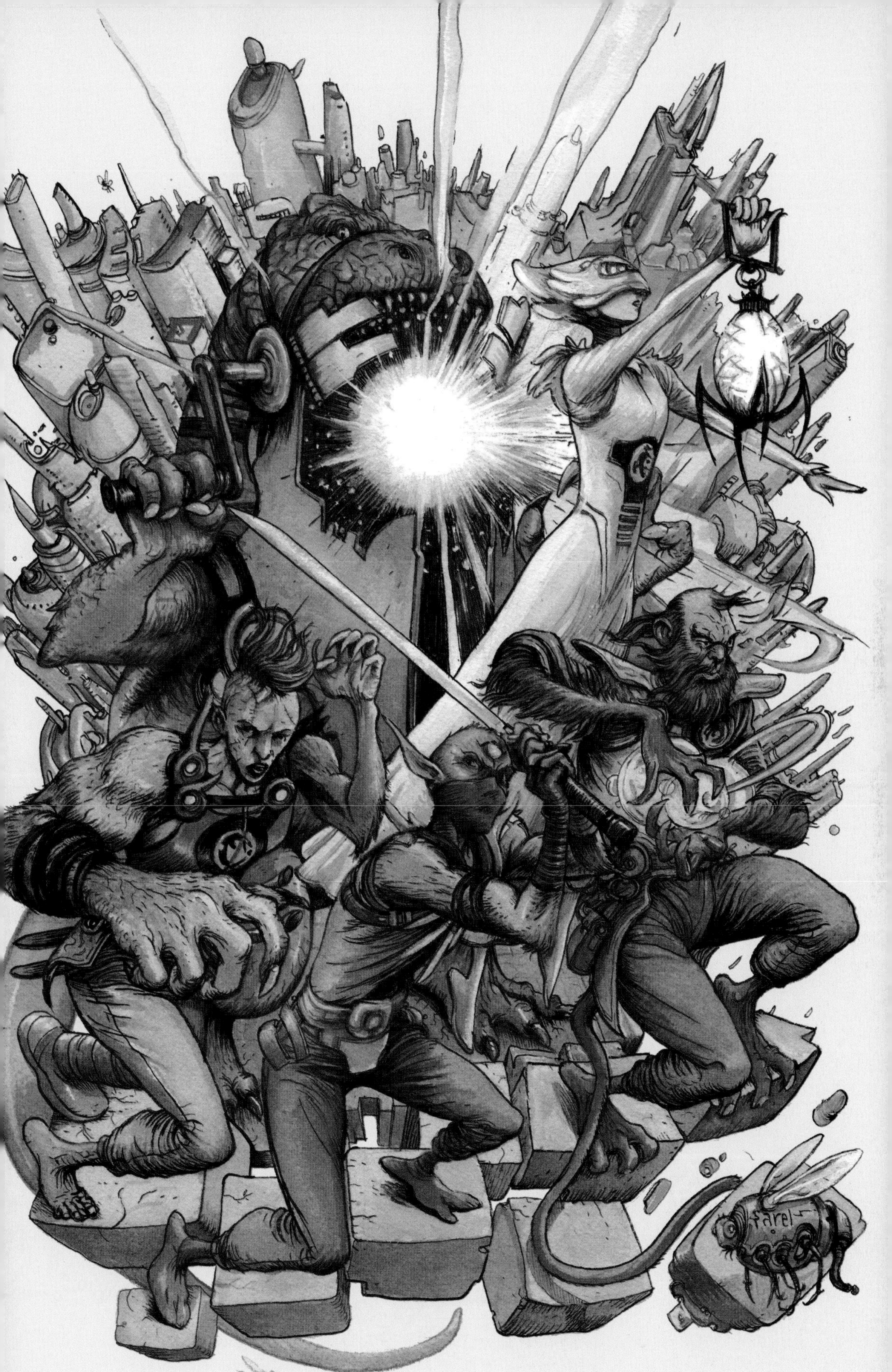

This and previous page are variant covers for Rick Remender and Jerome Opeña's excellent *SEVEN TO ETERNITY*.

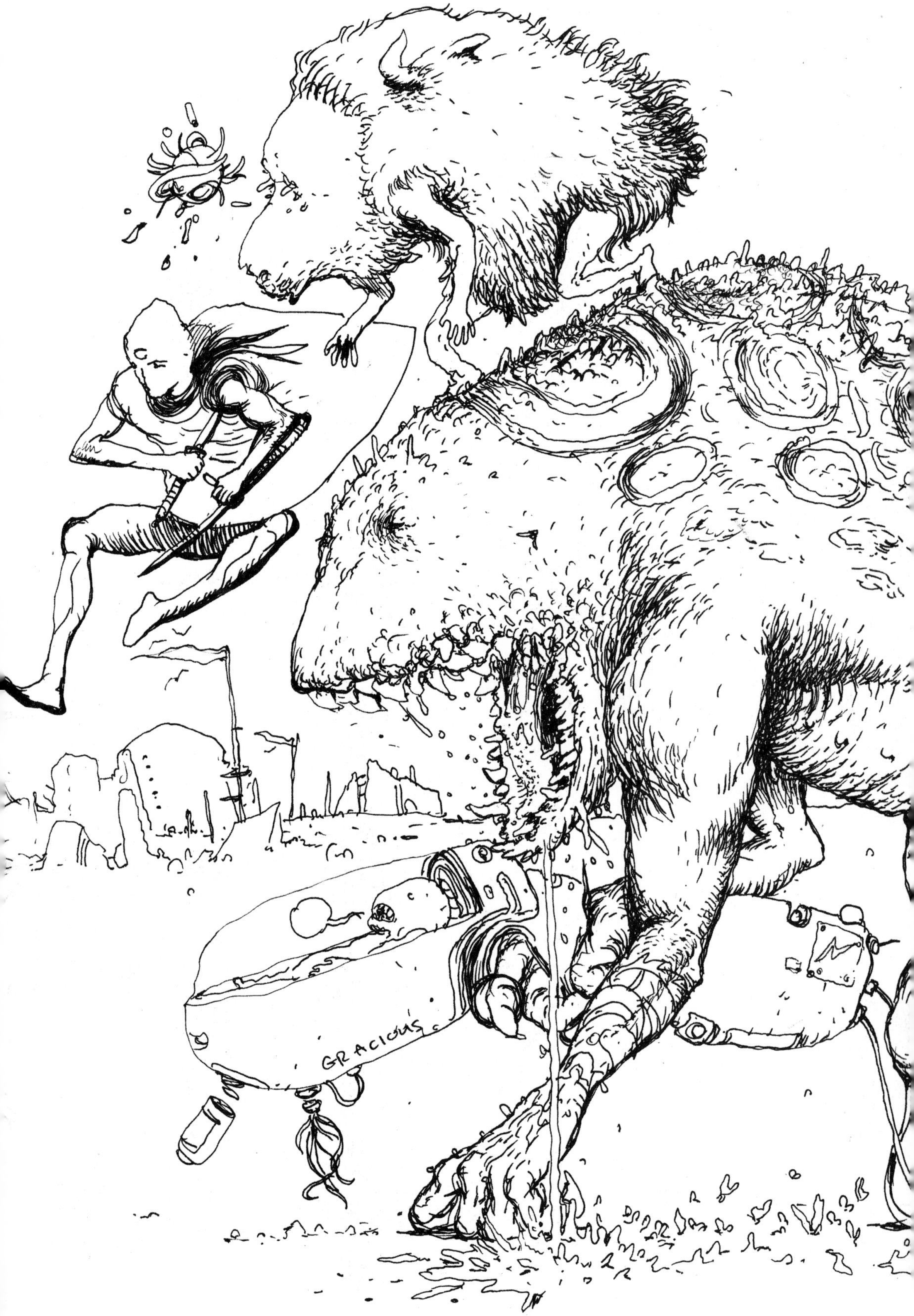
GRACIOUS

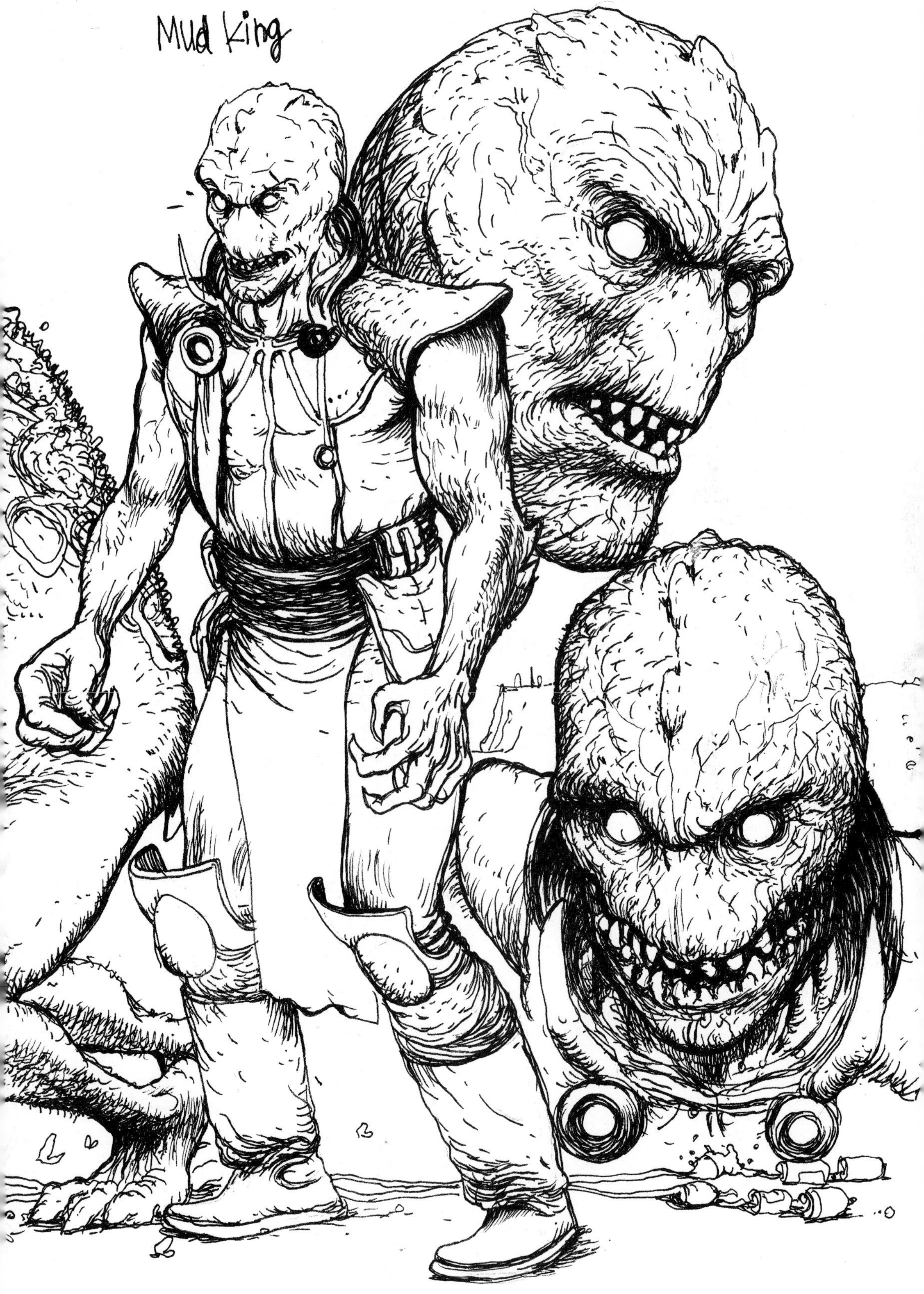
Mud King

The Mud King is a character from Rick Remender and Jerome Opeña's comic book epic *SEVEN TO ETERNITY*.

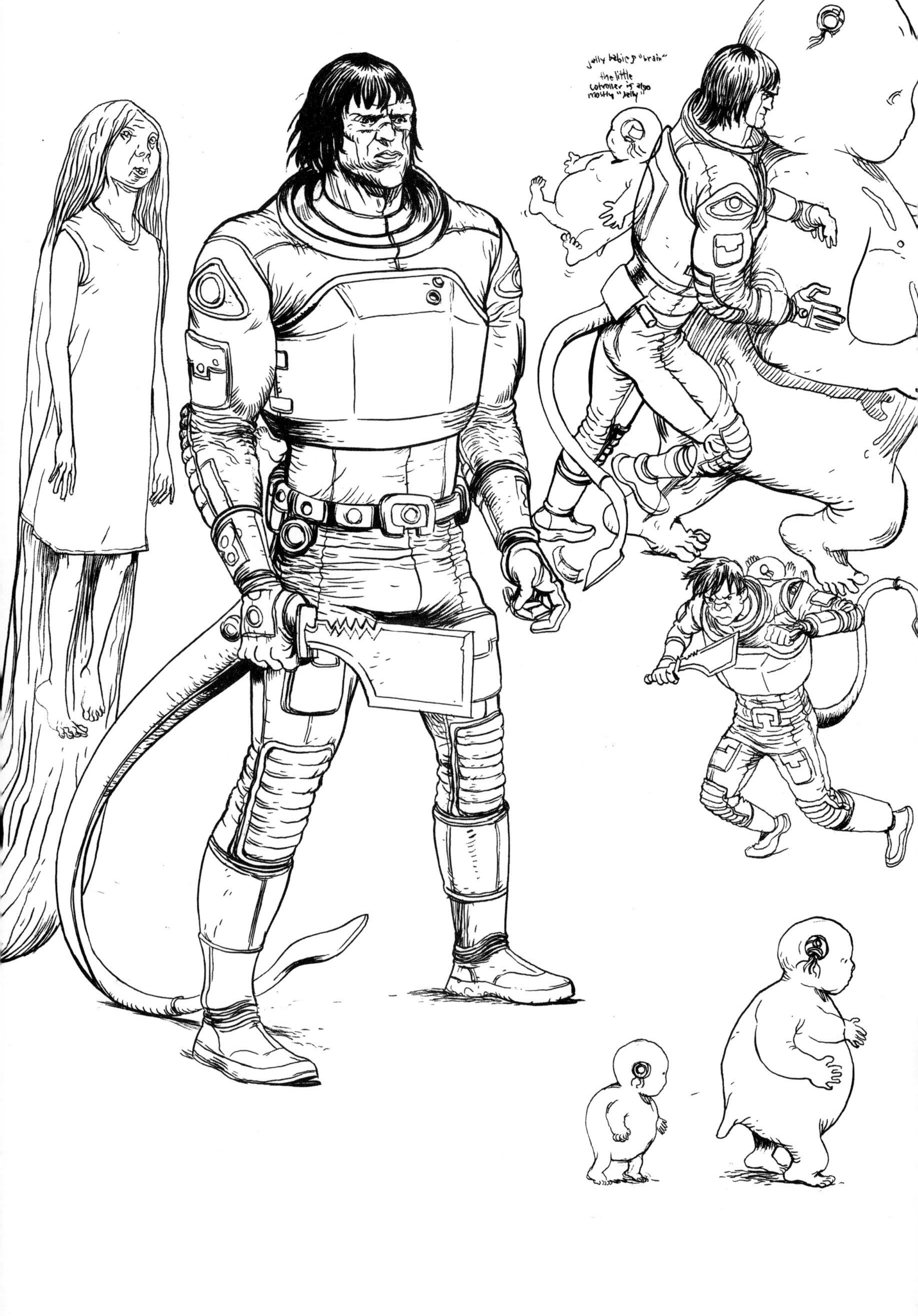
jelly babies "brain"
the little cotroller is also mostly "jelly"

A few years back Brandon Graham and Simon Roy created a reboot of Rob Liefeld's *PROPHET*.
I'm glad I was invited to contribute a few issues and some design work to their reimagined space barbarian epic.

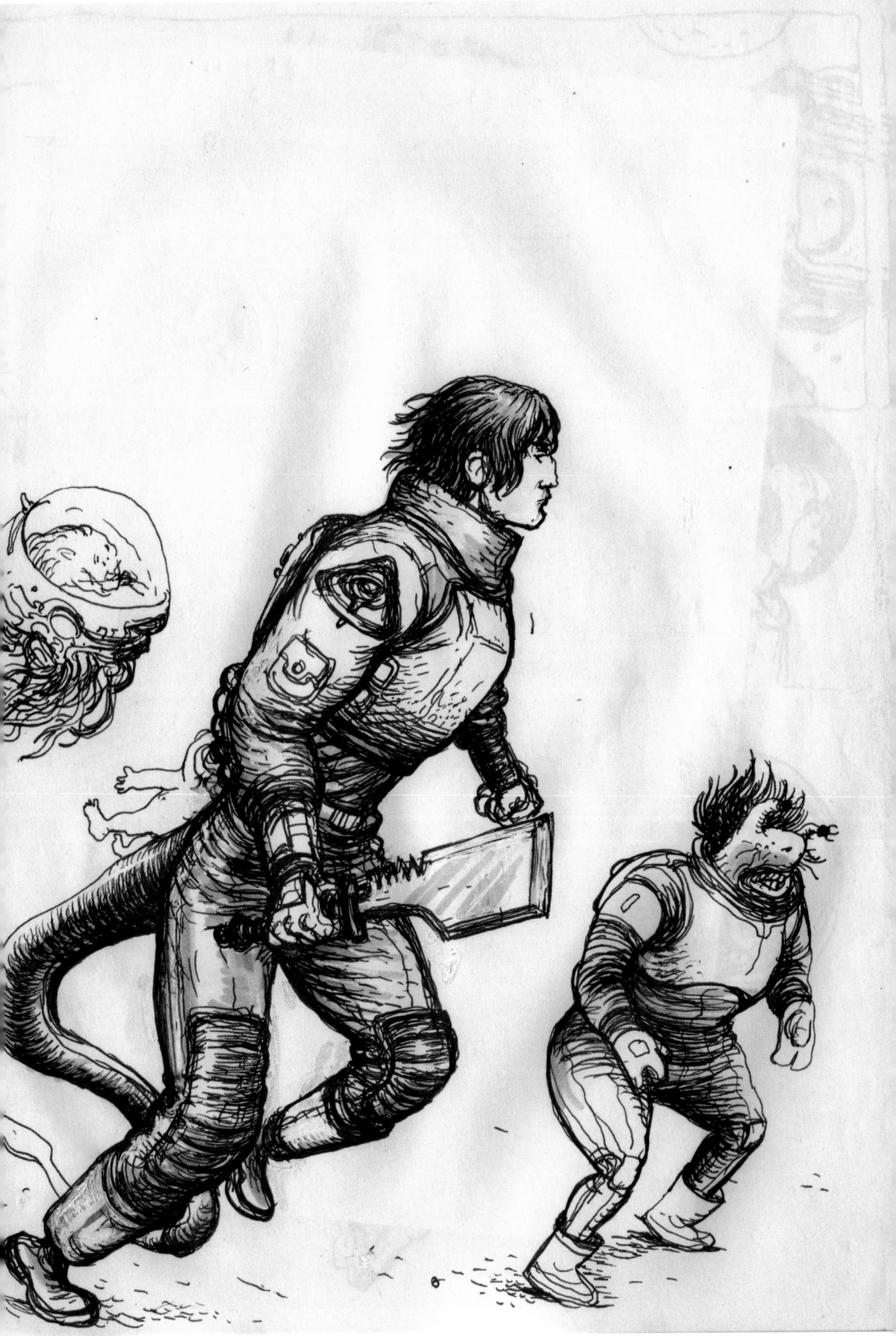

• prophet last issue •

- fighting monster
- gives spore dust

tail prophet

tail John

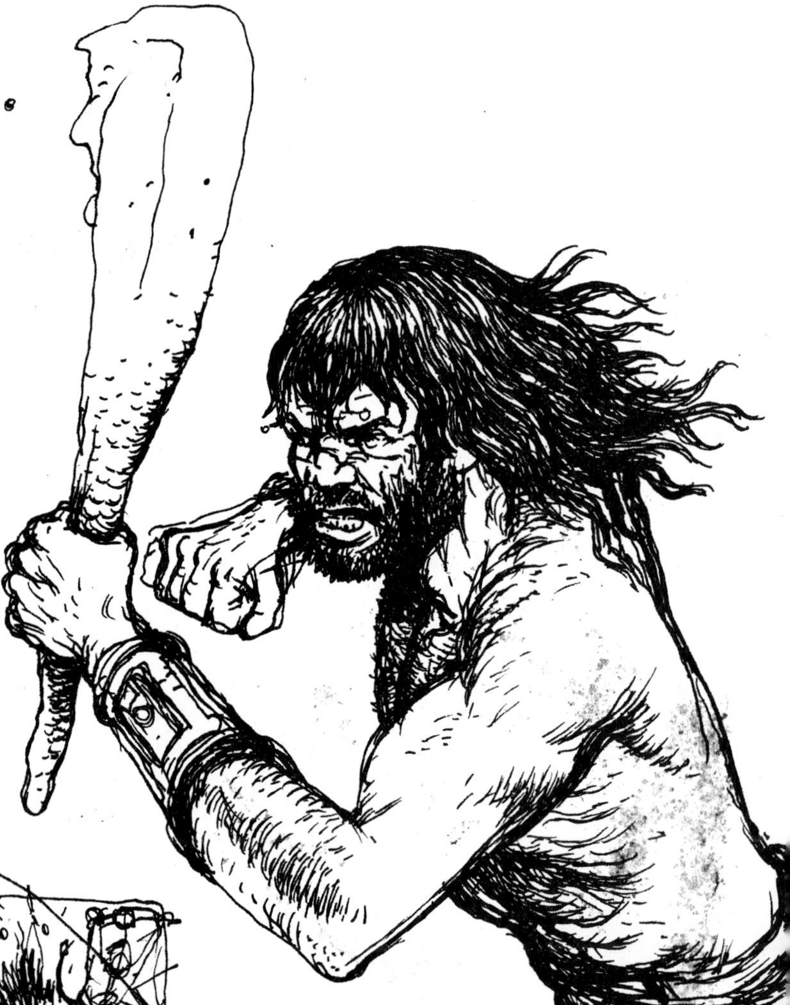

pg ①

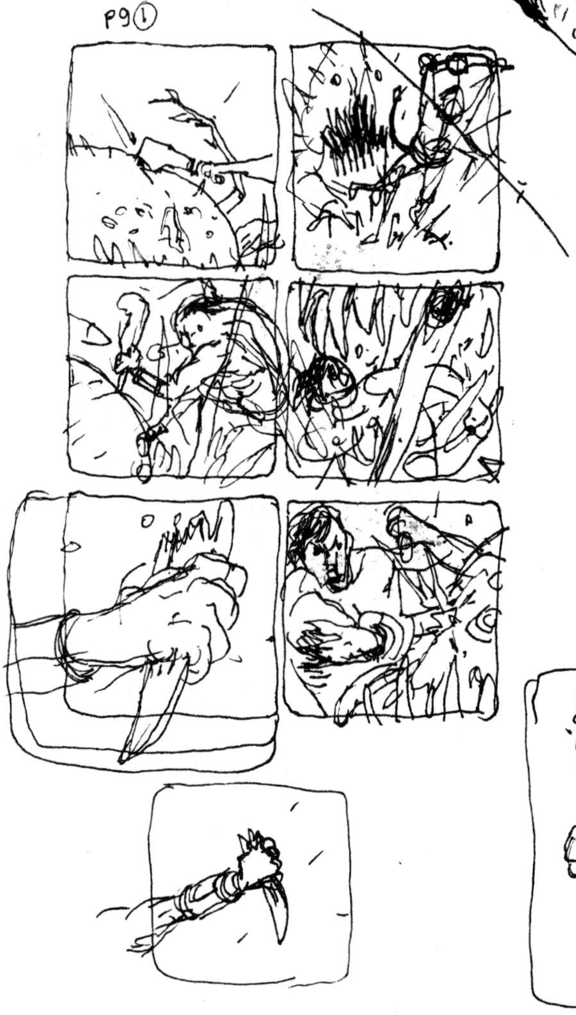

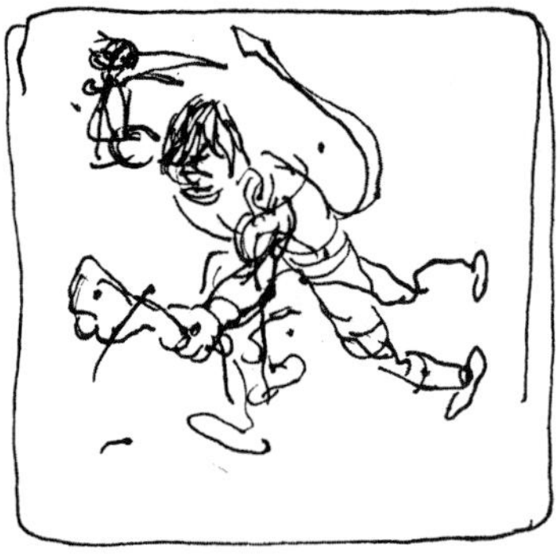

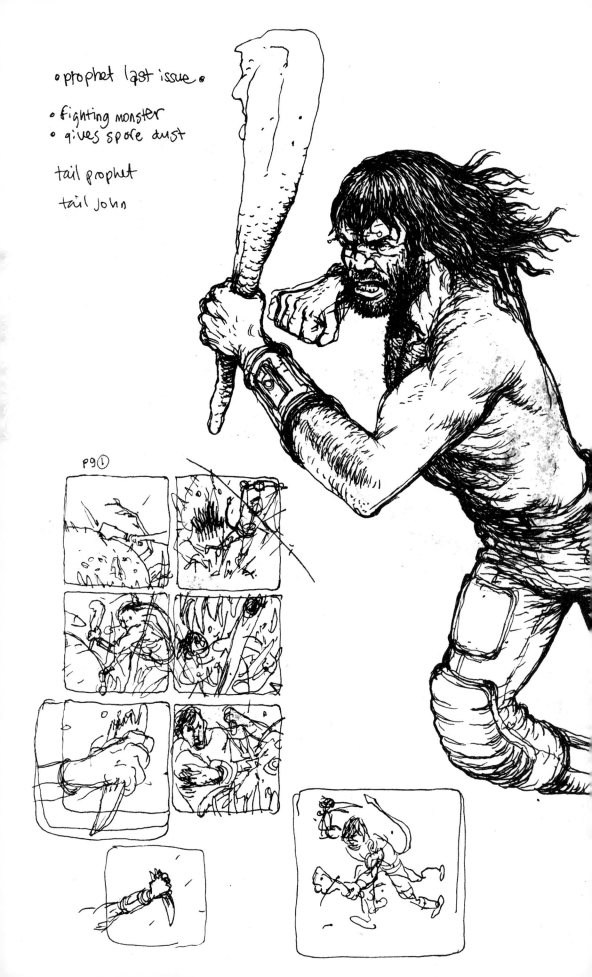

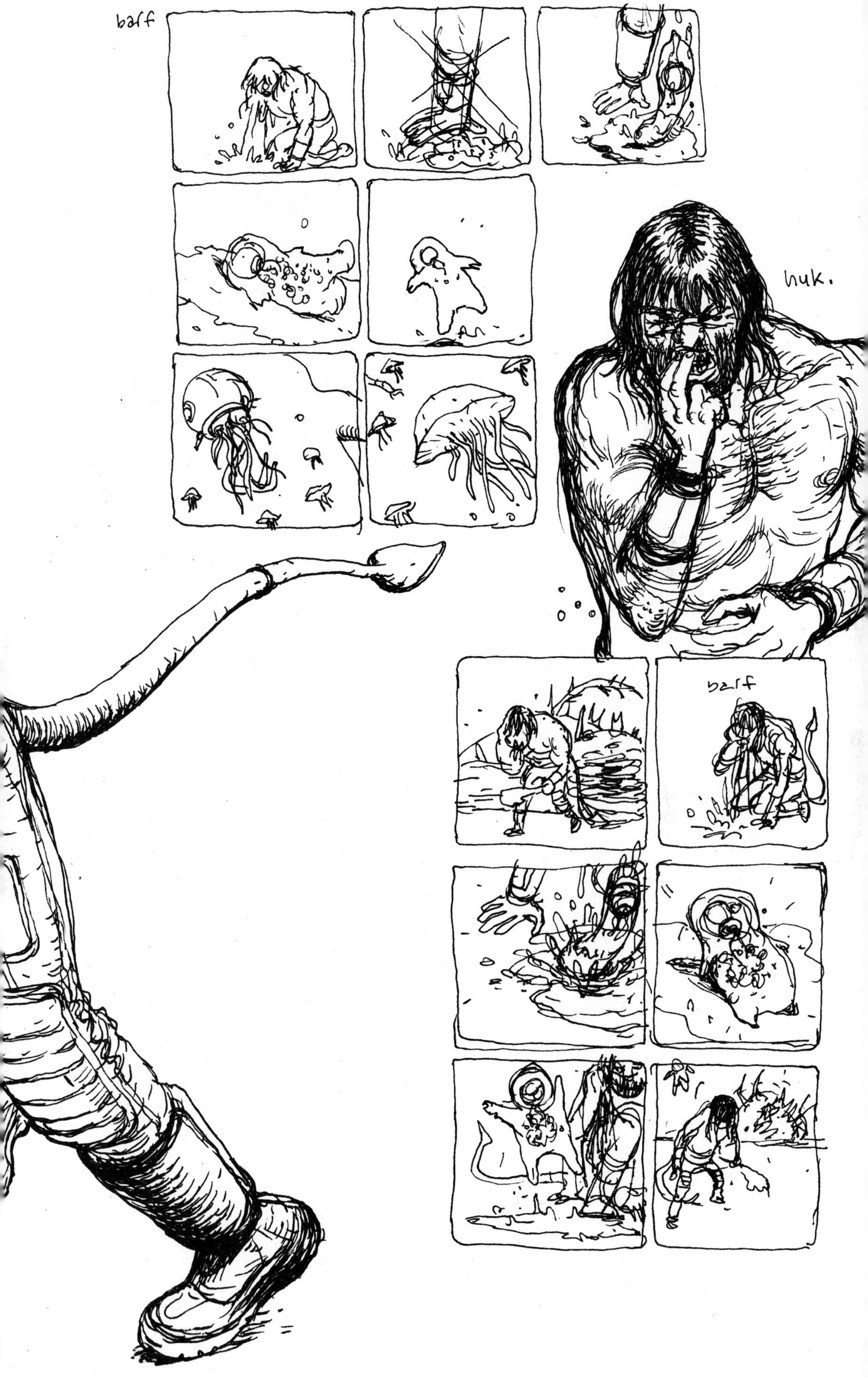
barf
huk.
barf

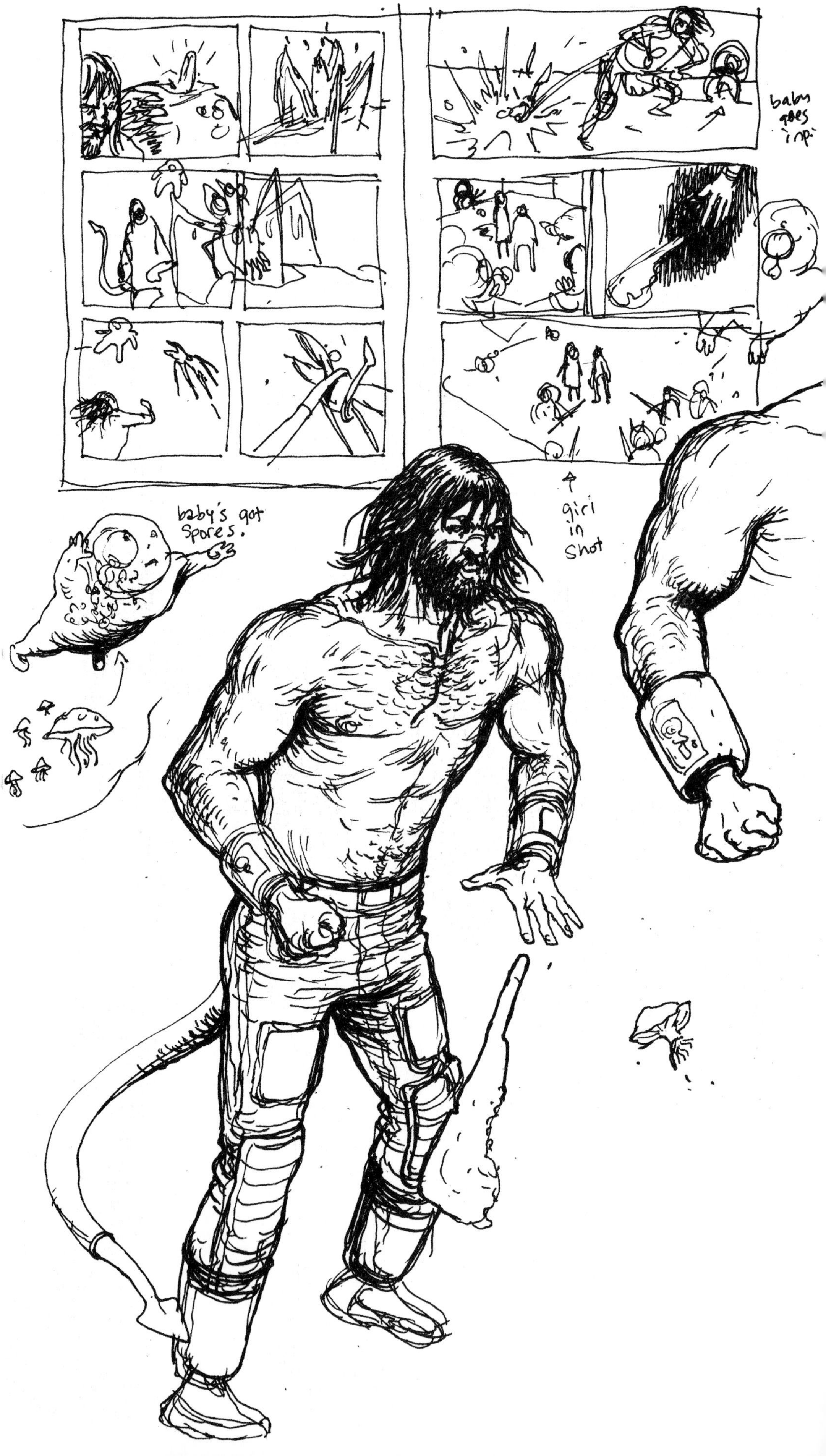
baby goes 'in'.
baby's got spores.
girl in shot

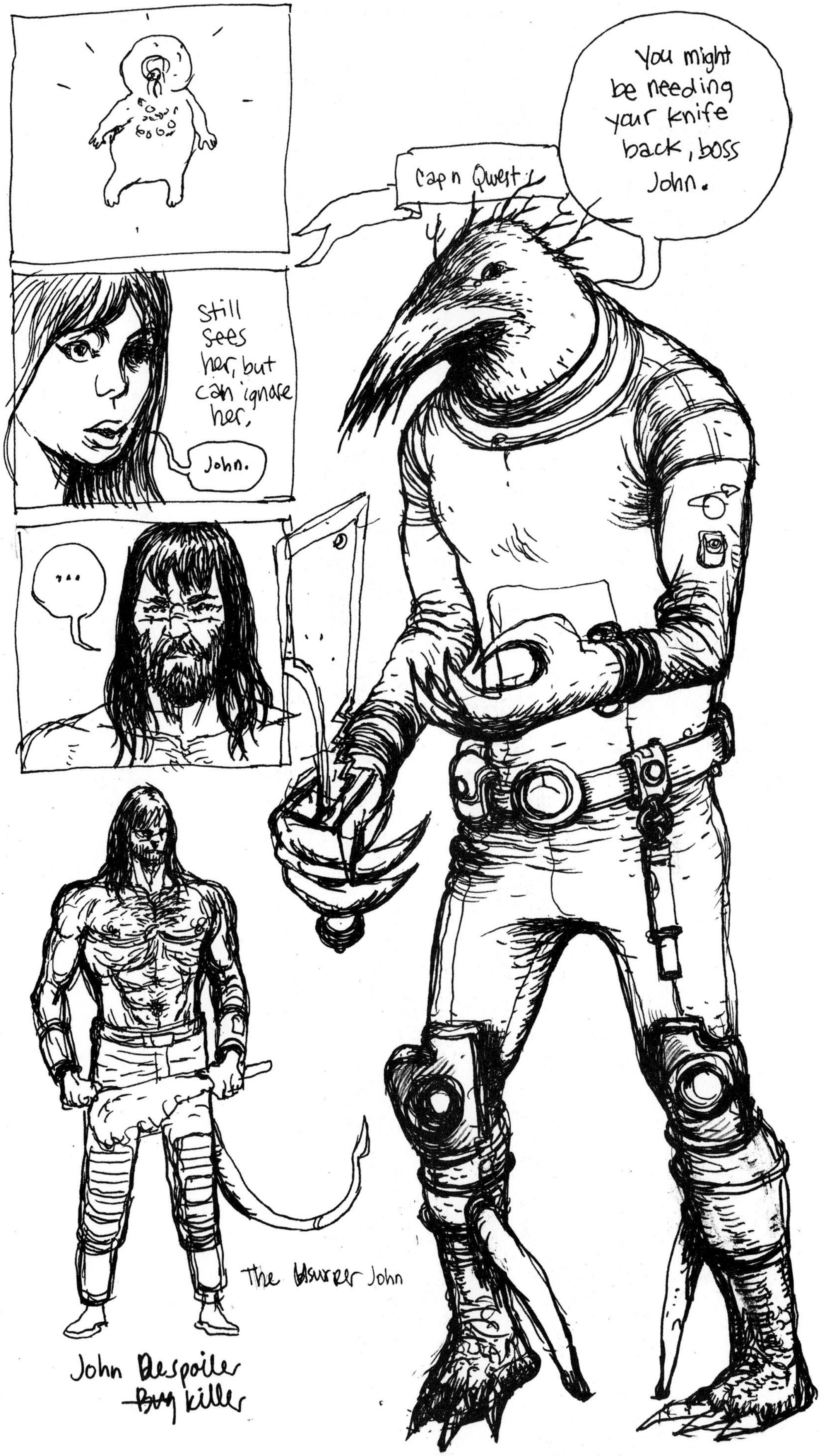
Still sees her, but can ignore her,
John.
...
Cap n Quest
You might be needing your knife back, boss John.
The Usurper John
John Despoiler
Bug killer

prophet pinups for strykefile

MYT

seadhear

- pirate crew - Quest et al
  =
- mushroom
  guy
- king man award guy/eyepatch who
  hurt tp

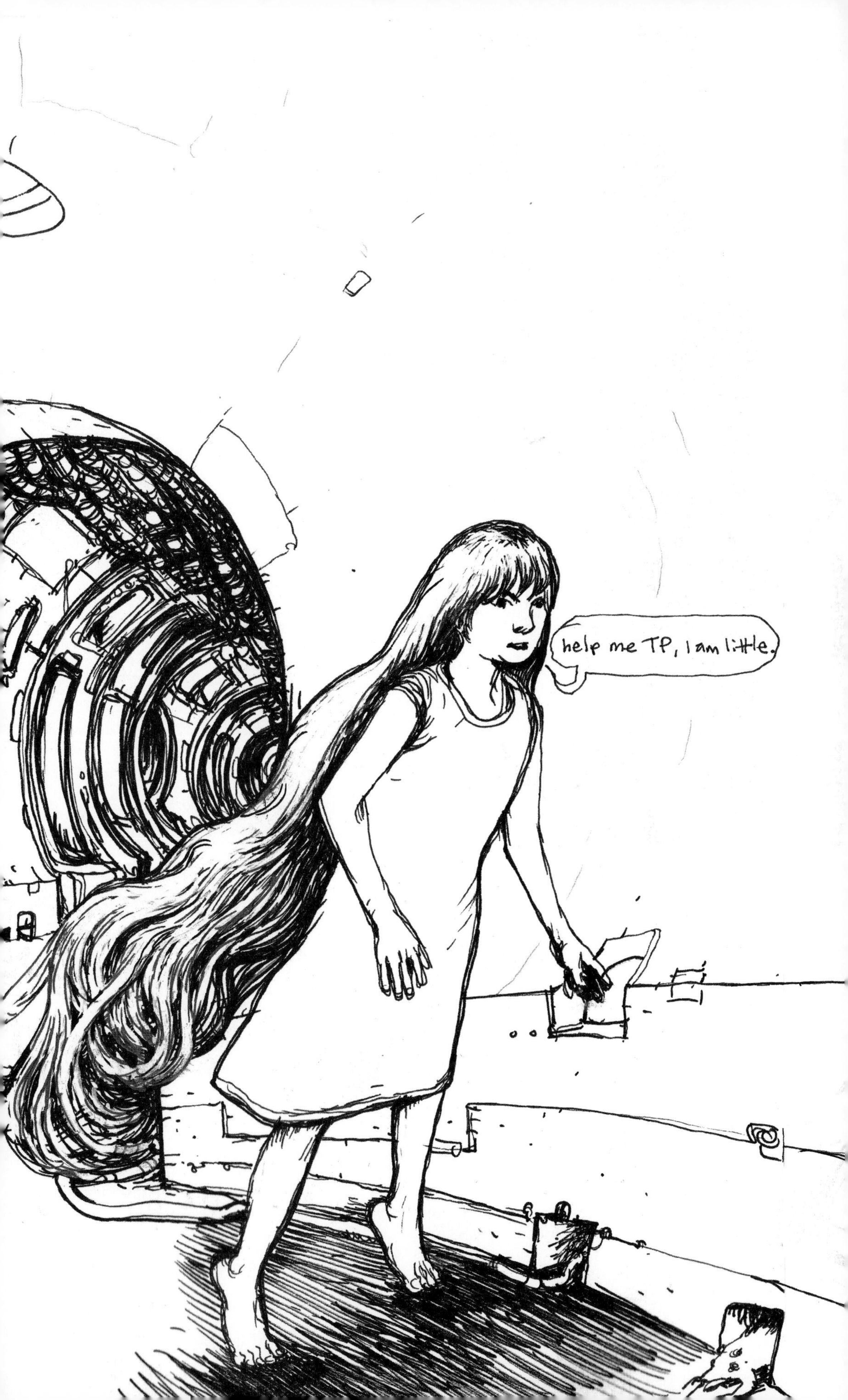
help me TP, I am little.

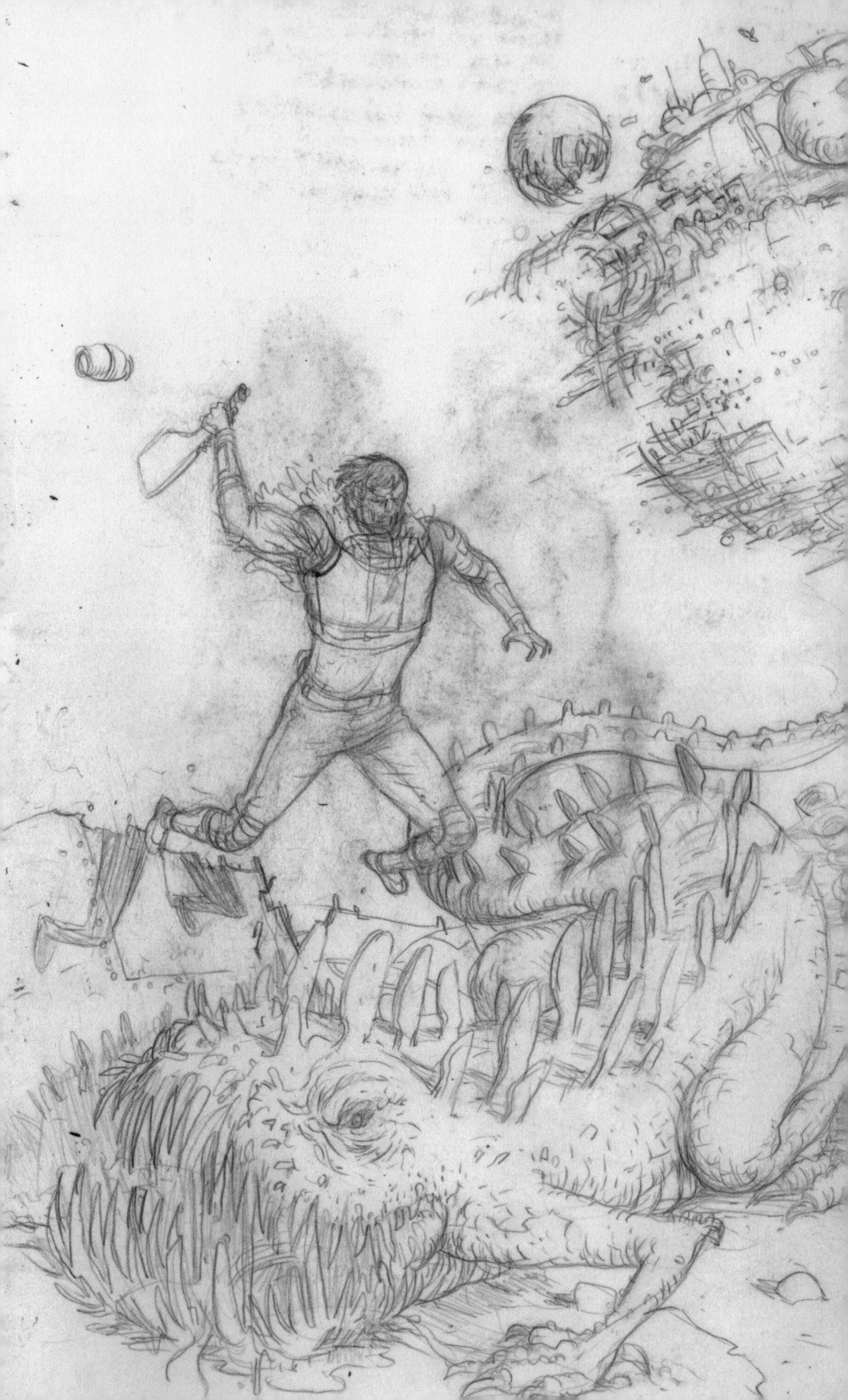

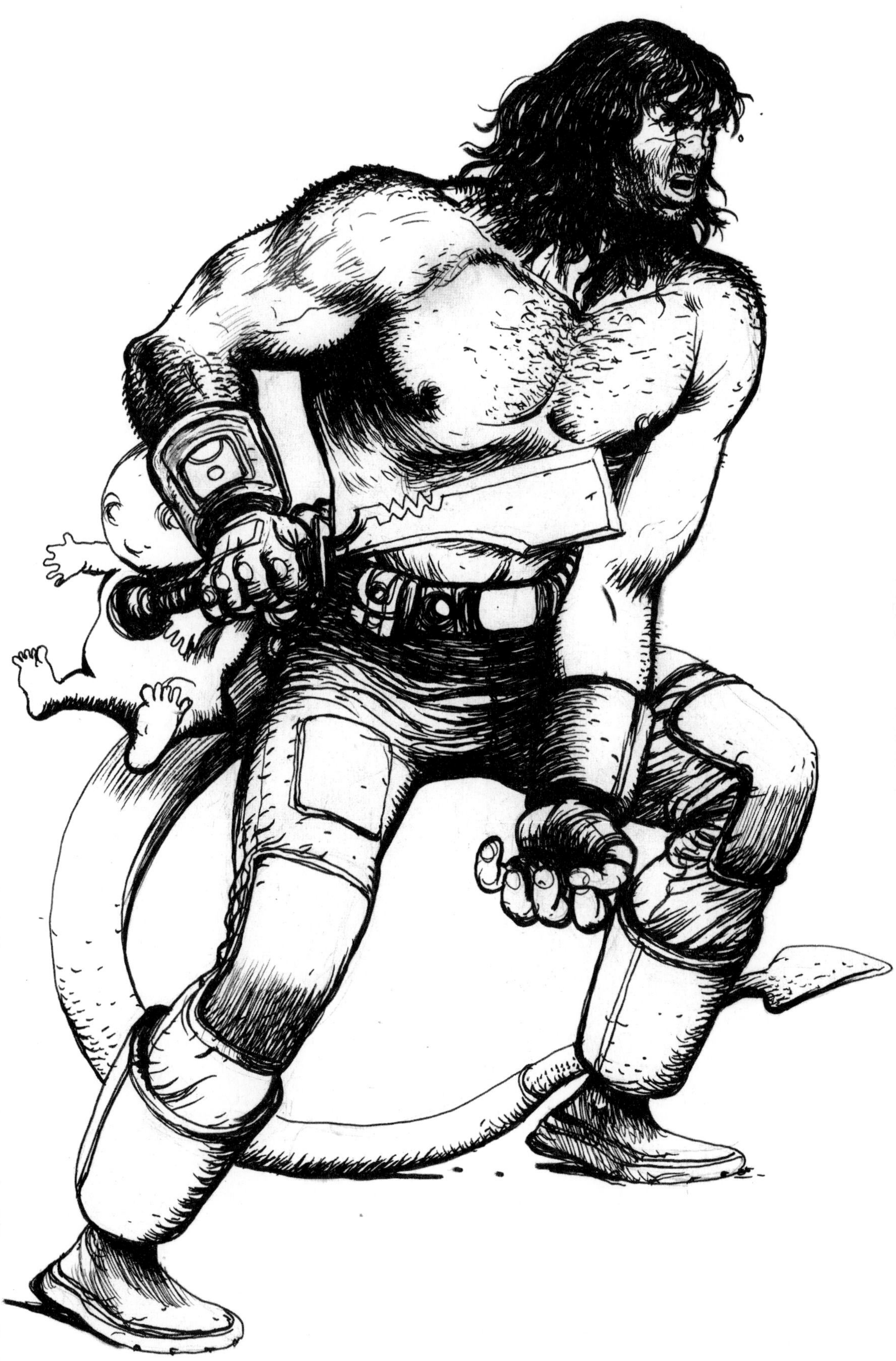

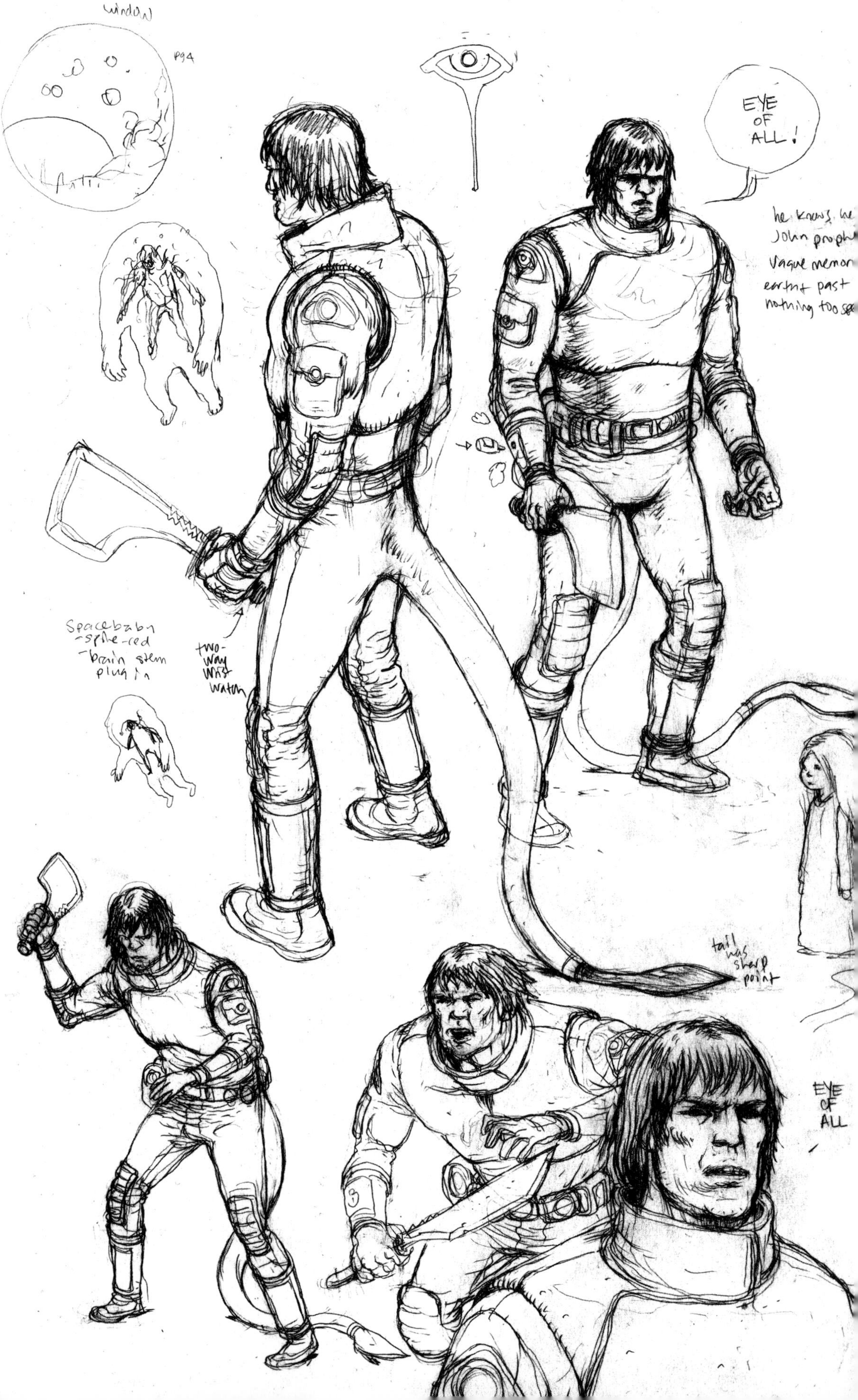
window
pg4
EYE OF ALL!
he knows, he
John proph
vague memor
earth past
nothing too se
Spacebaby
-spike-red
-brain stem
plug in
two-way wrist watch
tail was sharp point
EYE OF ALL

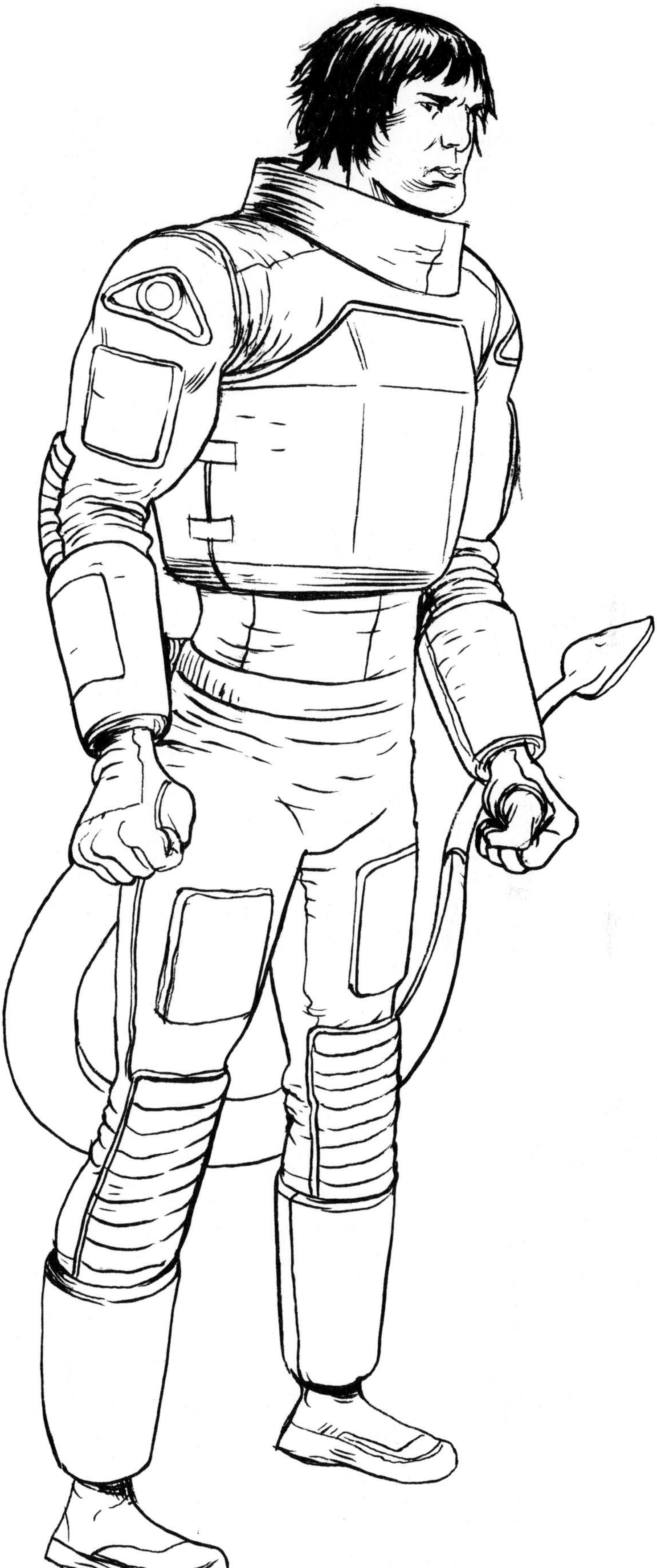

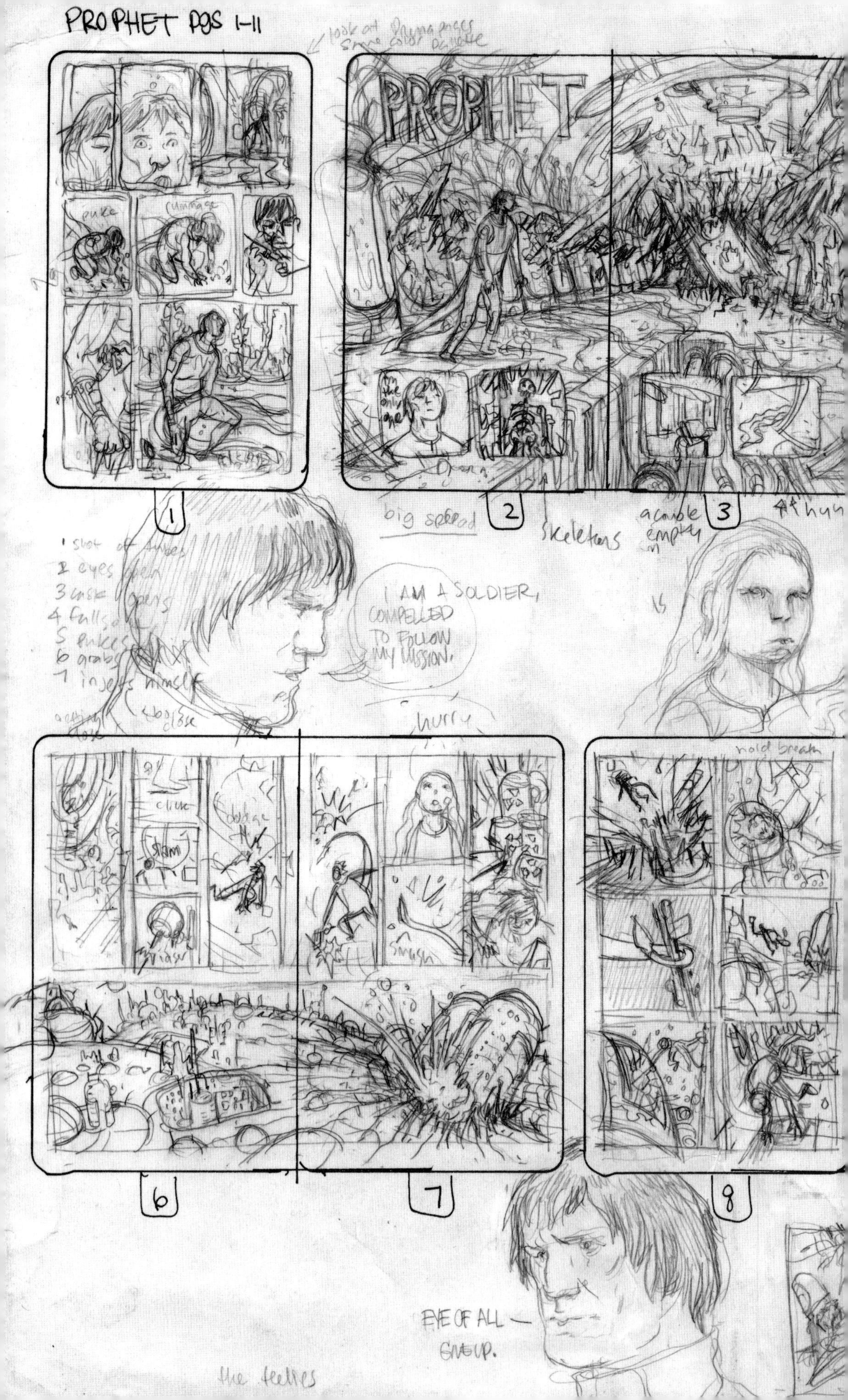
PROPHET pgs 1-11
puke
rummage
PROPHET
1
big spread
2
skeletons
3
1 shot of tubes
2 eyes open
3 cask opens
4 full shot
5 pukes
6 grabs
7 injects himself
I AM A SOLDIER, COMPELLED TO FOLLOW MY MISSION.
hurry
click
slam
smush
hold breath
6
7
8
EYE OF ALL — SIGN UP.
the feelies

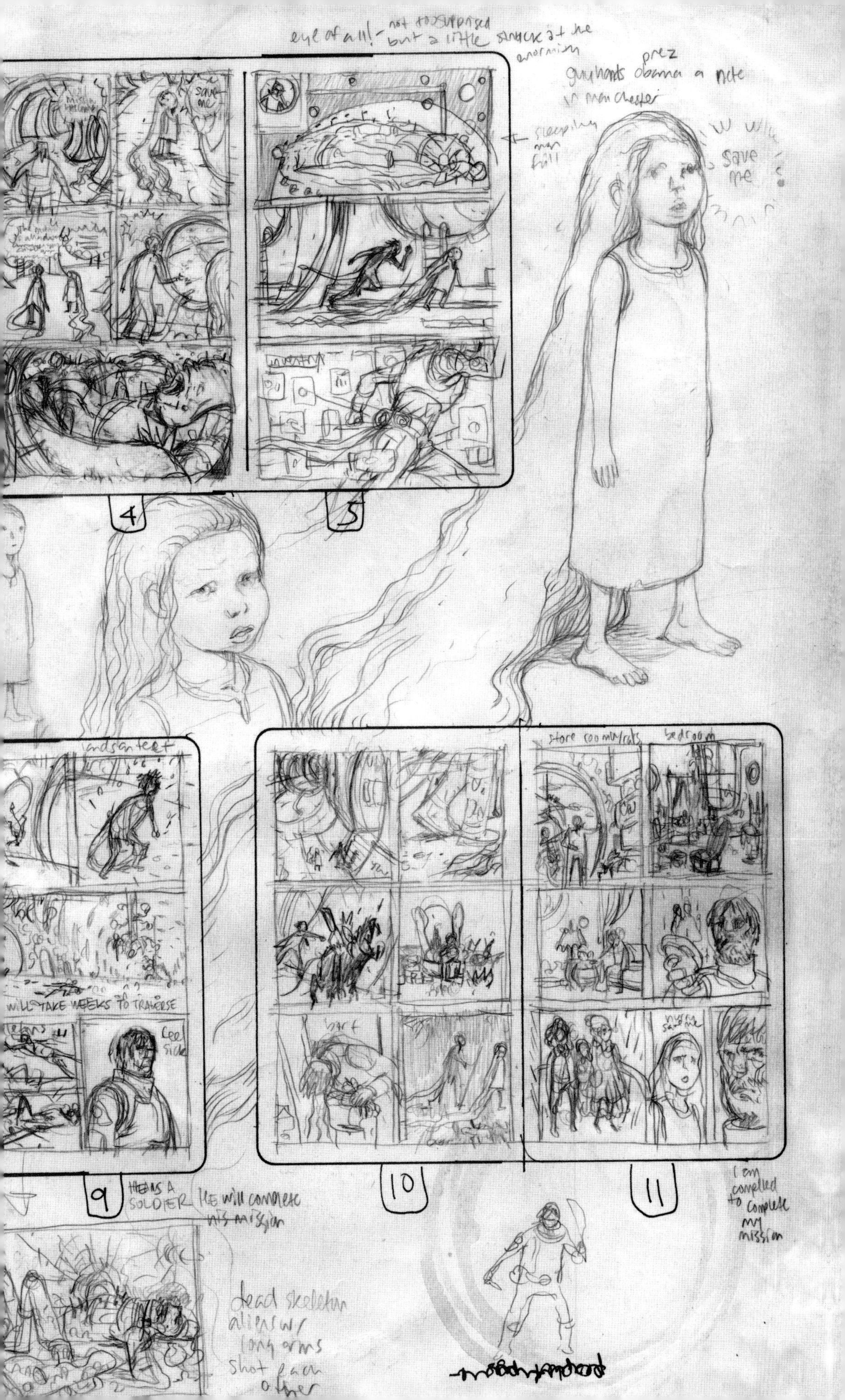
not too surprised but a little shock at the enormity
prez
guy hands obama a note in manchester
sleeping man fall
will you save me?
save me
4
5
WILL TAKE WEEKS TO TRAVERSE
feel sick
store room/cats
bedroom
9
HE IS A SOLDIER
he will complete his mission
10
11
I am compelled to complete my mission
dead skeleton aliens w/ long arms shot each other

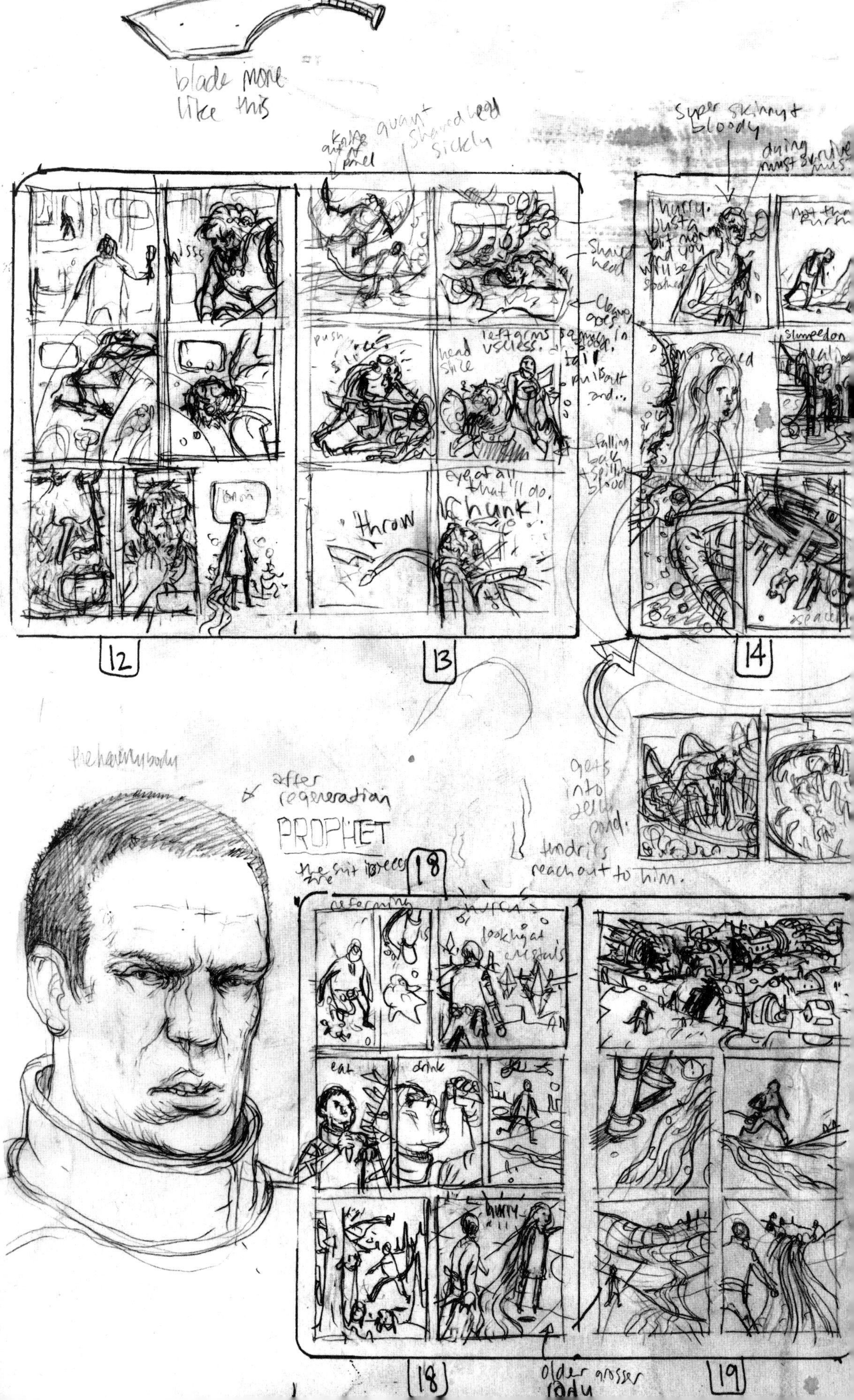

blade more like this
super skinny + bloody
dying must survive
hurry. just a bit more and you will be soothed
hisss
push
head slice
left arms useless
throw
chunk!
Shaved head
falling back spilling blood
12
13
14
after regeneration
PROPHET
gets into jelly pond.
tendrils reach out to him.
looking at crystals
eat
drink
hurry
older grosser body
18
19

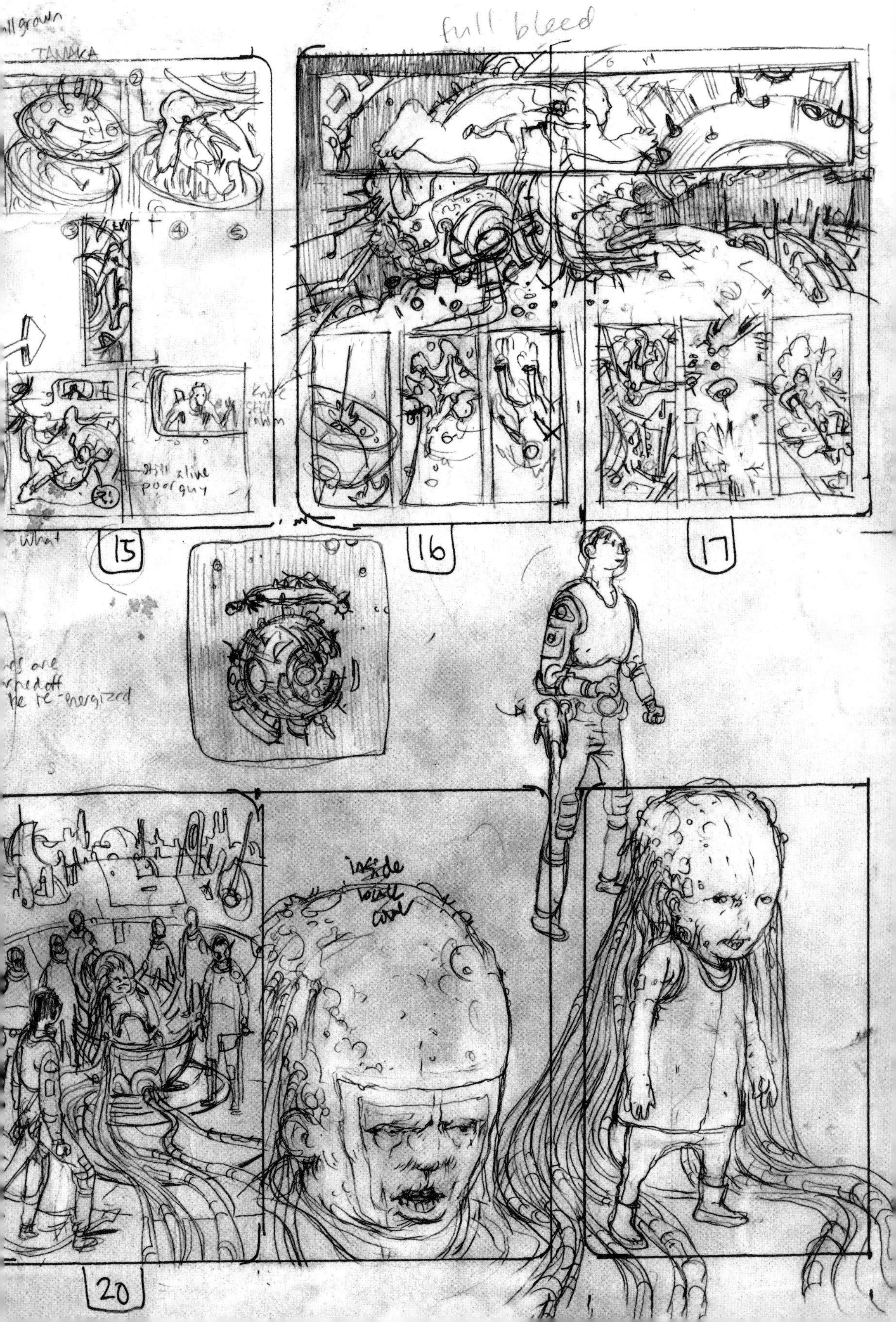

TANAKA
full bleed
still alive poor guy
what
15
16
17
20
inside

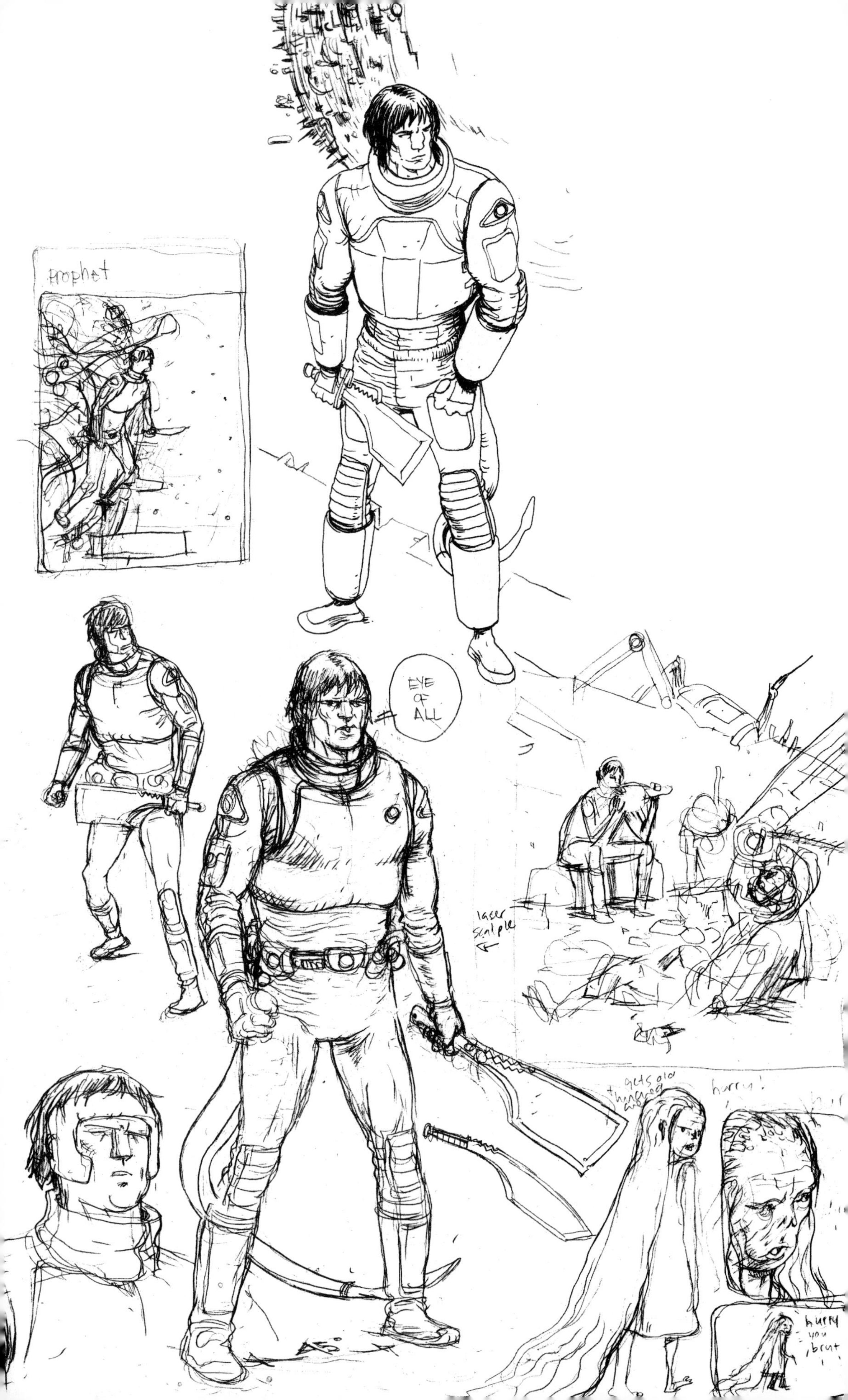
Prophet
EYE OF ALL
laser scalple
gets old
hurry!
hurry you brut

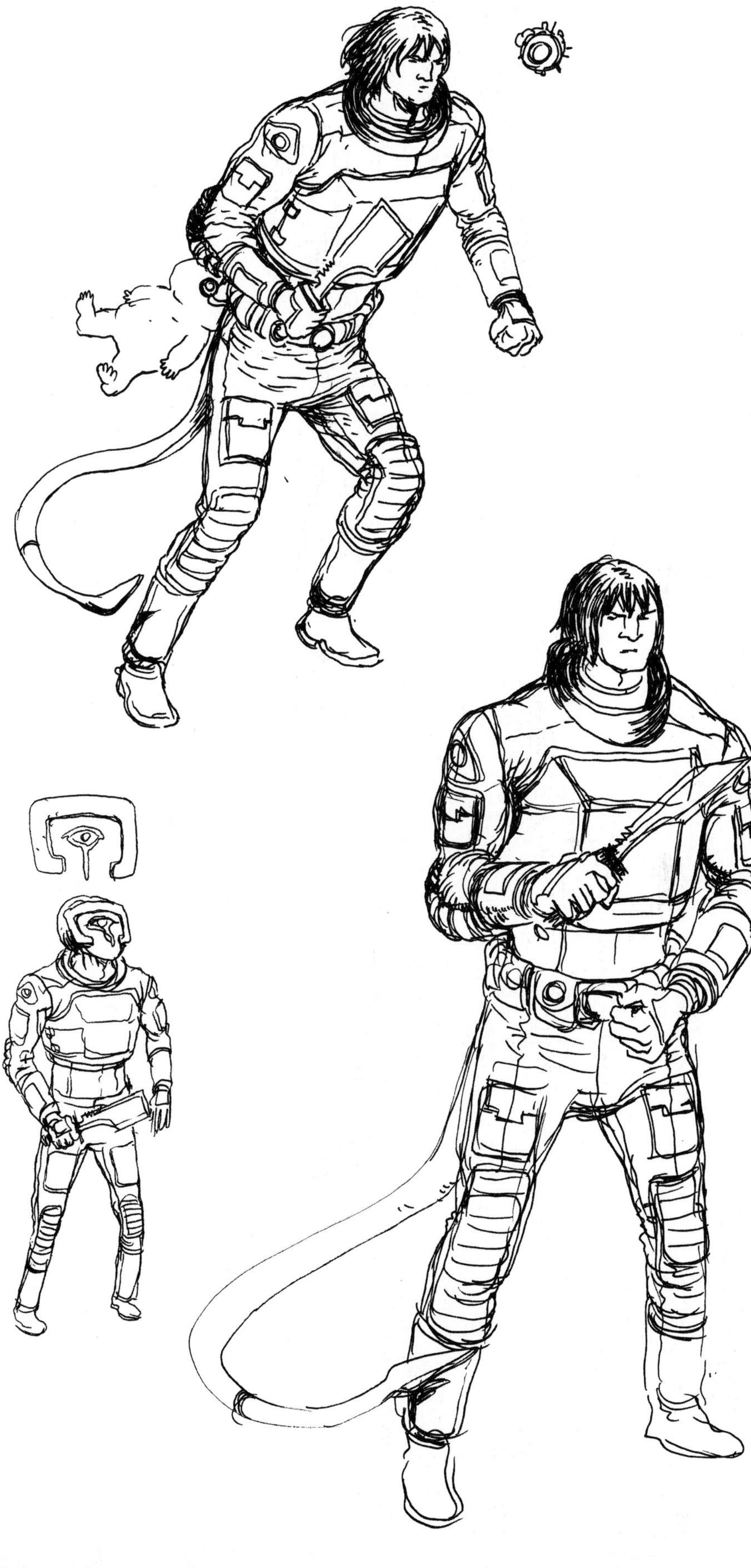

pg 2+3
2pg spread
characters →

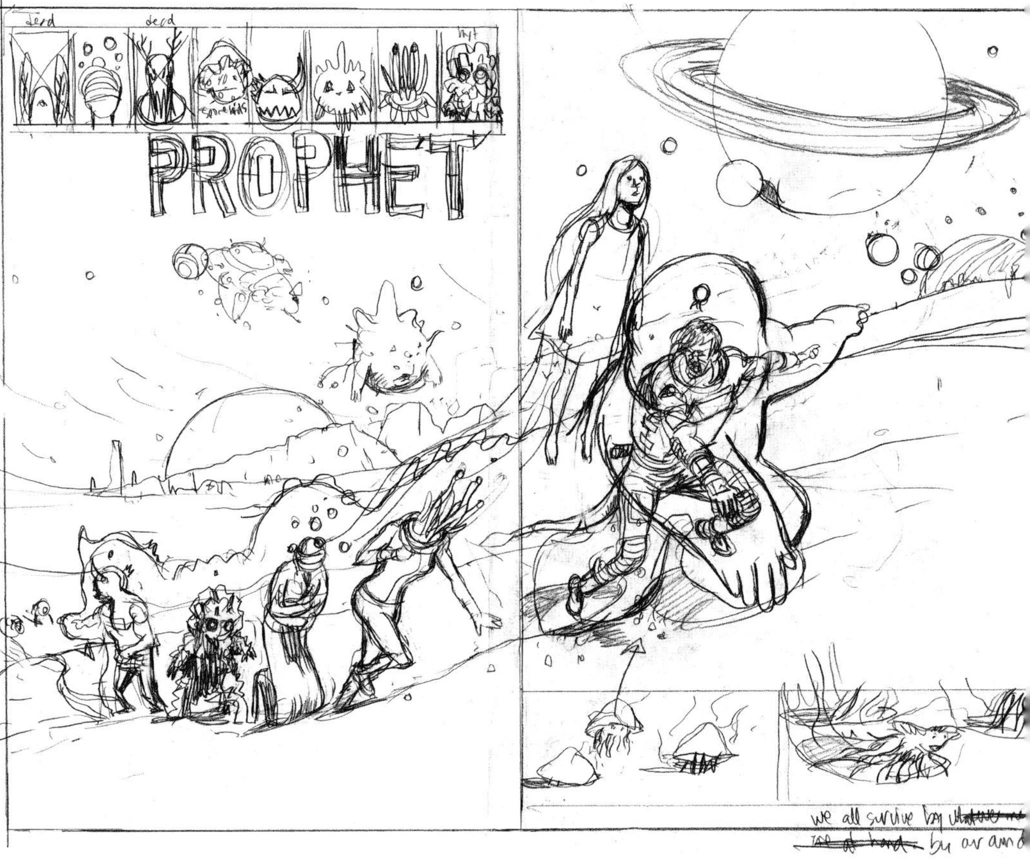
dead
dead
spore kids
PROPHET
we all survive by
by our and

Spread 6+7

moving too slow + never make it the wall before they are upon us.
prophet will lead them off our trail

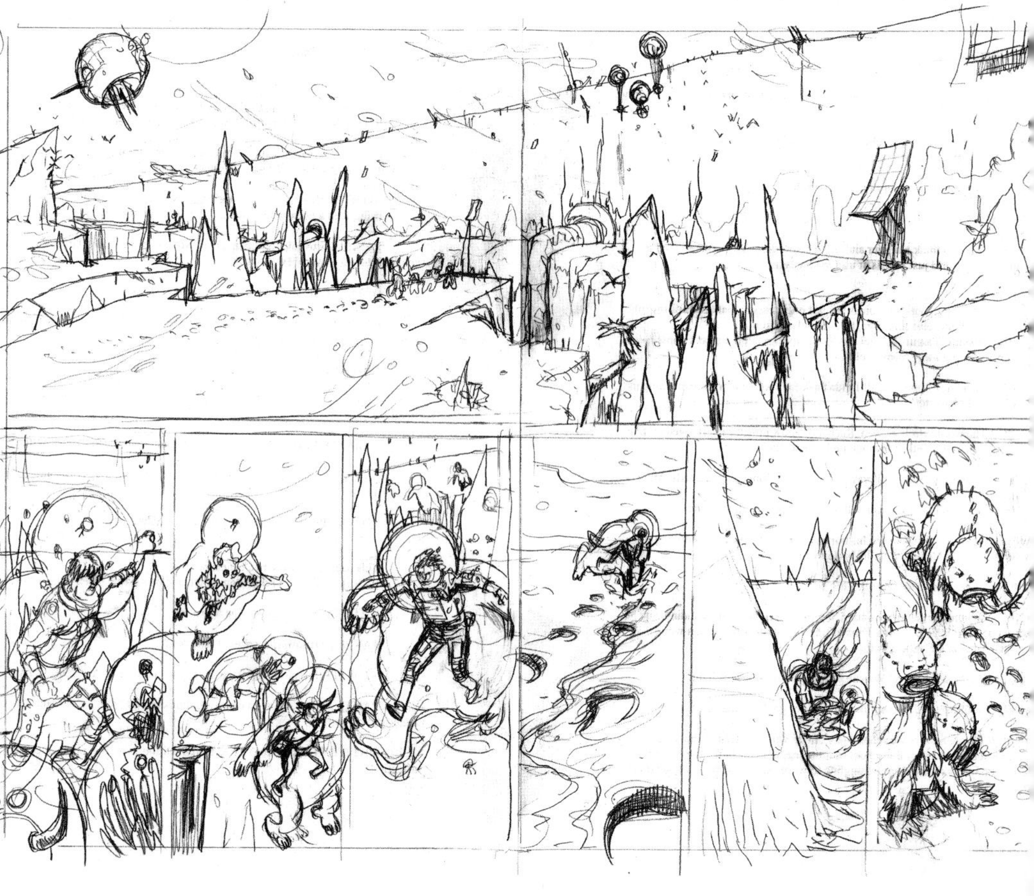

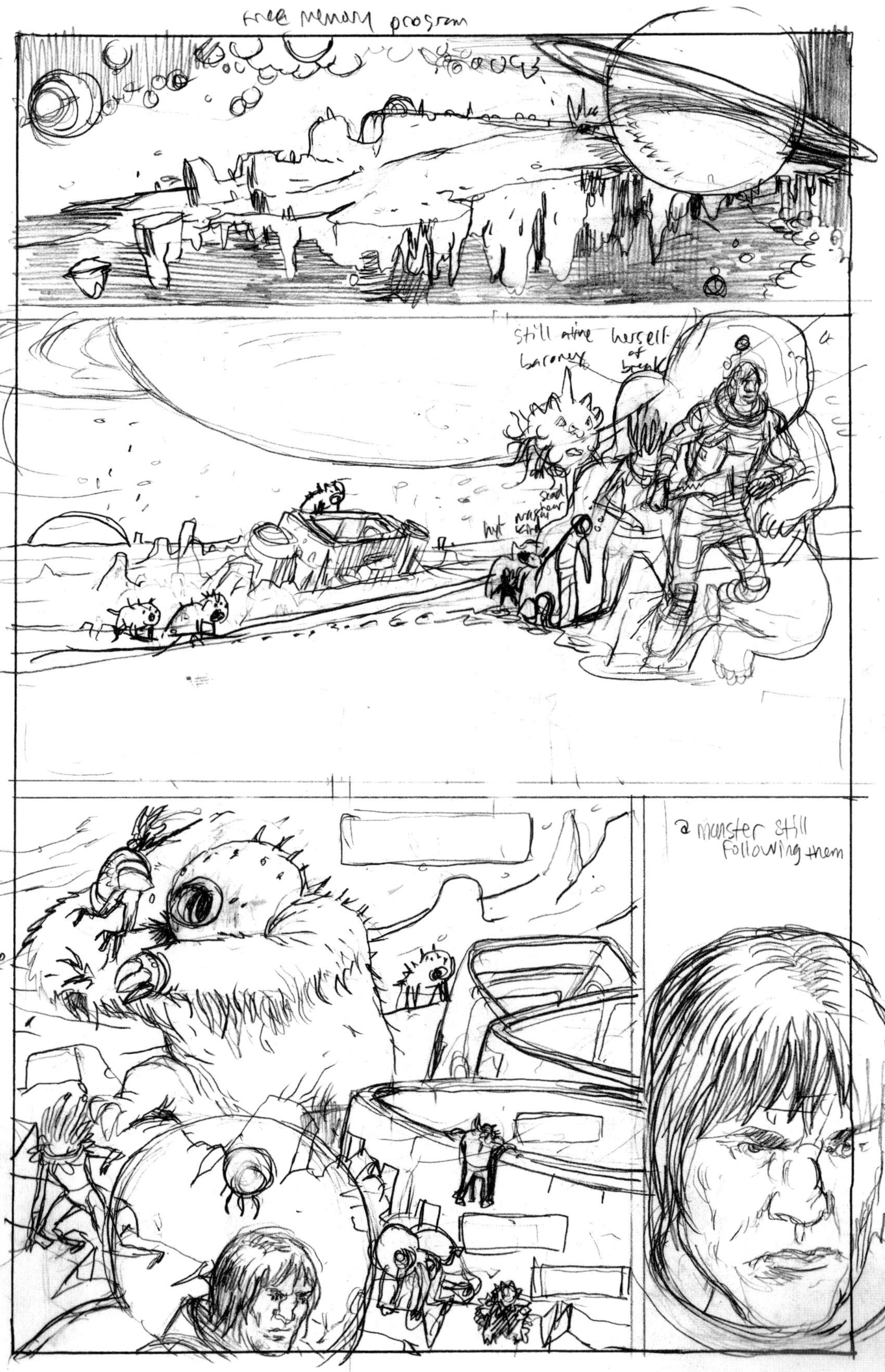
free memory program
still alive
baroness
herself
a monster still
following them

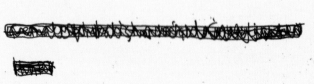

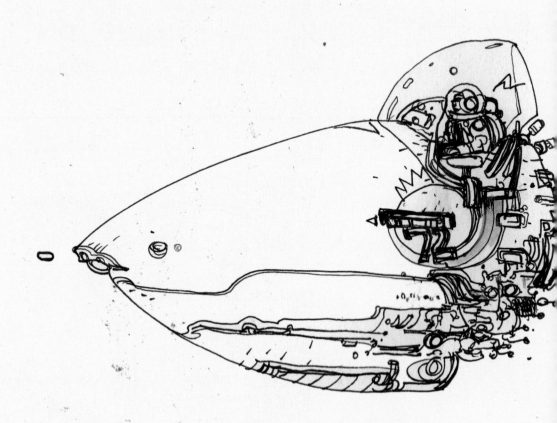

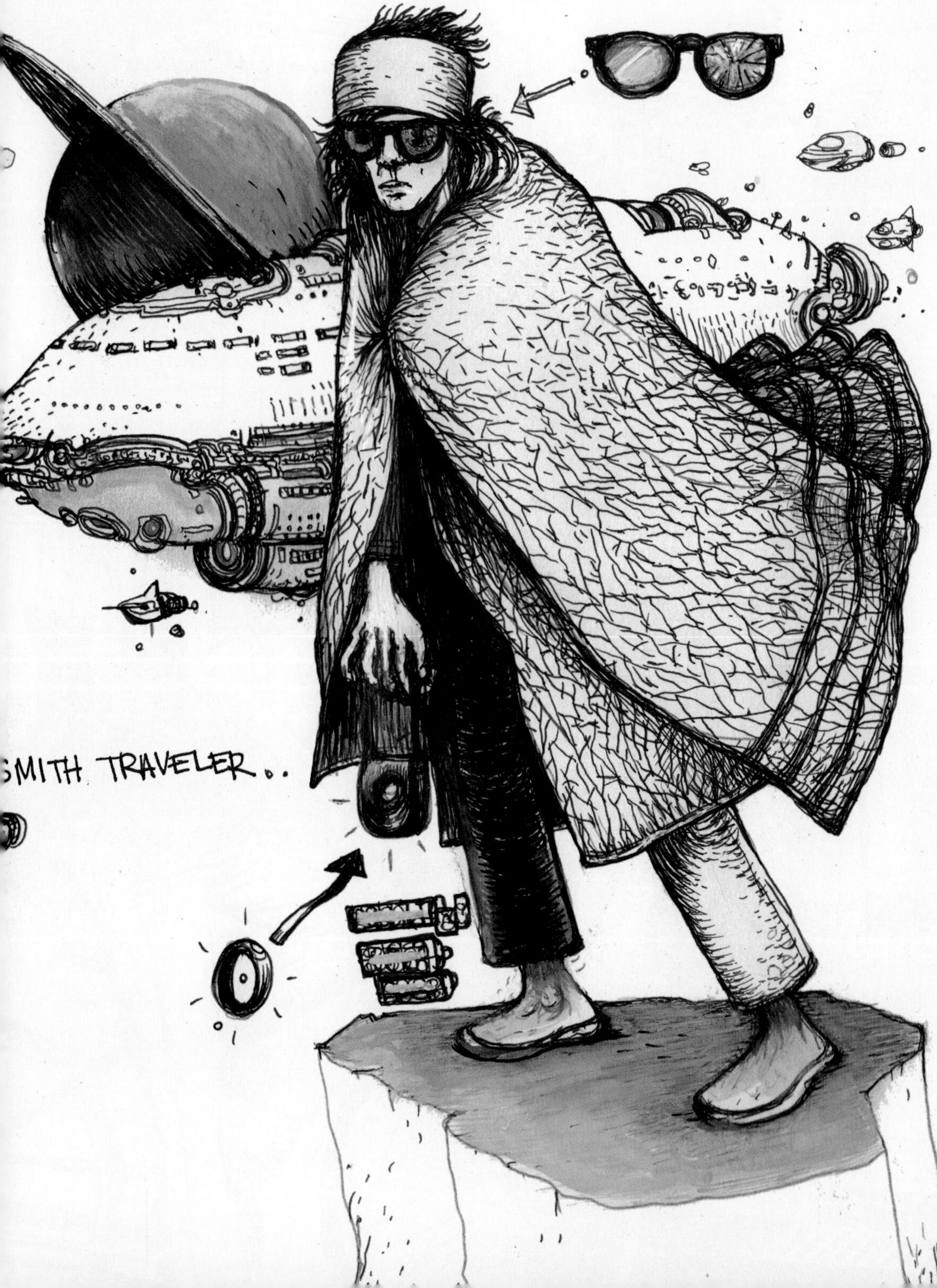
SMITH TRAVELER . .

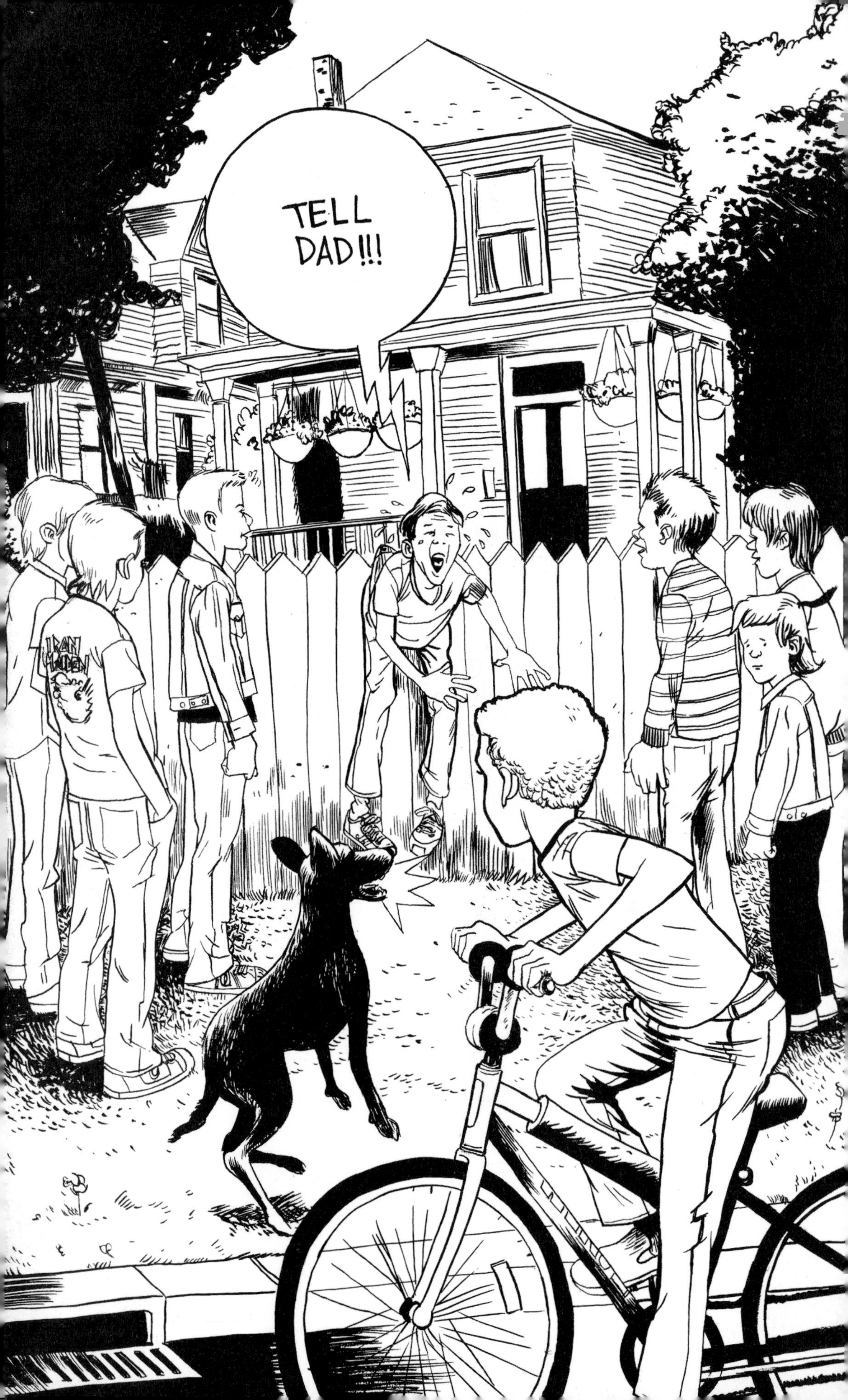
TELL DAD!!!

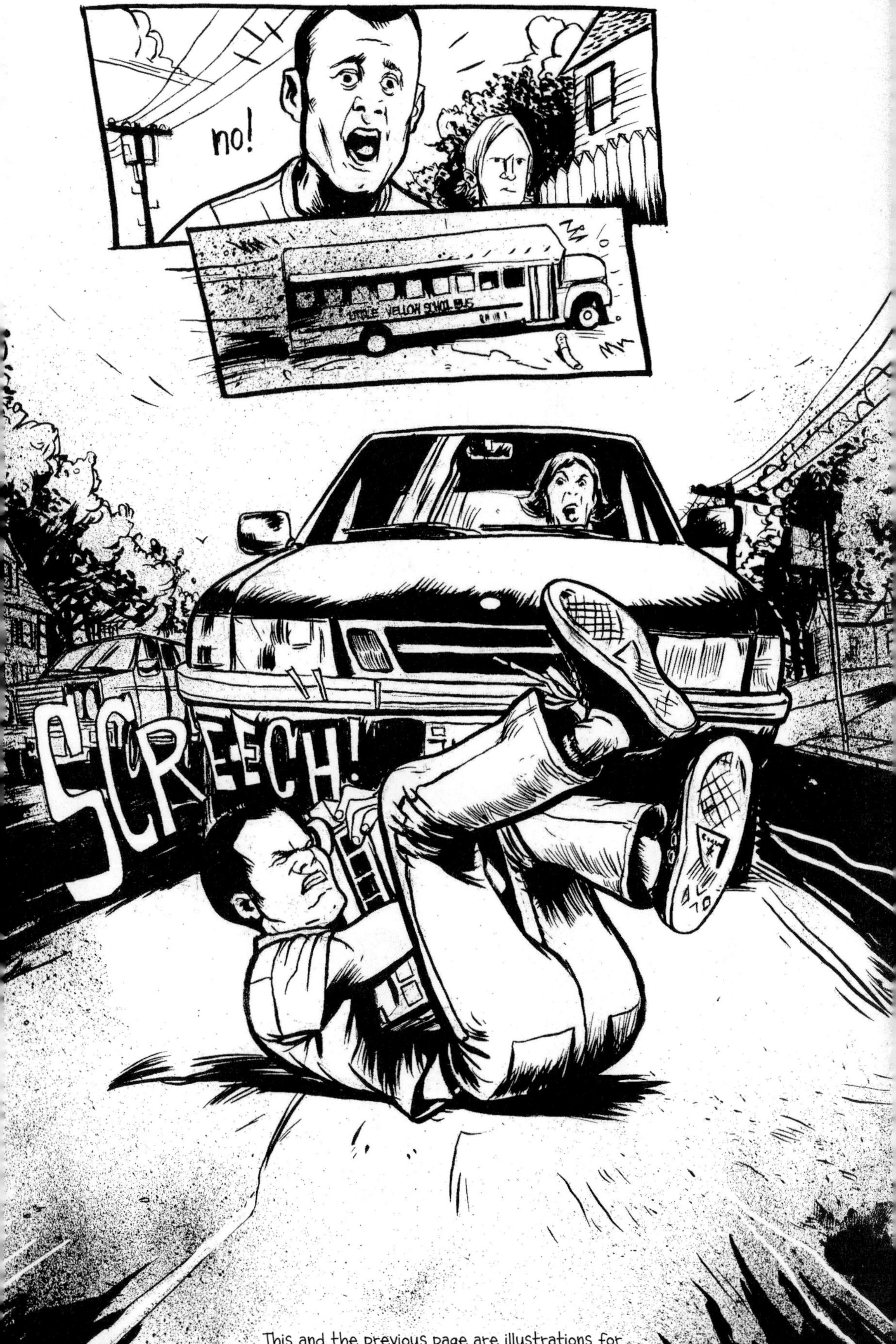
no!
LITTLE YELLOW SCHOOL BUS
SCREECH!

This and the previous page are illustrations for my good pal Roger Peffley's zine, *RHB ARCHIVES*, available at partykausa.com

the after wrong.

Thank you!

Rick and Danni Remender,
Valerie Dickie, John Arcudi,
Eric Stephenson, Brandon Graham,
Alejandra Gutiérrez, Shanna Matuszak,
Tricia Ramos, Craig Thompson, Chris Pitzer,
Cosmic Monkey Comics, MK Reed, Greg Means,
Nick Gazin, Andrew Nesbit, Scott Mills, Jasen Lex,
Andy Bodor, Gillian Robespierre, Diana Schutz,
Jonathan Lethem, Damon Gentry, Simon Roy, Wes Craig,
Nick Dragotta, Matthew Sheean, Malachi Ward, Demian Johnson,
Daniel Chabon, Matt Kindt, Zack Soto, Floating World Comics,
Cosmic Monkey Comics, Tim Goodyear, Corey Kalman,
Becky Cloonan, Michael Conrad, Andrew Carl, Chris Stevens,
Jason Sacher, Sandra Sue McVicker, Krista and David and family,
Sarah Palmer, Warren Ellis, Bernadette Baker-Baughman,
Brian Scott O'keefe, DJKG and CB3D, Pvvk, B-Side,
Meathaus people, Union Knott Gallery, Push/Pull in Ballard,
Multnomah County Library, all of the supporters of the scene,
Patreon pals, retailers, readers and friends.

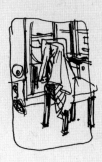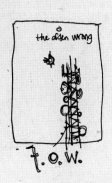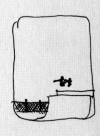

the risen wrong

f.o.w.

Farel Dalrymple was born in 1972.
He currently lives in Portland, Oregon, USA.

Other comic books and graphic
works from Farel Dalrymple:

PROXIMA CENTAURI (2019, Image)

IT WILL ALL HURT (2018, Image
and online at Studygroupcomics.com)

POP GUN WAR: CHAIN LETTER (2017, Image)

POP GUN WAR: GIFT (2016, Image)

PALEFIRE with MK Reed (2015, Secret Acres)

THE WRENCHIES (2014, First Second)

DELUSIONAL: THE GRAPHIC AND SEQUENTIAL WORK OF FAREL DALRYMPLE (2013, Ad House)

OMEGA THE UNKNOWN with Jonathan Lethem and Paul Hornschemeier (2010, Marvel)

PROPHET: VOLUMES 1-4 with Brandon Graham (2012-2015, Image)

MEATHAUS ANTHOLOGY: VOLUMES 1-9 (2000-2008, Meathaus)

Magazine interviews:
DRAW! MAGAZINE issue 28 (Two Morrows)
STUDYGROUP MAGAZINE issue 4 (Studygroup)

To purchase original art pages and covers:
The Beguiling Books & Art
store.beguilingoriginalart.com
319 College Street
Toronto, Ontario, Canada
M5T 1S2 Phone: 416-533-9168

Letterpress prints:
Dead Accents
deadaccents.bigcartel.com

fareldalrymple.com

patreon.com/fareldal